# CRIMINOLOGY

## Fourth Edition

**Piers Beirne**
*University of Southern Maine*

**James W. Messerschmidt**
*University of Southern Maine*

New York    Oxford
OXFORD UNIVERSITY PRESS

Oxford University Press, Inc., publishes works that further Oxford University's
objective of excellence in research, scholarship, and education.

Oxford   New York
Auckland   Cape Town   Dar es Salaam   Hong Kong   Karachi
Kuala Lumpur   Madrid   Melbourne   Mexico City   Nairobi
New Delhi   Shanghai   Taipei   Toronto

With offices in
Argentina   Austria   Brazil   Chile   Czech Republic   France   Greece
Guatemala   Hungary   Italy   Japan   Poland   Portugal   Singapore
South Korea   Switzerland   Thailand   Turkey   Ukraine   Vietnam

Published by Oxford University Press, Inc.
198 Madison Avenue, New York, New York 10016
http://www.oup.com

ISBN 978-0-19-533062-5

Printing number: 9 8 7 6 5 4 3 2 1

Printed in the United States of America
on acid-free paper

# Brief Table of Contents

# Table of Contents

## Part I
## Introduction to Criminology

# Part II
# Types of Crime

# Part III
# Criminological Theory

ix

# List of Boxes, Figures, and Tables

## Boxes

# Figures

# Tables

# Preface to the Fourth Edition

In this Fourth Edition of ***Criminology,*** we have tinkered with the original organization of chapters so that the structure of the book has an added coherence and a tighter feel. Where necessary, we have revised certain sections of the book, adding material in some cases and subtracting it in others. New and up-to-date empirical data are presented throughout the book, and we discuss types of crime that we did not properly address in the previous editions, including terrorism, globalization, cyberstalking, computer crime, animal abuse, the latest corporate scandals (Enron, Worldcom, etc.), violence by college athletes, and election fraud.

The aim of ***Criminology*** remains constant: to introduce the basic aspects of modern criminology to undergraduate students. This is no easy task in such a diverse discipline. All textbook authors have to make a number of hard choices. This book very much reflects our teaching experience in the undergraduate criminology program at the University of Southern Maine, where our introductory course in criminology both surveys the major areas of the discipline and provides an introduction to more specialized, upper-level courses in criminology. We have attempted both to strike a balance between depth of analysis and breadth of coverage and to make the book comprehensive in its presentation of the sociological aspects of criminology. Although we aim to survey all the major aspects of the field, we especially emphasize the importance of historical, feminist, and comparative perspectives on crime.

## Features of the Fourth Edition

This book is divided into three parts. Part One (Chapters 1–3) focuses on three questions: What is crime, and how are perceptions of it influenced by the mass media and by fear of crime? How can we measure crime? How are patterns of crime and victimization structured by the sociological variables of social class, gender, race/ethnicity, and age? Part Two (Chapters 4–8) examines specific types of crime, including property crime, interpersonal violence, syndicated crime, white-collar crime, and political crime. Part Three (Chapters 9–15) is a systematic guide to modern criminological theory and its historical development.

Part One serves as an introduction to some of the major themes of criminology. Chapter 1 outlines the major ways in which popular discourse about crime is articulated—through the mass media, through fear of crime, and through the pronouncements of the moral entrepreneurs of social problems. While the chapter summarizes the key elements of crime as a legal category, it stresses the importance of sociological definitions of crime. In so doing, it introduces the three key sociological concepts of criminology: crime, criminal law, and criminalization.

Chapter 2 outlines the major empirical sources of crime data. These include both official crime data (the FBI's Uniform Crime Reports, the National Crime Victimization Survey, and records of various federal agencies) and unofficial crime data (life-course and life-history data, criminal biographies, observation research and participant observation research, and comparative and historical research). We stress here that crime data can never represent criminal behavior objectively because there are inherent biases in the way that all data are conceived and constructed. Data do not speak for themselves! How crime data are explained, therefore, depends both on our concepts of crime and on the assumptions underlying our theories of crime. The importance of this point will become clear as the contents of the book unfold.

Chapter 3 offers the rudiments of a critical sociological perspective on the relationship between crime and structured social inequality. Here, we examine the influence of four major forms of social inequality—social class, gender, race, and age—on patterns of crime and victimization in the United States.

Part Two provides an introduction to various types of crime. Typologies of crime can be constructed in an infinite variety of ways. We have chosen a sociological typology that combines (1) those crimes usually defined in the legal codes and (2) those crimes and social harms outside the criminal law that have received much attention in the sociological and criminological literature. Because crime is found in every social institution, the chapters in Part Two offer a comprehensive understanding of the nature, extent, types, and costs of crime found not only in the street but also in the family, the workplace, and the state. In these chapters, we rely heavily on research done in the United States, but we also include material from other countries such as Canada, Australia, and Britain.

Part Three introduces students to criminological theory. Theories about crime can be greatly misunderstood by wrenching them from the context of the era in which they were conceived. Therefore, the seven chapters in Part Three unfold chronologically, with respect both to the contents of each chapter and to the position of each chapter in relation to the other six. We believe that all theories, including those popular today, should at first be understood historically. One virtue of this belief is the humbling discovery that our understanding of crime has advanced only very little beyond that of theorists of a century ago. In describing each theory, we try to show why it arose when it did, what theories it supplanted or modified, how it was understood and criticized by its competitors, and how it contributes to our understanding of crime today. The final chapter outlines the key concepts and sources of data in comparative criminology and assesses the merits of various cross-national generalizations about crime and crime rates.

We have avoided the common division in criminology textbooks between crime and corrections altogether by omitting the usual lengthy descriptions of the criminal justice system. Our focus in this book is not criminal justice but crime, and we have tried to discuss the complexity of the latter in the depth we believe it warrants. However, various aspects of social control (criminalization, labeling, police practices, comparative penal policies, and so on) naturally press their claims for attention, and we explore them here, especially when they affect the links between crime and structured social inequality.

## Chapter Previews and Chapter Reviews

Each chapter begins with a chapter preview of the main themes that follow. Included in the preview is a list of key terms that you should be especially aware of as you read the chapter. These terms are highlighted in the text and then followed immediately by a definition to help you understand them more easily. At the end of each chapter, a chapter review outlines the major points that have been discussed.

## Questions for Class Discussion and Suggestions for Further Study

Each chapter review is followed by several questions for classroom discussion. These questions are followed by a list of suggested readings that will be helpful for essays or term papers. Each of these suggested readings is then followed by several websites that offer additional information on specific crimes and theories.

## Websites

Because the Internet is an important source of information for criminology, we recommend that students explore the websites that we have listed at the end of each chapter. The use of these websites will allow students to expand and update their horizons somewhat beyond the information and analysis presented in any given chapter. For instance, if you are curious about recent data on workplace deaths and injuries, you can point your web browser to the site provided at the end of the chapter, search for the federal and state legislation governing workplace safety, and thereby begin to compile a report on the topic. Indeed, most government agencies maintain websites, and many activist organizations devote resources to their own websites.

## References and Glossary

After the main text, there is a comprehensive, alphabetical list of references cited in the book. In the body of the text, you will find the references cited in the following way: (Smith, 2005:21). This example begins with the last name of the author (Smith), then gives the year the material was published or written (2005), and ends with the page number of the citation (21). In the glossary, students will find brief definitions of all of the key terms used in the book.

## Acknowledgements

A book such as this inevitably incurs many debts. First and foremost, we thank our many students, who often forced us to clarify our ideas and who provided us with critical comments during our classroom presentations of the material.

Our colleagues in the Department of Criminology at the University of Southern Maine have contributed to various editions of the text, as has Rosemary Miller, the Department Administrative Assistant. Many colleagues at other institutions were kind enough to read portions of the manuscript. Their comments have undoubtedly turned it into a far better book than it otherwise would have been. In this regard, we would like to express our thanks to Kevin Bryant (Benedictine College), Suzette Cote (California State University-Sacramento), Joseph Franco (Pace University), Pamela Jenkins (University of New Orleans), Mark Mantyh (University of Wisconsin-Milwaukee), Ray Michalowski (Northern Arizona University), and David R. Simon (University of North Florida).

Finally, for their editorial skills and great patience we wish to thank the staff at Roxbury, especially Claude Teweles, Scott Carter, Jim Ballinger, Jackie Estrada, and Phong Ho. ✦

# About the Authors

**P**iers Beirne is Professor of Criminology and Legal Studies in the Criminology Department at the University of Southern Maine. He has also taught sociology and criminology in England, at the University of Wisconsin-Madison, and at the University of Connecticut-Storrs. His recent books include *Inventing Criminology* (1993), *Issues in Comparative Criminology* (1997, edited with David Nelken), and the forthcoming *Green Criminology* (coedited with Nigel South) and *Toward a Green Criminology* (coedited with Nigel South). His current research is in the area of nonhuman animal abuse.

**J**ames W. Messerschmidt is Professor of Sociology in the Criminology Department at the University of Southern Maine. His research interests focus on the interrelation of gender, race, class, sexuality, and crime. In addition to numerous articles and book chapters, he is the author of *The Trial of Leonard Peltier* (1983), *Capitalism, Patriarchy, and Crime: Toward a Socialist Feminist Criminology* (1986), *Masculinities and Crime: A Critique and Reconceptualization of Theory* (1993), *Crime as Structured Action: Gender, Race, Class, and Crime in the Making* (1997), *Nine Lives: Adolescent Masculinities, the Body, and Violence* (2000), and *Flesh and Blood: Adolescent Gender Diversity and Violence* (2004). Currently he is working on three research projects involving the sex-gender distinction and criminological theory, the gendered body and interpersonal violence, and global masculinities, political crime, and the state. ✦

# Part I

## Introduction to Criminology

# The Problem of Crime

## Preview

Chapter 1 introduces:

- The distorted images of crime projected by the mass media.

- How crime as a sociological problem differs from crime as a social problem.

- Three of the key concepts of criminology: "crime," "criminal law," and "criminalization."

- Various sociological definitions of crime, including crime as a violation of conduct norms, crime as social harm, crime as a violation of human rights, crime as a form of deviance, and crime as a violation of global conduct norms.

## Key Terms

| | |
|---|---|
| analogous social injury | globalization |
| conduct norms | global conduct norms |
| crime | human rights |
| criminalization | social control |
| criminal justice system | social harm |
| criminal law | social problem |
| deviance | sociological problem |
| fear of crime | the state |

## 1.1 Images of Crime

Our focus in this book is crime. What is crime? How much crime is there? How can we explain it? Even before reading this book, you probably have strong opinions about the causes of crime, its harmful effects, and how best to tackle it.

Let's start our journey into the study of crime with a brief discussion of how and why crime is viewed as a social problem.

### Crime as a Social Problem

Some of us have been directly affected by crime. Many others, because we are fearful of it, have been indirectly victimized by crime. Each of us already has a great store of knowledge about crime. We know, for example, that some areas of cities are not safe to walk in at night. We therefore avoid them. We go elsewhere, or we stay at home. We know that it is dangerous to leave infants unattended, front doors unbolted, cars unlocked, and bicycles unchained. We routinely process such knowledge, and we take defensive action accordingly. We know, or at least we think we know, what sorts of people are likely to commit crime. Each of us has an image of the typical criminal—perhaps a sick, degenerate, violent person who preys on the innocent and the vulnerable.

Crime exacts a high price on federal, state, and household budgets. According to the economist David Anderson (1999), the annual cost of crime in the United States is an astounding $1.7 trillion. This estimate includes crime-induced production, the opportunity costs of crime, the value of risks to life and health, and economic transfers (see Box 1.1). To put this figure in perspective, it is more than four times higher than the 2003 annual budget of the U.S. Defense Department. It represents a cost of $4,118 per person per year.

Partly because of its huge expense, and partly because of the fear that it produces, crime is regarded by the public as one of the leading social problems today. But what is a social problem? How is some social condition constructed as a social problem, by whom, and for what reasons? How and why is crime widely seen as a **social problem**?

We must stress that there is no objective set of social conditions whose harmful effects necessarily make them social problems. Something is a social problem only if it is perceived as such. What is regarded as a social problem thus varies over time. Child abuse, for example, has been seen as a full-blown problem only since the early 1960s (see Chapter 5.2). In some places and times marijuana use, prostitution, and gambling have been seen as social problems, even ones worthy of criminalization, yet in others the same social practices have been seen as private vices best regulated by individual morality rather than criminal law.

The perception of something as a social problem also varies from person to person and from one social group to another. For example, some people regard social inequality as a social problem; others see it as a virtue that encourages competition and economic responsibility. Some people regard the use of animals in laboratory experiments as a necessary step in the elimination of human diseases; others see it as unjustified abuse of our fellow creatures. And so on. Some social problems quickly capture public attention and remain as objects of national concern for a long time.

Several factors determine how a social problem is constructed and whether it is defined as a social problem in a particular society (Best, 2001). These factors include (1) the arguments, rhetoric, and power of claims makers and moral entrepreneurs, who may be as diverse as the U.S. Department of Justice, the pope, Pearl Jam, and the Reverend Jerry Falwell; (2) the pressure tactics of powerful private interest groups, such as the American Medical Association, the National Rifle Association, and Mothers Against Drunk Driving; and (3) the professional utterances of public officials such as politicians, judges, police and correctional officers, and, on occasion, those engaged in teaching, writing, and research in the social sciences, including criminology.

At least two additional factors are decisive in determining the meaning and seriousness of any given social problem. The first is the mass media. Successful claims makers are those who are able to use the mass media to broadcast their message that a certain

---

### Box 1.1  The Costs of Crime

1. **Crime-induced production.** The cost of goods and services that will not have to be produced in the absence of crime. It includes drug trafficking, police protection, corrections, judicial and legal services, DUI costs, etc.  $397 billion

2. **Opportunity cost.** The income that, in the absence of crime, criminals would be able to earn if employed in legitimate jobs. It also includes victims' lost workdays.  $130 billion

3. **The value of risks to life and health.** Refers to the value of lost life and the value of personal injuries.  $574 billion

4. **Transfers.** Criminals' costs, estimated as the value of the assets they receive through crime. Transfers include occupational fraud, unpaid taxes, health insurance fraud, business fraud, motor vehicle theft, shoplifting, household burglaries and larcenies, personal thefts, and robbery.  $603 billion

**Total annual gross cost of crime**  **$1,705 billion**

Source: Adapted from Anderson, 1999:611–642.

problem needs attention and amelioration. We will have much more to say about the images of crime in the mass media in the next few pages. The second factor is fear. Many of us fear crime. In our conversations with family and friends, on TV, and in our worst nightmares, our images of crime as a serious social problem are constantly fueled by our **fear of crime**. Given that our fear of it is seldom based on careful reflection, crime is a difficult phenomenon to explain. Let us therefore delve into the origins of the culture of fear that surrounds crime.

## Crime and the Culture of Fear

Nearly four decades ago, the National Commission on the Causes and Prevention of Violence made the following bleak predictions about the quality of life in large cities in the near future (1970:38–39):

High-rise apartment buildings and residential compounds protected by private guards and security devices will be fortified cells for upper-middle and high-income populations living at prime locations in the city.

Suburban neighborhoods, geographically far removed from the central city, will be protected mainly by economic homogeneity and by distance from population groups with the highest propensities to commit crimes.

Lacking a sharp change in federal and state policies, ownership of guns will be almost universal in the suburbs, homes will be fortified by an array of devices from window grills to electronic surveillance equipment, armed citizen volunteers in cars will supplement inadequate police patrols in neighborhoods closer to the central city, and extreme left-wing and right-wing groups will have tremendous armories of weapons that could be brought into play without any provocation.

High-speed, patrolled expressways will be sanitized corridors connecting safe areas, and private automobiles, taxicabs, and commercial vehicles will be equipped routinely with unbreakable glass, light armor, and other security features. Inside garages or valet parking will be available at safe buildings in or near the central city. Armed guards will ride shotgun on all forms of public transportation.

Streets and residential neighborhoods in the central city will be unsafe in differing degrees, and the ghetto slum neighborhoods will be places of terror with widespread crime, perhaps entirely out of police control during nighttime hours. Armed guards will protect all public facilities such as schools, libraries, and playgrounds in these areas.

Between the unsafe, deteriorating central city on the one hand and the network of safe, prosperous areas and sanitized corridors on the other, there will be, not unnaturally, intensifying hatred and deepening division. Violence will increase further, and the defensive response of the affluent will become still more elaborate.

Because of our great fear of crime, the Commission warned, we are in danger of closeting ourselves in anticrime fortresses. To a certain extent the Commission's terrifying images of life in large cities have not been contradicted, at least not in the minds of a fearful public. Both before and after September 11, 2001, the United States seems to have become a society whose increasing fears about crime, including its cost, reach into almost every corner of public and private life. Candidates for political office routinely campaign on the promise of restoring law and order to the nation's streets and of waging war against terrorism worldwide. Woe betide the politician who is perceived as "soft" on crime! Get-tough-on-crime rhetoric on the campaign trail and in Congress has led to a mass of new federal and state anticrime legislation, prominent examples of which include "three strikes" laws and minimum-sentence legislation. Nowadays, too, the government fights "wars" on crime—the war on drugs, for example, and wars on gangs, pornography, and terrorism. The prison population therefore expands year after year. In 2004, there were more than 2 million prisoners in the United States—more prisoners and at a higher rate than ever before in this country, and more than anywhere else on earth.

Despite the punitiveness of criminal justice in the United States or, as we will see later (Chapter 15.4), perhaps in part because of it, there is a widespread feeling that crime and violence are rapidly spinning out of control and that they are mostly unaffected by new anticrime legislation. Community crime watch programs, police-citizen action committees, and groups like the Guardian Angels have prospered across the country. Private video surveillance systems (CCTV), which were created in the 1970s to assist in road traffic management, have been rapidly extended to the workplace, city streets, stores, and sports stadiums. Whether these systems deter crime or, instead, increase fear of crime, is a matter of some debate (e.g., Ditton, 2000). The new "homeland security" legislation enacted after September 11, such as the U.S.A. Patriot Act and the Port and Maritime Security Act, have extended government surveillance to public transport and the approaches to many public buildings, including government offices and courts, airports, bus and train stations, ports and ferry terminals. Whether these policies will make the citizenry feel more secure, or simply more anxious, has not yet been determined (e.g., Simon, 2002).

According to opinion polls and victimization surveys, after September 11 members of the public transferred their highest level of fear from the violence of street crime to the violence of terrorism (e.g., Gallup, 2004). Thereafter, these two fears have been closely followed by concerns about unemployment, war, and health care. The list of crimes and criminals that the public fears is a lengthy one indeed. To this list must be added another—namely, our deep-seated, daily anxieties about environmental risks and hazards, about the dangers posed by technology's destructive effects on planet Earth, on humans, and on animals (Hollway and Jefferson, 1997; Hier, 2003).

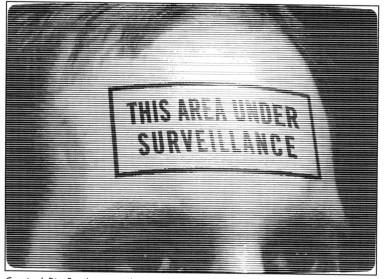

*Caution! Big Brother may be watching you. Protection of civil rights versus the need for national security is an intense debate in the post-September 11 world.*

Public fear of violent criminal acts is quite wide ranging and conjures up numerous images. Among these are terrorism, gang violence, carjackings, random muggings, road rage, "going postal," razor blades in Halloween cookies, drive-by shootings, child kidnappings, police brutality, plane crashes, and mutant microbes (Glassner, 1999). These acts are committed by killer kids, black males, Internet predators, pedophile priests, child pornographers, gun-toting madmen, crazed druggies, and serial murderers. Moreover, opinion polls today regularly show that about half of the public believes that crime rates continue to rise in the United States. (Ironically, as we will see in this book, they have been falling for more than a decade.)

What is the source of fear of crime? This is a complicated question, not the least because research has not devoted enough attention to exactly what "fear" of crime is and how often and how intensely it is felt (Lee, 2001; Farrall and Gadd, 2004). Fear of crime has numerous sources. Although criminologists may debate whether fear of crime accurately reflects the likelihood of victimization, it must be said that fear of crime stems partly from "American exceptionalism." This exceptionalism is the simple fact that crimes of violence, especially homicide, occur at a much higher rate in the United States than they do in other technologically developed societies (see Chapter 2.3 and Chapter 15).

Besides its problematic relationship with crime itself, including the cost of crime, fear of crime also derives from several other factors, both sociological and psychological. Research consistently shows that the relatively powerless sections of the community experience the greatest fear of crime and suffer the greatest psychological trauma from its effects (e.g., Stanko, 2000; and see Chapter 5.2). These relatively powerless groups are those with the least economic, political, and cultural assets. They include the elderly, females, and racial minorities. The elderly and youth are generally more fearful of crime than the middle-aged. Minorities are generally more fearful of crime than whites. Both males and females are most fearful of physical violence (Lane and Meeker, 2003b).

Fear of crime is therefore associated with one's position in society—with one's gender, for example, and with one's age, race, social class, and education. It also derives from people's lived experiences gained from where they reside and where they work, from their conversations with their family and their friends, and from the mass media.

Above all, it is through the self-interested and often distorted lenses of the mass media that most of us, most of the time, acquire our dominant images of crime. Mass media include TV and newspapers, in particular, but also the Internet, radio, advertising, movies, and videos. The mass media provide us with a certain knowledge of crime and, simultaneously, they generate fear of crime.

Media researchers have tended to assume that media images of crime are rather flat in their effects, affecting most people in the same way and with the same degree of intensity. This assumption is in the process of being undermined by new research on the relationship between audience characteristics and the content of the media's images of crime. Clearly, different social groups are affected differently by the everyday images of crime that they view in the mass media. Individuals differ in the specific crimes they fear. Three studies that have examined the link between audience characteristics and fear of crime are:

- Eschholz's (2002) study of TV content and TV audiences in a Southern state found that, overall, individuals who watched more TV were more fearful of crime. But when the audience was analyzed by race, this relationship was found to apply mostly to minorities, including African Americans, Hispanics, and Asians. Whites' levels of fear of crime rose, moreover, in proportion to the presence of minority offenders depicted on TV.

- Eschholz, Chiricos, and Gertz's (2003) research on TV viewers in Leon County, Florida, found that the strongest relationships between local news programs and tabloid TV programs, on the one hand, and fear of crime on the other, is found among those who perceive themselves to be living in a neighborhood with 25 percent or more black residents in it.

- In a study of residents in Orange County, California, Lane and Meeker (2003a) have found that whites, who rely more on newspapers for their crime news, have less fear of crime than Latinos, who rely more on TV for their crime news. They suggest that people probably fear crime more if the news story is about crime in their neighborhood, because their perceived risk of crime increases.

There is a triangular relationship among fear of crime, crime itself, and the images of crime constructed by the media. One of criminology's most important tasks is to examine the relationships in this triangle. If we experience heightened fear of crime, the quality of our lives is significantly reduced. If much of our fear of crime comes from the mass media's images of crime, we need to explore those images and try to determine whether they reflect or distort the nature and seriousness of crime in our lives. In short, fear of crime may be as costly as crime itself. Understanding the dimensions of a problem is of course a key first step in trying to solve it in an informed way.

## Crime in the Mass Media

Let us now provide a little more focus on the stereotypical images of crime routinely conveyed by the mass media. How much crime is portrayed in the media? How accurately do media portrayals of crime reflect the incidence of crime in real life?

We should not be too surprised to learn that the mass media's images of crime are almost never objective. After all, the mass media depend for their financial existence on reporting—or creating—the apparently unusual. When social life is routine and orderly, there is little news. Media executives know full well that nothing sells to advertisers quite so well as violence. To maximize their audience, the media feature unusual events rather than representative events. They emphasize the sensational rather than the mundane. The media's portrayal of violence feeds directly into viewers' fear of crime.

Reflect for a moment on how much crime is represented in the mass media, especially in print media and on TV. Though in the next chapter we directly examine how much crime there is in the United States, we should stress right away that neither the amount of crime nor the distribution of different types of crime depicted in newspapers and on TV bears much resemblance to what is reported in official crime data such as the FBI's Uniform Crime Reports (see Chapter 2.1). Yet it is chiefly from these two media that we acquire knowledge of what is newsworthy.

First, the mass media create the false image of a society with an enormous amount of violent crime, especially of murder, but also of assault and armed robbery. Indeed, from the 1940s to the present, the percentage of total TV program time devoted to crime-related shows has persistently increased; however, according to official crime data, the violent crime rate fell sharply in the 1980s and 1990s (see Chapter 2.1). Crime and justice topics occupy as much as 25 percent of all newspaper news space (Surette, 1998). Although in real life murders are only a tiny fraction of all serious crimes, the media researcher Doris Graber (1980; Heath and Gilbert, 1996) has found that it consumes 26.2 percent of all crime news reported in the *Chicago Tribune*. Moreover, whereas nonviolent crimes such as theft compose 47 percent of all crimes reported to the police, such crimes constitute only 4 percent of all crime items in newspapers (Graber, 1980; and see Chapter 2.1).

When media researchers have examined bias in what the media considers newsworthy, most of their attention has been directed to TV. It is well documented that a high percentage of stories in the evening and late-night local news programs concerns crime, as do their lead stories. Moreover, crime and justice topics occupy 10–13 percent of all national TV news and 20 percent of local TV news (Surette, 1998).

It has also been documented that 33 percent of total TV program time in the United States is devoted to crime or law-enforcement shows, with a concentration at prime time (Graber, 1980; Reiner, 2002). Among the numerous popular prime-time crime TV shows are *The Shield, CSI, Cold Case, Third Watch, The Sopranos, NYPD Blue, Law & Order,* and *Without a Trace.* Many topical TV shows also regularly concern crime, as do such documentary shows as *Unsolved Mysteries, 48 Hours, 60 Minutes,* and *Dateline.* New "reality-based" shows—some featuring talk-show interaction among police officers or even audience participation—include *Cops, World's Scariest Police Videos,* and *America's Most Wanted.*

Nearly all such prime-time crime shows have violent crime as their chief subject matter. According to a violence index used by researcher George Gerbner from 1967 to 1987, approximately 80 percent of all TV programs contain violence (Liebert and Sprafkin, 1988). In addition, at least 90 percent of children's cartoon shows contain violence. Although Gerbner's definition of violence may seem overly broad (it includes violence in humorous situations, for example), the fact remains that violence, however defined, is the staple of the crime-related TV diet. It has even been calculated that by the time they are 18 years old, children will have seen 200,000 acts of violence on TV, including 40,000 murders (Huston, Fairchild, and Donnerstein, 1992). In the news, as well, there is a strong bias toward coverage of murder, sexual crimes, and other forms of violence, often coupled with drug abuse (Surette, 1998; Welch, Fenwick, and Roberts, 1998).

Second, some types of violence are more likely to be reported in the mass media than others, often depending on the identity of offenders or victims. For example, in Chicago's two daily newspapers the homicides most likely to be reported are those occurring in middle-class neighborhoods; the least likely to be reported are those with African-American victims (Johnstone, Hawkins, and Michener, 1994; and see Beckett and Sasson, 2004). Another study examined the newspaper coverage of homicide between 1986 and 1994 in Houston, Texas, and found that black and Hispanic victims were the least likely to be mentioned (Paulsen, 2003). Similarly, of the homicides that were reported in national newspapers in England and Wales from 1993 to 1996, newspapers were quite selective about which murders they choose to cover (Peelo, Francis, Soothill, Pearson, and Ackerley, 2004). Those most likely to be reported were sexual homicides, homicides involving a clear motive for monetary gain or revenge, motiveless homicides, and those involving young children, though not infanticides. The homicides least likely to be reported were those involving marginalized groups, such as those of persons of color.

Besides bias in the actual content of media coverage of newsworthy events, bias is also seen in important news events that are not reported by the media. In general, white-collar crimes are the crimes least likely to be reported on TV (Ericson, Baranek, and Chan, 1991; Chermak, 1994). In a study of 878 chemical spills reported to the Environmental Protection Agency in Hillsborough County, Florida, between 1987 and 1997, Lynch, Stretesky, and Hammond (2000) found that only 9 (or 1.5 percent) were newsworthy enough to gain coverage in the county's largest newspaper, the *Tampa Tribune*. It was also found that this low frequency reflected the public's own low concern with environmental and corporate crimes such as environmental pollution and the dumping of hazardous waste (which can, of course, be every bit as deadly as street crime).

Sometimes, when the media accurately depict the volume of violent crime, they distort its seriousness. For example, one study has found that 84 percent of prime-time TV shows contain at least one episode of sexual harassment, which perhaps accurately reflects the commonplace nature of this violent crime (Grauerholz and King, 1997). But the depiction of sexual harassment in the media tends to reflect several myths, including the view that it is not a serious offense and that its victims can often remedy the situation themselves (pp. 142–143). Another study shows that *Time* and *Newsweek* cover stories misrepresent the problem of crime as primarily a problem of urban African Americans (Barlow, 1998).

Occasionally, the mass media will channel viewer attention toward particular sorts of immoral or criminal behavior. These episodic processes are known by criminologists as "moral panics" (Cohen, 1972 [1980]; Chapter 13.2). Well-documented examples of moral panics that are fueled and fanned by the media include the white slavers of the Progressive Era (c. 1890–1910), sex fiends in the 1940s, communists in the 1950s, serial murderers during the 1980s, youth crime and juvenile gangs in the 1990s, pedophile priests and illegal immigrants in the new millennium, and the ever-present druggie. It is unclear why moral panics arise when and as they do. But it is nevertheless true that every so often a society becomes engrossed in a process of public frenzy directed to certain forms of crime and deviance.

The media's distorted images of crime do not, of course, teach us much about the true nature of crime. To learn about this we must obtain a clearer idea of what crime actually is. In other words, we need a working definition of "crime."

## 1.2 Crime, Criminal Law, and Criminalization

The question "What is crime?" is a surprisingly difficult one to answer. Consider, for example, the events discussed in the book *Captain Kidd and the War Against the Pirates* (Ritchie, 1986).

During the early 1690s the soon-to-be-infamous Captain William Kidd was an obscure naval pirate who was based in New York and who operated in the Caribbean. In 1695 he obtained a commission as a privateer, which allowed him to engage essentially in the same piratical activities, but this time with the economic support and moral blessings of the king and of some of the most powerful families in England. Kidd's commission directed him to sail to the Indian Ocean and to end the practices of pirates from the North American colonies who were plundering British East India Company ships. For attacking and capturing one or more pirate ships and bringing some pirates to trial, Kidd, as well as the king and all the backers of the scheme, would earn a handsome profit.

But for doing roughly what he had been commissioned to do, Kidd did not earn the fame and fortune to which he believed he was legally entitled. In 1701, in London, Kidd was tried on charges of murder and multiple conspiracies, convicted after a farcical trial, sentenced to death by hanging, and—after a false start when the hangman's rope broke and the unfortunate Kidd lay stunned on the ground—he was duly executed. During his trial and execution—a dramatic time when convicts were expected to repent their sins, beg the indulgence of the Lord, and warn the many onlookers not to tread in their sinful footsteps—Kidd protested his innocence.

Kidd had been caught in the complicated and rapidly changing web of maritime trade and British imperialism of the late seventeenth century. Although there was little evidence that he had engaged in (illegal) piracy rather than (legal) privateering—and therefore British authorities had no proper reason to prosecute him—Kidd's activities in the Red Sea against the French and against the Dutch East India Company ensnared him in a larger movement that would find him a convenient symbol for a much broader problem, even though Kidd was never very successful either as a pirate or as a privateer.

Kidd was squeezed by the coincidence of two forces. On the one hand were thriving British companies such as the East India Company that needed order and regularity on the high seas for the profitable expansion of their commerce. On the other hand were the administrative and military apparatuses of the British state that, after tremendous expansion as a result of various European wars, could not tolerate maverick and unpredictable challenges to their power. Privateering, or legalized piracy, was therefore doomed. Kidd's activities as a privateer commissioned by royalty and by the rich were suddenly renamed piracy.

This story is a good example of how difficult it is to pinpoint the precise nature of crime. Clearly, Kidd's actions were defined as piracy rather than national heroics largely because of the changing fortunes of British imperialism. It is also clear that nothing in the nature of Kidd's actions was inherently criminal.

What, then, is crime? As a historical phenomenon, the concept of crime is of fairly recent origin. Prior to the eighteenth century, both in western Europe and in colonial North America, most offenses—when not handled privately—were typically the domain of either canon law (religious law) or civil law (especially the law of torts). Criminal law did not yet exist. Moreover, what constitutes crime varies from one culture to another. Thus, anthropologists have been unable to find any behavior that is universally defined as crime (see Chapter 15.3). For example, although all known societies have a concept of murder, societies differ in how they define the act of murder. Given such variation, it is nearly impossible for criminologists to agree either on a precise definition of crime or even on the definition of an act as seemingly simple to define as murder. Many sociologists and historians suggest that there is nothing in the nature of any behavior that makes it inherently criminal, because even what counts as crime changes over time within the same culture (see Chapter 7.3).

How, then, should crime be defined? Serious debate among criminologists about the proper definition of crime can be traced to the publication of a report initiated in 1933 by New York's oddly named Bureau of Social Hygiene (Michael and Adler, 1971). Written by lawyer Jerome Michael and philosopher Mortimer Adler, this report stressed that great confusion will arise unless criminologists can agree on a precise definition of crime. Only if crime is defined clearly and precisely can we distinguish criminal behavior from noncriminal behavior:

> The most precise and least ambiguous definition of crime is that which defines it as behavior which is prohibited by the criminal code. It follows that a criminal is a person who has behaved in some way prohibited by the criminal law. (pp. 2–3)

Agreeing with Michael and Adler's argument, Paul Tappan claimed that **crime** is an intentional act in violation of the criminal law (statutory and case law), committed without defense or excuse, and penalized by the state as a felony or misdemeanor (Tappan, 1947:100). In this view, therefore, crime is a legalistic category of behavior. Let us examine some of the major aspects of the legalistic definition of crime.

## Crime as a Legal Category

The preceding legalistic definition of crime contains several elements whose formal origins can be traced to the English common law (customary law) of the twelfth century. First and foremost, a crime must be forbidden by criminal law. So, too, criminal law must provide punishment for a crime—a basic principle expressed in the English common law doctrine *nullum crimen sine lege, nulla poena sine lege* (no crime without law, no punishment without law). The formal purpose of **criminal law** is to protect members of the public from the wrongdoing of others. Rules of criminal law can be found either in statutory law (enacted by legislatures) or in common law (judge-made decisions and opinions based on the principle known as *stare decisis*). Criminal law is distinguished from civil law—such as tort law and contract law—which deals with private wrongs. Whereas a violation of civil law leaves a defendant open to civil suit, a violation of criminal law potentially places a defendant at the point of entry into the **criminal justice system.**

The criminal law categorizes crime in two ways. First, crimes are either *mala in se* or *mala prohibita*. This old and somewhat artificial distinction refers to the apparent differences between "acts that are evil in themselves" (*mala in se*) and "acts that are merely prohibited" (*mala prohibita*). Lawyers take this distinction to mean that crimes *mala in se* are acts so inherently wrong that they are universally considered evil, whereas crimes *mala prohibita*, the list of which changes over time, are acts prohibited by statute. Second, the criminal law distinguishes between felonies and misdemeanors. Although these two categories of crime are often separated by procedural differences, the most important difference is that felonies are punishable either by death or by imprisonment in a state penitentiary for a term of not less than one year, whereas misdemeanors are punishable either by fine or by a term in a local jail of less than one year.

A second element of a crime is that it must be a voluntary illegal act or omission (an *actus reus,* some examples of which are given in Chapter 2 [Figure 2.1]). This means that no one can be prosecuted for bad or evil thoughts—although words (such as incitement to riot) can sometimes constitute a criminal act—and that failure to act (omission) can be criminal in situations where there is a legal duty to act. Leaving the scene of a traffic accident and failing to file an annual tax return with the Internal Revenue Service are examples of crimes by omission.

Culpability for a crime depends on a defendant's mental state, variously known as criminal intent or *mens rea.* According to the American Law Institute's Model Penal Code (§2.02), someone is not guilty of an offense unless he or she acted with purpose to do the forbidden act, or with knowledge of the nature of the act, or with recklessness or negligence. In some cases intent can be transferred, as, for example, when A intends to shoot B but misses and kills C.

To legal scholars, the precise meaning of the term "intent" is often quite elusive. For example, certain categories of individuals are judged legally incapable of forming intent: juveniles under the age of 14 and those certified as insane or severely retarded. Moreover, in cases of strict liability, intent is not a necessary requirement of guilt. Examples of strict liability offenses include felony murder (a murder committed during a serious felony such as rape or arson) and statutory rape (sexual intercourse with a juvenile, which usually means under age 16).

An act or omission is not a crime if a defendant has a socially legitimate justification for doing it or if the person lacks the criminal responsibility required by the element of mens rea. The defense of justification can be raised in three instances: duress, necessity, and duty. The defense of *duress* is typically limited to homicides. Thus, a killing may be justified if an individual reasonably believes that he or she is about to be killed or seriously harmed by another. The defense of *necessity* is available to defendants who are somehow threatened by natural circumstances over which they have no control, but this defense can be used only when there was no other reasonable course of action available. For example, one would not be guilty of vandalism if, trapped inside a burning department store, one smashed a window in order to escape. The defense of *duty* is typically raised by public authorities such as police officers. Many killings by police officers in the line of duty are therefore termed "justifiable homicides."

Finally, an act or omission may not be a crime if one lacks the necessary criminal responsibility, a condition that negates mens rea in several ways and that includes the controversial pleas of entrapment and insanity. The defense of *entrapment* is intended to discourage the state from creating a crime where none would otherwise have existed. According to the Model Penal Code (§2.13), entrapment occurs when police methods entice an average law-abiding citizen to commit a crime. The defense of *insanity* differs from all other defenses in that, if the plea is successful, in most jurisdictions the defendant is neither acquitted nor released but found "not guilty by reason of insanity." In some states defendants may be found "guilty but mentally ill," in which case they are confined to mental institutions until "cured," at which point they must finish their sentences in prison. This verdict almost always results in the commitment of defendants to mental institutions, often for a longer period than if they had been found guilty of the crime and sentenced to prison. In the United States the majority of states base the legal criteria of insanity on the definition contained in the Model Penal Code (§4.01):

1. A person is not responsible for criminal conduct if at the time of such conduct, as a result of mental disease or defect, he lacks substantial capacity to appreciate the criminality (wrongfulness) of his conduct, or to conform his conduct to the requirements of law.

2. The terms "mental disease" or "defect" do not include an abnormality manifested only by repeated criminal or otherwise antisocial conduct.

A key element of the legalistic definition of crime—*mens rea*—is based on the assumption that crime is behavior engaged in by individuals who are capable of exercising free will. As you progress through Part Two (Types of Crime) and Part Three (Criminological Theory) of this book, you will learn that such an assumption cannot be used to explain crime. Rather, we will suggest that the actions of individuals are, in varying degrees, influenced by their position in society.

At this point we would do well to ask, Why it is that for most nonsociological purposes crime is usually defined as behavior that violates criminal law? To put this question another way: Why is it that criminal law usually defines criminal behavior? As soon as we ask (dangerously circular) questions such as these, we should realize that criminology cannot be confined to the study of criminal behavior because the concept of criminal behavior depends for its meaning on the concept of criminal law.

A few introductory words about the role of criminal law in the process of criminalization are now appropriate.

## Law and State

Sociologically, the ideas and institutions of law vary greatly from one culture to another. Negatively, this means that law is not necessarily what some lawmakers or zealots claim it to be. Law is not an earthly expression of the will of God. It may not represent the interests of "the people." It has no necessary connection with justice. Law is above all else a social phenomenon created by members of society under specific historical conditions. Law has not always existed in the past. It might not exist in the future.

The great bulk of research in sociology and anthropology reveals that law originated with the emergence of social inequality and, specifically, that it accompanies the transition from stateless societies to state societies. Law has not always existed, because not all human societies have been characterized by social inequality. Indeed, until approximately 10,000 years ago, hunting and gathering societies were the dominant form of social organization, and these societies had egalitarian social, economic, and political relations. In these small-scale societies (about 50 members), property was communally owned, there were no social classes, and there was no organized state or societal ruler. Even in horticultural societies, which emerged after hunting and gathering societies, social relations were highly egalitarian, significant differences in wealth and power did not occur, and leaders typically had no coercive powers over others. Neither in hunting and gathering societies nor in horticultural societies did states exist, and a common morality was maintained by the authority of custom rather than by the rule of law (Diamond, 1973). Within these stateless societies, offenses and conflicts were managed informally in a variety of nonlegal ways such as self-help, avoidance, negotiation, settlement by a third party, and tolerance (Black, 1989; and see Durkheim's analysis in Chapter 10.2).

Not until the development of agricultural societies—in which economic productivity was expanded by new techniques such as the plow, fertilization, and irrigation—did class inequalities become prevalent. Increased productivity permitted new lifestyles that were not devoted solely to economic survival and subsistence. In some agricultural societies—such as in classical Greece—class relations developed in which slaves did most of the productive labor and slave owners dominated and appropriated the economic surplus. In other agricultural societies—such as those of medieval Europe—peasants made up most of the population, but the monarch, the nobles, and the church owned most of the land, which they obtained through military might and conquest. In both slave and feudal agricultural societies, a particular class controlled and appropriated the economic surplus, creating significant social inequalities.

An important feature of agricultural societies was the rise of states and legal systems. The **state** may be defined as the central political institution of a given society. Its major apparatuses are the government (legislative and executive), the legal system, the military, and a variety of public bureaucracies for the collection of taxes, the management of public health, the maintenance of law and order, and so on. The legal system is both a state apparatus and, through its constitutional and administrative branches, the chief mechanism for defining the sphere of state activities.

Rules of law have a variety of sources, such as superstition, divine oracles, religion, prophecy, charismatic leadership, court cases, and legislatures. Law differs from other rules of behavior—habit, convention, tradition, and custom—by its coercive nature and by the professional enforcement of its codes. Law's coercive nature can be expressed in shame, ridicule, censure, ostracism, imprisonment, torture, terror, and death. Law's professional interpreters and enforcers can comprise witches and wizards, kings and queens, popes and rabbis, village elders, chiefs, prophets, military warlords, federal judges, and state legislators, among others.

As a social phenomenon, law is a state form of **social control.** As such, its object is to manufacture conformity and to suppress what the state defines as deviance. In his classic book *The Behavior of Law,* Donald Black (1976:2) defined law as governmental social control and suggested that there are four basic styles of law, each corresponding to a broader style of social control: penal, compensatory, therapeutic, and conciliatory (p. 46). Each style defines deviant behavior in its own way, with its own logic, methods, and language.

In the penal style of social control, for example, the problem is to establish guilt when an offender has violated a prohibition, and the solution is punishment. Black argues that both the quantity and the style of law in a given society vary inversely with certain factors, such as the power of other forms of social control and the levels of social inequality. When other forms of social control—family ties, religion, and so on—are weak, for example, the power and the extent of law will be relatively strong (Black, 1976). Moreover, following the lengthy conflict tradition in the sociology and anthropology of law (see Chapter 13.3), Black argues that law varies directly with social inequality. That is, the societies with the most law are those with the most social inequality.

Many criminologists argue that the relationship between social inequality and crime is especially evident in the process of criminalization. We turn now to this important concept.

## Law and Criminalization

The term **criminalization** refers to the process whereby criminal law is selectively applied to social behavior. This threefold process involves (1) the enactment of legislation that outlaws certain types of behavior; (2) the surveillance and policing of that behavior; and (3) if detected, the punishment of that behavior. The study of criminalization is therefore an indispensable part of the study of crime, and in this book we offer frequent examples of this process.

The nature and contours of the criminalization process in Western industrialized societies is heatedly debated by criminologists. Argument rages over three wide-ranging questions. First, how did the criminalization process contribute to the rise of Western industrialized societies when they first emerged during the seventeenth century? Second, is criminalization today a neutral process, or does it generally serve the interests of the powerful? Third, does criminalization contribute to the maintenance of specific forms of contemporary social inequality?

The answers to these questions fall at or in between two extremes. One extreme claims that since its inception on a large scale (during the eighteenth century), the criminalization process has on the whole contributed to the rise of modern society in rational and humane ways. The other extreme suggests that criminalization has operated, in more or less subtle ways, as an instrument to defend the interests of powerful new social classes (for example, the capitalist class) and to undermine the interests of the powerless.

Our general view of criminalization, and thus also of criminal law itself, is that it tends to reflect the interests of the powerful. We will therefore often look at the ways in which the criminalization process tends to maintain unequal social relationships between the powerful and the powerless—especially in the areas of gender, class, race, and age. Sometimes, criminalization is a direct product of power struggles and inevitably reflects the political strengths of specific power groups. At other times, however, it is connected to power struggles only marginally. At still other times, it appears to transcend power struggles altogether.

## 1.3 Crime as a Sociological Problem

Neither the misleading images of crime manufactured by the mass media nor the definition of crime as a legal category can depict the complex social realities of crime. The purpose of criminology is to chip away at stereotypical or value-laden images of crime and then to try to explain what remains.

The academic discipline of criminology has a lengthy intellectual history. As we outline in Chapter 9, the origins of criminology can be traced to the rise of the classical (1760–1820) and the positivist (1820–1890) schools of thought, both of which, in certain key respects, flourish today. The term "criminology" derives from the Latin word *crimen*, meaning "judgment," "accusation," or "offense." Though the word "criminologist" appeared in Britain in the 1850s, "criminology" itself was first used to define the academic study of crime by the Italian sociologist Raffaele Garofalo in 1885. Establishing itself as a respectable academic discipline in the United States around 1900, criminology has since become an interdisciplinary field. Although most criminologists today are drawn from sociology, other academic disciplines are also well represented, including political science, law, economics, history, anthropology, psychology, biology, and geography.

We now explore five definitions of crime that are favored by sociological perspectives on crime:

1. Crime as a violation of conduct norms.

2. Crime as a social harm and analogous social injury.

3. Crime as a violation of rights.

4. Crime as a form of deviance.

5. Crime as a violation of global conduct norms.

## Crime as a Violation of Conduct Norms

In his influential book *Culture Conflict and Crime* (1938), Thorsten Sellin complained that "criminology as traditionally conceived is a bastard science grown out of public preoccupation with a plague" (p. 3). Sellin believed that it is unscientific for criminologists to study simply what the public happens to regard as a plague or as a social problem. Scientists should study objective facts as they occur in their natural states rather than as they are seen by the subjective concerns of the public, the government, powerful social groups, and the criminal law. As Sellin stated:

> The unqualified acceptance of the legal definitions of the basic units or elements of criminological inquiry violates a fundamental criterion of science. The scientist must have freedom to define his own terms, based on the intrinsic character of his material and designating properties in that material which are assumed to be universal. (p. 23)

Sellin urged that the basic units of criminological research be **conduct norms.** For every person there are normal (right) and abnormal (wrong) forms of conduct—and the norm depends on the social values of the group that formulates it. Such norms are the rules that govern appropriate behavior. Sellin insisted that there are different types of conduct norms, including custom, tradition, ethics, religion, and rules of criminal law. Conduct norms are found wherever social groups are found. They are not created by any one normative group, they are not confined within political boundaries, and they are not necessarily embodied in law. Sellin concluded therefore that a scientific criminology should focus on the violation of all forms of conduct norms and on the study of abnormal conduct in general. Crime is but one form of conduct norm, distinguished from others in that it violates the conduct norms specifically defined by the criminal law.

Sellin's rejection of the legalistic definition of crime and his advice about the proper subject matter of criminology are quite attractive. Clearly, criminologists would be foolish to limit their studies simply to what the criminal law happens to forbid. Imagine, for example, how hard it would be to study trends in the crime of marijuana use in a state where marijuana was constantly criminalized and decriminalized according to the changing whims of legislative and public opinion.

Sellin's advice has yet to exert much influence among criminologists, partly because they would be overwhelmed if they studied violations of all forms of conduct norms. However, Sellin's recommendation moves us to ask a question of much relevance to criminological research: Why are violations of one particular form of conduct regarded as crime and not others?

## Crime as Social Harm and Analogous Social Injury

A direct outgrowth of this debate about an appropriate definition of crime is Edwin Sutherland's position, voiced in his book *White Collar Crime* (1949). Sutherland was angry that many white-collar offenses were processed as civil violations rather than as crimes. He argued:

> The essential characteristic of crime is that it is behavior which is prohibited by the State as an injury to the State and against which the State may react, at least as a last resort, by punishment. The two abstract criteria generally regarded by legal scholars as necessary elements in a definition of crime are legal description of an act as socially harmful and legal provision of a penalty for the act. (1983:46)

To Sutherland it is unfair that white-collar offenders—for example, those found in civil suits to have violated regulatory laws such as the Sherman Antitrust Act or to have engaged in deceptive advertising—are not stigmatized as criminals. The behavior of white-collar offenders meets the two characteristics of his definition of crime: Their behavior is socially harmful, and they are punished for it (by fines). Because white-collar "offenses" are in fact crimes (however such behavior is defined by the state), they should be studied by criminologists. Although Sutherland's perspective on white-collar offenses has had great influence in criminology (see Chapters 11.4 and 7), his perspective is not opposed to the legalistic definition of crime. Rather, he suggests the use of an expanded definition of crime based on behavior prohibited by either criminal law or regulatory law.

Whereas Sutherland argues that any illegalities that cause **social harm** should be criminalized, others urge that any behavior should be criminalized if it causes social harm or analogous social injury. For Raymond Michalowski, for example, the concept of **analogous social injury** refers to "legally permissible acts or sets of conditions whose consequences are similar to those of illegal acts" (1985:317; and see Tifft and Sullivan, 2001). This extension of Sutherland's position has far-reaching implications. Under this view, crimes might include any violent or untimely death; illness or disease; deprivation of adequate food, clothing, shelter, or medical care; and the reduction or elimination of the opportunity for individuals to participate effectively in the political decision-making processes that affect their lives.

Consider some examples of injurious events that are not generally regarded as crimes by any legal system but that would be crimes if analogous social injury were the criterion of wrongful behavior:

- It is estimated that 4.83 million premature deaths in the world were attributable to smoking in the year 2000 (Ezzati and Lopez, 2003).

- Each year in the United States more than 200,000 citizens are injured or killed because of negligence by doctors (Jesilow, Pontell, and Geis, 1993).

- Each year approximately 6,000 workers are killed in job-related accidents in the United States, as many as 100,000 die because of exposure to dangerous substances, at least 10 million suffered injuries at work (at least 3 million of which are serious), and 390,000 workers contract new cases of job-related diseases (U.S. Department of Labor, 2004b; and see Chapter 7.2).

Expanded definitions of crime that include both social harm and analogous social injury are therefore fitting correctives to the biased values underlying the legalistic definition of crime. Of course, these expanded definitions leave themselves open to the objection that what counts as social harm or as analogous social injury is as value-laden a category as criminal law.

## Crime as a Violation of Rights

To some criminologists, crime is any behavior that violates **human rights**. In this view, simply because we are human beings we all have certain natural and inalienable rights. These include the rights to life, liberty, happiness, and so on. Violations of these rights, the argument continues, provide criminology with a more objective unit of analysis than does the legalistic definition of crime.

On this page are two depictions taken from the hundreds of photos and videos taken at the Abu Ghraib prison in late 2003. They depict American troops abusing Iraqis held at what was once a notorious center of torture and executions under toppled President Saddam Hussein. They show U.S. troops smiling, posing, laughing, or giving the thumbs-up sign as naked male Iraqi prisoners are stacked in a pyramid or positioned to simulate sex acts with one another. Calling for an independent inquiry, the human rights group Amnesty International said "there is a real crisis of leadership in Iraq with double standards and double speak on human rights" (Majendie, 2004).

A U.S. Army summary of deaths and mistreatment involving prisoners in American custody in Iraq and Afghanistan showed a widespread pattern of abuse from 2002 to 2004 (Jehl, Myers, and Schmitt, 2004).

Images of U.S. justice in Tehran, Iran.

The case that crime be defined in terms of human rights was first made by Herman and Julia Schwendinger (1975). For the Schwendingers there are two sorts of human rights: those personal rights that are absolutely essential to life (such as the right to good health) and those rights essential to a dignified human existence (freedom of movement, free speech, a good education, employment, the right to unionize, a certain standard of housing, and so on). The Schwendingers also argue that anything that causes a social injury should be considered a crime. Examples of social injury include imperialism, sexism, racism, and poverty. They suggest, too, that a government should be considered criminal if it does nothing to alleviate poverty.

To the importance of human rights in the definition of crime must be added the fact that humans frequently violate the rights of nonhuman animals to a natural and peaceable existence (Singer, 1990; Beirne, 1999). Since the middle of the nineteenth century, some animal rights have been recognized and secured both in state anticruelty laws and in federal legislation. Quite apart from the legal or illegal abuses routinely committed against them in factory farms, rodeos, circuses, zoos, and laboratories, animals are sometimes abused by humans in domestic households or in their wild or natural habitats. Violations of animal rights, we believe, are also harms that merit attention from criminologists (Chapter 4).

The suggestion that violations of rights should be the basis of criminology seems to offer criminology a less subjective definition of crime than the legalistic concept of crime. Moreover, the concept of rights opens up for analysis the obvious fact that legal categories themselves might sometimes be criminal—laws that detain people unjustly, that forbid freedom of speech, that limit opposition to political parties, and so on.

Let us point out, too, that a major difficulty for the human rights approach in criminology is that, as with the content of criminal law, the content of rights is culturally quite variable. In some societies human rights tend to be defined in individualistic terms—i.e., the rights of individuals to do certain things. In other societies human rights are defined in more social terms: the right to employment and to minimum standards of housing, health, and education. Given these differences of definition, it is hard to agree on which violations of what rights should constitute crime.

Moreover, though the last 50 years has seen a tremendous growth in human rights legislation (associated with the United Nations and the European Union, for example), many societies in the world reject the idea that human rights can or should be universal. In parts of Africa, the Middle East, Southeast Asia, and elsewhere, the attempt by outsiders to impose human rights is sometimes branded as just another form of imperialism. "Human rights imperialism!" is thus the angry chant of many members of Islamic countries against aid workers and foreign armies of occupation bent on implanting Western notions of democracy, governance, and the like.

## Crime and Deviance

Sociological theories of deviance have greatly influenced criminology. **Deviance** is any social behavior or social characteristic that departs from a society's conventional norms and standards and for which the deviant is sanctioned. Examples of deviant social behavior include witchcraft, bank robbery, picking one's nose in public, mental illness, and stuttering. Examples of deviant social characteristics are extremes of height and weight, aggressiveness, laziness, and beauty.

Several aspects of deviance shed light on the study of crime. Even from the few examples above, it is clear, first, that enormous variation exists in the practices and social characteristics regarded as deviant. What constitutes deviance varies from era to era and from society to society. What we call homosexuality, for example, was often regarded in classical Greece not as deviance but as a conforming social practice. Moreover, within the same society perceptions of deviance often vary by class, gender, race, and age. Second, deviance is commonplace. Each of us has committed a deviant act at one time or another. Some of us commit many deviant acts in the course of a single day! Third, all deviance is potentially subject to sanction. Deviant behavior can be subject to positive sanctions (such as winning a Nobel prize for promoting peace) or to negative sanctions (imprisonment for theft). Fourth, the norms and standards violated by deviant acts are quite diverse. They can originate in religion, custom, political belief, etiquette, fashion, and criminal law. Of course, not all deviant acts are criminal acts (and vice versa).

The deviance perspective implies that there is nothing in the nature of any act to identify it as deviant. Rather, deviance is in the eye of the beholder. This implication raises several important sociological questions for the study of crime. Although we explore these questions in greater depth later (Chapter 13.2), some should be mentioned now:

1. Who defines behavior as deviant? How? Why?

2. Why are some deviant practices defined as criminal but not others?

3. What are the consequences for an individual whose deviant behavior is subject to sanction?

## Crime, Globalization, and Global Conduct Norms

In several of the chapters that follow, we will discuss the extraordinary influence of globalization on crime, whose general importance to criminology has only recently begun to be understood (e.g., Findlay, 1999; Barak, 2001; Loader and Sparks, 2002). **Globalization** refers to the worldwide process whereby individuals, peoples, economies, and nation-states are becoming increasingly interconnected and interdependent. The driving engine of globalization is the movement of capital, credit, and cash that occurs as multinational corporations search for profit in the ever-expanding and seemingly infinite global economic market.

The rise of globalization has been facilitated by numerous factors—some large, some small, some arising from above, some from below. Perhaps the most important geopolitical factor in the rise of globalization is the end of the Cold War, which was marked around 1990 by both the collapse of communism in Eastern Europe and the political, economic, and military dominance of the United States and its allies.

An essential part of globalization's redrafting of political and geographical space is that the world seems much smaller. The sense that a global village is in the making has been greatly encouraged by new methods of communication, including CNN and other live-TV coverage of international events and crises, the Internet, and e-mail. Because of the growth of these mass media, it is much easier to see that what goes on in one part of the world often has ripple effects around the globe.

One obvious consequence of the globalizing process is crime. Crime is an integral part of the new global network because globalization promotes a host of new opportunities for crime. We will discuss the influence of globalization on crime, and vice versa, later in the book in our discussions of the commerce in illicit drugs; the traffic in women, children, and endangered species; the exploitation of cheap labor; the destruction of the environment; syndicated crime; white-collar crimes, including crimes involving electronic transfers of capital and credit; and political crimes, such as corruption and terrorism.

Consider September 11, 2001, as an example of how globalization affects crime. People of numerous nationalities were killed by the planes that were deliberately crashed into the World Trade Center, the Pentagon, and a field in Pennsylvania. They were killed on U.S. soil by terrorists of several nationalities, who were praised by their supporters as "Jihadists" or "liberation fighters" and who believed that this sort of action was their only effective recourse to U.S. foreign policies toward the Arab world, especially its interventions in the Israeli-Palestinian conflict. Thus, the catastrophic events of September 11th can only be fully understood by understanding events halfway around the world from the United States. So, too, the War on Terror is a global phenomenon fraught with difficulties of international cooperation, blurring of national boundaries, and ambiguities in the detection, detention, and prosecution of terrorists. Its battlefields are in the United States, Western Europe, the Middle East, Africa, and Southeast Asia.

Globalization has also been accompanied by the emergence of **global conduct norms** about certain sorts of serious crime. These are rules of conduct, agreed on by the international community, that allow for prosecution of certain coercive relationships between a state and its citizenry and between one state and another (Greer and Hagan, 2001; Passas, 2003). While these conduct norms are not yet truly global in their acceptance, with the growth of international criminal law since the end of World War II, they are certainly moving in that direction. This movement began in 1945–46 with the trial of leading Nazis in the Nuremberg war trials and the creation of the United Nations, and it was consolidated when nearly 100 nations ratified the powers of the International Criminal Court (ICC) as enacted in the Treaty of Rome of 2002. The ICC has jurisdiction over very serious international crimes, such as genocide, crimes against humanity, and war crimes. Those who are responsible for such crimes are now more likely to be held accountable for them.

Violations of global conduct norms will undoubtedly be embraced by criminology, and they will be written into its agenda. Perhaps the development of global conduct norms will provide a counterweight to the rise of ethnic politics and to atrocities committed in the name of racial, ethnic, and religious purity. But in a world where political borders and territorial integrity become ever more blurred, and where international organizations are still in such a rudimentary stage, it is unclear how global and normal global conduct norms will become. Will they be stamped "Made in the U.S.A."? Will they be genuinely democratic?

## Assessment

This book views crime as a **sociological problem,** and it surveys the various sociological approaches to crime that we term criminology. To focus on crime as a sociological problem is to explain how patterns of crime arise from the interplay of political, economic, social, and ideological forces. We do not therefore look at those explanations of crime that reduce its causes to the level of the individual. In pure form, examples of such reductionism are found, for example, in biological explanations of crime that emphasize the links between criminality and the physical constitution of the individual, as well as in psychological explanations that focus on the links between crime and such factors as defective character, loose morals, and so on.

Our chief task here is to understand crime as a sociological problem. Yet, we have already seen that criminologists disagree about the most suitable sociological definition of crime. This disagreement stems partly, we believe, from a mistaken search for a universal definition of crime that can be applied to all cultures, places, and times.

We hold to no fixed or dogmatic position concerning the definition of crime. Sometimes we agree with the way in which criminal law defines crime; at other times we simply question its adequacy. Occasionally we prefer and use other definitions of crime. For example, because we believe that nonhuman animals have the right to be considered "beings" or "persons," we consider animal abuse to be among the crimes of interpersonal violence (Chapter 5). In Chapter 5.1–5.2 we also point out that many women are victimized every year by the act of forcible rape, as it is defined by criminal law; but we also acknowledge that the traditional criminal law definition of rape—sexual intercourse obtained through the threat or actual use of physical violence—ignores acts that could be defined as rape, such as forms of nonphysical sexual coercion (for example, the male who informs his economically dependent mate: "If you don't put out, I'll leave you!").

In Chapter 7.2 we go considerably beyond the legalistic definition of crime (including both criminal and regulatory law), arguing that *corporate crime* is any illegal or socially injurious act of intent or indifference that occurs for the purpose of furthering corporate goals and that physically or economically abuses individuals in the United States or abroad. Finally, our definition of *political crime* (see Chapter 8) is somewhat broader than the legalistic definition, in that it includes not only crimes committed against the state but also crimes committed by the state. In the latter we include both domestic political crimes (unlawful or unethical acts committed by state officials and state agencies inside the United States) and international political crimes (violations of domestic and international law by state officials and agencies outside the United States).

## Review

This chapter introduced the different images of crime found in the discourses of social-problem movements, the culture of fear, the mass media, and sociology. The major task of the chapter was to introduce key sociological concepts of criminology.

## Images of Crime

1. Crime has become one of the leading social problems in the United States. But there is no objective set of social conditions whose perceived harmful effects necessarily make them social problems. What is regarded as a social problem varies over time and across cultures. What is defined as a social problem depends on numerous factors, including the activities of moral entrepreneurs.

2. There is a widespread culture of fear in the United States, and mass media undoubtedly contribute to fear of crime.

3. Mass media have become the most influential mechanisms for organizing public sentiment so that a certain social condition is perceived as a social problem.

4. Mass media routinely provide distorted information about the amount of crime, the most common types of crime, and who typically commits crimes.

## Crime, Criminal Law, and Criminalization

1. The term *criminalization* refers to the process whereby criminal law is selectively applied to social behavior. The sociological study of criminal law is therefore an integral part of criminology. Specifically, the criminalization process involves the enactment of legislation that outlaws certain types of behavior. It also provides for the surveillance, policing, and, if detected, punishment of that behavior.

2. Criminal law distinguishes between crimes *mala in se* and *mala prohibita* and between felonies and misdemeanors. To constitute a crime, behavior must be prohibited by law, must be voluntary, and must coincide with a defendant's mental state. An act or omission is not a crime if a defendant is justified in doing (or not doing) it, or if the person lacks the criminal responsibility required by *mens rea*.

3. Not all societies have had law. Law originated with the emergence of social inequality and accompanied the transition from stateless to state societies. The distinguishing features of law are its coercive nature, its reliance on a professional staff, and its use as a state form of social control.

4. In this book, the general view of the criminalization process, and thus also of criminal law, is that it tends to reflect the interests of the powerful (in terms of class, gender, race, and age).

## Crime as a Sociological Problem

1. This book views crime as a sociological problem. It surveys the various sociological approaches to crime found in the discipline of criminology. To focus on crime as a sociological problem is to explain how patterns of crime arise from the interplay of political, economic, social, and ideological forces in society.

2. The question "What is crime?" is difficult to answer because there is little agreement about the defining sociological characteristics of crime. Criminologists use a variety of sociological definitions of crime, including crime as a violation of

conduct norms, crime as a social harm, crime as a violation of human rights, crime as a form of deviance, and crime as a violation of global conduct norms.

## Questions for Class Discussion

1. Consider the facts in the following short story about cannibalism among a group of cave (speluncean) explorers caught in a life-threatening situation in the Commonwealth of "Newgarth." The story is adapted from a fictitious law case created by legal philosopher Lon Fuller (1949, excerpted in Schur, 1968:19–20). Although "The Case of the Speluncean Explorers" is fictitious, it is probably based on an actual case of cannibalism at sea in 1884 and on the bizarre trial that resulted from it in England.

### The Case of the Speluncean Explorers

Five members of an amateur cave-exploring society were trapped inside a deep and isolated cave following a landslide. After some time, through the efforts of relatives and the cave-exploring society, rescuers located the cave only to encounter repeated obstacles to removing the trapped men. At great monetary expense and the cost of ten rescuers' lives (in a subsequent landslide), the rescue operation finally succeeded thirty-two days after the men entered the cave. On the twentieth day, communication between the rescuers and the trapped explorers had been established, when it was discovered that the latter had with them in the cave a radio transmitter-receiver. At that time, the trapped men asked for medical advice as to whether they could live without food (there was none in the cave) for the time engineers had determined would be required to rescue them. A physicians' committee at the rescue site stated that they could not. When the trapped men later inquired if they could survive by consuming the flesh of one of their number, the reply (reluctant) was in the affirmative. But the explorers could get no guidance at all (from the physicians or from any clergyman or judge) when they went on to ask about the advisability of casting lots to determine who should be killed and eaten.

When the men were finally released, the rescuers learned that on the twenty-third day one of them, Whetmore, had been killed and eaten by the other four. Although originally it had been Whetmore's idea (at first resisted by his companions) that such an act might be necessary for survival, and also that a casting of lots would be the fairest means of selection, just before the dice were cast, Whetmore changed his mind. His companions disallowed this sudden switch, however, and cast the dice for him, after obtaining his agreement that this procedure was fair; he lost and was put to death and eaten by the others.

After they had recuperated, the four survivors were charged with Whetmore's murder.

Having read the facts in "The Case of the Speluncean Explorers," you should also know that Newgarth law commands, "Whoever shall willfully take the life of another shall be punished by death." In this case the defendants were charged with the crime of murder, convicted, and sentenced to death.

Assume that the defendants appealed the verdict and the sentence in "The Case of the Speluncean Explorers," and that you are a member of the appeals court. How would you decide the appeal? Are the defendants guilty of murder? What defense is available to them, if any? If their conviction in the lower court is upheld, would you recommend executive clemency (a pardon)?

2. It is estimated that each year nearly 5 million premature deaths in the world are attributable to smoking (Ezzati and Lopez, 2003). Do you think tobacco manufacturers and distributors should be held legally liable for these deaths? Should relatives of the deceased be allowed to sue them for damages? Should cigarette producers be prosecuted for murder?

3. According to criminologist Ray Surette (1998:68), "Criminals tend to be of two types in the news media: violent predators or professional businessmen and bureaucrats. Furthermore . . . they tend to be slightly older (20 to 30 years old) than reflected in official arrest statistics." How would you interpret such evidence?

## For Further Study

### Readings

Henry, Stuart, and Mark M. Lanier. 2001. *What Is Crime?* Lanham, MD: Rowman and Littlefield.

Jewkes, Yvonne. 2004. *Media and Crime.* London: Sage.

Vold, George B., Thomas J. Bernard, and Jeffrey B. Snipes. 2002. *Theoretical Criminology.* New York: Oxford University Press.

### Websites

1. <http://www.journalism.org>. This site is sponsored by the Project for Excellence in Journalism and the Committee of Concerned Journalists and is affiliated with the Columbia University Graduate School of Journalism. It reports results from a national study on local TV news programs and identifies the "bad habits" (or "six ways stations undercut their stories") of TV news broadcasting.

2. <http://www.law.cornell.edu/topics/state_statutes.html>. This useful site provides links to each state's laws, including criminal codes and procedures, and rules of evidence.

3. <http://www.amnesty.org>. This site for Amnesty International includes a general statement about the organization: its history, mission, and current activities. You may want to click on some of Amnesty's campaigns, including:

   • Stop violence against women.
   • Control arms.

- Death penalty.
- Stop torture.
- Refugees have rights.
- International justice.
- Economic globalization and human rights.
- Human rights defenders in Latin America and the Caribbean.
- Child soldiers.
- Treaty bodies.
- Human rights education.
- Health Professional Network.

4. <http://www.iccnow.org>. This is the website of the Coalition for the International Criminal Court, a network of over 2,000 nongovernmental organizations advocating for a fair, effective, and independent International Criminal Court (ICC). ✦

# The Measurement of Crime

**2.1 Caution: Data Do Not Speak for Themselves!**

**2.2 Official Crime Data**
- Police-Based Data: Uniform Crime Reports (UCR)
- Police-Based Data: National Incident-Based Reporting System (NIBRS)
- Evaluation of the UCR
- Victimization Data: National Crime Victimization Survey (NCVS)
- Evaluation of the NCVS
- Federal Data on White-Collar Crime, Corporate Crime, and Internet Fraud

**2.3 Unofficial Crime Data**
- Self-Report Data
- Life-Course Data
- Life-History Data
- Criminal Biographies
- Observation Research and Participant Observation Research
- Comparative and Historical Research

## Preview

Chapter 2 introduces:

- The major sources of official crime data.

- The major sources of unofficial crime data.

- The idea that crime data do not have a factual, objective existence independent of concepts about crime.

## Key Terms

| | |
|---|---|
| comparative criminology | criminal biographies |
| crime rate | historical data |

life-course data
life-history studies
methodology
official crime data
participant observation

positivist criminology
self-reports
unofficial crime data
victimization surveys

Chapter 2 outlines the major sources of crime data; precisely what such data tell us about specific types of crime is outlined in later chapters (Chapters 4–8).

Criminologists often distinguish between official crime data and unofficial crime data. **Official crime data** are those collected by the government and by government agencies, such as the Federal Bureau of Investigation (FBI) and the Department of Justice. **Unofficial crime data** are the nongovernmental data usually collected by private or independent agencies and researchers. Thus, the sources and types of unofficial crime data are quite varied. In distinguishing between official and unofficial sources of crime data, we do not imply that one data source is in principle better than another—although in practice this is often the case. Rather, official and unofficial crime data typically construct crime differently.

The majority of crime data are presented in the form of statistics. The term *statistics* derives from the mid-seventeenth-century English term "state-istics," which referred to state data about births, marriages, and deaths. Because contemporary statistical data are so extensively used for social purposes, we tend to be lulled into thinking that they represent objective facts. However, neither statistics nor data nor facts can ever be entirely free of the biases inherent in how they are constructed. The implications of this crucial point will soon become clear.

## 2.1 Caution: Data Do Not Speak for Themselves!

In the following pages we describe the major sources of data for studying crime today. But before we describe these types of data we must discuss how they are influenced by concepts and theories.

In the early nineteenth century, when official crime data were first systematically recorded, positivist criminologists such as Adolphe Quetelet believed that crime could be observed directly by using the procedures of the natural sciences (see Chapter 9.2). In this view, crime—like rocks, plants, and insects—exists in a natural state independent of the concepts and the theories of the criminologist. **Positivist criminology** is based on the idea that the collection of data about human beings follows the same scientific procedures as the collection of data in the natural sciences. This view, however, greatly distorts the process of scientific investigation. Why this is so can be understood by an analogy with astronomy.

Suppose that two astronomers are examining the surface of the moon through a telescope. Suppose also that one of the astronomers is peering into her telescope in the year 1500 (pre-Copernicus) and the other in the year 1900 (post-Copernicus). Would the two astronomers see the same thing? It can be argued that both astronomers would see the same image projected by the moon: a roundish, bright, yellowish object in the sky.

But beyond the optico-chemical level of sensory perception, would our two astronomers really "see" the same image? The answer is probably "no." The astronomers would see lunar data in terms of (1) their respective concepts of "the moon," of "optics," and so on, and (2) their theories of planetary motion. The early-sixteenth-century astronomer would see a roundish, bright, yellowish object that moves in orbit around the Earth. The twentieth-century astronomer, relying on modern theories of astronomy, would see a roundish, bright, yellowish object that not only moves in orbit around the Earth but that has a certain alignment with the Earth and the sun. The astronomers' perceptions of lunar images, in other words, would be structured by their respective astronomical concepts and theories.

This example demonstrates that data are not objective facts that exist independently of the concepts and theories of those who observe them. Data do not speak for themselves!

Let us apply this heavenly insight to the world of crime. When studying crime, it would be wrong to believe that we can simply observe, measure, and collect the facts and nothing but the facts about crime. We do not—indeed cannot—collect facts about crime through direct observation. What constitutes a fact about crime depends on our concepts and theories of crime. Crime data, like all other data, are structured by concepts and theories. What count as crime data are therefore very much open to debate.

In Chapter 1.2, we noted that the recognition of certain behavioral data (such as killing someone) as crime depends on whichever concept of crime is accepted as authoritative. According to the legalistic concept of crime, for example, murder is limited to those killings that are contrary to rules of criminal law. Thus, if a police officer kills someone, the killing is not murder, according to criminal law, if it is reasonable under the circumstances and if it occurs in the lawful execution of police duties. Another concept of crime, such as human rights (a concept that is itself quite culturally variable), yields very different crime data. Thus, to some proponents of human rights, murder might also include negligent surgery, workers' deaths caused by an employer's neglect of safety conditions, smoking-related deaths resulting from the commercial activities of tobacco companies, and the like.

## 2.2 Official Crime Data

The publication of national crime statistics was pioneered in France in 1827 (see Chapter 9.2). A century later, in 1927, a committee on Uniform Crime Records was set up in the United States. In 1930, after some bureaucratic wrangling between the FBI and the Bureau of the Census, 400 cities representing 20 million inhabitants in 43 states began to participate in the FBI's Uniform Crime Reports (or UCR) program.

The UCR, which has been published under congressional mandate each year since 1930, is popularly regarded as the most reliable set of crime data in the United States. Our task now is to examine what the UCR measures and then to assess its reliability.

### Police-Based Data: Uniform Crime Reports (UCR)

The UCR is compiled each year in Washington, D.C., by FBI statisticians. The FBI receives data from crime reports submitted voluntarily by more than 17,000 city, county, state, tribal and federal law enforcement agencies. In 2003 these agencies had jurisdiction over more than 260 million U.S. inhabitants, or 93 percent of the total population. The coverage is 94 percent in large cities and 90 percent in rural areas.

The meaning of much UCR data hinges on a distinction drawn by the FBI between Part I and Part II crimes. The UCR provides diverse statistical information about eight Part I crimes, which the FBI regards as the most serious: murder and nonnegligent manslaughter, forcible rape, robbery, aggravated assault, burglary, larceny-theft, motor vehicle theft, and arson (see Figure 2.1 for definitions of these offenses). It provides much less information about the 21 Part II crimes, which include simple assault; forgery and counterfeiting; fraud; embezzlement; buying, receiving, and possessing stolen

---

**Figure 2.1   Uniform Crime Reports—Part I Crime Definitions**

- **Murder and Nonnegligent Manslaughter:** The willfull (nonnegligent) killing of one human being by another.

- **Forcible Rape:** The carnal knowledge of a female forcibly and against her will. (Attempts are included, but statutory rape [without force] and other sex offenses are not.)

- **Robbery:** The taking of or attempting to take anything of value from the care, custody, or control of a person or persons by force or by threat of force or violence and/or by putting the victim in fear.

- **Aggravated Assault:** The unlawful attack by one person upon another for the purpose of inflicting severe or aggravated bodily injury. (This type of assault is usually accompanied by the use of a weapon, and it includes attempts.)

- **Burglary:** The unlawful entry of a structure to commit a felony or theft. (Three subdivisions include forcible entry, unlawful entry where no force is used, and attempted forcible entry.)

- **Larceny-theft:** The unlawful taking, carrying, leading, or riding away of property from the possession or constructive possession of another. (Included are shoplifting, pocket-picking, purse-snatching, thefts from motor vehicles, thefts or motor vehicle parts and accessories, bicycle thefts, and so forth, in which no force. violence, or fraud occurs.)

- **Motor Vehicle Theft:** The theft or attempted theft of a motor vehicle. (Included are the stealing of automobiles, trucks, buses, motorcycles, motorscooters, and snowmobiles.)

- **Arson:** Any willful burning or malicious burning or attempt to burn, with or without intent to defraud, a dwelling house, public building, motor vehicle or aircraft, personal property of another. . . . (Excluded are fires of suspicious or unknown origin.)

Source: Federal Bureau of Investigation, 1998, adapted from pp. 15–64.

property; carrying and possessing weapons; prostitution and commercialized vice; sex offenses (except forcible rape and prostitution); drug abuse violations; gambling; offenses against family and children; driving under the influence; liquor law offenses; drunkenness; disorderly conduct; vagrancy; all other offenses (except traffic); suspicion; curfew and loitering law violations; and runaway persons under age 18. The UCR also presents data on hate crimes, including the number of hate crime offenses and their motivation.

In addition to the FBI's view that Part I crimes are more serious than Part II crimes (a subject to which we return in a moment), UCR crime data are distinguished by their source. Data about Part I crimes derive from information that comes to the attention of police departments provided by victims of crime and other members of the public. Part II crime data are limited to cases involving actual police arrests.

The UCR focuses primarily on trends of the Part I crimes. In this regard the UCR tabulates:

1. The number of offenses.

2. The offense rate per 100,000 population.

3. The percentage change from the previous year.

4. The offense rate by region (for example, South, North, Northeast, Midwest).

5. The nature of the offense (age, gender, and race of offenders and victims).

6. The arrest (or clearance) rates for the offense.

The UCR displays the following data: relative frequency of Part I crimes; changes in the number and in the rate of violent crime (see Figure 2.2) and of property crime (see Figure 2.3); and the respective crime rates of the four regions—Northeast, Midwest, South and West (see Figure 2.4), of individual states, and of cities and towns of varying size. In addition, the UCR provides data about arrest trends by state, city, and suburban and rural areas, as well as about police employment by region, state, cities, suburban and rural counties, and universities and colleges.

Now that we have introduced the concept, and because of its importance, let us pause briefly to explain exactly what is meant by a **crime rate.** To understand this concept, let us talk in terms of "percentages" and "rates." A percentage is simply a proportion (or "rate"), a number per 100 (*centum* is Latin for 100).

A basic reason for using percentages is that they give us a feel for proportion. This feel is actually an implicit comparison with other known proportions. For instance, how are we to interpret the results of a survey reporting that 2,000 persons in California and 500 persons in Maine are afraid of crime? Does this mean that persons in California are four times more fearful of crime than persons in Maine? Answering this latter question requires a common scale—a proportion or rate of those surveyed. A percentage is the most commonly used scale to establish the rate of people in both states who report that they are afraid of crime. Thus, 90 percent translates easily into nine of ten. But when we want to know something such as the prevalence of crime relative to the population, the rate is extremely low.

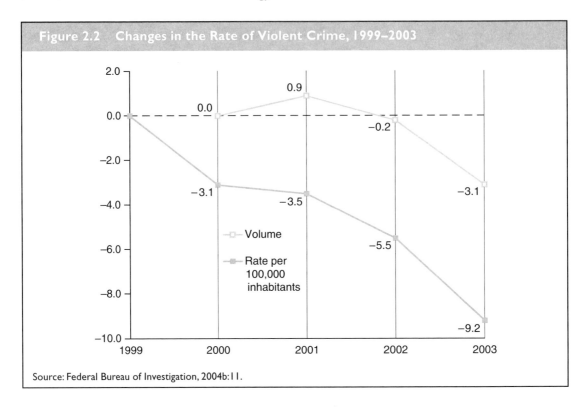

Figure 2.2   Changes in the Rate of Violent Crime, 1999–2003

Source: Federal Bureau of Investigation, 2004b:11.

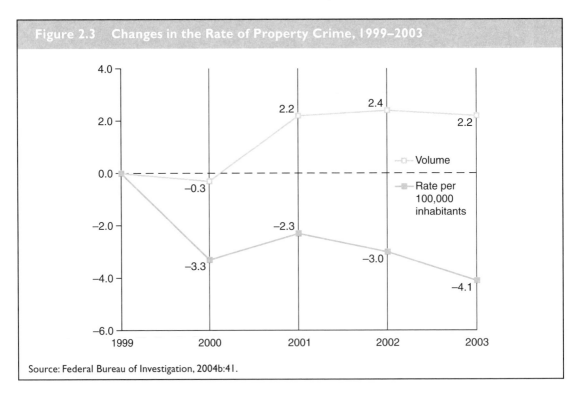

Figure 2.3   Changes in the Rate of Property Crime, 1999–2003

Source: Federal Bureau of Investigation, 2004b:41.

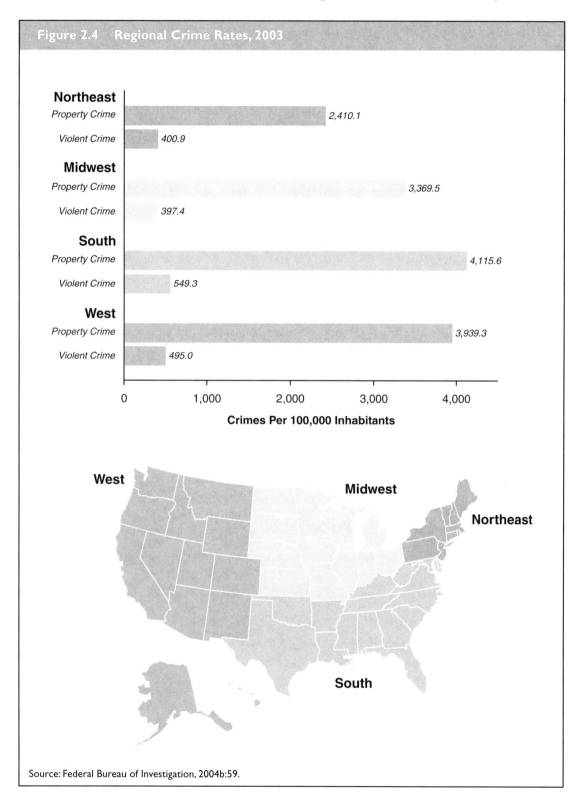

**Figure 2.4    Regional Crime Rates, 2003**

**Northeast**
- *Property Crime* — 2,410.1
- *Violent Crime* — 400.9

**Midwest**
- *Property Crime* — 3,369.5
- *Violent Crime* — 397.4

**South**
- *Property Crime* — 4,115.6
- *Violent Crime* — 549.3

**West**
- *Property Crime* — 3,939.3
- *Violent Crime* — 495.0

**Crimes Per 100,000 Inhabitants**

West    Midwest    Northeast    South

Source: Federal Bureau of Investigation, 2004b:59.

This concept can be illustrated with the following example in the UCR. In Figure 2.5 you can see the number of murders and also the murder rates per 100,000 inhabitants reported in the UCR for 2002 and 2003, when the population was an estimated 290,809,777. Given that the number of murders in 2003 was 16,503, the murder rate per 100,000 population was 5.7. This murder rate for 2003 is calculated as follows:

$$\frac{16,503 \; x \; 100,000}{290,809,777} = 5.7$$

Moreover, if the murder rate in 2003 was 5.7, and if in 2002 it was 5.6, then there was an increase of 0.1 murders per 100,000 inhabitants between 2002 and 2003. Thus, the murder rate in 2003 was 1.7 percent higher than the 2002 rate (although still 36.7 percent lower than the rate recorded for 1994).

Before examining the actual reliability of the crime data provided by the UCR, we emphasize how important the UCR program is as a source of crime data. In the words of the FBI itself:

The Program's primary objective is to generate reliable information for use in law enforcement administration, operation, and management; however, its data have over the years become one of the country's leading social indicators. The American

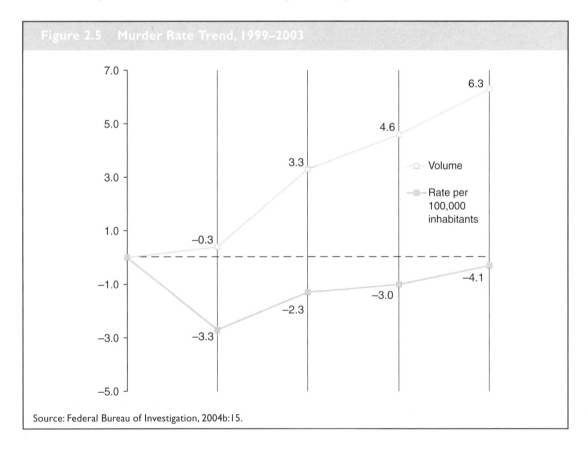

**Figure 2.5    Murder Rate Trend, 1999–2003**

Source: Federal Bureau of Investigation, 2004b:15.

public looks to the Uniform Crime Reports for information on fluctuations in the level of crime, and criminologists, sociologists, legislators, municipal planners, the media, and other students of criminal justice use the statistics for varied research and planning purposes. (Federal Bureau of Investigation, 2004a:3)

---

**Box 2.1     Murder in the United States, 2003**

In 2003 the UCR recorded 16,503 murders—a rate of 5.7 murders per 100,000 population. Although the annual number and rate of murders have decreased since 1993, many of the patterns and characteristics of murder victims have remained about the same. According to UCR Supplementary Homicide Reports, in 2003:

- 90.6 percent of murder victims were adults.

- 77.5 percent were males.

- 90.1 percent of murderers were male, and 92 percent were over 18 years of age. 51.3 percent of murderers were black, 45.9 percent were white, and 2.8 percent were of other races.

- One in eight murder victims was under age 18.

- Whites accounted for 48.7 percent of murder victims, African Americans for 48.5 percent.

- Firearms were used in 70.9 percent of murder incidents.

- For those murders in which the victim-offender relationship was known (55.5 percent):
    - 22.4 percent of victims were murdered by strangers.
    - 77.6 percent of victims knew their assailants.
    - Among those cases where victims knew their assailants, 70.9 percent were acquainted with their assailants, 29.1 percent were killed by family members. Husbands and boyfriends murdered 32.3 percent of female victims; wives and girlfriends murdered 2.5 percent of male victims.

- The murder rate was highest in the South and lowest in the Northeast.

- The murder rate was higher in large cities than in smaller cities and rural areas.

Source: Adapted from Federal Bureau of Investigation, 2004b:15–25.

---

## Police-Based Data: National Incident-Based Reporting System (NIBRS)

Working with state and local law enforcement agencies, the FBI is developing a new supplementary reporting system. Known as the National Incident-Based Reporting System (NIBRS), it is a modified and far more detailed version of the traditional UCR (to be renamed the "Summary UCR"). Not yet fully operational, NIBRS is a computerized system whereby local agencies report data to the national UCR program on each single incident and arrest within 22 offense categories comprising 46 crimes (the 8 index offenses and 36 other crimes). These are known as Group A offenses (see Table 2.1). The NIBRS collects details about the time, date, place, and circumstances of the crime; information about offenders' and victims' age, gender, race, and relationship to each other; the presence of guns or drugs; details of property loss; and whether hate/bias motivation was involved.

Because the new NIBRS system records all crimes committed in a crime incident

| Table 2.1   NIBRS: Group A Offense Categories | |
| --- | --- |
| Arson | Homicide offenses |
| Assault offenses | Kidnapping/abduction |
| Bribery | Larceny/theft offenses |
| Burglary/breaking and entering | Motor vehicle theft |
| Counterfeiting/forgery | Pornography/obscene material |
| Destruction/damage/ vandalism of property | Prostitution offenses |
| Drug offenses | Robbery |
| Embezzlement | Sex offenses, forcible |
| Extortion/blackmail | Sex offenses, nonforcible |
| Fraud offenses | Stolen property offenses |
| Gambling offenses | Weapon law violation |

(and not just the most serious, as traditionally recorded in the UCR), one effect of NIBRS is slightly to raise the number of officially recorded crimes, perhaps by 1 percent (Bureau of Justice Statistics, 2000; FBI, 2004). The numerous new empirical data produced in the still-incomplete NIBRS have already had considerable effects in the new technology of crime mapping; (see Chapter 8.2) and in the development of the theory of routine activities and crime (Chapter 14.1).

## Evaluation of the UCR

Criminologists often debate the question of how well the UCR measures the crime rate. Answers to this question tend to be twofold. First, some critics claim that although the UCR does a commendable job of measuring the crime rate, it could do even better with more sophisticated or more sensitive "methodological" techniques. **Methodology** involves the techniques of measurement used to collect and manipulate empirical data. Two examples of methodological techniques are opinion polls and statistical analyses.

Second, other critics claim that because of various "conceptual" biases in its methodological techniques, the UCR does not and cannot measure "the crime rate" very accurately. A *concept* describes a property of an empirical datum or a relation among empirical data. A concept is usually a part of a *theory* that is used to generate hypotheses. The United States is an example of a concept; some of the properties of the concept of the United States are sovereignty, 50 states, part of North America, and so on.

There are numerous methodological criticisms of the UCR. Here are four of the most important ones:

1. An unknown, but probably massive, amount of crime goes unreported to the police and therefore never shows up in the UCR. This unknown component is often termed "the dark figure" of crime. Methodologically, as we shall see, the

size of the dark figure of crime can to a certain extent be estimated with the use of victimization surveys and self-report studies.

2. Because participation in the UCR program is voluntary, not all police departments send crime reports to the FBI. Consequently, the FBI attempts to estimate crime rates in such jurisdictions. It is, of course, difficult to assess the accuracy of their estimates.

3. The UCR does not include federal crimes (such as blackmail), an omission that tends to underestimate the crime rate.

4. In any single criminal event, only the most serious crime reported to the police is included in the UCR. This is known as the "hierarchy rule." For example, if an armed man breaks into a person's home (burglary or criminal trespass), forces a woman inside to engage in sexual intercourse with him (rape), kills her (murder), and escapes with some of her belongings (robbery), only the murder is reflected in the UCR. Arguably, this practice understates the volume of crime.

In addition to these methodological problems, the UCR is open to at least three major conceptual criticisms. First, the UCR records only legally defined categories of crime (see Chapter 1.2). It must be stressed that UCR categories are not scientific or objective categories—they reflect the biases enshrined in the rules of criminal law and in the values of legislatures and the judicial system. Given one's personal viewpoints, UCR's biases may be seen as good, bad, or neutral. But biases they undoubtedly are.

The ramifications of such biases are examined in greater detail in Section 2.3 of this chapter. But consider a simple example of UCR's vulnerability to this sort of criticism. If you believe crime is less a violation of law than a breach of human rights, the UCR does not and cannot measure what constitutes crime. Whether or not they are defined as such in criminal law, if sexism and racism are crimes, the UCR—which counts neither of these as crimes—does a poor job of measuring crime.

A second conceptual criticism of the UCR is that the composition of Part I crimes imparts a distorted image of the seriousness of crime. Recall that the Part I crimes include murder, rape, robbery, aggravated assault, burglary, larceny, motor vehicle theft, and arson. The FBI apparently counts these as Part I crimes because they occur in large numbers and because the public regards them as the most serious crimes. But these two reasons are rather flimsy. There is considerable agreement that murder, rape, robbery, aggravated assault, and arson are very serious crimes and that they should be recorded as such. But are all burglaries, larcenies, and motor vehicle thefts sufficiently serious to warrant inclusion in Part I? How is it that the theft of a bicycle (a larceny) is recorded as a serious crime but child abuse is not? Moreover, with the exception of larceny, the crimes recorded in the greatest numbers (for instance, fraud, drug abuse violations, driving under the influence) are actually Part II crimes.

The FBI is also often accused of omitting a variety of serious crimes from Part I. With the exception of arson, all Part I crimes are typically committed by members of relatively powerless sections of society. White-collar, corporate, and political crimes—which the public increasingly views as serious crimes—committed by members of the more powerful sections of society are given relatively little attention by the FBI. Why the FBI omits these latter crimes from the index is a matter of broad speculation, including:

1. The FBI recognizes the fact that crimes typically or exclusively committed by the powerful are difficult to detect, are often covered up, and are seldom reported to the police.

2. The FBI is insensitive to the plight of the powerless.

3. The FBI is politically biased in favor of the powerful.

The third conceptual criticism of the UCR takes several forms. However, most approaches cluster around an intriguing question: Does the UCR actually measure criminal behavior (whether defined in terms of legal categories or human rights) or, instead, the bureaucratic activities of official agencies such as the police and the FBI?

Countless factors influence how official crime data are socially constructed. Consider for a moment the situation of the police. Quite apart from a change in actual criminal behavior, official crime statistics can be altered by changes in police reporting procedures, by improved or faster technological assistance, by changes in relations between the police and the citizenry, by crusades against particular crimes, by an increase in the ratio of police officers to population, and even by simple manipulation of crime reports. On this last point, we must stress that all police agencies are faced with two contradictory pressures in the representation of their activities to the FBI, to the media, and to the public:

1. It is in the best interests of police departments to ensure that officially recorded crime rates are low, thereby suggesting that the police are successfully doing their job of fighting crime.

2. It is in the best interests of police departments to ensure that officially recorded crime rates are high, thereby allowing the police to ask for larger budgets and more personnel.

All police departments operate at some point between these two pressures. The precise situation of any given police department depends on many factors, including levels of criminal activity, the honesty of police chiefs, local and national politics, media crusades, and pressure from the public.

Some time ago, sociologists John Kitsuse and Aaron Cicourel (1963) suggested that criminologists should be concerned chiefly with how crime rates are constructed by official agencies. Rather than searching for some mythical crime rate independent of how it is socially constructed, criminologists should examine the bureaucratic practices of agencies that record crime. The starting point of criminology, their argument implies, is understanding the behavior of those who define, classify, and record certain behavior as crime (see Chapter 13.3).

If we apply this method to the process by which criminal behavior enters the UCR, we find that for a crime report to enter the UCR, at least five things must happen:

1. Someone must perceive an event or behavior as a crime.

2. The crime must somehow come to the attention of the police, either through police observation, which is rare, or through a report from a victim, a confession, or detective work.

3. The police must agree that a crime has occurred.

4. The police must code the crime on the proper UCR form and submit it to the FBI.

5. The FBI must include the crime in the UCR.

---

**Box 2.2   Manipulating the UCR**

"Senior police officials around the nation are concerned that the sharp drop in crime in recent years has produced pressure on police departments to show ever-decreasing crime statistics and might be behind incidents in several cities in which commanders have manipulated crime data.

"So far this year, there have been charges of falsely reporting crime statistics in Philadelphia, New York, Atlanta, and Boca Raton, Fla., resulting in the resignation or demotion of high-ranking police commanders.

"Experts say they believe these incidents do not mean that the nationwide drop in crime since 1992 is illusory. But they are beginning to question whether politicians seeking office, the news media and the public should attach so much importance to the annual, and sometimes monthly, release of the latest crime figures" (*New York Times*, August 3, 1998:A1).

---

Each of these events is subject to enormous social interpretation and negotiation. The facts in these events, in other words, do not speak for themselves; each event is socially constructed.

An excellent example of how crime rates may reflect official activity more than they reflect criminal behavior is provided by Philip Jenkins's (1988, 1994) controversial research on serial murder. Jenkins was initially puzzled by the substantial and well-publicized increase in the serial murder rate that apparently occurred between 1983 and 1985. According to Jenkins, it was the mass media that first presented the volume of serial murders in the United States as an "epidemic" unknown in other societies. This epidemic was often tied to the growth of the pornography industry, whose sexually explicit materials allegedly tended to arouse the aggressive nature of certain individuals who had been abused as children. Harrowing TV interviews with convicted serial killers— Ted Bundy, Edmund Kemper, and Henry Lee Lucas—added fuel to media fires. Jenkins quoted a Justice Department claim that as many as 4,000 Americans a year, half of them under the age of 18, are murdered by serial killers.

Jenkins suggests that although serial murder may well represent a growing and heinous menace to society, the mass media and Justice Department officials grossly inflated their estimates of the annual total of serial murders. According to Jenkins's analysis, serial killers account for no more than 350–400 murders each year.

How, then, is it possible to distort and exaggerate UCR homicide data? What motives prompt such distortions? Jenkins describes the bureaucratic process that makes homicide data especially susceptible to manipulation. Whenever a murder is committed, the police department of jurisdiction is required to complete a lengthy UCR report and submit it to the FBI. But the police must also

> submit a supplementary homicide report, addressing topics like characteristics of the victim and offender; weapon; relationship of victim to offender; circumstances surrounding death; and so on. "Offenders" can be single, multiple or unknown. At this early stage, the police might well know neither the offender, a motive, nor the exact circumstances of the death. All these would thus be recorded as unknown.
>
> Weeks or months later, the situation might well change, and the correct procedure would be for the department to submit a new report to amend the first. Here, though, there is enormous room for cutting corners. The death has been notified, and whether a further correction is submitted depends on many factors. A conscientious officer in a professional department with an efficient record system would very probably notify the reporting center that the murder was no longer "unsolved" or "motiveless," especially in an area where murder was a rare crime. Other officers in other departments might well feel that they have more important things to do than to submit a revised version of a form they have already completed. This would in fact represent a third form on a single case.
>
> The chance of follow-up information being supplied will depend on a number of factors: the frequency of murder in the community; the importance given to record-keeping by a particular chief or supervisor; the organizational structure of the department (for instance, whether records and data are the responsibility of a full-time unit or of an individual); and the professional standards of the department. The vast majority of departments are likely to record the simple fact of a murder being committed; only some will provide the results of subsequent investigations, though these are crucial to developing any kind of national statistical profile of American homicide. (Jenkins, 1988:4)

The result of this bureaucratic process is that for many cases of homicide, even though an offender and a motive were subsequently discovered, the FBI will have only a "motiveless/offender unknown" entry in its records. In 1966 the UCR recorded 11,000 murders in the United States; of these, 644 (5.9 percent) were "motiveless." In 1982 there were 23,000 murders, with 4,118 (17.8 percent) "motiveless." By 1984 the motiveless category had risen to 22 percent. As Jenkins described it, there was an alarming tendency on the part of the media and the Department of Justice to assume that all or most motiveless murders were the work of serial killers.

Why would the Justice Department continue with this fabrication? Jenkins opposes the idea of a conspiracy, with the Justice Department seen as responsible for creating the illusion of an epidemic of serial murders. Nevertheless, he claims, the serial murder "epidemic" served certain organizational goals of the Justice Department. Although some FBI officials placed the number of serial murders at several hundred rather than several thousand, the latter figure was never properly contradicted by the FBI. Why not? According to Jenkins (1988), the serial murder "epidemic" was used as a justification for a new Violent Criminal Apprehension Program (VICAP) at a new proposed

National Center for the Analysis of Violent Crime at the FBI Academy in Quantico, Virginia.

Jenkins' account of this transformation of "unsolved" homicide data into data about serial murders is a wonderful example of the way in which crime data are socially constructed. Of equal interest, and perhaps even more compelling, are the ways in which crime data are routinely constructed by the public and the police.

In this respect, consider the findings of Donald Black's well-known study (1970; Avakame, Fyfe, and McCoy, 1999; Manning, 2003; Spano, 2003; Campbell, 2004) of members of the public who report crimes to the police. Whether or not police agree that a crime has occurred and, if so, whether they formally record it as a crime are outcomes preceded by complicated processes of social interpretation and negotiation. Black investigated these processes in his study of routine police work in predominantly working-class residential areas of Boston, Chicago, and Washington, D.C. He noted that after a victim or an observer of a crime (a complainant) has reported the crime to the police, five conditions influence whether a crime is actually accepted and formally recorded as a crime by the police:

*1. The legal seriousness of the crime.* The police are more likely to write a crime report if the crime is a felony rather than a misdemeanor. In Black's study, 72 percent of felonies but only 53 percent of misdemeanors were written up as reports. "It remains noteworthy," wrote Black, "that the police officially disregard one-fourth of the felonies they handle in encounters with complainants" (p. 738).

*2. The complainant's preferences.* When called to the scene of a crime the police are extremely dependent on a complainant's definition of the situation. Does the complainant want the police to take official action? Does the complainant want the matter settled informally and outside official channels? Is the complainant indifferent as to further action? Black found that the police almost always agree with a complainant's preference for informal action. In situations where a complainant wished official police action, the police complied in 84 percent of felony situations and 64 percent of misdemeanor situations.

*3. The relational distance.* How seriously the police regard a complainant depends partly on the relational distance between the victim and the alleged offender. The social relationship between a crime victim and an offender can be of three types: (1) fellow family members; (2) friends, neighbors, or acquaintances; and (3) strangers. Black found that when a complainant expresses a preference for official action, the police are least likely to comply in type 1, more likely in type 2, and most likely in type 3. Black also found that relational distance is often more important than the legal seriousness of the crime: "The police are more likely to give official recognition to a misdemeanor involving strangers . . . than to a felony involving friends, neighbors, or acquaintances" (p. 740).

*4. The complainant's deference.* Not surprisingly, Black found that the more deference or respect shown police by a complainant, in both felony and misdemeanor situations, the more likely police are to file an official crime report. As Black puts it: "Official crime rates and the justice done through police detection of criminal offenders, therefore, reflect the politeness of victims" (p. 744).

*5. The complainant's status.* Do the police discriminate in favor of complainants of high social status? In trying to answer this question, Black considered both social class and race as aspects of status. For class, Black found that the police tend to discriminate in favor of white-collar complainants in felony situations. Thus, the higher a complainant's social status, the more likely it is that police will respond to a complaint that a crime has been committed. For race, however, Black found it almost impossible to reach a solid conclusion about discrimination, because most crime is intraracial (for instance, whites tend to commit crimes against whites, blacks against blacks, Hispanics against Hispanics, and so on). Suppose, for example, that the police tend to respond more often to a white complainant than to a black complainant. It is hard to know whether this response is discriminatory because, given that whites tend to commit crimes against whites more often than against minorities, in favoring a white complainant the police would also be more likely to be pursuing a white offender. Similarly, if the police are less likely to respond to a black complainant, they are more likely to be discriminating in favor of a black offender.

## Victimization Data: National Crime Victimization Surveys (NCVS)

We have seen that the size and content of the unreported "dark figure" of crime shed an interesting light on the statistical data present in the UCR. We have implied that the actual size of the dark figure is unknowable and that there is no good reason to suppose either that it is constant from year to year or that it has a fixed ratio with reported crime. Moreover, because the volume of crime reported in the UCR depends as much on police activity as it does on the actual amount of criminal activity, the size of the dark figure of crime is, in principle, infinite. Simply put, there is as much officially recorded crime as the criminal law defines, as the public reports, and as the police acknowledge.

Criminologists have increasingly turned to **victimization surveys** to understand more about the volume and the rate of crime. Victimization surveys examine representative samples of a general population in an attempt to discern what crimes have been experienced in a given period. In the United States a victimization survey of a large national sample has been conducted by the Bureau of Justice Statistics each year since 1972. This is the National Crime Victimization Survey (NCVS).

The NCVS is based on a representative sample of 43,000 households, which include about 80,000 persons aged 12 and over. The entire sample is interviewed by rotation twice each year for three and a half years. In person and by way of computer-assisted telephones, interviewers ask the household residents about their victimization histories during the previous year. One of the NCVS's intended advantages over the UCR is its ability to discover information about crimes not reported to the police—or, in other words, about the "dark figure" of crime. The crimes examined by the NCVS include rape, robbery, aggravated and simple assault, robbery or assault resulting in personal injury, personal theft, burglary, household larceny, and motor vehicle theft.

The NCVS is designed more as a substitute for the UCR program than as a complement. Indeed, direct comparisons of NCVS and UCR data are of dubious value, because the sources from which they derive are quite different. Whereas crime rates in the UCR derive from reports of incidents of crime to the police, the rates in the NCVS derive from reports of victimizations to survey interviewers. In other words, NCVS data are based on individuals actually victimized; UCR data are based on reported criminal acts. Because their sources of data differ, the UCR and the NCVS tend to tell us rather different things about crime.

Some of the main findings of the NCVS (Bureau of Justice Statistics, 2004a, 2004b; and see Figures 2.6 and 2.7) for 2003 are:

- Only 44.5 percent of all NCVS victimizations were reported to the police; 49.7 percent of violent victimizations and 58.6 percent of property victimizations went unreported.

- U.S. residents age 12 or older experienced approximately 24 million crimes.
  - 77 percent (18.6 million) were property crimes.
  - 22 percent (5.4 million) were crimes of violence.
  - 1 percent were personal thefts.

- Violent victimizations were at the lowest levels ever recorded.

- Property victimizations continued a more than 20-year decline.

- Between 1973 and 2002, males had significantly higher victimization rates than females for all violent crimes except rape/sexual assault. Males were twice as likely to experience robbery and aggravated assault. In about half of all violent victimizations, the victim knew the offender.

- African Americans had higher violent crime victimization rates than whites or other races, and they experienced the highest rates of overall property crime, burglary, and motor vehicle theft. Hispanic households (at 12 percent of the

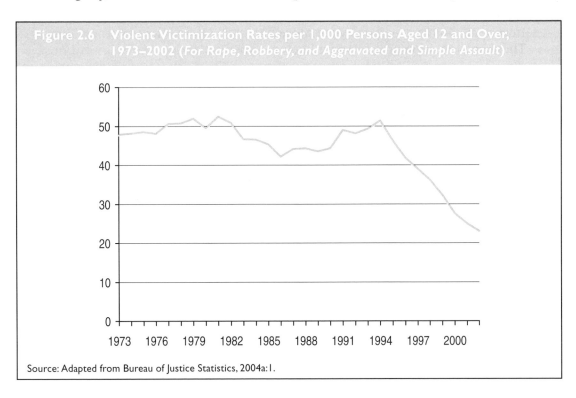

**Figure 2.6   Violent Victimization Rates per 1,000 Persons Aged 12 and Over, 1973–2002 (For Rape, Robbery, and Aggravated and Simple Assault)**

Source: Adapted from Bureau of Justice Statistics, 2004a:1.

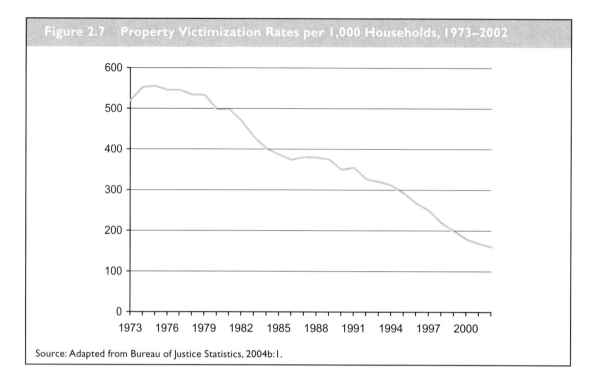

**Figure 2.7   Property Victimization Rates per 1,000 Households, 1973–2002**

Source: Adapted from Bureau of Justice Statistics, 2004b:1.

U.S. population) experienced 12 percent of all violent victimizations but had disproportionately high property victimizations.

* In general, younger persons were more likely to suffer violent victimizations. Those aged 65 or older were more likely to experience property victimizations.

## Evaluation of the NCVS

The NCVS was originally devised to provide a better idea of the size of the dark figure of crime unreported in the UCR. In this task it has been reasonably successful: NCVS data document that a massive amount of crime is not reported to the police. Additionally, despite consistent increases in the rates of UCR Part 1 during the 1980s and early 1990s, NCVS data reveal that victimization rates remained remarkably stable during the same period. Throughout the 1990s, both the NCVS and the UCR showed that crime and victimization declined to almost all-time measured lows (Blumstein, 2002; Conklin, 2003).

But the NCVS has its limitations. There are three problems in particular: underreporting to interviewers, response bias, and time-in-sample bias (Sparks, 1981; Cantor and Lynch, 2000):

1. Although victimization surveys always reveal more crime than that recorded in police-based documents such as the UCR, the NCVS also understates the crime rate. For example, because many crimes are often somewhat insignificant to their victims, they tend to be forgotten. The tendency to forget increases as the time between the crime and an NCVS interview increases.

Reflect, too, on how reluctant a female interviewee will be to report her domestic victimization to a telephone interviewer if her abuser is within earshot or if her telephone line is shared with another party—as sometimes happens, especially in rural areas.

2. The rate of underreporting is distributed unevenly throughout the class structure. Irrespective of actual victimization, whites are more likely than blacks to report having been victimized, as are college graduates compared to those with less formal education.

3. NCVS respondents are supposed to be interviewed every six months for a total of seven interviews. As interviewee participation in the NCVS increases, reported victimization rates decrease consistently. This decrease may arise because respondents, having been made more aware of victimization simply by exposure to interviewers' questions, take greater precautions against victimization. The reported victimization rates of often-interviewed participants also might fall because respondents are less cooperative and less candid in later interviews.

In light of these problems, the Bureau of Justice Statistics has made several important changes to the NCVS. The redesigned NCVS now has better strategies for improving the accuracy of victimization-incident recall; for easing respondents' fears about anonymity, with the use of computer-assisted interviewing, for example; and for expanding the scope of crimes covered, including vandalism. The redesigned NCVS also includes a strategy for dealing with changing victimization rates over a longer period of time (a longitudinal design), so as to permit analysis of such issues as:

- Whether crime victimization is a factor in the geographic mobility of respondents.

- Long-term health and economic consequences of victimization.

- Victim contacts with the criminal justice system over an extended period of time.

- The characteristics of victims, including victims who experience one-time, periodic, or relatively continuous victimization, together with such factors as the type of crime and victim (or offender characteristics) that vary across these different temporal patterns.

- The degree to which respondents in one year also account for victimizations in other years.

## Federal Data on White-Collar Crime, Corporate Crime, and Internet Fraud

Neither the UCR nor the NCVS contains data about corporate crime. Though we discuss corporate crime at some length in Chapter 7.2, it is worth mentioning here that important sources of official data about corporate crime are the deliberations of various federal agencies and regulatory bodies such as the Environmental Protection Agency and the Occupational Safety and Health Administration. Corporate violations become known to these agencies in many ways, including consumer complaints, government investigations, congressional committees, and complaints made by corporate competitors. However, it is important to realize that the amount of corporate misconduct not reported in the documents of federal agencies is enormous. Such data thus suffer from some of the same problems encountered by police-based data.

---

**Box 2.3   Sources of Corporate Crime Data**

Among the federal agencies from which information about corporate crime can be gathered are:

- For financial violations, the Securities and Exchange Commission.

- For environmental violations, the Environmental Protection Agency.

- For labor violations, the Equal Employment Opportunity Commission, the Occupational Wage and Hour Division of the Department of Labor.

- For manufacturing violations, the Consumer Product Safety Commission, the National Highway Traffic Safety administration, and the Food and Drug Administration.

- For unfair trade practices, the Federal Commission.

- For administrative violations, U.S. federal courts.

In addition, some data about transnational corporate crime are contained in the reports and activities of a variety of international agencies, such as the World Health Organization.

---

Data on Internet fraud have been collected since 2001 by the Internet Fraud Complaint Center (IFCC), which is a joint venture of the FBI and the National White-Collar Crime Center. The stated goal of the IFCC is to act as a repository for Internet fraud and to provide strategies for consumers to avoid Internet scams. According to its *Internet Fraud Report* (2003), the IFCC received 48,252 complaints in 2002 (a 300 percent increase over 2001). These complaints, amounting to a total of $54 million defrauded, included auction fraud (46 percent of referred complaints), nondelivery of merchandise and payment fraud (31 percent), credit/debit card fraud (12 percent), and about 1 percent each for investment fraud, business fraud, confidence fraud, and identity theft. The IFCC also publishes information on patterns of fraud, including the age, gender, and geographical location of victims and offenders.

## 2.3 Unofficial Crime Data

In addition to the official crime data just described, there are several unofficial (i.e., nongovernmental) sources of crime data: self-reports, life-course data, life-history data, biographies, participant observation, and comparative and historical research. We shall refer often to these data sources in this book.

## Self-Report Data

Given that the volume of crime is always underestimated by official crime statistics such as the police-based UCR and the victim-based NCVS, criminologists have long felt that a more complete picture of criminal activity can be had by using information provided by offenders themselves. Offender-based data typically derive either from analysis of offenders' responses (**self-reports**) to anonymous questionnaires or from personal interviews with offenders.

In many self-report studies, researchers distribute questionnaires to respondents and ask them to admit anonymously whether they have committed certain offenses and, if so, how often. In his study of delinquency among male and female Texas college students, Austin Porterfield (1946), was probably the first researcher to use a self-report questionnaire. Porterfield found no significant difference between the delinquent involvement of the students and that of a group of youths who had been processed by the juvenile court. But he also found a significant difference in court appearances between the two groups and that this difference grew out of both the powerlessness of the court children—who were overwhelmingly of low socioeconomic status—and the social disruption of their families.

Self-report studies have shown that police-based data seriously underestimate the criminal activity of certain segments of the population. Thus, whereas police-based data show that those who commit crimes are disproportionately young, male, and black, self-report studies have typically found far fewer differences among offenders, especially in terms of their social class.

For example, from a self-report study of middle-class delinquency Weis (1976) found that "the often-cited 1:6 ratio of male to female arrestees is twice as large as the mean ratio of 1:2.56 self-reported participants in delinquent behavior" (p. 23). However, Weis also discovered large gender differences in the prevalence (the proportion of a given population that commits crime), incidence (the rate at which a given criminal population commits crime), and seriousness of delinquent involvement: Young males are more often involved than young females in the most serious offenses. A large-scale, international self-report study has also found that in 13 Western countries boys commit more offenses than girls (Junger-Tas, 1994:374–375).

Moreover, using self-report data between 1976 and 2000, numerous National Youth Survey studies (e.g., Elliott and Ageton, 1980; Paternoster and Brame, 1997) have found that for adolescents between the ages of 11 and 17, middle-class youths (both males and females) are less likely to be involved in serious offenses than working- or lower-class youths. Even when they are involved in serious crimes, middle-class youths commit fewer offenses than working- and lower-class youths. There are substantial class differences in both the prevalence and incidence of serious crime.

When the focus is shifted from serious offenses to delinquent acts in general, few significant class differences occur in the proportions of youth reporting one or more delinquent acts. The frequency at which delinquent acts are committed does vary by class for males, however. Middle-class males commit substantially fewer delinquent acts each year than working- and lower-class males. Females of all classes have relatively low rates of offending compared to working- and lower-class males, but there is no consistent pattern of class differences in female incidence rates.

Critics point out that self-report studies have several methodological defects. First, young males, especially, often exaggerate the extent of their delinquency, even on anonymous questionnaires. Second, some respondents forget their delinquent acts, especially the more trivial ones. Third, until quite recently most of the items on self-report questionnaires concerned relatively minor offenses. They tended to ignore the more serious offenses involving violence. Fourth, the respondents in many self-report studies are sometimes drawn not from a representative sample of the population but from a group easily accessible to researchers, such as prisoners and high school or college students.

Each of these problems casts doubt on the findings of self-report studies, especially about serious crime. We should stress, too, that the interpretation of self-report findings is open to considerable debate. It is one thing to show empirically that males, African Americans, and members of the lower class tend to commit serious crimes more often than females, whites, and members of the middle and upper classes do. But it is another matter altogether to explain why this might be so.

## Life-Course Data

The last decade has seen great interest in the collection and interpretation of data about patterns of crime over the course of offenders' lives. These **life-course data** include official crime data, self-reports, psychological evaluations, IQ tests, criminal histories, court records, incarceration records, and coroners' reports.

Life-course data are typically collected and then integrated through large-scale longitudinal studies that look backwards over offenders' lives. They are used to try to explain why some adolescents do commit crimes and others don't, and then subsequently to examine the factors that lead to the onset of criminality; the differing social characteristics of those who commit trivial and serious offenses, respectively; the continuance, persistence, and escalation of crime; desistance from crime; and the consequences for offenders and their families of a career in crime (e.g., Laub and Sampson, 1993, 2001; Moffitt, 1993; Loeber and Farrington, 2001; Farrington and Coid, 2003; Sampson and Laub, 2003). Ongoing longitudinal life-course research includes the Cambridge Study in Delinquent Development, the Denver Youth Survey, the Pittsburgh Youth Study, and the Rochester Youth Development Study.

Although the life-course perspective has been applied to offenders of various types, a useful orientation to the life-course (or "developmental") perspective on youth gang membership is provided in a book by the Rochester Group (Thornberry et al., 2003), *Gangs and Delinquency in Developmental Perspective*. They suggest that in order to examine issues of the life-course and crime, it is necessary to

> identify a community sample of adolescents—some of whom will become gang members and some of whom will not—and trace their growth and development beginning prior to their age of joining the gangs. Doing so allows us to identify antecedent risk factors and the causal processes associated with gang membership. Following the sample during their gang-involved years allows us to gauge the contemporaneous impact of gang membership on behavior, attitudes, and social relations. Finally, by continuing to follow the sample—both gang members and nonmembers—after the peak years of gang membership, the longer-term consequences of gang membership on life-course development and adjustment can be assessed. In

other words, the way in which the trajectory of gang membership relates to other trajectories—both prosocial (e.g., schooling) and antisocial (e.g., drug selling)—can be more properly studied. (p. 9)

A major question posed by life-course researchers is whether there is a small group of chronic offenders who continue to offend during and even after middle age. Finding an answer to this question has been bedeviled by a number of problems, including relatively small offender samples and the inability to track a large number of offenders over their entire life course, both backward and forward. Recent research by Robert Sampson and John Laub (2003; and see Glueck and Glueck, 1930, 1950) has managed largely to overcome these obstacles. They have been able to do follow-up studies on a group of 500 men who were committed to Massachusetts reform schools in their adolescence in the 1940s. Among their findings is that, even for chronic offenders, crime does indeed decline with age in aggregate (see Figure 2.8), though property offenses, violence, and alcohol/drug offenses peak at somewhat different ages. Crime declines, of course, not only because offenders age but also because, as they age, offenders achieve greater stability and more responsibilities, jobs, children, and mortgages (but, see Hagan and Parker, 1999; Gadd and Farrall, 2004).

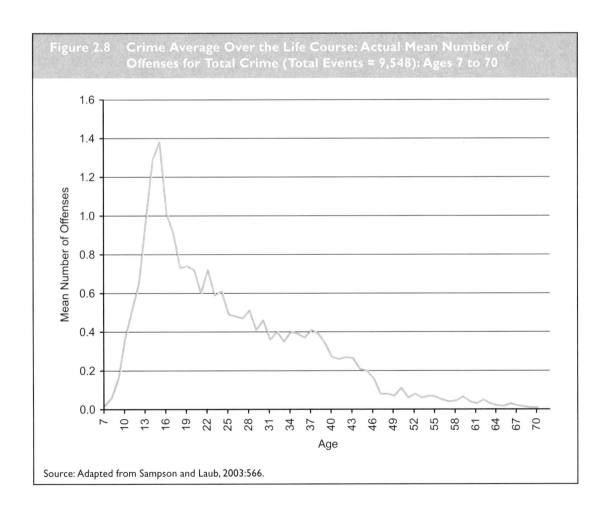

Figure 2.8    Crime Average Over the Life Course: Actual Mean Number of Offenses for Total Crime (Total Events = 9,548): Ages 7 to 70

Source: Adapted from Sampson and Laub, 2003:566.

## Life-History Data

Another way of looking at crime over the life course is with the gathering of information in the life history. The goal of **life-history studies** is to craft a rich document of offenders' changing personal choices and life experiences over time. Some life histories (or "life stories" or "pathways") are mainly sociological, while others, like Tony Jefferson's (1996) work on the boxer Mike Tyson's life history ("From 'Little Fairy Boy' to the 'Compleat Destroyer' ") are more psychosocial in their perspective. But all life histories try to uncover the continuous "lived experiences" of individuals. They involve a close evaluation of the meanings and contradictions of social life for those who enact it— revealing their choices, experiences, practices, and social world.

Messerschmidt (2000, 2004; and see Goetting, 1999; Totten, 2000; Burman, Batchelor, and Brown, 2001; Flavin, 2003; Chesney-Lind and Shelden, 2004, especially Chapters 3 and 6), for example, has investigated adolescent perpetrators of sexual and assaultive violence in the context of their entire lives, from their earliest memories to the point at which he encountered them. Such life-history accounts lead to an understanding of the stages and critical periods in the processes of violent and nonviolent development and of how particular individuals are both enabled and constrained by their position in society. As an example, consider a segment of Messerschmidt's (2000) dialogue on gendered power with "Hugh" (age 15), a gang member and incarcerated assaultive offender. Their dialogue explores Hugh's admission that he sometimes "stomped" the girls who were occasionally in his gang (when he was 12–15):

Q.  Can you further explain that?

A.  You know, we'd all help cook and clean the apartment and shit like that, guys and girls together. But if a girl talk trash to you or if a girl was like running a mouth to you, we wouldn't have it. She'd just get slapped down till she didn't know where she was.

Q.  It's okay to "slap down" girls in the gang?

A.  Oh yeah, if they get out of hand.

Q.  How often did that occur?

A.  It wasn't like everyday because they knew who they were and they knew what they had to do, you know. They knew where they stood and they knew where we stood.

Q.  Is "slapping a girl down" a form of violence?

A.  No, it's not violence because violence is not the way it should be. When you keep a girl in check, that's the way it should be. If she talks shit and you slap her down, that would not be violence.

Q.  Is it ever appropriate to have sex with a girl if she does not want to?

A.  No, that's not right. We'd bust them out if they did that. Once we heard about a kid who raped his sister, so we went and found him and broke both his arms. There was like bone coming out. We fucked him up bad. That just don't happen, you know. We don't like rapists.

Q. When is violence against women appropriate?

A. Women should get respect from men unless they deserve to lose that respect.

Q. What would cause a woman to lose that respect?

A. Like being a bitch, talking shit. But then they wouldn't get raped, you know. They'd just get slapped down and told to shut the fuck up and get out of the house.

## Criminal Biographies

**Criminal biographies** are another source of life-course data. Criminal biographies are criminals' own personal accounts of their activities, largely written by the offenders themselves. They were popularized in the 1920s and 1930s by Chicago criminologists who encouraged researchers to mix with the people they were studying (see Chapter 11.2).

Although one must be cautious in generalizing from the experiences of one criminal to an entire segment of society, biographies of criminals can be a fertile source for further investigation. Each of the studies shown in Box 2.4 adds relevant information to our stock of knowledge about the social world of the professional criminal.

---

**Box 2.4    Biographies of Crime**

Well-known biographies in the literature of criminology include the following:

- Edwin Sutherland, *The Professional Thief* (1937; see Chapter 5.4), based on the recollections of Broadway Jones, alias Chic Conwell, a professional thief, ex-drug addict, and ex-convict from Philadelphia who worked for twenty years as a pimp, pickpocket, shoplifter, and confidence man.

- Carl Klockars, *The Professional Fence* (1974; see Chapter 4.3), based on Vincent Swaggi's story of his life as a fence (one who receives and sells stolen goods); the book discusses the methods Swaggi used to obtain stolen goods for as little money as possible, as well as the elaborate rationalizations he developed to justify his career as a fence.

- William Chambliss, *Box Man* (King and Chambliss, 1984), an account of Harry King's career as a boxman (safe cracker), his philosophy of life, and his lavish consumerism.

- Darrell Steffensmeier and Jeffrey Ulmer, *Confessions of a Dying Thief* (2004), based on Sam Goodman's life as a fence; Goodman used his antique shop as a front to deal in stolen merchandise. In the book, Goodman discusses the relationships among fences, thieves, customers, and criminal justice personnel, and the skills required to perform fencing activities.

- Laurie Taylor, *In the Underworld* (1984), written after Taylor was introduced to the London underworld by John McVicar, an infamous gangster of the 1960s who, while in prison, graduated with a degree in sociology from the United Kingdom's Open University.

- Stuart Hills, *Tragic Magic* (Hills and Santiago, 1992), records the escapades of recovering addict Ron Santiago, a 42-year-old black male of Cuban ancestry. Set in New York, this is a harrowing and engrossing story of robberies, burglaries, drugs, and prison.

## Observation Research and Participant Observation Research

Observation research is a type of field study whereby researchers focus on observing people in their natural settings. Sometimes, the people they are studying fully know they are being observed. For instance, Jill McCorkle (2003) spent considerable time as a researcher—known as such to all—inside a women's medium-security prison, examining the effects of gender-neutral policies and initiatives on inmates' daily lives there.

At other times, however, to gain authentic or natural data, observation researchers go "underground" and try to blend into or with their subjects as unobtrusively as is possible. This type of observation research—**participant observation**—is especially useful for observing the behavior of people who, for one reason or another, usually resist the participation of outsiders in their social world. Examples include members of criminal syndicates such as the Hell's Angels and paramilitary survivalists. Ideally, participant observation requires that the subjects of study be unaware that the observer is in fact an observer.

The actual practice of participant observation is plagued with difficult questions. Some questions concern objectivity. For example, how can one study something objectively if one is a part of what one studies? Other questions concern ethics. Where is the dividing line between the appropriate gathering of data about human subjects and the invasion of their right to privacy? Does the researcher have an ethical obligation to report a crime when he or she witnesses one? Both Humphreys' (1970) research on homosexual encounters and Douglas and Rasmussen's (1977) observation of nudists have

---

**Box 2.5   Participant Observation Studies**

Among the many participation studies in criminology and the sociology of deviance are the following:

- Laud Humphreys, *Tearoom Trade* (1970). Humphreys' account of impersonal homosexual encounters in public facilities was the result of field research, during the course of which he gained entry into the subculture by posing as a lookout.

- Jason Ditton, *Part-Time Crime* (1977a). The English criminologist Ditton went undercover as a dispatch operative, observing the routine fiddles to which sales operatives in Wellbread's Bakery were prone.

- Jack Douglas and Paul Rasmussen, *The Nude Beach* (1977). Douglas and Rasmussen observed the complicated interaction among bathers on a nude beach in La Jolla, California.

- Marc Reisner, *Game Wars* (1991). Reisner takes us inside the underworld of Cajun alligator poachers and ivory importers, focusing on the dangerous investigations of undercover U.S. Fish and Wildlife game warden Dave Hall.

- Jeff Ferrell and Mark Hamm, *Ethnography at the Edge* (1998). In this edited collection 12 authors describe their observation and participant observation studies, including encounters with street gangs, the homeless, paramilitary units, sex work and gender work, drug subcultures, and sky divers and motorcyclists.

been attacked for being unethical. Still other questions concern danger. What happens if researchers' true identities are detected by their subjects?

Largely because of the effect of questions such as these, neither courts of law nor university institutional review boards look with much favor on participant observation studies. Indeed, in a tragic example of what Patricia and Peter Adler (1998) refer to as "the Dark Ages" for ethnographers, Rik Scarce, a graduate sociology student at Washington State University, served six months in prison in the early 1990s for contempt of court for refusing to reveal information about the activities of a group of radical environmentalists and animal rights activists with whom he had mixed in the course of his research.

## Comparative and Historical Research

The great French sociologist Émile Durkheim (1984:157) once remarked that comparative sociology is not a special branch of sociology, it is sociology itself. So it is, too, with criminology. **Comparative criminology** is an indispensable aspect of criminological inquiry and a rich source of data for its theories.

The focus of comparative criminology is the systematic comparison of crime in two or more societies (see Chapter 15). Comparative studies allow us to compare present crime rates in the United States, for example, with those in other cultures, places, and times. Does the United States have a higher homicide rate, for instance, than Japan, Canada, or England? If it does, why? Using Figure 2.9 you can compare cross-national homicide rates of selected cities. Note, for example, that in 2000, Washington, D.C., had a homicide rate of 41.78 per 100,000, compared with rates of 2.59 in London, 2.0 in Stockholm, and 1.24 in Tokyo. Comparative criminology also enables us to examine the effectiveness of social and government policies toward crime. For instance, to what extent does gun control legislation affect the number of murders in which firearms are used?

Comparative crime data, like other crime data, have both official and unofficial sources. Official comparative crime data derive from the activities and reports of national governments and government agencies. Such data can be found in the reports of international agencies such as the United Nations, the World Court, the World Health Organization, and the International Police Organization (Interpol). Some organizations, such as the United Nations, the Dutch Ministry of Justice, and the U.K. Home Office, also sponsor and conduct cross-national victimization surveys. Unofficial comparative crime data can be gleaned from the reports and findings of such private organizations as Amnesty International, Doctors Without Borders, and Human Rights Watch. These data are often especially useful for documenting crimes committed by governments or by the military against their own populations.

As we will see in some depth in Chapter 15, the use of national crime data for cross-national purposes is not without difficulty. Crime data are not items that can simply be pried loose from one culture and compared with those of another. For example, societies differ in how they define crime and in the degree of seriousness with which they regard certain types of crime, making simple comparisons of crime rates hazardous.

## Figure 2.9    Comparison of Homicide Rates in Selected Cities, 1999–2000

| City | Number of Homicides | | Homicides/100,000 Population | |
|---|---|---|---|---|
| | *1999* | *2000* | *1999* | *2000* |
| Washington, D.C. | 241 | 232 | 46.4 | 41.7 |
| Vilnius, Lithuania | 54 | 59 | 9.3 | 10.2 |
| New York City, USA | 671 | 673 | 9.0 | 8.6 |
| Belfast, N. Ireland | 11 | 21 | 3.8 | 7.4 |
| Warsaw, Poland | 80 | 88 | 4.9 | 5.4 |
| Paris, France | 43 | 88 | 2.0 | 4.1 |
| Amsterdam, Netherlands | 22 | 29 | 3.0 | 3.9 |
| Madrid, Spain | 90 | 100 | 3.1 | 3.4 |
| Brussels, Belgium | 33 | 26 | 3.6 | 2.7 |
| London, England | 190 | 189 | 2.4 | 2.5 |
| Berlin, Germany | 86 | 76 | 2.5 | 2.2 |
| Helsinki, Finland | 16 | 11 | 2.9 | 2.0 |
| Stockholm, Sweden | 29 | 15 | 3.9 | 2.0 |
| Dublin, Ireland | 24 | 16 | 2.2 | 1.4 |
| Sydney, Australia | 67 | 55 | 1.6 | 1.3 |
| Rome, Italy | 29 | 36 | 1.1 | 1.3 |
| Tokyo, Japan | 157 | 151 | 1.3 | 1.2 |
| Oslo, Norway | 9 | 6 | 1.7 | 1.1 |
| Edinburgh, Scotland | 11 | 5 | 2.4 | 1.1 |
| Ottawa, Canada | 12 | 8 | 1.4 | 0.9 |
| Berne, Switzerland | 4 | 1 | 3.1 | 0.8 |

Source: Adapted from Barclay and Tavares, 2003.

Other types of comparative studies can be based on **historical data**, including official statistics (on crime, prison populations, health, and so on), court records, books, newspapers, journals, pamphlets, plays, and oral histories. Historical data help us examine the past in order to understand how we have arrived at the present. Ideally, they allow us to make generalizations about crime that stand outside the peculiarities of any given era. Historical studies of crime are therefore also implicitly comparative. Douglas Hay's (1975) study of crime and criminal law in eighteenth-century England, for example, revealed that in societies where the criminal justice system is based on terror—in this case, execution for the most petty of offenses—a national police force might be quite unnecessary. Occasionally, historical studies of crime are also cross-cultural. A classic example of a study that is both historical and cross-cultural is *The Politics of*

*Crime and Conflict* (Gurr, Grabosky, and Hula, 1977; and see Godfrey, Emsley, and Dunstall, 2003). This study revealed that the relationship between public policies and crime rates in Calcutta, London, Stockholm, and Sydney during a 150-year period was in many ways strikingly similar, despite the enormous social, economic, and political differences among these disparate cities.

## Assessment

In this chapter we have described the major sources of crime data. We stress that crime data can never represent criminal behavior, however defined, in a neutral or unbiased way. Data do not speak for themselves! A particular crime rate identified and measured by official crime data, for example, depends on the legalistic concepts that guide the process of measurement. We do not, of course, mean to suggest that criminologists intentionally distort data to suit their own purposes. Rather, we mean that data are identified and defined by concepts and that criminologists naturally differ in the concepts of crime they hold appropriate for the study of crime.

This point is important. As you read this book, you will learn that how criminologists explain or interpret crime data depends both on their concepts of crime and on the assumptions underlying their theories of crime. Theories are sets of assumptions, mediated by concepts, that guide the interpretation of data. Theories try to explain both regularities and irregularities in data. In the same way that what constitutes crime data depends on any given concept of crime, so, too, how we explain crime data depends on the assumptions of our theories.

## Review

This chapter has outlined the major sources of crime data. Official crime data are published by the state and by state agencies. In the United States such publications include the Uniform Crime Reports (UCR), the National Crime Victimization Survey (NCVS), and federal records of corporate crime. Unofficial crime data include self-report data, life-course and life-history data, criminal biographies, participant observation, and comparative and historical data.

In this chapter you also learned that crime data can never represent criminal behavior in a neutral or unbiased way. We now review the major points of the chapter.

### Caution: Data Do Not Speak for Themselves!

1. Data are not objective facts that exist independently of the concepts and theories of those who observe them. Data can never represent criminal behavior in a neutral or unbiased way.

2. Data are identified and defined by concepts, about whose appropriateness criminologists naturally differ in their perceptions. In the same way that what constitutes crime data depends on any given concept of crime, so, too, how we explain crime data depends, to a certain extent, on the assumptions of our theories.

## Official Crime Data

1. The UCR distinguishes between eight Part I and 21 Part II crimes. Data about Part I crimes derive from reports to the police. Data about Part II crimes derive from police arrests.

2. The UCR and NIBRS annually tabulate data about the number and rate of crimes; crime trends by year and region; the age, sex, and race of offenders and victims; and offense clearance rates.

3. There are both methodological and conceptual criticisms of the UCR. Among the latter is the limitation that the UCR records only legally defined categories of crime. Ultimately, we cannot be sure if the UCR measures criminal behavior or, rather, the bureaucratic activities of official agencies. Whether or not police officers accept a crime report depends on the legal seriousness of the crime, the complainant's preferences, the relational distance between victim and offender, and the complainant's deference and social status.

4. The NCVS is based on reports of victimizations. It is designed to complement the UCR, but comparisons between the NCVS and the UCR are of dubious value because each tool attempts to measure different entities.

5. The NCVS indicates that only 39 percent of all crimes are reported to the police, that females and black males are among the most victimized groups in the population, and that nearly one-third of all households suffer some form of victimization annually.

6. Problems with NCVS data include underreporting to interviewers, response bias, and time-in-sample bias.

7. Neither the UCR nor the NCVS contains any data about corporate crime. However, various federal agencies and regulatory bodies are important sources of such data.

## Unofficial Crime Data

1. Self-report data are offender-based data obtained from questionnaires. These data tend to show that middle-class youth commit as much crime as working-class youth but that there are large gender differences in the prevalence, incidence, and seriousness of crime. Critics argue that self-report data suffer from exaggeration by young males, from biases due to the failure of some interviewees to recall delinquency, and from a concentration on relatively minor juvenile offenses.

2. Life-course and life-history studies collect and interpret patterns of crime over the course of offenders' entire lives.

3. Criminal biographies are accounts of personal activities given by criminals to criminologists. Biographies can be a fertile source for further investigation but are notoriously resistant to generalization.

4. Participant observation is a form of field research. Its goal is to observe people as unobtrusively as possible in their natural settings. Its actual practice is plagued with difficult questions, including the problem of where to place a dividing line between the appropriate gathering of data about human subjects and the invasion of their right to privacy.

5. Comparative and historical data are closely related. Comparative data derive chiefly from the activities and reports of national governments and such international agencies as the United Nations, the World Health Organization, and Interpol. Such data are typically used to compare crime in two or more countries at one point in time. Historical data derive from a great diversity of sources and allow us to generalize about crime free from the peculiarities of any given era. Occasionally, historical data are also cross-cultural.

## Questions for Class Discussion

1. What does the UCR measure: activities of offenders, activities of complainants, or activities of the police?

2. Do victimization surveys help us understand the true extent of the "dark figure" of crime?

3. Can crime data ever represent objective facts?

## Web Exercises

1. This exercise asks you to compare police-based crime rates in different parts of the United States. First, find the most recent UCR on the Internet. You can do so by going to <www.fbi.gov> and clicking on "UCR" and "year." Then, select one type of crime in any two cities—for instance, robbery in Boston and San Francisco. Next, produce two printed pages with statistics from a table titled "Offenses Known to the Police [time frame], Cities over 1,000,000 in Population." Which city had more reported robbery? Did the robbery rates in either city change from one year to the next? What factors might explain differences in the two cities' robbery rates?

2. Visit the website of the Internet Fraud Complaint Center (IFCC): <www.ifccfbi.gov>. Click on "Fraud Tips." Read and then discuss the adequacy of the advice on the "Nigerian letter" scam and on identity theft.

## For Further Study

### Readings

Godfrey, Barry, Clive Emsley, and Graeme Dunstall. 2003. *Comparative Histories of Crime*. Portland, OR: Willan.

Maguire, Mike. 2003. The 'Data Explosion' and Its Implications. In *The Oxford Handbook of Criminology,* edited by Mike Maguire, Rod Morgan, and Robert Reiner, 322–375. Oxford: Oxford University Press.

Manning, Peter K. 2003. *Policing Contingencies.* Chicago: University of Chicago Press.

Pogrebin, Mark, ed. 2004. *About Criminals: A View of the Offender's World.* Thousand Oaks, CA: Sage.

## Websites

1. <http://www.fbi.gov/UCR/ucr.htm>: This site provides open access to the Uniform Crime Reports, the major official data source from the U.S. government.

2. <http://www.ojp.usdoj.gov/bjs/nibrs.htm>: This link from the U.S. Department of Justice (DOJ) homepage offers access to a variety of governmental reports issued by the DOJ, including the National Crime Victimization Surveys. To get to the NCVS, go to the Bureau of Justice Statistics site and select "publications."

3. <http://www.nibrs.search.org>: This is the homepage for the National Incident-Based Reporting System (NIBRS) project from the U.S. government. It is an alternative to the UCR, taking into consideration many of the UCR's weaknesses. There is a set of links to all 50 states, updating readers on each state's activities with the NIBRS. Students may examine their own state's involvement with the NIBRS here.

4. <http://www.vera.org/section1/section1_5.asp>: The Vera Institute of Justice has compiled 18 sources of crime data. It also allows users to specify particular sorts of data. For example, national data and specific state data are both available; the American Bar Association is linked here, as are the Federal Bureau of Prisons and the Office for Victims of Crime. ✦

# Inequality, Crime, and Victimization

## Preview

Chapter 3 introduces:

- Social inequality and its relation to crime.

- How social position both permits and prevents criminal opportunity.

- Patterns of crime and victimization in the United States.

## Key Terms

| | |
|---|---|
| age | social class |
| gender | social inequality |
| race | social position |

As emphasized in Chapters 1 and 2, crime is a sociological problem. To understand the varieties of crime, then, it is essential to establish their sociological context—how crime is shaped by the social factors of society. Accordingly, in this chapter we discuss the considerable sociological research that is necessary to grasp the patterns of crime in the United States.

The chief social factor underlying crime is structured **social inequality.** All industrialized societies are marked by social inequalities. Critical aspects of life—such as economic benefits, life chances, social privileges, and political power—are intimately connected to the social inequalities that structure society. Inequality is a sociological question, a product of human history.

At least four major forms of inequality influence crime: class, gender, race, and age. These inequalities create different life experiences for people, depending on their class, gender, race, and age characteristics, and they also shape patterns of crime and victimization. In other words, criminal opportunities and victimization are intimately related to social position in the class, gender, race, and age hierarchies of society. **Social position** thus refers to one's individual location in society based on the social characteristics of class, gender, race, and age.

Some scholars try to explain why one individual commits crime and another individual in the same social position does not. Although this is an intriguing question, our focus is on explaining sociological patterns of crime. Why do members of one class disproportionately commit a certain type of crime? Why do men commit more crimes than women? To answer such questions we must analyze those inequalities in the social structures that shape our lives. Social position—in terms of class, gender, race, and age—influences, limits, and structures human behavior, whether that behavior is legal or illegal, harmful or safe. Social position permits and precludes criminal opportunities. The patterns of crime therefore reflect the broader inequalities embedded in society.

In this chapter, for analytical purposes, we discuss class, gender, race, and age separately. However, in the real world, social inequities are actually interrelated. As participating members of society, each of us has simultaneously a class, gender, race, and age social position. All four positions interact to structure society and its accompanying patterns of crime and victimization. Unfortunately, in an introductory textbook it is impossible to provide a complete picture of the relationship between social inequality and crime. Thus, our discussion is limited to an examination of why and how general patterns of crime and victimization occur in the United States.

## 3.1 Class and Crime

In the United States sharp class divisions exist, and inequalities structure the patterns of crime and victimization. Although class position is associated with level of income, occupation, and education, it is determined chiefly by the way in which the production system of a society is organized. Historically, societies have organized production in different ways, which in turn has created different types of social classes. Class, then, is an important sociological concept for understanding patterns of crime. We define a **social class** as a group of people who share the same position in the same economic system. Class influences both economic relationships and inequalities, as well as the *type* and *seriousness* of crime.

## Patterns of Crime and Victimization

The Uniform Crime Reports do not rank the crime rates for various social classes. However, John Braithwaite (1981) reviewed a significant number of studies that used official statistics to generate data on the relationship between class and crime, and he concluded that they all "showed lower-class juveniles to have substantially higher of-fense rates than middle-class juveniles. Among adults, all . . . studies found lower-class people to have higher crime rates" (p. 38). Moreover, Braithwaite's earlier review (1979b) of nearly 300 studies based on official statistics *and* self-reports concluded that

1. Lower-class adults commit those types of crime handled by the police (con-ventional crimes) at a higher rate than middle-class adults do.

2. Adults living in lower-class areas commit those types of crime handled by the police at a higher rate than adults living in middle-class areas.

3. Lower-class juveniles commit crime at a higher rate than middle-class juve-niles.

4. Juveniles living in lower-class areas commit crime at a higher rate than juve-niles living in middle-class areas.

Regarding specific offense types, self-report studies indicate that class differences exist for both serious property crime and interpersonal crimes of violence. A delin-quency study by Elliott and Huizinga (1983) is of particular importance because it ana-lyzed both the percentage of a social class committing certain offenses at a specific time (*prevalence*) and the frequency with which these class members commit crimes (*inci-dence*). For status offenses and general delinquency, class differentials in prevalence were practically nonexistent. Elliott and Huizinga did, however, find significant class differentials for youth in the serious conventional crimes: Middle-class youths were far less likely to report committing such crimes than lower- and working-class youths were. Regarding incidence, the same pattern held: Both male and female middle-class youth were much less likely than other youths to report committing serious crimes.

But conventional crimes are only one aspect of the entire range of crimes. Unfortu-nately, criminological studies of class and crime have concentrated on class differences in conventional crimes, ignoring white-collar and political crimes. Although poor and working-class people may commit the more serious conventional crimes handled by the police, members of the professional-managerial class (traditionally seen as the middle class) have greater opportunities to commit white-collar and political crimes. In fact, when we consider this class/crime link, it is clear that the vast bulk of avoidable harm and economic loss originates from the professional-managerial class. Consequently, the *type* and *seriousness* of crime are associated with social class position: Conventional crimes tend to be committed more often by the poor and working classes, while white-collar and political crimes tend to be committed more often by the profes-sional-managerial class.

The National Crime Vic-timization Survey provides information on victimization and in so doing helps us understand the *intra-* and *interclass* nature of conventional crimes. As Table 3.1 shows, for rape, robbery, assault, and purse snatching/pocket-picking in 2002, the lower the family income, the greater the chance of victimization. The most frequent victims of such crimes were those with an annual family income of less than $15,000. We can conclude that such crimes tend to be *intraclass:* Both the *offenders* and the *victims* are usually members of the same class.

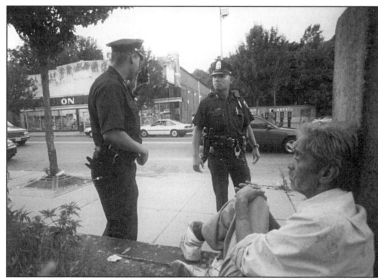

*Unemployment and crime: Historically, criminological research has found a correlation between unemployment and street crime. Despite the economic 'boom' of the 1990s, many U.S. citizens lack access to the legitimate labor market.*

Table 3.2 shows victimization rates for the category termed property crimes—household burglary, motor vehicle theft, and theft. Each crime shows a different pattern: Household burglary victimization declines with annual family income; motor vehicle theft victimization remains relatively stable between incomes of $25,000 and $75,000; and theft victimization remains relatively stable throughout all income levels.

With the exception of theft and motor vehicle theft, conventional crime victimization is therefore an intraclass phenomenon. In other words, the poor tend to victimize the poor, but they are *also* more susceptible to syndicated, corporate, and political crime victimization. Consequently, the poor face crime from all directions.

In Chapter 2 we outlined some longitudinal data sets with which criminologists are trying to determine why some offenders continue to offend while others desist from doing so. On the other side of this equation, research is also being conducted to determine why some victims are repeatedly victimized and others are not (Farrell and Pease, 2001; Tseloni and Pease, 2003). Using data in the 1994 National Crime Victimization Survey, these authors have identified two factors that are crucial in repeat victimizations. One is what they term "event dependence," in which an initial victimization increases the probability of subsequent victimizations. Simply, offenders are more likely to prey on victims if they have already successfully victimized them. The other is "heterogeneity," by which they mean that some households are more likely to be victimized irrespective of their past history of victimization. The victimization-prone households are characterized by factors related to gender, race, age, marital status, lone parenthood, educational level, employment status, and length of residence. But they also include lifestyle indicators, such as patterns of shopping and evenings outside the home. Using cross-national data, other researchers have found that youth, residence in large cities,

**Table 3.1 Personal Crimes, 2002: Victimization Rates for Persons Age 12 and Over, by Type of Crime and Annual Family Income of Victims**

| Type of crime | Less than $7,500 | $7,500–$14,999 | $15,000–$24,999 | $25,000–$34,999 | $35,000–$49,999 | $50,000–$74,999 | $75,000 or more |
|---|---|---|---|---|---|---|---|
| **All personal crimes** | **47.2** | **32.0** | **30.8** | **27.4** | **28.0** | **19.3** | **19.7** |
| Crimes of violence | 45.5 | 31.5 | 30.0 | 27.0 | 25.6 | 18.7 | 19.0 |
| Completed violence | 18.7 | 12.0 | 11.4 | 9.3 | 6.7 | 4.9 | 5.6 |
| Attempted/threatened violence | 26.8 | 19.5 | 18.6 | 17.7 | 18.8 | 13.8 | 13.4 |
| Rape/sexual assault | 2.5* | 3.2 | 2.1 | 1.2* | 0.9* | 0.2* | 0.4* |
| Rape/attempted rape | 2.3* | 2.7 | 1.3 | 0.8* | 0.3* | 0.1* | 0.2* |
| Rape | 0.6* | 1.4* | 1.0* | 0.3* | 0.1* | 0.1* | 0.1* |
| Attempted rape[a] | 1.7* | 1.3* | 0.2* | 0.5* | 0.2* | 0.0* | 0.1* |
| Sexual assault[b] | 0.3* | 0.4* | 0.8* | 0.4* | 0.6* | 0.1* | 0.2* |
| Robbery | 6.3 | 4.1 | 2.9 | 2.9 | 2.2 | 2.1 | 1.0 |
| Completed/property taken | 5.0 | 2.4 | 2.4 | 1.9 | 1.9 | 1.5 | 0.8 |
| With injury | 2.4* | 1.3* | 1.1* | 0.8* | 0.5* | 0.3* | 0.4* |
| Without injury | 2.7* | 1.1* | 1.3 | 1.1* | 1.4 | 1.2 | 0.4 |
| Attempted to take property | 1.3* | 1.7* | 0.5* | 1.0* | 0.3* | 0.6* | 0.2* |
| With injury | 0.3* | 0.9* | 0.1* | 0.4* | 0.0* | 0.2* | 0.1* |
| Without injury | 1.0* | 0.8* | 0.4* | 0.6* | 0.3* | 0.4* | 0.1* |
| Assault | 36.7 | 24.2 | 25.0 | 22.9 | 22.4 | 16.5 | 17.6 |
| Aggravated | 11.2 | 5.8 | 6.1 | 4.1 | 5.2 | 2.5 | 2.8 |
| With injury | 4.2 | 2.4 | 1.8 | 1.5 | 1.3 | 0.5* | 0.9 |
| Threatened with weapon | 7.0 | 3.3 | 4.3 | 2.5 | 3.9 | 2.0 | 1.9 |
| Simple | 25.5 | 18.4 | 18.9 | 18.9 | 17.2 | 14.0 | 14.8 |
| With minor injury | 8.6 | 5.6 | 5.7 | 5.2 | 3.1 | 2.8 | 3.7 |
| Without injury | 16.9 | 12.8 | 13.3 | 13.7 | 14.1 | 11.2 | 11.2 |
| Purse snatching/pocket picking | 1.7* | 0.5* | 0.8* | 0.3* | 0.4* | 0.6* | 0.7 |
| **Population age 12 and over** | 8,347,650 | 15,608,210 | 23,872,200 | 24,104,810 | 31,655,160 | 33,713,640 | 43,139,380 |

*Rate per 1,000 persons age 12 and over*

Note: Detail may not add to total shown because of rounding. Excludes data on persons whose family income level was not ascertained.
*Estimate is based on about 10 or fewer sample cases.  [a]Includes verbal threats of rape.  [b]Includes threats.
Source: Department of Justice, 2003.

and high income are also important factors in repeat victimization (van Dijk, 2000). However, which of these several factors is more important than others is not yet known.

Let us now consider theory and research on class and crime.

## Class and Varieties of Crime

Unequal class relationships help explain the class patterns of crime and victimization in the United States. Regarding the conventional crimes handled by the police, research has shown that economic conditions associated with the poor and working classes—in particular, unemployment and income inequality—play a significant role in the perpetuation of these crimes. Notwithstanding the inconsistencies in research on the relationship between unemployment and conventional crime, the majority of studies report a link between the two. M. Harvey Brenner's (1976) pioneering work in the 1970s, for instance, found that when the unemployment rate increased 1 percentage point, a corresponding 4 percent increase occurred in homicides and a 6 percent increase occurred in robberies.

In the 1980s, research again uncovered a link between unemployment and

### Table 3.2   Property Crimes, 2002: Victimization Rates by Type of Crime and Annual Family Income

| Type of crime | Less than $7,500 | $7,500–$14,999 | $15,000–$24,999 | $25,000–$34,999 | $35,000–$49,999 | $50,000–$74,999 | $75,000 or more |
|---|---|---|---|---|---|---|---|
| | | | | Rate per 1,000 households | | | |
| **Property crimes** | **188.9** | **166.7** | **172.1** | **161.7** | **175.4** | **158.3** | **169.8** |
| Household burglary | 51.4 | 31.8 | 33.8 | 27.8 | 27.3 | 24.6 | 21.0 |
| Completed | 39.1 | 27.0 | 25.8 | 24.2 | 23.0 | 21.8 | 18.6 |
| Forcible entry | 16.8 | 11.9 | 12.4 | 9.3 | 8.6 | 7.0 | 4.5 |
| Unlawful entry without force | 22.3 | 15.1 | 13.5 | 14.9 | 14.4 | 14.8 | 14.1 |
| Attempted forcible entry | 12.3 | 4.8 | 7.9 | 3.7 | 4.2 | 2.8 | 2.4 |
| Motor vehicle theft | 3.2* | 8.1 | 9.9 | 12.6 | 11.3 | 9.2 | 5.9 |
| Completed | 3.2* | 6.8 | 8.2 | 9.2 | 8.6 | 7.0 | 4.5 |
| Attempted | 0.0* | 1.3* | 1.7* | 3.5 | 2.7 | 2.1 | 1.4* |
| Theft | 134.3 | 126.8 | 128.5 | 121.2 | 136.9 | 124.5 | 142.9 |
| Completed | 130.9 | 124.1 | 125.6 | 116.4 | 133.1 | 119.0 | 138.6 |
| Less than $50 | 34.5 | 37.5 | 42.0 | 40.2 | 44.7 | 40.2 | 44.4 |
| $50–$249 | 55.1 | 46.6 | 44.7 | 40.8 | 43.8 | 39.9 | 44.1 |
| $250 or more | 32.8 | 28.7 | 30.1 | 26.3 | 33.8 | 26.1 | 36.5 |
| Amount not available | 8.4 | 11.3 | 8.8 | 9.0 | 10.8 | 12.9 | 11.5 |
| Attempted | 3.4* | 2.7* | 2.8 | 4.8 | 3.8 | 5.5 | 6.3 |
| **Total number of households** | **5,157,750** | **9,038,820** | **12,231,090** | **11,586,530** | **14,391,310** | **14,283,610** | **17,532,840** |

Note: Detail may not add to total shown because of rounding. Excludes data on families whose income level was not ascertained.
*Estimate is based on about 10 or fewer sample cases.

Source: Department of Justice, 2003.

conventional crime. James DeFronzo's (1983) study of 39 U.S. metropolitan areas found that "unemployment rates had statistically significant positive effects on rape, burglary, and larceny" (p. 128). Thornberry and Christenson (1984) investigated the employment history of 1,000 boys born in 1945 and related this to the boys' involvement in conventional criminality. They concluded that "unemployment has significant instantaneous effects on crime" (p. 408). In other words, crime seems to follow the onset of unemployment.

Cook and Zarkin (1985) investigated the business cycle and its relationship to conventional crime from 1933 to 1980. They concluded that "an increase in the unemployment rate from, say, 7 percent to 8 percent will result in a 2.3 percent increase in the robbery rate and a 1.6 percent increase in the burglary rate" (p. 126). More recent studies have shown a positive and significant relationship between unemployment and conventional crime (Carlson and Michalowski, 1997; Shihadeh and Ousey, 1998). Consequently, when large numbers of people are unemployed, there appears to be an increase in the conventional crime rate.

In addition to the above, some studies examining the relationship between unemployment and crime suggest that although unemployment increases the *motivations* for crime, it may simultaneously decrease the actual *opportunities* to offend (Britt, 1997; Elliott and Ellingsworth, 1997). That is, unemployment increases the incentive to engage in crime, yet because of the downturn in the economy, fewer concrete targets of crime exist. However, Kleck and Chiricos (2002), in the most rigorous study to date, show that "opportunity levels" are specifically unrelated to property crime rates and, therefore, do not mediate the relationship between unemployment and crime.

Given the correlation between unemployment and conventional crime, we cannot forget that other characteristics—such as gender and age—play an equally significant role in the patterning of conventional crime. Indeed, as we discuss later in this chapter, both the elderly and women have high unemployment rates yet do not commit conventional crimes at the rate, for instance, that young males do. Consequently, gender and age mediate the unemployment/crime association.

In addition to unemployment, income inequality significantly affects conventional crime. Braithwaite's (1979b) study of 193 U.S. metropolitan areas found "strong and consistent support for the hypothesis that cities in which there is a wide income gap between poor and average-income families have high rates for all types of crime" (p. 216). Jacobs (1981) studied property crimes and income inequality in some 200 cities and established a strong relationship between economic inequality and the crimes of burglary and larceny. Jacobs' study is important because it helps us understand why high rates of property crime victimization occur in higher income groups. As Jacobs points out:

> When there are large differences in resources in a metropolitan area, those with little to lose and much to gain will find that potential victims with more to steal are located only a limited distance away. . . . The less successful can readily observe the fruits of affluence in unequal metropolitan areas. It follows that in a society where there is a great cultural emphasis placed on economic success, pronounced differences in resources seem to result in more property crimes. (pp. 22–23)

In other words, relative class deprivation and inequality seem conducive to higher rates of conventional property crime.

Other research demonstrates that income inequality directly affects both the rate of property crimes and the rate of violent crimes. Blau and Blau's (1982) classic study found that in the 125 largest metropolitan areas, high rates of interpersonal violence result largely from economic inequalities. Income inequalities in cities promote interpersonal violence because "in a society founded on the principle 'that all men are created equal,' economic inequalities rooted in ascribed positions violate the spirit of democracy and are likely to create alienation, despair and conflict" (p. 26). Other studies have made similar conclusions about violent crime. For instance, Stack and Kanavy (1983) investigated the relationship between economic conditions and rape, reporting strong support "for an economic theory of crime based on unemployment as well as income inequality. Both variables exert positive, independent effects on rape" (pp. 71–72). More recent work (e.g., Shover, 1996; LaFree, 1999; Lee and Bankston, 1999) shows a relationship between neighborhood poverty, relative deprivation, and convention crime.

These unequal economic conditions are also associated with crimes of the *hidden economy*—those economic transactions that are unreported and often illegal. For instance, babysitting for a friend is a *legal* part of the hidden economy. Illegal transactions of the hidden economy consist of conventional property crimes—from robbery to fencing—and such crimes as illegal drug distribution, gambling, prostitution, and employee theft. The hidden economy entails large numbers of people participating in economic activity—working, buying, selling—outside the view and control of the state. Employee theft and the amateur trade in stolen goods are examples of activities within this hidden economy. Moreover, when the legitimate labor market offers few attractive alternatives, illicit work—selling drugs, running numbers rackets, engaging in prostitution, and organizing criminal syndicates—likewise becomes relatively inviting.

Conventional crimes of the hidden economy are not found solely on the street. Most crime actually occurs in the workplace. Economic conditions such as inflation can affect the working class by pushing people into higher tax brackets and reducing the overall purchasing power of their remaining income. The result is that those who experience reduced standards of living and are not prepared to endure it sometimes turn to tax evasion, embezzlement, fraud, and other forms of occupational crime and off-the-books income.

However, occupational crimes cannot be explained solely by economic deprivation. Closer examination of crimes such as employee theft reveals that the *internal* structure of the work-

*Quality of work and crime: Even those who do find work may turn to crime. The quality of work available in lower- and working-class communities is a consistent influence on the street crime rate.*

place is equally important. Hollinger and Clark's (1983) study of employee theft in three industries concluded that this crime "is best understood within the social context of the work environment that includes perceived job dissatisfaction as a principal component" (p. 86). Dissatisfaction includes not only job quality but also such issues as *perceived inequality*. Many workers, when belittled by employers and thus reminded of the inequality in the workplace, turn to employee theft to "get back" at the boss or company.

Jerald Greenberg (1997) has called employee theft "the motive to even the score" (p. 94). In other words, employee theft is designed to bring harm to employers who are believed to have harmed employees. Thus employee theft is used to establish equity in an unequal relationship. Indeed, in a series of recent studies, Greenberg demonstrated that the more inequality in the workplace between employer and employee, the greater the likelihood of employee theft. Moreover, the *amount* of employee theft depends on the nature of interpersonal treatment: Inequality is "magnified by the insult of insensitive treatment" by employers to employees (Greenberg, 1997:96). The unequal relationships within the workplace and the workers' resentment of that inequality often trigger employee theft.

Thus far we have looked at crimes largely associated with the poor and working classes and how social position permits and precludes opportunities for committing conventional crimes. However, with the development of large corporations, financial institutions, and the state, a corresponding consolidation of a professional-managerial class has emerged. Members of this class can of course commit conventional crimes, but their structural position also provides the opportunity to engage in corporate and political crimes. The remainder of this section is devoted to a brief discussion of each of these crimes.

Corporations in a capitalist economy endure only if they make a profit. Yet profit making is not simply a matter of individual corporate greed. Rather, the pressure to make profits is created and enforced by the competitive structure of capitalism as an economic system. Corporations that do not continually reinvest their capital are likely to be "eaten up" by those that do. This pressure for profit drives corporate executives to engage in corporate crime. Moreover, in the pursuit of profit, corporate executives must overcome several obstacles, such as minimizing costs and creating demand, to succeed at profit making. Corporate executives can increase profits by keeping costs down. The lower the cost to the corporation for labor, tools, machinery, and so on, the higher the profits. Many corporate executives secure profits by minimizing the costs of worker, consumer, and environmental safety. The pressure to minimize costs helps create the conditions for corporate crimes (such as unsafe working conditions, unsafe products, environmental pollution, and sub-minimum wages) and global corporate crimes (such as dumping unsafe products and moving unsafe working conditions to more favorable environments).

A corporation has difficulty making a profit if it fails to sell what it produces. Thus, in addition to minimizing costs, corporate executives must create a demand for their product. This necessity is conducive to corporate deception in marketing, especially when demand for the product is erratic and variable. Corporate executives thus may conquer this obstacle by engaging in such corporate crimes as consumer fraud, false advertising, and other deceptive practices.

In sum, then, although not every corporation is criminal, in a profit-driven society corporations are inherently criminogenic because of the intrinsic aspects of profit making and the obstacles a corporation must overcome to achieve its primary goal. Because of such corporate priorities, incentives exist that make corporate crime the logical outcome. In fact, sociological studies have shown that when corporate profits decline, corporate crime occurs more often (Friedrichs, 2004). Thus, the structural position of corporate executives in the professional-managerial class and the necessity of profit making help us understand corporate crime.

The constant requirement for profit making is also related to the corporate association with criminal syndicates (traditionally known as "organized crime"). Profits from the illegal sale and distribution of goods and services are often laundered through large financial institutions, providing profits for both the syndicate and these corporations. There is, then, a close relationship between the hidden economy and the formal economy. Through labor racketeering, criminal syndicates also serve corporate interests by providing a means for preventing unionization and for controlling labor organizing, which helps minimize costs. In short, the symbiotic relationship between criminal syndicates and legitimate businesses serves both interests by helping them achieve their common goal of profit making (Simon, 2002a).

Members of the professional-managerial class employed in the political arena can use their position for personal ends. For instance, politicians can gain financially by engaging in a variety of corrupt practices such as bribery and the misuse of state funds. Political crimes for personal economic gain provide another example of how class position influences the type of crime.

We must note, too, that the state operates in certain ways to serve the economic interests of corporations. Although the managers of the state have historically come from the capitalist and the professional-managerial classes, the state is not simply an *instrument* of any class. In a capitalist economy the state operates to protect and support a corporate-dominated economy. As noted in Chapter 1.3, the state came into being with the development of social classes in agricultural societies; since then, the economically dominant class has usually been the most politically powerful class. However, this does not mean the state operates in a monolithic manner. Rather, state actions result from political conflicts among classes and also within the capitalist class. Nevertheless, these conflicts are embedded in an overall state policy of maintaining a viable capitalist economy.

Inasmuch as the major corporations (Fortune 500) dominate the U.S. economy, the state has a particular interest in their viability. This intimate relationship between state and the economy often leads to political crime. For example, those who manage the state are interested in bolstering a healthy capitalist economy, not only for generating state revenues but also for their own continued political futures. Consequently, state managers take actions that facilitate corporate investment.

Corporations base their foreign investment decisions on such things as the cost of labor and raw materials, the size of the market, and the political climate (stability) of the society receiving the capital. Is the working class under control? Will the state raise taxes? Does the state support business freedom? If the answers to such questions are negative, it is unlikely that corporations will invest. Consequently, U.S. foreign policy has supported global practices that permit the greatest opportunity for corporations to invest in other countries. Revolutionary movements in Africa and Central and Latin America, for example, that challenge the status quo also threaten corporate profits. The result is that the U.S. government has supported reactionary and oppressive regimes to quell such movements—as in Iran under the Shah and in Chile under Pinochet—and the CIA and National Security Council have moved to overthrow democratically elected governments. In other words, the state sometimes engages in global political crimes because of its inherent need to protect and maintain a capitalist economy.

The preceding discussion has provided selected examples of the relationship among class inequality, social position, and the types and seriousness of crime. Class position and inequality, however, provide only a partial understanding of how the patterns of crime and victimization occur in the United States. We now turn to a second, although equally important, sociological factor—gender inequality and crime.

## 3.2 Gender and Crime

**Gender** refers to historically and culturally developed behavior resulting from relationships between males/males, females/females, and males/females. Gender relations have developed sociologically into unequal relationships between males and females. This inequality has profound consequences for patterns of crime and victimization. In fact, gender is probably the best predictor of crime and victimization.

### Patterns of Crime and Victimization

Arrest data, self-report studies, and victimization surveys help us form a picture of which gender commits the greatest number of conventional crimes and what *types* of conventional crimes are associated most often with each gender. Consider arrest data. According to the Uniform Crime Reports (UCR), males clearly outnumber females in terms of arrest numbers. Men compose the overwhelming majority of those arrested for the eight major felonies. Indeed, in every case except larceny, men account for 80 percent or more of the arrests. The most significant crimes committed by females, according to the arrest data, are larceny (37 percent), forgery and counterfeiting (40 percent), fraud (45 percent), embezzlement (50 percent), and prostitution and commercialized vice (66 percent) (Federal Bureau of Investigation, 2004b).

Numerous researchers have used self-report studies to generate data on gender and crime. Although we cannot discuss all aspects of this work here, Douglas Smith and Christy Visher (1980; also see Steffensmeier and Allan, 1995a; Broidy and Agnew, 1997) reduced a large portion of this research (44 studies) to a single database from which they determined the magnitude of the relationship between gender and crime. Smith and Visher concluded that the findings of the self-report studies are remarkably similar to arrest data. Thus, males reported much more involvement in conventional crimes, especially in serious felonies. Moreover, in number and type, the female contribution to conventional crimes was found to be quite similar to the arrest data. However, Smith and Visher established that arrest data underreport women's involvement in nonserious property crimes such as shoplifting and fraud, particularly for female youth. In other words, according to self-report studies, adult involvement in conventional crimes seems more male dominated than youth crime, especially for property crimes.

Thus, arrest, self-report, and victimization data all suggest that both male adults and youths commit more conventional crimes and more serious types of conventional crimes than female adults and youths. When women commit conventional crimes, they are primarily less serious offenses against property. Women are most likely to commit larceny, fraud, and embezzlement (Belknap, 2000; Chesney-Lind and Pasko, 2004). Males disproportionately commit interpersonal crimes of violence and property crimes, especially the more serious ones. Moreover, males have a virtual monopoly on the commission of syndicated, corporate, and political crime. Thus males commit the greatest number of crimes and the most serious types of them.

As Table 3.3 shows, males also have the highest rate of victimization for interpersonal crimes of violence (except rape and purse snatching/pocket picking). Consequently, for interpersonal crimes of violence, the highest victimization rate is *intragender:* males victimizing males. Nevertheless, there is substantial *intergender* victimization: males violating women through such offenses as rape and violence against women in the family.

## Gender and Varieties of Crime

The patterns of crime and victimization identified above reflect broad social inequalities between men and women. Unequal relations between men and women are evident most clearly in the fact that men control the institutional structures of society and, therefore, also control women. Patterns of crime and victimization in contemporary U.S. society reflect these unequal gender relations. We consider first how these gender relations are structured and then relate that structure theoretically to the empirical evidence on gender and crime.

As industrialization has developed, women have been drawn out of the home and into the labor market in increasing numbers. More women today work in the labor market than ever before. For example, in 1970, 32 percent of all women 16 years and older were in the labor force; by 2002 this figure had risen to 60 percent (*Statistical Abstract of the U.S.*, 2003). Yet, as women enter the labor market they are segregated into certain "feminine" occupations. Most women are concentrated in service, retail, and clerical jobs. These occupations are among the lowest-paid positions in the labor market and provide little opportunity for advancement. Women make up 93 percent of nurses; 98 percent of pre-kindergarten and kindergarten teachers; 77 percent of cashiers; 98 percent of secretaries, stenographers, and typists; 89 percent of clerks; 87 percent of bank tellers; 98 percent of child-care workers; and 78 percent of waiters and waitresses. At the other end of the job hierarchy, women make up only 11 percent of engineers; 19 percent of dentists; 31 percent of physicians; and 32 percent of lawyers and judges (*Statistical Abstract of the U.S.*, 2003).

Women's position in this unequal gendered labor market helps explain their patterns of crime. For example, as women experience economic pressure from increasing inflation and low pay, they are more likely to engage in crimes such as embezzlement. Moreover, the gender division of labor identified above determines the type of embezzlement women are most likely to commit. Although women make up slightly more than one-third of all embezzlers, they are primarily petty embezzlers (Chesney-Lind and Pasko, 2004). The gendered nature of embezzlement relates to women's subordinate position in the gender division of labor. As is clear from the foregoing evidence, the occupations in which women are employed today are ones that handle large quantities

**Table 3.3   Personal Crimes, 2002: Number of Victimizations and Victimization Rates for Persons Age 12 and Over, by Type of Crime and Gender of Victims**

| | Rate per 1,000 persons age 12 and over | | | | | |
| Type of crime | Both genders | | Male | | Female | |
| --- | --- | --- | --- | --- | --- | --- |
| | Number | Rate | Number | Rate | Number | Rate |
| **All personal crimes** | **5,496,810** | **23.7** | **2,927,520** | **26.1** | **2,569,300** | **21.5** |
| Crimes of violence | 5,341,410 | 23.1 | 2,857,930 | 25.5 | 2,483,480 | 20.8 |
| Completed violence | 1,753,090 | 7.6 | 816,240 | 7.3 | 936,850 | 7.8 |
| Attempted/threatened violence | 3,588,320 | 15.5 | 2,041,690 | 18.2 | 1,546,630 | 13.0 |
| Rape/sexual assault | 247,730 | 1.1 | 31,640 | 0.3 | 216,090 | 1.8 |
| Rape/attempted rape | 167,860 | 0.7 | 22,610* | 0.2* | 145,240 | 1.2 |
| Rape | 90,390 | 0.4 | 4,100* | 0.0* | 86,290 | 0.7 |
| Attempted rape[a] | 77,470 | 0.3 | 18,520* | 0.2* | 58,950 | 0.5 |
| Sexual assault[b] | 79,870 | 0.3 | 9,030* | 0.1* | 70,840 | 0.6 |
| Robbery | 512,490 | 2.2 | 323,530 | 2.9 | 188,960 | 1.6 |
| Completed/property taken | 385,880 | 1.7 | 237,350 | 2.1 | 148,530 | 1.2 |
| With injury | 169,980 | 0.7 | 102,860 | 0.9 | 67,130 | 0.6 |
| Without injury | 215,890 | 0.9 | 134,490 | 1.2 | 81,400 | 0.7 |
| Attempted to take property | 126,610 | 0.5 | 86,180 | 0.8 | 40,430 | 0.3 |
| With injury | 42,600 | 0.2 | 31,470 | 0.3 | 11,130* | 0.1* |
| Without injury | 84,020 | 0.4 | 54,710 | 0.5 | 29,300* | 0.2* |
| Assault | 4,581,190 | 19.8 | 2,502,760 | 22.3 | 2,078,440 | 17.4 |
| Aggravated | 990,110 | 4.3 | 588,430 | 5.2 | 401,670 | 3.4 |
| With injury | 316,260 | 1.4 | 166,930 | 1.5 | 149,330 | 1.3 |
| Threatened with weapon | 673,850 | 2.9 | 421,510 | 3.8 | 252,350 | 2.1 |
| Simple | 3,591,090 | 15.5 | 1,914,320 | 17.1 | 1,676,760 | 14.0 |
| With minor injury | 906,580 | 3.9 | 405,670 | 3.6 | 500,910 | 4.2 |
| Without Injury | 2,684,510 | 11.6 | 1,508,650 | 13.4 | 1,175,860 | 9.9 |
| Purse snatching/pocket picking | 155,400 | 0.7 | 69,590 | 0.6 | 85,810 | 0.7 |
| **Population age 12 and over** | **231,589,260** | ... | **112,241,930** | ... | **119,347,330** | ... |

Note: Detail may not add to total shown because of rounding.

*Estimate is based on about 10 or fewer sample cases.        [a]Includes verbal threats of rape.        [b]Includes threats.        ... Not applicable.

Source: Department of Justice, 2003.

of money. Not surprisingly, research on gender and bank embezzlement shows that since women are more likely to be bank tellers and men bank officers, women embezzlers tend to "take cash from the till" whereas men have greater opportunity to "manipulate the books." In addition, women's motivation to engage in bank embezzlement and other white-collar crimes differs from that of men:

> Although women and men do share motives, women are more likely than men to commit their crimes to improve their family's economic status, fulfill a care-taking role, or maintain a love relationship. They are less likely than men to commit their crimes to advance a career or to obtain some long-desired status symbol. (Bartol, 2001:284)

Women's position in the gender division of labor also helps explain their involvement in other property crimes, such as larceny and fraud. The literature on the *feminization of poverty* indicates that "the fastest growing population living in poverty today is made up of women and children" (Sidel, 1998). The increasing impoverishment of women is caused by such factors as (1) rising divorce rates and the attendant rapid development of female-headed households; (2) the gender division of labor, which continues to discriminate against women; (3) the lack of adequate child care; and

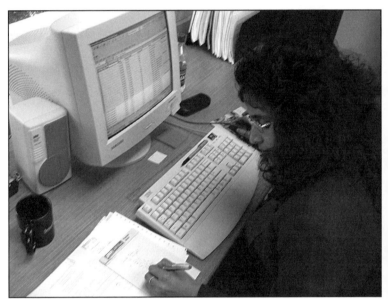

*Women and crime: Petty forms of property crime are the crimes commited most frequently by women. One such crime is embezzlement from institutions such as banks—a crime often committed to help solve unexpected financial problems arising in the family.*

(4) a welfare system that maintains its recipients below the poverty line. Not surprisingly, most female offenders are either unemployed or working in low-paying, menial jobs (Maher, 1997). Research has confirmed this relationship between the feminization of poverty and women's property crimes. For example, increasing economic marginalization of women places them in circumstances where they are more likely to offend. In particular, Holtfreter, Reisig, and Morash (2004) have found that poor women are most likely to commit crimes if they do not receive government-sponsored benefits such as subsidized housing and training for jobs that raise the quality of their lives.

Although segregation into the "pink-collar ghetto" structures women's conventional criminality, women are largely absent from the major professions. Given that more women have become corporate managers in recent years, women managers are still systematically segregated into such lower-status managerial positions as personnel, re-

---

**Box 3.1    Sexed Work**

Lisa Maher's *Sexed Work: Gender, Race, and Resistance in a Brooklyn Drug Market* (1997) provided considerable support for the links between gender, race, and class inequality. Maher undertook an ethnographic study of homeless women drug users and their relation to the street-level drug economy of the Bushwick section of Brooklyn, New York. She examined three major options for women's survival in the poverty-ridden section of New York City: "drug-business hustles," "nondrug hustles," and "sexwork." Drug-business hustles include the provision of goods and services necessary for the distribution and consumption of illicit drugs. Nondrug hustles are acts of income generation not directly related to distributing and selling drugs, such as robbery, burglary, and larceny. Sexwork is confined to prostitution at the street level.

Maher found that men dominated at the highest levels of drug dealing and of all nondrug hustles; women were limited to the lowest positions of street-level drug sales and sexwork. Since women were viewed by men as unreliable, untrustworthy, and incapable of demonstrating an effective capacity for violence, they were used primarily as "informal steerers," which involved recommending to drug buyers a particular drug "in return for 'change,' usually a dollar or so" (pp. 88–89). As Maher stated, it is institutionalized sexism of the street culture that is "the most powerful element shaping women's experiences in the drug economy: It inhibited their access to drug-business work roles and effectively foreclosed their participation as higher-level distributors" (p. 106).

Consequently, sexwork was the only survival activity consistently available to homeless women drug users in Bushwick. However, this street-level prostitution was far from financially lucrative. Because prostitution was the only consistently available option for these women to survive, a flood of female sexworkers led to the lowering of the going rate for sex transactions, "encouraged 'deviant' sexual expectations of the part of dates, engendered relations of competition and hostility, and promoted the atomization and social isolation of women drug users" (p. 130).

One of the most interesting findings of Maher's research was the interrelation between gender and race. Maher found that this intersection positioned women differentially with respect to opportunities for income generation in the street culture. For example, being white and a woman proved to be advantageous in one aspect of the culture but a disadvantage in another. Indeed, white women had the least opportunity to participate in drug dealing because they would "stand out like a sore thumb" in relation to the Latino and African-American women and thus would have a much greater chance of drawing police attention. However, regarding sexwork, white women had the advantage. As Maher put it, "European American women retain a relative advantage in that their skin color allows them to cater to the racial prejudices of clients which devalue the sexual services of minority women" (p. 186). Thus opportunities to survive economically in Bushwick were both race-bound and gender-bound.

---

search, affirmative action, and equal employment (*Statistical Abstract of the United States,* 2003). These jobs do not lead to decision-making positions within the corporation. In other words, the gender division of labor within the corporate managerial structure effectively segregates women from, but places men in, positions of power where corporate crimes are contrived. This process is often referred to as the *old-boy network,* a sponsorship system that recruits junior male executives into the upper ranks of the managerial divisions of the corporation. Consequently, corporate crime is a male-dominated activity. And studies examining gender and corporate crime have found that men's financial gains from such crimes are much larger than women's, that women usually work alone when committing these crimes whereas men usually work with others, and that women's share of corporate crime is only 1 percent of women's white-collar crime cases (compared to 14 percent of men's) (Belknap, 2001; Friedrichs, 2004).

In the political arena, the gender division of labor likewise guarantees that political crime is dominated by men. There has never been a female president or vice president of the United States, and in 2004 only 60 of the 435 representatives in Congress and 14 of the 100 senators were women. Thus, women constitute more than 50 percent of the U.S. population yet hold approximately 12 percent of the seats in Congress. This absence of women from top governmental positions also results from an old-boy network. The gender division of labor within mainstream political parties—the Democratic and Republican parties in the United States—makes it extremely difficult for women either to reach positions of party responsibility or to be supported as candidates by parties. Thus, historically, women have been involved in political crimes from "below"—such as Susan B. Anthony being convicted of voting in 1872 (women were not granted the right to vote in the United States until 1920) and Angela Davis being arrested for conspiracy to free revolutionary George Jackson (she was acquitted in 1972 in a highly publicized political trial) (Turk, 2000).

An old-boy network also functions in criminal syndicates and street gangs. Steffensmeier (1983) has shown that women are excluded or underrepresented in criminal syndicates and, if present, are allocated less-valued roles. Criminal syndicates are masculine dominated because of what Steffensmeier termed "homosocial reproduction," "sex-typing," and the "task environment of crime."

*Homosocial reproduction* refers to the ways in which those in powerful positions fill positions with men like themselves. Because men dominate (control and populate) criminal syndicates, they prefer to work, associate, and do business with other men. This homosocial reproduction works in tandem with *sex-typing*. According to Steffensmeier (1983), males in criminal syndicates stereotype women and criminal work in certain ways that effectively discriminate against women. Males in criminal syndicates, for example, see their work as (1) too hard, heavy, and dangerous for women and (2) too degrading and cheapening for women, leading to a loss of women's dignity. Steffensmeier added that men view "women as not as *capable,* or not as skilled, or not as stable; and believe that, while women *take orders* from men, men do not take orders from any woman" (p. 1013). Finally, the *task environment of crime* refers to the fact that to survive in the world of crime, a criminal syndicate must deal with the threat of arrest and imprisonment as well as threats from other criminal groups. Consequently, because both *secrecy* and *violence* are inextricable aspects of criminal syndicates, they recruit people who the leaders feel certain can help satisfy these needs. As Steffensmeier stated:

> A premium is placed on attributes such as trust and reliability and on physical characteristics such as strength and "muscle"—the capacity for force or violence. These characteristics have not been the prerogative of females. Furthermore, there is an almost inexhaustible pool of males to fill openings in crime groups; there are few empty places left for females. (p. 1014)

The three factors identified by Steffensmeier show that the structure of criminal syndicates tends to reflect the broader gender inequalities of society.

All this does not mean, of course, that women are never involved in important roles within professional and syndicated crime. Clearly, throughout history some women have been involved in such criminal activities. The important point is that these activities are highly dominated by men, a phenomenon that is socially determined by gender relations in the broader society. Nevertheless, more recent research indicates that women involved in syndicated crime are not simply subordinate to men but engage in a variety of activities in syndicated crime. For example, women who are wives, daughters, and sisters to men who are involved in syndicated crime often are not happy with their life, feel manipulated by "their men," and often "rebel against their lifestyle, usually by way of arguments, separations, divorces, and occasional violence" (Albanese, 2004:13). Moreover, some women have become involved in criminal syndicates without any type of dependent status to men—such as operating in the illegal gambling, loan sharking, and drug markets (Carson, 2000).

Not surprisingly, males also dominate street gangs. Within a culture based on gender inequality, parents tend to control the spare time of young females more closely than that of males, leaving males freer to explore the outside world and to come into contact with one another (Hagan, McCarthy, and Foster, 2002). Young male criminality is therefore much more likely than female criminality to be collective in nature. And as Box (1983) has pointed out, females are seen by male gang members as emotional, unreliable, illogical, and untrustworthy—"not the type of person you want along on an armed robbery" (p. 182). Thus the old-boy network also infiltrates street gangs. When girls are members of street gangs, they usually inhabit powerless positions. For example, Jody Miller (2001) reported in her book *One of the Guys* that gender inequality is rampant in mixed-gender gangs, such as male leadership, a double standard with regard to sexual activities, the sexual exploitation of some girls, and most girls' exclusion from serious gang crime.

Interpersonal violence against women is also closely associated with gender inequalities. Although some rapists actually may be psychopathic, research indicates that the vast majority are not emotionally disturbed (Walklate, 2004). Moreover, most assumptions about rape held by the public—such as that rape is impossible; that women want to be raped; that "no" means "yes"—have been disproven by research (Belknap, 2001). Most criminologists therefore view rape as the result of the structural subordination of women in contemporary society.

The United States has been described as a rape-prone society. In her research of 186 tribal societies, social anthropologist Peggy Sanday (1981) found that high rape rates occur in societies that are dominated by males and that feature male violence. Rape-prone societies, then, are those in which males dominate politically, economically, and ideologically and that glorify male violence. Rape-free societies, Sanday found, are marked by relative gender equality, the belief that the sexes are complementary, and a low level of interpersonal violence overall. Thus Sanday's work helps us understand why the United States can be considered a rape-prone society. Not only is U.S. society dominated politically, economically, and ideologically by males, but it also glorifies male violence in the street, in sports, in the state, and so on.

Indeed, the assertion of dominance enables rape. The rapist uses sex as a violent attack on the integrity of the woman as a person. In a rape, what is normally understood as an act of affection becomes an act of hate. This act destroys the woman's integrity by denying the victim her own will to engage, or not to engage, in sexuality as she pleases. By prohibiting this freedom, the rapist creates conditions of dominance and subordination.

Rape reflects the dominance/subordination gender relationships in society. This was evident in Philippe Bourgois' (1996) study of inner-city Puerto Rican men. Because of economic marginalization, these men were unable to become "head of the household" like in their grandfathers' generation. Consequently, Bourgois found that many of these men took "refuge" in a drug economy that celebrated misogyny and in a predatory street culture that normalized gang rape. As Bourgois stated, "Marginalized men lash out against the women and children they can no longer support economically nor control patriarchally" (p. 412).

Like rape, violence by men in the family (wife rape, wife battering, and child sexual abuse) reflects gender power and inequality. The structure of the traditional nuclear family encourages the husband/father to view "his" wife and children as under his control. Violence in the family is intimately linked to the cultural expectation that males are authority figures within monogamous relationships. Some men therefore feel they have the right to dominate and control their wives, and wife battering serves to ensure continued compliance with their commands. If a wife questions such authority in any way, a violent husband turns to force simply to "get his way" (Ptacek, 1998).

Women's subordinate social position reinforces masculine dominance and violence in the family. If a wife is unemployed or works in a low-paying job, as is all too typical nowadays, it is easier for a husband to control her. In this type of society a husband usually has the economic power and the wife is dependent, often even if she works outside the home. Such conditions make it difficult for her to leave a violent relationship, especially if she has children.

Economic dependency and powerlessness in the family also affect the likelihood of wife rape. Because of this unequal economic familial relationship, wife rape may not be physically violent. If she is unwilling to "oblige" him, a husband can obtain access to "his" wife's body by threatening a beating, loss of affection, or loss of economic support. The wife may thus conclude that unwanted sexual intercourse is not as harmful as the alternative—poverty and distress. This situation is exacerbated for women with children or without skills.

Gender inequality is also related to wife killing. For example, Bailey and Peterson (1995) found that the rate of women being killed by their husbands is significantly higher in cities where the college education gap between males and females is greater, where women experience higher levels of unemployment than men, and where a positive association exists with male-female inequality in income. As Bailey and Peterson concluded, "The overall pattern of findings for wife killings suggests that gender inequality breeds violence against wives" (p. 202).

Similarly, child sexual abuse results from the powerlessness of children (especially young girls) in the family and their economic and emotional dependence. Children are essentially a captive population; they are economically and emotionally dependent on parents. Particularly at young ages, children do what is necessary to maintain a supportive relationship with their parents, even to the extent of keeping the assault secret. Consequently, this dependency and powerlessness makes child sexual abuse highly exploitive and nonconsensual. In other words, to understand child sexual abuse it is essential to understand power within the family. This type of abuse primarily entails a father as perpetrator and his daughter as victim. The power and authority claimed by the father structures the offender/victim relationship. Believing that women's role is to serve the needs of men—including their sexual needs—the male authority figure uses his power to assault his daughter incestuously.

Our discussion points to the fact that analysis of gender inequality adds considerably to our understanding of the patterns of crime and victimization in U.S. society. As with class position, gender position structures the opportunities for engaging in crime and the possibilities of being victimized by crime.

In addition to class and gender, racial inequality also structures patterns of crime and victimization. Let us now turn to this topic.

## 3.3 Race and Crime

Genetic differences in skin color assume social significance when they are used to justify unequal treatment of one race by another. **Race** relations, like class and gender relations, have developed into unequal relations in which one race (white) uses skin color to legitimize domination and control of other races. Simultaneously, this inequality has important consequences for the patterns of crime and victimization in the United States.

Although whites continue to dominate several racial and ethnic groups in the United States—such as Native Americans, Asians, Mexican Americans, and African Americans—we focus on the inequality between whites and African Americans and the relationship of that inequality to crime and victimization. We concentrate on these two groups because, unfortunately, criminologists generally have ignored other racial and ethnic groups; therefore, insufficient data are available with which to make comparisons (but see Hawkins, 2003; Criminal Justice Collective, 2000). We begin with a discussion of racial patterns of crime and victimization and then turn to a discussion of race and varieties of crime.

### Patterns of Crime and Victimization

The UCR indicates that whites account for approximately 71 percent of all arrests; African Americans account for 27 percent; the remainder are of other races (Federal Bureau of Investigation, 2004b). Racial arrest disparities are evident when we take population into account. African Americans constitute only 13 percent of the U.S. population (Current Population Reports, 2004), yet they account for 38 percent of violent crime arrests and for over 29 percent of property crime arrests (Federal Bureau of Investigation, 2004b).

Although arrest data show striking differences in rates for adults, self-report studies show that African-American and white youths report similar involvement in youth crime (LaFree and Hussong, 2001). When specific offenses are analyzed, however, it appears that African-American adults and youths report more involvement in the most serious conventional crimes, especially crimes of interpersonal violence. Summing up their analysis of arrest, self-report, and victimization data on race and crime, Hagan and Peterson (1995) stated the following: "These data reflect a crucial aspect of crime and race in America: not only are rates of offending and arrest high in African-American communities, but so too are rates of victimization. That is, crime is predominantly intraracial" (p. 23).

Thus, the higher *arrest* rate for African Americans is probably the result of *both* the criminal justice system's selection bias and a greater involvement of African Americans in conventional crimes. Criminologists have known for quite some time that when individuals of different social classes and races come into contact with the criminal justice system *for the same crime,* young, lower-class, minority males are more likely to be arrested, prosecuted, convicted, and sentenced to prison for longer terms (Reiman, 2004). Moreover, this criminal justice system racial bias seems to occur at an even higher frequency in cities with the most pronounced racial segregation (Stolzenberg, D'Alessio, and Eitle, 2004). Because of racial inequality in U.S. society, African Americans indeed suffer considerable discriminatory and oppressive conditions that whites do not. It is this disadvantageous social position that most likely results in a higher crime rate by African Americans than might otherwise be expected for their population size.

African Americans are also more often the victims of violent crime. As Table 3.4 shows, in 2002 African Americans were victimized at a greater rate for all personal crimes—in particular, for robbery and assault. Moreover, as Table 3.5 shows, African Americans are victimized at a higher rate than whites for all household property crimes—in particular, for both household burglary and motor vehicle theft. Thus we can conclude that conventional crimes—especially crimes of interpersonal violence and property crimes—are *intraracial.* Nevertheless, there seems to be an increasing rate of *interracial* violence directed by whites *against* African Americans (see Chapter 5.1).

Conventional crimes are only one aspect of criminality, and, unfortunately, criminologists have concentrated their analysis of race and crime only on racial differences in rates of conventional crimes. However, whites clearly dominate in corporate and political positions where corporate and political crimes are committed. Therefore, although conventional crimes may be committed more often by African Americans than by whites, the more harmful and economically damaging white-collar and political crimes are disproportionately committed by whites.

## Race and Varieties of Crime

As we point out in our discussion of "hate crimes" (see Chapter 5.1), African Americans are among the most frequent victims of interracial violence. However, they are also the primary victims of conventional crime. Discrimination continues to worsen the disadvantages African Americans already suffer, creating conditions for high rates of intraracial crime. Obstacles experienced by the white working class are greater for African Americans because of racial discrimination. As Hagan and Peterson (1995) have pointed out, numerous studies have shown that racial discrimination, segregation, and concentrated poverty produce "pervasive family and community disadvantages as well as educational and employment difficulties, which in turn cause delinquent and criminal behavior among young minority males" (p. 16):

- Overall, African Americans account for one-third of all arrests and one-half of all incarcerations in the United States.

**Table 3.4    Personal Crimes, 2002: Number of Victimizations and Victimization Rates for Persons Age 12 and Over, by Type of Crime and Race of Victims**

| Type of crime | White | | Black | | Other | |
|---|---|---|---|---|---|---|
| | *Rate per 1,000 persons age 12 and over* | | | | | |
| | *Number* | *Rate* | *Number* | *Rate* | *Number* | *Rate* |
| **All personal crimes** | **4,525,090** | **23.5** | **824,530** | **28.6** | **147,190** | **15.1** |
| Crimes of violence | 4,392,620 | 22.8 | 805,440 | 27.9 | 143,350 | 14.7 |
| Completed violence | 1,430,510 | 7.4 | 271,200 | 9.4 | 51,380 | 5.3 |
| Attempted/threatened violence | 2,962,110 | 15.4 | 534,230 | 18.5 | 91,980 | 9.4 |
| Rape/sexual assault | 163,790 | 0.8 | 72,020 | 2.5 | 11,920* | 1.2* |
| Rape/attempted rape | 103,350 | 0.5 | 55,460 | 1.9 | 9,050* | 0.9* |
| Rape | 65,440 | 0.3 | 20,980* | 0.7* | 3,980* | 0.4 |
| Attempted rape[a] | 37,910 | 0.2 | 34,480 | 1.2 | 5,070* | 0.5* |
| Sexual assault[b] | 60,440 | 0.3 | 16,560* | 0.6* | 2,870* | 0.3* |
| Robbery | 370,800 | 1.9 | 118,040 | 4.1 | 23,650* | 2.4* |
| Completed/property taken | 275,550 | 1.4 | 98,310 | 3.4 | 12,020* | 1.2* |
| With injury | 119,810 | 0.6 | 43,780 | 1.5 | 6,390* | 0.7* |
| Without injury | 155,740 | 0.8 | 54,520 | 1.9 | 5,630* | 0.6 * |
| Attempted to take property | 95,250 | 0.5 | 19,740* | 0.7* | 11,630* | 1.2* |
| With injury | 34,750 | 0.2 | 5,230* | 0.2* | 2,620* | 0.3* |
| Without injury | 60,490 | 0.3 | 14,510* | 0.5* | 9,010* | 0.9* |
| Assault | 3,858,030 | 20.0 | 615,370 | 21.3 | 107,790 | 11.0 |
| Aggravated | 788,040 | 4.1 | 192,900 | 6.7 | 9,170* | 0.9* |
| With injury | 267,900 | 1.4 | 45,960 | 1.6 | 2,390* | 0.2* |
| Threatened with weapon | 520,140 | 2.7 | 146,930 | 5.1 | 6,780* | 0.7* |
| Simple | 3,069,990 | 15.9 | 422,480 | 14.6 | 98,620 | 10.1 |
| With minor injury | 780,230 | 4.0 | 93,360 | 3.2 | 32,990 | 3.4 |
| Without injury | 2,289,760 | 11.9 | 329,110 | 11.4 | 65,630 | 6.7 |
| Purse snatching/pocket picking | 132,460 | 0.7 | 19,100* | 0.7* | 3,840* | 0.4* |
| **Population age 12 and over** | **192,956,980** | ... | **28,871,440** | ... | **9,760,850** | ... |

Note: Detail may not add to total shown because of rounding.
*Estimate is based on about 10 or fewer sample cases.       ... Not applicable.
[a]Includes verbal threats of rape.       [b]Includes threats.
Source: Department of Justice, 2003.

**Table 3.5   Property Crimes, 2002: Number of Victimizations and Victimization Rates by Type of Crime and Race of Head of Household**

| Type of crime | All Races | | White | | Black | | Other | |
|---|---|---|---|---|---|---|---|---|
| | *Number* | *Rate* | *Number* | *Rate* | *Number* | *Rate* | *Number* | *Rate* |
| **Property crimes** | **17,539,220** | **159.0** | **14,527,440** | **157.6** | **2,434,780** | **173.7** | **576,990** | **139.8** |
| Household burglary | 3,055,720 | 27.7 | 2,396,810 | 26.0 | 578,880 | 41.3 | 80,030 | 19.4 |
| Completed | 2,597,310 | 23.5 | 2,080,340 | 22.6 | 444,040 | 31.7 | 72,930 | 17.7 |
| Forcible entry | 1,017,660 | 9.2 | 727,180 | 7.9 | 260,680 | 18.6 | 29,800* | 7.2* |
| Unlawful entry without force | 1,579,650 | 14.3 | 1,353,160 | 14.7 | 183,360 | 13.1 | 43,130 | 10.4 |
| Attempted forcible entry | 458,410 | 4.2 | 316,470 | 3.4 | 134,840 | 9.6 | 7,100* | 1.7* |
| Motor vehicle theft | 988,760 | 9.0 | 695,410 | 7.5 | 241,670 | 17.2 | 51,670 | 12.5 |
| Completed | 780,630 | 7.1 | 549,730 | 6.0 | 191,610 | 13.7 | 39,300 | 9.5 |
| Attempted | 208,120 | 1.9 | 145,690 | 1.6 | 50,060 | 3.6 | 12,380* | 3.0* |
| Theft | 13,494,750 | 122.3 | 11,435,220 | 124.1 | 1,614,240 | 115.2 | 445,290 | 107.9 |
| Completed | 13,039,920 | 118.2 | 11,054,970 | 119.9 | 1,556,620 | 111.1 | 428,320 | 103.8 |
| Less than $50 | 4,186,570 | 37.9 | 3,646,500 | 39.6 | 409,720 | 29.2 | 130,360 | 31.6 |
| $50–$249 | 4,455,080 | 40.4 | 3,717,980 | 40.3 | 598,290 | 42.7 | 138,810 | 33.6 |
| $250 or more | 3,270,530 | 29.6 | 2,766,820 | 30.0 | 396,330 | 28.3 | 107,390 | 26.0 |
| Amount not available | 1,127,740 | 10.2 | 923,680 | 10.0 | 152,290 | 10.9 | 51,760 | 12.5 |
| Attempted | 454,830 | 4.1 | 380,240 | 4.1 | 57,620 | 4.1 | 16,970* | 4.1* |
| **Total number of households** | **110,323,840** | ... | **92,182,320** | ... | **14,013,850** | ... | **4,127,670** | ... |

*Rate per 1,000 households*

Note: Detail may not add to total shown because of rounding.
*Estimate Is based on about 10 or fewer sample cases.
... Not applicable.
Source: Department of Justice, 2003.

- About one-fifth of all 16- to 34-year-old black males are under justice system supervision.

- Half of all African-American school dropouts, and three-quarters of dropouts who are between 25 and 34 years old, are under justice system supervision.

- Three-quarters of all black prison inmates have less than 12 years of schooling.

- African-American prisoners between 25 and 34 years of age report preprison incomes that average $11,368, compared with $20,175 for this age group in the general population.

- Homicide is the leading cause of death among African-American youth.

The relationship between unemployment and crime we discussed in the class and crime section is especially helpful in understanding the high crime rates of African-American male and female youth. Research has shown consistently that the overrepresentation of African-American adults and youths in conventional crime statistics is the result of racial and economical inequalities (Anderson, 1999; Hawkins, 2003; Sampson and Wilson, 1995). Indeed, the 1954 official unemployment rates of African-American and white 16- to 19-year-olds were almost identical: 15.4 and 14.0 percent, respectively (Duster, 1987). By 2004, however, 27 percent of African-American 16- to 19-year-olds and 10 percent of white 16- to 19-year-olds were officially unemployed (Department of Labor, 2004). In other words, increasing economic inequality between white and African-American youth has occurred since the mid-1950s. The high rate of crimes committed by African-American youths has thus stemmed from their deteriorating economic situation (McNulty and Bellair, 2003).

Although the African-American female violent crime rate is high, within the African-American community the vast majority of criminal violence is committed *by* African-American men *against* African-American men. For African-American men ages 15–44, homicide is the leading cause of death, and African-American men are eight times more likely to die by murder than are white males.

The work of Bruce, Roscigno, and McCall (1998) and Bruce and Roscigno (2003) has likewise shown the relationship between racial inequality and violence by African Americans. Specifically, they demonstrated that a link exists between structural racial disadvantage and the perpetuation of interpersonal violence in inner-city African-American communities. Growing up in disadvantaged communities, African Americans become aware of the structural constraints of their existence, such as the lack of educational and job opportunities. Bruce and his colleagues argued that these constraints shape social and psychological well-being and lead to anger, frustration, and despair.

Moreover, because of the lack of legitimate economic opportunities, many poor inner-city African Americans participate in the informal economy of drugs and weapons trafficking. The combination of illegal activities and the availability of weapons increases the potential for gun use to solve conflicts. The result is the transformation of nonviolent neighborhoods into communities gripped by the ever-present threat of violent confrontation. Such a threat of danger can result in interactional rituals that lead to violence:

The reality of living in an area where individuals have to depend on illegitimate activities for survival can have negative consequences for social psychological processes which, in turn, may increase the potential for violence. . . . Because gang members hold such grim prospects for life, minor incidents such as accidentally bumping into someone or wearing a particular color create the possibility that an individual will be attacked. (Bruce, Roscigno, and McCall, 1998:44)

Thus, these authors have shown how violence among African Americans results from the intersection of racial and economical disadvantage, local context, and individual social action.

In summary, racial inequality structures conventional crime, both interracial and intraracial. Interracial violence results from extreme racist beliefs in a racially segregated and unequal society. Crime by African Americans is the product of their positions in class and racial hierarchies, which are, of course, mediated by gender.

Still, we must remember that the vast majority of those who commit interpersonal violent crimes are young white males and that every year approximately 70 percent of *all* conventional crimes are

*Racism and the criminal justice system: For the same crime, young, lower- and working-class, racial minority males are more likely than other males to be arrested, prosecuted, convicted, and sentenced to prison for longer terms.*

committed by whites (Gould, 2000). Moreover, combined class, gender, and racial inequality also determine who can engage in white-collar and political crimes. African Americans hold only 7.6 percent of executive, administrative, and managerial positions and only 8 percent of professional positions (*Statistical Abstract of the U.S.*, 2003). Additionally, there has never been an African-American president or vice president, and in 2004, African Americans held no seats in the U.S. Senate and only 37 of the 435 seats in the House. Thus, racial inequality determines that whites hold more of those positions in which the most serious and harmful crimes occur—white-collar and political crimes. Racial inequality—as with class and gender inequality—governs social position in society and, therefore, criminal opportunities.

## 3.4 Age and Crime

Economic benefits, social privileges, and political power are based not only on class, gender, and race but also on **age.** Even such basic rights as sexual activity, voting, and drinking alcohol are conferred by age. Thus, age inequality and age discrimination exist in U.S. society. These phenomena are most pronounced for youth, but they also affect the elderly. Unequal generational divisions between young and old are prevalent, and social behavior—including crime—is linked to the aging process. One's position in the age hierarchy permits or precludes opportunity for engaging in crime. Consider the patterns of crime and victimization based on age.

## Patterns of Crime and Victimization

According to arrest data in the UCR (Federal Bureau of Investigation, 2004b), participation in conventional crime rises with age, peaks in the teenage and early adulthood years, then declines. Two important age patterns for conventional property and violent crimes emerge: (1) Property crime arrest rates peak between the ages of 13 and 17, and then decline rather quickly, and (2) for violent crimes the rate peaks at around the ages of 18–19 and declines much more slowly.

Some criminologists have questioned arrest data on age. For example, because youths tend to commit conventional crimes in groups, they are allegedly more visible to the police and thus more likely to be arrested. Also, some criminologists argue that youths are less skilled than are adults in committing crime and, therefore, more likely to be arrested. It may be, then, that arrest statistics on age are biased; this would explain the overrepresentation of youth in UCR data. However, self-report studies report similar age patterns for conventional crimes (Warr, 2001). We conclude therefore that arrest data are reliable evidence of the age distribution of conventional crime.

Tables 3.6 and 3.7 show victimization rates for conventional crimes by age. For crimes of violence, young persons aged 16–19 have the highest rates of victimization. For victims over the age of 19, violent crimes decline with age, so that those aged 65 and older have the lowest victimization rates for violent crimes. Moreover, as Table 3.7 shows, property crime victimization rates are highest for the youngest heads of household and decline with age. For conventional crimes, then, the highest victimization rates are *intra-age*.

## Age and Varieties of Crime

David Greenberg (1977) has shown that during the transition from childhood to adolescence, the links between children and parents decrease (yet economic dependence remains), while receptivity to peers and peer evaluation increases. Being popular and connected with the "right" groups becomes critically important for most youths. The partial disengagement from family and the heightened closeness to peers, combined with advertising directed toward the teenage market, create the conditions for youthful involvement in pleasure-seeking, consumption-oriented social lives. Indeed, participation in this teenage social life requires money for buying the "right stuff": clothing, cosmetics, cigarettes, alcoholic beverages, narcotics, CDs, CD players, gasoline for cars and motorcycles, tickets to films and concerts, and meals in restaurants. However, because teenage labor force participation has declined drastically, youths are finding it more and more difficult to support their participation in teen life. Thus, the high rate of property crimes for teenagers is, according to Greenberg, "a response to the disjunction between the desire to participate in social activities with peers and the absence of legitimate sources of funds needed to finance this participation" (p. 197). Because of teenage social position, property crimes increasingly serve as an alternative to work.

**Table 3.6   Personal Crimes, 2002: Victimization Rate for Persons Age 12 and Over, by Type of Crime and Age of Victims**

| Type of crime | Rate per 1,000 persons in each age group | | | | | | |
| --- | --- | --- | --- | --- | --- | --- | --- |
| | 12–15 | 16–19 | 20–24 | 25–34 | 35–49 | 50–64 | 65 and over |
| **All personal crimes** | **45.3** | **58.8** | **49.0** | **26.8** | **18.8** | **11.0** | **4.0** |
| Crimes of violence | 44.4 | 58.2 | 47.4 | 26.3 | 18.1 | 10.7 | 3.4 |
| Completed violence | 12.8 | 20.7 | 16.4 | 9.0 | 5.5 | 3.5 | 1.2 |
| Attempted/threatened violence | 31.7 | 37.6 | 31.0 | 17.3 | 12.6 | 7.2 | 2.2 |
| Rape/sexual assault | 2.1 | 5.5 | 2.9 | 0.6* | 0.5* | 0.2* | 0.1* |
| Rape/attempted rape | 0.8* | 4.6 | 2.0 | 0.6 | 0.3* | 0.0* | 0.1* |
| Rape | 0.5* | 2.7 | 1.4* | 0.2* | 0.1* | 0.0* | 0.0* |
| Attempted rape[a] | 0.2* | 2.0 | 0.6* | 0.4* | 0.2* | 0.0* | 0.1* |
| Sexual assault[b] | 1.3* | 0.9* | 0.9* | 0.1* | 0.2* | 0.2* | 0.1* |
| Robbery | 3.0 | 4.0 | 4.7 | 2.8 | 1.5 | 1.6 | 1.0 |
| Completed/property taken | 1.8* | 3.1 | 3.6 | 2.1 | 1.2 | 1.2 | 0.8* |
| With injury | 0.9* | 1.6* | 1.8 | 0.7* | 0.5 | 0.6* | 0.2* |
| Without injury | 0.9* | 1.5* | 1.8 | 1.4 | 0.7 | 0.6* | 0.6* |
| Attempted to take property | 1.2* | 0.9* | 1.1* | 0.7* | 0.3* | 0.4* | 0.2* |
| With injury | 0.2* | 0.4* | 0.1* | 0.4* | 0.2* | 0.0* | 0.1* |
| Without injury | 1.0* | 0.5* | 1.0* | 0.3* | 0.1* | 0.3* | 0.1* |
| Assault | 39.3 | 48.6 | 39.8 | 22.8 | 16.1 | 8.9 | 2.2 |
| Aggravated | 5.0 | 11.9 | 10.1 | 5.2 | 3.5 | 1.7 | 0.7* |
| With injury | 1.0* | 3.9 | 3.8 | 1.9 | 0.9 | 0.6* | 0.1* |
| Threatened with weapon | 4.0 | 8.0 | 6.3 | 3.3 | 2.5 | 1.0 | 0.6* |
| Simple | 34.3 | 36.7 | 29.7 | 17.6 | 12.7 | 7.2 | 1.5 |
| With minor Injury | 8.8 | 10.2 | 6.7 | 4.7 | 3.2 | 1.5 | 0.3* |
| Without injury | 25.6 | 26.5 | 23.0 | 12.9 | 9.4 | 5.7 | 1.3 |
| Purse snatching/pocket picking | 0.9* | 0.6* | 1.6* | 0.5* | 0.7 | 0.3* | 0.6* |
| **Population in each age group** | **16,676,560** | **16,171,800** | **19,317,740** | **37,329,720** | **65,263,580** | **43,746,850** | **33,083,000** |

Note: Detail may not add to total shown because of rounding.
*Estimate is based on about 10 or fewer sample cases.   [a]Includes verbal threats of rape.   [b]Includes threats.
Source: Department of Justice, 2003.

**Table 3.7    Property Crimes, 2002: Victimization Rates by Type of Crime and Age of Head of Household**

| Type of crime | *12–19* | *20–34* | *35–49* | *50–64* | *65 and over* |
|---|---|---|---|---|---|
| | *Rate per 1,000 households* | | | | |
| **Property crimes** | **389.0** | **208.6** | **194.7** | **131.1** | **64.6** |
| Household burglary | 64.1 | 35.4 | 32.2 | 23.4 | 14.7 |
| Completed | 51.1 | 29.1 | 27.6 | 20.5 | 12.7 |
| Forcible entry | 12.0* | 13.1 | 11.3 | 7.1 | 3.7 |
| Unlawful entry without force | 39.2 | 16.0 | 16.3 | 13.4 | 9.1 |
| Attempted forcible entry | 12.9* | 6.2 | 4.6 | 3.0 | 2.0 |
| Motor vehicle theft | 10.3* | 13.9 | 10.9 | 6.2 | 3.3 |
| Completed | 8.2* | 11.1 | 8.7 | 4.6 | 2.6 |
| Attempted | 2.0* | 2.8 | 2.1 | 1.6 | 0.8* |
| Theft | 314.7 | 159.3 | 151.6 | 101.5 | 46.6 |
| Completed | 312.2 | 153.2 | 146.5 | 98.3 | 45.3 |
| Less than $50 | 99.6 | 40.0 | 50.6 | 32.6 | 17.9 |
| $50–$249 | 90.5 | 56.3 | 49.8 | 32.3 | 13.7 |
| $250 or more | 96.3 | 45.2 | 33.7 | 24.2 | 8.3 |
| Amount not available | 25.8* | 11.7 | 12.3 | 9.2 | 5.4 |
| Attempted | 2.5* | 6.1 | 5.2 | 3.3 | 1.2* |
| **Total number of households** | **1,041,190** | **25,241,920** | **36,311,160** | **25,786,270** | **21,943,300** |

Note: Detail may not add to total shown because of rounding.
*Estimate is based on about 10 or fewer sample cases.
Source: Department of Justice, 2003.

When youths leave high school—and when their social position changes accordingly—peer evaluation decreases and opportunities for becoming financially self-sufficient expand. This situation reduces teenagers' motivation to engage in property crimes, and their involvement in property crimes drops off rapidly at post-high school ages. As Greenberg (1983) stated: "Employment, leaving school, military enlistment, and marriage eliminate major sources of criminogenic frustration, and at the same time supply informal social control" (p. 33).

Steffensmeier and Allan (1995b) expanded on Greenberg's thesis, arguing that five major changes mark the transition from late adolescence to early adulthood:

1. Greater access to legitimate sources of material goods and excitement: jobs, credit, alcohol, sex, and so forth.

2. Age-graded norms: externally, increased expectation of maturity and responsibility; internally, anticipation of assuming adult roles, coupled with reduced subjective acceptance of deviant roles and the threat they pose to entering adult status.

3. Peer associations and lifestyle: reduced orientation to same-age/same-sex peers and increased orientation toward persons of the opposite sex and/or persons who are older or more mature.

4. Increased legal and social costs for deviant behavior.

5. Patterns of illegitimate opportunities: with the assumption of adult roles, opportunities increasing for crimes (for example, gambling, fraud, and employee theft) that are less risky, more lucrative, and/or less likely to be reflected in official statistics.

Greenberg also attempted to explain the high rates of interpersonal violence committed by youth and young adults. As discussed earlier in this chapter, interpersonal crimes of violence are committed primarily by males. Traditional gender ideology calls for males to work outside the home and support a family. However, lower- and working-class males have less of a chance than other males of fulfilling these activities. This situation, Greenberg (1977) reasoned, generates a masculine status anxiety in which such men

> may attempt to alleviate their anxiety by exaggerating those traditionally male traits that *can* be expressed. Attempts to dominate women (including rape) and patterns of interpersonal violence can be seen in these terms. In other words, crime can . . . provide a sense of potency that is expected and desired but not achieved in other spheres of life. (p. 207)

Greenberg pointed out that arrest rates for interpersonal crimes of violence peak in the immediate post-high school age brackets when primarily lower- and working-class males—who do not attend college—anticipate or actively seek full-time work. He argued that masculine status anxiety helps us understand not only age variations in interpersonal crimes of violence but class, gender, and race as well. Greenberg concluded that the variable relationship between age and crime depends on historical, cultural, and economic factors. Patterns of crime in the United States therefore reflect the particular development of age segregation and of the social position of youth in U.S. society.

Not everyone agrees that age is an important factor in explaining patterns of crime. Hirschi and Gottfredson (1983), for example, have agreed that the age distribution of crime depicted in the UCR is accurate and that it "represents one of the brute facts of criminology" (p. 552). But, whereas Greenberg argued that the age distribution of crime varies with social conditions, Hirschi and Gottfredson have contended that the age distribution of crime is *invariant* across all social and cultural conditions. For them the shape and form of the age distribution remains "virtually unchanged" from time to time and place to place. Criminological theory and research therefore need not consider age as an important variable in explaining crime.

Greenberg (1985) has countered this argument with considerable historical and cross-cultural evidence. He has shown that today there is less adult crime relative to juvenile crime in the United States than there used to be. Similarly, an analysis of other societies—both industrial and preindustrial—displays a noticeable shift toward younger ages involved in criminality once industrialization occurs. For example, in contemporary Norway, the age distribution of crime is similar to that in the United States. Yet as criminologist Nils Christie pointed out, speaking of Norway: "Police statistics for 1870 showed no peak for teenagers. They did not exist at that time. A hundred years ago, the peak was somewhere in the middle twenties and with a *slow decrease* in criminal activity among the older groups" (cited in Greenberg, 1985:12, emphasis added). For the Banyoro and Basoga (two preindustrialized Bantu-speaking peoples of Uganda), the peak age of those who commit homicide is 35, and rarely are homicides committed by teenagers (Greenberg, 1985).

The emergence of the life-course perspective in criminology has encouraged further discussion of the link between age and crime (Warr, 2001). For example, Sampson and Laub (1993, 2003) and Warr (2002) argue that the transition to adulthood and its accompanying conforming practices—e.g., marriage and employment—"wean" youths from teenage peer influence and encourage desistance from crime.

In addition, race and class can affect an individual's ability to move out of crime; that is, race and class inequality limit access to legitimate resources—such as college attendance or employment at adequate wages—that allow "maturation" out of crime. Steffensmeier and Allan (1995b) provided one example:

> For black inner-city youths, the high level of youth inequality that characterizes modern societies is compounded by the problems of living in a racist society, and they are less able to leave behind the inequality of youth status. As they move into young adulthood they continue to experience limited access to the adult labor market. (pp. 103–104)

In a similar vein, Hagan (1991) has shown that crime rates for working-class youth decline less slowly than rates for middle-class youth.

The segregation and subordination of youth in society as a whole are not the only factors that generate specific age patterns of crime. The subordination of youth within specific institutions also plays a role. Unequal relationships between parents and children can set the stage for generational conflict and at least three types of crime: child physical abuse, child sexual abuse, and youth crime. Child abuse results from power relations across generations and the accompanying ideology that children should at all times be subordinate to parents. A thin line separates authoritarian, punitive, and harsh forms of discipline, on the one hand, and child abuse on the other; indeed, they seem to coexist.

Moreover, research reveals a strong relationship between child sexual abuse and future delinquency. The vast majority of victims of child sexual abuse (both girls and boys) report severe forms of trauma, leading many to run away from home. In particular, girls on the street report high rates of physical abuse and sexual abuse (Chesney-Lind and Pasko, 2004). Running away from sexual abuse and a violent home, these young women and men turn to crime to survive. After reviewing the literature on young women, Meda Chesney-Lind and Lisa Pasko pointed out that sexually abused female runaways are "significantly more likely than their nonabused counterparts to engage in delinquent or criminal activities, such as substance abuse, petty theft, and prostitution" (p. 27).

## Box 3.2    Youth Crime and Homelessness

John Hagan and Bill McCarthy used observational, survey, and interview data obtained in two Canadian cities, Toronto and Vancouver, to examine the family and school histories, living conditions, and the criminality of youth who live on the street. In their book *Mean Streets: Youth Crime and Homelessness* (1997), Hagan and McCarthy documented that the vast majority of street youth who engage in crime have recently run away from explosive, sexually and physically violent parents; as a result these youth are not committed to school and schoolwork. Once on the street they experience the day-to-day problems of finding food, shelter, and work. Not surprisingly, Hagan and McCarthy's data provided consistent evidence of a relationship between the involvement of these youth in street crime and their lack of food, shelter, and work.

Interestingly, there is an important difference between Toronto and Vancouver regarding street youth involvement in theft, prostitution, and the drug trade. According to Hagan and McCarthy, Toronto has a social welfare orientation toward street youth, whereas Vancouver provides few social services for the homeless. The result is more crime by street youth in Vancouver than by the street youth in Toronto. "The implication is that an absence of social capital in the form of services and support in Vancouver encourages street youth to capitalize on opportunities that they encounter to become involved in theft, prostitution, and the drug trade" (p. 232). Moreover, for street youth in both cities who were eventually able to find employment, they were much more likely than nonemployed street youth to move away from the street and, thus, crime. "They spent less time hanging out, panhandling, searching for food and shelter, using drugs, stealing with other youth, or pursuing other kinds of criminal activities" (p. 234).

Consequently, the powerlessness of children in the home and the extreme results of that subordination (child physical abuse, child sexual abuse, and neglect—along with the lack of community social services for homeless youth) contribute to crime both quantitatively and qualitatively. These findings demonstrate the important ties between social position, victimization, and subsequent crime.

In addition to the home, the school is an institution that structures aged social position, victimization, and subsequent crime. For example, in the 1990s several school homicides occurred in the United States, and nearly all the "school shooters" were boys. These boys had all been bullied consistently, primarily concerning their bodily appearance, by bigger and stronger boys. Research on these shootings has concluded that the killers viewed their subsequent violence as a means of retaliating against the peer abuse at school and thereby a way of gaining masculine respect (Kimmel and Mahler, 2003).

Although the social position of youth presents young people with opportunities for committing certain crimes, it also precludes them from committing others. Systematically denied access to the labor market, youths are effectively segregated from positions where workplace-related crimes—such as embezzlement and corporate crimes—and political crimes occur. For corporate and political crimes, the ages 30–60 clearly dominate; these are the prime ages of employment, and individuals of these ages make up the most powerful age group in society.

As we stated earlier, the elderly are also increasingly segregated and subordinated in the United States. Not surprisingly, in the 1980s criminologists became interested in the topic of crime and the elderly. An important article by Cullen, Wozniak, and Frank

*From home to street: Many young people have run away from physical and sexual abuse at home. Once on the street, they turn to variety of crimes to survive.*

(1985), for example, concluded that the majority (78 percent) of elderly arrests are for larceny, which is almost six times higher than the next highest category, aggravated assault. Elderly males and females seem to commit larceny in equal proportions (Mandino, 2000). Moreover, the elderly tend to steal household and personal necessities of low value—such as toothpaste, cigarettes, and tools (Brogden and Nijhar, 2000). It should be noted, however, that although larceny seems to be the crime most frequently committed by the elderly, they are much less likely to commit larceny than any other age group (Klemke, 1992).

As would be expected from our earlier analysis, elderly property crime rates are correlated with adverse economic conditions. In fact, those above the age of 55, and especially 65, have an economic situation similar to that of youth. The labor force participation rate for people 55 and older has decreased since 1980: In particular, for males ages 55–64 it fell from 72.1 in 1980 to 69.2 in 2002; for ages 65 and over it fell from 19.0 to 17.9 (*Statistical Abstract of the United States,* 2003). This decreasing labor force participation rate for males may help explain the high rate of larceny by males over 65.

## Review

This chapter discussed considerable empirical research to help explain the patterns of crime and victimization in the United States. Of primary importance is structured inequality: Class, gender, race, and age hierarchies determine social position and thus criminal opportunities.

### Class and Crime

1. Arrest data, self-report studies, and victimization surveys all show that conventional crimes by adults and youth are disproportionately concentrated in the lower and working classes.

2. White-collar and political crimes are disproportionately committed by members of the professional-managerial class.

3. Victimization data show that all conventional crimes—except personal larceny without contact and motor vehicle theft—are likely to be intraclass.

4. Unemployment and income inequality are associated both with conventional crimes and with nonoccupational crimes of the hidden economy.

5. Both economic conditions such as inflation and perceived inequality within the workplace itself are conducive to occupational crimes such as employee theft.

6. Corporate crimes are caused chiefly by the desire of corporate executives to overcome obstacles to profit making.

7. Because of their position within the state, politicians have opportunities to gain financially by engaging in a variety of corrupt practices.

8. The close association between the state and the economy creates conditions for systematic state crimes—such as global political crimes.

## Gender and Crime

1. Arrest data, self-report studies, and victimization surveys show that male adults and youths are the chief perpetrators of almost all forms of conventional crime.

2. Males have a virtual monopoly on the commission of syndicated, corporate, and political crimes.

3. When females commit crime, they engage mostly in petty forms of theft such as shoplifting, fraud, and minor embezzlement, and in prostitution.

4. Victimization data on conventional crimes suggest that males victimize other males.

5. Women's subordinate position in the gender division of labor structures the type of embezzlement women commit.

6. The feminization of poverty is associated with female fraud, shoplifting, and other forms of petty theft.

7. Males dominate in syndicated, corporate, and political crimes because of their power to exclude women systematically from positions where these crimes originate.

8. Male violence toward women derives from gender inequality, the structural subordination of women, and the power and dominance accorded men in U.S. society.

## Race and Crime

1. Data on race and crime suggest that African-American adults and youths commit a disproportionate amount of conventional crimes for their population size—especially interpersonal crimes of violence.

2. Whites clearly commit the vast majority of conventional crimes and dominate the more harmful and economically damaging white-collar and political crimes.

3. Victimization data show that conventional crimes are intraracial (e.g., African Americans typically victimize African Americans and whites typically victimize whites).

4. Because racial oppression multiplies African Americans' disadvantages, they experience a disproportionate number of economic and social obstacles.

5. Overrepresentation of African-American adults and youth in conventional crime statistics—both property crimes and interpersonal crimes of violence—is the result of racial economic inequality.

6. The racial hierarchy results in white domination of the positions where white-collar and political crimes occur.

## Age and Crime

1. Conventional crime arrest rates vary with age. Property crimes peak between 13 and 17 years of age and decline rapidly with age; violent crimes peak at around 18 or 19 years of age and decline much more slowly.

2. Victimization rates for conventional crimes show that young persons ages 12–24 have the highest rates of conventional crime victimization.

3. The high rate of property crime for youths results from their desire to participate in social activities and from a lack of adequate funds to pay for them.

4. Not all criminologists agree that age is an important factor in crime; the life-course perspective has added new insights to this relationship.

5. Power and inequality within institutions, such as the family and the school, can create social positions leading to the victimization of youths. This victimization has implications for future involvement in crime.

6. White-collar and political crimes are committed by the most powerful age group, those 30–60 years of age.

7. Elderly crime consists mostly of petty forms of theft, such as shoplifting, and is caused by their decreasing participation in the labor market.

## Questions for Class Discussion

1. Choose several crimes, then explain how social position permits and prevents opportunities for their commission.

2. Discuss how the interaction of class, gender, race, and age affects criminal opportunities. Cite several examples.

3. How does the discussion of the varieties of crime in this text differ from those offered by the media?

4. Identify other forms of inequality in society that have not been examined in this chapter, then discuss how they may be related to crime and victimization.

## For Further Study

### Readings

Barak, Gregg, Jeanne M. Flavin, and Paul S. Leighton. 2001. *Class, Race, Gender, and Crime: Social Realities of Justice in America.* Los Angeles: Roxbury Publishing.

Hagan, John, and Bill McCarthy. 1997. *Mean Streets: Youth Crime and Homelessness.* New York: Cambridge University Press.

Maher, Lisa. 1997. *Sexed Work: Gender, Race, and Resistance in a Brooklyn Drug Market.* New York: Clarendon Press.

Mann, Coramae Richey, and Marjorie S. Zatz, eds. 2002. *Images of Color, Images of Crime: Readings.* 2nd ed. Los Angeles: Roxbury Publishing.

### Websites

1. <http://www.americanhumane.org>: The American Humane Association operates this website, which provides reliable information on child abuse and neglect. It also provides information on the abuse of animals.

2. <http://www.interactivetheatre.org/mav/>: This site, titled "Men Against Violence Webring," offers some action-oriented solutions to male violence. Useful links are provided, with a goal for men to take greater responsibility for violence.

3. <http://www.fbi.gov/ucr/ucr.htm#hate>: This site provides statistics on hate crimes reported to the police from 1995 to 2002. The data cover incidents, offenses, victims, and offenders that were motivated by bias against the victim's perceived race, religion, ethnicity, sexual orientation, or disability. ✦

# Part II
# *Types of Crime*

# Property Crime

## Preview

Chapter 4 introduces:

- What sociologists mean by property crime.

- The various types of property crime.

- The difference between amateur and professional property offenders.

- The nature, extent, and costs of property crime.

## Key Terms

| | |
|---|---|
| armed robbery | automobile theft |
| arson | burglary |

| | |
|---|---|
| carjacking | larceny |
| check fraud | motor vehicle theft |
| credit-card fraud | property crime |
| fencing | robbery |
| identity theft | shoplifting |
| income-tax fraud | strong-arm robbery |

Most conventional "street crimes" entail the taking of property. Indeed, according to National Crime Victimization Survey (NCVS) data, property crimes make up more than 77 percent of all victimizations (Department of Justice, 2003).

In addition to being more frequent, property crimes differ from crimes of interpersonal violence in another significant way: Offender and victim are, in most cases, strangers. For crimes such as burglary, automobile theft, and arson, no direct interaction between offender and victim usually takes place. And in those crimes where interaction does exist—such as check fraud—it is not immediately apparent that a crime has been committed.

We define **property crime** as the unlawful damage to or taking of the property of another, regardless of whether the threat of or actual use of physical violence occurs. In this chapter we discuss seven types of property crimes: robbery, burglary, shoplifting, automobile theft, fraud, fencing, and arson. While discussing each, we examine the similarities and differences between professional and amateur property offenders. Professional and amateur property offenders are similar in that each commits the same type of crime. In other words, there are both professional and amateur robbers, burglars, auto thieves, and so forth. However, professionals and amateurs differ in important ways. Professionals carefully plan and execute their crimes, using sophisticated techniques and skills. They are committed to crime as a lifestyle and tend to specialize in one particular form of property crime. Amateurs engage in crime when the opportunity arises, do not extensively plan their crime, do not always think of themselves as criminals, and do not usually specialize in one type of property crime.

## 4.1 Robbery and Burglary

Our discussion of property crime begins with what most of us—including criminologists—consider to be the two most serious forms of theft: robbery and burglary.

### Robbery

**Robbery** has been defined in various ways. Some states define it as a property crime, although other states and the FBI see it as a violent crime. The FBI defines robbery as "the taking of or attempting to take anything of value from the care, custody or control of a person or persons by force or by threat of force or violence and/or by putting the victim in fear" (see Chapter 2, p. xx). In historical fiction and by contemporary media, robbers are often depicted as romantic heroes—professional thieves who are willing to go all the way in their quest for gold and booty.

Robbery ranks among the most feared of crimes because it entails both threatened or actual use of violence and loss of property to the victim. Moreover, unlike the other property crimes discussed in this chapter, robbery involves a direct confrontation between offender and victim. Robbery also differs significantly from other interpersonal crimes of violence, in that it is more likely to involve two or more offenders; the majority of robberies are committed by strangers to the victim, and robbers are more likely to use weapons. Moreover, the primary motive of the robber is not violence but economic gain.

If priority is given to an offender's motive, as most sociologists do, it makes sense to see robbery as a property crime rather than as a violent crime. In robbery, violence is secondary to the taking of property: when violence is used, it is a means to an end.

More than 90 percent of robbers are male, and their often unsophisticated crimes are disproportionately committed by members of minority groups, such as African Americans in the United States and Franco-Canadians in Canada (Desroches, 2002). The robbery rate has been steadily declining in the United States since 1990; part of this "decline" may be because street robbers' victims are nowadays more likely themselves to be criminals, such as drug dealers, and thus are unlikely to report their victimization to the police (Jacobs, 2000). In 2002 420,637 robberies were reported to the police, or 146 per 100,000 inhabitants (Federal Bureau of Investigation, 2003), though the NCVS reveals that about 40 percent of all robberies are never reported to the police (Department of Justice, 2002). About 53 percent of all robbery victims require some form of medical treatment; 25.1 percent are either treated in a hospital emergency room or admitted to hospital (Simon and Mercy, 2001).

## Typologies of Robbery

Scholars have developed several typologies of robbers. Some typologies focus on the level and type of violence used by robbers, some on robbers' skill and foresight, and some on whether the victim is an individual or an institution, such as a bank or a commercial enterprise (Gill, 2000).

Whether violence and personal injury occur during a robbery depends on the type of robbery. **Strong-arm robbery** (sometimes referred to as "unarmed robbery" because the offender robs without the use of a weapon) is actually much more dangerous than **armed robbery** (the display of a deadly weapon to carry out the robbery). Approximately twice as many strong-arm robbery victims, compared to armed-robbery victims, are injured (Wright, Rossi, and Daly, 1983). Armed robberies are not only less dangerous than strong-arm robberies, they also occur more often and are more likely to be successful (Department of Justice, 2002).

One of the most successful typologies is Conklin's (1972) separation of *professional robbers* and *opportunist robbers*. Both types can be involved in similar robbery scenarios. But professional robbers carefully plan and execute their crimes, exhibiting greater skill than other robbery offenders and, usually, operating with accomplices (Conklin, 1972). Walsh (1986) found that when professionals operate with accomplices, they commonly are people "recommended" to them. The professional commits to robbery as a lifestyle, engages in sophisticated planning, neutralizes security, and investigates all possible escape routes (Conklin, 1972). Thus, professional robbers are considerably more skilled and conduct more extensive planning than other robbers.

Conklin identified two types of professional robbers. The first commits robbery almost exclusively. The second commits other types of crimes but occasionally commits robbery with professional skill. In addition to these "solo professionals," Walsh (1986) found two other types of professionals: criminal syndicates that assemble teams of robbers, and independent, small, professional teams of two or three robbers.

The opportunist robber is probably the most common type of robber. Opportunists do not commit to robbery on a long-term basis such as professionals do. Rather, these individuals rob infrequently, choosing such easily accessible and vulnerable victims as the elderly, public drunks, taxi drivers, and people walking alone on unlit streets. Opportunists are sometimes involved in other forms of conventional property theft, such as burglary (Conklin, 1972).

When we commonly think of "street crime" or "muggings," we have opportunistic robbery in mind. Such haphazard, random, and spur-of-the-moment robberies generally net only small amounts of cash.

Four of every five opportunistic robberies are the work of strangers to the victim(s) (Bureau of Justice Statistics, 1993a). Moreover, opportunists rob their victims—more than half the time—on the street or in some outdoor area near their own home, such as a park, a playground, or a parking lot. Opportunistic robberies occur more often in inner districts of the largest cities. As shown in Table 4.1, street/highway robberies reported to police increase as size of city population increases. The table also shows that although street robberies increase with city size, other forms of robbery actually decrease with city size.

## Robbery as Transaction

Robbery is similar to murder and assault in that it involves a face-to-face confrontation between offender and victim. In fact, Luckenbill's (1981) research on robbery suggests that it involves a four-stage "transaction" between offender and victim. Each stage consists of important tasks that the offender and victim execute together. First, once a victim has been selected, the offender creates "copresence" with the victim by moving into striking range without causing suspicion. In other words, the robber attempts a "normal appearance" while maintaining an appropriate position for the imminent robbery. Second, after establishing copresence, and after the offender decides and subsequently initiates the robbery, the victim determines whether to resist. At the same time, the offender considers how much force, if any, is required to obtain the desired property. It is this interaction, and acknowledgment by both offender and victim, that creates a "common robbery frame" to which each, Luckenbill argues, most likely adheres. Third, once a common robbery frame is established, the property is transferred. Although the transfer is usually controlled by the offender, several obstructions may occur: The victim may not adhere to the robbery frame, outsiders may disrupt the robbery, or the offender may not have the knowledge and skill required to complete the transfer. Assuming transfer of the property is successful, in the fourth stage the offender tries to escape, such as by jumping into a getaway car or containing the victim in some fashion.

**Table 4.1  Robbery: Percent Distribution by Population Group, 2003**

| Type | Group I (58 cities, 250,000 and over; population 37,217,317) | Group II (146 cities, 100,000 to 249,999; population 21,875,380) | Group III (353 cities, 50,000 to 99,999; population 24,412,026) | Group IV (684 cities, 25,000 to 49,999; population 23,742,865) | Group V (1,512 cities, 10,000 to 24,999; population 23,834,682) | Group VI (5,925 cities, under 10,000; population 19,204,778) | County Agencies (58 cities, 250,000 and over; population 37,217,317) |
|---|---|---|---|---|---|---|---|
| Total[1] | 100.0 | 100.0 | 100.0 | 100.0 | 100.0 | 100.0 | 100.0 |
| Street/highway | 51.7 | 43.6 | 42.2 | 33.4 | 28.6 | 25.4 | 31.2 |
| Commercial house | 12.3 | 16.6 | 15.3 | 16.5 | 17.5 | 14.9 | 17.9 |
| Gas or service station | 1.7 | 2.8 | 3.3 | 4.2 | 4.8 | 4.4 | 3.7 |
| Convenience store | 4.5 | 6.6 | 7.0 | 8.6 | 8.5 | 10.1 | 7.9 |
| Residence | 12.6 | 13.1 | 12.0 | 12.7 | 14.6 | 14.3 | 19.5 |
| Bank | 1.5 | 2.5 | 2.7 | 3.6 | 3.9 | 3.6 | 2.7 |
| Miscellaneous | 15.6 | 14.8 | 17.5 | 21.1 | 22.1 | 27.3 | 17.0 |

[1]Because of rounding, the percentages may not add to 100.0.

Source: FBI (2004) *Crime in the United States: 34.* Washington, DC: U.S. Government Printing Office.

Luckenbill's research shows that robbery is more than just an offender's illegal behavior. It is an interaction involving joint contributions by both offender and victim. However, although both offender and victim contribute, it is hardly a simple "transaction" between equal partners, as Luckenbill suggests. The key point in a robbery scenario is that the interaction is coercive. One party—the offender—exercises dominance over the victim. "Transaction" implies equality, yet equality does not exist between robbery victim and offender.

It is also questionable whether Luckenbill's model applies to all robbery types. For instance, it does not apply especially well to the robbing of banks and armored cars, to muggings and purse snatchings, and to robbery during a burglary. Yet these robbery types constitute the majority of all robberies. More than half of all robberies are committed against persons who, as part of their employment, are in charge of money and goods (for example, banks and armored cars); 20–25 percent of robberies occur in the open following a sudden attack (such as muggings and purse snatchings); and 12–17 percent of robberies occur on private premises (for instance, during a burglary) (Walsh, 1986).

Moreover, Luckenbill's research ignores the similarities and differences between male and female robbers. In an important study, Jody Miller (1998) found that male and female robbers have similar motives: both want to obtain money to purchase status-enhancing commodities, such as jewelry and illegal drugs. Male and female robbers differ, however, in the way they accomplish the robbery transaction. Males use guns placed on the body of the victim, or in close proximity to the victim, in a confrontational manner. Female robbers engage in three much less confrontational forms of interaction. First, they are more likely than male robbers to choose females as victims because, from their point of view, they are easier to rob—i.e., women victims rarely fight back. Second, female robbers often promise men sexual favors and, when the male is in a vulnerable position and his guard is down, run off with his money or goods. Finally, female robbers will work with male robbers as subordinate accomplices to robbery.

## Robbers on Robbery

Richard Wright and Scott Decker's (1997) study of "active armed robbers" sheds light on the processes involved in committing the crime of armed robbery. Unlike previous studies of robbery, which have focused on incarcerated offenders, these criminologists interviewed 86 offenders who were actively involved in robbery on the streets of St. Louis, Missouri. The interviews generated data from the robbers' perspective on (1) why they commit robbery, (2) how they choose the target, and (3) how they commit the offense. Regarding the first, the vast majority of the offenders committed robbery because of deep involvement in self-indulgent activities promoted by street culture, such as gambling, alcohol use, and drug use. When faced with a pressing need for cash, these individuals turned to robbery as the quickest and easiest way out of financial difficulties.

In choosing a target, most of the robbers reported that they preferred victims in close proximity to where they lived, typically preying on local criminals, especially street-corner drug dealers. Drug dealers are "good robbery victims" because they carry plenty of cash and are in no position to report their victimization to the police. Of course, these robbers also robbed law-abiding citizens, choosing victims who indicate through their demeanor and dress that they have a supply of easily available cash. A few of the robbers Wright and Decker interviewed victimized small commercial establishments, such as liquor stores, gas stations, taverns, and pawn shops. These businesses were chosen because they also had cash readily available.

Having decided to rob and having settled on a particular target, the robber must next "pull it off"—that is, commit to the robbery and carry it out. Here Wright and Decker's data correspond with Luckenbill's perspective discussed earlier. First, robbers approach the victim, announcing the robbery and allowing victims no room for negotiation by "creating an illusion of impending death" (p. 96). Robbers attempt to catch victims off guard and, through tough talk, a fierce demeanor, and the display of a deadly weapon, usually scare people into compliance. Once dominance over the victim is established, the robber attempts to manage the transfer of goods. Many armed robbers simply order victims to "hand over the money," whereas some choose to actually search their victims. Only if victims fail to comply with demands do robbers turn to violence. As Wright and Decker explain,

> faced with a recalcitrant victim, most of the offenders responded with severe but nonlethal violence in the hope of convincing the person to cooperate. Often this violence involved smacking or beating the victim about the head with a pistol. (p. 113)

Finally, the offender must escape. Most of the robbers in this study preferred to be the first to depart the robbery scene. However, before making their escape, these robbers once again made verbal threats, such as "If you come out of this alley . . . I'm gonna shoot the shit out of you" (p. 116). Such threats are designed to continue the illusion of impending death from the beginning of the robbery to its completion.

In many accounts, robbers seem to be involved in a precisely calculated strategy of cause and effect (see also Chapter 15.1). They appear as actors who, despite the illegality of their actions, pursue their aims with considerable choice and rational calculation. However, this image of the reasoning criminal is far less neat and tidy in the messiness of real life. For example, from their reading of 5,000 police statements and from several interviews and group discussions with perpetrators of street robbery in the city of Amsterdam, de Haan and Vos (2003) show that "rationality" is not the only thing to consider when trying to understand what robbers do. Robbers routinely act inconsistently. They stumble around impulsively. They operate with emotions such as guilt and shame. Moreover, from interviews with 350 armed robbers in Britain, Roger Matthews (2002) concluded that many robbers are drunk or on drugs just before or during their robberies.

## Burglary

**Burglary** is defined as unlawful entry of a house, business, or other structure with the intent to commit a felony. Whereas robbery entails theft through the threat or actual use of violence, for burglary to occur someone must actually enter a structure unlawfully with the intent to commit a felony. Moreover, burglary—like the other property crimes to be discussed in this chapter—differs from robbery in another critical way: It seldom involves a direct, face-to-face confrontation between offender and victim.

*Burglars on the job: Professional burglars consider themselves specialists who have considerable skill, such as dismantling alarm systems or telephone lines.*

In 2003, 2,153,464 burglaries were reported to the police, or approximately 741.5 per 100,000 inhabitants (Federal Bureau of Investigation, 2004b). However, the NCVS reported that only about 60 percent of all burglaries are reported to the police. Consequently, the NCVS typically reports almost 1 million more burglaries as the FBI, for a total of a little over 3 million. As with robbery, the police probably know about no more than 60 percent of all burglaries.

Burglars can also be classified as amateurs or professionals. Both are similar in that they may burglarize houses or businesses and may operate alone or work with others in a team (Cromwell and Jolicouer, 2001). However, they also differ in important ways. *Amateur burglars* enter a structure when they "feel the need." Their style of intrusion is unsophisticated—perhaps simply breaking a window or breaking down a door. Because amateurs are more interested in volume of burglaries than in quality, little planning is involved. Amateur burglars rarely specialize in theft of specific items but rather steal a variety of merchandise as opportunities arise, usually accessible goods such as televisions, stereos, VCRs, CD players, silverware, jewelry, and money. Thus, amateurs are usually juveniles or young adults who lack a commitment to crime and do not think of themselves as "thieves." Moreover, the vast majority come from economically deprived backgrounds, are undereducated, and are often addicted to drugs (Mawby, 2001).

*Professional burglars* are specialists who use considerable skill and planning. Professionals have "external contacts" about specific goods to steal, are systematic in their offenses, and plan their crimes carefully (Cromwell and Jolicouer, 2001). A good example of a professional burglar is Harry King, a "boxman" (safecracker) who reported to Chambliss (King and Chambliss, 1984) all the intrigues and skill required to enter a building successfully, open or "kidnap" a safe, and efficiently escape. King's activities closely followed Sutherland's model of the professional thief outlined in Chapter 11.4. King learned his trade from another professional boxman, working initially as an apprentice. He eventually made his living from burglary, engaging in extensive planning and never feeling the need to carry a weapon during a "caper." Moreover, he kept up with the latest technology applicable to his trade. According to King, it is essential for the professional to be familiar with the latest "burglary tools," such as drills and saws, and to spend time practicing and preparing for future capers (p. 35).

Professional burglars also rely on contacts with tipsters, or persons who identify possible targets for the burglar. In addition to tipsters, professional burglars establish important contacts with police, attorneys, and judges. This liaison with members of the criminal justice system frequently allows professional burglars to "fix" their cases prior to committing the burglaries. King found it easy to fix cases because "the only people that really profit from theft are the fix, the judge, and the district attorney" (King and Chambliss, 1984:84).

Burglary is usually classified as either residential or commercial. The majority of residential burglaries (60 percent) occur during the day when residents are not usually at home, whereas the majority of commercial burglaries (65 percent) take place in the late evening or early morning when businesses are closed (Cromwell and Jolicouer, 2001). Moreover, whether residential or commercial, 60 percent of all burglaries involve forcible entry, 27 percent involve attempted forcible entry, and the remainder entail an illegal entry with no force.

### Burglars on Burglary

Several researchers have interviewed active residential burglars who are not currently incarcerated (Cromwell, Olson, and Avary, 1991; Wright and Decker, 1994). The major conclusions of these studies of "burglars on burglary" include the following:

- Need for money is the primary motivation for involvement in burglary. A legitimate job, when available, does not adequately satisfy the immediacy of desire of cash.

- The majority of burglars cannot compete in the labor market, because they are poorly educated, unskilled, and heavy illicit drug and alcohol users.

- Burglars use their proceeds for food, shelter, and clothing, yet most of their gain goes toward the maintenance of a "partying" lifestyle based in illicit drug and alcohol use.

- Burglary is a means for a burglar to "be somebody" by successfully completing a dangerous act.

- Most burglars watch potential targets before committing a burglary.

- Burglars choose residences to burglarize because of "external cues"—such as the size and condition of the dwelling and type of cars in the driveway—suggesting that there are goods worth stealing inside.

- Once a residence is chosen as a possible target, burglars use a decision-making strategy consisting of three questions: (1) Can the residence be entered without the burglar being seen and reported? (2) Is the residence currently occupied? (3) Can the residence be broken into easily? If the answer is "yes" to all three questions, the burglar will probably proceed.

- Most burglaries are committed during daytime hours when victims usually are at work.

- Situational factors, such as the presence of a dog, an alarm system, and alert neighbors, are the most effective deterrents to burglars.

None of the studies we cited so far examines how gender affects residential burglary. However, a recent study by Mullins and Wright (2003) compared the similarities and differences between male and female burglars. Their data are drawn from interviews with currently active (not incarcerated and interviewed on the street) young adult residential burglars—18 females and 36 males—and reveal some interesting findings. First, the vast majority of all burglars were initiated into burglary through interaction with intimate groups, committing their first burglary with friends, family members, or street associates. However, men were more likely to have been introduced to burglary by same-sex friends, while the women often were initiated to burglary through interaction with their boyfriends. Second, both male and female burglars reported similar motives for engaging in residential burglary—to finance a "party" lifestyle that centers on illicit drug use and flamboyant display of designer clothing and jewelry. However, once again differences were found: Female burglars committed the crime to also help provide the basic necessities for others (such as food, shelter, and clothing for children), while the male burglars emphasized protecting their street status by satisfying their own needs.

Third, during the commission of the crime, males prefer to burglarize alone or with other men because they feel that women are untrustworthy. When men and women work together on a burglary, the female usually takes on a subordinate role, seldom planning the crime or entering the residence, but rather serving as the "lookout" and the "get-away driver." Finally, regarding desistance from residential burglary, the men claimed that a good legal job or a stable relationship with a woman would deter them from committing this crime. In contrast, the vast majority of female burglars stated that for them to refrain from engaging in this crime they would need to sever their relationship with criminally involved males. Thus, Mullins and Wright conclude that the social processes involved in residential burglary—initiation, commission, and potential desistance—are heavily structured by gender and that, in particular, women must "negotiate male-dominated networks and landscapes in accomplishing their crimes" (p. 833).

---

**Box 4.1   Persistent Property Offenders**

An important question asked by criminologists is why offenders persist in committing crime; that is, even after arrest, conviction, and incarceration, many continue to engage in property crime. Why?

Kenneth Tunnell (1992), in his book *Choosing Crime*, examined this question by interviewing sixty chronic repeat property offenders. These were individuals who had committed a great number of crimes (mostly robbery and burglary) and with considerable frequency. In questioning these offenders about their motivation to continually commit property crimes, Tunnell found that 88 percent engaged in crime for "quick, easy money" to be used for living expenses and pleasurable commodities, such as illicit drugs (p. 39). In addition, many property offenders commit these crimes for a sense of accomplishment, to gain power over someone, for revenge, or simply as a sport.

This engagement in property crime primarily for money is related to their class position and, therefore, limited access to legitimate alternatives. As Tunnell found through his interviews, repetitive offenders choose "the best alternative available to them since crime often allowed them to obtain satisfaction of their immediate needs" (p. 70). Indeed, these offenders spent money as quickly as it came in and therefore had little to show for their risky criminal activity. Since the immediate need for drugs and easily consumable commodities continued, along with a lack of legitimate legal options, these criminals persisted in property crime.

An interesting aspect of this study considered whether the decision to commit crime was related to possible negative consequences of their illegal actions—getting caught. As Tunnell reported:

> Nearly all sixty reported they rarely considered the threat of capture, arrest, and imprisonment and that risk was considered a nuisance rather than a real, tangible threat. Risk-related thoughts were considered distracting from their prime objective—committing the crime. Thus, many were simply able to not think about risks and put them out of their minds. (p. 100)

Thus, crime control policies based on severe penalties (such as lengthy prison sentences) that attempt to scare criminals to "go straight" do not seem to have an impact on persistent property offenders.

A more recent study of street robbers and burglars is Neal Shover's (1996) similar exploration of why property offenders persist in committing crime. Shover has shown how the class background of persistent robbers and burglars limits their legitimate occupational options and, therefore, their ultimate choices. Born into a life of poverty, lower-working-class children are prepared to accept these limited legitimate choices. After dropping out of school, many are attracted to the local street culture, making it even more difficult for them to "defer gratification" in favor of long-term goals. Shover has shown that the street culture is much too attractive because of its emphasis of "life as party":

> The hallmark of life as party is enjoyment of "good times" with minimal concern for obligations and commitments external to the person's immediate social setting. Those who pursue life as party are

determined to suspend concern for serious matters in favor of enjoying the moment. . . . Life as party is enjoyed in the company of alcohol and other drugs. In bars and lounges, on street corners, or while cruising in automobiles, party pursuers celebrate and affirm values of spontaneity, independence, and resourcefulness. (pp. 93–94)

The pursuit of life as party quickly exhausts one's meager financial resources. Consequently, members of the street culture oscillate in and out of financial desperation. Robbery and burglary, then, become solutions for obtaining the badly needed "fast money" to adequately participate in the party. Thus, the cycle continues, and members of the street culture become persistent property offenders.

## 4.2 Varieties of Larceny

In Chapter 7.1 we discuss employee theft—workers who take merchandise and job-related items from their workplace. Our concern here, however, is with nonoccupational theft, or what is commonly referred to as larceny. **Larceny** is the unlawful taking of property from the possession of someone other than one's employer. A larceny does *not* involve the threat of actual use of force (robbery)—with the exception of carjacking—or breaking and entering (burglary). In 2002, 7 million larcenies were reported to the police, or approximately 2,415 per 100,000 inhabitants (Federal Bureau of Investigation, 2003).

The NCVS does not use the term *larceny* but rather *theft,* which refers to personal larcenies without contact, such as theft of an umbrella from a restaurant, a radio from the beach, or a bicycle from a schoolyard. Only 17 percent of such thefts valued at less than $50 were reported to the police in 2002. However, in the same year, for thefts of $250 or more, 56 percent were reported to the police. Thus, the greater the value of the merchandise stolen, the greater the likelihood the theft will be reported to the police. Finally, given these reporting figures, we should not be surprised to find that the NCVS reported more than twice as many victimizations as the UCR: In 2002 there were 17.4 million (Department of Justice, 2003).

In this section we discuss three major types of larceny: shoplifting, motor vehicle theft, and fraud.

### Shoplifting

One particular type of larceny—shoplifting—has been accorded considerable attention by sociologists and criminologists. **Shoplifting**—theft of property from a retail store by "customers"—results in approximately $31 billion of lost merchandise each year (Klemke, 2001).

One of the earliest efforts by a sociologist to study shoplifting is the classic work by Mary Owen Cameron (1964), *The Booster and the Snitch.* Cameron divided shoplifters into two types: "boosters," who steal merchandise to sell it, and "snitches," who steal for their own consumption. In other words, the booster is a professional who steals for the purpose of making money; the snitch is an amateur who steals for personal use.

According to Cameron, boosters—composing about 10 percent of shoplifters—possess five characteristics:

1. Boosters work a large number of stores rather than a few large stores.

2. Boosters use considerable planning and skill to execute their theft.

3. Boosters steal only expensive merchandise and, like professional robbers and burglars, sell it to a professional fence.

4. Boosters often easily "fix" their cases if caught.

5. Boosters use sophisticated methods and devices for engaging in shoplifting.

These devices include "booster bloomers," garments especially designed to hold stolen merchandise, and "booster boxes," specifically designed to look like wrapped packages but that actually contain secret openings into which items can be placed quickly and easily.

A more recent study of boosters found that they usually operate as a team, in which one member distracts sales associates, a second takes the item and surreptitiously passes it to a third, who then takes the item(s) out of the store (Klemke, 2001).

The other 90 percent of shoplifters, according to Cameron, are snitches, or amateurs, who possess the following characteristics:

1. They are "respectable" members of the community.

2. They do not think of themselves as criminals.

3. They have no criminal associations or connections.

4. They steal from a store when the opportunity arises.

5. They do not plan extensively but enter the store "prepared" to shoplift (equipped with "shopping lists," large handbags, briefcases, shopping bags, and scissors and razor blades for snipping off price tags).

Snitches simply place items in pockets or inside coats, sometimes actually wearing the stolen merchandise under their clothing, or engage in such activities as price-tag switching, in which they pay less for merchandise. Recent examinations of snitches confirm Cameron's initial insights (Klemke, 2001).

Cameron's findings about boosters and snitches are important because they show shoplifting to be a frequent crime and one that is not primarily committed by professionals, "lower-class" people, or a unique "criminal element." Rather, shoplifting is committed by "normal" and "ordinary" individuals. However, the most active shoplifters seem to be teenagers, with activity peaking at age 17, when approximately 39 percent of males and 23 percent of females admit having engaged in this crime at least once during the previous year. The percentage declines rapidly with age, so that by age 23 only 11 percent of males and 7 percent of females admit having shoplifted in the previous year (Klemke, 2001).

## Motor Vehicle Theft

**Motor vehicle theft** is the unlawful taking of or attempting to take a motor vehicle such as an automobile, a van, a truck, or a motorcycle. In 2003, 1,260,471 motor vehicle thefts were reported to the police, or approximately 433 per 100,000 inhabitants (Federal Bureau of Investigation, 2004b). In 2003, the estimated national loss from reported motor vehicle theft was $7.6 billion, and at the time of the theft the average value per vehicle stolen was $4,713.

The NCVS found that for 2002, 96 percent of completed motor vehicle theft victimizations were reported to the police. Not surprisingly, the NCVS reported a figure close to the FBI total: approximately 990,000 motor vehicle thefts in 2002.

Most scholars have concentrated on one type of motor vehicle theft, **automobile theft.** This is probably the best reported of all property crimes (90 percent) because of (1) the high value of vehicles, (2) insurance requirements, (3) the assistance needed from police to recover stolen cars, and (4) the high probability that stolen cars will actually be located.

As with robbery, burglary, and shoplifting, sociologists have divided auto thefts into the primary types of amateur and professional. One of the earliest applications of this typology is in Jerome Hall's (1952) well-known book, *Theft, Law, and Society.* For Hall, most auto thieves are amateur joyriders who steal automobiles for excitement and to "show off," quickly abandoning the car after a short time. According to Hall, joyriders mostly steal cars with unlocked doors, open windows, keys in the ignition, and sometimes even the motor running. Professional auto thieves steal automobiles in more indirect and skillful ways. According to Hall, many simply work with repair-shop employees who secure duplicate keys for the thief. Others steal cars advertised in newspapers by providing the owner with a "down payment," never to be heard from again. Once an automobile is stolen, many professionals work with or personally control a "chop-shop," in which stolen automobiles are stripped of all sellable accessories. These accessories are sold to dealers, repair shops and garages, and professional fences.

McCaghy, Giordano, and Henson (1977) argue that Hall's typology is too simplistic for this crime. According to these sociologists, auto thieves "are a more complex lot" (p. 377), and they have suggested a typology that includes five categories: (1) joyriding, (2) short-term transportation, (3) long-term transportation, (4) commission of another crime, and (5) profit. We now examine each.

McCaghy, Giordano, and Henson agree with Hall that joyriding auto theft signifies recreational, nonutilitarian, short-term use of cars. For the joyrider, the primary goal is not simply to obtain transportation; rather, "automobile symbolism is predominant: the car is stolen not for what it does, but for what it means" (p. 378). The second type—short-term transportation—is similar to joyriding in that it clearly involves short-term use of a stolen automobile. It differs, however, in that the thief's primary interest in the car is its ability to provide transportation from one location to another—from one place in the city to another, or even from one state to another. As with joyriding, many juveniles are involved in short-term auto theft.

The third type—long-term transportation—involves thieves stealing the vehicle with the intent of keeping it for long-term personal use. This type of auto thief usually steals automobiles outside his or her state of residence and, on returning home, if not before, repaints the vehicle. Most long-term auto thieves are adults. Some auto thieves—the fourth type—steal cars to aid them in the commission of another crime, such as robbery or burglary. This fourth type represents only a small portion of all auto thefts, even though the scenario is depicted over and over again on prime-time television. Once again, the motivation is utility of the automobile.

Finally, the fifth type identified by McCaghy, Giordano, and Henson is theft for profit, which is somewhat similar to Hall's professional theft. However, for McCaghy, Giordano, and Henson, this fifth type of automobile thief includes a wide variety of individuals whose motive is not to keep the car but rather to resell it, or its parts, for profit. They identify two forms of this type: amateurs and professionals. Amateurs steal a car to strip it of easily accessible components such as batteries, tires, and a variety of engine parts. They sell these parts to friends, acquaintances, or amateur fences, or they re-equip their own cars using some of the parts. Professionals, however, are highly organized, reselling expensive stolen cars in the United States and internationally. Professionals alter the vehicle registration numbers and falsify registration papers. Many purchase expensive wrecked vehicles and their ownership documents for a low cost, then steal an identical car (year, make, model), replacing the vehicle identification number plate with that of the wrecked vehicle and making other minor alterations. Subsequently, the converted vehicle is sold to an unsuspecting party who registers and retitles the vehicle in his or her name, giving it a legitimate identity virtually impossible to trace to the thief. McCaghy, Giordano, and Henson argue that professionals are also involved in the chop-shop business, specializing in the sale of specific parts to fences: hoods, fenders, bumpers, grills, and other hard-to-obtain parts.

Although amateurs and professionals clearly differ in skill and quality of theft, they both consider the automobile a valuable piece of property. Auto theft for profit differs from the other types of auto theft identified by McCaghy, Giordano, and Henson—joyriding, short- and long-term transportation, and aiding in the commission of another crime—because those who commit these latter types consider the automobile either a symbol or a form of transportation.

Ronald Clarke and Patricia Harris (1992) have provided a typology of auto theft that includes three types:

1. Thefts for temporary use, such as joyriding and short-term transportation.

2. Professional thefts intended to deprive the owner permanently of the vehicle, which is used for resale, for export, or for chopping.

3. Thefts from vehicles, such as CD players, radios, and batteries.

Clarke and Harris' typology differs from those of other researchers in one basic way: It includes "theft from vehicles" as a category of auto theft.

Claire Corbett (2003) has most recently constructed a typology of auto theft similar to Clarke and Harris' that includes the three following types:

- Theft for contents and parts.

- Joyriding.

- Professional theft.

In the past, auto thieves stole "internal parts" of the automobile—such as CD players and speakers—but Corbett records that today "external parts," such as bumpers, wheels, and license plates, are mostly targeted by auto thieves. Regarding "joyriding," Corbett notes that this form of auto theft does not actually maintain much joy for the rider once it is recognized that joyriders are 200 times more likely than other drivers to become crash-involved. Moreover, teenage males are by far the most frequent offenders, being six times more likely to have stolen an automobile than any-age female. Finally, professional auto thieves usually began as joyriders, work together in teams, and normally have some type of connection with the legitimate auto trade.

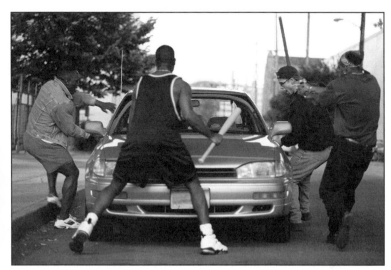

*The most dangerous auto theft: Although carjackings are the least frequent of all types of auto theft, they are the most dangerous. Carjacking is a form of auto theft in which the perpetrator uses direct physical force to steal a car from the driver.*

All of the above examples of auto theft usually occur without direct contact between offender and victim. However, during and since the 1990s a new type of auto theft began to be discussed in the media, **carjacking**, in which the auto thief uses direct physical force to steal a car from a driver. In a carjacking, automobiles are stolen from drivers at such places as rest stops, service stations, car washes, red lights, and shopping mall parking lots. Some facts on carjacking include (Copes and Wallace, 2001):

- The rate of carjacking is approximately 25 per 100,000 population.

- 50 percent of carjackings are successful.

- Victims are injured in 23 percent of completed carjackings and in 10 percent of attempted carjackings.

- Offenders use a weapon in 83 percent of all attempted and completed carjackings.

## Fraud

In Chapter 7.1 and 7.2 we discuss occupational fraud and corporate financial fraud; here we focus on nonoccupationally related frauds such as check and credit-card fraud and income-tax fraud. We begin with an examination of check fraud.

*Check fraud.* The crimes thus far analyzed—robbery, burglary, shoplifting, and motor vehicle theft—are clearly recognizable as crimes by an offender against a victim. In contrast, **check fraud**—deliberately deceiving someone for personal economic gain by producing a counterfeit or forged check—has little in the act to identify it as a crime. In other words, check fraud is not at the time of its commission easily recognizable as a crime. Indeed, this holds true for all forms of fraud discussed in this section; it is not until sometime later that the event is determined to be a crime.

Individuals can even engage in check fraud without knowing it. For instance, if someone continually writes checks against his or her account at a time when that account does not hold sufficient funds to cover the checks, the checks are normally returned with the designation "Nonsufficient Funds" (NSF), and the individual could be prosecuted for fraud. Other forms of check fraud include altering checks, forging someone else's personal checks, producing counterfeit personal and payroll checks, stealing government checks (checks rendering a salary, tax refund, pension, welfare allotment, and/or veteran benefit), and forging a signature.

Lemert's (1967) classic study of "naive" and "systematic" check forgery remains the most extensive examination of check fraud. *Naive check forgers* are amateurs who commit the crime only when they have an urgent need for money and who are unfamiliar with "criminal techniques." The naive check forger, Lemert found, ordinarily has completed more years of school than the general population and works in a clerical, skilled, or professional occupation. Lemert also established that a majority of naive check forgers reside in the community in which their crimes are committed.

*Systematic check forgers* view themselves as forgers, regularly use a special technique to pass bad checks, and organize their lives around check fraud. Some systematic check forgers view their fraud as a "regular business," but most do not, engaging in it for the alleged "fast and luxurious" life. These forgers give special attention to such details as banking hours and the best places to present checks; yet, according to Lemert, such details serve only as "guides" for the fraud. Moreover, systematic check forgers are less likely than other professional property offenders to use the "fix" because they simply have "too many bad checks outstanding and too many victims to mollify by offering restitution" (p. 111). The systematic check forger is different from other professional property offenders in another way. According to Lemert, check forgery requires neither a high degree of technical skill nor a long learning "apprenticeship"; you simply "learn as you go." However, systematic check forgery does require the ability to impersonate someone else, and therefore success is based on development of expertise in assuming fictitious roles. Finally, although the systematic check forger tends to be migratory (like other professional property offenders), most tend to work alone, avoiding contact with a network of illegitimate and legitimate people. Lemert found that some systematic check forgers work in "check passing gangs" and a few "contract out" their services; however, the majority operate on a solitary basis. These forgers manufacture or steal checks (usually personal or payroll checks) and then work alone to pass them illegally.

*Credit-Card and Related Fraud.* Lemert's discussion of check fraud identified fraudsters as amateurs and professionals; the same classification holds for **credit-card fraud.** The typical perpetrator of credit-card fraud is someone of modest means who finds himself or herself in need of money and subsequently views illegal credit-card use as the easiest way of satisfying that need (Scarpitti and Lenhart, 2001). Professionals usually work in groups who move from town to town in order to avoid detection and who concentrate on elaborate methods of stealing and manufacturing illegal credit cards.

Other methods of professional fraudsters include check guarantee fraud, purchase credit-card fraud, and purchase check fraud. The first, *check guarantee fraud*, occurs when individuals "ride" a stolen credit card—or several cards—by cashing checks (also stolen) in numerous bank branches in the shortest possible time. The term "ride" refers to the total number of banks visited by fraudsters with just one credit card; "the take" is the total amount of cash withdrawals per ride. *Purchase check* and *purchase credit-card fraud* simply entail using stolen checks and credit cards to purchase goods from retail stores. A group network of fraud usually consists of thieves (people who steal the checks and cards), riders (people who use the checks and cards in banks and stores), and fences (who buy the fraudulently obtained merchandise). Research indicates that large organized schemes account for half the total dollar loss due to credit-card fraud.

***Income-Tax Fraud.*** The government is also a potential victim of fraudsters. Indeed, the potential for defrauding the government is actually limitless because of the vast number and variety of government programs. To fraudsters, the federal government is a bottomless financial pit. **Income-tax fraud**, however, is probably the most prevalent form of defrauding the government. Cheating on one's income tax is made possible in the United States because of the following (Mattera, 1985):

1. The complexity of the tax codes.

2. The seemingly infinite number of deductible expenses.

3. The Internal Revenue Service's reliance on a system in which taxpayers calculate their own tax bill.

4. The small number of returns actually scrutinized by the IRS.

Two major forms of income-tax fraud are tax avoidance and tax evasion. In *tax avoidance*, individuals may underreport wages by, for example, working a second job—for which earnings are paid in cash—but filing an income-tax return only for wages earned from the first job. Another type of tax avoidance is to earn wages and salaries in a variety of ways but file no income-tax return for *any* portion of it. This completely off-the-books employment is not uncommon among restaurant and construction workers, as well as among providers of personal services, such as house painters and appliance repair persons.

*Tax evasion* involves intentionally paying less of one's tax bill than is legally required, through the understatement of tax liability (Thurman and Vose, 2001). Approximately 80 percent of lost federal tax revenue results from underreporting of income, while overstating deductions and failing to file a return account for the remaining 20 percent. The most recent research on income-tax fraud indicates that:

- It is one of the most serious types of fraud because of the size of the tax gap it produces.

- Most taxpayers do not engage in income-tax fraud.

- Taxpayers are most compliant when they feel a moral obligation to pay what they owe.

- Taxpayers who engage in tax avoidance and evasion usually subscribe to excuses to neutralize any moral guilt.

---

### Box 4.2   Identity Theft

**I**dentity theft occurs when someone adopts another person's identity, usually to facilitate further crime. The identity thief essentially steals the personhood of another by asserting in various ways to be that person. Thus, identity theft entails the fraudulent use of personal information to pretend to be someone else.

Emily Finch (2003) has developed an interesting typology of identity theft. She distinguishes two types of identity theft that differ in three major ways: duration, level of immersion, and motivation. *Duration* refers to the amount of time one fraudulently adopts another identity—from a few minutes to lifelong use. *Level of immersion* is "the depth with which the imposter delves into the victim's life and to the range and extent of the personal details that are misappropriated" (p. 90). Level of immersion, then, varies from illegally possessing and using someone's name and date of birth to more complex situations involving financial, employment, and education details to masquerade as the victim.

A combination of duration and level of immersion establishes the two major types of identity theft—*total identity theft* and *partial identity theft*. When someone permanently adopts all the details of another persons life, the offender has engaged in total identity theft, whereas the temporary use of someone's personal information is classified as partial identity theft.

*Motivation* is related to both types of identity theft in various ways. For example, partial and total identity theft often involve the adoption of the victim's identity solely for the commission of a crime, such as fraudulently obtaining access to goods and services. According to Finch, this is "the most prevalent form of identity theft as it accounts for the vast majority of partial identity theft and a significant proportion of cases of total identity theft" (p. 90). Moreover, adopting another person's identity—either for temporary or lifelong duration—can help an offender avoid detection by ensuring that his or her criminal acts (otherwise unrelated to the identity theft) are attributed to someone else. In these types of cases the motivation is to use another's identity to avoid detection should the identity thief be caught engaging in other criminal activities.

Nevertheless, identity theft does not always entail attempts to avoid detection or to facilitate fraudulent behavior; it also can provide a means to escape an unsatisfactory life and obtain the opportunity to begin anew. As Finch puts it:

> This urge to reinvent oneself may derive from a general sense of dissatisfaction with one's own identity or be a way to escape from some particularly problematic aspect of life such as debt or a traumatic relationship. Identity theft provides both a practical and symbolic respite from a life that has gone wrong by enabling the individual to escape the problem and to acquire a legal identity that is in accord with his or her perceived or desired individual identity. (p. 91)

Given that everything the identity thief requires to select a victim and fraudulently appropriate his or her identity is now available on the Internet, identity theft has been labeled by the Federal Trade Commission as "the fastest growing crime of our time" (p. 94).

## 4.3 Dealing and Damage

Fencing and arson, although property crimes, are somewhat different from robbery, burglary, and larceny. Fencing is buying and selling—or dealing in—stolen goods, and arson involves damage to property of another.

### Fencing

As stated above, **fencing** is buying, selling, or dealing in stolen goods. A fence's sources of goods include robbers, burglars, shoplifters, auto thieves, fraudsters, and employee thieves (whom we examine in Chapter 7.1). Once a thief successfully steals "the goods" and does not plan to make personal use of them, he or she must dispose of the goods as quickly as possible. Some thieves engage in "self-fencing"—that is, selling the stolen goods to people who do not know the goods are stolen or selling them to consumers who are unconcerned with their origin. Many people jump at the opportunity to buy items at a discount; consequently, thieves find accessible outlets for stolen merchandise in friends, acquaintances, and on the street generally.

In their interviews with burglars, Cromwell, Olson, and Avary (1991) found that the market for stolen property is both diverse and ubiquitous, including

> schoolteachers, social workers, plumbers, operators of small business establishments, attorneys, bail bond agents, drug dealers, systems analysts, college professors, high school and college students, and other individuals who regularly or occasionally purchased merchandise they knew or believed to be stolen. (p. 80)

Most of the individuals interviewed in this study reported that they bought stolen goods for personal use—and did not resell the goods—and, thus, technically, can be considered "receivers," rather than fences.

Some thieves, however, sell their goods to amateur fences. Stuart Henry's (1976, 1978) classic work on the amateur trade in stolen goods is interesting in this regard. Henry (1976) defined amateur fencing as "the activity of regular part-time purchase of genuine quality merchandise (usually, though not necessarily stolen) for the purpose of selling cheaply for the interest of those involved" (p. 794). Most amateur fences *say* they participate in the trade of stolen goods for personal economic gain. Notwithstanding, it seems that amateur fences rarely make money. Henry found this to be the case because amateur fences are unlikely to come into contact with either highly valued articles or large quantities of these items, or, if they do, find it is difficult to resell them. But more important, the price charged by the fence is determined by the nature of the relationship between the fence and the buyer. Most stolen goods go from the amateur fence to relatives and friends who "are often given the goods and not even charged cost price," and when friends and relatives are charged, it is rarely more than the fence actually paid for the items (p. 798).

Thus, even though amateur fencing is structured in terms of economic exchange, Henry concluded that in actuality, the majority of deals are made for the purpose of reaffirming established relationships. Amateur fencing provides the individual fence with status, prestige, and reciprocal social favors. As Henry (1976) stated, "The social content of the relations surrounding amateur exchange outweighs the material value of the goods involved" (p. 801). Amateur trade in stolen goods becomes a means of sustaining a network of communal relations among relatives, friends, and acquaintances. Consequently, amateur trade in stolen goods is quite informal and even takes place in people's homes. Henry (1978) provided an example: "Whenever Jim, a shoplifter, supplied cheap goods to Freddy, a plumber, there would be a Sunday-morning knock at the door: 'I got some suits: Do you want them?' " (p. 18).

Many thieves, however, sell their stolen merchandise to a professional fence. For example, burglars prefer a professional fence because professionals can purchase large amounts of merchandise, tend to ask fewer questions than other buyers of stolen goods, and are motivated to be discreet about their business dealings (Wright and Decker, 1994).

Several classic studies have examined professional fencing operations in relation to property theft. Within such literature the consensus seems to be that most professional fences have strong ties to the legitimate business community. As Hall wrote in his book *Theft, Law, and Society* (1952), the professional fence is "an established participant" in the legitimate "economic life of society" (p. 155). Professional fences are "offshoots from legitimate businesses," frequently specialize in a chosen field, and thus are "able to evaluate merchandise expertly and to compete generally on the basis of their special skills" (p. 157).

Marilyn Walsh (1977) reported that the average professional fence in her study was "a 45- to 55-year-old white, male businessman. As such, he looked strikingly similar to most managers and administrators in wholesale and retail trades." For Walsh, then, the professional fence is "strikingly dissimilar" to the thief and is "demographically a very ordinary man" (p. 15).

Finally, a study by Darrell Steffensmeier (1986) confirms that the "overwhelming majority of fences . . . are simultaneously proprietors or operators of a legitimate business which provides a cover or front for the fencing" (p. 20). "Sam Goodman," the main character of Steffensmeier's book, is a legitimate and successful businessperson who also—as part of his business—sells stolen merchandise. In Sam's view, it is difficult for anyone to succeed in business without "chiseling" in some form or fashion; professional fencing is simply his type of chiseling.

The legitimate business identity of the professional fence covers the comings and goings of thieves, making thieves indistinguishable from customers and legitimate delivery persons (Klockars, 1974). In short, the evidence on fencing shows that, as Henry (1977) put it,

> It is not the case that one species of actor, the 'fence,' buys stolen goods, whereas another, the 'businessman,' buys legitimate ones. Rather it demonstrates that businessmen buy cheap goods in order that they may sell at a profit; a greater or lesser proportion of their purchases may be illicit. (p. 133).

The professional fence is "in the shadow of two worlds" (the subtitle of Steffensmeier's book), providing legitimate and illegitimate goods in the business world while simultaneously buying stolen goods in the criminal world. Professional fencing is in fact indistinguishable from legitimate business activity. The professional fence may also develop a special relationship with the police:

> Fences are able to offer various "perks" or payoffs to the police and other legal officials. . . . In return for these perks, the police may be less zealous in responding to

complaints against the fence or may sabotage an ongoing investigation. (Steffensmeier, 1986:152)

Most detectives who frequented Sam's shop were simply recipients of Sam's generosity, yet a few were "actively on the take" (p. 153).

In Klockars' (1974) earlier case study of the fence "Vincent Swaggi" it was found that the largest single group of buyers were in some way connected to the criminal justice system: police officers, detectives, lawyers, judges, customs officials, insurance adjusters, and crime reporters. The relationship between Swaggi and these buyers was quite comfortable and friendly. As Klockars pointed out,

> A joking atmosphere prevails, with "What's hot today, Vince?" as a standard opening from Vincent's law enforcement customers. Although Vincent has heard that question a thousand times he always answers, "Everything," and laughs. (p. 104)

Thus, both amateur and professional thievery, as well as amateur and professional fencing, must be understood as being embedded in a network of relations with other legitimate and illegitimate people.

More recent discussions of fencing confirm the conclusions of this earlier research, suggesting that both amateur and professional fences continue to exist (Head, 2001). However, the role of the professional fence may be changing as most thieves today dispose of their stolen merchandise themselves. Moreover, an increased reliance on "anonymous outlets" such as the Internet "may unintentionally lead to the demise of traditional fencing operations, or it may serve to enhance the ability of fences to dispose of merchandise more efficiently and effectively" (Head, 2001:229).

### Arson

**Arson** is the willful or malicious burning of a house, public building, motor vehicle, aircraft, or other property of another. In 2003, 74,921 arson offenses were reported to the police, or approximately 32 per 100,000 inhabitants (Federal Bureau of Investigation, 2004b). The vast majority of arsons occur in cities with populations of over 250,000. However, it should be pointed out that only fires determined through investigation to have been willingly or maliciously set are classified as arsons by the FBI. Fires of suspicious or unknown origins are excluded. In addition, it is not simply in big cities but specifically in the economically declining inner-city neighborhoods of big cities that the most common arsons occur.

When we think of arson, what commonly comes to mind is the deranged pyromaniac depicted on prime-time television. Clearly, there are cases of individuals who engage in this behavior for the excitement and mere "pleasure" of setting fires and watching structures burn; however, their number is indeed small when compared with other types of arsonists. Excluding pyromaniacs, four major types of arson have been identified by sociologists, police officials, and firefighters. The types are based on arsonists' motives and include crime concealment, revenge, vandalism, and profit. We briefly consider each type.

*Crime concealment* refers to the use of fires to destroy evidence—for example, of a burglary, a larceny, or a murder. In such cases individuals use arson to remove any evidence connecting the perpetrator to the crime or to prevent identification of the victim.

In addition, people set fires to destroy records that contain evidence of other crimes, such as fraud and white-collar crimes such as embezzlement and corporate crime.

*Revenge arsons* result from quarrels, hatred, and jealousy among lovers, neighbors, employees, family members and relatives, and persons motivated by racist and religious contempt. Children sometimes express resentment against siblings who receive greater attention by burning a brother's or sister's bed; they may indicate incest victimization by setting afire the bed in which they were victimized. Similarly, women who are the victims of physical or sexual abuse in the home may obtain revenge by setting the bed afire. The church arsons that occurred in the mid-1990s are examples of arson resulting from racial and religious contempt. According to the National Church Arson Task Force (1997), between 1995 and 1997 approximately 429 church arsons were committed. Of these incidents, 162 involved African-American churches, more than three quarters were located in the southern United States, and the vast majority of offenders were white.

The third type of arson—*vandalism*—is usually associated with youths who set fires in schools, automobiles, and vacant buildings. Vacant buildings often serve as playgrounds for inner-city youths, some of whom may rationalize that a fire in such a building will not hurt anyone. Watching the building burn, as well as the fire department extinguishing it, can be "exciting" to some youth. However, it is difficult to determine whether such fires are actually the result of arson. Determining criminal intent of youth is based on age and the motive behind the fire setting. If the youth is under the age of consent and there is insufficient evidence indicating malicious and willful fire setting, the youth most likely will not be labeled an arsonist (Garry, 1997).

Finally, the most costly arson—in terms of property damaged and lives lost and injured—is for *profit*. Individuals can profit from arson in several ways: "stop-loss" arson—in which businesses on the verge of great financial loss or even financial ruin "sell" the business to an insurance company by setting it ablaze to obtain the coverage proceeds; "property improvement or rehabilitation" arson—in which property owners improve a structure or replace deteriorating furnishings from the proceeds of small fire insurance claims; "elimination of competition" arson—where a business eliminates its competition by setting it afire; and "extortion, coercion, and intimidation" arson—in which criminal syndicates use the threat of arson to extort money from businesses.

Arson for profit: This type of arson frequently occurs by defrauding insurance companies. Individuals may set a structure on fire to obtain insurance coverage money or to improve the quality of the structure with the financial return on an insurance claim.

However, arguably the most lucrative and destructive form of arson-for-profit occurs when individuals purchase a particular property—usually in an economically depressed area of a city—and insure the property for more than its value. By setting the property ablaze, the owner can reap a substantial profit.

Brady's (1983) classic study of arson concentrated on this latter type of arson-for-profit. His research went considerably beyond an examination of individuals, connecting arson-for-profit to major banks and criminal syndicates in one particular city, Boston. Brady showed that there was, in the late 1970s and early 1980s, a pattern to the fires occurring in Boston, with arson being demographically concentrated within certain poor Boston neighborhoods, such as Roxbury, North Dorchester, East Boston, and Jamaica Plain. Within these economically depressed areas, arson was more common in buildings owned by absentee landlords than in either owner-occupied tenements or public housing projects. Many of these privately owned buildings had been abandoned, and between 1978 and 1982 more than half of Boston's 3,000 arsons occurred in abandoned buildings. These buildings were not abandoned because of a "natural process of neighborhood evolution" but because of "discriminatory mortgage-lending policies of banks that deny credit to certain districts of the inner city in order to invest in more profitable suburban real estate" (p. 10). This latter practice, known as redlining, devastates neighborhoods by forcing small businesses to close because they cannot secure bank loans. Moreover, landlords fail to repair their buildings, eventually abandoning them, because property values decline drastically. This type of situation sets the stage for arson-for-profit. For example, property owners hire a criminal syndicate to "torch" their buildings as way to avoid losing on unprofitable property. Since the criminal syndicate offers to buy the building at a price far greater than market value—which the bank has agreed to mortgage—the syndicate arranges for insurance well above the actual value of the property. The overmortgaged and overinsured property is then set fire and both the criminal syndicate and the bank profit because "the new mortgage paid by the insurance company greatly exceeds the old bad debt assumed under foreclosure" (p. 11).

A recent discussion of arson confirms that the different types discussed above continue to be committed (Goetz, 2001). Yet it seems that "many arsons-for-profit go unchecked, with local law enforcement agencies unwilling or unable to do much about this problem" (p. 27). Nevertheless, Goetz argues that much of the arson-for-profit identified by Brady and others occurred in the 1970s and 1980s, in which a postindustrial transformation was taking place in local real estate economies (such as massive gentrification), which wreaked havoc on many working-class and poor neighborhoods. Thus, it remains unclear whether arson-for-profit will be as widespread in the future as it was in the 1970s and 1980s.

## Review

This chapter examined seven types of property crimes: robbery, burglary, shoplifting, motor vehicle theft, fraud, fencing, and arson. These property crimes are different from crimes of interpersonal violence in certain ways:

- They occur much more frequently.

- Offender and victim are usually strangers.

- In many cases no direct interaction occurs between offender and victim.

- In some cases—as in most frauds—it is not immediately apparent that a crime has been committed.

## Robbery and Burglary

1. Robbery is a unique property crime involving direct interaction between offender and victim. It also entails both the threatened or actual use of physical violence and property loss to the victim.

2. Because robbery differs from crimes of interpersonal violence in significant sociological ways, it is labeled a property crime.

3. Strong-arm robbery is considerably more dangerous than armed robbery.

4. Robbery can be classified in terms of both incidents and offenders. The two major types of robbery offenders are professionals and opportunists.

5. Burglars can be classified as professionals and amateurs.

6. Important information on robbery and burglary has come from interviews with criminals who are not incarcerated but are actively involved in these crimes.

7. Property offenders persist in their crimes because of their desperate economic situation and pursuit of "life as party."

## Varieties of Larceny

1. One type of larceny—shoplifting—has received the most attention by criminologists.

2. There are two major types of shoplifters: boosters (professionals) and snitches (amateurs).

3. Individuals steal automobiles for joyriding, for short- and long-term transportation, for commission of another crime, and for profit.

4. Check fraud consists of drawing checks on insufficient funds in a checking account, forging someone else's personal checks, producing counterfeit personal and payroll checks, altering payroll checks, and stealing government checks and forging a signature.

5. Two major types of check fraud are naive forgers (amateurs) and systematic forgers (professionals).

6. Systematic forgers differ from other professional property offenders in significant ways.

7. Check and credit-card fraudsters may work alone or in groups.

8. The government is the victim of substantial fraud, such as income-tax fraud.

9. Identity theft is the fastest growing crime of our time.

## Dealing and Damage

1. Fencing is the buying and selling of stolen goods and is conducted by both professionals and amateurs.

2. The majority of amateur fences sell their goods to relatives, friends, and acquaintances—not for purposes of economic gain but to enhance established relationships.

3. Most professional fences have strong ties to the legitimate business community and are part of a loosely structured, yet mutually supportive, network of individuals involved in acquiring and distributing stolen property.

4. This network consists of thieves, fences, criminal justice personnel, criminal syndicates, goods transporters, and buyers.

5. Arson causes more injury, death, and property loss than any other of the UCR index offenses.

6. There are four major types of arson: crime concealment, revenge, vandalism, and profit.

7. The most costly type of arson—in terms of property damage and lives lost and injured—results from profit-making ventures.

## Questions for Class Discussion

1. This textbook argues that robbery is a property crime. Examine that assessment of robbery and present an argument for or against its conclusion.

2. Most research on property offenders comes from incarcerated individuals. However, we presented research of "robbers on robbery" and "burglars on burglary." What are some of the advantages and disadvantages of this type of approach to gathering data on crime and criminals?

3. What are the major differences between professional and amateur property offenders?

4. Using examples, describe how "dealing" and "damage" are different from the varieties of larceny discussed.

5. How have modern forms of technology—such as computers and the Internet—changed the nature of property crime?

## For Further Study

### Readings

Jewkes, Yvonne, ed. 2003. *Dot.cons: Crime, Deviance and Identity on the Internet.* Portland, OR: Willan.

Wright, Richard T., and Scott H. Decker. 1997. *Armed Robbers in Action: Stickups and Street Culture.* Boston: Northeastern University Press.

### Websites

1. <http://www.whitehouse.gov/fsbr/crime.html>: This site contains some general statistical information regarding conventional crime. Of particular interest with regard to this chapter are the plummeting rates of property crime graphically displayed on the relevant chart.

2. <http://www.ojp.usdoj.gov/bjs/glance/mvt.htm>: From the Department of Justice, this graphic shows the rates of motor vehicle theft declining, according to the National Crime Victimization Survey.

3. <http://www.usfa.fema.gov/fire-service/arson/arson.shtm>: From the U.S. Fire Administration, this site provides prevention efforts in the United States. There are also links to community programs aimed at preventing arson.

4. <http://www.privacyrights.org/identity.htm>: This site educates users about identity theft. It contains numerous fact sheets on identity theft in the United States. ✦

# Interpersonal Violence

**5.1 Murder, Assault, Hate Crimes, and Rape**
- Murder and Aggravated Assault
- Hate Crimes
- Rape

**5.2 Interpersonal Violence in the Family**
- Heterosexual Wife Rape and Battering
- Gay and Lesbian Partner Battering
- Child and Elder Abuse
- Animal Abuse

**5.3 Interpersonal Violence in the Workplace**
- Murder and Assault
- Sexual Harassment

## Preview

Chapter 5 introduces:

- The various types of interpersonal violence.

- The nature and extent of interpersonal violence.

- The varying definitions of interpersonal violence.

## Key Terms

| | |
|---|---|
| aggravated assault | hate crimes |
| animal abuse | interpersonal coercion |
| battering | manslaughter |
| child abuse | mass murder |
| elder abuse | murder |

professional murder

rape

serial murder

sexual harassment

social coercion

victim precipitation

wife rape

Interpersonal crimes of violence have affected the way many of us live. We fear the streets, fear being home alone, fear being by ourselves in the center of the city, and fear specific acts, such as murder, assault, and rape. Fear of crime alters our lifestyles significantly.

Moreover, we are particularly afraid of strangers. In 1967 the President's Commission on Law Enforcement and the Administration of Justice reported that "the fear of crimes of violence is not a simple fear of injury or death or even of all crimes of violence, but at bottom, a fear of strangers" (President's Commission, 1967a:52). There is no reason to believe this situation has changed. Many of us assume that most violent crimes are committed on the streets by strangers. We fear most of all the random, unprovoked attack on the street by a stranger.

Much of this fear (see Chapter 1.1) is created by the mass media, for it is from the media that most people develop their comprehension of where, by whom, and how often violent crime is committed. Magazines, newspapers, and television focus on dramatic, violent crimes such as murder; "prime-time criminals," usually strangers to their victims, commit their crimes on the street. A distorted view of crime is thus encouraged.

Indeed, most conventional crime is not violent. There are many more crimes against property than crimes of interpersonal violence. And crimes of interpersonal violence occur most frequently indoors and, therefore, are more or less invisible to the public; the perpetrators—although sometimes strangers—are usually relatives, friends, or acquaintances of the victims. This is not to say, however, that crimes of interpersonal violence in the United States are not a substantial problem. As citizens, we are rightly concerned about a major social cancer: The United States has a higher level of interpersonal violence than any other industrialized country.

With this in mind, we turn now to a discussion of certain specific acts of interpersonal violence. We discuss the nature, extent, and types of three categories of interpersonal violence: (1) murder, assault, hate crimes, and rape; (2) violence in the family; and (3) violence in the workplace. These crimes are often referred to as "one-on-one" or "person-to-person" crimes because one person inflicts violence on another. Interpersonal violence therefore differs from other types of violence—such as corporate violence (see Chapter 7.2)—that inflict harm on larger numbers of people and do not entail direct face-to-face interaction.

## 5.1  Murder, Assault, Hate Crimes, and Rape

When we think of violent crimes, what commonly comes to mind are the crimes of murder, assault, and—for women, in particular—rape. In this section we look at the nature and extent of four forms of interpersonal violence. We begin with a discussion of murder and aggravated assault.

## Murder and Aggravated Assault

**Murder** is defined as "the willful (nonnegligent) killing of one human being by another" (Federal Bureau of Investigation, 2004b:3). Individuals can also be charged by the state with manslaughter for killing another person through gross negligence. The difference between murder and manslaughter is based on intent, or what is referred to as *mens rea* (a guilty mind is present in the offender)—the conscious intent of the murderer is to kill. In murder, malice is always present, although the degree of murder is based on the level of premeditation (essentially, to what extent the murder is plotted beforehand). **Manslaughter** is divided into two types: voluntary and involuntary. Voluntary manslaughter occurs when the death is the result of a sudden passion arising from an immediate adequate cause. If the victim does not die but sustains serious injury, the crime is defined by the state as assault. Involuntary manslaughter results when one individual unintentionally kills another through recklessness or gross negligence, such as might happen during an automobile accident.

As we noted, the most comprehensive source for determining the number of murders in the United States is the Uniform Crime Reports (UCR), published by the Federal Bureau of Investigation. Obviously, it is impossible to conduct victimization surveys on murder. Although it is difficult to conceal a killing from official investigation, a number of murders may be ignored, overlooked, or disregarded; coroners may err in ruling an accidental death or a suicide as a murder, and some bodies simply may be hidden. Thus, although we must rely on police data as our source for determining the nature and extent of murder in the United States, these data must be viewed with some degree of skepticism.

In 2003 there were 16,503 murders in the United States. This means that approximately 6 of every 100,000 people were victims of murder (Federal Bureau of Investigation, 2004b). Although murder is the most serious form of crime, it fortunately occurs the least often, accounting for only 0.1 percent of all index crimes. Moreover, the murder rate continues to decline in the United States—in 2003 it was 37 percent lower than the rate recorded for 1994.

Murder also occurs primarily in big cities and in the South. Generally, the larger the city in terms of population, the higher the violent crime rate. Studies over several decades have consistently shown a close relationship between city size and murder rates. That is, the larger the city, the higher the murder rate.

The typical killing—whether in large cities or small—results from a disagreement between individuals who know each other. Approximately 43 percent of murders involve family members, friends, or acquaintances, while 13 percent involve strangers; in the remaining 44 percent the relationship between victim and offender is unknown.

Moreover, most murders involve arguments over romantic triangles, property and money, and other issues. The typical murder, then, involves family, friends, or acquaintances who are engaged in an argument—usually over a trivial matter—that eventually leads to a killing. Consequently, we have more to fear from those to whom we are close than from strangers.

It is therefore not surprising to find that the typical murder is also related to routine social activities among family, friends, or acquaintances. Murder is most likely to occur during times when routine activities are more concentrated around the home. For example, murder occurs most often during summer vacations (July and August) and holiday seasons (December and January), which are traditionally a time when family members, neighbors, and friends are together (Federal Bureau of Investigation, 2004b). Moreover, weekend murders are more likely to occur at home, among family members, and during the early evening hours.

Although the typical murder discussed thus far is characteristic of the largest proportion of murders, there are other types. For example, **professional murder** takes place when one individual kills another for personal profit. An unwritten "contract" is arranged, such as over the telephone or the Internet, between people who have never met personally. The victim, or "hit," is normally unknown to the killer, which makes it easier for the killer to engage in the crime. By conceptualizing the killing as a "business" or as "just a job," professional murderers can deny wrongfulness and thus justify their behavior even further.

Another type of murder, **serial murder**, occurs when an individual kills two or more people over a period of time. In serial murder there is generally no prior relationship between offender and victims, the subsequent murders often have no connection to the initial murder, and the victims usually hold some type of symbolic value to the murderer (e.g., prostitutes, homosexuals, hospital patients, children) (Egger, 2001).

There are two types of serial murderers. First, there are those killers who murder within the general area of their residence. An example of this type of serial murderer is John Wayne Gacy, who in 1979 murdered 33 young boys in or near his home and then hid their bodies in the crawlspace of his home, inside the walls, and under the patio and driveway. Another example is Donald Harvery, a nurse's aide in Cincinnati. In the late 1980s, Harvery systematically killed 21 patients to allegedly relieve them from their suffering. Second, there are murderers who kill outside the proximity of their own residences. Examples of this type are Theodore Bundy, who was found guilty of killing more than 20 women in Washington, Utah, and Colorado, and Henry Lee Lucas, who *admitted* killing 365 people in 25 states. According to some researchers, at least 142 of Lucas's killings have been verified (Holmes and DeBurger, 1985). More recent examples include the case of the "Unabomber," or Theodore Kaczynski, who over the course of 17 years (1978–1995) killed three people and injured 22 by sending bombs through the mail (in 1998 he pleaded guilty to 13 federal bombing offenses) and the "sniper" case of Lee Boyd Malvo and John Allen Muhammed, who in 2002 killed 10 people in the Washington, D.C. and northern Virginia suburbs.

Finally, a **mass murder** is committed when an individual kills two or more people at once, rather than singly over time. An example of a mass murder is a husband/father who kills his wife and children at the same time. The various in-school killings of students and teachers that occurred in the 1990s provide another example. Some of the better-known of these "school shootings" include:

- On February 2, 1996, in Moses Lake, Washington, Barry Loukaitus (age 14) shot and killed a teacher and two students at his junior high school.

- Eight months later, in Pearl, Mississippi, Luke Woodman (age 16) shot and killed two students in his high school.

- Two months later, in West Paducah, Kentucky, Michael Carneal (age 14) shot and killed three students in his high school.

- On March 24, 1998, in Jonesboro, Arkansas, Michael Johnson (age 13) and his accomplice, Andrew Golden (age 11), shot and killed a teacher and four students in their junior high school.

- On April 20, 1999, in Littleton, Colorado, Eric Harris (age 18) and Dylan Klebold (age 17) shot and killed a teacher, 12 students, and themselves.

In a recent study of these "school shooters," Kimmel and Mahler (2003) show that the media distorted the facts regarding these killings by suggesting that (1) they resulted from an increase in violent media content (when in fact school violence has actually decreased as violent media content has increased), (2) the school shooters came from unstable/dysfunctional families (the truth being that almost all the school shooters came from intact "stable" families with no history of child abuse), and (3) the killings were simply "kids killing kids" (yet all the school killings involved *boys* killing boys and girls). Kimmel and Mahler go on to show that the vast majority of the school shooters were victims of severe in-school bullying because they were defined as "different," such as being shy, bookish, artistic, nonathletic, and geekish. Kimmel

HARRIS                    KLEBOLD

*The school shootings: From 1997 to 2005 there was a 'wave' of school shootings in the United States. On April 20, 1999, the worst school shooting ever took place when two students at Columbine High School in Littleton, Colorado, killed 12 students, a teacher, and themselves. On March 21, 2005, a student at Red Lake High School on Minnesota's Red Lake Indian Reservation killed nine people and wounded seven others before killing himself.*

and Mahler conclude that the bullying challenged the school shooters' masculinity and thus motivated them to adopt a practice that is culturally defined as "acceptable" for restoring their masculinity—interpersonal violence.

Undoubtedly the most horrific and unique case of mass murder in the United States (because of the number of people killed and because it also entailed mass suicide) occurred on September 11, 2001. On that day, 19 individuals connected to the Al Qaeda terrorist network hijacked four U.S. commercial airplanes and murdered close to 3,000 people by flying the airplanes into the twin World Trade Center towers in New York City, the Pentagon Building in Arlington, Virginia, and a field in rural Pennsylvania. We will more thoroughly discuss and contextualize this mass murder/suicide in Chapter 8 because it also represents an example of political crime.

The most common weapon used to commit murder in the United States is a firearm. In 2003 approximately 71 percent of all murders were committed with a firearm, 53 percent with a handgun (Federal Bureau of Investigation, 2004b). Many people argue that because of the relationship between firearms and murder, firearms (especially handguns) should be controlled rigidly by the state. Others, in particular members of the National Rifle Association (NRA), argue that "Guns do not kill, people do."

Although the debate over firearm ownership and murder is likely to continue for some time, sociologists and criminologists have generated some interesting information that sheds light on the subject. First, the risk of death from a firearm is not uniformly distributed throughout the U.S. population: "The highest fraction of homicides committed with firearms peaks for 15- to 19-year-olds, at 81 percent of homicides, and consistently declines relative to other weapons used as the offender age increases" (Iadicola and Shupe, 1998:107). Second, firearm ownership varies by region, which correlates with the regional murder rates. The South has both the highest murder rate and the highest rate of firearm ownership. The Northeast, on the other hand, has the lowest murder rate and the lowest rate of firearm ownership (Federal Bureau of Investigation, 2004b). Third, the chance of dying from a firearm wound is much higher than from assault with a knife, club, or fist. In fact, assaults with firearms are two to six times more likely to result in death than assaults with knives. Fourth, increases in murder are correlated with increases in firearm ownership (Iadicola and Shupe, 1998). Fifth, because of easy availability of firearms, more accidental deaths and injuries occur.

All of this does not mean that firearms *cause* murder. However, it is obvious that households with firearms present are more likely—during a family argument, for instance—to experience a firearm death than households without firearms. Thus, although scant evidence exists to suggest that firearm ownership deters crime, by assuming it does and then purchasing guns, households actually become less, rather than more, safe and secure.

In 1958 criminologist Marvin Wolfgang coined the term "victim-precipitated murder," applying it to those murders in which "the victim is a direct, positive precipitator in the crime" (p. 252). In victim-precipitated murder, the victim is the first to display and use a deadly weapon or to strike a blow and, therefore, "the first to commence the interplay of resort to physical violence" (p. 252). For example, such a murder may involve two people having an argument during which the victim threatens the offender with a knife. Responding, the offender pulls out a gun and fires a fatal bullet. Wolfgang estimates that in one of every four murders, the victim precipitates the killing.

Some criminologists have questioned the thesis of **victim precipitation**, suggesting that the interaction between offender and victim actually involves challenges and provocations by *both* participants that lead up to the killing. In his research, David Luckenbill (1977) found that murder results from an "intense interchange" between offender, victim, and sometimes an audience and parallels a "character contest" wherein both offender and victim attempt to maintain "face" at the other's expense. This interchange between offender and victim takes place as follows:

1. The victim makes what the offender perceives as an offensive move, gesture, or remark.

2. The offender then retaliates with a verbal or physical challenge.

3. The victim then retaliates, creating a "working" agreement that commits both parties to a violent resolution of the conflict.

4. The battle eventually results in the death of the victim.

In 63 percent of Luckenbill's cases such an exchange between offender and victim took place. Additional research has reported similar results, concluding that the typical murder involves both offender and victim contributing to the violent conflict (Polk, 1994).

Although Luckenbill's theory is intriguing, it is certainly not applicable to all forms of murder. Obviously, it offers little help in understanding professional, serial, and mass murder. Moreover, Nancy Jurik and Peter Gregware (1992) have shown that for female-perpetrated murder, the idea of a character contest does not seem to hold in many cases, such as murder resulting from child abuse and killing in self-defense (to avoid wife beating). Thus, Luckenbill's theory may help us understand some male offender/male victim murder but is inadequate when applied to typical female offender/male victim murders. Whereas Luckenbill emphasizes a character contest, Jurik and Gregware's data on women "suggest the salience of strategic, life-saving dimensions and an imposed—rather than consensual—characterization of the violence in these homicides" (p. 196).

**Aggravated assault** is "an unlawful attack by one person upon another for the purpose of inflicting severe or aggravated bodily injury" (Federal Bureau of Investigation, 2004b:29). Aggravated assault is usually accompanied by the use of a weapon or by other means likely to produce death or great bodily harm.

Aggravated assault and murder are closely related crimes. In fact, much of what has already been discussed regarding murder can also be applied to aggravated assault. However, there are some differences between the two crimes. The first and most obvious difference is that an assault does not result in an actual death. Although the typical aggravated assault and the typical murder are similar in most major respects, it is the existence of a dead body that creates the major difference between them. If a killing does not occur, the crime is some type of assault.

A second difference is that there are more aggravated assaults in the United States than murders. In 2003 there were approximately 857,921 reported aggravated assaults, resulting in a rate of about 295 per 100,000 individuals (Federal Bureau of Investigation, 2004b). This rate is nearly fifty times the murder rate. However, in its National Crime Victimization Survey (NCVS), the Department of Justice (2003) found that only 57 percent of the victims of aggravated assault reported the crime to the police. Consequently, aggravated assault occurs more often than the UCR data indicate. Indeed, the NCVS estimates that almost 2 million aggravated assaults occurred in 2003.

Finally, according to the NCVS, aggravated assault—unlike murder—involves strangers more often (57 percent of the time) than relatives, friends, or acquaintances (Department of Justice, 2003). However, victims may be less likely to report assaults by people they know. Thus, it could well be that regarding the victim/offender relationship, aggravated assault is similar to murder. Nevertheless, studies of aggravated assault show that males are more likely to be victimized by strangers and females victimized by husbands and boyfriends (Bachman, 2001). Moreover, the location of assault victimization corresponds to the gender patterns just noted: Females are more likely to be assaulted at or near a private residence while males are usually assaulted in a public setting.

## Hate Crimes

A pervasive fact of life in industrialized societies is the existence of **hate crimes**, or violence perpetrated on people because of their race, religion, disability, ethnicity, or sexual orientation. Hate crimes differ from other forms of interpersonal violence in at least three distinct ways (Martin, 2001): (1) victims face greater difficulty coming to terms with their victimization, (2) communities face higher levels of fear and heightened intergroup tensions, and (3) labeling such incidents "hate crimes" increases attention to these harms by the criminal justice system.

In 2003, 8,706 hate crimes were reported to the FBI, of which 4,574 were motivated by racial bias, 1,426 by religious bias, 1,430 by sexual-orientation bias, 1236 by ethnicity bias, 40 by disability bias, and nine by multiple biases (Federal Bureau of Investigation, 2004b). Moreover, a study by the National Coalition of Anti-Violence Programs (2004) found that in 2003 there were 2,057 reported incidents of violence against lesbian, gay, bisexual, transgender, and HIV-positive people. This represents an 8 percent increase in hate crimes over the previous year, yet only approximately 50 percent were reported to the police. Moreover, in 2003, 70 percent of all victims identified as lesbian or gay men and heterosexuals comprised only 9 percent of the reported victims of anti-lesbian, gay, bisexual, and transgender violence. This shows that hate crimes are crimes of perception: Victims are chosen not necessarily because they are, for example, lesbian or gay, but because the perpetrator perceives them to be such.

Despite the many positive changes resulting from the civil rights movement, racism persists in the United States, expressing its extreme form in racist attacks on African Americans and other racial and ethnic minorities. The 1970s saw increasing reports of racial violence against African Americans by white youth. In 1980, the Subcommittee on Crime of the U.S. House of Representatives investigated this violence. In its report, *Increasing Violence Against Minorities*, the Subcommittee found anti–African-American attacks both by individuals (primarily young white males) and by groups such as the Ku Klux Klan. The report concluded that there "is abundant evidence of a marked increase in the incidence of criminal violence directed against minority groups" (U.S. House Subcommittee, 1980:2). Today, 60 percent of reported hate crimes are motivated by racial bias (Federal Bureau of Investigation, 2004b).

Consider skinheads, who hold extremely conservative and neo-Nazi views. They routinely target racial and ethnic minorities and homosexuals for violent attacks. Indeed, Mark Hamm's (1993) important study *American Skinheads: The Criminology and Control of Hate Crime* reported that the defining characteristics of skinhead ideology are racism, homophobia, and anti-Semitism.

Hate crimes differ from other forms of interpersonal violence in three important ways: They are more vicious, extremely brutal, and frequently perpetrated at random on total strangers (commonly a single victim) by multiple offenders (usually groups of white, working-class male teenagers). For hate crimes perpetrated in 2003 against specifically lesbian, gay, bisexual, transgender, or HIV-positive people, offenders were strangers in 45 percent of the incidents. Comparing 2002 with 2003, there was a 20 percent increase in incidents involving four to nine offenders and an 83 percent increase in those involving 10 or more offenders (National Coalition of Anti-Violence Programs, 2004).

Why do hate crimes occur? One of the better explanations is offered by Levin and McDevitt (1993), who have argued that this type of crime is the result in the United States of a "growing *culture of hate:* from humor and music to religion and politics, a person's group affiliation—the fact that he or she *differs from people in the in-group*—is

*Hate groups: Hate groups like the Ku Klux Klan and skinhead gangs have mobi-lized to perpetrate violence on people because of their perceived race, religion, disability, ethnicity, and sexual orientation. The KKK holds white-supremacist views and has historically targeted people of color and non-Christian religions for violent attacks.*

being used more and more to provide a basis for dehu-manizing and insulting that person" (p. 34). Although this "culture of hate" does not actually cause hate crimes, in a social context of growing unemployment and hard economic times, coupled with an influx of recent immigrants from Eastern Europe, Southeast Asia, Africa, and Latin America, as well as a visible gay/lesbian rights move-ment, a culture of hate pro-vides "support and encour-agement to those who seek to express their personal version of bigotry in some form of criminal behavior" (pp. 42–43). Indeed, Barbara Perry's (1998) research on hate groups in the United States found that such groups facilitate a negative politics of difference:

> Hate groups have mobilized in an effort to reassert a narrow, exclusive understand-ing of national identity. In particular, they provide a menu of ideologies which pre-sume the hegemony of white, heterosexual, Christian male power. . . . To the extent that hate groups define their collective identity as the norm, they necessarily engage in a politics of difference which seeks to negate, exclude and repress those groups that fall outside of that norm, namely non-Whites, non-Christians, non-heterosexu-als, even non-males. And they do so by invoking ideological claims to superiority and power. (p. 32)

And as Stephen Tomsen (2002) has reported in his important work on anti-homo-sexual homicides:

> Savage gang attacks that are carried out in public locations with an expected avail-ability of homosexuals often closely approximate the typical pattern of hate crime. But perpetrators are also preoccupied with attaining a heightened male status for themselves and with policing the acceptable patterns of public male sexual identity. (p. 99)

## Rape

**Rape**, as traditionally defined in criminal law, is "the carnal knowledge of a female forcibly and against her will" (Federal Bureau of Investigation, 2004b:19). By concen-trating on "against her will," the criminal law makes it imperative that the threat or ac-tual use of physical violence by the offender be present to constitute proof that the victim did not consent. Consequently, this traditional definition of rape actually means, in practice, sexual intercourse obtained by the threat or actual use of physical violence. Hence, the criminal law labels rape "forcible rape."

However, many scholars have argued that the traditional criminal law definition of forcible rape is inadequate, for it recognizes only one type of force—sexual intercourse obtained through the threat or actual use of physical violence. Some scholars argue that this definition does not provide for rape resulting from intimidation or pressure other than the threat or actual use of physical force. For example, a rape omitted from this traditional definition involves a woman who is coerced *economically*—"If you don't 'put out' you'll be fired"—where her overt genuine consent is absent.

Moreover, some criminologists have pointed out that the traditional definition of rape does not include *all* rapes that occur through the threat or actual use of physical violence. These criminologists note that in many states the violent forcible rape of a wife is simply not considered rape. Although in 1993 wife rape became a crime in all 50 states, in 33 states certain exemptions from rape prosecution exist for husbands. For example, in the majority of these states a husband cannot be prosecuted for wife rape if the woman "is unable to consent because she is mentally or physically impaired, asleep, or unconscious. In these states husbands are held to a lesser standard than other assailants" (Bergen, 1998, p. 22).

Nevertheless, because of feminist criticism, state definitions of rape have been expanded in certain ways: They are now gender neutral, meaning either men or women can be victims of rape; they cover anal and oral penetration by a penis or other objects; and they include nonforcible intercourse with someone unable to consent (e.g., unconscious, mentally incapacitated) (Koss and Cook, 1998).

Not everyone agrees with expanding the definition of rape to include "economic coercion," however. Some argue that an important distinction should be made between those who are coerced physically and those who may be coerced in other ways. For example, David Finkelhor and Kersti Yllö (1985) have argued that although labeling sexual assault obtained through economic force as rape highlights how oppressive and coercive sex is under certain circumstances, it simultaneously expands, and therefore dilutes, the meaning of the word "rape." Moreover, they have argued, it is extremely difficult to determine when force or coercion is being used in a relationship. For these two reasons, then, Finkelhor and Yllö have contended that the term "rape" should be used only for situations of actual or threatened physical force. This does not mean that other kinds of force are not used. Indeed, Finkelhor and Yllö held that

> a woman whose husband tells her he is going to humiliate her publicly if she won't perform some sexual act, for instance, may be making a more fearsome and devastating threat than a man who threatens only to push himself on his wife. We would be prepared to call this type of coercion forced sex, but not rape. (pp. 89–90)

Thus, Finkelhor and Yllö suggested that there are two types of sexual coercion in the United States but that sexual coercion, although frightening and traumatic, is clearly not, and should not be considered, rape. They distinguished "social coercion" from "interpersonal coercion." **Social coercion** occurs, for example, when women feel they should have sex with their husbands because it is their wifely "duty." Many women feel they cannot say no because they are married, or because her husband pays the bills, or because of religious authority. Thus, there exist social pressures on women to have sex with their husbands even if they do not want to do so. **Interpersonal coercion** occurs when a woman has sex with her husband or an employer in the face of nonviolent threats. For example, a wife may have sex with her husband "to keep peace in the house," or an employee may have sex with her boss to gain a promotion or just simply to keep a job.

Whether we agree with Finkelhor and Yllö or with the expanded definition of rape, the important point to understand is that sexual coercion can, and in fact does, occur in ways other than through the threat or actual use of physical violence.

In 2003 there were 93,433 reported forcible rapes, representing a rate of 32 per 100,000 people (Federal Bureau of Investigation, 2004b). However, we must view the police data with caution, inasmuch as the majority of rapes are not reported to the police. Indeed, only approximately 10 percent of rapes and attempted rapes are reported each year to the police (Department of Justice, 2003). This situation is due not only to fear of retaliation but to the trauma that rape victims experience, the shame they are often made to feel, and the perception that getting involved with the criminal justice system would itself be traumatic and possibly futile. Moreover, women have a far greater chance of being raped by someone they know rather than by a stranger, which clearly affects the victim's decision to report the crime to the police. Victims may feel (1) embarrassed, (2) that they should have been able to prevent the rape, (3) that they want to protect the offender, or (4) that they will not be believed. Consequently, for all these reasons, the number of rapes in U.S. society is much larger than statistics in the Uniform Crime Reports indicate. Indeed, the National Crime Victimization Survey estimated that 247,730 forcible rapes occurred in 2002, suggesting that only about 30 percent of incidents were reported to the police (Department of Justice, 2003). Paralleling murder, then, rape is more likely to be committed by someone the victim knows. Women are more likely to be raped by a husband, an ex-husband, a boyfriend, an acquaintance, or a date than by a stranger.

Popular culture often represents rape as "victim precipitated"—that is, the eventual victim is seen as "attracting" victimization by, for example, wearing certain clothing (e.g., a miniskirt), frequenting particular places (e.g., a fraternity party), and engaging in specific practices (e.g., hitchhiking). However, the concept of "victim-precipitated rape" asks us to identify with the rapist because it fails to acknowledge the victim's rights—in particular, the right to change one's mind whenever one pleases. This situation is collusion, which is exactly what the rapist has done—namely, refused to recognize the victim's right to change her or his mind. Moreover, by shifting blame from offender to victim, the idea of victim-precipitated rape diverts attention from the rapist as well as from the broader social factors forming the context in which rape occurs. Thus, although the idea of victim precipitation may be relevant to the crime of murder, it is mistaken to apply the concept to rape.

In addition, the idea of victim-precipitated rape is based on the pervasive myth in our society that men have a special and overwhelming "urge" or "drive" toward heterosexual intercourse. According to this myth, men have virtually an uncontrollable sexual need that, once "sparked," must find instant satisfaction, regardless of the consequences. Thus, if a woman awakens this sexual desire by engaging in provocative behavior, it is argued, the man cannot be held responsible for his behavior because the "urge" will be too strong for him to control. However, rapists rarely randomly and spontaneously assault their victims. Most stranger rapists spend time looking for women in locations most likely to be immune from surveillance, such as inside a home, an apartment or a motor vehicle. Thus, stranger and date rape are not explosive acts, the result of sudden and uncontrollable sexual desire. Rape is an act of violent sexual domination intended to devalue and humiliate the victim. It is not simply an expression of sexual desire.

Rapists are also portrayed in popular culture as "crazy." However, empirical research has been unable to confirm this belief (Belknap, 2001). Indeed, studies comparing male "rapists" and male "nonrapists" indicate that often they are indistinguishable regarding (1) blaming women for "turning them on," (2) linking sex with violence, and (3) wanting to be violent toward women whom they perceive as "teasing" them (p. 234). As Joanne Belknap (2001) concludes with regards to this crime:

> Just as with sexual-assault victims, rapists come from every racial, ethnic, and economic group. They include doctors, lawyers, ministers, priests, professors, politicians, and many others. Thus, just as anyone can be a rape victim, so too, can anyone be a rapist. (p. 234)

An example is the case of a group of teenage middle-class white male athletes who lured a "retarded" girl into a basement in Glen Ridge, New Jersey (Lefkowitz, 1997; Messner, 2002). The rapists were the most popular high school athletes in the town and the gang rape was carefully planned. Chairs were set up in the basement for an "audience" of boys (13 boys were involved as rapists or voyeurs) to watch other boys induce the victim into various sexual acts. Eventually six of the 13 boys left—but did not notify the police—and seven remained in the basement. Messner (p. 31) explains what happened next:

> While the girl was forced to continue giving oral sex to the boy, other boys laughed, yelled encouragement to their friends, and derisively shouted, "You whore!" at the girl. One boy decided it would be amusing to force a baseball bat up her vagina. When he did this (and followed it with a broomstick), the girl heard one boy's voice say, "Stop. You're hurting her," but another voice prevailed: "Do it more." Later, the girl remembered that the boys were all laughing while she was crying. When they were done, they warned her not to tell anyone. (p. 31)

Messner points out that four factors enabled this gang rape to occur:

1. The key role of competitive, homophobic, and misogynistic talk and joking as the central, most honored form of dominance-bonding in the athletic male peer group.

2. The group practice of "voyeuring," whereby boys set up situations where they seduce girls into places and situations in which their friends can watch the sex act and sometimes take an active part in it.

3. The suppression of empathy toward others—especially toward the girls who are the objects of their competitive dominance bonding—that boys learn from each other.

4. The enabling of some men's sexual violence against women by a "culture of silence" among peers, in families, and in the community.

In the traditional definition of rape, the victims of forcible rape are always female. However, there are cases of males being forcibly raped by both males and females. When women are arrested for forcible rape, they are usually an accomplice to a man, assisting him in raping a female.

Male rape of another male is also rare, except in prison. In prison a male's chances of being a rape victim increase. It has been estimated that in U.S. prisons approximately one of every four male inmates has been raped (Kupers, 2001). Rape as an act of violent sexual domination intended to devalue and humiliate the victim is a widespread practice in male prisons. Young men in U.S. prisons must seek protection from stronger, older, and more powerful inmates, and many of them become sexual slaves to their "protectors." Others are forced into prostitution and are traded for such prison commodities as cigarettes. Rape in prison is a masculine confirming act. Stephen Donaldson (2001: 118) argues that at the top of the prisoner classification system are the

> so-called "Men," and they are defined by a successful and continuing refusal to be sexually penetrated. A single instance of being penetrated, whether voluntary or not, is universally held to constitute an irreversible "loss of manhood." The "Men" rule the roost and establish the values and behavioral norms for the entire prison population; convict leaders, gang members, and the organizers of such activities as the smuggling of contraband, protection rackets, and prostitution rings must be and remain "Men." (p. 118)

Rape in male prisons involves a power dynamic among men. A "Man" who engages in rape is considered a "booty bandit," and a "real man," not a homosexual. Booty bandits rape "punks"—those who are young, small in stature, inexperienced in personal combat, and first timers—who are forced into sexually submissive roles and thus become slaves to the booty bandits, who in turn have the power to sell, trade, rent, or lend them at a whim. In other words, the social dynamics of prison rape are extremely instructive in understanding the rape of women in the larger society.

Moreover, it is quite unlikely that a male will be the victim of a rape unless he is incarcerated, and even then, once he has reached adulthood, he is virtually safe from any form of sexual assault.

Finally, the discussion in Box 5.1 points to the fact that certain institutions—such as college campuses—may create forms of social interaction conducive to rape and other types of violence against women. Another institution is the military. As Peter Iadicola and Anson Shupe (1998) have shown, throughout history rape has often been an institutionalized component of war:

> The systematic rape by soldiers of innocent women in towns and villages in the United States during the American Revolution, during the conquest and attempted genocide of native people on the North American continent, during the American Civil War, during World Wars I and II in Belgium, France, China, and Germany, and during the most recent wars of our time in Korea and Vietnam, Bangladesh, Nicaragua,

El Salvador, Russia and the former Yugoslavia, are just a few examples. Rape has been used to punish the enemy and as a reward for the victors. (p. 127)

---

**Box 5.1   College Male Athlete Violence Against Women**

Violence is a common feature in men's sports culture. "Legitimate" forms of violence are characterized through such practices as tackles, blocks, body checks, collisions, hits, and jabs, and are officially sanctioned in a variety of college sports. Some acts that are prohibited by official rules of a given sport are still accepted and occur routinely, such as fistfights and avoidable boarding in hockey, the late hit in football, the wandering elbow in basketball and soccer, and the "beanball" and "knockdown" pitches in baseball.

In addition, athletes are encouraged to ignore pain ("no pain, no gain") and college sports reward men for physically dominating others, hiding their fears, and distinguishing themselves from all that is feminine. Consequently, the world of college male sports *may* motivate men to construct a violent masculinity, because such sports are predicated on the successful utilization of violence; that is, sport activities routinely turn the human body into a weapon to be used against other bodies, resulting in pain, serious injury, or death. Men's college sports are key institutional sites for the reflection of violent masculinity (Messner and Stevens, 2002).

Although college male sports culture institutionalizes a hypermasculinity in which violence is an essential part, does the empirical research support the conclusion that it is simultaneously a breeding ground for rape and other forms of violence against women? Some studies, using both official college police data as well as self-reports, have concluded that male college athletes are more likely to be violent toward women than other college males are (Fritner and Robinson, 1993; Koss and Gaines, 1993; Boeringer, 1996; Crosset et al., 1996). However, other studies have found no significant difference between college male athletes and nonathletes in sexual violence reports to campus police and self-report studies (Crosset, 1995; Schwartz and Nogrady, 1996). Thus, it is difficult to simply conclude that athletic participation in college predisposes men toward violence against women.

Nevertheless, researchers have also investigated whether specific types of male college athletes are more often violent against women. The conclusion of several studies is that college males involved in especially high-contact sports—such as football, hockey, and lacrosse—have higher rates of violence against women (in particular group rape) than other athletes and nonathletes (Koss and Gaines, 1993; Crosset, et. al., 1996; Sanday, 1996; Nixon, 1997; Curry, 2000). The conclusion of this research is straightforward: Male college athletes who participate in the above contact sports use violence as a customary and institutionalized strategy during competition and that this violence *may* carry over to other social situations outside the sporting context. However, these studies still leave unanswered the important question of which male college contact-sport athletes are also involved in violence against women outside the sport context. Do you think certain college contact-sport males are violent toward women while other college contact-sport male athletes are not? If so, why do those that are violent toward women engage in different types of violence?

---

## 5.2 Interpersonal Violence in the Family

The family is, on the one hand, a "haven in a heartless world," a place where love and security prevail. On the other hand, it is a site of conflict among its members. Unfortunately, for many family members this conflict turns into violence. Although considerable violence occurs among family members (as we have seen), violent crimes such as murder, assault, hate crimes, and rape are not specific to the family and can occur outside its boundaries. In this section we focus on those types of interpersonal violence that occur only within the family setting. An accurate measure of interpersonal violence specific to the family is difficult to establish, but sociologists estimate that the problem is widespread for families throughout Western industrialized societies. We discuss five types of interpersonal violence specific to the family: wife rape, battering, child abuse, elder abuse, and animal abuse.

### Heterosexual Wife Rape and Battering

"It is within marriage," wrote sociologists Russell Dobash and Rebecca Dobash over 25 years ago, "that a woman is most likely to be slapped and shoved about, severely assaulted, killed or raped" (1979, p. 75). In fact, sociologists and criminologists have shown since 1977 that wife rape is more common than rape by dates, acquaintances, and strangers. Following Patricia Peacock (1998), we define **wife rape** as any sexual activity by a legal spouse that is performed against and without the consent of the other spouse. In the section on rape we showed that women are more likely to be raped by someone they know. Adding to this, women can likewise be raped by an acquaintance, friend, date, relative, authority figure, or stranger. However, wife rape is different in the sense that *only* women who have ever been married can actually be raped by their husband or ex-husband. Thus, Russell (1990) calculated rates of rape and attempted rape based on the percentage of women who had ever been married—rather than as a percentage of the entire sample—and found that "the prevalence of wife rape increases from 8 percent to 12 percent. This percentage places rape and attempted rape by husbands second only to rape and attempted rape by acquaintances" (p. 62).

When Russell looked only at *completed* rapes (rather than the combination of completed and attempted rapes), she found that more women had been victimized by their husbands than by any other type of perpetrator. Although only 3 percent of the women in her sample were victims of a completed rape by a stranger, 5 percent were victims of a completed rape by lovers or ex-lovers, and 8 percent were victims of a completed rape by husbands or ex-husbands. One could therefore conclude from Russell's data that the more intimate the relationship between the victim and the offender, the greater the chance that a rape attempt will be completed.

Similarly, Finkelhor and Yllö (1985) surveyed 323 Boston-area women to determine the extent of wife rape there. They found that 10 percent of these women had experienced a rape by a husband or ex-husband, whereas only 3 percent had been raped by a stranger. In addition, another 10 percent of the women had been raped by a date. Finkelhor and Yllö concluded that "sexual assaults by intimates, including husbands, are by far the most common type of rape" (p. 7). It is estimated that 14 percent to 25 percent of married women are forced by their husbands to have sexual intercourse against their will during the course of their marriage (Bergen, 1998).

In Patricia Peacock's (1998) survey of 278 women, she found that 40, or 14 percent of the sample, reported at least one incident of wife rape. The following are the sexual activities that husbands forced their wives to participate in: intercourse (88 percent);

perpetrator fondling victim (48 percent), victim forced to fondle perpetrator (45 percent), victim forced to perform oral sex on perpetrator (45 percent), perpetrator engaging victim in anal sex (40 percent), and perpetrator performing oral sex on victim (17 percent).

Moreover, the victims of wife rape report not only that the rape by their husbands is frightening and brutal but that it involves humiliation, degradation, and hatred (Bergen, 1998; Peacock, 1998). And a large proportion of wife rapists use "sexual coercion"—"If you don't 'put out' I'll divorce you"—rather than direct physical violence to obtain sexual access to a wife's body, and because of such coercion many women "give in" to unwanted sex with their husbands for the following reasons (Basile, 1999; Belknap, 2001):

1. *Unwanted turns to wanted.* The woman did not initially want to have sex but was able to enjoy it ultimately.

2. *It's my duty.* The woman has sex because she believes it is her marital obligation, not because she wants to have sex.

3. *Easier not to argue.* The woman has sex because she can't tolerate any more verbal or nonverbal behavior from her partner, and sex is the easiest way out of the situation.

4. *Don't know what might happen if I don't.* The woman has sex because she is afraid of a negative consequence if she doesn't.

5. *Know what will happen if I don't.* The woman knew from experience that, if she didn't comply, she would be raped and/or experience other serious forms of violence.

It is clear, then, that the sexual assault of a wife may also occur in marriages with little or no physical violence. However, there also seems to be a close relationship between wife rape and wife beating. Studies indicate that between 30 and 50 percent of all wife beating involves some form of sexual abuse (Bergen, 1998; Belknap, 2001). This physical violence against women was not always illegal. Throughout the seventeenth, eighteenth, and nineteenth centuries in western Europe, it was legal for men to beat their wives, as long as the method used, and the extent of the violence, remained within certain limits. For example, in eighteenth-century France the law restricted violence against wives to "blows, thumps, kicks, or punches on the back if they leave no traces." Moreover, the law did not allow for the use of "sharp-edged or crushing instruments." The phrase "rule of thumb" is derived from English common law, which specified that a man could beat his wife—for disciplinary reasons—as long as he used a stick no thicker than his thumb.

Although ideas on wife **battering** have changed considerably—it is now socially abhorred and illegal—it still occurs more frequently than most people believe. It is impossible to generate useful statistics on wife battering, because the beating most likely has taken place in isolation from the community and most victims are too embarrassed to report the assault to the police, social service agency, or shelter. Therefore, to understand the prevalence of wife battering, we must rely on estimates provided by researchers in the field.

Estimates of the amount of wife battering in the United States vary. For instance, *Time* magazine reported in 1983 that 6 million women are physically abused each year by their husbands, battery being the "single major cause of injury to women, more significant than auto accidents, rapes, or muggings" (p. 23). According to the National Coalition Against Domestic Violence, more than 50 percent of women will be battered in their lifetime, and every 15 seconds a woman is battered in the United States (Bergen, 1998; Belknap, 2001). However, most women battered by their husbands do not report the incident. Thus, the amount of wife battering is higher than the above figures indicate.

Research on battering in heterosexual couples suggests there are four major types (Johnson and Ferraro, 2000; Johnson, 2001):

1. *Common couple violence.* This type is not connected to a general pattern of control but arises in the context of an argument in which both partners lash out at each other. Common couple violence has a low per-couple frequency, does not escalate over time, does not involve severe physical violence, and it is likely to be mutual.

2. *Patriarchal terrorism.* This type involves violence as only one aspect of a general pattern of control—the violence is one of the means to control a partner. Patriarchal terrorism has a high per-couple frequency and is likely to escalate over time, to involve serious physical injury, and to be perpetrated by exclusively only one of the partners. Men are approximately 97 percent of patriarchal terrorists.

3. *Violent resistance.* This type is perpetrated almost entirely by women who are primarily the victims of patriarchal terrorism.

4. *Mutual violent control.* This type involves partners in which both are controlling and physically violent. This type is rare (see Table 5.1) and little research has been done on mutual violent control.

The vast majority of research on battering in heterosexual couples has concentrated on patriarchal terrorism. This research indicates that, although patriarchal terrorism transcends class, race/ethnicity, and neighborhood boundaries, not all groups of women are equally at risk of victimization. Indeed, a recent study of how each of these variables plays a role in patriarchal terrorism concluded the following (Benson and Fox, 2004):

- Patriarchal terrorism occurs more often and is more severe in economically disadvantaged neighborhoods. Women living in disadvan-

| Table 5.1 | Individual Violent Behavior in Heterosexual Couples | |
|---|---|---|
| **Types of Violence** | **Husbands** | **Wives** |
| Common couple violence | 56% | 44% |
| Patriarchal terrorism | 97% | 3% |
| Violent resistance | 4% | 96% |
| Mutual violent control | 50% | 50% |

Source: Johnson, 2001:1000.

taged neighborhoods are more than twice as likely to be the victims of intimate violence compared with women in more advantaged neighborhoods.

- For the individuals involved, both objective (being unemployed or not making enough money to meet family needs) and subjective (worrying about finances) forms of economic distress increase the risk of intimate violence against women.

- Women who live in economically disadvantaged communities and are struggling with money in their own relationships suffer the greatest risk of patriarchal violence.

- African Americans and whites with the same economic characteristics have similar rates of patriarchal violence, but African Americans have a higher overall rate due in part to higher levels of economic distress and their location in disadvantaged neighborhoods.

- Women whose male partners experienced two or more periods of unemployment (during the five-year study) were almost three times as likely to be victims of patriarchal terrorism as women whose partners were in stable jobs.

- Women in disadvantaged neighborhoods are more likely to be victimized repeatedly or to be injured by their domestic partners than women who live in more advantaged neighborhoods.

An important question always asked by students of patriarchal terrorism is, "Why doesn't she leave?" In fact, most victims of battering do leave violent relationships (Johnson and Ferraro, 2000). Nevertheless, Angela Browne (1995) has argued that asking "Why don't battered women leave?" assumes that leaving an abusive relationship will end the violence. Indeed, battered women who leave a violent relationship are more likely to experience more violence. Yet several researchers have answered this question, reporting that women stay in a violent relationship for a number of reasons. First, of course, is fear. The wife fears that if she leaves, the husband will find her and injure her even more severely. As Browne reported, based on interviews with battered women: "Many of the women stayed because they had tried to escape and been beaten for it, or because they believed their partner would retaliate against an attempt to leave him with further violence" (p. 232). Many women also fear for the safety of others (such as children), and they fear being without a home and losing the status of "wife."

Second, most battered women do not have the material resources to survive. Many are normally full-time homemakers, with few marketable skills and several children to provide for. Third, Browne (1995) reported "practical problems" faced by battered women in effecting a separation from an abusive relationship, such as where to live, how to obtain legal help, and how to plan for continued safety (e.g., can she go to work, or will the batterer find her there and cause her further harm?). Finally, women in abusive situations adopt "coping" strategies—similar to prisoners of war—evaluating which particular method will allow survival with the least amount of violence. As Browne found in her study of battered women, the women . . . often attempted to appease the aggressor by compliance, and to work through the relationship to obtain leniency and safety. Their primary concern during assaultive incidents was to survive. Their main concern after abusive incidents was to avoid angering the partner again. (p. 239)

However, because of the existence of shelters, more and more women are able to leave such situations. There are more than 2,500 women's shelters and service programs in the United States offering short-term refuge for women and their children, and every state has legislation against wife battering (Bergen, 1998). Moreover, in 1994 Congress passed the Violence Against Women Act, establishing the Office in Domestic Violence within the Department of Justice and appropriating $1.5 billion to eliminate violence against women.

We should mention, also, that wife battering is related to spouse killings. The case of O. J. Simpson serves as an example. In 1995 O. J. Simpson was found not guilty for the murders of his ex-wife Nicole Brown Simpson and her friend Ronald Goldman. However, in a subsequent civil trial, Simpson was found liable for the two deaths and ordered to pay $33.5 million in damages to the Brown and Goldman families. The heart of the civil case against Simpson was that the deaths resulted from a pattern of continued wife battering, with Goldman caught in the crime by chance. As one example of this wife battering, on New Year's Day 1989, Nicole Brown Simpson suffered a split lip, a red welt over one eye, and scratches and bruises, including a handprint on her neck. Police charged Simpson with wife battering, he pleaded no contest to the charge, and the judge found him guilty (Berry, 1998).

The Simpson case is not unique, as husbands/boyfriends are much more likely to murder wives/girlfriends than wives/girlfriends are to murder husbands/boyfriends (Federal Bureau of Investigation, 2004b). Moreover, husbands often kill wives after lengthy periods of prolonged physical violence, yet the roles in such cases are seldom if ever reversed for wives. Husbands and wives also do not initiate similar acts of murder, as men are more likely than women to kill their spouse and children together, to stalk and kill a spouse who has left them, to kill their spouse as part of a planned murder-suicide, or to kill their spouse in response to a revelation of wifely infidelity. Unlike husbands, wives kill their spouses after years of suffering physical violence, after all

*Wife rape and battering: They occur much more often than is commonly assumed, in part because of the myth that they are victim-precipitated. In effect, this myth blames women and removes responsibility from men, the community, and society.*

attempts for assistance have been exhausted, when they feel trapped by the violence, and because they fear for their own and/or others' lives.

---

### Box 5.2    Offline and Online Stalking

*Offline stalking* normally refers to repeatedly pursuing someone offline (or physically) in a harassing or threatening manner. In popular culture, offline stalking is frequently associated with celebrities—such as the case of Jody Foster being stalked by John Hinckley—but criminologists have shown that it is also highly correlated with patriarchal terrorism (Belknap, 2001:270):

> Increasingly researchers and the general public are aware that not only are noncelebrities also at risk of being stalked but that the vast majority of stalking is perpetrated in the context of intimate partner relationships and often those that already exhibit other forms of victimization and abuse.

One study has revealed the following information regarding offline stalking (Tjaden and Thoennes, 1998):

- Over 1 million women are stalked each year in the United States.

- One in 12 women are stalked in their lifetime.

- 77 percent of women know the stalker.

- 87 percent of stalkers are men.

- 59 percent of women are stalked by a current or former intimate partner.

- 81 percent of women stalked by an intimate partner are also physically assaulted by that partner.

- The average duration of stalking involving intimate partners is 2.2 years.

- 61 percent of stalkers make unwanted phone calls; 33 percent send or leave unwanted letters or items; 29 percent vandalize property; and 9 percent kill or threaten to kill a family pet.

- 56 percent of women stalked take some type of self-protective measure, such as relocating.

- 26 percent of women stalked lose time at work.

- Gay men are more likely to be stalked than straight men.

A study (McFarlane et. al., 1999) that examined women who have been stalked offline and then became victims of attempted or actual femicide, found that

- 76 percent of femicide victims and 85 percent of attempted femicide victims were stalked by the person who killed them.

- 67 percent of femicide victims and 71 percent of attempted femicide victims had been physically abused by their intimate partner, and 89 percent of all victims were stalked in the 12 months prior to the murder.

- 79 percent of physically abused victims reported stalking during the same period as the physical abuse.

*Online stalking,* or "cyberstalking," refers to repeatedly pursuing someone online in a harassing or threatening manner. Online stalking takes many forms, such as unsolicited hate, obscene, or threatening e-mail, malicious messages posted in newsgroups, "mail bombs," e-mail viruses, and electronic junk mail or "spam" (Joseph, 2003). The vast majority of online stalkers seem to be men, and their victims are women. Online stalking has a more global dimension than offline stalking—the cyberstalker and victim may even be located in different countries when the stalking takes place. Moreover, in online stalking a victim may not even know who the perpetrator is. Joseph provides an example of how "cyberstalking hackers" can "mask" their identities:

> A hacker may gain access to an e-mail account of an "innocent" user and use this address to send messages that may be threatening or offensive. From his or her home computer in Toronto, for example, a person can hack into the computer server at a university in Australia. From the account at the university in Australia, he or she can hack into a university in Japan. From this new account he or she can then hack into the University of Arizona, choose a user name and send threatening messages to his or her next-door neighbor in Toronto. The message will appear to have come from Arizona, but in fact it is coming from their neighbor in Toronto. (p. 108)

Popular culture suggests that another form of online stalking—Internet-initiated sex offenses against young people—is primarily committed by strangers who are pedophiles and who (1) pretend to be peers to victims, (2) initiate relationships with very young children, and (3) persistently stalk these children into abduction and then rape them. However, a study examining 129 sexual offense cases involving juvenile victims that originated through online interaction found that the victims primarily were 13- to 15-year-old girls who met adult male offenders in online chat rooms (Wolak, Finkelhor, and Mitchell, 2004). The offenders therefore were not found to be pedophiles, since pedophilia is defined as having a sexual attraction to prepubescent children. Although the offenders did manipulate the youths in various ways, only 5 percent represented themselves as peers; thus, the vast majority did not deceive victims about being older men (76 percent were older than 25) who were interested in sexual relationships. Moreover, the vast majority of offenders did not use physical force or coercion to abuse victims, and they did not abduct victims. Rather, victims "typically agreed to meet these adults, knowing of their sexual interest. They engaged in sexual intercourse, or other sexual activity, with the adults, often on multiple occasions" (p. 16). Finally, the authors of this study argue that it is misleading to characterize these offenders as "strangers," because in the majority of cases they had communicated extensively with victims (both online and offline), establishing "romantic or otherwise close relationships before they first met victims face-to-face" (p. 16). Consequently, most of the Internet-initiated sex crimes in this study involved teenagers who were too young to legally consent to sexual intercourse.

## Gay and Lesbian Partner Battering

Most research on battering concentrates on heterosexual relationships. However, recent studies suggest that battering is not only found in heterosexual monogamy but also occurs in other family forms, such as gay and lesbian relationships.

Like heterosexual wife battering, homosexual partner battering is difficult to document, especially because homosexuals remain an even more hidden population. Nevertheless, the studies that have been done (and based on small samples) report rates of domestic violence within lesbian and gay families as similar to those found in hetero-sexual families (Mahoney, Williams, and West, 2001; McClennen, 2005). In 2003 the National Coalition of Anti-Violence Programs (NCAVP) documented 6,523 cases of lesbian, gay, bisexual, and transgender domestic violence. Of these cases, the vast majority involved lesbians and gay men, males and females (as opposed to intersexed and transgender people), and white individuals between the ages of 30 and 44 (NCAVP, 2004).

Additionally, the dynamics of homosexual partner battering are similar to those for heterosexual wife battering. For example, both involve similar types of violence, such as pushing, shoving, slugging, threats, and demeaning forms of behavior, as well as similar motives, such as manipulation, control, coercion, and punishment (Cruz, 2000; Renzetti, 2000). Moreover, as in heterosexual wife battering, in homosexual partner battering the violence increases in frequency and severity over time, and most victims of homosexual partner battering remain in abusive relationships for similar reasons as those for heterosexual wife battering victims (McClennen, 2005). Thus, overall, gay and lesbian partner battering is in many ways similar to heterosexual wife battering.

However, there is one important difference, which derives from the homophobic culture we live in: The abuser may threaten to reveal to others that the partner is lesbian or gay. This practice, labeled "outing," can result in shunning by relatives and friends, the loss of a job, and a range of other discriminatory consequences with little or no legal recourse for victims (Renzetti, 2000; Mahoney, Williams, and West, 2001). This form of abuse does not exist with heterosexual couples.

### Child and Elder Abuse

Prior to the 1960s, no laws existed that criminalized child abuse—not because child abuse did not exist but because it was not in the interests of medical doctors to "see" it. According to Stephen Pfohl (1984), four factors impeded the recognition of child abuse by the medical profession:

1. Physicians were unaware of the possibilities of an abuse diagnosis.

2. Many physicians were unwilling to believe that parents would abuse their own children.

3. The "norm of confidentiality" created an obstacle for an abuse diagnosis.

4. Physicians were reluctant to become involved with the criminal justice system because it was time-consuming and hindered their ability to control the consequences of such a diagnosis.

However, for a specific specialty within medicine—pediatric radiology—these four barriers, Pfohl argued, did not apply. Abuse diagnosis was in fact an ultimate consequence of their mission: Pediatric radiologists constantly viewed children's X-rays and thus observed broken bones and other abnormalities. Pediatric radiologists were also removed from direct contact with the patient's family and thus had no need to be fearful of confidentiality. Most important, the "discovery" of child abuse provided pediatric radiologists—working in a low-profile specialty—the possibility of greater recognition within the medical community, as well as an opportunity to coalesce with more academic segments of that community, such as psychiatrists. Thus, as Pfohl pointed out: "The organizational advantages surrounding the discovery of abuse by pediatric radiology set in motion a process of labeling abuse as deviance and legislating against it" (p. 61). Indeed, in a four-year period beginning in 1962, all 50 states passed laws against child abuse. Consequently, the "discovery" of child abuse "manifestly contributed to the advancement of humanitarian pursuits while covertly rewarding" pediatric radiology with enhanced status (p. 45).

After its discovery, public concern about child abuse increased dramatically, so that by the mid-1980s, 90 percent of the U.S. population considered it a serious national problem (Wolfe, 1985). Moreover, although more people today seem concerned about child abuse, the media have helped perpetuate the myth that most abuse of children—especially sexual abuse—occurs outside the home by day-care workers and child molesters lurking around elementary school playgrounds. However, most physical and sexual abuse of children actually occurs within the family (Bergen, 1998).

Researchers tend to agree that **child abuse** takes four forms—physical, sexual, emotional, and neglect (inattention to a child's basic needs for health, nutrition, shelter, education, affection, and protection). Approximately 1 million cases of child abuse are reported each year, or a rate of approximately 12 per 1,000 children (National Center on Child Abuse and Neglect, 2003). Of these cases, 20 percent entail physical abuse, 60 percent neglect, 10 percent sexual abuse, and 7 percent emotional abuse; the remainder are classified as "other" types of abuse.

Regarding the perpetrators of child abuse, the National Center on Child Abuse and Neglect (2003) reports that more than 80 percent are parents; other relatives account for 7 percent, and unmarried partners account for 3 percent. The remaining perpetrators include people with other (e.g., camp counselor) or unknown relationship to victims. Regarding parents, both men and women commit child abuse. However, although women perform most of the child care in U.S. society, they commit only about 50 percent of the *physical abuse* and neglect of children. In other words, 50 percent of those who physically abuse and neglect children are men, who have on average little responsibility for children.

Important gender differences are found regarding abuse and neglect: Females are more likely to be abused and to suffer injuries due to abuse than males; females experience more abuse than males, whereas males experience more neglect than females; and for both males and females, abuse and neglect increase with age (National Center on Child Abuse and Neglect, 2003).

Because sexual abuse has tended to be surrounded by extreme secrecy, it is hard to document its incidence. Nevertheless, it is estimated that approximately 20 percent of women and 10 percent of men in the United States were sexually abused as children (Bergen, 1998). In *The Secret Trauma,* Diana Russell (1986) examined incestuous abuse and found that 16 percent of the 930 women interviewed reported at least one experience of incest before the age of 18. Of these women, 12 percent (152) had been sexually abused by a relative before their fourteenth birthday. Thus, incestuous abuse is by no means rare.

Most incestuous abuse is committed by an adult male (usually the father), with the likely victim a child (usually the daughter) under the age of 18. Certain "typical characteristics" of incestuous assault include the following (Chesney-Lind and Pasko, 2004; Hunter, 2000):

- Approximately 70 percent of incestuous abuse victims are female.

- At least one-third of all female victims are younger than 11 years old.

- Incestuous abuse usually begins earlier for girls than for boys, and victimization of girls lasts longer than for boys.

- Assaults commonly take place repeatedly, lasting three years or more.

- The assault involves not only "sexuality" but also betrayal of trust by an adult on whom the child depends and exploitation of power differences in terms of gender as well as age.

As with other sexual assaults, victims experience incestuous abuse as coercive. At first—because of her young age—the victim may be unable to comprehend what is happening. However, as she suffers the assaults over time, she eventually understands that something "different" and wrong is happening to her. She feels guilty and humiliated and blames herself for the continued assaults. Many such victims not only experience fear, anxiety, depression, anger, and difficulties in school; they also often run away from home (Chesney-Lind and Pasko, 2004). Incestuously abused women also reveal that they remain frightened and upset years later (Kendall-Tackett, 2000). Moreover, prostitutes have informed sociologists that as victims of incestuous assault, they were first bribed by an adult family male (sex for clothes, toys, and affection, for example), only later to be forced into sexual intercourse with him (Chesney-Lind and Pasko, 2004). Consequently, they learned they could obtain commodities by making their bodies available to men and thus turned to prostitution on the street to survive once they ran away from an incestuously abusive home.

Like child abuse, **elder abuse** involves physical abuse (use of physical force that may result in bodily injury, physical pain, or impairment), sexual abuse (nonconsensual sexual contact of any kind), and emotional abuse (infliction of anguish, pain, or distress through verbal or nonverbal acts), as well as neglect (refusal or failure to fulfill any part of a person's obligations or duties to an elderly person). But elder abuse differs from child abuse in that it also includes financial or material exploitation. This latter form of abuse involves illegal or improper use of an elder's funds, property, or assets.

There are two major types of elder abuse—domestic and institutional. *Domestic* elder abuse generally refers to any of the above abusive behaviors committed by someone who is a spouse, sibling, child, friend, or caregiver in the elder's home or in the home of a caregiver. *Institutional* elder abuse involves any of the above-mentioned forms of abuse that occur in a residential facility, such as a nursing home or group home, and committed by someone who has a contractual relationship with the victim (i.e., paid caregiver, staff, or professional).

According to the National Center on Elder Abuse (2004):

- Women disproportionately constitute the victims of elder abuse (56 percent).

- 66 percent of all victims are Caucasian and 17 percent are African Americans.

- 47 percent of elder abuse victims are 80 years of age or older.

- 66 percent of all victimizations are domestic and 10 percent occur in institutional settings (in the remaining 24 percent, the setting is unknown).

- The majority of victimizations entail neglect (49 percent), followed by emotional abuse (36 percent), financial/material exploitation (30 percent), physical abuse (25 percent), and sexual abuse (0.5 percent).

- The majority of perpetrators (52 percent) are males between the ages of 36 and 50.

- Typically, perpetrators are family members (for domestic elder abuse), with the highest percentage being a spouse to the victim, followed by an adult child.

- Domestic abusers tend to be dependent—usually financially—on the victim, which challenges the popular culture ideology that domestic elder abuse is primarily caused by frail elderly people who are dependent on others for care.

- In an institutional setting, the vast majority of perpetrators are "institutional staff."

Most domestic forms of elder abuse are similar to interpersonal violence in the family in the sense that husband or adult son uses the abuse to wield control over the wife/mother (Vinton, 2001). In addition, victims often are isolated from people they might report the abuse to, and victims fear further physical or emotional abuse should they mention it to others.

Studies of elder abuse in nursing homes report practices that result in chronic neglect, substandard care, overcrowding, authoritarian practices, and failure to protect residents from abusive staff (Nerenberg, 2002). Regarding perpetrators, research shows that 10 percent of nurses and aides *admit* committing physical abuse, and 40 percent *admit* committing emotional abuse against nursing home residents. The most common forms of physical abuse in nursing homes include unnecessary restraints, pushing, grabbing, shoving, punching, hitting with an object, and throwing something at a resident. The most common forms of emotional abuse in nursing homes are yelling at, swearing at, and insulting residents; denying them privileges; and threatening to throw something at or hit residents. Moreover, approximately 36 percent of nurses and aides report witnessing other employees physically abusing residents, and 81 percent have observed at least one incident of emotional abuse. Finally, the perpetrators tend to be much younger than nonperpetrators, and they view the victims as residents who "need to have everything done for them," "are waiting to die," and "are like children who sometimes need discipline."

## Animal Abuse

The cruel treatment of certain species of animal has been outlawed in Maine since 1821, in England since 1822, and in most other U.S. states since the second half of the nineteenth century. Yet, as we saw in Chapter 1.2, criminal law is sometimes not a useful point of reference from which to look at this crime, let alone to understand it or to reduce its incidence. Indeed, animal anticruelty statutes are often species-biased and ineffective.

Anticruety statutes are often species-biased (i.e., "speciesist" or "anthropocentric") because the range of animals that they typically define as capable of being abused is narrow and highly selective. Among the numerous species excluded from the reach of many current anticruelty statutes are "wild" animals, birds, fish, reptiles, invertebrates, "vermin," and "pests." More favored species include popular, endangered, and exotic species such as whales, wolves, and eagles, the abuse of which often carries considerable criminal sanctions.

Moreover, even when they are occasionally enforced, **animal abuse laws** tend not to be effective—chiefly because in most jurisdictions animal cruelty and neglect are not regarded as serious offenses. In the United States, for example, animal cruelty is classified as a misdemeanor (rather than a felony) in about half of the states, with maximum penalties (which are almost never imposed) of a few days in jail and a fine of less than $500. Typically, even when it is criminalized, animal abuse tends to be limited to those one-on-one situations of cruelty where animals are abused by human members of their households.

Indeed, one of the least recognized forms of interpersonal violence in the family is violence against nonhuman animals. When they are regarded as "pets," nonhuman animals (hereinafter, "animals") are typically treated as family members. Like other family members, they have names, they eat (but are not eaten), they play and sleep indoors, they receive affection and love, and sometimes they are abused. Like humans, animals may be abused physically, sexually, emotionally, and psychologically, and they may be neglected. Like human infants and young children, domesticated animals are completely dependent on humans for food and shelter. Significantly, animals are for the most part unable either to deter humans who intend to abuse them or to report their abuse to authorities who might aid them.

Animal abuse tends to coexist with other forms of family violence. If one human member of a household is abusing another, animal abuse is also more likely there—and vice versa. Animal abuse has been found to be disproportionately present in situations of partner abuse (both heterosexual and homosexual), child physical abuse, child sexual abuse, and sibling abuse (Flynn, 2000; Ascione, 2001; Baldry, 2003). Somewhat piecemeal findings about the presence of animal abuse in families have come from a variety of sources. These include the records of Societies for the Prevention of Cruelty to Animals, victimization surveys, and structured interviews with battered women and abused and neglected children. In addition, reports of animal abuse are made to veterinarians, women's shelters, animal shelters, animal control officers, police, and staff in various government agencies such as the Department of Human Services.

However, the exact prevalence of animal abuse is not known. Perhaps because animal abuse is not generally regarded as a serious crime, the amount of solid information on it is quite thin. We cannot analyze official (i.e., government-generated) data on animal abuse—there is none. In its compilation of crime data for 17,000 police departments, for example, the FBI's Uniform Crime Reports has no entries on animal abuse, although it does refer—next to "office equipment" and "televisions"—to "livestock" and "clothing and furs" stolen and recovered. In no technologically advanced societies do there exist large-scale, police-based data on the incidence and prevalence of animal abuse. There are no large-scale self-report studies of animal abuse. There are no household victimization surveys of animal abuse.

Our sociological knowledge of the hows, the whys, and the whens of animal abuse is therefore quite rudimentary. We know very little, for example, about how animal abuse is related to the key sociological variables of social class, gender, race/ethnicity, and age. At present, we can really only speculate that some of the sociological dimensions of animal abuse mirror those on interhuman violence. For example, young males probably commit animal abuse far more frequently than young females, and, when they do, their abuse is often considerably more violent.

Animal sexual assault is one of the few crimes against animals that has gained some attention recently, although it is still regarded as so distasteful and controversial that even *The Jerry Springer Show* refused to air a segment filmed on it. Beirne (2002) has argued that "bestiality" should be renamed animal sexual assault, because human-animal sexual relations almost always involve coercion, often cause animals pain and even death, and because animals are unable either to communicate consent to us in a form that we can readily understand or to speak out about their abuse.

Beirne offers a fourfold typology of animal sexual assault, based on a combination of humans' motives and the degree of harm suffered by the abused animals:

1. *Sexual fixation.* This form of animal sexual assault occurs when animals are the preferred sexual partners of humans. Sexual fixation with animals is probably the least common form of animal sexual assault. Dekkers (2000) estimates that much fewer than 1 percent of humans have sex exclusively with animals.

2. *Commodification.* This is the main aspect of animal sexual assaults—packaged as commodities for sale in a market. It often involves a twofold assault: one by a man on a woman who is assaulted and humiliated by being forced to have sex with an animal, the other on the animal who is coerced into having sex with a human. Examples include live shows of women copulating with animals in bars and sex clubs or depictions of animal sexual assaults in pornographic films such as *Barnyard Love* and *Deep Throat* and at numerous Internet pornographic websites.

3. *Adolescent sexual experimentation.* This is probably the most prevalent form of animal sexual assault. It can occur either alone or with other adolescents who either watch or participate. In a group context, some boys of necessity teach how it is done while others learn. It can be performed for a variety of reasons, including curiosity, cruelty, showing off for other boys, and acquiring the techniques of intercourse for later use on girls (or on boys). Presumably, too, there is some point toward the end of adolescence when young males desist from experimental sexual activities with animals because such practices are regarded as unmanly or perhaps as perverse and ridiculous.

4. *Aggravated cruelty.* Besides the possibility of cruelty during adolescent sexual experimentation, aggravated cruelty can be a major element in animal sexual

assault in other ways. In mid-nineteenth century England, for example, one case was reported in which two-foot-long knotted sticks were thrust into mares' wombs, which were then vigorously rent, and another where the penises of cart horses and donkeys were cut off (Archer, 1985: 152). Multiple cases of such atrocities were confirmed in several English counties in 1993 (Yates, Powell, and Beirne, 2001). Similarly, in 1991 at a zoo in New Bedford, Massachusetts, a deer was found with fatal wounds that included a fractured jaw and extensive bleeding from the rectum and vagina (*Standard Times*, 1991). Sometimes, aggravated cruelty against animals takes place in conjunction with the humiliation of women. This has been documented in Nazi concentration camps and in the course of partner abuse.

In the past decade many well-publicized claims have linked animal abuse with subsequent interhuman mass murders committed by adolescent and adult males. Claims about this human-animal link have been put forth by journalists in the mass media, and by philanthropic and charitable groups such as the Humane Society of the United States and the American Humane Association. For example, several journalists reported that before the school shootings of two high school girls in 1997 the teenage murderer Luke Woodham had gruesomely tortured his own dog. Woodham repeatedly beat the dog with a club, wrapped it in garbage bags, torched it with a lighter, listened to it whimper, and tossed it in a pond (*New York Times*, October 15, 1997). After describing the sight of the dog sinking beneath the surface of the pond, Woodham added, "[I]t was true beauty" (p. A10). In another report of a school-shooting mass murder (of two classmates and both his parents) in Springfield, Oregon, in 1998, it was revealed that 15-year-old Kip Kinkel had earlier enjoyed shooting squirrels, setting off firecrackers in cats' mouths, and stuffing firecrackers down gopher holes (Associated Press, May 23, 1998).

At a similarly anecdotal level, the truth of this "progression thesis" from animal abuse to interhuman violence has been claimed for the life histories of a number of serial killers in the United States, including Thomas Lee Dillon, Ted Bundy, Alberto DeSalvo, and Jeffrey Dahmer.

There is an obvious commonsense appeal in the idea that animal abuse and interhuman violence are linked. Perhaps children who abuse animals, or children who witness animal abuse, become desensitized to violence and abuse in general. Or, perhaps, they develop a taste for it.

However, claims about the nature of this link have sometimes been made prematurely and are therefore easily contradicted by counterexamples. Consider the anecdote that the young Jeffrey Dahmer (the "Milwaukee cannibal") used to roam his neighborhood for roadkill and that he had a little graveyard with animals buried in it. Add, for good measure, the widespread report that as a boy Dahmer had impaled or staked frogs and cats to trees. However, nothing in either description indicates that Dahmer himself ever tortured or killed live animals (Beirne, 2004), and Dahmer's father (1994) has stated that his adolescent son even rescued several at-risk animals.

So, suppose a given adolescent is fascinated with dead animals—why should we infer that she or he is a serial killer in-the-making rather than a budding zoologist or forensic scientist? And what about serial murderers who have no animal abuse in their background—such as Myra Hindley, the infamous "Moors Murderess"?

A key aspect of the human-animal cruelty link is the "progression" or "graduation" from animal abuse to interhuman violence. Confirmation of the progression thesis ultimately depends on the successful combination of two quite separate propositions. Chronologically and causally, one proposition looks forward, the other backward. In the first, those who abuse animals must be more likely than those who do not to subsequently act violently towards humans. In the second, those who act violently toward humans must be more likely than those who do not to have previously abused animals. Most assessments of the progression thesis, extended or brief, currently lie on a continuum between possible disconfirmation (e.g., Miller and Knutson, 1997; Arluke et al., 1999) and a cautious attitude of wait-and-see (e.g., Dadds, Turner and McAloon, 2002). Few would subscribe to the ironclad determinism embedded in the view of David Farrington (2002) that

> [p]eople graduate from hyperactivity at age 2 to cruelty to animals at age 6, shoplifting at 10, burglary at 15, robbery at 20, and eventually spouse assault, child abuse and neglect, alcohol abuse, and employment and later health problems later in life. (p. 58)

Moreover, the links between animal abuse and interhuman violence are surely present not only in the personal biographies of those individuals who abuse or neglect animals but also in those institutionalized social practices where animal abuse is routine, widespread, and often defined as socially acceptable. These practices are exemplified in the multiple sites of violence condoned in slaughterhouses. Consider how these might lead (or "progress") to extra-institutional violence. There is, first, the abrupt, unnatural, and sometimes painful death of billions of terrified animals. Second, and less acknowledged, is the awesome physical and psychic toll on slaughterhouse workers who, among all employees in private sector U.S. industries, suffer the highest annual rate of nonfatal injuries and illnesses and repeated-trauma disorders (U.S. Department of Labor, 2004b: Table 1). And third, less documented, is the violence visited on those beings—human and animal—with whom slaughterhouse workers interact outside their work sites.

Whenever human-animal relationships are marked by authority and power, and thus by institutionalized social distance, there is an aggravated possibility of extra-institutional violence. Gail Eisnitz's (1997) book *Slaughterhouse* graphically uncovers this human toll. One worker interviewed by Eisnitz—"Van Winkle"—believed that it is not uncommon for slaughterhouse workers to be arrested for having assaulted humans. Describing the mental attitude developed from "sticking" hogs (i.e., slitting hogs' throats in the often-botched attempt to kill them), he divulged that "[M]y attitude was, its only an animal. Kill it" (p. 88). Then:

> I've had ideas of hanging my foreman upside down on the line and sticking him. I remember going into the office and telling the personnel man I have no problem pulling the trigger on a person—if you get in my face I'll blow you away. . . . Every sticker I know carries a gun, and every one of them would shoot you. Most stickers I know have been arrested for assault. A lot of them have problems with alcohol. They have to drink, they have no other way of killing live, kicking animals all day long. (p. 88)

---

**Box 5.3   Defining Animal Abuse**

There is still very little agreement about what animal abuse is. A radical, animal rights' definition of animal abuse might be (Beirne, 2004):

Any act that contributes to the pain, suffering or death of an animal or that otherwise threatens its welfare. Animal abuse may be physical, psychological, or emotional, may involve active maltreatment or passive neglect or omission, and may be direct or indirect, intentional or unintentional. Some forms of animal abuse are socially acceptable.

This definition sees as abusive many human-animal practices that are widely seen as socially acceptable. These practices include the use of animals in slaughterhouses (to consume as food or to wear as items of clothing), in entertainment and education, in scientific and commercial laboratories, in sports, and in zoos and aquaria. Is this definition too radical for most of us?

---

## 5.3 Interpersonal Violence in the Workplace

In Chapter 7.2 we discuss some of the environmental hazards in the workplace, such as unsafe working conditions because of inadequate protection from dangerous substances. Although workplace dangers such as environmentally unsafe working conditions are impersonal, murder, assault, and sexual harassment are different, entailing violence perpetrated in a personal manner. For these reasons we discuss murder, assault, and sexual harassment as forms of interpersonal violence rather than as occupational crime.

### Murder and Assault

The most common type of workplace violent crime is simple assault (Duhart, 2001). Each year, approximately 1.3 million simple assault victimizations occur in the workplace, followed by 325,000 aggravated assaults and 900 murders. Workplace violence accounts for approximately 18 percent of all violent crime. Police officers experience workplace violent crime at rates higher than any other occupation, whereas university professors are victimized the least often. The workplace violent crime rate for whites is 25 percent higher than that for African Americans and 59 percent higher than the rate for other races (although most workplace victimizations are intraracial). Finally, the male workplace violent crime victimization rate is 56 percent higher than the female rate (and men and women are primarily victimized by men), and mostly people between the ages of 20 and 34 are victimized.

Although a large majority of workplace violence occurs among strangers, personal disputes among coworkers have received the most attention by criminologists. Indeed, this type of workplace murder is classified by researchers as "murder by proxy," in which victims are chosen by a vengeful employee because of their association with the revenge target. The vengeful employee—usually a middle-aged white male who is "falling down" (was recently fired or reprimanded by a boss or lost his "status" or job to younger competitors, racial minorities, women, or immigrants)—responds by "getting back" at those seen as causing his frustration or as simply being an employee at his place of work where the painful event occurred. Some recent cases include the following:

- Four state lottery executives killed by a Connecticut lottery accountant (March 1998).

- Seven coworkers killed by a Xerox technician in Honolulu (November 1999).

- Seven coworkers killed by a software engineer at Edgewater Technology Company in Massachusetts (December 2000).

- Four coworkers killed by a former forklift driver at the Navistar Plant in Chicago (February 2001).

- Three coworkers killed by an insurance executive at Empire Blue Cross and Blue Shield in New York City (September 2002).

- Three coworkers killed by a manufacturing plant worker in Jefferson City, Missouri (July 2003).

- Six coworkers killed by a Lockheed-Martin aircraft plant worker in Meridian, Mississippi (July 2003)

Regarding workplace assaults (both simple and aggravated) by occupation, law enforcement officers again suffer the largest amount of assault victimization on the job, followed by those working in mental health, retail sales, medical health, teaching, and transportation occupations (Duhart, 2001). Additionally, transportation workers (such as taxi drivers) suffer more aggravated, but not simple, assault than those who work in medical health and teaching.

## Sexual Harassment

Whereas males are much more often the victims of murder and assault at work, female workers have more often been victims of sexual harassment. But it was not until the mid-1970s that sexual harassment was recognized as a social problem (Benson and Thompson, 1982), and it was not until 1980 that sexual harassment actually became a crime. The Equal Employment Opportunity Commission issued guidelines in 1980 for determining sexual harassment as a violation of Title VII of the U.S. Civil Rights Act. This act was intended to prohibit discrimination on the basis of gender, and its guidelines apply to federal, state, and local government agencies as well as to private employers with 15 or more employees. The guidelines specify that employers have an "affirmative duty" to prevent and eliminate sexual harassment on the job and that "unwelcome sexual advances, requests for sexual favors, and other verbal or physical conduct of a sexual nature" are offenses if submission is explicitly or implicitly a condition of the individual's employment. When the submission or rejection affects one's employment or work performance by creating a working environment that is intimidating, hostile, and offensive, a violation of Title VII has also occurred. Thus, following this definition, **sexual harassment** includes not only attempted and completed forcible rape and

"interpersonal coercion" but also sexist jokes and in-
nuendos, "accidental" collisions and fondling, and
constant ogling and pinches.

Myths about sexual harassment—that it affects
only a few women, that women really "ask for it," and
that charges of sexual harassment are commonly
false, for example—continue to be perpetuated.
However, studies of sexual harassment indicate the
prevalence of *nonconsenting* interpersonal sexual violence in the workplace. For example, in 1981 the
Merit System's Protection Board conducted a study
of sexual harassment among federal employees for
the Subcommittee on Investigations of the House
Committee on Post Office and Civil Service (Russell,
1990). The board found (in their random sample of
over 20,000 federal employees) that 42 percent of all
female employees reported being sexually harassed
at work. The number of sexual harassment complaints filed with the Equal Employment Opportunity Commission jumped from 5,694 cases in 1990 to
10,900 cases in the first eight months of 1993, most
likely because of the national "teach-in" on sexual
harassment following the confirmation hearings of
Supreme Court Justice Clarence Thomas. Surveys
continue to show that prevalence rates of sexual harassment have *not* decreased over time—approximately 40 percent of U.S. women report every year

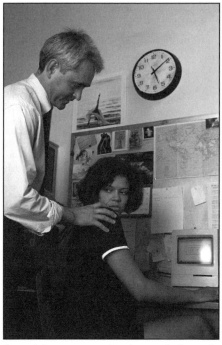

*Sexual harassment in the workplace: As
women gain positions of expertise, responsibility, and power, their presence is threatening to
some men, and these men may respond by engaging in sexual harassment to 'put women in
their place.'*

that they experienced a legally actionable form of sexual harassment (Morgan, 2001).
What this information reveals is that sexual harassment in the workplace is likely widespread.

Why does such harassment occur? Some have argued that certain organizations
maintain value systems, communicative processes, rituals, and organizational symbols
that create a sexist culture at work (O'Toole and Schiffman, 1997). Many organizations
use sexual metaphor in communicative processes that may be conducive to sexual harassment. For example, female employees at Stroh's Brewing Company brought a sexual harassment suit against the company, charging that the Swedish Bikini Team advertising campaign in the early 1990s contributed to a sexualized work environment in
which women were subjected to daily verbal and physical abuse by male employees.

Studies of sexual harassment also indicate that rape and interpersonal coercion
exist within the workplace. Approximately 37,000 rapes and sexual assaults occur at the
workplace every year (Duhart, 2001). Interpersonal coercion (recalling our earlier discussion in this chapter) involves economic threats made by a male supervisor to the effect that, if the female employee or possible employee does not engage in sexual intercourse with him, she either will not be hired, retained, or promoted or else will be fired,
demoted, or transferred to a more unpleasant position. If we assume that the female

employee or possible employee does not secretly desire sexual intercourse with the male supervisor, such threats can be coercive. In other words, economic deprivation is a serious and expensive cost even when set beside unwelcome and undesired coitus.

Indeed, sexual harassment has similarities with incestuous assault: The victim of incest, like the sexually harassed woman, is economically, if not emotionally, dependent on the offender. Sexual harassment is likewise humiliating, and paralleling incestuous assault, there is motivation to keep it a secret. In fact, only approximately 12 percent of sexually harassed women at the workplace report the offense (Morgan, 2001). Sexual harassment, like incestuous assault, often continues for a long time and is experienced as an abuse of power and a betrayal of trust.

Finally, the risk of sexual harassment is highest in male-dominated workplaces. For women in military, coal mining, construction, and criminal justice system occupations, the rate of sexual harassment is approximately 30 percent higher than in the general population.

Victims of sexual harassment suffer severe consequences. The majority of women report emotional stress, such as nervousness, fear, and sleeplessness, as well as interference with their job performance, and many also find it necessary to obtain psychological help. Moreover, victims of sexual harassment at work report higher rates of absenteeism and low productivity, thereby adversely affecting their own financial situation as well as that of their employer.

## Review

In this chapter we have discussed interpersonal crimes of violence—murder, assault, hate crimes, rape, wife and gay/lesbian partner battering, child abuse, elder abuse, animal abuse, and sexual harassment. These crimes create extensive public concern and fear—and rightly so, inasmuch as the United States has one of the highest levels of violent crime in the industrialized world. However, crimes of interpersonal violence occur most often indoors—not on the streets—and are usually committed by relatives, friends, and acquaintances of the victims.

### Murder, Assault, Hate Crimes, and Rape

1. Murder is the most serious form of interpersonal violence; fortunately, it occurs the least often. Murder is primarily a big-city crime and occurs most frequently in the South. There is little evidence suggesting that owning a firearm is the chief cause of murder. In some cases the interaction between offender and victim involves threats and retaliation by both participants to the murder. There are important similarities and differences between murder and aggravated assault.

2. Hate crimes differ from other forms of interpersonal violence in that they are more vicious, are excessively brutal, are frequently perpetrated at random on total strangers (commonly a single victim) by multiple offenders, and victims face great difficulty coming to terms with their victimization.

3. Rape occurs much more often in the United States than most people recognize. Sociologists, criminologists, and feminists are currently debating the appropriate definition of rape. Women are more likely to be raped by someone they know than by a stranger. The idea of victim-precipitated rape is a myth. Although there are a few reported cases of women raping men, males are relatively safe from sexual assault unless they are in prison. Throughout history, rape has been an institutionalized component of war, and institutions—such as universities—may create conditions conducive to rape.

## Interpersonal Violence in the Family

1. Women of completed rapes are victimized more by their husbands than by any other type of perpetrator. Victims of wife rape feel humiliated and degraded and experience psychological trauma for years afterward.

2. Between 30 and 50 percent of battered women are also raped by their husbands. Wife battering was legally and socially acceptable for centuries. Research on battering in heterosexual couples identifies four major types: common couple violence, patriarchal terrorism, violent resistance, and mutual violent control. Many women, because of social and economic pressures, feel they cannot leave an abusive relationship.

3. Stalking occurs both online and offline.

4. Homosexual battering—in lesbian and gay male relationships—seems to occur at a similar rate as wife battering in heterosexual relationships. The dynamics of battering in lesbian and gay male relationships are similar to those in heterosexual relationships, although there are some important differences.

5. Most physical and sexual abuse of children occurs within the family. Men and women each commit 50 percent of the physical abuse and neglect of children. Incestuous abuse is by no means rare in the United States; it is usually committed by an adult male (usually the father), and the victim is usually a child under 18 (generally a daughter). Incestuously assaulted girls and women find the encounter coercive, and years later many report still being frightened and upset.

6. Elder abuse involves physical, sexual, and emotional abuse, as well as neglect and material and financial exploitation. There exists two major types of elder abuse—domestic and institutional.

7. As a form of family violence, animal abuse is one of the least recognized. Its several forms include cruelty, abuse, and neglect. There are no large-scale sources of data on animal abuse, though an in-depth discussion of some of the sociological characteristics of animal sexual assault has been presented in this chapter.

8. The chapter uses an animal rights definition of animal abuse as any act that contributes to the pain, suffering, or death of an animal or that otherwise threatens its welfare. Animal abuse may be physical, psychological, or emotional; may involve active maltreatment or passive neglect or omission; and may be direct or in-

direct, intentional or unintentional. Some forms of animal abuse are socially acceptable.

## Interpersonal Violence in the Workplace

1. The most common form of interpersonal violence in the workplace is assault; retail sales and law enforcement suffer the most victimizations. The typical violent person in the workplace is a vengeful middle-aged white male.

2. Sexual harassment includes behavior ranging from sexist jokes to interpersonal coercion and rape. Sexual harassment in the workplace is not uncommon. Sexual harassment causes emotional stress and interferes with job and nonoccupational performance.

## Questions for Class Discussion

1. The media foster the image that most interpersonal violence occurs in the streets; as we have seen, it primarily takes place indoors. Discuss why you think the media distort the reality of interpersonal violence and why most violence occurs indoors.

2. Is there a "culture of hate" in North America? If so, what type of policy would you create to curb that culture?

3. Is the legal definition of rape too narrow, or is it satisfactory as it stands?

4. Identify the similarities and differences between child and elder abuse and then explain why these forms of abuse exist.

5. Consider the problematic case of Deena the stripping chimpanzee reported in Adams (1990). For $100 Deena and her trainer would appear at a social gathering, during which Deena would perform a striptease act for the partygoers. Is this animal sexual assault?

## For Further Study

### Readings

Bergen, Racquel Kennedy, ed. 1998. *Issues in Intimate Violence.* Thousand Oaks, CA: Sage.

Brogden, Mike, and Preeti Nijhar. 2000. *Crime, Abuse, and the Elderly.* Portland, OR: Willan.

Tomsen, Stephen. 2002. *Hatred, Murder and Male Honour: Anti-Homosexual Homicides in New South Wales, 1980–2000.* Canberra: Australian Institute of Criminology.

Websites

1. <http://www.ojp.usdoj.gov/vawo>: The Department of Justice Violence Against Women Office's website provides links to federal legislation and current research on violence against women.

2. <http://www.abanet.org/domviol/home.html>: The American Bar Association's Commission on Domestic Violence provides excellent and up-to-date statistics on intimate violence. Especially useful is the "Myths vs. Facts" page.

3. <http://www.ncavp.org>: The website of the National Coalition of Anti-Violence Programs provides useful information on violence committed against and within the lesbian, gay, bisexual, and transgender communities.

4. <http://www.hsus.org>: The website of the Humane Society of the United States (HSUS), a pro-animal organization. The website provides information about human-animal interaction, animal rights and animal welfare, and current campaigns against a variety of forms of animal abuse.

5. <http://nccanch.acf.hhs.gov>: The website of the National Clearinghouse on Child Abuse and Neglect provides information on research, legislation, and research related to child abuse and neglect.

6. <http://jan.ucc.nau.edu/~pms/icash.html>: The International Coalition Against Sexual Harassment website provides useful links to the most current issues related to sexual harassment, including "facts about sexual harassment." ✦

# Syndicated Crime

## Preview

Chapter 6 introduces:

- A history of syndicated crime in the United States.

- The structure and extent of syndicated crime in the United States today.

- The principal forms of syndicated crime and their social costs.

## Key Terms

| | |
|---|---|
| crime networks | mafia |
| criminal syndicates | money laundering |
| direct investment | patron-client relations |
| globalization | Prohibition |
| illicit drug business | prostitution |
| labor racketeering | |

The core of syndicated crime (commonly referred to as "organized crime") is the pro-vision of illegal goods and services in a society that displays a continued and considerable demand for such goods and services. Syndicated crime has developed a structure that makes it possible to provide such goods and services on a regular basis. This structure can best be understood as a variety of **criminal syndicates**—associations of individuals such as businesspeople, police, politicians, and criminals—formed to conduct specific illegal enterprises for the purpose of making a profit. These enterprises include, for example, illegal drug distribution, illegal prostitution, and such other illegal activities as money laundering and labor racketeering. However, the structure of a syndicate depends on its specific illegal activity. Thus, although criminal syndicates are highly organized, a syndicate engaged in the distribution of illegal drugs, for example, is structured differently than one engaged in illegal prostitution.

In this chapter we examine three major aspects of syndicated crime: its history, its structure, and its principal activities today. We begin with a history of syndicated crime.

## 6.1 A History of Syndicated Crime

When people commonly think of "organized crime" (what we call syndicated crime), the first term that usually comes to mind is "the Mafia." However, people rarely ask where this term originated or whether it is appropriate to use such a term to describe syndicated crime in the United States. In this section we attempt to answer these two questions.

### 'Mafia' in Sicily

The word "mafia" is not found in Italian or Sicilian writings until the nineteenth century, and even then it designated a *method* rather than an *organization* (Albini, 1971). To understand this method, we must look at Sicily during the 1800s. In this period, Sicilian peasantry lived on land controlled by absentee landlords. The centralized Italian state attempted to curb the power of feudal landlords and emancipate its peasantry from traditional feudal obligations (Blok, 1974). Not surprisingly, the landlords did not cooperate with the centralized power in Italy and sought to maintain control over both the feudal estates and the peasantry. To accomplish this the landlords worked with a group of ambitious middle-class persons—the *gabelloti*—who paid the "absentee feudal owners a lump-sum rent for the whole estate" and then "sublet it at a profit to the peasantry" (Hobsbawn, 1959:38). The *gabelloti* ensured continued payment to the landlords while providing protection over the estates. In this way they served as mediators between the landlords and the peasantry. Moreover, because of their geographic location vis-à-vis the peasantry and landlords, the remoteness of a centralized power (in Italy), and the rural character of feudal Sicily, the *gabelloti* were the only authoritative "organ" for local law and order. In short, they controlled and monopolized the links between peasant, landlord, and a remote centralized government. As Eric Hobsbawn pointed out in his important work *Primitive Rebels* (1959), the *gabelloti* provided a parallel machine of law and organized power; indeed, so far as the citizen in the areas under its influence was concerned, the only effective law and power. In a society such as Sicily, in which the official government could not or would not exercise effective sway, the appearance of such a system was as inevitable as the appearance of gang-rule, or its alternative, private posses and vigilantes in certain parts of *laissez-faire* America. (p. 35)

The *gabelloti* in Sicily then played an important role as an organ of social control—in the absence of official bodies—and in fact enjoyed a high degree of social acceptance within Sicilian communities. Consequently, a *method* of patronage developed whereby the *gabelloti* held sufficient power to maintain law and order and to control feudal estates, whereas the peasantry (in return) offered services and loyalty to the *gabelloti*. As Albini explained, a *gabelloti*

entrenched himself in a patronage system which continues today. As a client to his landowner in return for certain favors he promised continued suppression of the peasant. As a patron to the peasant he promised work and the continuation of contracts. (1971:133)

It was this method of patronage that came to be identified as "mafia," and the role of the *gabelloti* as "mafioso." Because it represents a system of patron-client relationships, mafia is a method, not an organization. As Dwight Smith (1976) noted:

Events in Sicily that we have subsequently called Mafia were essentially localized patron-client relationships . . . to which the word "Mafia" was generally applied. It existed in the absence of a strong governmental presence. The mafioso person served to mediate, in a heavily stratified economy, between absent landlords and landless peasants; inevitably, men of a mafioso character obtained influence that extended also into political affairs. The system was dependent upon patronage and upon the ability of a "man of respect" to utilize violence when necessary, to maintain his authority as middleman. (pp. 82–83)

Other historical research supports this conclusion (see, for example, Hess, 1973; Blok, 1974).

## Syndicated Crime in the United States, 1800–1930

Thus, *mafia* evolved from certain political, economic, and social conditions. Not being an organization per se, it was not "imported" to the United States. Yet, this fact does not mean that syndicated crime was not an important phenomenon in the United States during the 1800s and early 1900s. In fact, crime was clearly organized in the various vice districts of the growing urban centers. As Samuel Walker (1980) argued: "There was a large demand for liquor (regardless of the day or hour), gambling, and prostitution. To meet this demand vice districts flourished in every major city" (p. 107). Syndicates providing these illegal goods and services blossomed everywhere. They were well organized and run primarily by Irish, Jewish, and Italian working-class entrepreneurs.

Policy gambling provides an example. Policy gambling is based on the illegal drawing of numbers—usually around twelve—upon which players place bets, hoping that from one to four numbers of their choosing will be among the twelve drawn. This form of illegal gambling was a well-organized part of criminal syndicates early in U.S. history. For instance, at about the time of the Civil War, a number of politicians, gamblers, and businesspeople in New York City accumulated $1 million to organize policy shops in that city (Haller, 1976). Moreover, by 1900 other large cities (like Chicago) had policy writers in a sizable number of stores, saloons, and barbershops; policy writers collected bets and delivered the money twice daily to a headquarters where the winning numbers were then "drawn" by means of a wheel. During this time, criminal syndicates made substantial profits from policy gambling, and "the policy runners or writers operating on commission could be assured of a steady income" (p. 105).

Similarly, the cocaine trade was organized and coordinated by a variety of criminal syndicates. As a trade it was decentralized into importers, wholesalers, and retailers "who formed, re-formed, split, and came together again as opportunity arose and when they were able" (Block, 1979:94). Criminal careers in the cocaine trade were not structured in one centralized and particular organization but rather in an increasing network of small but efficient criminal syndicates. Some of these syndicate members had interests in other drug-related illegal syndicates as well as in other types of syndicates, such as gambling. The cocaine trade was not structured along ethnic lines; Block found substantial evidence of interethnic cooperation between cocaine importers, wholesalers, and retailers.

The vice districts, and subsequently syndicated crime, flourished because corruption pervaded city government and everyone involved benefited: Citizens had their liquor, gambling, sex, and drugs; ethnic groups had a means of social mobility; police and city officials benefited through financial gain (Walker, 1980). Thus, from the Civil War onward (perhaps even earlier), provision of illegal goods and services was *syndicated*, having well-established political and police connections. In fact, as time went on, the boundary between politician and syndicated criminal became more and more obscure as "ward bosses were in a good position to engage in racketeering, and racketeers and their nominees could move into political positions" (McIntosh, 1973:56). As Haller (1976) has shown concerning gambling during this period:

> It was not simply that gambling syndicates influenced political organizations, but that gambling syndicates sometimes were the local political organizations. Local bookmakers or policy writers served as precinct captains, and the leaders of syndicates became ward leaders and often won election as alderman or state representatives. By the

Bootlegging: With the passage of the Volstead Act in 1919, the U.S. government attempted to limit the production and distribution of alcoholic beverages. With continued widespread demand for such beverages, however, 'bootlegging' became a major activity for criminal syndicates.

early twentieth century it would not be possible to understand the structure of local politics without a knowledge of the structure of gambling syndicates. (p. 106)

In short: "The operations of the early criminal syndicates were carefully coordinated with, and often even controlled by, local machine politicians and police" (Nelli, 1987:16-17).

---

**Box 6.1    Prohibition**

Enactment of the Volstead Act in 1919 made it illegal to produce, distribute, or sell alcoholic beverages. With law enforcement effectively neutralized and the demand for alcohol continuing unabated, **Prohibition** (1920–1933) provided the context for the rapid development of a new illegal enterprise: importing, manufacturing, bottling, wholesaling, distributing, and retailing illegal alcoholic beverages. Initially, bootlegging was chaotic and uncoordinated. By the middle of the 1920s, however, syndicates grew in strength and increasingly coordinated the bootlegging activities. In fact, bootlegging, like the cocaine trade, became regional, national, and international.

To supply the large urban markets, bootlegging syndicates required improved coordination and organization. For example, Max Hassel—an owner of breweries in Reading, Pennsylvania, and Camden and Atlantic City, New Jersey—provided beer throughout the Delaware Valley and Philadelphia (Haller, 1976). Similarly, in a single four-month period in 1926 and 1927, "Boo Boo" Max Hoff's bootlegging syndicate produced and diverted 350,000 gallons of pure alcohol throughout the Northeast and Midwest (p. 115).

The Mill Creek Distillery, established in Cuba in 1929, further illustrates the national and international ties of bootlegging syndicates:

> Investors in the distillery included Leon Gleckman, perhaps the leading bootlegger in Minneapolis; representatives of Ansonia Copper and Iron Works of Cincinnati, a manufacturer of stills and other apparatus for making alcohol; G. L. Bevan of Montreal, through whom there were ties with major Canadian distilleries that exported for the American market; Charles Haim of New York, who may also have been a partner in "Boo Boo" Hoff's enterprises in Philadelphia. Mill Creek manufactured both Scotch and rye whiskey. To transport the liquor into the United States, Mill Creek owned or chartered ships to take the liquor off ports such as New Orleans, from which contact boats carried the liquor to shore. Mill Creek also exported liquor directly to ports such as New York in cartons labeled ink or canned fruit. And Mill Creek sold liquor to George Gough of Belize, British Honduras. . . . Thus, the investments in Mill Creek were part of a complex set of relationships that linked New Orleans, Minneapolis, and New York bootleggers with Canadian and West Indian smugglers. (p. 116)

During Prohibition, criminal syndicates grew into larger organizations involving more participants than any other criminal grouping. They also developed a much more complex division of labor. As depicted by Mary McIntosh (1973), criminal syndicates developed "the form that any organization theorist would suggest was most appropriate to their kind of business, that is, to coordinate and control one or a series of complex but routinized and continuous activities" (p. 42).

This development does not mean that criminal syndicates became highly centralized into one organization, under the direction of an alleged Italian mafia. All evidence indicates the contrary. In fact, data on individuals considered to be the leading syndicate criminals during Prohibition indicate that they included a variety of ethnic groups—from Jews and Italians to the Irish and Polish (Haller, 1976; Block, 1983; Nelli, 1987).

Some criminologists argue, however, that although criminal syndicates grew into larger organizations during Prohibition (see Box 6.1), toward the end of that era syndicated crime became extremely centralized and controlled chiefly by Italians. According to this view, a national crime syndicate controlled by a small group of Italians was the "final product of a series of 'ganglord wars' in which an alliance of Italians and Sicilians first conquered other groups and then fought each other" (Cressey, 1969:9). It is to the validity of this argument that we now turn.

## A National Crime Syndicate?

Donald Cressey argued in his classic book *Theft of the Nation* (1969) that a nationwide, centralized control of illegal goods and services came into existence in 1931. As a result of the so-called Castellammarese War, "in 1931 leaders of Sicilian-Italian organized crime units across the United States rationally decided to form monopolistic corporations, and to link these corporations together in a monopolistic cartel" (p. 35).

Basing his account "principally on the memoirs of one soldier, Joseph Valachi," Cressey has presented the following argument. In 1929, Giuseppe Masseria controlled Sicilian-Italian syndicated crime in New York City. A group called the "Castellammarese" (named after a specific geographical area in Sicily) rebelled against this control, Salvatore Maranzano becoming the leader of the rebels. Throughout 1929 and 1930 a series of feuds and assassinations occurred between the two groups, Masseria declaring war against the Castellammarese on November 5, 1930. Within five months, Masseria's "soldiers" realized they were outnumbered, and some of his "key men"—including Charles "Lucky" Luciano—secretly surrendered to Maranzano. To demonstrate their new loyalty, these men successfully arranged to have Masseria executed in April 1931.

According to Cressey, Maranzano immediately appointed himself the "Boss of Bosses" ("Godfather") and "established the notion that there would be bosses beneath him, each with an underboss and a *'caporegima,'* or 'lieutenant,' who, in turn, would have 'soldiers' working for him" (p. 42). Luciano was allegedly rewarded with a position as a boss, with Vito Genovese becoming Luciano's underboss. However, within five months, so the argument goes, Luciano and Genovese grew disenchanted with Maranzano's demands for unquestionable allegiance, eventually aligning themselves with "four Jews"—Louis Buchalter, Meyer Lansky, Benjamin "Bugsy" Siegel, and Jake Shapiro—as well as Al Capone from Chicago. On September 11, 1931, Maranzano was assassinated, this day becoming the so-called Mafia Purge Day because, as Cressey has argued:

> On that day and two days immediately following, some forty Italian-Sicilian gang leaders across the country lost their lives in battle. Most, if not all, of those killed on the infamous day occupied positions we would now characterize as "boss," "underboss," or "lieutenant." Perhaps it is for that reason that the "purge day" terminology emerged. (p. 44)

Luciano then substituted the "Boss of Bosses" position with the *"consigliere* of six," which consisted of the six most influential syndicated criminals in the United States. Thus, what had previously been, according to Cressey, a local alliance of gangsters in

Charles 'Lucky' Luciano (1897–1962): Lucky Luciano was one of the most powerful syndicate criminals in New York City during the 1920s and 1930s. In 1936, he was found guilty of compulsory prostitution and was sentenced to 30 to 50 years in prison.

the major U.S. cities became, in 1931, a nationally organized network under the control of an exclusive Italian "board of directors."

In 1951 this conspiracy theory was officially recognized by the U.S. government when it was crystallized in the infamous Kefauver Committee (1951) report, which examined the possibility of a national crime syndicate in the United States. Even though *all* the syndicated criminals testifying before the committee denied membership in, or knowledge of, a "mafia" (Albanese, 1985:31), the committee concluded that there "is a nationwide crime syndicate known as the Mafia, whose tentacles are found in many large cities"; it centralizes and controls syndicated crime in the United States, and its leadership is found in "a group rather than in a single individual" (Kefauver Committee, 1951:150).

In 1963, Joseph Valachi testified before the Senate Subcommittee on Investigations and outlined the Mafia Purge Day story to the committee. In addition, Valachi gave his view of the structure of syndicated crime at that time, arguing that it was centrally controlled by an Italian organization, "Cosa Nostra."

Cressey (1969) echoed Valachi, arguing that "the Mafia" was superseded by Cosa Nostra ("our thing") and had the following structure:

1. A nationwide alliance of at least 24 tightly knit "families" of criminals exists in the United States. (Because the "families" are fictive, in the sense that members are not all related, references to them are within quotation marks.)

2. Members of these "families" are all Italians and Sicilians, or of Italian and Sicilian descent; those on the Eastern Seaboard, especially, call the entire system "Cosa Nostra." Each participant thinks of himself as a "member" of a specific "family" and of Cosa Nostra (or some equivalent term).

3. The "families" are linked to each other, and to non-Cosa Nostra syndicates, by understandings, agreements, and "treaties" and by mutual deference to a "Commission" made up of the leaders of the most powerful "families."

4. The "boss" of each "family" directs the activities, especially the illegal activities, of the members of his "family."

The President's Commission on Organized Crime (1986a), although recognizing the existence of a wide variety of criminal syndicates, simply echoed Cressey—and thereby Valachi—by arguing (without evidence to support it) that an alleged "Cosa Nostra" is the largest and most influential criminal group in the United States.

However, several criminologists question these conclusions. Alan Block (1983), for instance, has criticized Cressey for relying on the testimony of *one* gangster, Valachi. Also, he has reinvestigated the so-called Mafia Purge Day story. Block therefore went beyond simply questioning the competence of Cressey's source, investigating whether the event actually took place. Block surveyed newspapers in eight cities—New York, Los Angeles, Philadelphia, Detroit, New Orleans, Boston, Buffalo, and Newark—for any stories (two weeks before and two weeks after Maranzano's death) of gangland murders "remotely connected" to the Maranzano assassination. Block found various accounts of the Maranzano murder but could find only three murders of "gangsters" that might have been connected to the Maranzano killing. Thus, Block concluded that the killing of three gangsters did not constitute a purge and he was perplexed as to the origin of Cressey's figure of 40 killings. Additionally, in newspaper stories reporting the killing of Maranzano, it was disclosed that Maranzano was killed for simply *informing* on fellow gangsters for illegally importing aliens, not to rid the "Boss of Bosses" of power. Similarly, research by Nelli (1981) uncovered no evidence to support the Mafia Purge Day thesis.

Beyond questioning evidence on the so-called Mafia Purge Day, Block also analyzed syndicated crime in New York City between 1930 and 1950. These two decades are critical because this is the period between the alleged purge of "the Mafia" and the rise of the so-called Cosa Nostra (1930s) on the one hand, and the Kefauver Committee's endorsement of the centralization thesis (1951), on the other hand. What did Block find?

First, although it was clear that some criminal syndicates became increasingly centralized and hierarchically controlled between 1930 and 1950, Block found *no* evidence indicating the emergence of a national crime syndicate in the sense of Cosa Nostra. Instead, two types of criminal syndicates operating in New York City during this time period were uncovered: *enterprise* syndicates and *power* syndicates. Enterprise syndicates are groups of people organized into illegal enterprises; power syndicates are "loosely structured, extraordinarily flexible associations centered around violence and deeply involved in the production and distribution of informal power" (p. 13). Enterprise syndicates organize the production and distribution of illegal goods and services, such as narcotics and gambling. These syndicates tend to be large, with a complex division of labor, a centralization of authority, and a hierarchy of command. In contrast, power syndicates have no clear division of labor, as their specific purpose is to maintain power over others through extortion-obtaining control through the use or threat of violence.

Block has demonstrated that certain of the more energetic power syndicates—controlled by such people as Charles "Lucky" Luciano, Arthur "Dutch Schultz" Flegenheimer, and Louis "Lepke" Buchalter—attempted to exploit enterprise syndicates for extortionary purposes. However, rather than resulting in a centralized Cosa Nostra, this move by the power syndicates was *disruptive,* creating the conditions for the gangsters' eventual downfall. The case of "Lucky" Luciano is illustrative.

Prior to 1933 in New York City, prostitution was well organized and centralized in enterprise syndicates. There were approximately six "bookers" (individuals who organized the prostitution business and "booked" prostitutes into brothels) who had numerous brothels—and the madams and prostitutes who staffed them—under their control. Luciano's power syndicate "conspired to carry this centralization to an extreme," attempting to control the entire operations of "bonding" (providing bail for arrestees) and "booking."

A prostitute made approximately $85 for a week's labor. However, a prostitute had to pay $10 each week to a bonder, who would then guarantee bail if she were arrested. In 1933, Luciano forced the bonders out of business, and his organization took control. The elimination of the bonders led to centralization and control of the bookers. As Block (1983) pointed out, Luciano's power syndicate used extortion, such as terrorizing

> booker Dave Miller with threats of murder unless he paid $10,000. . . . Pete Harris was similarly threatened and told he must pay $250 a week to "a 'mob' being formed to 'protect' the bookers." Harris settled his problem by paying $100 a week to stay in business. The other major bookers including Weiner, Charlie Spinach, and Montana were also "taken over.". . . By the end of 1933 . . . the bonders had been totally replaced and the bookers were now employees of the Luciano syndicate. (p. 144)

Once in control, however, Luciano's power syndicate became rapacious. For instance, with regard to posting bond, the syndicate decided to put up only half of the bond, with the other half coming from the particular madam affected. When the defendant (prostitute) appeared at trial—and the bond money was returned—the syndicate kept the entire amount, returning nothing to the madam. This "exploitation of madams was one of the key disruptive issues under the new syndicate" (Block, 1983:147). As time passed, madams were less and less likely to cooperate (bookers joined them), and they attempted to conceal brothels from the syndicate. This rebellion by madams and bookers was so strong that by 1935 Luciano reportedly wanted out of the prostitution business because the profit was not worth the trouble. Indeed, Luciano's power base was reduced considerably, and in February 1936 he was successfully prosecuted by Thomas Dewey for compulsory prostitution. Luciano received a sentence of 30 to 50 years. As Block concluded, the Luciano power syndicate:

> took a fairly centralized operation, the booking system, and subjected it to intense pressures which threatened to disrupt the entire trade. It turned on the key personnel in the trade with the exception of the prostitute herself who was already cruelly exploited, and initiated various methods of financially squeezing both bookers and madams who resorted to cheating and ultimately to testifying against their bosses. . . . It was clearly an effort at extreme centralization that attacked what was already a stable system of organized prostitution. . . . As neither the price structure nor the volume of trade changed under the Luciano syndicate, profits for the entrepreneurs of violence could only come from the pockets of the formerly independent syndicate leaders and madams. Indeed, one might want to argue that without substantial changes in the economics of organized prostitution, it had about all the centralization it could take by 1933. (pp. 147–148)

Syndicated prostitution continued, "but never under the centralized direction of a power syndicate" (p. 148). Overall, Block found no evidence of the emergence of a national crime syndicate in New York between 1930 and 1950.

Frank Pearce's (1976) important examination of the legendary Al Capone provides yet another example of historical inaccuracy. Although it is clear that Capone was a central figure in such illegal activities as bootlegging and labor racketeering, there is no evidence that he became a "boss" in an alleged national crime syndicate in the early 1930s. In fact, Pearce has shown that syndicated crime's involvement in corruption and, therefore, its close relationship with the police and politicians, undermined "legitimate" business endeavors at the time. It was this phenomenon that actually led to Capone's downfall. Pearce wrote that:

> Many businessmen had begun to feel that City Hall could no longer be relied upon to provide the "rational legal" form of administration that they required to run their businesses. Chicago's judges were corrupt, her administration was inefficient, civic contracts were awarded to the highest briber; the infrastructure was starting to break down. The true magnitude of the city's crisis became clear in 1930 when it was found to be $300 million in debt. (pp. 128–129)

In addition to a corrupt and bankrupt state, businesspeople were also concerned about Prohibition and supported its repeal. Legal alcohol, they argued, would relieve social tensions, lessen class hatred, and provide tax revenues for the state. Thus, businesspeople appealed to the federal government to intervene in Chicago, and in 1929 federal proceedings began against Capone for tax evasion (Eliot Ness and his Justice Department Raiders soon destroyed his breweries). Three years later—in 1932—Capone was sentenced to 10 years in Alcatraz; in 1933, Prohibition was repealed.

As with New York then, Pearce found no evidence of leading syndicate criminals in Chicago becoming involved in a national crime syndicate. Moreover, with the downfall of Capone—as with Luciano—criminal syndicates were not even bruised, continuing to operate such activities as extortion, loan sharking, gambling, drugs, and labor racketeering.

Given that it is highly unlikely that a national crime syndicate emerged between 1930 and 1950, most criminologists have also argued that it is doubtful such a syndicate emerged after 1950. Numerous scholars—such as William Moore (1974), Joseph Albini (1971), and Daniel Bell (1961)—found no evidence of a na-

*Al Capone (1899–1947): Al Capone is probably the most famous syndicate criminal in the United States. He was a central figure in the bootlegging activities in the Chicago area during Prohibition. In 1932, Capone was convicted of tax evasion and sentenced to 10 years in Alcatraz.*

tional crime syndicate in the 1950s, arguing that the Kefauver Committee's "Mafia" conclusion was based simply on assumptions and conjecture, not empirical evidence. Moreover, from Kefauver to the present, no reliable evidence indicates the existence of a national crime syndicate. For it to exist, one criminal syndicate would have to retain monopoly control over all syndicated criminal activity—from illegal gambling to the illegal drug trade, from labor racketeering to the illegal disposal of hazardous wastes. Although there is evidence of some large-scale syndicates—some of which are dominated by Italians and call themselves "Mafia" (there are also syndicates other than Italians that use this designation, such as the "Black Mafia" and "Mexican Mafia")—no such monopoly exists (Block, 1991; Lyman and Potter, 2004). As Jay Albanese (1985) concluded after an exhaustive review of research on syndicated crime: "It is difficult to understand, therefore, the continuing belief in a nationwide criminal conspiracy when no one has been able to produce reliable evidence of it" (p. 64).

## 6.2 Syndicated Crime Today

The endless demand for illegal goods and services in the United States creates perfect conditions for criminal syndicates to flourish and prosper. These syndicates are not controlled by an Italian-dominated national crime syndicate. Rather, they are diverse and autonomous. In fact, researchers have found a wide variety of racial and ethnic groups involved in syndicated crime, including Chinese, blacks, Mexicans, Italians, Vietnamese, Japanese, Cubans, Colombians, Irish, Russians, Canadians, and a number of others. Thus, there is no specific ethnic stereotype synonymous with syndicated crime. Several sociological studies help us further understand the structure of syndicated crime in the United States today. We briefly summarize their conclusions.

### Patron-Client Relationships

Albini (1971) has argued that syndicated crime in the United States is characterized by **patron-client relationships.** Syndicated criminals differ in the kinds of relationships they establish among themselves, between themselves, and with those who protect them. For Albini, no rigid formal structure is prevalent; syndicated criminals simply make use of whatever resources or persons are necessary to accomplish their goals. Moreover, every criminal syndicate has several powerful individuals who serve as "patrons" to the criminal clientele; these patrons wield force and deliver favors. Yet, as Albini further argued:

> A powerful syndicate leader in the west at a particular time may be influential in his area because he has excellent protection in his city and because he provides funds for a multitude of new criminal enterprises, giving other syndicated criminals continued sources of revenue. Yet he may have no power whatsoever over other syndicated criminals in other parts of the country. (p. 265)

In addition, powerful syndicate figures may serve as "clients" to others more powerful, especially those with legal power to offer protection in return for payoffs. In other words, the entire system involves various levels of patron-client relationships that are constantly permeated with conflict, cooperation, and accommodation (Albini, 1971). Syndicated crime therefore is never formally or rigidly bureaucratized; rather, it maintains numerous and complex criminal and noncriminal patron-client relationships. As Albini concluded, syndicated criminal enterprises

> are generated at all levels of patron-client relationships and they are primarily held together by the fact that each participant is basically motivated by his own self-interest. Power within the system depends upon the individual's rise in the number of significant patron-client relationships he is able to establish. (p. 300)

Albini's perspective on the structure of syndicated crime is supported by other research that uses a variety of methodologies, such as participant observation, interviews with informants, and analysis of the government's syndicated crime files (Bynum, 1987).

## Crime Networks

In his book *On The Take*, Chambliss (1988a) has extended Albini's thesis a little further. He has documented how businesspeople, politicians, and members of the criminal justice system are involved in "the subterranean, often invisible" industry built on, for example, illegal gambling, illegal drugs, business fraud, and illegal prostitution. Chambliss studied syndicated crime in Seattle, finding that the vice district was prospering and controlled not by "Cosa Nostra" but by

> a loose affiliation of businesspeople, politicians, union leaders, and law-enforcement officials who cooperate to coordinate the production and distribution of illegal goods and services, for which there is substantial demand. (p. 151)

Thus, financiers (who finance the operations) and middle-level organizers (who supervise the racketeers) unite in a loosely structured **crime network** for the purpose of financial gain. Rather than the existence of a highly centralized "Cosa Nostra," Chambliss's research indicates that criminal syndicates are organized by those who primarily benefit from criminal activities—those "legitimate" members of society who hold business, political, and criminal justice positions.

Similarly, Gary Potter (1994) investigated syndicated crime in "Morrisburg" (a pseudonym for a city in a Mid-Atlantic state). In this town of approximately 95,000 residents, one major syndicate and two smaller syndicates dominate the illegal distribution of goods and services, such as illegal drugs and illegal prostitution and pornography. None of the syndicates has a monopoly on the illegal activities, and none could exist without the close cooperation of "legitimate" members of the community. As Potter stated,

> The overt connections between the leaders of political parties, officeholders of both parties, and the organized crime network is the central theme in "Morrisburg's" organized crime. The system of political payoffs and the active connivance of local business people add the final elements needed to organize crime. (p. 105)

Indeed, Morrisburg's syndicates have extensive holdings in legitimate businesses, such as vending companies, the garment industry, and the coal industry. As Potter concluded, "Crime, politics, and finance all clearly form part of a peculiar milieu. They are not separate activities, they are not distinct from one another—they are only different areas of a single economic spectrum" (p. 114).

Jeffrey Scott McIllwain (1999) likewise argues that "organized crime" is more accurately characterized as "criminal networks," composed of relationships engaged in a process of social interaction for the purpose of providing illicit goods and services for a profit. Such criminal networks

> create a social system of organized crime, a system which explains the remarkable consistency of the process of organizing crime across time and space. Social networks encompass underworld and upperworld actors who benefit from this social system of organized crime. (p. 319)

McIllwain shows that this networking is not static but constantly changing, evolving and adapting to new social conditions, consequently manifesting itself in "different ways for different reasons in different cultures."

Finally, Albanese (2004) discusses recent Russian criminal syndicates operating as "networks" in New York City. These networks are not centralized or dominated by a few leaders but, rather, are composed of individuals who "have many indirect connections to others and take on partners as they are needed for a criminal activity, but there is no hierarchy that exists independent of the crime" (p. 193). The partnerships that develop to accomplish certain forms of criminal activity do not endure and do not form ongoing criminal groups.

The importance of the research on patron-client relations and crime networks, then, is that it shows that the overall structure of syndicated crime has changed little since the 1800s. Syndicated crime is not centrally organized in a national crime syndicate, and "upright" businesspeople and public officials often continue to play a regular and significant role in the organization and perpetuation of criminal syndicates.

## 6.3 Principal Forms of Syndicated Crime

In this section, we consider the principal forms of syndicated crime. Specifically, we examine the following:

1. Two types of illegal sale and distribution of goods and services—illegal drugs (a good) and illegal prostitution (a service).

2. Syndicated crime's involvement in legitimate business through direct investment, racketeering, and money laundering.

3. Syndicated crime's involvement with the state, such as corruption and performance of political favors.

4. The globalization of syndicated crime.

### Illegal Goods and Services

Drugs and prostitution are the two main types of illegal goods and services in which syndicated crime is involved.

***Illicit drugs.*** The **illicit drug business**  (primarily heroin, cocaine, and marijuana) reaps tremendous profits for syndicated crime—approximately $110 billion each year—and accounts for 40 percent of all syndicated crime activity (Albanese, 2004).

Psychoactive drugs—alcohol, tobacco (nicotine), amphetamines, tranquilizers, marijuana, cocaine, heroin—are chemicals capable of altering and affecting mental processes and states. Historically, humans have found an interest in ingesting such chemicals to obtain their effects. In this section we first provide a historical sketch of the stated reasons why the production, distribution, and use of marijuana, cocaine, and heroin have been criminalized. Second, we examine the extent and use of these three illegal drugs today. Finally, we discuss the structure of the illegal business that distributes these drugs.

Throughout much of the 1800s, U.S. residents purchased opiates (opium, morphine, and heroin) over the counters in pharmacies, groceries, and general stores and obtained them from physicians for tranquilization and the relief of pain. In fact, opiates "were as freely accessible as aspirin is today" (Breacher, 1972).

In 1875, however, the city of San Francisco enacted an ordinance outlawing opium "dens" (smoking houses). Prior to that time Chinese laborers, working for low wages building U.S. railroads, were "free" to smoke opium as they pleased and their dens were not illegal. With the onset of the 1875–1880 depression, Chinese laborers became an obstacle to white workers' economic survival. As a result, whites organized against the opium-smoking Chinese. Consequently, the San Francisco ordinance—and several other anti-opium laws enacted in other cities—legally repressed the Chinese, thus serving the interests of the white working class (Helmer, 1975). Eventually (in 1909) Congress enacted the Opium Exclusion Act, thereby prohibiting importation of opium and/or its derivatives, except for medical purposes.

Similarly, in the early 1900s cocaine was widely used in the United States (it was a major ingredient of Coca-Cola). Yet racist beliefs that African Americans were especially prone to cocaine use—causing them to be particularly violent, criminal, and dangerous—grew widespread at the turn of the century. As David Musto (1973) argued, however:

> Evidence does not suggest that cocaine caused a crime wave but rather that anticipation of black rebellion inspired white alarm. Anecdotes often told of superhuman strength, cunning, and efficiency resulting from cocaine. One of the most terrifying beliefs about cocaine was that it actually improved pistol marksmanship. Another myth, that cocaine made blacks almost unaffected by mere .32 caliber bullets, is said to have caused Southern police departments to switch to .38 caliber revolvers. These fantasies characterized white fear, not the reality of cocaine's effects, and gave one more reason for the repression of blacks. (p. 7)

In addition to white fear, this association of African Americans with cocaine use and the Chinese with opium use tended to mystify the actual drug users during the early 1900s. Most persons addicted to opiates and cocaine were not African Americans and Chinese, but rather white, middle-aged, middle-class women. Moreover, their addiction resulted largely from "medical problems" rather than, as today, from a search for euphoria and excitement; furthermore, it was as frequent in rural areas as in urban areas (Goode, 1984).

Eventually, because of such racist fears, the Harrison Narcotics Act of 1914 was enacted. This act taxed those who produced, imported, dispensed, and sold opium and cocaine (and their derivatives, such as heroin) and required these individuals to register with the Treasury Department. The act was aimed primarily at regulating and controlling the traffic in narcotics. However, a series of Supreme Court decisions between 1919 and 1922 also made it illegal for physicians to prescribe narcotics to patients. Thus, it was the combination of these events and the act itself that, as Oakley Ray (1983) pointed out, took "the first step toward making it impossible for addicts to obtain their drugs legally. The result was the development of an illicit drug trade that charged users up to 50 times more than the legal retail drug price" (p. 36).

And as Erich Goode (1984) added, following passage of the Harrison Act and the Supreme Court decisions, the United States

> witnessed the dramatic emergence of a criminal class of addicts—a *criminal class that had not existed previously*. The link between addiction and crime—the view that the addict was by definition a criminal—was forged. The law itself created a new class of criminals. (p. 221, italics in original)

Not only was a criminal class of opiate and cocaine users created by the Harrison Act and the Supreme Court decisions (a class composed primarily of lower- and working-class individuals—middle-class women turned to legal drugs, such as tranquilizers [Goode, 1984:221]), but those who inhaled marijuana also became victims of the law. Although marijuana was smoked for years by U.S. citizens and was not considered a social problem, all of a sudden in the 1930s it began to receive considerable attention. As with the Chinese during the 1875-1880 depression, Mexicans during the depression of the 1930s were seen as a threat to white survival because they worked for lower pay. As a result, whites began to link marijuana use with the "degenerate and violent Mexican" and called for legal intervention. Politicians, police, and prosecutors likewise "protested constantly to the federal government about the Mexicans' use of the weed" (Musto, 1973:220). Thus, by the summer of 1936 it became obvious that the only way to appease whites in the Southwest was to enact some type of federal legislation. The result was the 1937 Marijuana Tax Act, which regulated importation and use of marijuana and, as its own product, created a criminal class of marijuana users (Helmer, 1975). The possession of marijuana became a criminal act in the same way that possession of opiates and cocaine did—not because of a thorough examination of the effects of marijuana on human behavior but because of racist attitudes toward minorities thought to be its typical users (Goode, 1984).

By 1951, not only were an illegal drug market and a drug-using subculture firmly established in the United States, but Congress was well on its way to repressing that subculture. In that year it enacted the Boggs Amendment to the Harrison Act, which introduced a law-and-order stance on illegal drug use (including marijuana) by instituting minimum mandatory sentences and prohibiting suspended sentences and probation for second offenses (Ray, 1983). Numerous laws enacted since then have continued to increase existing controls over the production, distribution, possession, and sale of what had been judged to be illegal drugs. Thus, behavior previously considered legitimate and legal was subsequently outlawed, the result being the creation of a new class of criminals.

Eventually, the Comprehensive Drug Abuse, Prevention, and Control Act of 1970 repealed, replaced, or updated all preexisting laws dealing with "dangerous drugs." This law placed all drugs controlled by the act under federal jurisdiction (by the Justice Department rather than the Treasury Department), regardless of involvement in interstate commerce. The law did not, however, "eliminate state regulations; it just makes clear that federal enforcement and prosecution is possible in any illegal activity involving the controlled drugs" (Ray, 1983:40). In addition, the law determined once and for all which drugs in circulation were to be considered dangerous, as well as who would make up the criminal class of drug users.

As Graham (1975) argued in his analysis of the events leading to passage of the 1970 act, its original intent was to control the distribution and use of *all* dangerous drugs. Nevertheless, after considerable lobbying by the pharmaceutical industry, the act concentrated exclusively on drugs imported or produced easily by individuals (such as marijuana and heroin). Dangerous drugs produced by pharmaceutical manufacturers (such as amphetamines and tranquilizers like Valium and Librium) were not controlled, even though considerable congressional testimony indicated their use to be more widespread, incapacitating, dangerous, and socially disrupting than narcotic use.

In the 1980s, the United States witnessed new efforts by the federal government to control illegal drugs. Congress enacted the Comprehensive Crime Control Act of 1984 and the Anti-Drug Abuse Act of 1986. Each law strengthened existing drug statutes. In the 1980s, Congress also created the federal position of "drug czar," appointed by the president to oversee policies for marijuana, heroin, and cocaine.

The National Household Survey on Drug Abuse, published annually by the U.S. Department of Health and Human Services, provides data about illicit drug use. This survey is a nationally representative sample of the U.S. population (noninstitutionalized) age 12 and older. According to its most recent report (U.S. Department of Health and Human Services, 2004):

- In 2003, an estimated 20 million Americans were current illicit drug users. The number of current illicit drug users was at its highest level in 1979, when there were 25 million.

- No change occurred in the overall rate of illicit drug use between 2002 and 2003.

- Marijuana is the most commonly used illicit drug (14.6 million past-month users). In 2003, it was used by 75 percent of current illicit drug users.

- In 2003, an estimated 2.3 million people were cocaine users, and 119,000 were heroin users.

Overall, the illegal drug industry that profits from this illicit drug-use population operates like other importing, wholesaling, and retailing businesses. It is organized and coordinated by a variety of criminal syndicates—not one exclusive criminal elite.

Specifically regarding the structure of the heroin, cocaine, and marijuana distribution systems, heroin seems to be the most organized of the three, with a few criminal syndicates sharing in monopolizing *importation* of heroin into the United States. The United States contains a variety of small syndicates, creating a long vertical distributional structure. Even though these syndicates are small, they maintain separate levels between production and sales, with each level relatively insulated from other levels. At the top are the heroin *importers,* who coordinate large shipments of heroin into the United States. Importers have high operating costs because success is somewhat based on employing skilled smugglers. Importers rarely see or touch the actual heroin; they simply coordinate the shipment of uncut and undiluted heroin to a criminal syndicate in the United States, which then distributes it to a variety of *wholesalers.* The wholesalers dilute the purity of the heroin—usually with quinine, mannite, and/or lactose—thereby doubling the volume and weight of the heroin mixture. Eventually the heroin is reduced in purity to approximately 25 percent and then divided into "street-ounce" packets (a little less than one full ounce). These packages are then sold to a variety of what may be called "street syndicates," which also dilute the purity, reducing it to approximately 10–15 percent heroin, selling "half-ounces" or "bundles" to users (Simon and Witte, 1982; Lyman and Potter, 2004).

Frederick Desroches' (2003) important work on wholesalers found that they work in small groups, are flexible in their organization and division of labor, have a small number of clients, insulate themselves from their illegal activity, and function as independent entrepreneurs. Indeed, these individuals view drug trafficking as a business enterprise that requires a "business sense"—the provision of a quality product at competitive prices and a reputation of reliable service. In fact 60 percent of the wholesalers Desroches interviewed had operated a small business prior to becoming a drug dealer, such as an auto body shop, a fruit and tobacco business, a used car dealership, or a trucking company. The wholesaling syndicates ranged in size from only three to nine members, consisting of the "dealer," one or two "partners" who would oversee the drug distribution, and paid employees who moved the drugs to various street syndicates. Wholesalers would also employ "legitimate" people—such as airline employees and truckers—to store, hide, and transport the drugs, as well as lawyers, bank employees, and accountants to help establish the means to launder profits.

Mieczkowski's (1986) work on heroin street sales uncovered three major players in street syndicates, all of whom are not heroin users: "runners," "guns," and "crew bosses." Runners are given allocations of heroin from the crew boss to sell on the street at a variety of locations. Runners maintain a specific "selling position" on the sidewalk or in an alley and sell their heroin to customers. Guns are armed members of the syndicate who station themselves close to the sales areas to provide security for runners. As Mieczkowski stated: "Guns observe and monitor the street transactions. Should anything go awry, guns are expected to intervene" (p. 652). The crew boss manages the street syndicate, distributes the heroin to runners, and collects funds obtained by runners. Crew bosses either go "into the field" to collect the money, or runners report to crew bosses at specific locations. The average "wage" of a runner is approximately $800 per week (if the runner works a five-day week); crew bosses average almost $1,500 per week. The crew bosses in Mieczkowski's study were approximately 18 to 19 years of age; the runners were several years younger. It is also the job of crew bosses to obtain quantities of heroin on a regular basis. Doing so requires coming into contact with wholesalers, who either require payment for the heroin up front or after the street sales are completed.

Overall, Mieczkowski's research is important because it reveals that the overall structure of the heroin distribution system is based on patron-client relationships. The runner requires the patronage of a crew boss, and the crew boss the patronage of a supplier; in turn, the supplier (or wholesaler) requires the patronage of an importer.

The cocaine and marijuana distribution systems in the United States are similar to the heroin system in that they maintain a long vertical distribution system with well-insulated syndicates, each servicing a small number of customers—or clients—below them. For cocaine, each participant dilutes the drug, thereby increasing its volume and price. By the time the mixture reaches the street, it is rarely over 5-10 percent pure. Marijuana is seldom diluted but is repackaged into smaller parcels as it passes from one level to the next (Lyman and Potter, 2004).

In "Morrisburg," Potter (1994) found that the largest syndicate imports drugs from Toronto, Canada, and then supplies approximately 20 wholesalers, who in turn sell the drugs to about 200 street dealers. The Morrisburg drug operation, as Potter observed,

The drug economy: A large portion of crime syndicate activity revolves around the supplying of illegal drugs. Since the criminal justice system seems unable to control illegal drug use, many criminologists suggest decriminalization or legalization as alternatives to prohibitive drug laws.

> is set up in such a way as to minimize contact between layers of the operation. Street-level pushers have no information on the activities of wholesalers. Dealers have no knowledge of financing and/or sources of supply. In addition, on a horizontal axis, people performing similar functions often do not have contact with each other. A built-in system of compartmentalization separates operatives. (p. 87)

The vast majority of heroin, cocaine, and marijuana sold in the United States comes from foreign countries. The major heroin producers are the countries of the "Golden Crescent" area of Southwest Asia (Afghanistan, Iran, and Pakistan), Mexico, Colombia, and the "Golden Triangle" area of Southeast Asia (Laos, Burma, and Thailand). The major cocaine producers are Bolivia, Colombia, and Peru, and of marijuana, Colombia and Mexico (Lyman and Potter, 2004).

***Illegal prostitution.*** The second type of illegal sale and distribution of goods and services is illegal prostitution. In the United States, as in most industrialized societies, there is a hierarchical system of sexual value. In other words, some forms of sexuality are defined as "normal" and "natural"; others are deemed "deviant." Marital, reproductive heterosexuals are at the top of the sexual hierarchy, followed closely by unmarried heterosexuals. Further down are those who prefer solitary sexuality, lesbians and gay men, bisexuals, prostitutes, transvestites, transsexuals, transgenderists, and sadomasochists. Heterosexuals are rewarded with certified mental health, respectability, legal-ity, social and physical mobility, institutional support, and material benefits. Those below heterosexuals in the hierarchy are often presumed to be mentally ill, disreputable, and sometimes criminal. Their social and physical mobility is restricted, they have no institutional support, and they face economic sanctions. In other words, U.S. culture emphasizes that "there is only one way to do it, and that everyone should do it that way." In this section we examine one type of sexual activity that is subordinated in U.S. society, prostitution (for money).

Most people commonly think of prostitution simply as accepting payment for sexual services. However, this definition is so broad that some monogamous relationships (such as marriage) could be defined as prostitution. Indeed, some define *all* marriages as a form of prostitution. As one radical feminist states, "We have long held that all women sell themselves: that the only available roles of a woman—wife, secretary, girlfriend—all demand the selling of herself to one or more men" (cited in Jaggar, 1983:264). We agree that *some* women (and men) may marry for money and that *some* spouses may sexually service their husband/wife in order to receive some type of remuneration. However, we focus our definition of **prostitution** on the consensual grant of *illegal* and *nonmonogamous* sexual services to clients for payment. Although both males and females may become prostitutes, it is in the illegal female prostitution business where we find the vast majority of "organized" prostitution. Before we discuss this organization, let us briefly examine how this organization historically emerged in the United States.

Female prostitution, throughout the 1800s, was condemned in the United States but was not classified as a criminal offense. In the early 1800s, community gangs engaged in the infamous "whorehouse riots," demolishing houses of female prostitution and battling female prostitutes in the streets. These riots did not end female prostitution but helped segregate it within the "red-light districts" of the growing urban slums (Rosen, 1982). As a result, in the 1860s and 1870s a reform movement emerged that concentrated on regulation of female prostitution. These "regulationists" argued for medical control, maintaining that such control would contribute to overall public health. During this period men were thought to possess an excessive sexual "drive"; women were considered to be asexual. Regulated female prostitution would therefore serve as an "outlet" for those men who could not control their alleged special "drive." Regulation involving both police and medical supervision was seen by its supporters as being in the best interests of both society and the prostitutes. Compulsory medical examinations for female prostitutes rather than the complete suppression of prostitution itself was viewed by regulationists as the answer to prostitution (Messerschmidt, 1987).

However, not everyone agreed with the regulationists. Women involved in the late nineteenth- and early twentieth-century feminist movement opposed regulation. Feminists argued that regulation forced female prostitutes into vaginal examinations and licensing, thus providing men with the freedom to engage in sex with female prostitutes without acquiring venereal disease. They further showed that by not inspecting the men, regulation failed to reveal those men who were carriers of venereal disease—therefore not really protecting anyone. According to feminists, then, regulation actually served the interests of the men (customers) rather than the women (prostitutes). In the end, the movement *against* regulation in the United States proved so strong and so successful that only one city (St. Louis) ever tried it, and the experiment there lasted for only four years.

In spite of the "regulation" victory, feminists united with the conservative social purity movement of the time (a movement to reform sexual mores) to press for the actual *abolition* of female prostitution itself. This motley group consolidated into an abolitionist movement that embraced a program of social purity measures. Feminists argued that the alleged male "excessive drive" had to be eliminated. The abolition of female prostitution would contribute to this end by forcing men to control their "drive" and thereby raising men to the level of purity of women.

Subsequently, in the early 1900s state legislatures began enacting laws aimed at closing down red-light districts. Iowa enacted the first law in 1909—the Red-Light Abatement Act—making it illegal to maintain a building for "immoral purposes." By 1917, 31 states had enacted similar laws (Rosen, 1982). However, these laws failed to reduce female prostitution. On the contrary, because female prostitutes could not find "respectable work," new forms of prostitution emerged. As Rosen reported:

> Since brothels and parlor houses could no longer advertise their wares, rooming houses, flats, hotels, and massage parlors became the predominant sites for prostitution. To avoid detection, madams and prostitutes who had once catered to a wealthy clientele began to rely on the "call girl" system of prostitution, in which customers call to see a particular prostitute. In this way, connections could be made secretly without danger of police harassment. . . . For the majority of poor women, however, the closing of the houses meant increased streetwalking, which was immediately noticed in most American cities. Without recognized districts or brothels, prostitutes could no longer receive customers in the semiprotected environment of the brothel or district. Instead, they had to search for business in public places—hotels, restaurants, cabarets, or on the street. (p. 32)

This search for customers in public places made female prostitutes vulnerable to violent clients and police harassment. Consequently, control of female prostitution began to change hands. Because of the new conditions resulting from the abolitionist movement, working-class and street female prostitutes turned to male pimps to help them ward off dangers, provide legal assistance, and offer some additional support. Eventually, the overall female prostitute/male "john" transaction became dominated by individual pimp entrepreneurs or male-dominated criminal syndicates (Rosen, 1982).

Today, female prostitutes continue to search for customers in such public places as streets, bars, and hotels, and they work in a variety of private settings, such as massage parlors or even customers' homes. The contemporary illegal female prostitution business is stratified in the following way (Caputi, 2000; Simon, 2001):

1. *Call girls.* Call girls are so named because they do not solicit clients on the street or in a massage parlor but rather make appointments through the telephone. These prostitutes are at the top of the hierarchy, cater to upper- and upper-middle-class clients, and command high fees relative to other prostitutes. Since they work in secret, usually with a Madam, they are less vulnerable than other prostitutes to police actions, harassment, and violence. Some call girls are also "corporate prostitutes" in the sense that they are hired by a

corporation to "reward" customers, partners, or employees and to "help" in business transactions, such as closing deals or mergers, lobbying, and undercutting competitors.

2. *Working-class prostitutes.* This level of prostitution usually involves working in an established business, such as a massage parlor. These prostitutes are at a middle level of the prostitution hierarchy; cater mostly to lower-middle-class and working-class males such as cab drivers, truck drivers, and factory workers; and do not command as high fees as call girls. A specific type of working-class prostitute is labeled a "lot lizard" who solicits primarily truck drivers at freeway truck stops.

3. *Streetwalkers.* The most common form of prostitution is the streetwalker who is poor and engages in prostitution to survive economically. Many streetwalkers are teenage girls who have run away from abusive homes. U.S. society has defined youthful women as desirable and, consequently, girls on the street exchange their bodies for economic survival. Streetwalkers receive the least amount of pay of all prostitutes and are at the greatest risk of violent victimization from the "pimps" (who usually control them) and the "johns" (who are their "clients").

The syndication of prostitution varies according to the above hierarchy. Regarding call girl syndicates, the case of Heidi Fleiss is probably the best known. Fleiss maintained an exclusive brothel in Los Angeles, and her "girls" made as much as $50,000 per month providing sexual services to politicians, film personalities, and businessmen. It is alleged that actor Charlie Sheen spent as much as $53,000 in one year on the "Hollywood Madam's" call girls. As the Madam, Fleiss hired the call girls, collected the clients' fees, kept the books, and paid each call girl after taking a hefty percent. Fleiss' father, Dr. Paul Fleiss, allegedly helped her launder her tremendous earnings. Fleiss was eventually convicted of pandering, conspiracy, income-tax evasion, and money laundering and was sentenced to three years in prison (Meier and Geis, 1997).

Working-class prostitution is usually organized as a business (i.e., massage parlor or escort service) in which the prostitute is hired and controlled by an "employer" (Lyman and Potter, 2004). These employers often disguise their prostitution business as legitimate in various ways. Jay Albanese (2004) provides an example:

> Penelope Hatteras operated several businesses in Houston, Dallas, Atlanta, and Denver. These businesses were advertised as "nude modeling and escort services." Customers would call these businesses, and "models" would be dispatched directly to the customer's location. The customer paid by cash or credit card. What was actually occurring was organized prostitution. Once the "model" reached the customer, she would negotiate a monetary agreement in exchange for sex acts. (p. 50)

An increasing number of women who work in these establishments are recruited and transported across international borders for the purpose of engaging in prostitution. A large portion of the estimated 4 million women who are annually moved around the globe are imported from Asia to countries with well-established sex industries, such as Japan and the United States (Miller and Jayasundara, 2001). Some of these women find themselves the victims of deception—hired to be a domestic worker, only later to be forced into prostitution—and eventually of coercion, dependence, debt bondage, and violence. Miller and Jayasundara explain "debt bondage":

> This occurs when women borrow money for the cost of travel, visas, false documents, and employment location; they are, then, charged exorbitant interest and required to work off the debt before accumulating their own earnings. (p. 474)

Although Asian women involved in prostitution in the United States are often subjected to deceptive, exploitive, and eventually debt-contract arrangements, research indicates that many leave Asia with the explicit purpose to engage in prostitution and thus consent to do so because of its promised financial rewards (Thorbek and Pattanaik, 2002). In other words, these Asian women are "opportunity seekers" who use migration-related prostitution as a means to escape from oppressive local conditions.

*Streetwalkers are the most common type of prostitutes, yet receive the least amount of pay of all prostitutes, and face the greatest risk of violent victimization.*

The prostitute working in a street context is usually one of a "stable" of women controlled by a single pimp (Simon, 2001). Simon further describes the streetwalker-pimp relationship in organizing this form of prostitution:

> Pimps take a portion of the prostitute's earnings (sometimes more than 60 percent). In return, the pimp provides legal protection when the streetwalker is arrested or obtains a doctor if she is sick or injured. Pimps sometimes make recruiting trips to certain cities, like Miami and Minneapolis, that are known havens for runaway young women. Pimps often have been reported to sexually exploit and regularly physically abuse their prostitutes. (p. 265)

Indeed, street walking is the most dangerous form of prostitution. The vast majority of streetwalkers experience rape and assault by clients, pimps, and drug dealers (Miller and Jayasundara, 2001; Williamson and Cluse-Tolar, 2002).

In the mid-1980s, crack cocaine emerged on the streets of the United States and led to research interest in the relation between crack and participation in street prostitution. Some criminologists argued that selling crack provided a new opportunity for women on the street, generating a larger share of street women's income than in the past and, simultaneously, decreasing women's reliance on prostitution (Inciardi, Lockwood, and Pottieger, 1993; Fagan, 1994; Mieczkowski, 1994). As Fagan (1994) has argued, "the expansion of drug markets in the cocaine economy has provided new ways for women to escape their limited roles, statuses and incomes" (p. 210).

However, other research challenges this "new opportunity" perspective, arguing that not much changed in the 1980s (and since) for street-level prostitutes (Maher and Curtis, 1992; Maher and Daly, 1996; Maher, 1997). Although in theory we might expect that an expansion of the cocaine market would provide more opportunities for street women to earn money, the real world of gender inequality suggests this is not the case—it is men who control the selling of crack on the street. As Maher and Daly (1996), Maher and Curtis (1992), and Maher (1997) have shown in studies of street women in New York City, the only consistent economic option for women on the street is prostitution. What has changed, then, is not "new opportunities" to move out of prostitution but, rather, increased adverse effects on their working lives from widespread crack consumption in poverty-ridden neighborhoods:

> The streetwalking market became flooded with novice sex workers, the going rates for sexual transactions decreased, and 'deviant' sexual expectations by dates increased, as did the levels of violence and victimization. (Maher and Daly, 1996:484)

Many of these women engage in prostitution to support their crack use and are independent from pimp control. Nevertheless, they experience disempowerment and dependence in relation to male cocaine dealers; thus, a change has taken place in the *content* of gendered dominance but not the overall *form* (Miller, 1995).

Very little research has been done on the buyers—or "johns"—of prostitution services. However, we do know that buyers of all three types of prostitution are less likely than the prostitutes to be criminalized by the criminal justice system, even though their behavior is likewise illegal. As Lynn Chancer (1998) has pointed out, prostitution entails a buyer-seller interaction in which the buyer is essential to the transaction.

> The sexual demands (and economic resources) of a primarily male clientele could even be said to be more important to the system than prostitutes entering this profession on the side of supply: men's desire precedes, and functions as a necessary condition for sustaining, prostitution's existence. (p. 181)

Thus, the buyers are an equally important aspect to the illegal sex business.

Only one state in the United States has legalized prostitution. In 1971 the Nevada state legislature legalized regulated prostitution within licensed brothels (Chapkis, 1997). Only smaller counties in Nevada (rather than the large tourist cities, such as Reno, Las Vegas, and Lake Tahoe) were authorized to license brothels. However, this rule did not eliminate prostitution in the tourist areas: "Illegal prostitutes continue to far outnumber those working legally in the state's licensed brothels" (p. 62). Moreover, the working conditions at Nevada's brothels are oppressive:

- The prostitutes are defined as "independent contractors" with no claim to health benefits, vacation pay, or retirement benefits.

- The prostitutes are required to live on premises while working and must register with the police.

- A standard shift runs 12–14 hours a day, seven days a week, for 21 days.

- Half of prostitutes' earned income goes to brothel management, and women's incomes are additionally reduced through brothel fees for room, board, and supplies (including condoms).

- Prostitutes cannot refuse customers unless management agrees.

---

**Box 6.2   Is Prostitution a Victimless Crime?**

D iffering opinions exist regarding whether prostitution is a *victimless* crime. Some maintain that the female prostitute is clearly the victim of prostitution, being exploited and treated simply as a sexual object by the Madam, "employer," pimp, and "client" alike. Kathleen Barry (1979) has gone so far as to refer to female prostitution as "female sexual slavery":

> Because it is invisible to social perception and because of the clandestine nature of its practices, it is presently impossible to statistically measure the incidence of female sexual slavery. But considering the arrested sexual development that is understood to be normal in the male population and considering the numbers of men who are pimps, procurers, members of syndicate and freelance slavery gangs, operators of brothels and massage parlors, connected with sexual exploitation entertainment, pornography purveyors, wife beaters, child molesters, incest perpetrators, johns (tricks) and rapists, one cannot help but be momentarily stunned by the enormous male population participating in female sexual slavery. The huge number of men engaged in these practices should be cause for a declaration of a national and international emergency, a crisis in sexual violence. But what should be cause for alarm is instead accepted as normal social intercourse. (p. 220)

Thus, some people argue that society should find a way for female prostitutes to "escape their plight."

However, others respond by arguing that prostitutes are not helpless victims who must be "saved." In her book *Live Sex Acts: Women Performing Erotic Labor*, Wendy Chapkis (1997) has documented, through the words of prostitutes themselves, the oppressive and often violent conditions they face in their everyday working lives. Yet these prostitutes do not criticize prostitution per se but, rather, attribute their plight to the poor working conditions experienced and the illegal nature of their "profession." Thus, rather than criminalizing sex workers through the legal system, Chapkis has called for guaranteed full workers' rights and benefits for all prostitutes and the decriminalization of this consensual sexual activity.

Similarly, Margo St. James (1987), founder of Call Off Your Old Tired Ethic (COYOTE)—a female prostitute union that provides such legal services as bail and counseling for arrestees, as well as child-care services for prostitutes—has said that the view of the female prostitute as "victim" and "sexual slave" is patronizing and condescending. St. James has argued that

> in private the whore has power. She is in charge, setting the terms for the sexual exchange and the financial exchange. In public, of course, she has absolutely no rights—no civil rights, no human rights. Prostitution laws are how women are controlled in this society. (p. 82)

Given the evidence on violence perpetrated against primarily prostitutes who work in a street context, it is difficult to assume that St. James speaks for *all* prostitutes. Nevertheless, other female prostitutes have added to St James' argument by declaring that a democratic morality should be used to judge all sexual acts. Many female prostitutes do not see themselves as sexual objects but rather as engaging in a specific type of sexuality that is stigmatized in this society.

Increasingly, some sociologists are supporting many of these views held by activist female prostitutes. Although opposing gender inequality and, therefore, the male-dominated nature of the female prostitution "business" (just as they oppose gender inequality in other areas of society), these sociologists do not argue for the criminalization, and therefore the dissolution of commercial sex, because it does not benefit the women involved. As Lenore Kuo (2002) has shown, criminalizing prostitution reinforces the "whore stigma" and it subjects women to discriminatory arrests and a reliance on pimps for "protection" and legal support. Thus, sociologists emphasize the need for society to provide all women with equal opportunities to enter any type of employment they wish. As Lynn Chancer (1998) argues, society should concentrate on "guaranteed jobs and income support for all women (including health and child care, and family allowances where applicable). Under such conditions, women would never have to become sex workers out of necessity rather than interest" (p. 196). Moreover, rather than viewing female prostitution as degrading and the prostitute as a passive victim, more and more people regard female prostitution as a legitimate form of sexuality. Accordingly, they argue that we should work to empower women within the sex industry itself.

## Legitimate Businesses

In addition to illegal sale and distribution of goods and services, criminal syndicates work with legitimate businesses. There are three major means by which syndicated crime effects this involvement: direct investment, money laundering, and labor racketeering.

*Direct investment.* Criminal syndicates often reinvest their profits from the illegal sale and distribution of goods and services in legitimate enterprises. Numerous studies have reported syndicate **direct investment** in (1) construction; (2) waste removal; (3) garments; (4) food processing, distribution, and retailing; (5) legal gambling; (6) hotels; (7) bars; (8) liquor retailing and wholesaling; (9) entertainment; (10) business and personal services; (11) motor vehicle sales and repair; (12) real estate; (13) banking; and (14) various other wholesale and retail businesses (Lyman and Potter, 2004). The advantages of investing in legitimate businesses include less risk than expanding an illegal operation, opportunities for concealing illegal activities, and avenues for paying income taxes.

Legitimate businesspeople may also become involved in working relationships with syndicate-owned businesses. In the "Morrisburg" study, Potter (1994) found that syndicated crime and legitimate businesses were "cozy partners" in illegal transactions—businesses provided the sites for illegal gambling bets, illicit pornographic film distribution, and fencing and loan sharking operations.

*Money laundering.* Much of what is earned by criminal syndicates from the illegal sale and distribution of goods and services is in cash, and usually in small bills. Before this "dirty" money (illegally earned) can be spent or invested in legitimate businesses, it must be turned into "clean" money. Criminal syndicates accomplish this task by engaging in **money laundering**, or the process by which individuals conceal the illegal source of income and then disguise that income to make it appear legitimate. Those engaged in money laundering range from the small individual drug dealer who wishes to exchange smaller-denomination bills for larger ones to the large criminal syndicate that obtains enormous sums of money from numerous illegal activities.

Money laundering generally involves a series of transactions that are used to disguise the source of the income. These transactions typically occur in the following way:

1. *Placement:* The first stage of the money laundering process involves placing illegitimate money into a legitimate financial institution through, for example, direct deposit, wire transfers, or other means.

2. *Layering:* The second stage involves numerous and complex financial transactions that move the money so as to obscure a "paper trail"—such as moving money from one bank to other banks numerous times through electronic funds transfer.

3. *Integration:* The final stage involves using a legitimate transaction—such as buying and then reselling a house—to disguise the illicit proceeds. In this way, the initial dirty money becomes clean as it is integrated into the legitimate economy.

***Labor racketeering.*** In addition to direct investment and money laundering, criminal syndicates are involved with legitimate businesses through **labor racketeering**, or the infiltration, domination, and use of unions for personal benefit by illegal, violent, and fraudulent means. Traditional forms of racketeering that continue to proliferate include (1) entering into "sweetheart contracts" with employers, (2) looting workers' benefit funds, and (3) extorting "strike insurance" payments from businesses.

A "sweetheart contract" results from a criminal syndicate's extensive infiltration of a union, ensuring it the opportunity to control the union and consequently to collude with management, permitting employers to violate collective bargaining provisions. In return for payoffs to syndicate figures who negotiate such contracts, the employers have, for example, the privilege of using nonunion labor, a guarantee that workers will not be organized by specifically unwelcome unions, and the right to select union representatives with whom to negotiate.

Concerning workers' benefit funds (which cover pension, health, and welfare benefits for retired, disabled, and needy workers), infiltration of unions by criminal syndicates has resulted in the systematic looting of these funds to provide syndicate figures and their friends with such perks as "no show" jobs, homes, automobiles, travel expenses, stocks and bonds, and capital for legitimate investment. The International Brotherhood of Teamsters (IBT)—which has a long history of benefit-fund abuse—provides a shocking example. In the early 1960s, Jimmy Hoffa (then president of the Teamsters Union) shared pension-fund kickbacks with Allen Dorfman, a former asset manager and service provider to the Teamsters Central States Pension Fund. Other presidents of the Teamsters Union—such as Roy Williams and Jackie Presser—in association with criminal syndicates, have similarly looted the Teamsters pension fund. For example, Jackie Presser placed his uncle, Allen Friedman, on the union payroll at a $1,000 a week, even though Friedman did not work for the union. In addition, Presser arranged to pay a syndicate-controlled firm—Hoover-Gorin and Associates—$1.3 million per year and a $350,000 yearly retainer to do advertising and public relations work that was never performed. Even before assuming the Teamsters' presidency, Presser had compiled an extensive record of syndicate crime associations, benefiting from their support in his elevation to the IBT presidency.

Criminal syndicates may also extort "strike insurance" from employers in return for the promise to keep the business "running as usual" (namely, free from labor strife). In other words, the employer pays a criminal syndicate a fee to keep labor peace. For example, syndicate figures in the past created and owned a series of labor-leasing companies throughout the country. These companies provided workers and labor peace to the corporations that hired them. Criminal syndicates received contractual payments, and the corporations minimized their labor costs. If a corporation did not voluntarily hire one of these syndicate companies, corrupt union officials created labor disputes to suggest the need for labor peace and, therefore, syndicated crime's leased labor. A related example is the 2 percent "organized crime tax" imposed on construction contracts in New York City:

> Failure to pay this extortion demand means work stoppages and interruptions and an inability to get services from organized crime-controlled subcontractors. In particular, construction projects find it virtually impossible to get concrete poured at construction sites in New York City without paying this tax. (Lyman and Potter, 2004:204)

## The State

Criminal syndicates are involved with the state in two essential ways: providing political favors for the state and colluding with state officials (such as the police and politicians). We consider each of these.

*Political favors.* The use of syndicate figures to perform political favors for the state goes back to the time of "Lucky" Luciano. As David Simon (2002a) pointed out, this practice began during World War II when the underworld figures in control of the New York docks were contracted by navy intelligence officials in order to ensure that German submarines or foreign agents did not infiltrate the area. It was thought that waterfront pimps and prostitutes could act as a sort of counterintelligence corps. The man whose aid was sought for this purpose was Lucky Luciano; he was reportedly very successful in preventing sabotage or any other outbreaks of trouble on the New York docks during the war. . . . Luciano was granted parole and given exile for life in 1954 in exchange for the aid he provided during the war (p. 82).

Other historical examples abound (McCoy, 1972; Church Committee, 1975; Pearce, 1976; Hinckle and Turner, 1981):

- In France in 1950, the CIA recruited syndicate figures to create a "criminal terror squad" to force recalcitrant Marseilles dockers to load ships with arms for use in Vietnam. For their assistance to the state, these syndicate figures were "allowed" to continue refining heroin in Marseilles and then export it to the United States.

- In the 1960s the CIA recruited anti-Castro, right-wing, syndicate figures to assassinate Fidel Castro. Such notables as John Roselli, Sam Giancana, and Santo Trafficante, Jr., as well as Rafael "Chi Chi" Quintero, Felix Rodriguez,

Frank Sturgis, and E. Howard Hunt were all involved in the assassination plans.

• In the middle to late 1960s, syndicate figures worked together with the CIA to develop the Golden Triangle area as a major source for growing opium. In return for fighting the Pathet Lao opposition forces, the Meo tribespeople of the area were compensated by the CIA's own airline—Air America—which helped transport the opium to heroin laboratories and, ultimately, into the arms of GIs in Vietnam and users in the United States.

*Collusion.* The overall viability and profitability of criminal syndicates have been based historically on a symbiotic relationship between syndicate figures and state officials. Earlier in the chapter we discussed this close relationship during the 1800s and early 1900s. Since then, this relationship has continued, as a variety of governmental commissions and academic researchers have uncovered widespread corruption between state officials and criminal syndicates. For example, in 1931 the National Commission on Law Observance and Enforcement found that "nearly all of the large cities suffer from an alliance between politicians and criminals" (cited in Chambliss and Seidman, 1982:278). John Gardiner's (1970) study of Reading, Pennsylvania, found that for decades criminal syndicates in that city systematically worked closely with mayors, city council members, police officers and chiefs, and judges.

After an investigation of police corruption in New York City, the Knapp Commission (1972) concluded:

> We found corruption to be widespread. . . . In the five plainclothes divisions where our investigation was concentrated we found a strikingly standardized pattern of corruption. Plainclothesmen, participating in what is known in police parlance as a "pad," collected regular biweekly or monthly payments amounting to as much as $3,500 from each of the gambling establishments in the area under their jurisdiction, and divided the take in equal shares. The monthly share per man . . . ranged from $300 and $400 in midtown Manhattan to $1,500 in Harlem. When supervisors were involved they received a share and a half. . . . Evidence before us led us to the conclusion that the same pattern existed in the remaining divisions we did not investigate. . . . Corruption in narcotics enforcement lacked the organization of the gambling pads, but individual payments . . . were commonly received and could be staggering in amount. . . . Corrupt officers customarily collected scores in substantial amounts from narcotic violators. . . . They ranged from minor shakedowns to payments of many thousands of dollars, the largest narcotics payoff uncovered in our investigations having been $80,000. . . . The size of this score was by no means unique. (p. 22)

Chambliss' (1988a) study of Seattle demonstrated that syndicated crime in that city flourished with the support and cooperation of a number of state officials. Block and Chambliss (1981) showed that criminal syndicates have been linked with leading political and legal figures in Detroit, Chicago, Denver, Columbus and Cleveland, Ohio, Miami, Boston, and a hoard of other cities. Finally, in the "Morrisburg" study, Potter (1994) found that collusion "extends from the cop on the beat to the most senior political officials" (pp. 101–102).

This intimate and symbiotic relationship may even reach the White House. Some researchers have argued that since at least the 1940s, former President Richard Nixon socialized with and was involved in business endeavors with a number of syndicate members (Block et al., 1972). Nixon, however, is not the only president implicated by researchers and journalists as a "friend" of shady individuals and dealing. Former President Ronald Reagan had certain associations with people reportedly connected to syndicated crime. As Lyman and Potter (2004) have argued, syndicated crime

> played a major role in putting Ronald Reagan in the White House. He received support from organized crime, and his administration reciprocated and gave organized crime's representatives seats on the highest councils of the U.S. government. Persons with clear and compelling connections to organized crime were appointed to important governmental positions. (p. 458)

Moreover, Reagan had an intimate relationship with Walter Annenberg, son of Moses Annenberg, the previously powerful and economically successful publisher of the Nationwide News Service that, in the 1920s, catered to bookies (Haller, 1976). In 1939, Moses and Walter were indicted for federal tax evasion and for selling pornography illegally through the mail. Moses eventually agreed to divest control of the "news" wire, settle his tax liabilities by paying $8 million, and go to prison for three years. Moses' son, Walter, became publisher of the *Philadelphia Inquirer, Seventeen,* and *TV Guide* and was appointed ambassador to Britain by Richard Nixon (Block et al., 1972). In addition, when he was president, Ronald Reagan spent almost every January 1 at Walter Annenberg's Palm Springs estate to celebrate the New Year (Scott, 1988).

White House crimes: Numerous U.S. presidents have been involved in illegal and/or unethical behavior. Ronald Reagan is a recent example of a president who had certain associations with people allegedly connected to syndicated crime.

Finally, former Senator Paul Laxalt of Nevada, Reagan's close associate and friend as well as past chair of both the Republican National Committee and the 1984 Reagan-Bush re-election committee, has allegedly had certain close associations with syndicate figures. As Robert Friedman (1984) reported, Morris "Moe" Dalitz (named by the Kefauver Committee as being involved in syndicate activities), Al Sachs (alleged to be involved in illegal casino profiteering operations), and Rudy Kolod (convicted in an extortion-murder plot) all contributed generously to Laxalt's campaigns for governor and senator. When governor, Laxalt allegedly helped Howard Hughes—whose corporation collaborated with criminal syndicates in several casino and resort speculations in Las Vegas and the Caribbean (Simon and Eitzen, 1986)—"become the largest landowner and casino operator in Clark County, Nevada," and "Governor Laxalt's Gaming Control Board waived investigations of Hughes' finances required by the state gaming and control board" (Friedman, 1984:36). Finally, Laxalt had a close relationship with Allen Dorfman, "the man who had supervised the use of the Teamsters' Central States Pension Fund as a private bank for organized crime figures" (Lyman and Potter, 2004:458).

## Globalization

In Chapter 1 we defined **globalization** as the worldwide process whereby individuals, peoples, economies, and nation-states are becoming increasingly interconnected and interdependent. Although syndicated crime has been transnational since at least the emergence of Prohibition in the United States, globalization has promoted new opportunities for syndicates to flourish. The global trafficking in illicit drugs provides an example.

Approximately 80 percent of all cocaine imported to the United States is controlled by two Colombian syndicates—the Medellin and Cali cartels—and these syndicates connect with thousands of people in a variety of syndicates internationally to process, ship, smuggle, and distribute the cocaine into and throughout the United States (Albanese, 2004). For example, the two Colombian cartels use Mexican syndicates to transport cocaine shipments across the southwest border of the United States; once across, these Mexican smugglers transfer the cocaine to Colombian-connected syndicates in the United States that specialize in transportation, local distribution, and money movement (Lyman and Potter, 2004).

How are such complex arrangements coordinated? One way is that drug traffickers take advantage of globalization. An important element driving globalization has been the expansion of communication around the globe. Today, individuals are linked to any part of the globe through cell phones, fax machines, the Internet, and e-mail. These relatively new forms of technology allow individuals from distant places to communicate and interact on a whim. Indeed, drug traffickers—such as the Colombian cartels—now rely on these new forms of technology to coordinate their illegal activities, as Chepesiuk (1999) reports in his study of globalization and drug trafficking:

> [I]nternational drug-trafficking syndicates have been able to take advantage of the revolution in global communication and transportation. Traffickers now use sophisticated technology such as sign interceptors to plot radar and avoid monitoring, and they can now move their illicit drug profits in seconds to almost any place in the world and use computers, faxes, and cellular phones to coordinate their activities and make their businesses run smoothly. (p. 205)

In addition to globalization making it easier for syndicates to run their businesses, it has also contributed to their money laundering necessities. Technological developments have led to e-money, e-commerce, and the globalization of financial and banking services. These developments have in turn permitted criminal syndicates expanded opportunities to disguise their illegitimate money as legitimate. Indeed, the vast amount of money circulating around the globe not only creates a "global electronic economy," it also makes the movement of dirty money less noticeable. Moreover, syndicates have integrated such efforts into their businesses by using a variety of experts in the fields of accounting, law, and e-systems to help them grant legitimacy to their money. As Lyman and Potter (2004) put it:

> The present-day global financial network makes the transfer of profits from illegal transactions easy, fast, and virtually immune from discovery. Money laundering, already an art form, is now conducted at warp speed. The internationalization of finance has rendered state law and state economic policy impotent. (p. 319)

In addition to using new forms of technology, syndicates can simply deposit "dirty" money directly into financial institutions, often with the help of the financial institution itself. Under the Bank Secrecy Act, financial institutions must report all currency transactions of $10,000 or more. When a financial institution fails to do so, it is engaging in money laundering.

Syndicated crime's involvement in the illegal flow of drugs provides an excellent example of how direct deposit money laundering occurs, benefiting both financial institutions and criminal syndicates. For example, in one case, certain New York City heroin dealers deposited tens of millions of dollars in cash at banks in New York City. The New York banks then transferred the funds to a variety of banks in other countries, such as Switzerland. From these foreign banks the money was channeled to various narcotic sources to pay for conversion of opium to heroin, to finance additional "drug" laboratories, and to support and profit the overall network of heroin trafficking. By transferring the funds around the world via modern technology, the process of money laundering is considerably more difficult to detect.

One of the couriers in this particular case, Franco Delle Torre, deposited almost $5 million (in $5, $10, and $20 bills)—over a six-week period—into an account at the brokerage firm Merrill Lynch Pierce Fenner and Smith. The deposits apparently were so important to the brokerage firm that Merrill Lynch's security employees determined that Delle Torre's funds could not be afforded proper security, and arrangements were made to escort the money from Delle Torre's hotel directly to Bankers Trust, where Merrill Lynch maintained accounts. Eventually, however, Merrill Lynch closed the account, and Delle Torre simply moved his laundering operation to the Manhattan offices of the brokerage firm E. F. Hutton and Company. Delle Torre made 18 different cash deposits totaling $13.5 million in a Hutton account. Security personnel at Hutton similarly provided Delle Torre protection from his hotel room to the depository institution. In sum, this case reveals not only the close relationship between syndicated crime and legitimate businesses but also the *global* nature and context of this relationship.

## Review

This chapter examined the nature, extent, types, and costs of syndicated crime in the United States. The first section outlined a brief history of syndicated crime. The second section discussed the structure of syndicated crime in the United States today. The third described in greater depth the structure of various syndicates, examining this structure in light of the principal activities of syndicated crime.

## A History of Syndicated Crime

1. The term "mafia" originally described a method rather than an organization.

2. Syndicated crime can best be conceptualized as a variety of criminal syndicates, or associations of people (from all walks of life), formed to conduct specific illegal enterprises.

3. Early in U.S. history criminal syndicates were local in scope, primarily involved in such illegal enterprises as gambling and prostitution, and worked in a symbiotic relationship with state officials.

4. The passage of the Volstead Act in 1919 provided the context for the rapid development, increased size, and more complex division of labor of criminal syndicates.

5. It is quite unlikely that a national crime syndicate has ever existed in the United States.

## Syndicated Crime Today

1. The work of sociologists such as Joseph Albini, William Chambliss, Gary Potter, and Jeffrey Scott McIllwain reveals that criminal syndicates flourish and prosper today and that businesspeople and state officials continue to play a regular and significant role in them.

2. Albini argues that syndicated crime in the United States today is characterized by "patron-client" relationships. Chambliss, Potter, and McIllwain document how numerous businesspeople, politicians, and members of the criminal justice system are involved in crime networks.

## Principal Forms of Syndicated Crime

1. The illegal drug industry (heroin, cocaine, and marijuana) operates like legitimate importing, wholesaling, and retailing businesses, while the illegal prostitution business primarily maintains three major types of syndication—call girl operations, working-class massage parlors and escort services, and pimp-controlled streetwalking.

2. Criminal syndicates directly invest some of their profits in legitimate businesses and are also extensively involved in labor racketeering and money laundering.

3. Criminal syndicates provide political favors for the state, continue to maintain a symbiotic relationship with state officials, and benefit from the processes of globalization.

## Questions for Class Discussion

1. How did the term "mafia" originate? Is it applicable today?

2. Summarize Cressey's argument concerning the national crime syndicate, then outline the major criticisms of his position. Explain which position you support and why.

3. We presented evidence on the structure of syndicated crime in the United States today. Why do you think such a structure exists?

4. In the media, locate examples of syndicated crime, then compare them to our analysis here. How are they similar? Different?

5. Identify and discuss other ways than those mentioned in this chapter that syndicated crime has benefited from globalization.

## For Further Study

### Readings

Albanese, Jay. 2004. *Organized Crime in Our Times.* Cincinnati: Anderson.

Block, Alan, and Constance A. Weaver. 2004. *All Clouded by Desire: Global Banking, Money Laundering, and International Organized Crime.* Westport, CT: Praeger.

Lyman, Michael D., and Gary W. Potter. 2004. *Organized Crime.* Upper Saddle River, NJ: Prentice Hall.

Simon, David R. 2002. *Tony Soprano's America: The Criminal Side of the American Dream.* Boulder, CO: Westview.

Thorbek, Susanne, and Bandana Pattanaik, eds. 2002. *Transnational Prostitution: Changing Global Patterns.* New York: Zed Books.

### Websites

1. <http://www.yorku.ca/nathanson/default.htm>: The home  page for York University's Nathanson Center for the Study of Organized Crime and Corruption provides readers with current bibliographies on syndicated crime and links to other related websites.

2. <http://www.laundryman.u-net.com>: This site, titled "Billy's Money Laundering Information Website," is managed by Billy Steele, an attorney with a keen interest in studying the extent and techniques of money laundering. ✦

# White-Collar Crime

## 7.1 Occupational Crime
- Occupational Theft
- Occupational Fraud

## 7.2 Corporate Crime
- Corporate Violence
- Corporate Theft

## 7.3 Transnational Corporate Crime
- Bribery
- Dumping
- Dangerous Working Conditions

## Preview

Chapter 7 introduces:

- What sociologists mean by white-collar crime.

- The various types of white-collar crime.

- The nature, extent, and costs of white-collar crime.

- How white-collar crimes differ from other crimes.

## Key Terms

| | |
|---|---|
| collective embezzlement | embezzlement |
| corporate crimes | employee theft |
| corporate theft | financial fraud |
| corporate violence | insider trading |
| deceptive advertising | occupational crimes |

occupational fraud                                    price-fixing
occupational theft                                    transnational corporate crime
physician fraud                                       white-collar crime

W hen we think of crime, we usually focus on the types of crimes already discussed
    in this book—property crimes, interpersonal crimes of violence, and syndicated
crime. This thinking is inevitable because official agencies of social control (police and
courts) concentrate on these behaviors (thus attracting media attention) and because
these crimes are the most frequently studied by sociologists and criminologists. However, although the crimes discussed in Chapters 4, 5, and 6 generate considerable fear
and suffering in society, the white-collar crimes discussed in this chapter are much
more harmful.

Edwin Sutherland (see also Chapter 5.4) was the first sociologist in the United
States to conceptualize the problem of **white-collar crime**. Given the contemptuous attitude toward the law and business ethics displayed by the "robber barons" (such as
Daniel Drew and John D. Rockefeller) in the late 1800s and the widespread and publicized corporate fraud of the 1920s and 1930s, Sutherland (1949) focused his classic
study on "crime committed by a person of respectability and high social status in the
course of his occupation" (p. 2). Demonstrating that white-collar crime was widespread
and endemic to U.S. business, Sutherland's findings led him to concentrate almost exclusively on one type of white-collar crime: corporate crime. However, later, sociologists
and criminologists expanded the definition of white-collar crime to include not only
corporate crimes but also occupational crimes and transnational corporate crimes.

**Occupational crimes** are committed by individuals in the course of their occupations for direct personal gain. These crimes are usually committed against an employer. Embezzlement is an example of an occupational crime.

**Corporate crimes** differ from occupational crimes in that they are not committed
for direct personal gain—although certain individuals may benefit indirectly from
them. Rather, these crimes primarily benefit the corporation. We define corporate
crimes as illegal and/or socially injurious acts of intent or indifference that occur for
the purpose of furthering corporate goals and that physically and/or economically
abuse individuals in the United States and/or abroad. Collusion of top executives of
utility corporations to fix prices is an example of corporate crime.

**Transnational corporate crimes** constitute the third type of white-collar crime.
Many corporations conduct their business operations in more than one country.
Consequently, this transnational character of U.S. corporations sometimes results
in crimes perpetrated on the people of other societies, ranging from bribery, to export of hazardous products, to dangerous working conditions.

These three types of white-collar crime are both similar to and different from the
crimes already discussed in Chapters 4, 5 and 6. Like other crimes, white-collar crimes
also involve theft and violence. That is, commission of white-collar crimes results in loss
of property and/or physical injury and death. But white-collar crimes differ from other
crimes in two important ways. First, white-collar crimes entail far more victimization—

in terms of economic loss and lives injured and lost—than the crimes discussed earlier. Second, victimization resulting from white-collar crimes is less apparent—although once again, far more severe—than the one-on-one type of victimization resulting from interpersonal crimes of violence. Indeed, most of us who suffer the pains of white-collar crimes—corporate crimes in particular—are unaware of our own victimization.

## 7.1 Occupational Crime

Occupational crime occurs in the workplace and is motivated by direct personal gain; it has two main forms: occupational theft and occupational fraud. **Occupational theft** stems from an abuse of trust between the employee and employer. We examine two types of occupational theft: employee theft and embezzlement. Both types affect consumers by increasing the cost of goods and services; they also affect some businesses negatively. **Occupational fraud** is a deliberate workplace deception practiced for the purpose of obtaining personal financial gain. This type of fraud is ubiquitous; we explore the major aspects of occupational fraud with examples from the fields of medicine and securities.

### Occupational Theft

In preindustrialized societies—such as feudal England in the seventeenth century—people had common rights to such necessities as the gathering of wood, the killing of game, and the grazing of animals. But with the transition from feudalism to capitalism, these "rights" were translated into "property." As Jason Ditton (1997b) has stated: The "annexation of common rights . . . naturally culminated in the simultaneous creation of 'property,' and the propertied classes, and the ultimate criminalization of customary practices" (p. 41). As land previously open to everyone's use became the private property of a few, wood gathering became wood theft, game rights became poaching, and grazing rights became trespassing. In addition, this privatization, as Ditton explains,

> released into urban life a working population not only used to receiving part of their "wages" in kind . . . but also one still stinging from the effects of the abrupt and cruel negation of those practices in the countryside. As one might expect, and empirical evidence supports this, a major source of irritation to factory owners who took on such "idle" rural labourers was their penchant for making off with parts of the workplace or the fruits of their labour there, in addition to their wages. (p. 43)

Indeed, the preindustrial cultural tradition of common rights was carried over into industrialized society. Workers expected "wages-in-kind"—extras to supplement their actual earnings. In eighteenth-century England, for instance, workers in manufacturing industries "constantly borrowed, bartered, and sold small quantities of materials among themselves," a good portion of which was stolen from the workplace (Henry, 1987:142). As Stuart Henry argued,

> criminalization of the consumption of a part of one's daily labor was redefined in conjunction with capitalist development of the factory to become employee theft and embezzlement; the trading of embezzled goods came to constitute a hidden economy. (p. 142)

In other words, accompanying the rise of capitalism was the emergence of two major forms of occupational theft: employee theft and embezzlement. We consider each in turn.

**Employee theft**—stealing merchandise and job-related items from one's workplace—is one of the most pervasive and costly crimes in the United States. Self-report studies suggest that 75 percent of employees *admit* to some sort of theft from the workplace (Greenberg, 1997).

The cost of employee theft is enormous. Most employees steal minor items; yet when these items are multiplied by many workers, the cost becomes substantial. "Inventory shrinkage" (loss from employee theft, shoplifting, poor paperwork, and vendor theft) adds approximately 15 percent to the price of all retail goods, and most of this loss is attributable to employee theft (Coleman, 2002). Overall, researchers estimate that employee theft costs $400 billion annually (Greenberg, 2002).

Research indicates that perceived unfairness in the workplace (i.e., being underpaid) is the main reason for employee theft. Moreover, interpersonally insensitive treatment on the part of managers and supervisors provide individuals with rationalizations for engaging in theft at the workplace. As Jerald Greenberg puts it, "People who feel underpaid are inclined to steal and to engage in other types of deviant behavior when company agents display indifference regarding the suffering they experience as a result of underpayment" (p. 986).

Employee theft: Stealing merchandise and job-related items from the workplace is one of the most pervasive and costly crimes in the United States.

Two classic studies by Jason Ditton (1977a) and Gerald Mars (1983) enhance our understanding of the relationship between employee theft and occupation. Ditton considered employee theft a form of what he called "part-time crime." However, part-time crime is not simply a matter of time commitment inasmuch as a part-time criminal may well

> spend more hours and minutes breaking the law than somebody involved full-time in crime. The crucial distinction is that whereas the full-time criminal's legitimate occupation is perceived by him [or her] to be merely nominal, the part-time criminal sees his [or her] illegitimate activities in the same way, as nominal. (p. 91)

In other words, part-time criminals may spend more hours planning and executing their crime than full-time criminals, but this activity is *perceived* by them as inconsequential to their full-time legitimate activity at work.

In a participant observation study of bread salesmen at "Wellbread Bakery," Ditton found that part-time employee theft entailed three activities: fiddling, stealing, and dealing. "Fiddling" is the practice by salespeople (those who sell and deliver bakery goods) of overcharging customers by either increasing the price or reducing the number of items for the standard price. Ditton found that fiddling was tolerated—even overtly recommended—by management because the loser is the customer rather than the company.

"Stealing" is theft from the company itself. Although production workers have "pilfering rights" to a daily loaf of bread, salespeople are excluded from this dubious privilege. As Ditton explains:

> It is assumed that production staff have no outlet other than domestic consumption of pilfered loaves, and that this empirical feature of the practice will de facto limit the amount of bread that they will take. Salesmen, on the other hand, are assumed to have guaranteed occupational access to facilities (a round of customers) which would encourage them systematically to escalate their thefts beyond tolerable levels. Thus, for salesmen at Wellbread's, we may define a successful steal as the removal of some sort of asset skillfully, unobserved, and without permission. Salesmen steal both convertible consumer goods, for resale to their customers, and nonconvertible assets, such as plastic bags and clipboards, which, as tools of the trade, make occupational life easier. (p. 101)

"Dealing"—the third employee theft activity identified by Ditton—is the clandestine unofficial "distribution of other people's goods to the mutual interest and profit of those covertly involved" (p. 106). Dealing involves the collusion of salespeople and other employee staff in arranging a profit-making venture. For example, the bread dispatcher may provide extra trays of bread to salespeople without "booking it." Subsequent to the sale of the extra trays, both the salespeople and the dispatcher share the profits. Dealing then involves the amateur trade (or fencing) in stolen goods from the workplace.

Ditton's book describes how crime can provide an outlet for creativity in monotonous and alienated work environments, as well as challenge the official view of crime as being predominantly a lower-class, nonoccupational phenomenon.

Gerald Mars distinguishes between various types of employee theft and links these to types of jobs. Mars divided workers into four types (hawks, donkeys, wolves, and vultures) distinguished by such elements as the amount of job autonomy, extent of isolation from others, and degree of control over one's labor power. Mars also examined the amount of collectiveness in the workplace, which varies according to how a workplace prioritizes the interests of the group over the individual and is distinguished by such elements as the frequency with which people interact with others, whether contacts occur within a mutually interconnecting network, and the scope of group social life outside the workplace.

"Hawks" are professionals, executives, and small-business persons who maintain individuality, autonomy, and control over their labor power but have infrequent contact with others. Therefore, it is much easier for hawks to "bend the rules" to their personal advantage. Work-related expenses provide an example. A journalist, for instance, may claim first-class travel but actually go second class, or may falsify costs of entertainment and meals as business expenses. More extreme, one journalist said: "It's not uncommon for you to say you're dashing . . . somewhere for a story. You look up fares plus a few beers for fictitious informants and a taxi or two and bang it in for expenses" (cited in Mars, 1983:47).

"Donkeys" have little autonomy, are not isolated from others, and have no control over their labor power. Moreover, donkeys do not work within a group setting with frequent interaction. Supermarket cashiers and workers "on long and noisy mass-production belts" are examples of donkeys. Because of the structured nature of these jobs, employee theft is more restricted than it is for hawks. Supermarket cashiers, for instance, are limited to undercharging—or not charging at all—friends and family who frequent the store where they work, or to simply "taking from the till." As one cashier expressed to Mars: A theft may occur "when your mother or friend comes in. Then they get away with a load of stuff and you put hardly anything through the till" (p. 66).

"Wolves" are similar to donkeys in the sense of having little autonomy and lacking control over their labor power, but they differ in that their jobs require a group of workers. For both hawks and donkeys, control over theft belongs to the individual. For wolves, however, theft is under group control. Airport baggage handlers and longshoremen are examples of wolves. If dockworkers, for example, want to steal cargo, they need the support of the group to do so. This is so both because they work as a group and because they must divide their labor so that some workers steal cargo while others distract supervisors. As Mars explained:

> Theoretically, all these men can pilfer cargo. Yet supervision of unloading by the ships' officers at one end and the shed superintendent at the other greatly reduces *individual* opportunities. Those with *access* therefore need the *support* of those who do not have access, to distract the attention of the supervisors, to provide cover, to "clear" documents and to enable the swift removal and distribution of goods once they have been pilfered. (p. 103)

Finally, "vultures" have considerable individual autonomy, yet that autonomy operates within a loosely structured work group setting. Waiters, truck drivers, and hotel workers are examples of vultures. Such occupations enjoy a degree of independence yet rely on support from coworkers. For example, Mars found a coordinated group of truck drivers who arranged the "private delivery" of stolen company goods on company time.

Mars' work thus identifies how type of occupation and workplace setting help determine type of occupational theft. Indeed, his classification of hawks, donkeys, wolves, and vultures involves a combination of employee theft and embezzlement.

**Embezzlement**, like employee theft, involves a violation of employer-employee trust. However, embezzlement differs from employee theft in that it involves taking money—rather than merchandise and job-related items—for one's personal use. The supermarket cashier "donkey," for example, has the opportunity to steal both merchandise (employee theft) and money (embezzlement).

Embezzlement ranges from simply "taking from the till" to "manipulating the books," but people in certain occupations can embezzle more easily than those in other jobs. Individuals who occupy top business or bank positions—such as loan officers, accountants, computer operators, and CEOs—have a much greater opportunity for embezzling large sums of money than cashiers, bank tellers, sales clerks, or other lower-level employees do. Consequently, individuals in the position to embezzle, and who actually do embezzle large sums of money, frequently are viewed by employers as some of the most important people in the company.

Most embezzlers turn to this crime because they are living beyond their financial means, and in some cases the problem involves large gambling debts or family emergencies (such as unexpected medical bills not covered by insurance) (Coleman, 2002).

Much embezzlement results from the use of computers: Computer technology makes it easier to manipulate books because manipulations are so difficult to detect and trace. Moreover, only about 15 percent of computer embezzlements are ever reported. According to one estimate, the average computer crime nets approximately $500,000, and most computer embezzlement is committed by authorized users, trusted insiders, and skilled employees (Rosoff, Pontell, and Tillman, 2004). The most common method of computer embezzlement is to divert cash into fraudulent accounts. A variation of this method is called "salami slicing," in which many small amounts of numerous private accounts are "sliced off" and diverted to the fraudulent account. Coleman (2002) provides an example of this technique of computer embezzlement:

> [T]wo computer programmers at a large New York garment firm instructed the company computer to increase each employee's income tax withholding by two cents a week and to deposit the money in the programmer's withholding accounts. At the end of the year, the embezzlers planned to receive their profits in the form of refund checks from the Internal Revenue Service. However, those giant-size refunds touched off an IRS investigation that uncovered the crime. (p. 22)

---

**Box 7.1    Collective Embezzlement**

The text identifies embezzlement as a crime committed by employees *against* the company. However, a new type of embezzlement has emerged from the savings and loan scandal, what Kitty Calavita, Henry Pontell, and Robert Tillman (1997) term **collective embezzlement.** This type of embezzlement entails the theft of funds from savings and loan institutions for personal gain, at the expense of the institutions and with the approval of management. In other words, like traditional embezzlement, collective embezzlement is a crime against the company. Yet collective embezzlement differs from traditional embezzlement in that it is endorsed, approved, and accomplished by management itself. It is, in short, "crime *by* the corporation *against* the corporation" (p. 63).

The savings and loan scandal is the most expensive white-collar crime in U.S. history and will likely eventually cost the U.S. government between $300 and $500 billion. Ultimately, U.S. taxpayers are the victims of this crime because the money embezzled did not belong to the embezzlers. The reason that taxpayers are the victims is that in 1980, Congress increased the amount for which the Federal Savings and Loan Insurance Corporation (FSLIC) would insure S&L accounts from a maximum of $40,000 to $100,000 per deposit. Additionally, Congress phased out controls on interest rates. Subsequently, S&Ls raised their interest rates, thus attracting wealthy depositors who did not face any risk of loss; should an S&L fail, the U.S. government (and therefore taxpayers) would reimburse depositors up to $100,000 per deposit. This new opportunity, when combined with the Reagan administration's deregulation policies of "getting government off our backs," created the perfect conditions for this new form of occupational crime.

According to U.S. government reports, crime or misconduct played a crucial role in 70 to 80 percent of the S&Ls bailed. The vast majority of these bailouts were the result of embezzlement. The case of Erwin "Erv" Hansen's "shopping spree," or embezzling S&L funds to finance a lavish lifestyle, is one example of collective embezzlement. Hansen, president of Centennial Savings and Loan in northern California, embezzled S&L funds to purchase such things as antique furniture ($130,000), a penthouse in San Francisco ($773,487), a Mercedes limousine ($77,000), five cars for his family ($90,000), and a $137,000 Rolls Royce for himself. Hansen also gave a Christmas party for his friends based on the theme of a "Renaissance Faire." Couples were "proclaimed" as jesters announced their entry into the hall, which was transformed into an Elizabethan forest of 300 living trees sparkling with 75,000 tiny white lights. Candlelight shimmered through piped-in fog that simulated medieval moors and woods. Oriental rugs covered the floor. Because of this embezzlement, Centennial eventually became insolvent, costing the FSLIC an estimated $160 million.

Other types of collective embezzlement include such group behavior as "land flips," "nominee loans," "reciprocal lending," and "linked financing." A *land flip* is described as follows:

> A sells a parcel of real estate to B for $1 million, its approximate market value. B finances the sale with a bank loan. . . . B sells the property back to A for $2 million. A finances the sale with a bank loan, with the bank relying on a fraudulent appraisal. B repays his original loan and takes $1 million in "profit" off the table, which he shares with A. A defaults on the loan, leaving the bank with a $1 million loss. (p. 49)

Thus, this type of collective embezzlement requires three participants: two people to "flip" the money and a corrupt appraiser.

In the case of *nominee loans*, the owner/officer of an S&L will extend a loan to a "straw borrower"—someone indirectly connected to the S&L—who receives a kickback for obtaining the loan and then returns the remaining money to the lender. One such owner/officer, Don Dixon (owner of all the stock in Vernon S&L in Texas), put together a network of some 30 companies for the purpose of making illegal loans to himself, costing taxpayers approximately $1.3 billion.

*Reciprocal lending* refers to executives from at least two different S&Ls making loans to each other. One investigation in Wyoming revealed a chain of reciprocal loans among four S&Ls that resulted in a $26 million loss to taxpayers.

Finally, *linked financing* involves someone depositing money in a S&L (insured by the FSLIC) under the condition that they receive a loan in return. Subsequently, the loan is defaulted on, the S&L becomes insolvent, and the federal government pays back the deposit because it was insured. Thus, both the depositor and the owner of the S&L make money.

## Occupational Fraud

In Chapter 4.2 we discussed various types of fraud committed against the government and through the use of checks and credit cards. We now discuss two types of occupational fraud—physician fraud and insider trading—committed for direct personal gain in the course of one's occupation.

Most physicians are honest. Some, however, commit **physician fraud** through unnecessary prescription of pharmaceutical drugs, unnecessary surgical procedures, and overtreatment of Medicare and Medicaid patients. Approximately 22 percent of all antibiotic prescriptions in U.S. hospitals are prescribed unnecessarily, and adverse drug reactions result in more than 100,000 hospitalized patient deaths each year (Coleman, 2002). Some physicians even perform unnecessary surgeries, which cost the people of the United States approximately $4 billion annually, and it is estimated that 2.4 million unnecessary surgeries are performed in the United States each year. Moreover, estimated deaths each year from unnecessary surgeries range from 12,000 to 16,000 (Reiman, 2004).

Physician fraud occurs in Medicaid (for the poor) and Medicare (for the elderly) programs, costing an estimated $100 billion a year (Coleman, 2002). When physicians know that medical costs will be paid for the poor and elderly, there seemingly exists much to be gained by fraudulently increasing the amount of medical work performed and doing it at a minimum cost. A prominent example of Medicaid fraud is that of a California ophthalmologist found guilty of performing unnecessary cataract surgery on poor patients to obtain Medicaid fees. For the affluent the surgery was performed skillfully and successfully; for the poor it was performed in "slipshod fashion." In one case the physician totally blinded a 57-year-old woman when he performed unnecessary surgery on her one *sighted* eye (p. 28).

Paul Jesilow, Henry Pontell, and Gilbert Geis (1993) investigated Medicaid fraud in the early 1990s. For their book *Prescription for Profit,* they drew on case file material from California and New York (the two states with the largest number of violators) and found four primary categories of crimes committed by physicians caught violating Medicaid programs:

> (1) billing schemes, which include billing for services not rendered, charging for nonexistent office visits, or receiving or giving kickbacks; (2) poor quality of care, which includes unnecessary tests, treatments, and surgeries as well as inadequate record keeping; (3) illegal distribution of controlled substances, which include drug prescriptions and sales; and (4) sex with patients whereby physicians under the guise of "therapy" received payments for sexual liaisons with their patients. (p. 105)

Psychiatrists constitute a disproportionate share (in relation to other medical specialists) of Medicare and Medicaid fraud. Examples of physician fraud by psychiatrists include charging patients for individual therapy when patients are actually involved in group therapy, charging a fee for "treatment" that is in reality sexual relations between psychiatrist and "patient," and charging for therapy that simply constitutes the prescription of pharmaceutical drugs (Jesilow, Pontell, and Geis, 1993). Moreover, psychiatrists represent approximately 8 percent of all physicians but about 20 percent of all physicians suspended from Medicaid for fraud (Rosoff, Pontell, and Tillman, 2004).

A second type of occupational fraud is insider trading, a form of securities fraud. **Insider trading** occurs when one uses "inside information" (information unavailable to the public) to gain a personal advantage over others in the buying and selling of stock. Individuals obtain such inside information because of their occupational position. For example, if one company plans to take over another, a large number of people are usually involved in the decision-making (lawyers, corporate executives, and others). All these people know that if the takeover occurs, the value of each company's stock will change. Thus, prior to takeover, some of these people may take advantage of their "inside information," using it to buy or sell stock prior to public disclosure. This trading is illegal.

One of the earliest insider trading cases involved the Texas Gulf Sulfur Company. In 1963 large deposits of copper and zinc were discovered by company engineers. Employees with access to this information (prior to public disclosure) abused that privilege to profit personally by buying considerable amounts of the company's stock. The employees were convicted of insider trading; the court concluding that all potential investors should have equal access to this type of information and that company employees—"insiders"—should not have an advantage over the public at large.

Some of the better-known insider trading cases in recent years include the following:

- Paul Thayer, official of LTV Corporation and former deputy secretary of defense, admitted committing insider trading in 1985.

- Thomas Reed, former Reagan national security aide, used inside information to convert a $3,000 stock option into a $427,000 gain in two days.

- Dennis Levine, managing director of Drexel Burnham Lambert (an investment banking firm), and Ivan Boesky, Wall Street's most successful arbitrageur—two of the major actors in an informal 1986 network—exchanged information on mergers, takeovers, and corporate restructurings in order to execute trades prior to public disclosure. It is alleged that Boesky profited more than $50 million and Levine almost $13 million from this insider trading network.

- Part of the Levine/Boesky network was Martin A. Siegel, who sold takeover information to Boesky from August 1982 until February 1986.

- In 1987 it was uncovered that Timothy Tabor (ex-vice-president of Kidder, Peabody), Richard Wigton (Kidder vice-president), and Robert M. Freeman (head of arbitrage at Goldman, Sachs) were also involved in the network, exchanging takeover information that allegedly earned its participants millions of dollars.

- In 1994 it was shown that an investor paid a Keystone mutual fund analyst $700,000 for insider information on the fund's future investments.

- In 1995, a Time Warner employee had advance information that company stock was about to fall in value. Subsequently, this employee sold 20,000 shares of Time Warner stock and avoided $413,700 in losses.

- In 2002, the founder of ImClone Systems, Inc., Sam Waksal, pleaded guilty to insider trading because he provided advance information to several family members that the FDA was about to disapprove for sale a new Imclone cancer drug. Waksal and his family made approximately $10 million through this insider fraud.

The case of Martha Stewart—the "queen of perfection"—who is a friend of Sam Waksal, recently increased public awareness of insider trading. On December 27, 2001, Stewart sold 3,928 shares of ImClone stock at $58 per share, earning $230,000 on the sale. The following day the FDA refused to approve ImClone's application for a new cancer drug, and ImClone's stock immediately dropped to $45 per share. Thus, Stewart had made $51,000 by selling her stock prior to the FDA's report becoming public.

Stewart was originally charged with insider trading because it was alleged that she—like Waksal's family members had received "inside information" that Waksal was planning on selling a portion of his own stock. However, eventually Stewart was not charged with insider trading, but rather of making false statements to investigators and obstruction of justice. In March, 2005, she completed a sentence of five months in a minimum security prison and, as we write, is likely to become even richer and more powerful than she was prior to serving time in prison.

## 7.2 Corporate Crime

We define *corporate crime* as (1) illegal and/or socially injurious acts of intent or indifference (2) that occur for the purpose of furthering the goals of a corporation and (3) that physically and/or economically abuse individuals in the United States and/or abroad. Thus, corporate crime includes not only illegal acts but also socially injurious acts that lie outside the jurisdiction of criminal or regulatory law. Moreover, corporate crime includes harmful acts that result from indifference to the consequences of certain actions as well as from the deliberate intent to harm. By including "indifference," we follow Steven Box (1983), who explained that if

> a person intends doing *someone* harm, it cannot be assumed that s/he displays a disdain towards humanity, although it is clearly directed towards the particular intended victim. However, if indifference characterizes the attitude a person has toward the consequences of his/her action, then s/he is indifferent as to who suffers—it could literally be anybody—and this does display disdain for humanity in general. In this sense, the intent to harm someone may be less immoral (or at least no more immoral) than to be indifferent as to whom is harmed. (p. 21)

Finally, our definition notes that corporations perpetrate violence and theft at home and abroad. Corporate crime victimizes large numbers of people throughout the globe, and it is considerably more harmful and dangerous than the crimes we have already discussed in this and other chapters. We turn now to certain specific types of corporate violence and corporate theft.

### Corporate Violence

In this section we examine **corporate violence** against workers, consumers, and the general public. We begin with workers.

Every year approximately 32,000 workers die from work-related diseases and accidents, and approximately 3.6 million workers suffer new cases of job-related diseases and accidents in the U.S. (Friedrichs, 2004). Some criminologists have argued that workers are injured and die on the job not because of their own carelessness (although this does occur) but rather because of the conditions under which workers must labor, such as production quotas (Reiman, 2004). The organization of the workplace, then, primarily determines possible worker negligence and carelessness. However, we must note that all the preceding figures are based primarily on company reports. Because a company's insurance rating and costs are related to the frequency of injuries, illnesses, and deaths in the workplace, corporations have an incentive to hide accidents.

Consequently, the preceding figures most likely understate the seriousness of corporate violence. Even so, the figures clearly indicate that corporate violence in the workplace exceeds the amount of interpersonal violence in U.S. society. We pointed out in Chapter 5 that we are actually safer in the street than indoors; the evidence presented here suggests that we are safer almost anywhere than the workplace.

An example of corporate violence caused by the intentional violation of safety standards is the case of Film Recovery Systems, Inc. (Frank and Lynch, 1992). Workers at the Film Recovery plant who worked around cyanide—poisonous if swallowed, inhaled, or absorbed through the skin—were not protected with adequate equipment (gloves, boots, aprons, and so on) and effective ventilation. In fact, the plant air was thick with an odorous "yellow haze" of cyanide fumes. On February 10, 1985, Stephen Golab, a worker at the plant, collapsed on the plant floor and died. During the autopsy, when the

> medical examiner made the first incision, a strong almond-like smell came out of the body, indicating cyanide poisoning. Subsequent blood tests revealed that Golab had a blood cyanide level of 3.45 micrograms per milliliter, a lethal dose. (p. 22)

Three executives of Film Recovery were eventually convicted of murder and 14 counts of reckless conduct. The conviction of the Film Recovery executives was the first of its kind in this country. Moreover, state courts have upheld the principle that employers can be criminally prosecuted for unsafe working conditions (Friedrichs, 2004).

In a more recent case, McWane, Inc., a large Alabama-based sewer and water pipe manufacturer, maintained unsafe working conditions for years that resulted in the death of nine workers and more than 4,600 injuries since 1995 (Mokhiber and Weissman, 2004). For example, one worker died when "an industrial oven exploded after he was directed to use it to incinerate highly combustible paint" and another "was crushed by a conveyor belt that lacked a required protective guard" (p. 19). Although McWane, Inc. had been cited for 400 safety violations and 450 environmental violations since 1995, it only had to pay a fine of $500,000, and no McWane executives have been charged with murder.

Corporations also continue to expose workers to dangers, such as the "silent killers." Workers are sometimes victims of corporate violence simply because they hold a job with a company that does not adequately protect them from such dangerous substances as asbestos fibers, cotton dust, and chemical compounds. Asbestos, for example, was a suspected "silent killer" as early as 1918 when a number of life insurance companies disallowed policies to asbestos workers because of their high death rate (Epstein, 1978). In the 1950s a connection between asbestos and lung cancer was found by British epidemiologist Richard Doll. The asbestos industry funded eleven studies in an attempt to rebut this link; however, fifty-two independent studies found asbestos to pose a major threat to human health (Coleman, 2002). For decades asbestos producers hid from workers and the public the known dangers of the product, which has resulted in 100,000 deaths each year from asbestos-related disease and the medical costs for asbestos-related disease over the next 25 years is expected to reach $500 billion (Bowker, 2003). As sociologist James Coleman (2002) stated: "Such evidence suggests that the asbestos industry knowingly perpetrated a massive fraud on its workers and on the public" (p. 72).

Finally, countless asbestos victims exist who have not had direct connection to its production, such as spouses who wash asbestos-laden clothes (Rosoff, Pontell, and Tillman, 2004).

Other examples of corporations concealing the dangers of "silent killers" abound. Since at least the 1960s medical studies have shown that byssinosis (or brown lung disease) is a severe health problem for textile workers; yet the textile industry remains insensitive to worker health (some 85,000 textile workers suffer impaired breathing due to acute byssinosis) (Mokhiber, 1999). By the early 2000s textile workers continued to offer detailed testimony on the extreme levels of cotton dust that fills the mills (Friedrichs, 2004). Also, in the 1960s, the chemical industry knew of research indicating that vinyl chloride is linked to a degenerative bone condition, acroosteolysis, as well as a rare form of cancer, angiosarcoma, in workers exposed to the chemical. To keep this information concealed from workers and the public, chemical companies signed a joint secrecy agreement not to publicly reveal the conclusions of the research (Markowitz and Rosner, 2002).

As consumers, we are also subject to victimization from corporate violence. According to the National Commission on Product Safety, 20 million U.S. citizens have suffered injuries from using unsafe products, in which 110,000 are permanently disabled and 30,000 die from the injuries (Simon, 2002b).

The case of the Dalkon Shield, an IUD, is a telling example. The Dalkon Shield was manufactured, promoted, and marketed in the face of company files containing several hundred negative reports from physicians and others about its safety. Although these reports represented firm evidence linking the Dalkon Shield with 75 cases of uterine perforation, ectopic pregnancies, and at least 17 deaths, they were never made public (Braithwaite, 1984). Approximately 2.86 million Dalkon Shields were distributed in the United States, and the vast majority of women who used this IUD developed the dangerous infection known as pelvic inflammatory disease (Mintz, 1985).

Myriad products—from hazardous toys to dangerous automobiles—have been found harmful to consumers. A horrific example of corporate violence against youthful consumers is the drug thalidomide that was marketed as a safe treatment for "morning sickness" during the early stages of pregnancy. Approximately 8,000 pregnant women who took the prescription drug gave birth to terribly deformed babies. The corporation that patented and distributed the drug deliberately falsified test data and concealed the facts about the drug's serious side effects.

Production of an unsafe automobile, the Ford Pinto, is a notorious illustration of corporate violence against consumers. As David Simon (2002) points out, Ford knew that this car had a defective gasoline tank that would ignite even in low-speed rear-end collisions, yet the company "reasoned that 180 burn deaths, 180 serious burn injuries, and 2,100 burned vehicles would cost $49.5 million (each death was figured at $200,000). But doing a recall of all Pintos and making each $11 repair would amount to $137 million" (p. 123). It is reported that as many as 900 burn deaths occurred as a result of the exploding Pinto (Dowie, 1977).

In the early 1970s the Firestone 500 steel-belted radial tire was produced and sold, and throughout that decade the company continued to receive evidence of the tire's danger to motorists. It was plagued with sudden blowouts and the separation of its tread from the steel-belted inner layer. Although the tire had been linked to thousands of automobile accidents and at least 41 deaths, Firestone was fined $50,000 (Simon, 2002b).

In the 1990s, Ford was accused of legal responsibility for deaths resulting from "rollovers" by their Bronco II's, and General Motors was found liable for gas tank defects in some of their pickup trucks (Friedrichs, 2004). Moreover, in the same decade it became known that the tobacco industry had committed a horrendous fraud on consumers by (1) hiding unfavorable research indicating that nicotine is an addicting drug, (2) hiding their own studies indicating that smoking causes lung cancer and heart disease, (3) manipulating the nicotine level in cigarettes to make sure each "smoke" had enough nicotine to keep smokers hooked, and (4) creating covert campaigns to addict teenagers to nicotine in order to create lifetime smokers. The percentage of high school students who smoke now exceeds the percentage of smokers in the adult population (Rosoff, Pontell, and Tillman, 2004).

We turn now to a discussion of violence against the general public, not only specific consumers. Corporate pollution provides an easy illustration of this type of corporate crime. The case of Love Canal is no doubt the most familiar. From the late 1930s until 1953, Hooker Chemical Company dumped hundreds of tons of toxic waste into the abandoned Love Canal, near Niagara Falls, New York (Tallmer, 1987). In 1953, Hooker sold the dump site to the local school board, which in turn sold it to a private developer. The canal was filled in, and eventually houses were built on top of the chemical dump. Some 20 years later, "as leaching wastes began to be linked to miscarriages, birth defects, and other ailments, more than 200 families fled their homes" (p. 113).

U.S. corporations produce approximately 292 million tons of toxic waste each year, and the Environmental Protection Agency (EPA) estimates that 90 percent of this waste is disposed of improperly. Thus, Love Canal is not unique. In Times Beach, Missouri, the EPA found dioxin levels 100 times those considered safe, forcing the federal government to purchase the entire town and move the people out.

Probably the worst hazardous waste condition in the United States—more serious than Love Canal and Times Beach—is, as Russell (1988) reported, the chemical contamination of a small Arkansas community, Jacksonville, referred to by local residents as "Dioxinville." Approximately 20 chemicals have been found in Jacksonville's air, 12 of which were also found in the Love Canal area. But the major problem in Jacksonville is dioxin, one of the most lethal substances ever produced. Dioxin has been found to cause cancer and fetus-malforming effects in animals at concentrations as low as 10 to 100 parts per trillion; the EPA considers dioxin dangerous to humans when it measures one part per billion. As Russell pointed out, just "one part per million is therefore 1,000 times more toxic. In Jacksonville, dioxin was measured . . . at concentrations as high as 111 parts per million," or 111,000 times as toxic as the EPA danger level (p. 9).

Jacksonville is contaminated with at least 30,000 barrels containing dioxin waste. From 1946 to 1957, Reasor-Hill Chemical Corporation buried drums of chemical waste in an open field near its plant in Jacksonville. In 1961 the plant was acquired by the Hercules Chemical Corporation, which continued to bury drums of chemical waste and began discharging processed wastewater—from production of chlordane and Agent Orange—into a nearby creek. By 1979 it became known that the plant and surrounding area were contaminated with dioxin. Today, dangerous levels of dioxin (higher than one part per billion) have been found in soil samples (taken from residents' yards), as well as in the air, the city sewer system and lagoons, the sediments of the nearby floodplain, and fish and wood ducks (Russell, 1988).

This disaster could have been avoided. Dow Chemical Company knew as far back as 1965 about the dangers of dioxin. As Green and Berry (1985a) reported:

One memorandum from Dow's toxicology director warned then (1965) that the chemical could be "exceptionally toxic"; the company's medical director said that dioxin-related "fatalities have been reported in the literature." Dow's response was to discuss these problems with its competitors at a March meeting, but not to inform the government or public because the situation might "explode" and spur more federal regulation of the chemical industry. (p. 263)

Dow's cover-up contributed to the violence at Love Canal, Times Beach, and Jacksonville. Yet the story of hazardous waste does not end here. More recently, it has been estimated that approximately 30,000 waste sites pose significant health problems related to water contamination, and in Ponca City, Oklahoma, families were paid $40,000 to evacuate the town because of water contamination (Rosoff, Pontell, and Tillman, 2004).

Contaminated drinking water is only a tip of the corporate violence iceberg. As Jodi Seager (1993) noted, American chemical companies admitted that they annually leak or vent 196 "extremely hazardous" compounds into the air. The EPA cautiously estimates that as few as 15 to 45 of the hundreds of released air toxins directly cause up to 1,700 cases of cancer each year. American industry alone generates annually 280 million tons of lethal garbage and 10.3 billion pounds of toxic chemicals that are spewed each year into the air,

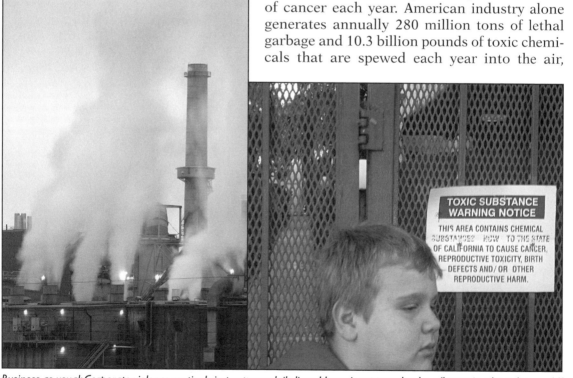

*Business as usual: Corporate violence routinely impacts our daily lives. Home is supposed to be a 'haven in a heartless world,' yet for many people—especially those of the working class—corporate violence invades their shelter.*

discharged into public waters, and flushed into the sewers—enough to fill 8,000 Love Canals. Some recent examples of violence against the public are provided by Simon (2002):

- The Louisiana-Pacific Corporation was fined $37 million and convicted of 18 felony counts, including conspiring to violate the Clean Air Act, lying to the Colorado Department of Public Health, and submitting nonrepresentative samples to the American Plywood Association.

- The Colonial Pipeline Company was fined $7 million after pleading guilty to spilling 1 million gallons of oil into the Reedy River in South Carolina, killing approximately 35,000 fish.

- Royal Caribbean cruise line was fined $18 million for dumping oil and other hazardous wastes (some mixed with ordinary garbage) into U.S. harbors and coastal areas.

## Corporate Theft

**Corporate theft** is similar to other forms of theft—in the sense that property is taken from people—yet it is significantly different, primarily because it does not entail a face-to-face confrontation and it is not easily apparent that a crime has been committed. Three of the most costly and prevalent forms of corporate theft are deceptive advertising, financial fraud, and price-fixing. We look briefly at each.

According to the Federal Trade Commission Act, **deceptive advertising** occurs when advertisements are "misleading in a material respect" (Coleman, 2002: 24). This means that advertising can in fact be false, as long as it is not deceptive. In other words, it is illegal for advertising to be both false and deceptive, or just simply deceptive. When Jell-O claims that "every kid in America loves Jell-O brand gelatin," that is clearly making a false statement. However, exaggerated claims (hype) such as this have been interpreted by the courts as not deceptive because it is believed that no reasonable person would take the statement seriously. Nevertheless, many corporations have simultaneously lied and deceived for decades. For example, Anacin was found to be the subject of deceptive advertising in that its manufacturer claimed that Anacin (Simon and Eitzen, 1986:88):

- Relieved nervousness, tension, stress, fatigue, and depression.

- Was stronger than aspirin.

- Brought relief within 22 seconds.

- Was highly recommended over aspirin by physicians.

- Was more effective for relieving pain than any other analgesic available without prescription.

Moreover, corporations have also violated the law by engaging in deception without outright lying. For example, the bottom of a bowl of Campbell's "chunky style" soup used in a TV commercial was lined with marbles, creating the illusion that the soup was much thicker and chunkier than it actually was (Coleman, 2002).

More recent cases include the following (Mokhiber and Weissman, 2004; Rosoff, Pontell, and Tillman, 2004):

- The Home Shopping Network was fined $1.1 million by the Federal Trade Commission for advertisements making unsubstantiated claims for skin care, weight loss, and PMS/menopause products.

- The manufacturer of No Nonsense Pantyhose was penalized for wrongly claiming that its hosiery was virtually indestructible.

- The Federal Trade Commission obtained a settlement agreement from Jenny Craig, Inc., in response to charges of deceptive advertising regarding Jenny Craig diet program's claims about weight loss, price, and safety.

- Providian Financial, one of the largest credit card issuers in the United States, agreed to pay $300 million to consumers for its deceptive advertisements promising lower rates on balance transfers when in fact they were higher.

- The Federal Trade Commission charged Kentucky Fried Chicken with making false claims that its fried chicken is both nutritious and compatible with certain weight-loss programs. Kentucky Fried Chicken stated in advertisements that Original Recipe fried chicken breasts are better for consumers' health than eating a Burger King Whopper, even though the chicken breasts have three times the trans fat and cholesterol and twice the sodium.

Corporate executives can engage in a form of fraud that serves the interests of the corporation, **financial fraud**. Such was the case with the firm E. F. Hutton and Company. Hutton officials pleaded guilty in 1985 to defrauding some 400 banks by writing checks in excess of amounts it had on deposit. Hutton officials then moved funds—to cover these amounts—from one bank to another, thereby avoiding overdrafts. In effect, what Hutton officials did was simply provide the company with interest-free loans (Nash, 1985; Claybrook, 1986). As Cullen, Maakestad, and Cavender (1987) pointed out, the entire "operation involved nearly $10 billion; on some days the company enjoyed $250 million in illegal 'loans' " (p. 56).

In 1988, E. F. Hutton pleaded guilty to two felony counts of laundering hundreds of thousands of dollars for criminal syndicate figures and businesspeople seeking to evade payment of taxes. According to the *Washington Post*, investigators found that "customers would bring suitcases full of cash to Hutton brokers," who would then transfer the money to secret overseas bank accounts (Kurtz, 1988:A3).

Both financial institutions and criminal syndicates profit from money laundering. It is against the law not to report cash transactions in excess of $10,000. Financial institutions evade this required federal disclosure by fraudulently converting large amounts of cash (sometimes provided by criminal syndicates) into bonds worth $9,999 or less, or they secretly launder it in foreign bank accounts. Financial institutions are attracted to obtaining money from criminal syndicates because large sums of money can be used for future investments or interest-earning loans. As pointed out in Chapter 6, criminal syndicates benefit from money laundering because, in essence, this process changes "dirty" money into "clean" money.

A recent example of financial fraud involves the now infamous Enron Corporation. Enron was formed in 1985 and quickly became the seventh-largest corporation in the United States. As an energy company involved in trading gas and electricity stock, Enron eventually found its profits squeezed from competing trading operations. After numerous years of complicated deals in an attempt to stay afloat, Enron was billions of dollars in debt. The entire debt, however, was concealed from shareholders by pumping up reported earnings and creating secret partnerships that "had the effect of grossly dis-

torting the relationship between Enron's assets and profits and its losses and debt" (Friedrichs, 2004: 80). The fraud was not revealed to the public until October 2001 when Enron announced that the company was actually worth $1.2 billion less than previously reported; as a result, in December of the same year, Enron filed for bankruptcy. Consequently, large numbers of Enron employees lost billions of dollars in retirement savings because their retirement accounts had been invested in Enron stock. Moreover, although

*Corporate theft: At one point vaunted as a model for American businesses of the future, instead Enron was artificially inflating profits, illegally manipulating U.S. energy markets, and lying to stockholders and its employees.*

employees knew Enron stock was drastically dropping in value, Enron executives prohibited them from withdrawing their retirement funds. At the same time, as Rosoff, Pontell, and Tillman (2004) point out, these same executives "literally made out like bandits." Indeed, 29 executives at Enron sold $1.1 billion worth of stock, including the major fraudsters: Andrew Fastow sold stock worth $23 million, Jeff Skilling sold his holdings for $67 million, and Kenneth Lay earned $146 million from options trades.

The case of Enron was only the beginning of a "corporate crime wave" that introduced the twenty-first century—Arthur Andersen & Company (a top accounting firm in the world), WorldCom (a large telecommunications company), Adelphia (a large cable company), Global Crossing (an international fiber-optic cable company), Qwest Communications (a long-distance telephone company), and Halliburton (an energy servicing company), are just a few of the corporations that have been implicated—but their cases unresolved at this writing—in various forms of financial fraud.

Finally, corporate theft may result in tremendous costs to unsuspecting taxpayers. For example, Wal-Mart has a notorious reputation for paying workers relatively low wages and inadequate benefits. Such practices harm workers directly but simultaneously indirectly harm taxpayers (Mokhiber and Weissman, 2004). As Mokhiber and Weissman point out, a 200-person Wal-Mart store costs taxpayers approximately $420,750 per year, or about $2,103 per employee, including:

- $36,000 a year for free and reduced lunches for just 50 qualifying Wal-Mart families.

- $42,000 a year for Section 8 housing assistance, assuming 3 percent of the store employees qualify for such assistance, at $6,700 per family.

- $125,000 a year for federal tax credits and deductions for low-income families, assuming 50 employees are heads of household with a child and 50 are married with two children.

- $100,000 a year for additional Title I [educational] expenses, assuming 50 Wal-Mart families qualify with an average of two children.

- $108,000 a year for the additional federal health-care costs of moving into state children's health insurance programs (S-CHIP), assuming 30 employees with an average of two children qualify.

In other words, corporations engage in a hidden form of theft that imposes costs on communities and taxpayers.

**Price-fixing** is probably the most expensive form of corporate theft. The basic purpose of antitrust laws is to impede corporations from colluding to fix prices (price-fixing) by ensuring that competition keeps prices as low as possible. Profits above those that would be produced in a competitive industry are illegal. Probably the most famous price-fixing incident is the case of Heavy Electrical Equipment, in which 29 corporations—including General Electric and Westinghouse—conspired to fix prices, primarily on government contracts (Green, Moore, and Wasserstein, 1972; Pearce, 1976). The illegal costs paid by purchasers of the electrical equipment in this case alone totaled $1.75 billion per year for seven years (Hills, 1987).

Recent cases of price-fixing indicate that this crime is widespread, occurring in such diverse industries as steel, glass, natural gas, infant formula, commercial explosives, athletic shoes, residential doors, scouring pads, plastic dinnerware, video games, white bread, and Passover matzo (Rosoff, Pontell, and Tillman, 2004). Some specific cases include the following (Friedrichs, 2004; Mokhiber and Weissman, 2004):

- Archer Daniels Midland Corporation paid a $100 million fine for fixing prices on feed additives, an illegal activity driving up prices of processed foods, soft drinks, detergents, and other widely consumed products.

- Two drug companies, Hoffman-LaRoche and BASF, were fined $752 million for fixing prices on vitamins.

- Nintendo, the video game maker, was fined $147 million for fixing prices on its products.

- Bayer agreed to pay the Federal Trade Commission $66 million to settle a price-fixing case related to chemicals used to make rubber.

## 7.3 Transnational Corporate Crime

Transnationals—large corporations that maintain business operations in more than one country—are a major factor in globalization. Because of advances in communication and transportation technology, as well as the establishment of "free" trade agreements (such as the Osaka Declaration and the North American Free Trade Agreement), transnationals have been able to accelerate the movement of capital over vast distances. Indeed, transnationals account for two-thirds of all world trade (Waters, 2001), and as Sarah Anderson and John Cavanagh (2000) have documented, transnationals—especially those based in the United States—are the key players of the global economy:

- Of the 100 largest economies in the world, 51 are now transnational corporations; only 49 are countries.

- The combined sales of the world's top 200 corporations are far greater than a quarter of the world's economic activity.

- The top 200 corporations' combined sales are greater than the combined economies of all countries minus the largest nine; that is, they surpass the combined economies of 182 countries.

- U.S. transnational corporations dominate the top 200 list, with 82 slots, or 41 percent of the total.

By 1975 three-fourths of all U.S. companies with sales over 100 million dollars had manufacturing facilities in other countries (Michalowski and Kramer, 1987). By 1977 developing nations had surpassed developed ones in dollar value as locations for manufacturing by U.S. industries. Re-importation of overseas assembly by U.S. companies increased fivefold between 1969 and 1983, and in the textiles and electronics industries more than half of all sales in the mid-1980s by U.S. corporations were assembled abroad. Transnationals expanded dramatically throughout the 1990s, so that by early in the twenty-first century few societies could claim isolation from the touch of transnational corporations.

A major aspect of this transnational global reach is transnational corporate crime. Indeed, criminologists have known since the early 1980s that transnational corporations are the worst corporate offenders. In one comprehensive study of corporate crime, Clinard and Yeager (1980) found that small corporations (annual sales of $300–499 million) accounted for only 10 percent of corporate violations, and medium-sized corporations (annual sales of $500–999 million) for 20 percent; however, large corporations (annual sales of $1 billion or more) accounted for almost 75 percent of all violations. Moreover, large corporations accounted for 72.1 percent of the serious and 62.8 percent of the moderately serious violations. Of the 15 largest corporations in the world in 1978 (the time of Clinard and Yeager's study), three were car manufacturers, eight were oil companies, and one was a chemical producer. The largest corporations, then, are the worst offenders in view of Clinard and Yeager's finding that "the oil, pharmaceutical, and motor vehicle industries" are the "most likely" to commit corporate crime (p. 119). Subsequent studies have likewise found that the largest corporations are the worst corporate offenders (Rosoff, Pontell, and Tillman, 2004). Indeed, it is the oil, auto, and chemical corporations that continue to dominate the top 200 transnational list (Anderson and Cavanagh, 2000).

Although transnationals are a *global* phenomenon, the most harmful consequences of transnational actions are found at the *local* level, victimizing real people and real environments far removed from U.S. society. Let us then turn to three major types of transnational corporate crime: bribery, the export of hazardous products, and the relocation of dangerous working conditions.

## Bribery

The transnational nature of U.S. corporations has resulted in considerable Third World corporate crime, ranging from bribery to export of hazardous products to dangerous working conditions. Regarding bribery, one study of 34 U.S. transnational corporations that admitted paying overseas bribes found that the bribes totaled $93.7 million and that the resulting sales revenues amounted to $679 billion (Coleman, 2002). As Coleman points out, "The bribe money constituted only 0.014 percent of the sales of those companies" (p. 41).

Because of the enormous volume of bribery, in 1977 Congress enacted the Foreign Corrupt Practices Act, which attempted to prevent such conduct. Yet transnational bribery continues. For example, in 1984 the Justice Department investigated the Bechtel Group for bid rigging and for illegal payments to a South Korean utility company that was awarding contracts for nuclear plant construction. The media continues to report violations of the Foreign Corrupt Practices Act (Simon, 2002b).

Bribery is profitable for transnationals and the political elites in Third World countries, yet it perpetrates serious harm on a good portion of the rest of the people in these countries. Braithwaite (1979a) convincingly argued that transnational bribery is one of the most destructive and injurious crimes today because of its unequal and antidemocratic consequences:

> When a government official in a Third World country recommends (under the influence of a bribe) that his country purchase the more expensive but less adequate of two types of aircraft, then the extra millions of dollars will be found from the taxes sweated out of the country's impoverished citizens. For a mass consumer product, the million dollar bribe to the civil servant will be passed on in higher prices to the consuming public. Although it is conceivable that bribes can be used to secure the sale of a better and cheaper product, the more general effect is to shift the balance of business away from the most efficient producer and in favor of the most corrupt producer. The whole purpose of business-government bribes is, after all, the inegalitarian purpose of enticing governments to act against the public interest and in the interest of the transnational. (p. 126)

## Dumping

Transnational corporations are also involved in "dumping" on other countries certain hazardous products banned or not approved for sale in the United States. U.S.-based transnationals frequently sell to other nations defective medical devices, lethal drugs, known carcinogens, toxic pesticides, contaminated foods, and other products ruled unfit for use and/or consumption in the United States. For example, the contraceptive Depo-Provera—banned in the United States because of its severe effects—was dumped in 70 foreign countries, especially in the Third World (Simon, 2002b).

A. H. Robbins dumped approximately 1.71 million Dalkon Shields in 40 foreign countries (Mintz, 1985), and the Agency for International Development (AID) purchased approximately 700,000 Dalkon Shields for distribution in the Third World (Mintz, 1986). These IUDs were sold by Robbins to the Agency for International Development at a 48 percent discount and were packaged *unsterilized* (Braithwaite, 1984). They were then distributed by AID to a variety of countries in Africa, Asia, the Middle East, the Caribbean, and Central and South America, where medical techniques are mostly underdeveloped and consumer protection laws are practically nonexistent. Obviously, tens of thousands of women worldwide have been victimized by this corporate crime, especially once we consider the fact that the Dalkon Shield "is still in common use in some countries" (Simon, 2002b: 175).

Corporations also dump chemicals, such as pesticides, on foreign markets. For example, DDT—a pesticide banned in the United States—in the mid-1980s was being sold particularly in Central and South America, only to return home on such imported food as bananas and coffee (Asinoff, 1985). Overall, more than 150 million pounds of "blacklisted" products worth up to $800 million are dumped each year, representing approximately 25 percent of U.S. pesticide production (Simon, 2002b).

---

### Box 7.2    Bhopal—1984 and Beyond

In 1984, Union Carbide Corporation (UCC) was one of the largest chemical transnational corporations in the world. Based in Danbury, Connecticut, UCC operated numerous chemical plants around the globe. These plants manufactured and processed chemicals to produce pesticides, insecticides, and other consumer products (Doyle, 2004).

One of the plants owned by UCC was constructed in Bhopal, India, in 1980 to produce a highly toxic chemical—methyl iso-cyanate (MIC)—for use in UCC's various products. The plant produced substantially more MIC than it could immediately process, so UCC installed bulk-storage tanks in the Bhopal plant. However, there existed critical differences in the design for the safety standards for UCC plants in the United States and UCC plants elsewhere. The table below compares the safety measures realized in two UCC plants, one in Institute, West Virginia, and the other in Bhopal, India. In particular, storing MIC in large tanks for long periods of time, coupled with inadequate investment in safety measures—such as no emergency scrubbers to neutralize leaks, inappropriate cooling systems, and a lack of continued refrigeration—increased the possibility of a toxic leak occurring.

| Institute, West Virginia, USA | Bhopal, Madhya Pradesh, India |
|---|---|
| Capacity ||
| High production of MIC matched with high processing capacity. MIC not stored for long periods of time. | High production capacity of MIC but low processing capacity. MIC stored in large quantities for long periods of time. |

| Institute, West Virginia, USA | Bhopal, Madhya Pradesh, India |
|---|---|
| **Emergency Scrubbers** | |
| MIC storage tank equipped with emergency scrubbers (to neutralize any escaping MIC) designed to operate under emergency conditions. | No emergency caustic scrubber to neutralize any MIC leak. |
| **Computerized Monitoring** | |
| Computerized monitoring of instruments (gauges, alarms, etc.) and processes to support visual observation. | No computerized monitoring of instruments and processes. Relied solely on manual observation. |
| **Cooling System** | |
| MIC field storage tanks used a cooling system based on chloroform (inert and nonreactive with MIC). | MIC tanks used a cooling system based on brine (highly reactive with MIC). |
| **Refrigeration Unit** | |
| Refrigeration unit to control temperature in the tanks was never turned off. | Refrigeration unit had been turned off since June 1984. |
| **Nitrogen Pressure** | |
| MIC was always maintained under nitrogen pressure. | MIC tanks had not been under nitrogen pressure since October 1984. |
| **Emergency Plan** | |
| An elaborate four-stage emergency plan to deal with toxic releases, fires, etc., including a general public alert linked to community police, river and rail traffic, and local radio stations. Various emergency broadcast systems in place to alert and disseminate appropriate information to the public. | No system to inform public authorities or the people living adjacent to the plant. No emergency plan shared with communities living adjacent to the plant; no system to disseminate information regarding emergency to the public with the exception of a loud siren. |
| **Maintenance Program** | |
| A maintenance program to determine and evaluate replacement frequency for valves and instrumentation and alarm systems. Weekly review of safety valves and reviews and maintenance recorded extensively. | No evidence of an effective instrument maintenance program. Safety valve testing program largely ineffective and no proper records maintained of reviews of instruments, valves and alarm systems, etc. |
| **Lab Analysis** | |
| A lab analysis of MIC was conducted to test quality and check for contamination prior to storage, processing, or distribution. | No lab analysis of quality was undertaken. MIC stored for long periods without testing for contamination. |
| **Training** | |
| Extensive employee training program to ensure high level of training and information among all employees of normal and emergency procedures. | Operators put in charge without sufficient training. |
| **Protective Equipment** | |
| Extensive provision of appropriate personal protective equipment to employees, including protective clothing, air respirators, etc. | Personal protective gear and breathing air equipment not easily accessible, inadequate, and of poor quality. |

Source: © Amnesty International, 2004:46–47.

In addition to poor safety measures, UCC management ignored warnings of ongoing safety problems at the Bhopal plant. For example, from 1982–1984 occupational safety survey teams from UCC headquarters in the United States warned management numerous times of the potential release of toxic substances at the Bhopal plant—such as MIC—because of equipment failures, operating and maintenance problems, and deficiencies in safety valves. No measures were taken by management to confront these safety issues, and UCC failed to implement an emergency plan in Bhopal to warn the community about leaks, even though it had such a plan in place in the United States (Amnesty International, 2004).

On December 2, 1984, the predicted nightmare occurred: An estimated 54,000 pounds of deadly MIC—together with 26,000 pounds of reaction products—silently leaked out of one of the tanks, killing close to 8,000 Bhopal residents within three days of the leak. Between 1985 and 2003 an estimated additional 15,000 people died because of the gas leak, and exposure to the toxin has resulted in chronic, debilitating illnesses for at least 120,000 people for whom treatment has proved largely ineffective (Amnesty International, 2004).

In response to the crime, UCC blamed India's "cultural backwardness" for the gas leak (Pearce and Tombs, 1999). This is an astonishing and racist claim given the fact that, as Pearce and Tombs rightly point out, UCC "possessed" the Bhopal plant in the sense that the parent company (1) dictated how and which chemicals were produced and stored, (2) monitored safety procedures at the plant, and (3) had the right to intervene if safety was ever affected. In short, UCC management is "responsible for both acts of commission and omission that created the Bhopal disaster" (p. 205).

The victims of this transnational corporate crime await just compensation and adequate medical assistance. The plant site has not been cleaned up, toxic waste continues to pollute the environment and the drinking water, and no one associated with UCC has ever been held responsible for the crime (Amnesty International, 2004).

## Dangerous Working Conditions

Transnationals have also—in addition to bribery and dumping—relocated dangerous working conditions to other countries. Transnationals search for areas of the world where pollution controls and worker safety regulations are minimal or nonexistent. For example, in the United States it is now illegal to expose workers to carcinogenic agents such as asbestos. However, in Mexico, the "law merely provides a light fine ($45 to $90) for the failure to warn workers that they are working around a health hazard" (Simon, 2002b:177). Consequently, U.S. asbestos makers have increasingly relocated plants to Mexico and other Third World countries where little control exists over workplace hazards.

Additionally, Mexico provides a good example of the harmful consequences of relocating dangerous polluting plants. Indeed, the U.S.-Mexico border has become "a two-thousand-mile Love Canal":

These plants have filled the sky and water with a staggering amount of chemical pollution. With this contamination have come all the accompanying human miseries. A disturbing pattern of deformities and mental retardation has been observed among children of this area. Their mothers had all worked in the *maquiladoras* zone [border area where U.S. companies invest] and had been exposed to toxic chemicals. (Rosoff, Pontell, and Tillman, 2004:158)

Economists have argued that the North American Free Trade Agreement (NAFTA), signed by Canada, the United States, and Mexico in 1994, has accelerated the trend toward expansion of the Mexican *maquiladora* industrial sector. Whereas the U.S. economy has lost approximately 450,000 jobs since the signing of NAFTA, foreign direct investment rose 64 percent in 1994, the first year after NAFTA's activation. This investment resulted in approximately 750,000 Mexican workers employed in some 2,500 export *maquiladora* plants (Burgoon, 1996). Moreover, a study of the effects of NAFTA on Mexico 10 years after its implementation found, for example: (1) 1.5 million Mexican farm livelihoods were destroyed because cheap U.S. corn was "dumped" in Mexico, (2) migration to the United States more than doubled because of low-paying jobs (i.e., the average wage in Mexico for manufacturing workers actually *declined* from $5.00 to $4.00 per day following NAFTA), (3) migration to the "maquila zones" has likewise doubled, overwhelming the outdated sewage systems and resulting in dramatic contamination of drinking water (i.e., hepatitis A infection rates in the "maquila zones" is more than double the national rate), and (4) increasing industrialization in the "maquila zones" has massively intensified toxic dumping (i.e., rates of birth defects and lupus in these zones have doubled) (Public Citizen, 2004).

## Review

This chapter examined various types of white-collar crime—occupational crime, corporate crime, and transnational corporate crime. These crimes are similar to crimes previously discussed because they also entail theft and violence. However, they differ from other crimes because (1) they cause far greater victimization and (2) the victimization they produce is less apparent.

### Occupational Crime

1. There are two major types of occupational crime: theft and fraud. Occupational theft includes employee theft and embezzlement, which differ in what is stolen—merchandise and job-related items or money, respectively.

2. Employee theft and embezzlement—two of the most costly crimes in the United States—occur in different ways depending on the type of job, and they range from simply stealing merchandise to "taking from the till" and "manipulating the books" to collective embezzlement.

3. Two types of occupational fraud are physician fraud and insider trading. The former occurs through prescription of pharmaceutical drugs, surgical procedures, and treating Medicare and Medicaid patients. Insider trading results when "insiders" gain special advantage in the buying and selling of stock.

### Corporate Crime

1. Corporate violence causes considerable worker illness, injury, and death; corporations also perpetrate violence on consumers and the general public.

2. Three of the most costly and prevalent forms of corporate theft are deceptive advertising, financial fraud, and price-fixing.

## Transnational Corporate Crime

1. Transnational corporations are the worst corporate offenders.

2. Three of the most costly and prevalent forms of transnational corporate crime are bribery, dumping, and relocating dangerous working conditions.

## Questions for Class Discussion

1. Why is it valuable to study white-collar crime?

2. How do various types of work help determine specific types of occupational theft? How do the arguments of Ditton and of Mars relate to your own job? Your parents' jobs?

3. Describe how corporate violence and theft differ from the types of violence and theft discussed in Chapters 4 and 5.

4. Discuss the differences and similarities between transnational corporate crime and the other types of white-collar crime examined in this chapter.

5. Are there other forms of white-collar crime not covered in this chapter? Would they fit into one of the three categories identified here?

## For Further Study

### Readings

Doyle, Jack. 2004. *Trespass Against Us: Dow Chemical and the Toxic Century.* Monroe, ME: Common Courage Press.

Friedrichs, David O. 2004. *Trusted Criminals: White-Collar Crime in Contemporary Society.* Belmont, CA: Wadsworth.

Markowitz, Gerald, and David Rosner. 2002. *Deceit and Denial: The Deadly Politics of Industrial Pollution.* Berkeley: University of California Press.

Pearce, Frank, and Steve Tombs. 1999. *Toxic Capitalism: Corporate Crime and the Chemical Industry.* Toronto: Canadian Scholars' Press.

Rosoff, Stephen M., Henry N. Pontell, and Robert Tillman. 2004. *Profit Without Honor: White-Collar Crime and the Looting of America.* Upper Saddle River, NJ: Prentice Hall.

## Websites

1. <http://www.citizen.org/trade>: This site provides valuable information on corporate globalization and its effects on health and safety, environmental protection, economic justice, and democratic, accountable governance in selected countries.

2. <http://www.osha.gov/oshstats/work.html>: From the Occupational Safety and Health Administration, this site provides current statistics on workplace deaths and injuries. It should be kept in mind that these are conservative estimates from the Bureau of Labor Statistics.

3. <http://www.natlconsumersleague.org>: The National Consumers' League compiles recent information on consumer fraud.

4. <http://www.pirg.org>: Public Interest Research Groups are nonprofit organizations that monitor the safety of consumer products. This site offers PIRG reports on child deaths from unsafe toys as well as some deadly consequences of illegal dumping of toxic chemicals. Readers may be interested to find out the contact information for the PIRG in their own state.

5. <http://www.multinationalmonitor.org>: This site is an online magazine, Multinational Monitor, which has articles documenting cases of corporate crime. Every year the magazine announces its 10 worst corporations of that year. ✦

# Political Crime

## 8.1 Political Crimes Against the State
- Violent Political Crimes Against the State
- Nonviolent Political Crimes Against the State

## 8.2 Domestic Political Crimes by the State
- State Corruption
- State Political Repression
- State Corporate Crime

## 8.3 Transnational Political Crimes by the State
- State Terrorism
- The State, Terrorism, and Globalization

## Preview

Chapter 8 introduces:

- What sociologists mean by "political crime."

- The extent, nature, and costs of political crime.

- The various types of political crime, including crimes against the state and crimes by the state.

## Key Terms

| | |
|---|---|
| civil disobedience | political repression |
| corrupt campaign practices | state-corporate crime |
| election fraud | state corruption |
| individual/group terrorism | state terrorism |
| international law | terrorism |
| political bribery | transnational political crime |
| political crime | |

Criminologists rarely recognize the category "political crime." When they do, however, they usually conceptualize political crime as crime committed against the state. However, as we show in this chapter, the state and its representatives often *initiate* illegal attacks on legally functioning—albeit politically challenging—subordinate groups. Moreover, criminologists' failure to label this conduct as harmful serves to obscure the real nature of such actions. As we assert in the following argument, the state's political actions not infrequently result in violations of domestic and international law.

Accordingly, our definition of **political crime** is threefold, entailing not only crimes *against* the state (violations of law for the purpose of modifying or changing social conditions) but also crimes *by* the state, both domestic (violations of law and unethical acts by state officials and agencies whose victimization occurs inside the United States) and transnational (violations of domestic and international law by state officials and agencies whose victimization occurs outside the United States).

## 8.1  Political Crimes Against the State

Political crimes against the state are carried out for the purpose of changing or modifying existing social conditions. When individuals or groups believe a particular social condition (or overall social structure) is problematic in some important way, they may attempt to modify the social order, or alter it entirely, by means that violate criminal law. Political crimes against the state differ from other crimes discussed in this book in that they are not engaged in for personal gain. Rather, they are committed on behalf of a specific group (class, race, gender, political party, for example). Moreover, political crimes against the state are usually intentionally overt and public, rather than covert and secret.

Political crimes against the state, then, involve intentional violations of criminal law for political purposes, as well as various acts criminalized by the state for the purpose of curbing political dissent. Political crimes against the state may also be violent or nonviolent. We consider first some examples of violent political crimes against the state.

### Violent Political Crimes Against the State

Throughout U.S. history, social groups have turned to violence in a bid to modify or change the social order. In fact, the United States was born of politically violent crimes against the British government. By encouraging, and then engaging in, the Revolutionary War (1775–1783), colonists violated the British law of treason, which made it illegal to levy war against the king.

Native Americans in the United States have likewise resorted to violence to oppose state policies and to change social conditions. Although the examples are legion, consider briefly the case involving the Lakota Sioux and General George Armstrong Custer. In 1868 the U.S. government signed the Fort Laramie Treaty with the Lakota, guaranteeing them tribal sovereignty and assuring them perpetual control over "unceded Indian territory from which whites are excluded, stretching from the Missouri River west to the Powder River hunting grounds into the Wyoming Big Horn Mountains and from the Canadian border South into Nebraska" (Garitty, 1980).

However, the treaty was repeatedly broken by the U.S. government. In 1874 Custer trespassed onto Lakota land to confirm the existence of gold in the Black Hills of South Dakota. Gold was indeed found, and Custer's cavalry allowed thousands of "gold-hungry miners" to scrape the Black Hills clean (Johansen and Maestas, 1979). As a result, in 1876 the Lakota, Cheyenne, and Arapaho assembled at Little Big Horn in Montana. This gathering has been reported to be "the largest gathering of native peoples ever to have taken place in the hemisphere" (Garitty, 1980:263). Led by Gall, Two Moons, Dull Knife, and Crazy Horse, the Native Americans responded to the trespassers by killing Custer and 204 of his men because they had "violated the sanctity of the Black Hills" (Johansen and Maestas, 1979:29). This did not stop the U.S. government from violating the treaty; it continued to do so until 1889, when the Great Sioux Nation was reduced, in violation of the treaty, to five small reservations in western South Dakota (Ortiz, 1977).

Overall, between 1776 and 1871 the U.S. government ratified 371 treaties with native Indian nations (Weyler, 1982). Figure 8.1 traces the results of U.S. government violations of those treaties. The Lakota example is important not only for indicating the use of violence to change social conditions and to oppose state policy but also for understanding that groups often resort to violence *in response* to state violence or criminality.

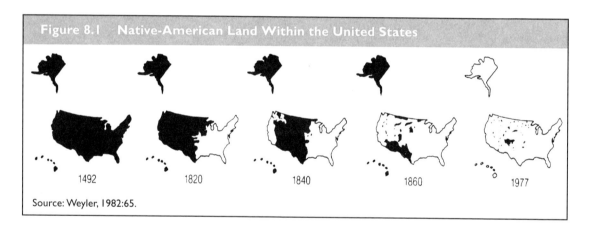

**Figure 8.1    Native-American Land Within the United States**

1492    1820    1840    1860    1977

Source: Weyler, 1982:65.

Similarly, farmers in the United States have engaged in violence to change existing conditions. Prior to 1800, farmers were involved in numerous rebellions, the Shays' Rebellion being one of the most famous. In the late 1700s many farmers experienced severe social and economic problems, forcing many to borrow money at extremely high interest rates to survive. Moreover, in order to meet their growing debts "they mortgaged their future crops and went still deeper into debt" (Parenti, 1983:63). And, as Parenti pointed out:

> Among the people there grew the feeling that the revolution against the English crown had been fought for naught. Angry armed crowds in several states began blocking foreclosures and forcibly freeing debtors from jail. They gathered at county towns to prevent courts from sentencing honest men to jail for being unable to pay mountainous debts and ruinous taxes. Disorders of a violent but organized kind occurred in a number of states. In the winter of 1787, debtor farmers in western

Massachusetts led by Daniel Shays took up arms. But their rebellion was forcibly put down by the state militia after skirmishes that left 11 men dead and scores wounded. (p. 64)

Workers have also historically engaged in violence to change certain working conditions. The extraordinarily unsafe, lengthy, and alienating working conditions in the 1800s and early 1900s led many workers to turn to labor violence to make their grievances effective. A good example was the 1886 struggle for the eight-hour day that resulted in substantial violence between striking workers and the police. In May of that year a major rally was held at Haymarket Square in Chicago; when the last speaker had finished, a bomb exploded among the police, killing one and wounding many others. The police responded by firing into the crowd. The labor movement in the late 1800s and early 1900s—for the eight-hour day and other job demands—resulted in many long and bloody battles (Lens, 1973; Brecher, 1980).

Women have also engaged in violence at times in an attempt to change social conditions. For example, during the U.S. suffrage movement (to give women the right to vote) a number of feminist marches turned to mob violence between the demonstrators and outside agitators (O'Neil, 1969). However, the suffrage movement in the United States was clearly not as militant as it was in England. The British suffragettes (the Women's Social and Political Union) engaged in a specific strategy of violence—such as arson and vandalism—to achieve political ends; their motto was "Deeds not Words" (Heidensohn, 1985).

In addition to the above, many of the African-American urban rebellions in the 1960s and 1970s were motivated by political concerns for civil rights. During the same period, groups such as the Weather Underground—an organization that broke off in 1969 from the Students for a Democratic Society—turned to violence as a means for political change. The Underground made the following announcement in 1969: "Kids know that the lines are drawn; revolution is touching all of our lives. Tens of thousands have learned that protest and marches don't do it. Revolutionary violence is the only way" (cited in Evans, 1983: 255).

Certain feminist groups in the United States have engaged in such violent acts as setting afire, or bombing, shops selling pornographic

*Striking back: Compelled by anger and frustration in confronting the overwhelming resources and structure of the state, some people advocate targeted violence and random violence as necessary to have their concerns addressed.*

materials. For example, in 1980 in Seattle, women's antipornography groups stink-bombed several pornography bookstores, and in that same year in New York City, "three porn movie houses were firebombed" (Morgan, 1980:138). In 1986, six members of the United Freedom Front were convicted of violent, politically motivated crimes. According to the *New York Times,* the six were found guilty of bombing (unoccupied) military centers and corporate buildings that were either defense contractors or companies doing business in South Africa (Buder, 1986).

Today, when most people think about political crimes against the state they think of terrorism. We define **terrorism** as the use of force or violence to intimidate, coerce, or change a government or a civilian population for political reasons. Terrorism may be perpetrated by a state through its political policies or by individuals and groups (not necessarily supported by a state) to oppose certain state policies. In Section 8.3 we discuss "state terrorism." Here we examine three types of **individual/group terrorism**: political assassination, domestic terrorism, and international terrorism.

Political assassination of members of the state for political reasons has occurred historically in the United States. Some of the better-known political assassins are John Wilkes Booth, Leon Czolgosz, Oscar Collazo and Griselio Torresola, and Sirhan Sirhan (Hagan, 1997). John Wilkes Booth murdered President Lincoln in 1865 in support of slavery and the Confederacy; Czolgosz murdered President McKinley in 1901 as part of an anarchist revolt; Collazo and Torresola's assassination attempt of President Truman in 1950 was in support of Puerto Rican independence; and Sirhan felt the assassination of Robert Kennedy in 1969 would help the Palestinian cause. Certainly the best-known political assassination in the United States is that of President John F. Kennedy. However, as David Simon (2002) pointed out, that assassination remains unsolved and is marked by considerable controversy:

- After the assassination, President Johnson, Assistant Attorney General Katzenbach, and FBI Director Hoover ordered a cover-up of the investigation. All three agreed that the public must be convinced that Lee Harvey Oswald was the lone killer.

- The House Special Committee on Assassinations found that President Kennedy's assassination most likely resulted from a conspiracy, not one individual. The committee pointed to syndicated crime as having the "means, motive, and opportunity" to assassinate the president, and/or anti-Castro Cubans killed the president because he did not support the Bay of Pigs invasion with air cover.

- Others have argued that the CIA killed President Kennedy because he was about to make peace with the Soviet Union, end the Cold War, and withdraw military personnel from Vietnam. Moreover, the CIA was allegedly upset because the Kennedy administration canceled covert operations against Cuba.

In addition to political assassinations, another type of individual/group terrorism is referred to as *domestic terrorism*, or violent acts committed against the U.S. state for political reasons by citizens of the United States. On April 19, 1995, the worst act of domestic terrorism was committed by Timothy McVeigh and Terry Nichols. As members of antigovernment paramilitary right-wing militia groups (approximately 850 such groups currently operate in 49 states), these two conspired and carried out the bombing of the Alfred P. Murray Federal Building in Oklahoma City, killing 168 people and injuring more than 500. Some 4,000 pounds of homemade explosives were packed inside a rental truck and detonated in front of the federal building. A large number of those killed were federal employees as well as 15 children under the age of 5 who were attending a day-care center in the building. McVeigh was found guilty of murder, conspiracy, and use of a weapon of mass destruction; Nichols was convicted of conspiracy and involuntary manslaughter in the bombing.

*International terrorism* refers to violent acts committed against the state for political reasons by citizens of other countries and is the most recent form of terrorism within the borders of the United States. The first bombing of the World Trade Center in New York City—which killed six people, injured over 1,000, and caused more than $500 million damage—is a prime example. On November 12, 1997, Ramzi Yousef and Eyad Najim were convicted of the 1993 bombing. Yousef directed and helped to carry out the bombing, while Najim drove the truck that carried the bomb. Four others had previously been convicted of the bombing. These men were working under the direction of Shaikh Omar Abdul Rahman (who was ironically recruited by the CIA to fight against the Soviet Union in Afghanistan in the 1980s, which we further discuss in Section 8.3) and allegedly bombed the World Trade Center building in order to punish the United States for its continued support of Israel (Hagan, 1997).

However, the most horrific international terrorist act in the United States occurred on September 11, 2001. As we pointed out in Chapter 5.1, this is a unique case of mass murder in the United States because of the number of people killed (more than 3,000) and because it also entailed a mass suicide (by 19 hijackers). These terrorists, who were connected to the Al Qaeda ("the base") network, hijacked four U.S. commercial airplanes and flew those planes into the twin World Trade Center towers in New York City, the Pentagon Building in Arlington, Virginia, and a field in rural Pennsylvania. Osama bin Laden—an exile from Saudi Arabia who also earlier worked with the CIA to fight the Soviets in Afghanistan—was the financier and mastermind behind this terrorist act. Bin Laden also organized the 1998 bombings of U.S. embassies in Kenya and Tanzania, killing 12 U.S. citizens and 300 Africans, as well as the 2000 bombing of the U.S.S. Cole, which killed 17 U.S. sailors. Most of the 19 hijackers were from Saudi Arabia, in their mid-twenties, and well educated (Hewitt, 2003). Al Qaeda operates in at least 35 countries and maintains "sleeper cells" that can be activated to carry out specific attacks. The motive behind the bombings as well as the September 11 attack was to punish the United States for its support of corrupt and authoritarian regimes in several Arab states, including Saudi Arabia and Egypt, and for the global dissemination of Western values. We will have more to say about Al Qaeda, bin Laden, and the terrorist attack of September 11 in Section 8.3.

## Nonviolent Political Crimes Against the State

Most political crime against the state is not violent. Individuals and groups in the United States historically have engaged in such actions as civil disobedience and demonstrations of a nonviolent nature, which sometimes result in criminalization by the state. Consider a few examples.

The efforts of Martin Luther King, Jr., and the civil rights movement of the early 1960s to end racial segregation in the United States were based on an explicitly nonviolent strategy. Dr. King's major weapon was **civil disobedience**, or refusing to obey certain laws seen as unjust. In his famous "Letter from Birmingham Jail," King put forth his arguments for such actions:

> There are two types of laws: there are *just* and there are *unjust* laws. I would agree with St. Augustine that "An unjust law is no law at all." Now what is the difference between the two? How does one determine when a law is just or unjust? . . . Any law that uplifts human personality is just. Any law that degrades human personality is unjust. All segregation statutes are unjust because segregation distorts the soul and damages the personality. It gives the segregator a false sense of superiority, and the segregated a false sense of inferiority. . . . So segregation is not only politically, economically, and sociologically unsound, but it is morally wrong and sinful. . . . So I can urge men to disobey segregation ordinances because they are morally wrong. . . . I hope you can see the distinction I am trying to point out. In no sense do I advocate evading or defying the law as the rabid segregationist would do. This would lead to anarchy. One who breaks an unjust law must do it *openly, lovingly,* and with a willingness to accept the penalty. I submit that an individual who breaks a law that conscience tells him is unjust, and willingly accepts the penalty by staying in jail to arouse the conscience of the community over its injustice, is in reality expressing the very highest respect for law. (Cited in Washington, 1986:293–294)

Individuals can also engage in civil disobedience not for the purpose of changing the law being broken but rather to protest—and hopefully put a stop to—particular state policies. For example, in 1976 members of the Clamshell Alliance engaged in civil disobedience by organizing a "sit-in" at the construction site of the Seabrook, New Hampshire, nuclear power plant. On May 1 of that year, 1,414 people occupied the construction site (for the purpose of halting construction of the plant) and were arrested for trespassing, more than half refusing bond and spending about two weeks in National Guard armories. The resulting publicity inspired other groups around the country, and a massive antinuclear movement eventually emerged (Dwyer, 1983).

Another example of this type of civil disobedience involved student and community demonstrators at the University of Massachusetts in the fall of 1986. The demonstrators—who included former President Carter's daughter Amy and ex-"yippie" leader Abbie Hoffman—engaged in a sit-in at a campus building used to recruit agents for the Central Intelligence Agency (CIA). Carter, Hoffman, and others, arrested for trespassing and disorderly conduct, were tried in April 1987. Although the demonstrators admitted at trial that they had trespassed on university property, they were nevertheless allowed by the judge to assert the criminal defense of "necessity" and won acquittal. This affirmative defense can be used to prove that a defendant's "illegal" acts were justified—in this case to stop a more dangerous crime: the recruiting of CIA agents who would, according to the demonstrators, most likely engage in significantly more heinous and illegal activities. After presenting the testimony of various experts on CIA criminality around the globe, the jury acquitted the demonstrators (Tushnet, 1988).

Individuals and groups may also engage in nonviolent protests and demonstrations against state policies that are not specifically directed at violating any law. Because the state regards such behavior as threatening, it enforces certain laws chosen for the purpose of curbing the dissent. For example, the trial of the Chicago Eight—which grew out of nonviolent demonstrations against the Vietnam War conducted at the 1968 Democratic convention—resulted in the demonstrators being charged with "conspiracy." The state does not have to prove that an activity was actually planned, only that the conspirators communicated in some way (Clinard and Quinney, 1973). All Chicago Eight defendants were acquitted of conspiracy but received numerous contempt citations because of their behavior during the course of the trial. As Clinard and Quinney noted, "Whether or not the defendants are convicted, the conspiracy law is an effective form of political harassment whereby those who threaten the system can be detained for long periods of time at great personal expense" (p. 156).

The most recent nonviolent demonstrations have been the anti-globalization protests that began in Seattle in 1999 but quickly moved to a number of other cities throughout the world, such as Prague and Melbourne. Approximately 100,000 people take part in these demonstrations, protesting against the policies of the World Trade Organization, the International Monetary Fund, transnational corporations, and governments in the Western world. The anti-globalization movement consists of people from a wide range of political and cultural persuasions, yet their message is the same: "Globalization worsens economic insecurity and deepens social inequality" (Ruggiero, 2002:48).

What is ironic about this new type of social movement is that although it is anti-globalization, it is an example of "globalization from below," or a global movement that challenges the negative aspects of "globalization from above" (Kellner, 2003), and its organizing efforts have benefited from globalization. For example, Ruggiero examined one organization in France that is part of the anti-globalization movement—Attac—and found that it uses 200 translators who make information material available in 10 languages through discussion lists that are available in six languages and accessible on their website:

*Nonviolent protest: Public demonstrations can be effective devices to bring media attention to a group or community's concerns; other times media coverage will be minimal if the position presented is deemed 'too radical' for the national agenda.*

Attac's web site was first seen as a source of information for experts, later as an activists' tool, and finally as the showroom of the association. Each month it hosts between 30 and 40 new documents and is contacted 800,000 times from 90 different countries. The site offers information about political activities and demonstrations, and also launches petitions and organizes conferences online. (p. 49)

Despite the fact that the vast majority of people demonstrate peacefully during anti-globalization protests, the police reaction to the protestors has grown stronger in terms of the number of police deployed and the tactics used. These demonstrations are now routinely met with police officers dressed in riot gear who outnumber the protestors and use pepper-spray, tear gas, truncheons, water cannons, and mass arrests to "control" the protestors. And this has simultaneously resulted in global communication and cooperation among police and immigration authorities. For example, two weeks prior to the Prague demonstration, the Czech border police had received from police in other countries the names and photos of foreigners who had participated in earlier anti-globalization protests, and they turned back approximately 600 of these people at the border (Vayrynen, 2004).

Another example of nonviolent political crime against the state is spying. There exist different types of political spies, which Hagan (1997) argued can be classified according to motivation. For example, there are "mercenary spies," which are the most common and provide intelligence secrets to a foreign government for monetary gain; "ideological spies," which provide secrets to foreign governments because of strong political or ideological beliefs; "alienated/egocentric spies," who provide secrets to a foreign government because they want to "get even" with the U.S. government or government agency; and finally, the "buccaneer spy," who provides secrets to a foreign government for adventure and for excitement.

Probably the best-known recent case of illegal spying is that of Aldrich Ames, a 32-year veteran of the Central Intelligence Agency (CIA). Beginning in 1985 and continuing until 1994, Ames stole intelligence secrets and sold them to the Soviet Union. Ames is probably the highest-paid known Soviet spy, earning between $1.5 and $2.5 million. He most likely got caught because of his lavish lifestyle—he paid $540,000 in cash for a home in Arlington, Virginia, bought two new cars (including a Jaguar), bought stock worth $165,000, and charged $455,000 on credit cards. Ames was sentenced to life in prison (Hagan, 1997).

"Computer spying" emerged as a growing security issue in the 1990s. Consider the following examples (Rosoff, Pontell, and Tillman, 2004):

- A 22-year-old former Harvard student allegedly used stolen university passwords to break into military computers.

- Two "hackers" penetrated seven computer systems, gaining access to all information at Griffis Air Base in New York. The spies copied files—including sensitive battlefield simulations—and installed devices to read the passwords of everyone entering the systems.

- A Washington, D.C., hacker was arrested for breaking into the Pentagon computer system and subsequently demonstrated his computer skills by cracking the Air Force computer system within 15 seconds while military officials watched.

## 8.2 Domestic Political Crimes by the State

Domestic political crimes by the state are violations of law and unethical conduct by state officials or agencies whose victimization occurs within the boundaries of the United States. We discuss three types: state corruption, political repression, and state-corporate crime. **State corruption** is illegal or unethical use of state authority for personal or political gain. **Political repression** is illegal or unethical conduct by state officials or agencies for purposes of repressing domestic political dissent. **State corporate crime** is illegal or socially harmful behavior that occurs at the intersection of state agencies and private corporations.

### State Corruption

State corruption exists at city, state, and national levels and involves a wide range of state-directed activities—such as purchasing goods and services, use of public funds and property, tax assessment and collection, regulation of commercial activity, zoning and land use, law enforcement, and so on. We focus on three types of state corruption: political bribery, election fraud, and corrupt campaign practices.

**Political bribery** is the acceptance of money or property by state officials in return for favors. Politicians, for example, have myriad opportunities for involvement in bribery, accepting money for such services as introducing special forms of legislation, voting a specific way on already-introduced legislation, and voting in favor of a government contract. One of the best-known cases of bribery of politicians is the ABSCAM case. This FBI "sting" operation, which took place in the early 1980s, resulted in the conviction of seven members of Congress for accepting bribes from undercover FBI agents posing as Arab sheiks. The "sheiks" met the members of Congress in hotel rooms, offering them substantial amounts of money or stock for favorable legislation on business ventures. Only one of the eight politicians refused the bribe.

Two recent examples of this form of state corruption involved the case of James Traficant, Jr. and Vincent "Buddy" Cianci. Traficant is an ex-Democratic congressperson from Ohio who was convicted in 2002 on 10 counts of bribery, tax evasion, and extorting money from his own staff (Rosoff, Pontell, and Tillman, 2004). Cianci is the ex-mayor of Providence, Rhode Island, who in 2002 was convicted and sentenced to five years and four months in federal prison for soliciting bribes for city contracts, jobs, and tax breaks. Testimony at his trial indicated, for example, that Cianci received a $10,000 bribe for reducing an individual's $500,000 tax bill to $100,000, and he received $5,000 for ordering the hiring of a woman's son on the city police force.

State officials, other than politicians, are also in a position to accept bribes. The police, for example, have a long history of involvement in corruption. From at least the 1890s, a legion of investigative committees have consistently unearthed substantial and wide-ranging forms of police bribery (Coleman, 2002). In the 1980s bribery in law enforcement once again came to national attention. In 1988, for example, seven Boston police detectives were convicted on 57 counts of bribery totaling $18,000 over an eight-year period (*Boston Herald,* 1988). Moreover, over 100 law-enforcement drug-related bribery cases came before state and federal courts in the 1980s (Shenon, 1988a). In the late 1990s an investigation uncovered numerous corrupt acts—including bribery—by some members of the Los Angeles Police Department (LAPD). Dozens of "anti-gang offi-cers" were implicated in drug dealing, making false arrests, shaking down drug dealers, bribery, giving perjured testimony, and framing innocent people (Coleman, 2002). As a result of this police corruption, over 100 criminal convictions were overturned, and the responsibility for making police reforms at LAPD was placed in the hands of a federal judge.

Judges and lawyers have similarly been found to be involved in bribery. An investi-gation of the Circuit Court of Cook County, Illinois, for example, revealed that judges were providing specific dispositions or consideration to a case in exchange for money or other things of value, and "lawyers would pay off judges for permission to 'hustle' cli-ents in large volume criminal courtrooms" (Valukas and Raphaelson, 1988:4). In one particular court,

> a corrupt chief judge assigned other judges to the "big rooms" (courts where driving under the influence cases were heard) based on their willingness to accommodate the corrupt defense lawyers who practiced there. These defense lawyers were called "miracle workers" because they never lost a case. These same lawyers got their re-sults by paying judges, often through middlemen, for favorable disposition of their clients' drunk driving cases. Often the arresting police officer was also paid to testify in a way that created a reasonable doubt. The weakened evidence gave the corrupt judge "something to hang his hat on" in finding the defendant not guilty. (p. 4)

Most recently, several Dade County, Florida, judges were found guilty of taking bribes from drug-trafficking defendants totaling $266,000; a federal district judge in Louisiana was convicted of accepting $16,500 from a convicted drug dealer to obtain a lighter sentence; and a judge in Chicago was found to have accepted eight automobiles and $400,000 in cash payoffs for dismissing drunk driving cases (Rosoff, Pontell, and Tillman, 2004).

Many politicians have also been involved in **election fraud**—illegal voting, false registration, stuffing ballot boxes, and the like—which had its beginning in the heyday of political machines in the late 1800s. Some presidential examples include the follow-ing (Douglas, 1977; Weld, 1988):

- Harry Truman likely would not have been elected senator from Missouri if he had not received 50,000 fraudulent votes provided by the "Pendergast Ma-chine" in Kansas City.

- John Kennedy was assured victory in 1960 when Chicago Mayor Richard Daley and his machine stuffed ballot boxes with Kennedy votes.

- Lyndon Johnson won his 1948 Senate race in Texas by 202 fraudulently ob-tained votes.

- Approximately $5,000 was allegedly used to purchase black votes for Jimmy Carter in the 1976 California primary.

- Election fraud can also occur through forgery and false accounting by elec-tion officials (Simon, 2002b).

As David Simon shows:

> corrupt election officials can (1) complete ballots when the voter has failed to vote for a particular office, (2) declare ballots for the opposition invalid by deliberately defacing them or making two preferences for a single office, (3) destroy ballots for the opposition, (4) add premarked ballots to the total, and (5) simply miscount. (p. 221)

In the 2000 presidential election between Vice President Al Gore and Texas governor George W. Bush, the outcome was determined by the vote in Florida, which Bush eventually won. However, investigations of the voting process in Florida reveal the strong possibility of fraud (Parenti, 2002; Corn, 2003):

- Punch-card ballots were printed in a confusing manner causing several thousand Gore supporters to mistakenly vote for another candidate; voters who realized they had made a mistake were denied a new ballot, even though the law stipulates up to three ballots in case of error.

- Punch-card ballots were nullified or disputed more often in pro-Gore precincts than in pro-Bush ones. Voting machines read nearly 4 percent of the punch cards as blank or invalid. By contrast, ballots read by modern optical scanning systems rejected only about 1.4 percent. The more-modern equipment tended to be in predominantly white pro-Bush precincts.

- The punch-card ballot counting machines have an error rate of between 0.1 percent and 1 percent. Given that these machines tallied 3.45 million votes in Florida, this suggests that between 3,450 and 34,500 votes could have been misread—which was many more votes than the actual margin between Bush and Gore.

- In Palm Beach, voters were required to use "butterfly" ballots that led to thousands of Gore voters either mistakenly voting for another candidate or disqualifying their ballots by errantly voting for two candidates.

- Some 10,000 primarily African-American voters were turned away in Seminole County and 22,000 in Duval County (Jacksonville) after they registered but were never added to the voter rolls.

- The telephone lines to the central registrar were continuously busy, so many voters were unable to confirm their registration status. To avoid the busy telephone lines, George W.'s brother and governor of Florida, Jeb Bush, dispatched laptop computers to counties that voted disproportionately for George Bush. Predominantly black counties that went heavily for Gore did not get computers despite the thousands of new registrants.

- In several heavily Democratic precincts, officials closed the polls early, leaving lines of would-be voters stranded.

- Ballots were misplaced and left uncounted; at least seven ballot boxes were found in unexplained places, and two bags of ballots were found in a poll worker's car trunk.

- An African-American church that had served as a polling place in numerous elections was unable to get anyone to come pick up its ballot boxes at the end of the day.

- Florida state troopers set up checkpoints near polling sites in predominantly black precincts, then stopped and held would-be voters for up to two hours while searching their cars.

- Many African Americans who had no police record were prevented from voting because they were incorrectly declared "convicted felons."

- Over 200 Puerto Rican voters in Orange County were required to show two photo IDs before being permitted to vote, which many did not have. The legal requirement under Florida law was only one photo ID. This law itself, passed just before the election, posed an added difficulty for low-income or elderly voters who did not own cars or have driver's licenses or any other photo ID.

- During the recount, Bush agitators, imported from out of state, stormed the Dade County Canvassing Board, punched and kicked one of the officials, and created a climate of intimidation that caused the board to abandon its recount and accept the original pro-Bush tally.

- Florida law required a vote recount if the margin is less than half of 1 percent. Because Bush's lead was 0.03 percent of the votes recorded, a mandatory recount was ordered by the secretary of state. But a full recount never occurred: 18 of the state's 67 counties did not reprocess their ballots; most of them merely rechecked the math from their tabulations, and these counties accounted for approximately one-quarter of the state's total vote.

Eventually, the U.S. Supreme Court heard arguments on the recount in the case of *George W. Bush v. Al Gore,* and in a five-to-four decision the Court ruled that because different counties might use different methods of tabulating ballots in a hand recount, the recount would violate the equal protection clause of the Fourteenth Amendment (Parenti, 2002). In ruling this way, the Court ignored the extensive evidence listed above as a violation of equal protection. As Michael Parenti states in his conclusion about this presidential vote:

> Every indication showed that an honest recount would have given the state of Florida and the presidency to the Democratic candidate, Vice President Al Gore, who at that point was behind by only a hundred or so votes in Florida and who was gaining ground with each attempt at a recount. By preventing a complete tally, the Court handed Florida's electoral votes and the presidency to Bush—a stolen election in which the U.S. Supreme Court played a crucial role. (p. 297)

Finally, **corrupt campaign practices** appear to be relatively widespread in the United States. For example, politicians tend to be extremely loyal to those who contribute to their campaign. In 1981, Senator Robert Dole, chair of the Senate Finance Committee, would not support tax loopholes for 333 Chicago commodity traders. Yet when these same traders contributed over $70,000 to Dole's 1984 campaign, he reversed himself and won the traders their loopholes (Judis, 1988). Moreover, all congressional members who received $30,000 or more in campaign contributions from the dairy industry lobby voted for dairy subsidies, and 97 percent of those members receiving $20,000 to $30,000 supported the bill.

In addition to the foregoing, in June 1972 a group of ex-CIA operatives was caught breaking into the Democratic party's national headquarters in the Watergate Building in Washington, D.C. Subsequent investigations revealed that the burglary was only part of an extensive campaign of political corruption "involving political espionage, electoral sabotage, wiretapping, theft of private records, and illegal use of campaign funds—planned and directed by members of Nixon's campaign staff and White House staff" (Parenti, 2002:173). In August 1974, in order to avoid an impeachment trial, Richard Nixon resigned from the presidency and eventually was pardoned of all crimes associated with Watergate by President Gerald Ford.

Corrupt campaign practices may also have been part of the 1980 Reagan-Bush campaign for the presidency. On November 4, 1979, the U.S. embassy in Tehran, Iran, was taken over by a group of students loyal to the Ayattollah Khomeini. Sixty-six U.S. citizens were held captive until, mysteriously, January 20, 1981. Only two hours after President Reagan's inauguration on that day—the 444th day of captivity—the hostages were released. Why were the hostages released at that particular time? Abbie Hoffman and Jonathan Silvers (1988) think they know why. Fearing in the final weeks of the 1980 presidential campaign that President Carter would come up with an "October Surprise"—somehow bring home the hostages, thus almost guaranteeing his re-election—the Reagan-Bush campaign, Hoffman and Silvers argued, quite possibly managed to stop such an event from occurring. What follows is a summary of Hoffman and Silvers' argument.

In May 1984 the House Subcommittee on Human Resources, investigating "Unauthorized Transfers of Nonpublic Information During the 1980 Presidential Election," concluded in its report that what began as a simple inquiry into the alleged theft of Carter's debate briefing book had unearthed an immense quantity of unethical—if not illegal—behavior by the Reagan-Bush campaign. For example, the subcommittee found that by October, 1980, senior Reagan advisers had informants at the CIA, the Defense Intelligence Agency, the National Security Council, the White House Situation Room, and military bases around the country for purposes of reporting any aircraft movements related to the hostages in any way. In short, by "the fall of 1980, the Carter White House was riddled with moles, spies, and informers" for the Reagan-Bush campaign (p. 151).

In addition to monitoring the possibility of a Carter "October Surprise," Reagan-Bush campaign officials may also have attempted to deal directly with the Iranians themselves. Basing their argument on anecdotal evidence, Hoffman and Silvers contend that in September, 1980, Richard Allen (who would become Reagan's first National Security Adviser), Robert McFarlane (then a consultant on Iran for the Senate Armed Services Committee), and campaign adviser Laurence Silberman met a representative of the Iranian government at the L'Enfant Plaza Hotel in Washington, D.C. According to Hoffman and Silvers, Allen and Silberman admitted that this meeting did take place, yet asserted that they specifically *rejected* an offer by the Iranian that Iran could obtain release of the hostages to the Reagan-Bush campaign prior to the election. In any event, it seems neither Silberman nor Allen reported the meeting to the Carter White House.

Moreover, others, according to Hoffman and Silvers, disagreed with these Reagan-Bush officials, arguing that a deal had indeed been made with Iran. For example,

Bassar Abu Sharif, Yasir Arafat's chief spokesperson, is on record saying that "Reagan people" contacted him during the first (1980) campaign, requesting "the PLO to use its influence to delay the release of the American hostages from the embassy in Tehran until after the election" (p. 152). Further, Barbara Honegger, a former policy analyst in the Reagan White House, has stated that Allen "cut a deal" with the Iranians on the hostages in Iran prior to the election. And former president of Iran Abolhassan Bani-Sadr (exiled in France) stated that those at the Washington meeting "agreed in principle that the hostages would be liberated after the election, and that, if elected, Reagan would provide significantly more arms than Carter was offering" (p. 153). In other words, prior even to taking office, Reagan-Bush campaign officials may have attempted to guarantee victory by "cutting a deal" with Iran. In exchange for keeping the hostages until Inauguration Day, Hoffman and Silvers argued, Reagan-Bush officials pledged that Iran would receive U.S. military arms and supplies. Others have supported Hoffman and Silvers' argument (Honegger, 1989; Sick, 1991). In particular, Gary Sick (1991) added that William Casey, Reagan's campaign manager, met with Iranian arms dealer Cyrus Hashemi in Madrid and Paris on July 26 and 27, 1980, to hammer out the deal.

The "October Surprise" argument is not without substance. The hostages were released on Inauguration Day, and that same year, on July 24, Israel contracted with Iran to sell them more than $100 million worth of U.S. arms (Marshall, Scott, and Hunter, 1987). Moreover, McFarlane, Casey, and Israel played important roles in the initial phases of the arms-for-hostages deal that eventually erupted as the Iran-Contra scandal.

The allegations we have outlined prompted investigations by both the U.S. Senate and the House. Neither inquiry found credible evidence of a secret deal. In fact, according to Lee H. Hamilton, chair of the House October Surprise Task Force, "There was virtually no credible evidence to support the accusations. Specifically, we found little or no credible evidence of communications between the 1980 Reagan campaign and the Government of Iran and no credible evidence that the campaign tried to delay the hostages' release" (1993:17).

Yet Sick responded to the House report by arguing that William Casey's activities were not adequately substantiated. For example, Sick has claimed that "the report says Mr. Casey could not have attended a Madrid meeting the weekend of July 26–27 because he was at the Bohemian Grove outside San Francisco. Yet the committee's own evidence places him at the Grove the following weekend, from August 1 to August 3" (p. 17). Casey's passport mysteriously vanished—and was therefore not available to the task force—and crucial pages were missing from his loose-leaf calendar. Thus, Sick concluded that questions remained, and he hoped "the task force will open its files to outside independent investigators to the maximum extent permissible by law" (p. 17).

## State Political Repression

Federal agencies such as the FBI and the CIA have been involved in numerous illegal activities, many of which relate to political repression. For instance, although legally the CIA has no domestic security or law-enforcement functions, it has (1) opened and photographed the mail of over one million private citizens for 30 years, (2) broken into homes and offices, stealing documents and installing illegal surveillance devices, and (3) equipped, trained, and supported local police forces (Parenti, 2002).

Similarly, since its inception in 1938, the FBI has been involved in a variety of illegal activities related to the repression of political dissent. Historically, one of the first responsibilities of the FBI was to investigate "subversion," which was entirely unrelated to the enforcement of federal criminal laws (Church Committee, 1976). In 1938, for instance, the FBI *illegally* investigated subversion in (1) the maritime, steel, coal, clothing, garment, fur, automobile, and newspaper industries; (2) educational institutions; (3) organized labor; (4) youth groups; (5) African-American groups; (6) government affairs; and (7) the military. Explicit illegality included wiretapping, bugging, mail openings, and breaking and entering. Through such illegal behavior the FBI gathered information on "radical" individuals and groups and forwarded it directly to the White House.

The major thrust of the FBI since at least 1941, however, has been its counterintelligence program, more commonly known as COINTELPRO. Although the FBI's counterintelligence function is restricted by law to "hostile foreign governments, foreign organizations, and individuals connected to them" (Churchill and Vander Wall, 1988:37), the FBI clearly went beyond that mandate to include not only intelligence gathering but also strategies and tactics for the purpose of disrupting and "neutralizing" organizations that the FBI felt were threatening to the social order. As William C. Sullivan, former head of the FBI Counterintelligence Division, stated in the mid-1970s (cited in Church Committee, 1976): "We were engaged in COINTELPRO tactics, to divide, conquer, weaken, in diverse ways, an organization. We were engaged in that when I entered the Bureau in 1941" (p. 66).

Between 1940 and the early 1960s, COINTELPRO activities were primarily directed at the U.S. Communist party and the Socialist Workers party (Church Committee, 1976). In the 1960s and early 1970s the FBI investigated new groups, implementing some 2,370 separate COINTELPRO actions (Kunstler, 1978). Some of the groups embraced by COINTELPRO activities were the Puerto Rican independence movement, the civil rights movement, Students for a Democratic Society, and the Black Liberation movement. Because of space limitation, it is impossible to discuss the effects of COINTELPRO on each of these movements. Therefore, we focus on one particular case, the FBI's campaign against Martin Luther King, Jr.

In 1962 the FBI claimed that Dr. King and the civil rights movement had been duped by the Communists. This claim was eventually proved false (Garrow, 1981). Nevertheless, in December 1963—four months after the famous civil rights march on Washington and King's "I Have a Dream" speech—a nine-hour meeting was convened at FBI headquarters to discuss various "avenues of approach aimed at neutralizing King as an effective Negro leader" (Church Committee, 1976:220). Agents throughout the country were instructed to continue gathering information on King's personal life "in order that we may consider using this information at an opportune time in a counterintelligence move to discredit him" (p. 220). According to David Garrow (1981), the FBI went through the Southern Christian Leadership Conference's (SCLC) trash in hope of finding incriminating evidence against that organization and King. The FBI investigated Dr. King's bank and charge accounts, instituted electronic surveillance of King's apartment and office, attempted to win cooperation with the bureau from certain SCLC employees, sent threatening forged letters in King's name to SCLC contributors, and attempted to intensify the well-known mutual dislike between King and NAACP head Roy Wilkins. However, the FBI was unable to produce any incriminating evidence against the SCLC or King himself.

Undaunted, on January 5, 1964, FBI agents planted a microphone in King's bedroom at the Willard Hotel in Washington, D.C. Over the next two years the FBI installed at least fourteen additional bugs in King's hotel rooms across the country, sometimes accompanied by physical and photographic surveillance (Church Committee, 1976). Alleging that the resulting tapes revealed "meetings" with prostitutes, the FBI then fabricated an anonymous letter to King, enclosing a copy of one of the tapes, and sent them to King on the eve of his receiving the Nobel Peace Prize (pp. 220–221). The letter, in part, reads as follows (cited in Garrow, 1981):

King,

In view of your low grade . . . I will not dignify your name with either a Mr. or a Reverend or a Dr. . . . No person can overcome facts, not even a fraud like yourself . . . I repeat—no person can successfully argue against facts. You are finished. . . .

King, there is only one thing left for you to do. . . . You are done. There is but one way out for you. You better take it before your filthy, abnormal fraudulent self is bared to the nation. (pp. 125–126)

When this effort by the FBI failed to force King to commit suicide—as he himself allegedly interpreted the purpose of the message (Church Committee, 1976)—the FBI "leaked" the tapes and photographs to a number of leading newspapers in the United States (Wise, 1976; Bray, 1980).

*Targeted by the state: National security and law enforcement agencies made intensive efforts to discredit or intimidate many left-wing leaders in the 1960s. Before his assassination Reverend Martin Luther King, Jr., suffered numerous state-sponsored smear campaigns.*

Unhindered by the FBI's virulent attacks and efforts to halt his political movement, King traveled to Sweden to receive the Nobel Peace Prize. During his stay in Europe, and upon his return to the United States, the bureau continued its activities (Church Committee, 1976). The "neutralization" program actually continued until King's death. As late as March 1968, FBI agents were instructed to neutralize King because he might, according to the bureau, become a "messiah" who could "unify and electrify the militant black nationalist movement" (p. 223). Moreover, as Churchill and Vander Wall (1988) pointed out: "Given the nature of the Bureau's campaign to neutralize King, there remain serious questions—unresolved by subsequent congressional investigations—as to the FBI's role in King's assassination in Memphis on March 31, 1968" (p. 57). Indeed, the FBI had long previously (1964) determined that New York attorney Samuel R. Pierce (an extreme conservative) should be

King's successor; he would be, according to one FBI document, the " 'right kind' of leader" (p. 395).

Most methods used by the FBI under COINTELPRO were, according to the Church Committee investigating FBI illegalities, "secret programs . . . which used unlawful or improper acts" to carry out desired goals (1976:137). Beyond falsification of information and documents and illegal surveillance, the FBI conducted hundreds of illegal burglaries against "threatening" individuals and organizations, stealing private files and documents. Moreover, through COINTELPRO the FBI conducted disinformation campaigns, used "agent provocateurs" to disrupt political (primarily leftist) organizations, and was implicated in the assassination of such dissident political group leaders as Fred Hampton of the Black Panther Party (Churchill and Vander Wall, 1988).

---

### Box 8.1   The Case of Leonard Peltier

Although COINTELPRO was allegedly abolished in 1971, FBI illegalities continued. The case of Leonard Peltier is extraordinary in this regard. Leonard Peltier is, and was in the 1970s, a member of the American Indian Movement (AIM), a national movement of Native Americans striving to restore their traditional culture and reclaim the rights guaranteed them by treaties entered into over a period of 100 years. In 1975, Peltier was living at the Pine Ridge Indian Reservation in South Dakota (along with approximately 30 other AIM members and supporters) when, on the morning of June 26, two armed FBI agents entered the reservation allegedly in search of a young Native American accused of stealing a pair of cowboy boots. A firefight occurred between members of AIM and the FBI. Shortly thereafter, both agents and an AIM member were dead. There was never an investigation of the killing of the AIM member, yet four Native Americans were charged with the murder of the two agents. Only one, Leonard Peltier, was convicted. The charges against one of the original defendants were dropped allegedly due to a lack of evidence; the other two were brought to trial in Cedar Rapids, Iowa, in the summer of 1976. Both were eventually acquitted amid controversy concerning FBI misconduct in the prosecution of their case (Messerschmidt, 1986a).

Prior to the Cedar Rapids trial, Peltier sought political asylum in Canada, where he was apprehended by the Royal Canadian Mounted Police at the request of the FBI. He petitioned the Canadian government to grant him status as a political refugee, contending that it would be impossible for him to receive a fair trial in the United States because of his political beliefs and activities. The FBI's response to Peltier's petition was to provide the Canadian authorities with two fabricated "eyewitness" affidavits signed by a Lakota woman, Myrtle Poor Bear. It was later revealed at Peltier's trial, but out of the presence of the jury, that Myrtle Poor Bear never knew Leonard Peltier, had never seen him before, was more than 50 miles away from the crime scene on the day of the firefight, and was most likely coerced by FBI agents to sign the affidavits. The Canadian government honored the U.S. extradition request.

Unhappy with the acquittal in Cedar Rapids, and thus the "performance" of the federal judge in that case, the federal government obtained a change of venue to Fargo, North Dakota. Here the FBI found the judge they wanted. Virtually the entire defense, which had justified an acquittal in Cedar Rapids, was ruled inadmissible by the judge in Fargo. But more important, according to a detailed examination of the trial record, the prosecution enjoyed free rein to manipulate highly inconsistent and contradictory circumstantial evidence, and the entire trial was saturated with the suppression of evidence, the coercion of testimony and, quite possibly, judicial impropriety. It was under these circumstances that Leonard Peltier was convicted and sentenced to serve two consecutive life terms for the murder of two FBI agents.

Peltier appealed the conviction to the Eighth U.S. Circuit Court of Appeals in St. Louis. Although noting, for example, that the Myrtle Poor Bear affair was "disturbing," the court upheld his conviction. Several more appeals were heard, each fruitless. In the final appeal to the Eighth Circuit, the judges stated the following in their decision: "We recognize that there is evidence in this record of improper conduct on the part of some FBI agents, but we are reluctant to impute even further improprieties to them" (cited in Churchill and Vander Wall, 1988). As Churchill and Vander Wall responded, "Thus, it was deemed more appropriate that Leonard Peltier remain locked away in a maximum security cell rather than expose the FBI to further scrutiny concerning the way in which it had obtained its conviction, even *after* a clear pattern of Bureau misconduct had been demonstrated" (p. 326).

Because of the foregoing, many people worldwide believe that Peltier's arrest, prosecution, and continued confinement are the result of his political activities as a leader of AIM. Although Peltier remains behind bars, (1) he was selected to receive the International Human Rights Prize by the Human Rights Commission of Spain, (2) over 50 members of Congress have twice signed "Friend of the Court" briefs supporting Peltier's right to a new trial, (3) over 50 members of the Canadian Parliament signed a petition asking the U.S. government to order a new trial (six of the Canadian endorsers held cabinet posts at the time of Peltier's extradition), (4) human rights organizations, such as Amnesty International, have supported Peltier's request for a retrial and have recommended that an independent Commission of Inquiry be established to look into the case, and (5) over 14 million people worldwide have signed petitions demanding a new trial for Peltier.

In the 1980s, the FBI was involved in intelligence gathering and overall monitoring of the Committee in Solidarity with the People of El Salvador (CISPES). Through the Freedom of Information Act, the Center for Constitutional Rights in New York obtained FBI files on CISPES, documenting political intelligence gathering and political harassment of individuals and groups associated with CISPES and working to change U.S. foreign policy in Central America. The files also reveal that 52 of the 59 FBI field offices were involved in the massive investigation. Initially the FBI attempted to substantiate that CISPES was an agent of a foreign government and, therefore, in violation of the Foreign Agents Registration Act. When this failed, the FBI—with approval from then-Attorney General William French Smith—mounted a new investigation on the premise that CISPES was probably a "terrorist" organization. The FBI, however, never found any evidence to support this thesis either. In fact, field reports came into FBI headquarters indicating that those involved in CISPES and related organizations were "legitimate" and "respectable" people involved in such activities as demonstrations, lobbying, protests, rallies, newsletters, and occasional nonviolent civil disobedience—all protected by the First Amendment.

The FBI, however, did not stop there but went on to develop two rationales that allowed the investigation to continue. Ann Buitrago (1988) summarizes the rationales:

*The "Covert Programs" Rationale:* To explain away its negative results, the FBI reasoned that all the peaceful legal activities on which CISPES' broad support was based merely represented an *overt* program designed to cover a sinister *covert* program of which most CISPES members were unaware.

*The "Front Groups" Rationale:* The old concept of "front groups" was dredged up to enable the investigation to expand beyond CISPES chapters and affiliates to any of the hundreds of organizations whose work brought them in touch with CISPES or its members. The usefulness to the FBI of the notion of "front groups" was that even though a given group was clearly not involved in terrorism but only in public education and/or protest, it could continue to be investigated because it might be a CISPES "front." (p. 3)

These rationales had the effect of driving the investigation further and deeper. Under the guise of looking for "fronts" and "covert terrorists," the FBI used the following techniques to investigate CISPES:

1. FBI informers infiltrated organizations and were sent to meetings and demonstrations.

2. Record checks were made of FBI files, other police records, school records, phone books, and student-faculty directories.

3. Frequent physical surveillance of people, residences, meeting places, offices, and demonstrations took place, often accompanied by photographic surveillance.

4. CISPES-related literature was collected and reviewed.

5. Radio programs were monitored.

6. License plate numbers of vehicles at or near demonstrations, public events, and conferences were traced, and the names of owners were investigated.

7. FBI interviews were attempted of CISPES leaders, members, former members, and members of other groups "knowledgeable" of CISPES.

In addition, the FBI worked closely with several right-wing groups, helping to develop further the privatization of intelligence gathering. For instance, right-wing groups—such as the Young Americans for Freedom (YAF) and CARP (followers of Sun Yung Moon)—would routinely gather "intelligence" and pass it on to the FBI. In one case a YAF document on the CISPES National Convention was sent to FBI headquarters, where it was disseminated to 32 field offices (Center for Constitutional Rights, 1988).

Ironically, the only "covert program" uncovered during this operation was conducted by right-wing groups and the FBI. In fact, the FBI's "terrorist" investigation was viewed by those investigating the case as simply a cover for conducting domestic security programs aimed at disrupting organizations critical of U.S. foreign policy. According to Buitrago (1988), hostility toward CISPES "pours out of these documents" (pp. 4–5). For example, the field office at "Dallas wrote frequently about the need to devise investigative activity '*against* this organization'; New Orleans fired off a tirade against CISPES and individuals who 'display contempt against the U.S. government,' calling for them to be deported or denied reentry if they ever left the country" (pp. 4–5).

At least one FBI agent refused to go along with this investigation. In January 1988, Jack Ryan, an FBI agent for 22 years, was fired because he refused to investigate peace groups opposed to U.S. policy in Central America. As Ryan stated: "Investigating this as domestic terrorism or domestic violence is absurd. . . . What our Government's doing is wrong in Central America. I don't want to be a part of it" (cited in Hopkins, 1988:14). Ryan was fired just 10 months before his retirement.

In 1978 a secret court was established by the Foreign Intelligence Surveillance Act (FISA) that had the power to authorize electronic surveillance requests of the FBI and the National Security Agency (NSA) (Parenti, 2002). In 1995, President Clinton signed an executive order that expanded the power of the FISA court, authorizing the above agencies to engage in "physical searches as well as electronic ones, without obtaining a warrant in open court, without notifying the target or providing an inventory of items seized. The target need not be under suspicion of committing a crime but might simply be deemed to have questionable associations that pose a 'threat to U.S. national security'" (pp. 140–141).

The most politically repressive form of legislation in recent years is the Uniting and Strengthening America by Providing Appropriate Tools Required to Intercept and Obstruct Terrorism Act (USA PATRIOT Act), which was passed by Congress just six weeks after the September 11, 2001, international terrorist attacks. The act sacrifices political freedoms in the name of national security by (1) limiting freedom of speech and political association, (2) denying U.S. entry to noncitizens simply on the basis of political ideology, (3) granting the state enhanced surveillance powers, such as tracking e-mail and Internet use, conducting sneak-and-peek searches (by postal workers, for example), obtaining sensitive personnel records, monitoring financial transactions, conducting nationwide roving wiretaps, and even monitoring library records (Chang, 2001). Within only two months of the act being signed into law by President Bush (on October 26, 2001), the Department of Justice admitted detaining more than 1,200 immigrants, none of whom were charged with terrorism. Moreover, most of these individuals were denied basic rights of due process, including the right to know the charges against them, the right to an attorney, and the use of prolonged solitary confinement (Platt and O'Leary, 2003).

## State Corporate Crime

State corporate crime generally is understood as illegal or socially harmful acts that occur at the intersection of state agencies and private corporations. However, research on state corporate crimes has uncovered two major types: (1) when a state agency utilizes a private corporation to achieve a state goal in an illegal or socially harmful way, and (2) when omissions by a state agency allow a private corporation to pursue illegal or socially harmful acts (Kramer and Michalowski, 1990; Aulette and Michalowski, 1993). We discuss one example for each.

On January 28, 1986, the space shuttle *Challenger* took off on its last mission, tragically exploding just 73 seconds into flight, killing all seven crew members, including a New Hampshire school teacher. This case is an example of the first type of state-corporate crime because a state agency, the National Aeronautics Space Administration (NASA), utilized a private corporation, Morton Thiokol, Inc. (MTI), to launch *Challenger* despite solid evidence indicating it was unsafe to do so (Kramer, 1992; Maier and Messer-schmidt, 1998).

In its final report, the Presidential Commission (1986) that investigated the *Challenger* tragedy found that it was in part caused by technical failure (of a rubber O-ring in one of the solid rocket boosters that failed to seal properly) due to freezing temperatures preceding lift-off. But the Commission also concluded that the decision-making process that led to the fatal launch was "seriously flawed." The string of warnings unheeded, of recommendations ignored—from the early developmental stages years prior all the way through the final decision processes—culminated in the crime. Indeed, the managers at both NASA and MTI agreed to allow the launch because the former was required to "stay on schedule" (to continue receiving congressional economic support) and the latter wanted to preserve a lucrative contract (NASA was seeking bids from competitors for MTI's $1 billion contract). Thus, both NASA and MTI agreed to the dangerous launch in order to satisfy their individual organizational needs.

The second type of state-corporate crime involves omissions by state agencies that allow a private corporation to pursue harmful acts. An example of this type of state-corporate crime occurred on September 3, 1991, when an explosion and fire occurred at the Imperial Food Products chicken processing plant in Hamlet, North Carolina, killing 25 workers and injuring another 56 (Aulette and Michalowski, 1993). Investigations of the explosion and fire revealed a pattern of failures by regulatory agencies—such as the Occupational Safety and Health Administration (OSHA)—that played a significant role in creating the conditions that led to this crime. As Aulette and Michalowski further point out: "This regulatory failure was facilitated by the state of North Carolina through its refusal to fund and support the state's Occupational Safety and Health Program even to the limits of *available* Federal monies" (p. 1710).

The technical cause of the fire was a rupture in a hydraulic line near a deep fryer, which resulted in the explosion. However, the killing of 25 workers at the Imperial plant is more complex than simply a technical failure. Indeed, historically state agencies developed a pro-business and an anti-labor climate in the state, resulting in underfunding and understaffing the North Carolina–OSHA program. In such a context, that state agency often overlooked dangerous working conditions in the interest of attracting business investments in the state. Consequently, it was such omissions by state agencies that led to the "single most important" cause of the killing: a lack of accessible routes to safety. In violation of OSHA regulations, Imperial plant managers had locked the exit doors to stop employees from stealing chicken nuggets. Consequently, 25 workers died from smoke inhalation.

## 8.3 Transnational Political Crimes by the State

In 1947, President Harry Truman signed into law the National Security Act, providing not only for the Central Intelligence Agency (CIA) but also the National Security Council (NSC). The primary responsibility of the CIA, according to this act, is to gather foreign intelligence and transmit it directly to the White House; the NSC was set up ostensibly as a civilian advisory group to the president on domestic, foreign, and military policies related to national security. However, both the CIA and the NSC have used their respective powers to go beyond their legislative mandates, engaging in a variety of covert operations almost from their inception. These covert operations have, at times, violated U.S. laws, such as the Neutrality Act, which makes it a crime to prepare a means for, or to furnish weapons for, military expeditions against any foreign country with which the United States is at peace.

In addition, both the CIA and the NSC have, at times, violated international law. **International law** embodies a variety of treaties, agreements, customary law principles, and general legal principles that serve to judge the actions and behavior of various states that have agreed to them. For example, the United Nations Charter is an essential part of international law. In particular, Article 2(3) of the U.N. Charter obligates member states to settle international disputes through peaceful means, and Article 2(4) provides that no country has the right to use force or the threat of force against the territorial integrity or political independence of any state (Buergenthal and Murphy, 2002). These provisions impose a general prohibition on the use of force in international relations, but the Charter also outlines two exceptions when use of force is permitted: (1) as self-defense in response to an armed attack, or (2) through the specific authorization by the U.N. Security Council as a last resort to maintain international peace and security. If the use of force or threat of force by one state against another does not meet these two exceptions, a violation of international law has occurred.

In this final section we present examples of violations of international law by the U.S. state. These violations represent transnational political crimes by the state because they violate international law, and the resulting victimization occurs outside of the United States. More specifically, since these violations of international law entail the use of force or violence to intimidate, coerce, or change a government or civilian population for political reasons, they also constitute examples of **state terrorism**. We first discuss numerous examples of state terrorism perpetrated by the U.S. government through its foreign policy, then we end the chapter with a discussion of the state, terrorism, and globalization.

## State Terrorism

In 1953 the U.S. state engaged in its first extensive operation to overthrow a democratically elected foreign leader. This situation occurred in Iran, where the legitimately elected and reform-minded prime minister, Mohammed Mossadegh, was toppled by the CIA. The CIA (along with British intelligence agencies) planned, funded, and implemented the operation (Gasiorowski and Byrne, 2004). Mossadegh had nationalized several large foreign-owned oil companies, thus challenging U.S. interests in the region (Prados, 1986). Even though Mossadegh offered compensation, Secretary of State John Foster Dulles, and his brother Allen Welsh Dulles (then director of the CIA), supported President Eisenhower's decision to reinstate the Shah as head of Iran. Once in power, the Shah—Reza Pahlavi—was considerably more favorable to U.S. economic interests. For example, he allowed U.S. oil companies to take over almost 50 percent of Iran's oil production, and U.S. arms merchants (such as Richard Secord, who would emerge as a leading figure in the Iran-Contra scandal in the 1980s) negotiated more than $18 billion in weapon sales over the next 20 years (Moyers, 1988).

In 1957 the CIA helped set up the Iranian secret police (SAVAK), which stalked Iranian dissidents and earned a worldwide reputation for extreme sadism and frequent use of torture. From its inception, SAVAK agents "received special training at the Marine base in Quantico, Virginia, and attended orientation programs at CIA headquarters in Langley, Virginia" (Chomsky and Herman, 1979:49). While the Shah was in power, close to 1,500 people were arrested *monthly*, and on only one day, June 5, 1963, SAVAK and the Shah's army allegedly killed as many as 6,000 citizens (Simon and Eitzen, 1986). Future Iran-Contra operative Richard Secord (working with Albert Hakim) was chief of the U.S. Air Force's Military Advisory Assistance Group in Iran in 1975, which represented U.S. defense contractors selling the technology of control to the Shah (Sheehan, 1988). Secord proved an excellent representative. In 1977 alone, Iran purchased $4.2 billion worth of arms, "making Iran the largest foreign buyer of U.S. arms"; in the entire decade, the Shah purchased more than $17 billion worth of military equipment (Marshall, Scott, and Hunter, 1987).

In addition, political prisoners (arrested and incarcerated because they disagreed with government policy) numbered as high as 100,000 each year in Reza Pahlavi's Iran. Amnesty International, the human rights organization, reported twenty years after the coup (when the Shah was still in power) that Iran "has the highest rate of death penalties in the world, no valid system of civilian courts, and a history of torture which is beyond belief. No country in the world has a worse record in human rights than Iran" (cited in Chomsky and Herman, 1979:13). Thus, this early operation in Iran violated the U.N. Charter and represents an example of state terrorism.

The Iranian people rebelled against the Shah in 1979, shouting such slogans during demonstrations as "Death to the Shah" and "Death to the American Satan." Historically, the emergence of the Shah's outrageous repression, the subsequent rise of Khomeini, the hostage crisis, and the subsequent Iran-Contra scandal can all be seen as direct outcomes of the 1953 U.S. state policy in Iran (see Box 8.2 later in this chapter).

In 1954 the U.S. state turned its attention to Guatemala, violating the U.N. Charter again by overthrowing its president, Jacobo Arbenz, who received 65 percent of the vote in a democratic election (Herman, 1982). Not only did Arbenz maintain democratic institutions—such as allowing workers the right to unionize—he also launched a massive land reform program. Given that less than 3 percent of the landowners held more than 70 percent of the land when Arbenz was elected, he nationalized more than 1.5 million acres—including land owned by his own family—and turned it over to peasants (Moyers, 1988).

A considerable portion of this land belonged to a U.S.-based corporation, United Fruit Company, which immediately worked with the Dulles brothers in Washington to remove Arbenz from office (Herman, 1982). The CIA organized a contingent of "rebels," led by Castillo Armas, who crossed over the Honduras border on June 18, 1954. Although Arbenz's military attempted to hold off the rebels, it was unable to defend against CIA B-26 and P-47 air raids on Guatemala City (McClintock, 1985). Arbenz fled the country, and on July 8, 1954, he was replaced by Armas, who immediately overturned the reformist policies of the Arbenz government, returning the land to United Fruit and other landowners. Virtually all beneficiaries of the agrarian reform movement under Arbenz were dispossessed, entire cooperatives dissolved, literacy programs suspended, teachers fired, and "subversive" books burned. As Moyers (1988) pointed out, the CIA's "Operation Success" was in reality an example of state terrorism:

> The CIA had called its covert action against Guatemala, "Operation Success." Military dictators ruled the country for the next 30 years. The United States provided them with weapons and trained their officers. . . . Peasants were slaughtered, political opponents were tortured, suspected insurgents shot, stabbed, burned alive or strangled. There were so many deaths at one point that coroners complained they couldn't keep up with the workload. "Operation Success." (p. 10)

Approximately five years after Operation Success, the U.S. state began planning another covert action that violated the U.N. Charter, this time in Cuba. Prior to 1959, syndicate figures—in particular, Santo Trafficante, Jr.—were heavily invested in narcotics trafficking, gambling, and prostitution in Cuba. Fulgencio Batista, then dictator of Cuba, profited substantially from these syndicate ventures (Kruger, 1980). On January 1, 1959, however, Fidel Castro's revolution forced Batista, and much of syndicated crime, out of Cuba. Immediately the CIA moved to overthrow the Castro government, recruiting right-wing anti-Castro Cubans who had fled the country to do the dirty work (Hinckle and Turner, 1981). Under the title "Operation 40," this group organized by the CIA carried out terrorist acts against Cuba and conspired to assassinate various leaders in the Cuban government. Part of the program involved hiring Robert Maheu—an associate of Howard Hughes and a private investigator who worked for the CIA—to recruit syndicate figures John Roselli, Sam Giancana, and Santo Trafficante, Jr. to orchestrate the assassination of Castro for $150,000 (Wyden, 1979). Also involved in Operation 40 were people later identified with the Iran-Contra scandal, such as Rafael "Chi Chi" Quintero and Felix Rodriguez (both anti-Castro Cubans working for the CIA) (Marshall, Scott, and Hunter, 1987). Thus, Operation 40 consisted of a well-organized sabotage, invasion, and assassination force, later known as Brigade 2506, which was based and trained by the CIA in both the United States and Guatemala. In short, Operation 40 and Brigade 2506 were U.S. state-sponsored terrorist organizations.

In mid-April 1961 a major invasion of the Bay of Pigs in Cuba took place but was unsuccessful (Hinckle and Turner, 1981). At the last minute President John Kennedy—fearing the attack would be identified as a U.S. operation if air cover were provided to the anti-Castro Cubans—halted the air strike, leaving Brigade 2506 defenseless upon landing at the Bay of Pigs (Ranelagh, 1987). Nevertheless, the plan to assassinate Castro continued.

The assassination operation became known as JM/WAVE, was based in Miami, and consisted of some 300 agents and 4,000–6,000 Cuban exile operatives (Kruger, 1980). In addition to at least eight attempted assassinations of Castro, this CIA-directed unit was involved in *daily violations* of the law—from the National Security Act to the Neutrality Act—as well as statutes involving firearms possession and perjury (Prados, 1986). JM/WAVE involved state terrorist attacks against Cuban infrastructure—such as railroads, oil and sugar refineries, and factories—as well as, for example, contaminating exported Cuban sugar with chemicals at San Juan, Puerto Rico, and at other ports, and sabotaging shipments of machinery and spare parts en route to Cuba (p. 212). Raids against Cuban targets continued until 1965.

When JM/WAVE was dismantled in 1965, the CIA left behind a highly trained army of 6,000 fanatically anticommunist Cubans allied to syndicated crime, who eventually merged into international terrorist organizations such as Alpha 66 and Omega 7 (Kruger, 1980). These organizations ultimately became known as the "Cuban Refugee Terrorist Network," involving overlapping memberships in the different groups. According to Edward Herman (1982) in his examination of terrorism, this network was responsible for a substantial number of terrorist acts in the Western Hemisphere. Trained by the CIA in the "arts of bomb construction, demolition, and efficient murder as part of the secret war against Cuba," the network was found to be responsible for 25 to 30 bombings in Dade County, Florida, in 1975 alone. In addition, Herman has argued that this network has assassinated diplomats in Lisbon, Mexico City, New York City, and Washington, D.C.

Ironically, certain Bay of Pigs veterans in this network financed their underground terrorist operations through involvement in the illegal drug trade. Indeed, according to Kruger, a primary reason JM/WAVE was closed down was "because one of its aircraft was caught smuggling narcotics into the United States" (p. 146). Criminologist Howard Abadinsky (1989) has added that certain of these anti-Castro Cubans "imported only enough cocaine to satisfy members of their own community, but by the mid-1960s, the market began to expand, and they began to import the substance in greater quantities" (p. 209). And, as Marshall, Scott, and Hunter (1987) have asserted:

> America's drug problem today is arguably, in large measure, an outgrowth of the "secret war" against Fidel Castro begun under Presidents Eisenhower and Kennedy. . . . The connection isn't fanciful. Over the years, federal and local law enforcement officials have found CIA-trained Cuban exiles at the center of some of this nation's biggest drug rings. They had the clandestine skills, the Latin connections, the political protection and the requisite lack of scruples to become champion traffickers. (p. 134)

In 1965 many of those involved in the Miami JM/WAVE operation were transferred to Laos, where the CIA organized its secret Meo tribe army (Kruger, 1980). CIA offices were set up in Vientiane and Long Tieng, both cities becoming new centers of the heroin trade. During this time, one of the most active heroin laboratories was in Vientiane and was under the direction of Huu Tim Heng, who also built a Pepsi-Cola bottling plant on the outskirts of the city (McCoy, 1972). This plant, however, never bottled a single Pepsi but rather served as a front for the purchase of chemicals vital to the processing of heroin. Moreover, one Vang Pao, head of the Meo secret army, was extensively involved in heroin production, operating a heroin plant at Long Tieng, in Laos.

The CIA used the Meo tribespeople to combat leftist Pathet Lao forces in Laos. The only air transport in the area was the CIA's Air America. These planes ensured an adequate food supply to the Meo tribespeople through regular rice drops, thus allowing the Meo to "devote all their energies to opium production" (McCoy, 1972:283). The opium was purchased by Vang Pao's officers and flown to heroin plants in Long Tieng and Vientiane by Air America. Ultimately, the heroin was distributed to GIs in Vietnam and users in the United States. Indeed, syndicate figures invaded Southeast Asia, helping create the then-major producer and exporter of heroin around the world—the Golden Triangle (Kruger, 1980) (see Figure 8.2). It is estimated that approximately 20 percent of

U.S. troops were addicted to heroin during their tour of duty in Vietnam (Stanton, 1976). Moreover, as Bellis (1981) has argued:

> Between 1965 and 1970 the estimated number of active heroin addicts in the United States grew from about 68,000 to some 500,000. Extremely high and rapidly spreading incidence and prevalence were taken as indicators of "epidemic" heroin abuse, which grew to peak rates in American cities between 1969 and 1972. (p. 19)

It has been alleged further by Sheehan (1988) that much of the money generated by this drug trade was laundered through the Nugan Hand Bank. Nugan Hand operated a branch in Chiang Mai, Thailand (in the Golden Triangle), and several of the bank's officials—such as former CIA director William Colby—worked for the U.S. government at one time.

In 1968, "Operation Phoenix" (in Vietnam) was orchestrated by William Colby, who at the time was working for the CIA (Branfman, 1978). Although "Phoenix" was originally formed to incarcerate and assassinate members of the Vietcong—the National

**Figure 8.2 CIA-Meo Tribe Rice-Heroin Connection in the Golden Triangle**

Source: Adapted from McCoy, 1972:249–281.

Liberation Front—it involved other state terrorist acts, such as the massive roundup, incarceration, murder, and torture of thousands of Vietnamese citizens. Colby, according to Branfman, established "quotas for the number of Vietnamese to be 'neutralized' each month" (p. 113). In the end, over 40,000 enemy civilians were murdered in a three-year period, 1968–1971, and thousands more tortured (Chomsky and Herman, 1979). This then is a clear example of state-organized terror in violation of the U.N. Charter.

By 1972 the U.S. state had moved its covert operations to Chile, once again violating international law by overthrowing the democratically elected socialist, Salvadore Allende. In the late 1960s the CIA had worked closely with International Telephone and Telegraph (ITT)—because of ITT's heavy investments in Chile—to prevent Salvador Allende from being elected president; if elected, Allende had pledged to nationalize ITT (Kornbluh, 2003). When this effort failed and Allende was elected in 1970, the CIA, working with the State Department, did all it could to destabilize the Chilean economy through such practices as reducing U.S. aid to Chile (while increasing aid to the Chilean military); eliminating loans from U.S. banks and encouraging international financial institutions, such as the World Bank, to do the same; cutting supplies of and parts for U.S.-made machinery in Chile; and organizing a worldwide boycott of all Chilean products (Coleman, 2002). In addition to destabilizing its economy, the CIA worked with high officials in the Chilean military to overthrow Allende, which it did in 1973, resulting in the death of President Allende himself. A military dictatorship under the direction of Augusto Pinochet subsequently came to power. Immediately, the nationalization policies of Allende were overthrown, many democratic institutions were dismantled, and repression by the Pinochet regime grew rampant. Between 1973 and 1976, for example, over 100,000 people were detained for political reasons in Chile—over 20,000 of them were eventually killed during incarceration, and an even larger number tortured (Herman, 1982). According to Amnesty International's *Report on Torture, 1975–1976*, in Chile under Pinochet:

> The most common forms of physical torture have been prolonged beating (with truncheons, fists or bags of moist material), electricity to all parts of the body, and burning with cigarettes or acid. Such physical tortures have been accompanied by the deprivation of food, drink and sleep. More primitive and brutal methods have continued to be used. On 19 December, one prisoner was found dead, his testicles burned off. He had also been subjected to intensive beating and electricity. One day later another prisoner who died from torture had the marks of severe burns on the genital organs. (1976:113)

During Pinochet's active and brutal repression of dissent in Chile, Congress approved George H. W. Bush, in 1976, to head the CIA (Maas, 1986). Under Bush's control, the agency continued its involvement in shady, covert operations, a few of which are listed below (Corn, 1988):

- The CIA secretly provided weapons and money to "our side of the Angolan war," much of the money never reaching the rebels but, rather, pocketed by President Mobutu Sese Seko of Zaire.

- The CIA secretly worked to destabilize the "democratic-socialist" Jamaican government of Michael Manly, spending an estimated $10 million trying to overthrow the prime minister.

• Bush allegedly met, and kept on the CIA payroll, General Manuel Noriega of Panama, even though the United States had evidence linking Noriega to drug dealing and other criminal activities.

Perhaps most disturbing of all is the CIA's possible connection to "Operation Condor" while Bush was at its helm. In 1976, six Latin American states—Argentina, Bolivia, Brazil, Chile, Paraguay, and Uruguay—"entered into a system for the joint monitoring and assassinating of dissident refugees in member countries" (Herman, 1982:69). The program was encouraged by the CIA and sponsored and organized by Pinochet's secret police, DINA, which provided the initial funding and centralized coordination for the operation. Herman illustrates how Condor initially worked in Uruguay and Argentina:

> Under Operation Condor, political refugees who leave Uruguay and go to Argentina will be identified and kept under surveillance by Argentinian "security" forces, who will inform Uruguayan "security" forces of the presence of these individuals. If the Uruguayan security forces wish to murder these refugees in order to preserve Western values, Argentine forces will cooperate. They will keep the Uruguayans informed of the whereabouts of the refugees; they will allow them to enter and freely move around in Argentina and to take the refugees into custody, torture and murder them; and the Argentinians will then claim no knowledge of these events. (p. 70)

Approximately 30,000 Latin Americans were abducted and subsequently murdered under Operation Condor, a state terrorist transnational program in which the CIA acted as a link in the Condor terrorist chain (McSherry, 2001; Dinges, 2004).

---

### Box 8.2   The Iran-Contra Scandal

In February 1979 the U.S. State Department, under President Jimmy Carter, recalled more than half its officials from Nicaragua and suspended all new economic and military aid to that country. In July of that year a revolution occurred in Nicaragua, whereby the dictator Anastasio Somoza was ousted and the Sandinista National Liberation Front (FSLN) assumed power (Black, 1981).

In early March 1981, President Ronald Reagan authorized covert CIA activities against Nicaragua (Oberdorfer and Tyler, 1983). The CIA worked with Argentinians and other governments in Central America to build a paramilitary force against Nicaragua, which became known as the Contras.

Toward the end of 1981, debate in Congress and throughout the country led to widespread criticism, and increasing scrutiny, of White House intentions in Central America, especially in Nicaragua. By December 21, 1982, Congress was so skeptical that it enacted the first Boland Amendment to the Defense Appropriations Act, terminating the use of any public money for the purpose of toppling or destabilizing the Nicaraguan government (Scheffer, 1987). Nevertheless, the Reagan administration chose to ignore the Boland Amendment by secretly seeking new ways to train and arm the Contras.

One such way was "Operation Elephant Herd" (Emerson, 1988), in which the CIA clandestinely obtained, on September 22, 1983, $12 million worth of military equipment (for deployment against Nicaragua) from the U.S. military. At least 40 attacks using Elephant Herd equipment against Nicaraguan targets occurred in 1984, the most well known being on March 7 and consisting of speedboats armed with Bushmaster 25-millimeter cannon-guns firing on and destroying numerous oil facilities and storage tanks at various Nicaraguan ports. Moreover, during this time the CIA also engaged in the mining of Nicaraguan harbors, resulting in the following:

> Two small fishing boats at the Caribbean port of El Bluff were the first to detonate the mines and sank on February 25. . . . A Dutch dredger was seriously damaged at Corinto on the Pacific coast on March 1; a week later a Panamanian freighter detonated a mine. On March 20, a Soviet oil tanker reported damage at Puerto Sandino on the Pacific coast. (Gutman, 1988:198–199)

In June 1986 the World Court (the United Nations International Court of Justice) ruled that these actions by the U.S. government violated the U.N. Charter. U.S. aid to the Contras, its support of attacks on Nicaraguan oil installations and ports, and the mining of Nicaragua's harbors constituted, according to the World Court, "force against another state." By organizing and supporting the Contras, the United States had violated Nicaraguan sovereignty, amounting "to an intervention of one state in the internal affairs of another." Finally, the World Court ordered the United States "to cease and to refrain" from violating international law, and held further that the United States was obligated to pay reparations to Nicaragua. The United States simply ignored the rulings (Pfost, 1987).

Largely because of the foregoing crimes, in August 1984 Congress enacted a stronger Boland Amendment, which prohibited any administrative agency or entity involved in "intelligence activities" from "supporting, directly or indirectly, military or paramilitary operations in Nicaragua by any Nation, group, organization or individual" (cited in Scheffer, 1987:714). Congress also halted all military aid to the Contras (Gutman, 1988).

The Contras, however, obtained funds in two ways. First, considerable evidence suggests that the Contras were involved from the beginning in the illegal drug trade to support their cause (Marshall, Scott, and Hunter, 1987). In April 1988, for example, Senator John Kerry's Senate Subcommittee on Terrorism, Narcotics, and International Operations began exploring Contra drug ties throughout the 1980s. One year later, the subcommittee—in its report "Drugs, Law Enforcement, and Foreign Policy"—concluded the following: "It is clear that individuals who provided support for the Contras were involved in drug trafficking, the supply network of the Contras was used by drug trafficking organizations, and elements of the Contras themselves knowingly received financial and material assistance from drug traffickers" (U.S. Senate Subcommittee on Terrorism, Narcotics, and International Operations, 1989). Second, Oliver North (NSC liaison to the CIA) worked with others to build a private funding and supply network for the Contras (Ignatius, 1986:D1). One method they used was to secretly sell arms to Iran and then divert the funds to the Contras.

Most distressing of all, of course, is the fact that as profits were secured in a variety of ways (such as illegally selling arms and drugs), the Contras conducted a campaign of terror. Certain organizations—from Witness for Peace (a religious group that maintained a permanent presence along the Nicaraguan border to monitor Contra-Nicaragua activity) to America's Watch and Amnesty International (two human rights organizations)—have documented atrocities committed by the Contras against Nicaraguan civilians.

Moreover, former Assistant Attorney General of the State of New York Reed Brody (1985) headed a fact-finding mission to Nicaragua in 1984 and 1985, which obtained testimony from victims and eyewitnesses of Contra attacks against civilians. His report concluded that Contra activity often included the following:

- Attacks on purely civilian targets that resulted in the killing of unarmed men, women, children, and elderly.

- Premeditated acts of brutality including rape, beatings, mutilation, and torture.

- Individual and mass kidnapping of civilians . . . for the purpose of forced recruitment into the Contra forces and for the creation of a hostage-refugee population in Honduras.

- Assaults on such economic and social targets as farms, cooperatives, food storage facilities, and health centers, including a particular effort to disrupt the coffee harvests through attacks on coffee cooperatives and on vehicles carrying volunteer coffee harvesters.

- Intimidation of civilians who participated or cooperated in government or community programs such as distribution of subsidized food products, rural cooperatives, education, and local self-defense militias.

- Kidnapping, intimidation, and even murder of religious leaders who supported the government, including priests and clergy-trained lay pastors.

Thus, although the Iran-Contra affair was a covert operation hidden from the people of the United States, it was clearly not secret to its victims—a frightening example of violating the U.N. Charter and of state terrorism.

United States foreign policy in Afghanistan during the 1980s contributed to the international terrorist acts of September 11, 2001. In 1979 the Soviet Union invaded Afghanistan to avoid having a fundamentalist Islamic state as its neighbor. The United States responded by covertly supporting the fundamentalist "Jihad" against the Soviet occupation. Douglas Kellner (2003:32) summarizes this support:

> During this period, the CIA trained, armed, and financed precisely those Islamic fundamentalist groups who later became part of the Al Qaeda terror network that is now the nemesis of the West, the new "evil empire." In the battle to defeat Soviet Communism in the Cold War, the U.S. poured billions of dollars into Afghanistan to train "freedom fighters" that would overthrow the purportedly communist regime. . . . The military aid went into training and arming radical Islamic groups who would emerge with a desire to fight other wars for Islam in the countries that had earlier supported them in their Jihad against the Soviet-backed regime in Afghanistan. Bin Laden and his Al Qaeda network thus emerge as a Frankenstein of U.S. policy. (p. 32)

Nevertheless, the "secret" support for the Afghan "Jihad" against the Soviet occupation was also in part financed through the heroin trade. In the 1970s most of the heroin in the United States, as pointed out, came from the Golden Triangle geographical region. At that time, Afghanistan and northwestern Pakistan were virtually untapped opium areas, and heroin use was practically unknown in these countries (Lamour and Lamberti, 1974; Lifschultz, 1988). However, CIA support for Afghan rebels involved the Golden Crescent region (see Figure 8.3), which became one of the major heroin-producing areas of the world. The CIA arms pipeline from Karachi in the south through Pakistan to the Afghan mujahedeen in the north, was "also one of the principal routes for the transport of heroin to Karachi for shipment to Europe and the United States" (Lifschultz, 1988:495). Moreover, a great deal of the poppy crop grew in areas controlled by Afghan rebels or in areas where they had influence (Sciolino, 1988). As Bellis (1981) reported,

**Figure 8.3    Probable CIA-Supported Arms-Heroin Pipeline in the Golden Crescent**

Source: Adapted from Bellis, 1981:86; Lifshultz, 1988:495–96; Sciolino, 1988:110.

Not surprisingly, the unleashing of this opium flow from Afghanistan coincided perfectly with the arrival of the CIA on the Afghan-Pakistan border—to support and arm the tribes who were both producing opium and fighting the Russian invaders. (p. 86)

According to a General Accounting Office (1988) 1980s status report on drug abuse and drug trade, in the first six months of 1986, of the heroin in the United States, 19 percent came from the Golden Triangle and 40 percent from the Golden Crescent. In other words, as the CIA moved its operations from Southeast Asia to Southwest Asia, so, it seems, did the heroin trade. Indeed, by 1995–96, production in Afghanistan had risen to 2,600 tons of raw opium, increasing to 2,800 tons in 1997 (Cooley, 2000).

The defeated Soviet troops left Afghanistan in 1989, and president George H. W. Bush immediately "decided to completely pull out of Afghanistan rather than build democracy and a viable government in that country" (Kellner, 2003:33). The result of that decision was a massive civil war that took place for years in Afghanistan, in which the notorious Taliban emerged as the victors in the mid-1990s. The Taliban, now in political control of Afghanistan, formed an alliance with bin Laden (who had also participated in the anti-Soviet "jihad") and his Al Qaeda group, who in turn "used Afghanistan to form networks that engaged in terrorism throughout the world" (p. 32). For example, in the late 1990s, Al Qaeda bombed two U.S. embassies in Africa—as we mentioned earlier in this chapter—and the Clinton administration responded by shooting missiles into a chemical weapons factory (allegedly owned by bin Laden) in the Sudan, and Al Qaeda training camps in Afghanistan. However, it turned out that the camps had long ago been deserted and that the chemical factory was actually a legitimate pharmaceutical plant. Indeed, this pharmaceutical plant provided approximately 90 percent of Sudan's pharmaceutical products, resulting in literally "tens of thousands" of people—many of them children—suffering and dying from malaria, tuberculosis, and other treatable diseases (Chomsky, 2002).

Once it was determined that Osama bin Laden and Al Qaeda were behind the September 11, 2001, international terrorist attacks, on October 7, 2001, the U.S. state launched a ferocious air assault on an almost defenseless Afghanistan. Although the Taliban was an extremely repressive "government," especially toward women and girls, this state terrorist attack led to a "wholesale panic amongst residents of villages and cities," as well as the large-scale killing of civilians (Jones, 2004). It is estimated that as many as 3,600 civilian deaths occurred in the first two and a half months of the U.S. air campaign against Afghanistan, a figure higher than all the civilians killed in the September 11th attacks (Mahajan, 2002).

Moreover, a large number of Al Qaeda and Taliban fighters escaped capture, including Osama bin Laden, yet U.S. state officials decided to detain over 500 of those captured in a makeshift prison at the U.S. military base at Guantanamo Bay, Cuba. Labelling those detained "enemy combatants," these individuals continue to be held without any formal charges filed against them, and they are being detained indefinitely without access to a lawyer (Gareau, 2004). The detainees have also suffered torture and other cruel, inhuman, and degrading treatment, such as the use of painful stress positions, extended solitary confinement, use of military dogs as a threat, and prolonged exposure to extremes of heat, cold, and noise (Human Rights Watch, 2005a).

Although Afghans approved a new constitution in January 2004 and elected Hamid Karzai to a five-year term as president in October 2004, warlords and armed factions, including remaining Taliban forces, dominate most of the country and routinely abuse human rights (Human Rights Watch, 2005b). As Human Rights Watch point out in its most recent report on Afghanistan:

> Political repression, human rights abuses, and criminal activity by warlords—the leaders of militias and remnants of past Afghan military forces, who were brought to power with the assistance of the United States after the Taliban's defeat—are consistently listed as the chief concerns of most Afghans. . . . Local military and police forces, even in Kabul, have been involved in arbitrary arrests, kidnapping, extortion, torture, and extrajudicial killings of criminal suspects. Outside Kabul, commanders and their troops in many areas have been implicated in widespread rape of women, girls, and boys, murder, illegal detention, forced displacement, and other specific

abuses against women and children, including human trafficking and forced marriage. . . . U.S. and coalition forces, active in Afghanistan under Operation Enduring Freedom since November 2001, continue to arbitrarily detain civilians, use excessive force during arrests of noncombatants, and mistreat detainees. (pp. 1, 3)

Finally, the Afghan drug economy continues to flourish. Afghanistan was the largest worldwide producer of opium and heroin in 2004, and opium cultivation in that year increased by two-thirds from the amount cultivated in 2003, resulting in an output of 4,200 tons (United Nations, 2004). Moreover, opium cultivation has now spread to *all* provinces in the country, up from 18 provinces in 1999 (when the Taliban was in power), 23 in 2000, 24 in 2002, and 28 in 2003 (p. 3).

In 1979 Saddam Hussein became president of Iraq and the Ayattollah Khomeini returned as the leader of Iran. Tensions arose between the Iranian Islamic republic and the secular nationalist Iraq. In mid-September 1980, Iraq attacked Iran and the two countries remained at war until 1988. The U.S. state supported Iraq in its war efforts (although see Box 8.2) through loan programs with financing as well as intelligence information and military hardware. This support took place even though the U.S. state had solid evidence indicating Iraq was using chemical weapons "almost daily" against Iranian forces (Battle, 2003). In 1983 and 1984 Donald Rumsfeld headed a presidential envoy to the Middle East, meeting with Saddam Hussein on both occasions, yet during these meetings he never made any reference to Hussein about Iraq's chemical weapon use. Instead, military equipment was exported to Iraq, such as Bell helicopters (which subsequently were used to spray mustard gas on the Kurds), as well as dual-use equipment in the fabrication of missiles and enhancing Iraq's nuclear, bacteriological, and chemical war capabilities (Battle, 2003; Gareau, 2004).

Although publicly the U.S. state condemned Iraq's use of chemical weapons, it made no actual diplomatic attempt to stop that use, nor did it seem at all concerned about Iraq's repressive internal policies. Indeed, the U.S. state supported a regime in which terror was a systematic part of state policy. In its 1985 report on torture, for example, Amnesty International listed 30 types of torture used in Iraq, including beatings, burning, electric shock, and mutilation, and U.S.-based corporations sold Iraq chemicals used in producing mustard gas, Sarin, and other toxic chemical agents (Bennis, 2003). As Frederick Gareau (2004) describes Hussein's terror:

> His victims were tortured, killed, and their bodies were either returned to their families or put on public display. Either method of exposure was intended to strike terror in the target audience. . . . [T]he Iraq air force dropped 13,000 chemical bombs on its victims in the period from 1983 to 1988. (pp. 175, 177)

In addition, Hussein was ruthless toward the Shiites and the Kurds—a ruthlessness that escalated during U.S. state support for this terrorist regime. Some 300,000 Shiites were forced out of Iraq to become exiles in Iran and other countries, and approximately 250 Kurdish cities were gassed, killing approximately 7,000 and injuring as many as 20,000.

President George H. W. Bush signed National Security Directive 26 on October 26, 1989, affirming that the goal of U.S. foreign policy was to achieve normal relations with Iraq (Gareau, 2004). This relationship of course changed when on August 2, 1990, Iraq invaded and occupied Kuwait. Four days later the U.N. Security Council imposed comprehensive economic sanctions banning all trade with Iraq, and the U.N. eventually authorized the use of "all necessary means" to reverse the occupation. Subsequently, in January, 1991, the U.S. state launched a bombing campaign against Iraq, targeting specifically civilian infrastructure, such as electrical plants, water treatment facilities, factories, roads, bridges, and telecommunications. The U.S. and its coalition forces dropped 84,200 tons of munitions on Iraq during 43 days of bombing, killing 110,000 civilians, including 70,000 children under the age of 5 and 7,000 elderly (Center for Economic and Social Rights, 2003). In addition, the comprehensive economic sanctions and embargo—sustained by a massive U.S. military presence in the Middle East—resulted in over 500,000 excess child deaths between 1991 and 1998 (UNICEF, 1999; Halliday, 2004). Indeed, former U.N. Assistant Secretary General Denis Halliday (2004) stated that although the invasion and occupation of Kuwait by Iraq was illegal under the U.N. Charter, so too was the bombing of civilians and civilian infrastructure by the U.S. as well as the economic sanctions and embargo: "There is no possible justification for the murder of Iraqi children and adults, innocent of that invasion, by the United States, United Kingdom, and other powers simply because they cannot punish the leadership of Iraq. That is morally and legally unacceptable on all counts" (p. 268).

In April 1991 a cease-fire resolution included Iraq's complete withdrawal from Kuwait and an acknowledgment from Iraq that it would eliminate all of weapons of mass destruction in its possession. From 1991 to 1998, and again in 2002, U.N. weapons inspection teams carefully monitored Iraq's elimination progress. Nevertheless, on March 19, 2003, the U.S. state once again invaded Iraq, allegedly because that country continued to illegally posses weapons of mass destruction and maintain a historical, and therefore dangerous, relationship with the terrorist organization Al Qaeda. These weapons, according to the U.S. state argument, could easily be made available by Saddam Hussein to Al Qaeda for use against the United States.

However, despite considerable effort by weapons inspectors prior to the invasion and now two years after the invasion, no weapons of mass destruction have been found in Iraq and no credible evidence exists indicating a link between Hussein and Al Qaeda (Clarke, 2004). Indeed, launching a massive invasion to overthrow a government and occupy its territory in response to an uncorroborated imminent threat—which also lacked U.N. Security Council authorization to invade—constitutes a serious violation of the U.N. Charter. In 1946 the International Tribunal at Nuremburg had concluded that Germany's invasion and occupation of Norway and Denmark—allegedly in self-defense to prevent future Allied invasions—actually violated international law and therefore constituted a war of aggression (Center for Economic and Social Rights, 2003). As the Tribunal stated in its decision:

> To initiate a war of aggression, therefore, is not only an international crime; it is *the supreme international crime* differing only from other war crimes in that it contains within itself the accumulated evil of the whole. (p. 7)

The *invasion* of Iraq in 2003 was illegal under the U.N. Charter and, as we write, it is estimated that between 20,000 and 100,000 Iraqi civilians, as well as over 1,600 U.S. soldiers, are the victims of the most recent *supreme international crime*. In addition, the *occupation* of Iraq by the U.S. military also violates international law. According to the

Geneva Conventions, an occupying power must quickly end its occupation (an occupation is always a temporary status), but in the interim it must (1) protect civilians and their property, (2) ensure the well-being of the occupied population, and (3) refrain from changing the country's legal and economic system. The U.S. state has systematically violated each of these. The following are a few examples (Center for Economic and Social Rights, 2004):

**Failure to provide public order and safety.** The United States allowed the wholesale looting of Iraq's public, religious, cultural, and civilian institutions and properties. The United States also created a climate of unbridled lawlessness by dismissing the entire army, security, and law enforcement personnel without a backup plan to maintain public safety—predictably resulting in a sharp increase in violent crime, especially directed against women.

**Unlawful attacks.** U.S. forces have routinely conducted indiscriminate attacks in populated areas of Iraq, causing widespread and unnecessary civilian casualties. Ambulances, medical staff, and facilities have been targeted by snipers and regular forces.

**Unlawful detention and torture.** It is regular policy for U.S. forces to indiscriminately arrest and detain Iraqi civilians without charge or due process. Up to 90 percent of the 43,000 Iraqis detained under the occupation are innocent bystanders swept up in illegal mass arrests. The much-publicized torture, rape, and murder of detainees—at Abu Ghraib prison, for example—is a systematic practice in U.S. prisons throughout Iraq, the result of decisions made at the highest levels of the Bush administration.

**Failure to protect the rights to health and life.** The United States is not ensuring access to health care and not preventing the spread of contagious disease. The health infrastructure is in disrepair, unsanitary conditions are widespread even in hospitals, drugs and medical supplies are in short supply, clean water and sanitation are largely unavailable, and medical staff report disease outbreaks and increased mortality throughout the country.

**Fundamentally changing the economy.** The Coalitional Provisional Authority, under the direction of the United States, has issued a number of executive orders that aim to privatize Iraq's economy for the benefit of U.S. corporations, with little consideration for the welfare and rights of the Iraqi people.

## The State, Terrorism, and Globalization

**Transnational political crimes** by the state must be understood in terms of their global context. Globalization is of course the process whereby individuals, peoples, economies, and states are increasingly interconnected and interdependent. One of the most important aspects of globalization, as we pointed out in the last chapter, is the movement of capital that results from transnational corporations' search for profit in the expanding global economic market.

However, some scholars of globalization argue that transnational corporations are not simply an "important aspect" but actually have now supplanted the state as the

*Because they are operating in an increasingly global world economic system, transnational corporations—such as the oil companies—are now often beyond the control of national governments, affording such corporations more power and opportunities to engage in questionable and illegal practices worldwide.*

major actor in the world. For example, Strange (1996) argues that "the impersonal forces of world markets" have now become "more powerful than the states to whom ultimate political authority over society and economy is suppose to belong" (p. 4). And Ohmae (1995) similarly put forth the position that we now live in a "borderless world" in which transnational capital is much more powerful than individual states. David Held and colleagues (1999) have described this conceptualization of globalization as "the hyperglobalist thesis" in which these scholars share the belief that:

> [G]lobalization is primarily an economic phenomenon; that an increasingly integrated global economy exists today; that the needs of global capital impose a neoliberal economic discipline on all governments such that politics is no longer the "art of the possible" but rather the practice of "sound economic management.". . . [T]he authority and legitimacy of the nation-state are challenged: national governments become increasingly unable either to control what transpires within their borders or to fulfill by themselves the demands of their own citizens. (pp. 4–5)

In short, state managers around the globe are allegedly finding that their control and power has declined in significance and influence.

Although we recognize the increasing power of transnational corporations in fashioning the "global village," we believe that the U.S. state has not decreased—but rather has increased—its power on a global scale. In fact, one of the most significant driving forces of globalization has been the collapse of communism in the former Soviet Union (now Russia) and in countries previously under its sphere of influence (such as Poland, Hungary, and the Czech Republic). The result has been a lessening of East-West political and economic differences, as well as a conceding of sole superpower status to the United States. To be sure, with this new global standing the door was opened wide for U.S. state managers to exercise dominance around the globe. Thus, Ronald Steel (2004) describes the contemporary U.S. state as one of the most powerful—if not the most powerful—empires the world has ever seen:

> A nation possessing this kind of power—the world's dominant economy, the currency with which the world reckons and pays its bills, the most powerful armed force with bases around the globe and a budget that nearly exceeds that of all other nations combined, and a messianic desire to spread its ideology and to mold the

lives and minds of the rest of the world in its image—is by honest reckoning an imperial state. (p. 29)

This is "globalization from above" (Kellner, 2003) at its most powerful, in which the current U.S. state maintains worldwide hegemony and virtually no states have the ability to challenge that global domination. A defining feature of sole superpower status is a unilateral militarism by which the U.S. state simply *shuns* international law and *overtly* engages in state terrorism. Kramer and Michalowski (2004) use the invasion and occupation of Iraq as an example of this unique historical phenomenon:

> The invasion and occupation of Iraq by the United States and its allies is a violation of International Law, and as such constitutes state crime. It is a state crime, however, over which there is no effective social control, and for which there is no likelihood of formal sanction. As the most militarily and economically powerful nation in the world system, it appears that the United States and its leaders can, if they choose, violate International Law with relative impunity. (p. 36)

But in addition to this negative aspect of "globalization from above," there is also a negative aspect of "globalization from below." We noted one positive expression of "globalization from below" in our discussion of the anti-globalization movement and its struggle to minimize the devastating effects of globalization from above. However, not only has the anti-globalization movement emerged as a form of globalization from below, but international terrorist groups such as Al Qaeda have intensified their attacks and made use of globalization to do so (Kellner, 2003). Just as advanced forms of technology—such as airplanes—can be used to move people and goods quickly around the globe for transnational corporations, they can also be turned into weapons of mass terror and destruction. Indeed, globalization makes possible

> global terror networks as well as networks of commerce and communication. The circulation of commodities, technologies, ideas, money, and people can facilitate networks of terror, as well as trade and travel. The Internet makes possible the spreading of hate and fear, as well as knowledge and culture. Computers can be an integral part of a terror network just as they are part of businesses everywhere and many of our own everyday lives. And biotechnology, which promises such extravagant medical advances and miracles, can provide weapons of mass destruction as well. (p. 43)

Thus, the negative aspects of globalization from above has generated both types of globalization from below—anti-globalization movements and international terrorism—and both have made use of globalization to fashion their unique responses.

## Review

This chapter examined the nature, extent, types, and costs of political crime in the United States in terms of (1) political crimes against the state (violations of the law for the purpose of modifying or changing social conditions), (2) domestic political crimes by the state (violations of the law by state officials and/or agencies whose victimization occurs *inside* the United States), and (3) transnational political crimes by the state (violations of domestic and international law by state officials and/or agencies whose victimization occurs *outside* the United States).

## Political Crimes Against the State

1. Political crimes against the state involve intentional violations of criminal law for political purposes, as well as various acts criminalized by the state for the purpose of curbing political dissent.

2. Political crimes against the state may be violent or nonviolent.

3. From the Revolutionary War onward, various groups in the United States have used violence in an attempt to modify or change the social order.

4. Historically, various groups in the United States also have been engaged in such nonviolent actions as civil disobedience and demonstrations, involvement that sometimes results in their criminalization.

5. Three types of terrorism have historically been directed at the state: political assassination, domestic terrorism, and international terrorism.

## Domestic Political Crimes by the State

1. Domestic political crimes by the state are violations of law by state officials and/or agencies whose victimization occurs inside the boundaries of the United States.

2. Two major types of domestic political crimes by the state are corruption (political bribery, election fraud, and corrupt campaign practices) and political repression (illegal repression of dissent).

## Transnational Political Crimes by the State

1. Transnational political crimes by the state are violations of domestic and international law by state officials and/or agencies whose victimization occurs outside the boundaries of the United States.

2. Historically, both the CIA and the NSC have been involved in transnational political crimes—including sabotage, assassinations, and state terrorism.

## Questions for Class Discussion

1. Should the concept of political crime encompass both crimes *against* the state and crimes by the state? Why?

2. Explain the difference between violent and nonviolent political crimes against the state. Discuss why you believe the state may be interested in criminalizing each.

3. Choose two examples from the category of domestic political crime by the state and explain why you think they occur in U.S. society.

4. Discuss some additional ways globalization may facilitate political crime.

## For Further Study

### Readings

Chomsky, Noam. 2003. *Hegemony or Survival: America's Quest for Global Dominance.* New York: Metropolitan Books.

Jones, Adam, ed. 2004. *Genocide, War Crimes, and the West: History and Complicity.* London: Zed Books.

Simon, David R. 2002. *Elite Deviance.* Boston: Allyn & Bacon.

### Websites

1. <http://www.freepeltier.org>: This site updates readers on Leonard Peltier's case. It also offers links to e-mail discussion groups and to the FBI files on Peltier.

2. <http://www.actupny.org>: From ACT UP! AIDS Coalition to Unleash Power, this site provides some basic information regarding the tactics and philosophy of nonviolent civil disobedience. Readers can learn about the typical scenario after arrests have been made and the many ways to practice nonviolent protest.

3. <http://www.cesr.org>: This is the site of the Center for Economic and Social Rights, which was established to promote social justice through human rights. It has a wealth of information on violations of human rights around the world.

4. <http://www.icdc.com/~paulwolf/cointelpro/cointel.htm>: This site offers a history of COINTELPRO, an operation of the FBI. Links to other sites are provided. ✦

# Part III
## Criminological Theory

# The Origins of Criminological Theory

## Preview

Chapter 9 introduces:

- The origins of modern criminological theory.
- The key writings of the early criminologists.

## Key Terms

| | |
|---|---|
| born criminal | Enlightenment |
| classical criminology | eugenics |
| dangerous classes | neoclassical criminology |

Panopticon                                    social contract
positivism                                    social mechanics
positivist criminology

The ideas and concepts of the first criminologists originated in response to a variety of social conditions. These conditions included the legal and penal practices of the era and the concerns of government and influential sections of European society regarding the perceived dangers posed by the "dangerous classes." We do not assess directly the merits of these writings here. Worthwhile though that task is, our chief focus is on the background and social context of the era in which modern criminology began.

## 9.1 The Enlightenment and Classical Criminology

The origins of modern criminological theory can be traced to the writings of **Enlightenment** philosophers in the second half of the eighteenth century. To understand why these writings arose when they did, we begin with the notorious case of Jean Calas, a prosperous French cloth merchant who was wrongly convicted and then executed in 1762 for the murder of his son. The sentence of execution required that Calas

> in a chemise, with head and feet bare, will be taken in a cart, from the palace prison to the Cathedral. There, kneeling in front of the main door, holding in his hands a torch of yellow wax weighing two pounds, he must make the amende honorable, asking pardon of God, of the King, and of justice. Then the executioner should take him in the cart to the Place Saint Georges, where upon a scaffold his arms, legs, thighs, and loins will be broken and crushed. Finally, the prisoner should be placed upon a wheel, with his face turned to the sky, alive and in pain, and repent for his said crimes and misdeeds, all the while imploring God for his life, thereby to serve as an example and to instill terror in the wicked. (quoted in Beirne, 1993:11–12)

The Enlightenment theorists opposed Calas's execution and all other punishments like it. They objected to the form of the punishment because it was cruel and inhumane. They also disagreed with prevailing views of the relation between crime and punishment. At this time, in much of Europe crime was defined as that which opposed the Word of God as it was revealed in the dogma of Roman Catholicism. Serious crimes were often seen to result from a pact made by individual sinners with supernatural forces such as the devil, demons, and evil spirits. Catholic doctrine held that the role of lawful authorities was to eradicate the devil from the body of the condemned so that others would not be infected with their sins. The application of physical pain took a great variety of forms and was widely used both as a method of punishment and as a form of inquisition to establish the innocence or guilt of the accused. Michael Kunze (1987) offers an example of this process, the barbarous forms of inquisition used to extract confessions of witchcraft from members of a peasant family in seventeenth-century Germany. Kunze reports that only after she was left dangling upside down in midair, her hands bound behind her back and fastened to a rope that ran over a pulley connected to the ceiling, did Agnes Pappenheimer (a girl of 10) confess that she and her mother were both witches.

---

**Box 9.1    Animals on Trial**

Even nonhuman animals were occasionally subjected to judicial irrationalities. Indeed, there is much evidence that until about 1800 in Europe and in colonial America pigs, horses, and a variety of other species were formally prosecuted in criminal courts for crimes and if convicted, were executed with the full majesty of the law. One such example is the public execution in 1386 of an infanticidal sow in the French city of Falaise. Having been duly tried in a court of law presided over by a judge with counsel attending, the sow was dressed in human clothes, mutilated in the head and hind legs, and executed in the public square by an official hangman on whom had been bestowed a pair of new gloves befitting the solemnity of the occasion (Beirne, 1994).

---

Throughout Europe those accused of crimes were overwhelmingly poor and enjoyed little or no protection from legal systems unashamedly designed to serve monarch, government, church, and men of property. In England, for example, even as late as 1820 there were as many as 200 capital offenses, the great majority for crimes against property. During these judicial dark ages, the precise punishments for many crimes were not even contained in the legal codes. The enormous discretionary powers of judges were exercised arbitrarily and were often open to bribery and corruption.

The Enlightenment's reforming spirit emerged in France in the middle of the eighteenth century and grew into a widespread philosophical and humanist movement. The movement believed that reason and experience, rather than faith and superstition, must replace the excesses and corruption of feudal societies. The Enlightenment's demands were guided by several new doctrines, one of the most important of which was the doctrine of the social contract. The Enlightenment's chief theorists included Voltaire, Montesquieu, Helvétius, Rousseau, and Diderot in France; Kant in Germany; and Ferguson, Adam Smith, and Hume in Scotland.

The doctrine of the **social contract** was an attempt to avoid Thomas Hobbes' (1588–1679) belief that society was based on the nasty and brutish fact of *bellum omnium contra omnes* ("the war of all against all")—all citizens pursuing their own narrow self-interests. How then could government be justified? What was the role of law in such a society? Enlightenment philosophers responded to such questions by asserting that society was held together by a contract between citizens and property owners. The fulfillment of this contract required a governmental authority. Only with such a contract could society exist. Citizens must surrender some measure of their individuality so that the government can enact and enforce laws in the interests of the common good; the government, in return, must agree to protect the common good but not to invade the natural, inviolable liberties and rights of individual citizens. The lives of the citizenry were to be regulated and protected not by theology but by "the rule of law." This utilitarian view further asserted that those who challenged the social contract, those who decided to break its rules, and those who pursued harmful pleasures and wickedness were liable to be punished for their misdeeds.

Some writers at this time also began to protest the specific barbarities and inequities characteristic of feudal systems of justice, such as the continued use of capital punishment. This classical criminology was part of the broad Enlightenment movement.

We now examine the writings of the two most influential classical theorists: Cesare Bonesana Beccaria (1738–1794) and Jeremy Bentham (1748–1832).

## Beccaria: *Of Crimes and Punishments* (1764)

At first glance it could not have been suspected that Cesare Beccaria's *Of Crimes and Punishments* (1764) would become so influential. Little of his book was original. Its proposals for reform borrowed heavily from the existing humanist and rationalist texts of Enlightenment philosophers. Even the idea for his book was suggested to Beccaria by his friend Pietro Verri. Beccaria knew very little about criminal law and punishment when he began to write *Of Crimes and Punishments,* and his ideas were developed only after long discussions and much prodding by Pietro and Pietro's brother, Alessandro. The finished product consisted less of reasoned arguments for reform than of a controversial program of reform. Because of Beccaria's singular and continuing importance in the history of criminology, we quote major points from *Of Crimes and Punishments* at length:

2. ***The Origin of Punishments, and the Right to Punish.*** No man ever freely sacrificed a portion of his personal liberty merely in behalf of the common good. That chimera exists only in romances. If it were possible, every one of us would prefer that the compacts binding others did not bind us; every man tends to make himself the center of his whole world. . . .

Laws are the conditions under which independent and isolated men united to form a society. Weary of living in a continual state of war, and of enjoying a liberty rendered useless by the uncertainty of preserving it, they sacrificed a part so that they might enjoy the rest of it in peace and safety. The sum of all these portions of liberty sacrificed by each for his own good constitutes the sovereignty of a nation, and their legitimate depositary and administrator is the sovereign. But merely to have established this deposit was not enough; it had to be defended against private usurpations by individuals each of whom always tries not only to withdraw his own share but also to usurp for himself that of others. Some tangible motives had to be introduced, therefore, to prevent the despotic spirit, which is in every man, from plunging the laws of society into

This engraving of 'Justice' appeared at the beginning of the a 1765 edition of Beccaria's Crimes and Punishments. It was probably completed by Beccaria himself in the same year. Notice that Justice herself recoils from the executioner's offering of three decapitated heads. Instead she gazes approvingly at various instruments of labor, of measurement, and of detection.

its original chaos. These tangible motives are the punishments established against the infractors of the laws. . . .

It was, thus, necessity that forced men to give up part of their personal liberty, and it is certain . . . that each is willing to place in the public fund only the least possible portion, no more than suffices to induce others to defend it. The aggregate of these least possible portions constitutes the right to punish; all that exceeds this is abuse and not justice. . . . (pp. 11–13)

6. *Imprisonment.* Detention in prison is a punishment which, unlike every other, must of necessity precede conviction for crime, but this distinctive character does not remove the other which is essential—namely, that only the law determines the cases in which a man is to suffer punishment. (p. 19)

12. *Torture.* A cruelty consecrated by the practice of most nations is torture of the accused during his trial. . . . No man can be called guilty before a judge has sentenced him, nor can society deprive him of protection before it has been decided that he has in fact violated the conditions under which such protection was accorded him. . . . (p. 30)

16. *The Death Penalty.* It is not the intensity of punishment that has the greatest effect on the human spirit, but its duration, for our sensibility is more easily and more permanently affected by slight but repeated impressions than by a powerful but momentary action. . . . The death penalty becomes for the majority a spectacle and for some others an object of compassion mixed with disdain; these two sentiments rather than the salutary fear which the laws pretend to inspire occupy the spirits of the spectators. But in moderate and prolonged punishments the dominant sentiment is the latter, because it is the only one. (pp. 46–47)

19. *Promptness.* The more promptly and the more closely punishment follows upon the commission of a crime, the more just and useful will it be. . . . (p. 55)

20. *The Certainty of Punishment.* One of the greatest curbs on crimes is not the cruelty of punishments, but their infallibility, and consequently, the vigilance of magistrates, and that severity of an inexorable judge which, to be a useful virtue, must be accompanied by a mild legislation. The certainty of punishment, even if it be moderate, will always make a stronger impression than the fear of another which is more terrible but combined with the hope of impunity. (p. 58)

23. *Proportion Between Crimes and Punishments.* It is to the common interest not only that crimes not be committed, but also that they be less frequent in proportion to the harm they cause society. Therefore, the obstacles that deter men from committing crimes should be stronger in proportion as they are contrary to the public good, and as the inducements to commit them are stronger. There must, therefore, be a proper proportion between crimes and punishments. . . . (p. 62)

24. *The Measure of Crimes.* The true measure of crimes is . . . the harm done to society. . . . (p. 64)

41. *How to Prevent Crimes.* It is better to prevent crimes than to punish them. This is the ultimate end of every good legislation, which, to use the general terms for as-

sessing the good and evils of life, is the art of leading men to the greatest possible happiness or to the least possible unhappiness. . . .

Do you want to prevent crimes? See to it that the laws are clear and simple and that the entire force of a nation is united in their defense, and that no part of it is employed to destroy them. See to it that the laws favor not so much classes of men as men themselves. See to it that men fear the laws and fear nothing else. For fear of the laws is salutary, but fatal and fertile for crimes is one man's fear of another. . . .

Do you want to prevent crimes? See to it that enlightenment accompanies liberty. . . . (pp. 93–95)

We must stress that the image of crime and punishment in Beccaria's book is not one based exclusively on a single assumption about human nature. Borrowing liberally from the emerging determinism of the Glaswegian philosopher Francis Hutcheson, Beccaria believed—as did many others of his era—that human action was based on both free will and determinism. Indeed, attached to his humanism was Beccaria's attempt to apply to the study of crime and punishment some of the deterministic principles found in natural science, mathematics, probability theory, and the early forms of psychology. This project Beccaria termed the "science of man." From the perspective of this new science, Beccaria identified some of the causes of crime as "tyranny," "inequality of wealth," and "poverty."

In Beccaria's recommendations are the seeds of policies present in criminal justice systems around the world today, including the system in the United States. His book was the first widely read text to urge that the machinery of criminal justice use rules of due process, that sentencing policies reflect the harm inflicted on society by a given crime (essentially, that punishment "fit" the crime), and that punishment be prompt, certain, and contain a measure of deterrence. His major recommendations can be summarized as follows:

- The right of governments to punish offenders derives from a contractual obligation among its citizens not to pursue their self-interest at the expense of others.

- Punishment must be constituted by uniform and enlightened legislation.

- Imprisonment must replace torture and capital punishment as the standard form of punishment.

- Punishment must fit the crime. It must be prompt and certain, and its duration must reflect only the gravity of the offense and the social harm it caused.

*Of Crimes and Punishments* had a great impact on much of Europe and colonial America. Part of Beccaria's fame doubtless derived from the fact that in 1766 his book was condemned for its extreme rationalism and placed on the *Index Prohibitorum* (the Papal Index of forbidden books) by the Catholic church. Beccaria's influence was most visible in the new classical legal codes of Austria, Denmark, France, Poland, Prussia, Russia, and Sweden. In the fledgling United States of America, the Constitution embraced Beccarian principles, as did the Bill of Rights. Beccaria's ideas were widely quoted by Thomas Jefferson, John Adams, and others. Upon reading *Of Crimes and*

*Punishments,* English reformer Jeremy Bentham was driven to declare: "Oh! my master, first evangelist of Reason . . . you who have made so many useful excursions into the path of utility, what is there left to do?—Never to turn aside from that path" (cited in Paolucci, 1963 [1764]:x–xi). These words bring us to the other pillar of classical criminology, Jeremy Bentham, and to his writings on punishment and prisons.

## Bentham: Punishment and the Panopticon

Jeremy Bentham was a gifted and passionate young man who graduated from Oxford University at the age of 12 and who later became a law student in London. Bentham never practiced law but instead became the prolific author of numerous texts on moral philosophy, punishment, jurisprudence, prison reform, and the police. A keen critic of the British constitution, and even more so of the U.S. Constitution, he traveled extensively throughout Europe and corresponded frequently with many leading intellectuals and political figures of his day.

Although much in his writing was original, Bentham owed intellectual debts to Beccaria, inevitably, and also to Scottish philosopher David Hume (1711–1776).

Bentham was inspired by Beccaria to campaign for a rational, humane, and codified system of law. However, whereas Beccaria had simply compiled a list of humane reforms to the barbaric practices of criminal justice, Bentham intended to place these reforms on a solid philosophical foundation. While a law student, Bentham first read Hume's moral philosophy and was greatly impressed by it. Hume argued that the basic quality of moral action was its tendency to produce happiness—but that, as social beings with free will, members of a society derive pleasure from the happiness of others. Thus individual members of society should pursue not only their own pleasure but that of others. He argued that the happiness, pleasures, and security of individuals are the sole ends that laws should protect and promote. This utilitarian principle—the greatest happiness to the greatest number—became the cornerstone of Bentham's writings. We now turn to his campaign to reform punishment and prisons.

*Jeremy Bentham (1748–1832): Jeremy Bentham was one of the chief architects of the 'inspection house' known as the Panopticon. In his will, he bequeathed his original manuscripts to the University College of London on the condition that the administrators there embalm his body and put it on permanent display for all to see. This is a photograph of Bentham in his wooden and glass box. There is no more perfect irony in the history of criminology!*

***Punishment.*** In the theory of punishment outlined in Bentham's 1780 book *Introduction to the Principles of Morals and Legislation,* he assumed that potential criminals consciously calculate the profits and losses that arise from committing a crime. Similarly, he suggested, lawmakers should calculate the measures required to prevent and punish crimes. Bentham argued that in promoting the law of utility, legislators should prevent mischiefs such as crimes by means of various sanctions, including punishment. Crimes, Bentham argued, could be prevented either through positive sanctions (rewards) or negative sanctions (punishment).

However, Bentham urged that punishment not be inflicted at all in certain circumstances (1973:170–178):

- Where it is groundless—where, on balance, the act itself is not really mischievous.

- Where it is inefficacious—where it cannot act so as to prevent the mischief.

- Where it is unprofitable, or too expensive—where the cost of the punishment outweighs the cost of the harm it seeks to prevent.

- Where it is needless—where the mischief may be prevented, or cease of itself, without punishment.

Bentham argued that when punishment is worthwhile, legislators should follow four rules of utility in calculating the proportion (balance) between crime and punishment. First, the ultimate goal is the prevention of all crime. To achieve this goal, legislators should ensure that the pleasure derived from any crime always be outweighed by the pain inflicted by the punishment for its commission. Second, a person about to commit a crime should be persuaded by the very threat of punishment either not to commit that crime at all or to commit a lesser offense. Third, a person who has actually decided to commit a crime should be persuaded by the threat of punishment to do no more mischief than is necessary. In no case should punishment for a crime be more than is necessary to prevent its occurrence. Fourth, legislators should try to prevent crime as cheaply as possible.

***The Panopticon.*** In criminology, Bentham is most famous for the invention of his macabre Inspection-House, otherwise known as the **Panopticon** (Greek, meaning "all seeing"). Bentham wrote in 1787 that the principles of his Panopticon represented an unequaled power of mind over mind. The Panopticon was explicitly created to be an engine of power that would discipline all of society.

We should remember that until the late eighteenth century, prisons were crudely designed and not intended for prolonged incarceration. Their uses were limited to holding institutions for torture before trial, for debtors, for confinement prior to exe-

---

**Box 9.2   The Panopticon**

The objectives of the Panopticon were to punish the incorrigible, guard the insane, reform the vicious, confine suspects, employ the idle, maintain the helpless, cure the sick, and offer training in any branch of industry and education. These objectives therefore embraced not only prisons but also workhouses for the poor, factories, madhouses, hospitals, and schools. Bentham believed that the ingenious architectural principles of the Panopticon would enable morals to be reformed and "health preserved; industry invigorated; instruction diffused; public burdens lightened; Economy seated as it were upon a rock; the Gordian knot of the Poor-Laws not cut but untied—all by a simple idea in Architecture!" (1971, 1:i)

*The Panopticon: This illustration shows an architectural cross-section of the original Benthamite Panopticon. It depicts the central guard tower, in which the guards remained hidden from view, and the individual cells in which inmates were exposed for inspection at any time of the day or night.*

cution, and (especially in England and France) for the period between conviction and transportation to a penal colony. Bentham argued that the prison must be transformed from its position as one among many marginal and temporary institutions within the system of criminal justice to its permanent center. His plan for a penitentiary Panopticon began with a three-storied circular or polygonal building. The circumference of the building contained the prisoners' cells, which were divided by partitions in the form of radii issuing from the circumference toward the center. The prisoners were thus isolated from one another. At the building's center was a three-storied central tower, the Inspectors' Lodge, for the prison guards. Because the tower's windows were draped with blinds, the prisoners were unable to see the inspectors. The prisoners were to be seen without seeing, subject to "uninterrupted exposure to invisible inspection" (Bentham, 1971, III:88). Moreover, Bentham planned for the Panopticon to be built at a strategic location in a metropolitan area—a visible reminder to free citizens of the foolishness of their wrongdoing.

To these architectural principles Bentham added a strict regimen of visits by prisoners to the prison chapel for moral and religious instruction. Every minute of the prisoners' day was subject to discipline, order, and isolation to encourage self-reflection and moral reformation of character. Bentham's plans included rules for a crushing uniformity: in the segregation of inmates by sex and class; in diet, clothing, and bedding; in the ventilation, shading, cooling, and airing of cells; in the health, cleanliness, and exercise of prisoners; in the precise distribution of time; and in forms of punishment.

The prison governor was charged with ensuring that all prisoners were taught some marketable skill. The profits from what the prisoners produced through a system of contract labor were to contribute to the financial management of the prison. Bentham also offered suggestions for the conduct of prisoners' lives after prison: Their release was made conditional on "acceptance by a bondsman" (payment of bail) and on successful fulfillment of apprenticeship in a worthy trade or occupation.

At first, Bentham's innovative plans were praised; they were debated in Parliament, and in 1794 several sites in England were purchased for the construction of his penitentiary houses. But no Benthamite Panopticon was ever completed in England, partly because, according to some (Phillipson, 1975), King George III opposed it and Parliament deemed it too expensive. Moreover, no pure Benthamite Panopticon was built in continental Europe—despite a frenzied program of prison construction between 1780 and 1840—and the two Panopticons undertaken in the United States (one in Pennsylvania, the other in Illinois) were eventually abandoned as impractical.

Bentham's writings on crime and criminal justice were ignored and forgotten in the 50 years after his death. However, Bentham's lasting influence lay less in the actual implementation of his architectural plans than in the widespread acceptance of his principles of punishment and prison.

### Toward the Disciplinary Society

Significant questions remain about the nature of the reforms initiated by classical writers such as Beccaria and Bentham. How progressive was **classical criminology**? Whose interests did its ideas serve? Why did the proposals of Beccaria and Bentham gain widespread acceptance?

The origins of modern criminology begin with the writings of Beccaria and Bentham. Clearly, their ideas about penal reform gained official attention and were implemented in practice. But ideas about penal reform are rarely implemented simply because they are believed to be better somehow than those of their competitors; they are implemented also because they tend to serve certain interests and to achieve certain aims. Doubtless, the humanism of the classical writers commanded a measure of respect among most, if not all, sections of society in Europe and in the United States. The insistence that law must be subject to rules of due process, for example, was a progressive idea, as was a revolutionary, if rather primitive, belief in the scientific study of society that implicitly placed the classical writers at odds with the Catholic church and all those who believed that free will is the basis of human action.

At the same time, Beccaria and Bentham also championed ideas that were conservative even for their era. Though Beccaria's *Of Crimes and Punishments* was a plea for the supremacy of law rather than of religion and superstition, his proposed legal and administrative solutions to the problem of crime left untouched the social conditions in which it occurred. Bentham planned to extend Beccaria's proposals far beyond the criminal justice system. His Panopticon was to be an engine of regulation whose architectural principles would be used for the design not only of prisons but also of factories, hospitals, and schools (see Garland, 1997; Mathiesen, 1997). The ultimate aim, then, of classical criminology was not to lessen punishment but to make it more efficient and to ensure that its principles applied to everyone.

## 9.2 The Emergence of Positivist Criminology

The second source of modern criminology was **positivism**, which is a method of analysis based on the collection of observable scientific facts. Its aim is to uncover, to explain, and to predict the ways in which observable facts occur in uniform patterns. Positivist analysis can thus be applied to such things as the movement of stars through the heavens, the fertility of rabbits, and, indeed, the entire subject matter of natural sciences such as physics, chemistry, and biology. Thus, the term **positivist criminology** is used generally to refer to the search for uniformities in the area of crime and criminal justice. Table 9.1 compares the major principles of classical criminology and positivist criminology.

| Table 9.1 Classical and Positivist Criminology—A Comparison | |
|---|---|
| *Classical Criminology* | *Positivist Criminology* |
| 1. The focus of criminological study should be the administration of justice and, especially, the prevention of crime. | 1. The focus of criminological study should be the criminal and the causes of crime. |
| 2. Human action is based on free will, the "motivation" for which can be determined by psychological factors. | 2. Human action is largely deterministic. |
| 3. Crime is an action voluntarily engaged in by free-willed individuals; their motivation can be determined by psychological and social factors. | 3. Crime is an action into which individuals are propelled by social, economic, and "mental" forces largely outside their control. |
| 4. The punishment should fit the crime. | 4. The punishment should fit the criminal. |

Positivist criminology emerged in the writings and observations of various European authors in the nineteenth century. One of its forerunners was phrenology, whose founders were the Germans Franz Joseph Gall (1758–1828) and his pupil John Gaspar Spurzheim (1776–1832). This movement focused on the psychiatric concern with relationships between the organic structure of the brain, illness, and social behavior. But the phrenologists never regarded crime or criminals as the focus of their studies.

As a self-conscious effort to apply positivist principles to the study of crime, positivist criminology began with the ideas of French and Belgian statisticians in the 1820s. These ideas responded to a perceived crisis in classical criminology, and it is to this crisis that we now turn.

## The Crisis of Classicism: The Dangerous Classes

The emergence of positivist criminology in early nineteenth-century France was an important response to changes in the system of criminal justice that occurred between the middle of the eighteenth century and the beginning of the nineteenth century.

On one side of this transformation were the barbaric practices of feudal society, especially in France. At the center of the new system was a network of institutions of confinement ushered in by classical writers such as Beccaria and Bentham. These institutions had been created to control and to oversee the entire population of society and to operate on their inmates with the same monotonous precision as schools, barracks, and monasteries. Their expanding inventory included hospitals, workhouses, asylums, reformatories, houses of correction, and prisons. Their official aim was moral reformation through the deprivation of liberty and the prevention of crime through deterrence. Their "delinquent" and "pathological" inmates included syphilitics, alcoholics, idiots and eccentrics, vagabonds, immigrants, prostitutes, and petty and professional criminals. Inaugurated in 1810, the French prison system was based on a complex classification of inmates and included military prisons, debtors' prisons, agricultural colonies, and the galleys. These components operated in concert with a new criminal code, a professional police force (*gendarmerie*), a system of passport and identity cards, and an extensive network of paid informers and spies (Foucault, 1979; Stead, 1983).

Positivist criminology itself emerged from the convergence of two areas of government activity in France. From the criminal justice system, criminology acquired a secure position of status, financial support, and, because of its pronouncements about the social distribution and causes of crime, considerable interest among the citizenry. From the statistical movement, criminology acquired its intellectual orientation and the recognition by the scientific community of its methods of analysis. During the Restoration (1814–1830), the activities of the criminal justice system and the statistical movement had a common concern: the failure of the new institutions of confinement (such as prisons) to regulate the conduct of the **dangerous classes**—a derogatory term used by law-abiding citizens to describe those members of the working classes, the unemployed, and the unemployable who seemed to pose a threat to law and order.

Criminals, especially thieves, formed a large part of the dangerous classes. That the expanding network of prisons had significantly failed to control the criminal activities of the dangerous classes was apparent in at least three ways (Beirne, 1987a). First was the growing presence in urban areas of large numbers of poor, unemployed, and working-class thieves whose desperate conditions were immortalized in such works as Victor Hugo's *Les Misérables* and Charles Dickens's *Oliver Twist*. For example, Paris, despite a doubling of its population between 1800 and 1850, remained structurally intact. It is not difficult to imagine how quickly this population explosion manifested itself in the incidence of infant mortality and related social problems of accommodation, food supplies, unemployment, public order, and crime. It has been estimated that in 1800 the only source of income for 30,000 Parisians was robbery; Balzac's *Code des gens honnêtes* recorded that twenty years later there were 20,000 professional criminals and as many as 120,000 "rogues" in Paris (Chevalier, 1973).

Second, the continued presence of the dangerous classes led to widespread fear of criminality. Reports of crime were widely circulated by newspapers and government inquiries—and eagerly devoured by their audiences. During certain winters of cold and destitution, the fear of crime turned to panic and terror. This widespread fear was heightened by working-class insurrections, and it quickly became an unquestioned tenet of middle-class thought that crime and revolution were symptoms of the same disease (Tombs, 1980).

Third, after 1815 increases in the official crime rate lent support to fearful public opinion. For example, in that year a sudden increase was recorded in felony offenses, primarily in theft and disturbances of public order (Duesterberg, 1979; Wright, 1983). Between 1813 and 1820, the number of convictions in the criminal tribunals nearly doubled. Even more telling was the fact that many members of the dangerous classes were continually shuttled back and forth between incarceration and free society. This process was apparent in rising rates of recidivism, which implied that prisons were failing in their duty to reform the moral character of their inmates and that deterrence itself was a failure. In 1820 it was already understood that the prisons, "far from transforming criminals into citizens, serve only to manufacture new criminals and drive existing criminals ever deeper into criminality" (Foucault, 1980:40).

The failure of the new system of prisons to regulate the conduct of the dangerous classes stimulated considerable statistical research into their lives, which, both inside and outside prison, were examined by government investigators and independent researchers from the public health movement. One question was central: "Should (or could) the prisoners be returned to society and, if so, how?" (Petit, 1984:137). It was soon obvious that this question could not be answered with information derived solely from prison conditions. Inquiry broadened, therefore, to consider the larger population that passed through the criminal justice system. In 1825 the French government commissioned the first national statistical tables on crime, the annual *Compte général* (*General Account*). These tables were first published in 1827, immediately after a winter during which crime and death rates both increased and public fear and terror were the major themes of police reports and newspaper articles throughout Paris (Chevalier, 1973). The *Compte* reported the annual number of known and prosecuted crimes against persons and property, whether the accused (if prosecuted) were acquitted or convicted, and the punishments awarded. It also recorded the time of year when the offenses were committed and the age, sex, occupation, and educational status of both accused and convicted.

The French government reasoned that the hard facts in the *Compte's* tables could be used to understand the causes of crime and how to ameliorate them. These hopes were echoed by a group of social statisticians who were busy collecting data on such items as births, marriages, and deaths. Among this group was André-Michel Guerry, who in 1829 produced a one-page sheet of three maps that allowed the reader to see some elementary relationships between property crimes and personal crimes. But the most influential member was the young Belgian astronomer Adolphe Quetelet (1796–1874). Quetelet's account of the "social mechanics of crime" is the place to begin an examination of the development of positivist analysis in criminology.

## Quetelet's Social Mechanics of Crime

Quetelet was a brilliant student of astronomy and mathematics at the University of Ghent in Belgium. In 1823, during a visit to Paris, he learned of the potential for applying algebra, geometry, and the principles of astronomy to the understanding of social conditions. Quetelet soon turned his attention to crime and crime rates. In his book *Research on the Propensity for Crime at Different Ages,* published in 1831, Quetelet stressed that **social mechanics** could never pretend to discover laws verifiable for all individuals. But he argued that the phenomena of crime—when observed on a large scale using such statistical records as the *Compte*—obeyed the same lawlike regularities as physical phenomena. In his early writings, Quetelet attempted to show that the lawlike regularity existing in the heavens and the world of nature also existed in society.

From the astonishing regularity in French crime rates between 1826 and 1829, Quetelet inferred that the ratio of unknown crimes to recorded crimes was in practice constant (see Table 9.2). He also noted constancy in the annual number of accused (tried) and convicted and in the ratios of accused to convicted, of accused to inhabitants, and of crimes against persons to crimes against property. Furthermore, Quetelet noted regularities in the number of accused who failed to appear in the courts, in the number of convictions in different types of courts, and in the number of convicts sentenced to death, imprisonment, or forced labor. Quetelet found even the different methods of murder to be constant from one year to another.

| Table 9.2 | The Constancy of Crime, France, 1826–1829 | | | | |
|---|---|---|---|---|---|
| | | Accused of Crimes Against | | Disposition | |
| Year Accused | Accused (Tried) | Persons | Property | Guilty | % Guilty |
| 1826 | 6,988 | 1,907 | 5,081 | 4,348 | 62 |
| 1827 | 6,929 | 1,911 | 5,018 | 4,236 | 61 |
| 1828 | 7,396 | 1,844 | 5,552 | 4,551 | 61 |
| 1829 | 7,373 | 1,791 | 5,582 | 4,475 | 61 |
| Totals | 28,686 | 7,453 | 21,233 | 17,610 | 61 |

Source: Quetelet, 1984 [1831]:20, amended.

From the apparent constancy of crime rates recorded in the *Compte*, Quetelet inferred that, even if individuals have free will, criminal behavior obeys scientific laws of the same sort as those governing the motion of inanimate objects such as stars. The disproportionate presence of certain categories of people in the *Compte* between 1826 and 1829 also indicated to Quetelet that young males, the poor, and those without jobs or in lowly occupations had a greater propensity (or probability) than others to commit crimes and to be convicted of them.

Quetelet reasoned that the many causes of crime could be divided into three types: (1) accidental causes such as wars, famines, and natural disasters; (2) variable causes such as free will and personality that can oscillate between greater or smaller limits; and (3) constant causes such as age, gender, occupation, and religion. Moreover, because he saw crime as a constant and inevitable feature of social organization, Quetelet (1842) further claimed that society itself caused crime:

> Every social state presupposes, then, a certain number and a certain order of crimes, these being merely the necessary consequences of its organization. . . . Society prepares crime, and the guilty are only the instruments by which it is executed. (pp. 6, 108)

Quetelet's placement of criminal behavior in a formal structure of causality was a remarkable advance over the unsystematic speculations of his contemporaries. Flying in the face of the theory that criminals freely chose to engage in wickedness, Quetelet's intuition that society somehow caused crime marked a profound theoretical departure from the crude realism of public opinion and classical criminology.

However, in the early 1840s, Quetelet began to contrast virtues of the average law-abiding citizen with the criminality of vagabonds, vagrants, "primitives," "gypsies," "inferior classes," certain races with "inferior moral stock," and persons of low moral character. Eventually, he came to believe that unhealthy morality was manifest in biological defects and that those with such defects had high criminal propensities. Crime, he concluded, was "a pestilential germ . . . contagious . . . [sometimes] hereditary" (Quetelet, 1848:214–215).

## 9.3 Criminal Anthropology: Lombroso's 'Born Criminal'

Into this climate the notion of the **born criminal** was first introduced by Italian army physician Cesare Lombroso (1835–1909), in his book *Criminal Man* (1876). Between 1852 and 1856, as a medical student and after studying anatomy and pathology, Lombroso became concerned about Italy's high incidence of such diseases as cretinism and pellagra. When he began to study delinquents in the 1860s, Lombroso was convinced that only a scientific criminology (anthropometry) could avoid classical criminology's superstitious belief in free will.

### Lombroso's *Criminal Man* (1876)

*Criminal Man* was written from within a diverse positivist landscape that included the new prominence of the scientific method in social investigations, the claim by statisticians that science is objective and therefore factual and free of values, and the evolutionism of Charles Darwin's *Origin of Species*. According to Lombroso's own account of his intellectual development, he began to realize gradually that the only scientific criminology was one based on an analysis of the individual criminal. This he realized after a series of revelations, one of which came during his postmortem examination of the convicted thief Vilella:

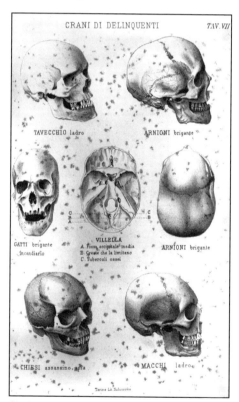

> On [Vilella's] death one cold grey November morning, I was deputed to make the postmortem, and on laying open the skull I found on the occipital part, exactly on the spot where a spine is found in the normal skull, a distinct depression which I named median occipital fossa, because of its situation precisely in the middle of the occiput as in inferior animals, especially rodents. . . .
>
> This was not merely an idea by a revelation. At the sight of that skull, I seemed to see all of a sudden, lighted up as a vast plain under a flaming sky, the problem of the nature of the criminal—an atavistic being who reproduces in his person the ferocious instincts of primitive humanity and the inferior animals. Thus were explained anatomically the enormous jaws, high cheek-bones, prominent superciliary arches, solitary lines in the palms, extreme size of the orbits, handle-shaped or sessile ears found in criminals, savages, and apes, insensibility to pain, extremely acute sight, tattooing,

*Skulls of criminals, from Cesare Lombroso, L'Uomo delinquente, 1876: These skulls were collected by the Italian army doctor Cesare Lombroso (1836–1909) and reproduced in his book Criminal Man. Lombroso believed that the signs of criminality are manifest in certain bodily deformities and in physical and mental illnesses.*

excessive idleness, love of orgies, and the irresistible craving for evil for its own sake, the desire not only to extinguish life in the victim, but to mutilate the corpse, tear its flesh, and drink its blood. (Quoted in Lombroso and Ferrero, 1972:xxiv–xxv)

The arguments of *Criminal Man* stemmed from Lombroso's autopsies of 66 male delinquents in Italian anatomical museums. He examined several aspects of the skulls of these corpses and found them to be similar to those of insane persons examined in his clinic, to those of "blacks" in the United States, to those of the Mongolian races, and above all, to those of "prehistoric man." Lombroso also studied the physiognomy of 832 living Italian delinquents. This second group of delinquents included both males and females selected from among the "most notorious and depraved" Italian criminals. Of this group, 390 of its members were compared with 868 Italian soldiers and 90 "lunatics." From these data Lombroso (1876) concluded that

many of the characteristics found in savages, and among the coloured races, are also to be found in habitual delinquents. They have in common, for example, thinning hair, lack of strength and weight, low cranial capacity, receding foreheads, highly developed frontal sinuses . . . darker skin, thicker, curly hair, large or handle-shaped ears, a great analogy between the two sexes . . . indolence . . . facile superstition . . . and finally the relative concept of the divinity and morals.

Lombroso's discoveries of the born criminal established his new school as an academic science. With the publication of its own journal and key supporting texts by Ferri ([1884] 1917) and Garofalo (1885), the *scuola positiva* formed an identifiable program. Although challenged by classical lawyers and by some socialists, Lombrosianism dominated public discussion of crime in Italy. Its reputation quickly extended beyond Italy to Germany, Russia, and France. Lombrosian findings were tested in the late 1880s and early 1890s and received favorably by converts in France and Italy (Gibson, 2002), the United States (Rafter, 1992), and elsewhere.

## Tarde's Criticisms of the 'Born Criminal'

Enthusiasm for Lombroso's concept of the "born criminal" was not universal. Criticisms of the concept were led by French sociologist Gabriel Tarde (1843–1904) and by a coalition of lawyers and anthropologists, including Topinard, Manouvrier, and Lacassagne. Criticisms were also made by criminologists in the United States, such as Frances Kellor, although somewhat later than those in Europe (see Chapter 11.1).

Three influential criticisms of the born criminal were put forward by Gabriel Tarde. First, he argued that there was no agreement about the characteristics of born criminals. In their anatomy, physiology, and pathology, born criminals were a mass of contradictory evidence. For example, one of Lombroso's disciples, Marro, having compared 456 "malefactors" with 1,765 "honest" persons, reported that criminals' cranial capacity, stature, and weight were sometimes greater than average and sometimes less (Tarde, 1890). The anthropologist Topinard reported that pictures of criminals collected by Lombroso reminded him of photos of his own friends!

Second, Tarde showed that one of the born criminal's key attributes—moral atavism (embracing lunacy, degeneracy, and epilepsy)—was absent in many cases. He noted that the Italian provinces registering the highest rates of bodily illnesses and deformities typical of degeneracy were in fact the most moral provinces—in northern Italy. Moreover, in the provinces with the highest crime rates—in southern Italy—the inhabitants had excellent health. "Does this mean," Tarde joked, "that degeneracy constitutes the best condition for the increase of morality?" (p. 237).

Third, Tarde attempted to shift the evidence from one field to another. He suggested, for example, that variations in crime rates in different areas of his native France were caused not by different concentrations of born or habitual criminals but by local variations in the incidence of such factors as poverty and alcoholism. Another example of this tactic was Tarde's attempt to reinterpret the finding that born criminals often indulged in the practice of tattooing.

However, Tarde's criticisms offered no alternative explanation of habitual criminality. Indeed, Tarde believed that individual criminals were sometimes abnormal, inferior, and degenerate beings. Tarde's contributions were his empirical criticisms suggesting that not all criminals were born to their misdeeds. His efforts led not to the complete defeat of Lombrosianism in France but to a serious decline in its intellectual influence.

In turn, the attempt to rescue the causal purity of the notion of the born criminal increasingly led Lombroso to a thoroughly eclectic notion of causality in which an infinite number of factors could predispose someone to criminality. Indeed, in one of his last major statements, Lombroso said that "[e]very crime has its origin in a multiplicity of causes, often intertwined and confused, each of which we must . . . investigate singly" (1918:1). These expanded causes included such factors as climate, temperature, age, poverty, occupation, race, and gender.

Lombroso also retreated from his claim that all criminals were atavistic beings. A new classificatory system recognized a variety of criminal types: the born, the epileptic, the criminaloid, the occasional, the passionate, and the female. Regarding the latter, Lombroso began with the idea that although female criminality increases with the advance of civilization and education, most women are not criminal (Lombroso and Ferrero, 1895) because women are both physically more "conservative" and socially more "withdrawn." Women are physically conservative—and, therefore, physically less ferocious than men—because of "the immobility of the ovule compared with the zoosperm" (p. 109), and they are socially withdrawn because they bear the larger share of childrearing and thus necessarily lead a more sedentary life. The physical characteristics of female criminals, such as prostitutes, tend to resemble those of male criminals. Extending this paternalistic logic, Lombroso argued that because most female criminals have their crimes suggested to them by men, the best deterrent to female criminality lies in an appeal to women's natural vanity—by threatening, for instance, to cut off their hair.

## Goring's *The English Convict* (1913)

Lombrosianism exercised little influence in England, but it was there that the most heralded refutation of it occurred: Charles Goring's (1913) *The English Convict: A Statistical Study*. In the history of criminology few books have commanded such high esteem. The eminent statistician Karl Pearson (1919), for example, suggested that "it is not too much to say that in the early chapters of Goring's work he clears out of the way forever the tangled and exuberant growths of the Lombrosian School" (p. xviii).

*The English Convict* combined the focal concerns of three hitherto more or less separate areas of activity. First, it continued the English tradition of prison research pursued by medical doctors such as J. Bruce Thomson, David Nicolson, and John Baker. This tradition involved the empirical calculation of "criminal propensities," often couched in the language and rhetoric of psychiatry: What mental and psychological factors distinguished prisoners from the law-abiding citizenry? Second, *The English Convict* extended the work of the British statistical movement. From the 1830s onward, the primary mission of many statisticians had been the quantification of social facts in order to address a wide range of controversial issues having to do with public health, child labor, factory conditions, education, and crime. Goring's contribution to these two traditions was the application of innovative statistical techniques to the study of criminals.

Goring's work was also strongly influenced by a third tradition, one that began with the publication of Darwin's *Origin of Species* in 1859 and that, in the 1890s, culminated in the findings of evolutionary and mathematical zoologists such as Francis Galton and W. F. R. Weldon. Galton's (1889) work on ancestral resemblance in sweet peas, for example, had shown that peas of a certain type, weight, and genetic structure tended to pass on their specific characteristics to their progeny. Weldon (1894–1895) found in his research on shrimps and crabs that creatures with deviant organs, such as long carapaces, tended to die early. Such findings led to the belief that the content of social action was itself inherited and that those with a genealogically deviant inheritance would be unable to adapt adequately to social life.

Straddling these three traditions was the desire of the professional middle class to stem the political and economic decline of the British Empire through rejuvenation of the physical stock and moral character of the British people. One platform in this social and political agenda was **eugenics** (Greek for "good genes"). It was hoped that eugenist principles could be used to eliminate a broad spectrum of social undesirables, including the physically unfit, alcoholics, the very poor, the morally and mentally depraved, and habitual criminals.

Eugenist proposals were of two sorts. Positive eugenics suggested that the middle and upper classes should be provided with incentives to intermarry and produce offspring, on the grounds that ordinarily only in these strata were intelligent and hard-

---

**Box 9.3   The Science of Eugenics**

The basic assumption of the eugenists was that the distribution of social, moral, and intellectual qualities could be discerned in humans with the same procedures used to identify the distribution of physical qualities in the world of nature. Francis Galton pioneered the view that in any nation the natural human talents that compose "civic worth" are distributed according to certain statistical laws. Galton assumed further that the distribution of worth was spread throughout society and that its presence or absence was manifest in such indicators as wealth and pathologies, respectively. In *Hereditary Genius* (1869), Galton argued—seeking retrospective confirmation from his cousin's *Origin of Species*—that it was almost exclusively the "naturally" worthy who achieved social prominence, conversely, the naturally "worthless" never succeeded in rising above their lowly positions, and this despite all government or private supports.

working citizens found. Negative eugenics demanded that social undesirables (such as habitual criminals) should be isolated, sterilized, or occasionally castrated, because their useless offspring were a drain on national resources.

These diverse traditions merged in Goring's *The English Convict.* In 1903, Charles Goring, a junior medical officer in the English prison service, was made coordinator of a government-sponsored project to test the factual reality of the concept of born criminals. Goring's tests involved three phases: (1) a statistical analysis to determine the presence of 37 Lombrosian characteristics in the criminal population, a group represented by 2,348 male convicts; (2) a comparison of the findings in the first phase with the characteristics of the "noncriminal public," represented by control groups including a company of soldiers, English and Scottish undergraduate students, and the staff and inmates of two separate hospitals; and (3) an analysis of the general physique of criminals. Goring (1913:173) concluded that in

> the present investigation we have exhaustively compared . . . criminals as a class, with the law-abiding public. . . . No evidence has emerged confirming the existence of a physical criminal type, such as Lombroso and his disciples have described—our inevitable conclusion must be that there is no such thing as a physical criminal type. (p. 173)

However, Goring did report that most criminals were physically inferior (in height and weight) to the general population. He reasoned that such differences could be explained perhaps by the process of "selection"; for example, those with inferior physiques were less likely to avoid arrest, given that the police were appointed only from among those with superior physiques. However, Goring suggested further that

> this physical inferiority, although originating in and fostered by selection, may tend with time to become an inbred characteristic of the criminal classes, just as, with the passage of generations, the upper classes of the noncriminal community have become differentiated in physique from those lower on the social scale. (p. 200)

By the early twentieth century, most European criminologists distinguished firmly between biological and sociological causes of crime. Although most eugenists dismissed altogether the relevance of sociological factors, Goring nevertheless engaged in an analysis of the relative importance of several "adverse environmental conditions"—including employment, education, family life, and social class—and of mental defectiveness and heredity on the recidivism of convicts and the types of their crimes. In this second line of analysis, Goring assumed that sociological factors, on the one hand, and mental capacities and heredity, on the other, were independent of each other. For Goring it followed that to measure the effect of one factor, the effect of others must be controlled or eliminated. He therefore assumed that maladaptive, deviant, or defective qualities of individuals in a given species were not influenced by social environment. "Our interim conclusion," he argued,

> is that, relative to its origin in the constitution of the malefactor, and especially in his mentally defective constitution, crime in this country is only to a trifling extent (if to any) the product of social inequality, of adverse environment, or of other manifestations of what may be comprehensively termed the 'force of circumstances.' (p. 288)

Goring also noted that as many as 68 percent of the male offspring of criminals became criminal themselves. Was this the result of the genetic inheritance of criminal propensities or of the influence of family? Controlling for the influence of family contagion—by eliminating it from his calculations—Goring found the intensity of the inherited factor in criminality to be extremely significant and the intensity of family contagion to be almost negligible. "Criminality," Goring concluded, is inherited "at much the same rate as are other pathological conditions in man. . . . The influence of inheritance, and of mental defectiveness [are] by far the most significant factors we have been able to discover in the aetiology of crime" (p. 368).

In sum, *The English Convict* failed to refute Lombroso's concept of the born criminal. Indeed, Lombroso's concept of born criminality still had fervent followers in the United States even in the 1930s (Rafter, 1997; and see Chapter 11.1). Goring's dubious achievement was simply to replace Lombroso's atavistic criminal with one born with inferior weight, stature, and mental capacity.

## 9.4 Neoclassical Criminology

Thus far we have described the origins of the two most influential forms of modern criminology, classicism and positivism. These two versions of criminology competed strongly for legislative and popular attention throughout Europe and North America. Yet in combination they produced unworkable dilemmas for the machinery of criminal justice.

### Penal Dilemmas

Classical and positivist criminology harbored fundamental differences of perspective on four key points (see Table 9.1). Especially after the rise of Lombrosianism in the mid-1870s, the classicists and the positivists engaged in a heated, bitter, and prolonged dispute. The outcome of this dispute—the precise contours of which varied from one country to another—had great significance for assumptions about criminal responsibility and the objectives and styles of punishment. In short, the intractable differences between classical and positivist criminologies, far from being confined to an academic arena, caused practical penal dilemmas whose resolution entailed a series of compromises agreed upon by the major institutions of criminal justice.

The serious implications of the conflict between the classicists and the positivists were best understood by Gabriel Tarde. In his 1890 book *Penal Philosophy*, Tarde (1912) took issue with the debate between the classicists and the positivists over the respective merits of free will and determinism. Neither doctrine, he argued, was justified either theoretically or practically. The doctrine of free will held that the individual, uninfluenced by any external factors, chose to do one thing rather than another with complete freedom and foresight. This position was clearly absurd, Tarde indicated, given the obvious truth of the positivist insight that crime varied according to such factors as gender, age, and socioeconomic position. The doctrine of determinism had arisen, Tarde continued, largely as a reaction to the exaggerated free-willed individualism of the classicists. Determinism viewed the individual as a machine incapable of free choice. But Tarde replied that quite apart from such factors as gender, age, and socioeconomic position, individuals were authentic beings who somehow were the "authors" of their actions. Tarde therefore concluded that neither doctrine was adequate as a basis for a coherent system of penal responsibility.

Tarde attacked certain effects classicism had on the style of criminal justice. First, he denied that free will as such should be the basis of criminal responsibility. Individuals should be held accountable for their actions whether or not they exercise free will. Every individual, Tarde asserted, has unique psychological, social, and familial characteristics. Therefore, the basis of criminal liability and the relation between liability and punishment should be a combination of the social harm caused by accountable offenders and the offenders' unique personal characteristics. Second, Tarde objected to many classical legal reforms as impractical. If individuals had unique characteristics, they should not be subjected to uniformity of treatment by the criminal justice system. Legal distinctions should be made, for example, between men and women, children and adults, violent offenders and property offenders, first-time offenders and habitual criminals, and the sane and the insane.

Tarde also attacked the positivists, chiefly because their determinism greatly contributed to the ineffectiveness of the criminal justice system. If the positivists' concept of the criminal was accepted as the basis of criminal law, Tarde believed, only two unacceptable strategies would be available for dealing with criminals: complete forgiveness of a crime or extermination of the criminal. Clearly, if the actions of criminals were "caused" by factors outside their control, rehabilitation was not a practical possibility—certainly not in the case of "born criminals." The influence of determinism was found in the increasing laxity with which prosecutors, judges, and juries treated criminals. Such leniency was apparent in the judicial tendency to reduce criminal charges from felonies to misdemeanors, which artificially reduced the crime rate and, in its turn, caused more than a threefold increase in the number of misdemeanors.

The key dilemma facing judges, legislators, and the criminal justice system, then, was this: How can justice be administered on a coherent and systematic basis? How can the partial truths of classicism and positivism be recognized without accepting the most dangerous implications of their respective extremes?

## Neoclassical Compromises

The typical response of the criminal justice system to these two critical questions was doctrinal and procedural compromise. The compromise—devised roughly between 1880 and 1920 and led by Tarde and his pupil Raymond Saleilles (1911)—is known as neoclassicism. In effect, **neoclassical criminology** has become the basis of criminal responsibility and punishment in most Western countries.

The exact terms of the neoclassical compromise between classicism and positivism varied from one country to another; nonetheless, wherever it was instituted the compromise has had six general features (Garland, 1985; Beirne, 1993):

1. The concept of character has replaced the extremes of free will and determinism as the source of criminality. An offender's character is open to analysis by experts from the fields of law, medicine, psychiatry, probation, criminology, and social work. Because the links between character and crime can

be influenced by an infinite variety of factors, crime should be understood through multicausal (multifactorial) analysis.

2. There should be an equivalence between the seriousness of crime and the degree of punishment pronounced. Punishment should be exemplary but not vengeful.

3. Imprisonment must be the normal method of punishment, and a variety of penitentiary systems should be used. The criminally insane and the recidivists should be segregated from other prisoners. There should be increased use of visitation and probation.

4. The treatment of the criminal character should not be uniform but individualized. Specific treatment, both in prison and during postrelease programs, should be administered to offenders according to the nature and the degree of an individual's incorrigibility of character.

5. Every punishment should include a measure of deterrence for future miscreants. Deterrence is unworkable only for the insane.

6. The death penalty should be abolished for nearly all crimes.

## Assessment

Classicism and positivism have been regarded as the two great systems of early criminological theory. In some ways they were quite different enterprises. Each identified a different object of analysis for criminology: the one, the application of criminal law; the other, the criminal. Each provided a different focus on punishment: Classical criminology demanded that punishment fit the social harm caused by the crime, whereas positivist criminology demanded that punishment fit the criminal. At the same time, as we have suggested, both were part of the same broad movement to apply scientific principles to the study of society. However, whereas Beccaria's criminology (and classicism in general) held that human action is based simultaneously on both free will and determinism, the positivists of the next century insisted that crime and criminality are determined, patterned, and regular events in which an individual's will is more or less irrelevant.

As the remaining chapters of Part Three argue, the intellectual history of modern criminology is largely one of positivism's triumph over classicism. So thoroughgoing has been this triumph that even neoclassical criminology—which emerged as a compromise to the extremes of both classicism and positivism—has developed in positivist terms. Most criminological theory is modeled on the positivist methods of the natural sciences. Thus criminal behavior tends to be viewed rather like the behavior of billiard balls (they move, predictably, according to certain laws of motion): The subject of criminology—the criminal—behaves according to certain sociological, historical, psychological, or economic laws. Most crime policies, likewise, are based on the assumption that individuals can be redirected toward lawful behavior, given changes in the sociological, historical, psychological, and economic causes that propel an individual into crime. The appeal of positivism in criminology is overwhelming.

But there have been mounting signs, in the last decade or so, that the fortresses of criminological positivism are not impregnable. Put simply, if positivist criminology has accurately identified the causes of crime, why do state anticrime policies repeatedly fail? Reflecting the pessimism that seems the obvious answer to this question (anticrime policies fail because we have failed to grasp the true causes of crime), criminologist James Q. Wilson (1985; and see Gottfredson and Hirschi, 1990) has gone so far as to suggest that we should perhaps abandon the search for the causes of crime. As policymakers, he reasons, all that criminologists can do today is devise anticrime policies that assume that potential criminals are rational actors who weigh the costs and benefits of engaging in crime. Wilson therefore asks us to return to the rational calculus of classical criminology. Let us devise policies that deter free-willed actors from committing crimes (and see Chapter 14.1).

Wilson's plea for the prudent use of the classical criminology of Bentham and Beccaria returns us to the beginning of this chapter. Although no modern criminological research adopts the pure model of free-willed classicism, many studies have appeared recently that focus on the deterrent effect of punishment. Although we cannot explore the complicated issues associated with deterrence in this book, we note the significant influence of classical deterrence in current research on topics as diverse as the death penalty for murder (Bailey and Peterson, 1987); the impact of gun control on violent crime (Kleck, 1997); and drinking and driving (Ross, 1992). We conclude by noting further that not one of the studies found sufficient evidence to support the view that specific legislation deters criminal behavior.

## Review

This chapter introduced the earliest theories of modern criminology, each of which has had a great impact on the subsequent development of criminological theory. Each theory defines certain ways that criminologists understand crime today.

### The Enlightenment and Classical Criminology

1. Classicism was the first form of modern criminology. It began as part of the Enlightenment's opposition to barbarism and arbitrariness in the criminal justice system.

2. Its principles are based in the belief that social action is influenced by both free will and determination.

3. The principles of utilitarianism were developed by Bentham. His views on punishment and imprisonment were widely accepted in theory, if not always in practice. Bentham is best remembered for his model prison, the Panopticon.

### The Emergence of Positivist Criminology

1. Positivist criminology began in France in the 1820s as a response to a breakdown in the classical penal system, chiefly evident in the failure of the new

systems of incarceration to regulate the conduct of the dangerous classes. Positivist criminology was (and is) based on the belief that criminal behavior is as regular, patterned, and predictable as is behavior in the world of nature and that it should be examined with the scientific method.

2. The most influential form of early positivism was Quetelet's social mechanics of crime, which derived from the convergence of the concerns of criminal justice, astronomy, and statistics.

3. Quetelet's criminology employed natural science methods to identify the constancy of crime rates, criminal propensities, and the causes of crime.

4. Although his criminology was in some respects far in advance of his time, Quetelet ultimately believed that crime has biological causes.

## Criminal Anthropology: Lombroso's 'Born Criminal'

1. In 1876, Lombroso popularized the concept of the "born criminal" in his book *Criminal Man*. This biological concept radically opposed the supposed free-willed individual of classicism.

2. Lombroso believed that born criminals have primitive features that distinguish them from the law-abiding citizenry.

3. The crusade against Lombrosianism was led by Tarde, whose critical endeavors in the 1880s and 1890s caused a decline in the influence of Lombrosianism throughout much of Europe.

4. Goring's *The English Convict* tried to disentangle the respective influences of heredity and social environment on the activities of criminals. Goring's analysis of the physical features of English convicts, and his comparisons between them and control samples of nonconvict populations, led him to decisively reject Lombroso's concept of born criminality. Through assumptions derived from eugenics, Goring also found that English criminals engaged in crime because of alleged mental deficiencies rather than for sociological reasons. This finding was quite compatible with Lombrosianism.

## Neoclassical Criminology

1. By the 1890s it was clear that a serious dilemma faced the machinery of criminal justice. Conflict between the classical and the positivist schools created a dangerous vacuum in penal policies.

2. The neoclassical school of criminology attempted to fill this vacuum with a coherent system of criminal responsibility based on accountability, individualization of punishment, and treatment programs.

3. Neoclassical criminology was led by Tarde and Saleilles. Although the exact terms of the compromise between classicism and positivism varied from one country to another, today its general outlines remain the dominant features of most Western systems of criminal justice.

## Questions for Class Discussion

Refer again to the grisly execution of Jean Calas in France in 1762, recounted at the beginning of this chapter. Less than a century later, in the 1830s, a very different penal style is visible in rules for the House of Young Prisoners in Paris. Some of these rules were as follows (cited in Foucault, 1979:6–7):

Art[icle] 17. The prisoners' day will begin at six in the morning in winter and at five in summer. They will work for nine hours a day throughout the year. Two hours a day will be devoted to instruction. Work and the day will end at nine o'clock in winter and at eight in summer.

Art. 18. Rising. At the first drum-roll, the prisoners must rise and dress in silence, as the supervisor opens the cell doors. At the second drum-roll, they must be dressed and make their beds. At the third, they must line up and proceed to the chapel for morning prayer. There is a five-minute interval between each drum-roll.

Art. 19. The prayers are conducted by the chaplain and followed by a moral or religious reading. This exercise must not last more than half an hour.

Art. 20. Work. At a quarter to six in the summer, a quarter to seven in winter, the prisoners go down to the courtyard where they must wash their hands and faces, and receive their first ration of bread. Immediately afterwards, they form into work-teams and go off to work, which must begin at six in summer and seven in winter.

Art. 21. Meal. At ten o'clock the prisoners leave their work and go to the refectory; they wash their hands in their courtyards and assemble in divisions. After the dinner, there is recreation until 20 minutes to eleven.

Art. 22. School. At 20 minutes to eleven, at the drum-roll, the prisoners form into ranks, and proceed in divisions to the school. The class lasts two hours and consists alternately of reading, writing, drawing and arithmetic.

Art. 23. At 20 minutes to one, the prisoners leave the school, in divisions, and return to their courtyards for recreation. At five minutes to one, at the drum-roll, they form into work-teams. . . .

Art. 28. At half-past seven in summer, half-past eight in winter, the prisoners must be back in their cells after the washing of hands and the inspection of clothes in the courtyard; at the first drum-roll, they must undress, and at the second get into bed. The cell doors are closed and the supervisors go the rounds in the corridors, to ensure order and silence.

1. What are the major differences between the assumptions of the two styles of punishment characterized respectively by the execution of Calas (in 1762) and by the rules for the House of Young Prisoners in Paris (circa 1837)?

2. This transformation of penal styles largely reflects changing theories on the causes of crime. Describe the broad transformation in such theories between the Enlightenment and Goring's *The English Convict* (1913).

3. Is one penal style more "humane" than the other?

4. What do these different penal styles imply about the possibility of the treatment and correction of criminals?

## For Further Study

### Readings

Beirne, Piers. 1993. *Inventing Criminology*. Albany: State University of New York Press.

Gibson, Mary. 2002. *Born to Crime: Cesare Lombroso and the Origins of Biological Criminology*. Westport, CT: Praeger.

Rafter, Nicole Hahn, and Mary Gibson. 2004. Editors' Introduction. In *Criminal Woman, the Prostitute, and the Normal Woman*, by Cesare Lombroso and Guglielmo Ferro, translated by Rafter and Gibson, 3–33. Durham, NC: Duke University Press.

Whitt, Hugh P. 2002. Inventing Sociology: André-Michel Guerry. In *Essay on the Moral Statistics of France* (1833) by André-Michel Guerry, edited and translated by Hugh P. Whitt and Victor W. Reinking, ix–xxxvii. Lewistin, NY: Edwin Mellen.

### Websites

1. <http://www.wsu.edu/~dee/ENLIGHT/ENLIGHT.HTM>: This site provides a history of the European Enlightenment as an intellectual and scientific revolution, including more detail on Descartes, Rousseau, and the philosophes.

2. <http://www.deathpenaltyinfo.org>: This is the site for the Death Penalty Information Center. Capital punishment was and remains one of the key points of debate between classical and positivist criminologists.  ✦

# The Emergence of Sociological Criminology

## Preview

Chapter 10 introduces:

- The major strands in the emergence of sociological criminology: Tarde's social psychology, Durkheimian sociology, and classical Marxism.

- The criminological theories of Gabriel Tarde, Émile Durkheim, Karl Marx, and Friedrich Engels.

## Key Terms

ideology                          restitutive law
imitation                         social classes
mode of production                social solidarity
repressive law

## 10.1 Toward a Social Psychology of Crime: Gabriel Tarde

In Chapter 9 we learned that French criminologist Gabriel Tarde believed that rising rates of recidivism were one of the most serious aspects of criminality. Departing from public opinion, Tarde did not think these rates could be explained by the criminality of Lombroso's born criminals (see Chapter 9.3). Attempting to devise a social theory of crime that would explain more about the incidence and causes of criminality than the notion of born criminals, Tarde began with the concept of "imitation."

### Imitation and Crime

Tarde reasoned that crime—like all other social phenomena—is influenced by the processes of imitation. **Imitation** is a mental process that he defined as "the powerful, generally unconscious, always partly mysterious, action by means of which we account for all the phenomena of society" (Tarde 1912:322). Imitation applies to the various psychological states and beliefs of individuals. It is a process in which individuals behave as if they were in a trance, as in sleepwalking. According to Tarde, the process of imitation always operates in a social context. Socially and historically it is present in the growth of cities, in national institutions, and even in international warfare. Imitation cuts across all social, racial, and religious boundaries. It infiltrates all aspects of social life, from art to architecture and from music to militarism. It produces both good and evil. It encourages crime.

Tarde (1903) argued that crime originates in the "higher ranks" and descends to the "lowest ranks." The masses are typically tied through imitative bondage to the ideas and fancies of their social superiors. Drunkenness, smoking, moral offenses, political assassination, arson, and even vagabondage are, according to Tarde, crimes that originated with the feudal nobility and were transmitted, through imitation, to the masses. Criminal propensities therefore typically travel downward and outward—from the powerful to the powerless, from urban centers to rural areas.

Why, then, despite a common exposure to the same set of imitative processes, do some people commit crimes while others do not? Tarde claimed that some people are born with psychological qualities that predispose them to crime. Those born with vicious dispositions, for example, are more likely to become violent. To the presence of predisposing qualities, Tarde added the necessary component of "a special kind of fever" (1912:261). This fever he variously described as a fermentation, an agitation, and a disturbance.

Despite his preference for an individualistic or psychological theory of crime, Tarde consistently identified two sociological factors that in practice had causal status in his criminology. First, he isolated *urbanism* as the greatest arena for the spread of crime through imitation. He showed that cities have the highest rate of homicide motivated by greed; it is there where murderer and victim are likely to be utter strangers, and where recidivism is most pronounced. Urban life encourages the greatest decadence in customs: the formation of political sects, increasing rates of assassination, murder and suicide, crimes against children and by children, rape, and vandalism.

For Tarde a second cause of crime was the violence fostered by *mass collective behavior.* Such violence exemplifies the processes of imitation and is closely tied to the impersonal social relations of modern urban life.

## Collective Behavior and Crime

Tarde's analysis of collective behavior reveals a frantic dislike of any body of people larger than a small and orderly gathering. For example, he suggested that "the crowd, even among the most civilized populations, is always a savage or a faun, still worse, an impulsive and maniacal beast, a plaything of its instincts and unconscious habits, occasionally an animal of a lower order" (Tarde 1892:358). Tarde often used such concepts as somnambulism (sleepwalking), paroxysm (a fit), and mental contagion (imitation) to explain the abnormality and the dangerousness of crowds in late nineteenth-century France. In his writings on collective behavior, Tarde tended to equate mob violence with organized activities of the French working class (such as strikes). "The conduct of a crowd," Tarde declared, "largely depends on the social origin of its members, on their profession, class or caste" (pp. 372–373). Moreover, "Urban crowds are those whose contagion achieves the highest degree of speed and intensity . . . their members . . . drawn from those detached from family and tradition" (p. 373). Appalled by events such as a strike by mill workers in his native region of Périgord, by anarchist uprisings in 1871 (the "Paris Commune"), and by a wave of bombings, Tarde (1893) asserted that the emotional turbulence of crowd behavior was perfectly expressed in the deluded actions of striking workers, rioters, and revolutionary political movements.

*Public execution in Paris, May 1, 1871: This photograph depicts the execution of 62 police officers by the communards of the Paris Commune during the civil war between the Third Republic and the Paris Commune. Events such as this aggravated the French public's fear of crime and fostered the analysis of mob behavior by Gabriel Tarde.*

Tarde shared certain prejudices with sociologist Émile Durkheim. Before considering Durkheim's analysis of crime, we briefly assess Tarde's contribution to the development of criminology.

## Evaluation of Tarde's Social Psychology

Tarde's criminology was an intriguing attempt to place both the sociological and the psychological dimensions of life into a unitary perspective. In his own era, Tarde's perspective was of enormous influence. His social psychology of crime forged a compromise between the classical and positivist schools of criminology. His theories on the causes of crime anticipated and influenced later developments in criminology (see Sasson 1995; Zimring and Hawkins 1997). Tarde's concept of imitation and his theories about urban life and crowd behavior, for example, explicitly influenced certain of the most important theoretical developments in criminology in the United States—among them the Chicago school of criminology (see Chapter 11.2), Merton's theory of anomie (see Chapter 11.3), Sutherland's theory of differential association (see Chapter 11.4), and subcultural perspectives on delinquency (see Chapter 12).

## 10.2 Toward a Sociology of Law and Crime: Émile Durkheim

Émile Durkheim (1858–1917) was one of the founders of sociological criminology, and his analyses of crime and punishment exert a powerful influence in the world of criminology today. Durkheim was a prodigious scholar whose innovative concepts and arguments spanned a great diversity of topics. The breadth of his interests is best seen in the titles of his major books: *The Division of Labor in Society* (1893), *The Rules of Sociological Method* (1894), *Suicide* (1897), *Professional Ethics and Civil Morals* (1900), and *The Elementary Forms of Religious Life* (1912).

Durkheim's writings on law and crime have had tremendous intellectual influence on the development of criminology. In much of his sociology, Durkheim tried to answer the difficult questions about how order and stability could be restored to France as it made the disruptive transition from a preindustrial social structure to modern and more complex forms of social organization in the nineteenth century: What are the preconditions of an ordered, stable, and moral society? What conditions produce social disorder? A logical consequence of Durkheim's search for the sources of

How is public order possible? A late-nineteenth-century French industrial scene.

social order was a concern with situations in which order and stability seemed to be lacking and that were manifest in such "pathologies" as crime and deviance.

Before outlining Durkheim's writings on law and crime, we emphasize a theme that spanned his entire work: a sociological method. For Durkheim, societies can be analyzed properly only through the scientific method of positivism. Like Quetelet's social mechanics (see Chapter 9.2), Durkheim's positivism involved a search for lawlike regularities in social behavior. Unlike Tarde, Durkheim insisted that generalizations about social behavior can be made independently of individual variations in free will, psychological state, and motivation.

Durkheim's positivist method stemmed from his insistence that "the first and most basic rule is *to consider social facts as things*" (1982:60). Durkheim's chief intention here was to distinguish sociology from such sciences as biology, politics, and psychology by making the "social fact" its object of study. But for Durkheim social facts were not to be confused with the psychic phenomena that exist only in individual consciousness; in reality, although we are often victims of the illusion that we act with free will, our actions are usually imposed on us externally. Durkheim defined social facts as "manners of acting, thinking and feeling external to the individual, which are invested with a coercive power by virtue of which they exercise control over him" (p. 52). Social facts are thus obligatory and coercive. They have this character not because they are practiced by many people but because they are practiced collectively. "Social phenomena," Durkheim wrote, should thus "be considered in themselves, detached from the conscious beings who form their own mental representations of them" (p. 70).

For Durkheim, then, social phenomena (such as law and crime) have an objective existence of their own and exist quite independently of the individuals who experience them. This is a crucial insight, as we shall learn.

## Law and Social Solidarity

Durkheim analyzed law in many of his writings. His most extended treatment occurs in *The Division of Labor* (1893). Here he tried to find the sources of social order ("social solidarity") in modern industrial societies and to determine the changes they undergo during evolution from lower to higher stages of civilization.

Durkheim argued that social development lies along a continuum, with primitive societies of "mechanical solidarity" at one end and modern societies of "organic solidarity" at the other. Mechanical solidarity is typical of simple societies with only a limited role specialization or division of labor. Members of such societies are quite similar to each other in their ways of acting, thinking, and feeling. They live within a shared consensus of beliefs and values—the "collective conscience"—in which collective life dominates and replaces individualism. During the course of social evolution, as roles within the division of labor became more specialized, **social solidarity** is transformed from a mechanical to an organic basis. Organic solidarity is thus typical of societies with an advanced division of labor and with members who have diffuse ways of acting, thinking, and feeling. Individualism dominates and replaces collective life. The cohesion of such societies derives from complex patterns of interdependence among the members and is based on the morals of various occupational categories and also on increasing respect for individual differences.

In his search for the sources of social order, Durkheim realized that social solidarity, which is abstract and internal to consciousness, does not lend itself to exact observation or precise measurement. Thus, to classify and compare the various forms of social solidarity he believed that it was necessary to use another, more visible aspect of social life that varies directly with solidarity. Durkheim argued that "to arrive at this classification, as well as this comparison, we must therefore substitute for this internal datum, which escapes us, an external one which symbolizes it, and then study the former through the latter" (p. 24). That visible symbol, he asserted, is law.

Durkheim never explicitly defined the essential qualities of law, but he implied that law differs from other forms of social regulation (including custom, ritual, ceremony, and professional obligation) because it alone exercises an organized pressure on individuals to conform to its commands. This pressure appears in the form of sanctions. To classify the different types of law, which themselves correspond to the different types of social solidarity, Durkheim reasoned that one must only classify different types of sanctions. Two forms of legal sanction correspond to the two forms of social solidarity: repressive sanctions and restitutive sanctions, which Durkheim termed respectively repressive law and restitutive law.

Durkheim held that **repressive law** is found chiefly in societies of mechanical solidarity. It is religious in origin and largely identical with penal and criminal law. The violation of repressive law results in the use of repressive sanctions. These sanctions consist of inflicting suffering or loss on individuals for having offended the strong sentiments of the collective conscience. Because repressive sanctions tend to be enforced by the whole of society, no special or organized institution (lawyers, courts, police, and so forth) is needed to enforce them. Durkheim provided numerous examples to show that the vast majority of the commands of ancient legal systems—such as the last four books of the Pentateuch (Exodus, Leviticus, Numbers, and Deuteronomy)—are solely directed to sentiments offended by crimes.

During the evolution from mechanical to organic solidarity, Durkheim argued, the volume of penal law in legal systems declines relative to other forms of law. He noted that certain crimes, such as those offending sexual and traditional sentiments, have nowadays almost disappeared (1984:109–110). With the decline of collective sentiments and the growth of individualism, repressive law is gradually ousted by **restitutive law**. This law consists not in the infliction of pain but in *"restoring the previous state of affairs, reestablishing relationships . . . disturbed from their normal form"* (p. 29). Restitutive law, growing continually in volume and intensity, results not from breaches of the collective conscience but from conflicts among occupational groups (for example, guilds, unions, and professional associations). Its violation involves enforcement of the *status quo ante* (previously existing state of affairs). Moreover, in contrast to repressive law, restitutive law is specialized through its two basic forms: (1) *Positive law* reflects the co-operation required in a complex division of labor and includes contract, administrative, domestic, and commercial legislation. (2) *Negative law* involves the rules between persons and objects that enjoin others not to interfere in certain proprietary rights of the owner and includes property and tort legislation.

## The Nature of Crime

Durkheim's analysis of relationships between law and sanctions was a critical tool for understanding social solidarity. In pursuing this goal he was led to analyze the nature of crime. As a sociologist, Durkheim rejected definitions of crime based on legalistic criteria. Such criteria—as well as criteria based on notions such as evil, social harm, violations of justice, and so forth—he regarded as inadequate for a scientific sociology.

What, then, is crime? To begin, no action is intrinsically or universally criminal. For Durkheim, the common denominator of all crimes is that they are "acts repressed by prescribed punishments" (1984:31). This is what distinguishes a crime from a minor offense such as a tort or a breach of etiquette. In societies of mechanical solidarity, an act is defined as criminal because of the universal social reaction that condemns it. As Durkheim argued in *The Division of Labor:* "An act is criminal when it offends the strong, well-defined states of the collective consciousness. . . . We should not say that an act offends the common consciousness because it is criminal, but that it is criminal because it offends that consciousness" (pp. 39–40). From this it seemed to follow that to investigate the nature of crime one must examine the nature of punishment.

What functions, then, does punishment serve? Central to Durkheim's criminology is his linking of crime and punishment. Thus: "If our definition of crime is exact it must account for all the characteristics of . . . punishment" (p. 44). Durkheim defined *punishment* as "a reaction of passionate feeling, graduated in intensity, which society exerts through the mediation of an organized body over those of its members who have violated certain rules of conduct" (p. 52).

Durkheim rejected popular beliefs that the function of punishment is simply revenge, deterrence, or the reformation of the character of criminals. The true function of punishment is to maintain and strengthen social solidarity. Each time a crime is committed, the subsequent condemnation of it by penal law reaffirms the values of the collective conscience or the shared consensus of a community's beliefs and values. In this way "honest people" are convinced of the moral righteousness of their conformity to law and of the "inferiority" of criminals. With great insight, Durkheim therefore concluded that "punishment is above all intended to have its effect upon honest people" (p. 63).

Durkheim made three specific claims about the nature of crime: (a) crime is normal, (b) crime is inevitable, and (c) crime is useful.

***Crime is normal.*** Durkheim caused considerable outrage by claiming that crime is a normal phenomenon, as normal as birth and marriage. Durkheim's discussion of this seemingly unusual claim is found in his 1894 book *The Rules of Sociological Method*, in which he tried to restructure "the fundamental facts of criminology." Durkheim's starting point—like the starting point of his sociology in general—was his concept of the social fact: "*A social fact is normal for a given social type, viewed at a given phase of its development, when it occurs in the average society of that species, considered at the corresponding phase of its evolution*" (p. 97; emphasis in original).

In other words, in a given social context and against the background of a given level of social development, the very generality of social facts indicates that they must be normal phenomena. At any given moment society has a "normal" or statistically average volume of births, for example, or of marriages and deaths. For Durkheim, it is only statistical deviations from such averages that are abnormal. Because crime is a social fact, Durkheim complained that criminologists err in seeing it only as a pathological or morbid phenomenon. Generally, crime should not be viewed as deviance or as sickness—what is abnormal to the biologist or to the pathologist is not necessarily so to the sociologist.

For Durkheim, then, crime as such is rarely abnormal. Crime occurs in all societies, it is tied closely to the facts of collective life, and its volume tends to increase as societies evolve from lower to higher phases. However, he was careful to add that although crime is a normal social fact, in a given context its rate might be abnormal.

***Crime is inevitable.*** To begin with, Durkheim admitted that his idea about the normality of crime surprised him. Eventually, he reasoned that no society can ever be entirely free of crime. To illustrate this point, Durkheim asked that we imagine a community of saints in a perfect and exemplary monastery: "In it crime as such will be unknown, but faults that appear venial to the ordinary person will arouse the same scandal as does normal crime in ordinary consciences" (1982:100). Moreover, universal and absolute conformity to rules is impossible because each member of society faces variation in "the immediate physical environment, . . . hereditary antecedents, . . . [and] social influences" (p. 100). Crime is therefore inevitable. Even if all the actions regarded as criminal at one moment suddenly disappeared, new forms of crime would be created at once.

***Crime is useful.*** Durkheim first claimed that crime is normal and inevitable in *The Division of Labor.* But in *The Rules of Sociological Method* he took the argument a stage further in suggesting that "to classify crime among the phenomena of normal sociology is not merely to declare that it is an inevitable though regrettable phenomenon arising from the incorrigible weakness of man; it is to assert that it is a factor in public health, an integrative element in any healthy society" (p. 98).

Besides claiming that crime is normal and inevitable, Durkheim thus argued that crime is useful because crime is indispensable to the normal evolution of law and morality. Indeed, if crime is not a sickness, punishment cannot be its remedy. The nature of crime and punishment must therefore lie somewhere else than in the area of wrongdoing and its correction. If there were no crimes—if there was no deviation from social norms—Durkheim reasoned, then the collective conscience would have reached an intensity, an authoritarianism, unparalleled in history. In other words, a society with "no crime" must be an extremely repressive one.

For Durkheim, crime is useful because it is often a symptom of individual originality and a preparation for changes in law and morality. He cited the fate of Socrates as an example of crime's utility. Socrates (470–399 B.C.), perhaps the most original of all Greek philosophers, committed the "crime" of independent thought. Having been convicted of not believing in the official gods of the Athenian state and of corrupting the minds of the young, Socrates committed suicide by drinking hemlock. Durkheim suggested that "Socrates' crime served to prepare the way for a new morality and a new faith—one the Athenians . . . needed [inasmuch as] the traditions by which they had hitherto lived no longer corresponded to the conditions of their existence" (1982:102). Today's criminal may be tomorrow's philosopher!

## Anomie, Egoism, and Crime

Durkheim applied his sociological insights to the analysis of two specific forms of deviance: suicide and homicide. First, he tried to show that suicide—usually regarded as the supreme act of individual deviance—has profoundly sociological rather than psychological or biological causes. Indeed, Durkheim (1951) claimed that variations in suicide rates can be explained only sociologically. His general concern was to show that the suicide rate of any society depends on the type and extent of social organization and integration. In any society each social group

> really has a collective inclination for the act, quite its own, and the source of all individual inclination, rather than their result. It is made up of the currents of egoism, altruism or anomie running through the society under consideration. . . . These tendencies of the whole social body, by affecting individuals, cause them to commit suicide. (pp. 299–300)

Durkheim's explanation of varying suicide rates hinges on four types of suicide:

1. *Egoistic suicide* results from a weakening of the bonds between an individual and society. It is a special type of suicide caused by excessive individualism. It recedes only with the sort of increase in collective sentiments produced by wars and political crises. Social groups prone to egoistic suicide include Protestants (whose religious beliefs foster individualism), the unmarried, the childless, and the widowed.

2. *Altruistic suicide* results when individuals have insufficient inner strength to resist the demands of a social group into which they are overly integrated. Examples include Hindu widows, who place themselves next to their husbands on their funeral pyre, and slaves, who are expected to die with their masters.

3. *Anomic suicide* results from a sudden crisis in economic or familial life. Thus, in situations such as sudden impoverishment or unexpected riches, or immediately after family members are divorced, an abrupt change in expectations causes massive personal or social upheaval. In the aftermath of these situations, those who cannot adjust to their suddenly altered position become more suicide-prone (and see Chapter 12.3).

4. *Individualized suicide* has particularized characteristics, either in the mental state that leads to the act or in the way it is achieved. These characteristics include melancholy, passion, and irritation, though these might also have social causes.

In addition to suicide, Durkheim (1958) analyzed the offense of homicide. He suggested that civilized peoples always consider three broad moral attitudes as duties: respect for life, respect for property, and the honor of others. In primitive societies, homicide is the most serious breach of moral duty because it is viewed as an offense against the whole of society, against what is sacred. Offenses against individual property or individual honor are seen as far less serious than offenses against the social order as a whole—and sometimes they are not considered offenses at all. In ancient Greece, Rome, and Judea, for example, victims of crimes other than homicide had to pursue their own redress and could allow the guilty party to pay a sum of money as a form of satisfaction.

Durkheim suggested that during social evolution, and especially with the onset of Christianity, something of a reversal occurs in the hierarchical order of these duties.

With the growth of modern societies, collective sentiments are generally reduced in intensity and sentiments centering on the individual achieve prominence. Homicide therefore remains the supremely forbidden act because it violates the individual. Given that homicide is so abhorred, Durkheim (1958) claimed that homicide rates tend to decline relative to the advance of civilization. At the same time, rates of other offenses against the individual, whether against person or property, tend to increase.

Durkheim was confident that homicide rates decreased with modernization because of the growth of the "cult of the individual" (namely, the great respect afforded the person by public opinion). But Durkheim knew that this explanation was too general:

> The decline in the rate of homicide at the present day has not come about because respect for the human person acts as a brake on the motives for murder or on the stimulants to murder, but because these motives and these stimulants grow fewer in number and have less intensity. (p. 117)

How, then, does one explain cases in which the general rule about declining homicide rates does not apply? To explain counterexamples, Durkheim introduced statistical evidence showing how other variables—including rural/urban differences, wars, religious membership, political crises, and state power—influence homicide rates. For example, he argued that Catholic countries tend to have higher homicide rates than Protestant ones because the latter's religious beliefs are more individualistic and, therefore, promote greater respect for the sanctity of individual life.

### The Evolution of Punishment

In his 1901 essay "Two Laws of Penal Evolution," Durkheim offered a sophisticated theory of the history of punishment, returning squarely to his earlier concern with law and crime in *The Division of Labor*. This final theory on the sources of punishment, and of changes in its justifications and forms, was a marked improvement on earlier analyses. Indeed, in his entire criminology it was only here that Durkheim considered that political factors sometimes influence the way in which certain behavior is defined as criminal.

In the essay, Durkheim modified his earlier argument to suggest that forms of punishment have varied historically in two ways, quantitatively and qualitatively. Each form is governed by a separate law, one quantitative in scope, the other qualitative (see Box 10.1).

Durkheim's first law contains two propositions. First, societies are more or less advanced according to their level of social complexity or to the intensity of their division of labor. Here Durkheim repeated his argument that less-developed societies are domi-

---

**Box 10.1  Durkheim's Two Laws of Penal Evolution**

Law 1: The intensity of punishment is greater the more closely societies approximate to a less-developed type—and the more the central power assumes an absolute character.

Law 2: Deprivations of liberty, and of liberty alone, varying in time according to the seriousness of the crime, tend to become more and more the normal means of social control.

nated by repressive laws and barbaric forms of punishment, especially capital punishment. In such societies punishment is severe because most crimes are seen as religious violations that threaten the collective conscience. The second proposition concerns absolutist forms of political power: the exercise of governmental power without checks and balances. This authoritarian form of power (hypercentralization) exists in different types of society, early and modern, but occurs only when it is seen as a right: "Such was the state of the criminal law until the middle of the eighteenth century. There then occurred, throughout Europe, the protest to which Beccaria gave his name" (1983:113).

Durkheim's first law implies that with social development the severity of punishment generally declines. This decline occurs not because authorities become more lenient but because the type of crime changes. In less-developed societies, crime is seen as a threat to collective life, and, therefore, punishment is severe; in more-developed societies, crime is seen as a threat to individuals only, and punishment is correspondingly less severe. However, by identifying the importance of the relationship between state power and punishment, Durkheim could now explain certain factual counterexamples to his earlier analysis. For example, he now claimed, interestingly, that in societies dominated by political absolutism, crimes retain a primarily sacrilegious character (1983). In other words, authoritarian societies act punitively and repressively not because they are not socially developed but because their organs of political power regard crime religiously—as an attack on the social order as a whole.

Durkheim's second law refers to qualitative changes in punishment. Durkheim illustrated the workings of the second law with examples from ancient Greece and modern France. He established that the death penalty had disappeared completely from some legal codes and had been taken over by incarceration. Durkheim explained this change by arguing that there is no need for incarceration in less-developed societies. There, a crime affects the entire community, and, because responsibility for it is communal, all members of the community ensure that the offender does not escape before trial. However, with the disintegration of ancient societies—after which crime became more of an offense against an individual rather than society as a whole—some method of pretrial detention was needed to ensure that offenders were held accountable.

Thus, Durkheim advanced the brilliant argument that the prison emerged from changing forms of crime. But he realized that this explanation was incomplete: "To explain an institution, it is not enough to establish that when it appeared it served some useful end; for just because it was desirable it does not follow that it was possible" (1983:117). Hence Durkheim proceeded to explain the growth of the prison in terms of his first law concerning the less repressive nature of punishment. Prisons arose because of the transformation in criminal responsibility from a collective to an individual basis. Some of the first prisons were "hole[s], in the form of a pit where the condemned wallow in refuse and vermin" (p. 119). But prisons, responding to the changed basis of criminal responsibility, gradually became milder, reflecting the general decline in the severity of punishment. As punishment as a whole became less severe, these new prisons became the typical form of punishment in developed societies.

Durkheim therefore concluded that "the qualitative changes in punishment are in part dependent on the simultaneous quantitative changes it undergoes" (p. 120). His two laws of penal evolution thus turn out to be interdependent. The very facts that bring about changes in the bases of criminal responsibility in early societies also create the apparent need for widespread use of imprisonment in modern societies!

## Evaluation of Durkheim

Quite aside from the power and scope of its analysis of crime, Durkheim's criminology has exerted tremendous influence on the development of sociological criminology. This influence has been most obvious in the writings of the Chicago school of criminology (see Chapter 11.2), Merton's theory of anomie and social structure (see Chapter 11.3), and Hirschi's theory of control and crime (see Chapter 12.3). Moreover, criminologists today continue to draw on Durkheim's insights.

More than anyone before him, Durkheim identified the sociological links among crime, law, punishment, and social organization. He showed that in any given society the amount and types of crime relate directly to the basic ways in which that society is organized. And societies, he insisted, should be understood historically. Durkheim also suggested that crime must be explained sociologically rather than in terms of an individual's psychological state or biological nature. Sociologically, crime is a normal and inevitable feature of social organization. Its functions lie not only in the area of sanctions but also in the creation and enforcement of solidarity.

Assessments of Durkheim's criminology tend to focus on three questions. Did he correctly describe the historical transformation in styles of punishment? Have homicide rates declined with modernization? How did his own personal and political agenda influence the propositions set forth in his various theories?

The first question has been debated largely in terms of whether the facts of the evolution of punishment fit Durkheim's theory of crime. In a well-known study that examined legal evolution in 51 societies, Schwartz and Miller (1964; see also Garland 1990) concluded that in simple societies restitutive law is more common than penal sanctions. This conclusion contradicts Durkheim's account of the evolution from repressive to restitutive sanctions. Therefore, it is reasonable to conclude that

> Durkheim may have derived his idea [of the evolution of punishment] from the fact that punishments in European societies were becoming much less severe at the time, due to the reforms introduced by Beccaria and other classical theorists. But the extremely harsh punishments that had been imposed prior to those reforms were not associated with simple, undeveloped societies, but rather with absolute monarchies. (Vold, Bernard, and Snipes, 2002:112)

In answering the second question, empirical researchers have reached quite opposing results. While some have found that homicide rates have declined with modernization (e.g., Quinney, 1965), others have found an increase (e.g., Ortega et al., 1992). Still others claim that most researchers have not really tested Durkheim's theory at all. Instead, as DiCristina (2004) points out, most commentaries on Durkheim's theory of homicide have been rather careless in understanding exactly what Durkheim meant by concepts like "societal complexity" and "modernization." Moreover,

> Overall, the empirical studies that attempt to assess Durkheim's theory of homicide require extensive reinterpretation since they misrepresent his theory and/or neglect its complexity. Indeed, in view of its complexity, its potential for extensive elabora-

tion, and the considerable data limitations researchers face when testing it . . . Durkheim's theory is not readily "falsifiable." (DiCristina, 2004:83)

Finally, we note that Durkheim is also frequently criticized for the biases that allegedly entered his sociological method in general and his criminology in particular. Durkheim has thus been scolded because his preoccupation with the sources of social order apparently led him to neglect the sources and expressions of social conflict. It is indeed true that Durkheim's criminology is based on certain assumptions: for example, that law tends to stem from and reflect widely held social values, that crime is a breach of these shared values, and that an examination of the political factors that influence the definition of certain actions as criminal is not necessary. A sustained disagreement with such assumptions was an important theme in the works of Marx and Engels. We now turn to their writings about the relationships between law, on the one hand, and power and domination on the other.

## 10.3 Classical Marxism: Marx and Engels on State, Law, and Crime

An introduction to the emergence of sociological criminology would be seriously incomplete without an analysis of the perspectives of the authors of classical Marxism: Karl Marx (1818–1883) and his colleague and friend Friedrich Engels (1820–1895). Before outlining the various claims Marx and Engels made concerning the nature of crime, we briefly consider certain key concepts of their writings.

### Key Concepts of Marxism

The development of Marxian theory can be traced to Marx and Engels' initial acceptance, subsequent rejection, and ultimate transcendence of early nineteenth-century German idealist philosophy. In his very first writings in the 1840s, Marx strongly opposed the idea that history and social change reflect such idealist factors as God, the intellect, reason, the spirit, and the progress of civilization. Marx gradually developed a materialist concept of historical change. His materialism combined the ideas of English political economists (such as Malthus, Ricardo, Bentham, and Say) and French socialists (including Saint-Simon, Lassalle, and Fourier), forging them into a new theory termed "historical materialism."

Marxism is based on the concept that although human beings make their own history, they do not do so entirely as they choose. "The history of all hitherto existing society," Marx and Engels famously declared, "is the history of class struggles" (Marx, 1969a:108). During such struggles **social classes** actively create and recreate the conditions of their existence. At the same time, the very existence of social classes means that members of a society cannot live exactly as they would choose. Social classes, therefore, also constrain social relationships. Class position is an important determinant of such basic life events as social mobility, consciousness, level and types of education and income, leisure patterns, and (as we see later) the likelihood of incarceration.

What, then, did Marx and Engels understand by the term "social classes"? To grasp this term properly we begin with their concept of **mode of production**, which Marx analyzes carefully in his lengthy book *Capital* (1868). Analytically, the concept "mode of production" entails two major elements: the means of production and the social relations of production.

"Means of production" refers to specific types of technology, capital, labor, tools, machinery and equipment, monetary systems, and land. In combination, these items are the necessary raw materials for producing commodities. All these materials, combined in various ways, are required to produce commodities as different as bicycles and criminology textbooks. They are subject to almost infinite variety. Commodities such as reading materials, for example, can be produced on stone tablets, papyrus, parchment, biodegradable paper, and computer discs. Commodities can also be produced, exchanged, and sold on a small or a large scale and by capital-intensive or labor-intensive means.

"Social relations of production" refers to the many ways in which members of a society relate both to the possession (legal or otherwise) of the means of production and to the distribution of the commodities that result from the process of production. For example, the productive process can occur in the institutional context of private or communal relationships; it can occur at home, in fields, or in factories; its participants can be slaves, free laborers, white-collar workers, bankers, landed gentry, industrialists, or state bureaucrats. The productive process can be more or less influenced by gender. It can be unaffected by or be dominated by political authority.

The means of production and the social relations of production, in combination, compose a mode of production. In their theory of history, Marx and Engels identified several distinct modes of production: primitive communal, slave, feudal, Asiatic, capitalist, socialist, and communist. Engels usually, but Marx almost never, saw such modes of production as definite stages through which all societies evolved. Several modes of production can exist in one society. For example, until at least the Civil War in the 1860s, slave, feudal, and capitalist modes of production all coexisted in the United States. Again, during the 1920s, feudal, capitalist, and socialist modes of production all coexisted in the USSR. However, in any given society, one mode of production tends to dominate and lend its character to other aspects of social relationships (Marx, 1973).

Any given society, depending on its dominant mode of production, has typical social classes. Under capitalism—Marx's primary focus—typical classes include the *lumpenproletariat* (the perennially unemployed, those "unfit" for work), the *proletariat* (skilled and unskilled workers), the *middle class,* and the capitalist class (those who own capital: industrialists, financiers, commercial speculators, and landlords). In capitalist societies the basic class struggle is between the capitalist class (bourgeoisie) and the working class (proletariat). The economic site of this particular struggle is the productive process; the struggle occurs over the distribution of the fruits of this process. The capitalist class, on the one hand, strives to maximize profit from the unpaid labor of the working class. Its income lies in rent, interest, and industrial profit. The working class, on the other hand, strives to maximize wages. It attempts to do so by reducing the length of the working day, by compelling employers to pay higher wages, and by wresting from the capitalist class such concessions as health insurance, work-safety regulations, and job security. The goals of the capitalist class and the working class are thus mutually exclusive. Typically, the one maximizes its return from the productive process at the expense of the other.

For Marx and Engels, then, social classes are determined chiefly by their economic position within a given mode of production. The relationships among classes are rarely fixed; they vary according to changes in the political and economic power of one side or another. However, in Marxian analysis the basic source of conflict in capitalist societies is between those who own the means of production and those who have no source of income other than their labor. This exploitive situation is inherently unstable and, Marx and Engels asserted, tends to lead toward socialism. Under socialism the means of production are socialized and class struggles begin to evaporate.

We note here the great importance of political power to the maintenance, development, or rupture of a mode of production and the class relationships associated with it. Maintenance of class relationships ultimately depends on coercion. Sometimes this coercion is quite naked; usually it is a subtler process. The relationship between economic position and political power—and, indeed, between economic position and many other aspects of social life—Marx often depicted in terms of the metaphorical "base and superstructure." He once described the relationship between economy and politics in the following terms:

> In the social production of their life, men enter into definite relations that are indispensable and independent of their will, relations of production which correspond to a definite stage of development of their material productive forces. The sum total of these relations of production constitutes the economic structure of society, the real foundation, on which rises a legal and political superstructure and to which correspond definite forms of social consciousness. The mode of production of material life conditions the social, political and intellectual life process in general. It is not the consciousness of men that determines their being, but, on the contrary, their social being that determines their consciousness. (1969c:503–504)

The mode of production thus conditions the life process in general. It does so with a mechanism Marx and Engels term ideology. **Ideology** has several meanings in their writings. First, it refers to any set of structured beliefs, values, and ideas. Examples include bourgeois ideology, proletarian ideology, and legal ideology. *Bourgeois ideology*, for example, refers to beliefs and values—such as thriftiness and respect for private property—typically held by bourgeois (capitalist) classes. In capitalist society, the ideas of the capitalist class tend to be the ruling ideas.

Second, ideology refers sometimes to a set of mistaken or false beliefs. "Ideology is a process," wrote Engels, "accomplished by the so-called thinker consciously, it is true, but with a false consciousness" (1970d:496). Marx often attacked religious beliefs ("the opium of the masses"), not only because he believed they alienated people from each other but also because religious beliefs wrongly assumed the existence of God. In the same context, Marx sometimes contrasted ideology with science: Ideology is false belief; science is correct belief.

Finally, and most difficult, the term "ideology" refers to a set of beliefs that both reflect social reality and simultaneously distort it. To help understand this dual process, think of a straight stick standing upright in a pool of water. In this situation the image conveys the appearance that the stick is bent. Thus, the image is both a reflection of physical matter (governed by the laws of optics) and a distortion of it (the stick is not actually bent). This final meaning of ideology, then, refers to a process whereby beliefs, deriving from real social relationships, hide or mask the precise nature of such relationships. Certain ideas, such as those associated with justice, fulfill the ideological function of masking from exploited classes the nature of their oppression and its precise source.

This final meaning of ideology was especially important for Marx and Engels's analysis of state and law. Here the institutions and doctrines of state and law play a key role in the dominance of bourgeois ideology.

## State and Law

Marx and Engels used the term "state" to refer broadly to the organs of political authority and to the ideological processes that underpin the legitimacy of this authority, including the standing army, police, bureaucracy, clergy, and judicature. Generally, Marx and Engels saw the state both as a product of society at a certain level of development and as an institution that seemingly stands above society. However, this apparent ability to stand above society and represent itself as neutral and independent of class struggles is in fact an ideological distortion, inasmuch as the state and its various components are actually manipulated by the dominant class.

***The state thus has a class character.*** In capitalist societies the state is typically a weapon or instrument manipulated by the capitalist classes, though Marx realized that state activities are not always so simple. For example, in one analysis of French politics, Marx (1969b) described how the French state represented the interests of millions of smallholding peasants. In this sort of scenario, the state can be a prize actively pursued by contestants in the class struggle.

***Law is a crucial component of the state apparatus.*** In class societies law is endowed by Marx and Engels with several functions (Cain and Hunt, 1979). First, law tends to reflect and promote the interest of the dominant class in private property. It does so by promoting and protecting all private property, thereby obscuring the fact that the vast majority of property is owned by only a tiny fraction of the population. Law fulfills this function through constitutions, through statutory and case law, and, with support from agencies of the criminal justice system, by enforcing compliance with its commandments. Second, law operates as a central mechanism of bourgeois ideology. Through such notions as "justice" and "fair play," law promulgates the idea that it is independent of economic and political interests and that it can mediate conflicts in the interests of the whole society. But in class societies law cannot do this: To apply law fairly and equally in a society of inequality is merely to perpetuate inequality. Legal doctrines such as "the rule of law" and "equality before the law" are thus no more than fictions designed to lull the populace into believing that law truly does stand above society as an impartial arbiter. Finally, law acts as a repressive apparatus. Typically, this function is activated when the legal system represses the working class and its organized political movements.

## Criminalization as a Violation of Rights

In certain of Marx's writings the process of criminalization was described somewhat moralistically as a violation by the state of some natural or inalienable human rights.

Thus, in commenting on a decrease in the official crime rate in Britain between 1855 and 1858, Marx complained:

> This apparent decrease of crime, however, since 1854, is to be exclusively attributed to some technical changes in British jurisdiction; to the Juvenile Offenders' Act . . . and to the Criminal Justice Act of 1855, which authorizes the Police Magistrates to pass sentences for short periods, with the consent of the prisoners. Violations of the law are generally the offspring of economical agencies beyond the control of the legislator . . . [but] it depends to some degree on official society to stamp certain violations of its rules as crimes or as transgressions only. This difference of nomenclature, so far from being indifferent, decides on the fate of thousands of men, and the moral tone of society. (Quoted in Cain and Hunt, 1979:189)

In one of his very first articles—written in 1842 when he was a radical journalist in Prussia—Marx (1975a) attacked censorship laws because they violated real freedom of expression. By "real" freedom Marx meant not only freedom to do certain things but also freedom not to be exploited by others. In another 1842 article—which led him eventually to study economic relationships—Marx (1975b) discussed a Prussian law, enacted by the Rhineland Assembly, on the theft of wood. Despite a serious shortage of firewood and a depression in the local wine industry, this draconian law made it a criminal offense for anyone to collect and pilfer fallen wood in private forests. Marx attacked this law as a blatant undermining of what had been a customary right of the Rhenish peasantry since the sixteenth century.

## Crime and Demoralization

There is another way in which Marxian writings argued that criminalization violates rights. Many of Marx and Engels's writings analyzed the capitalist mode of production, and it is difficult not to believe that they thought capitalist production was unjust. Thus Marx (1859) wrote in the *New York Daily Tribune,* commenting on the lot of the Irish peasantry: "There must be something rotten in the core of a social system that increases its wealth without diminishing its misery, and increases in crimes even more rapidly than in numbers." For Marx, the social system associated with capitalist production was unjust partly because it permitted others (namely, capitalists) to profit from workers' labors.

It is a simple matter of historical record that from the birth of industrialization to the time when Engels wrote *Condition of the Working Class in England* (1845), British capitalism spawned gruesome living and working conditions for the mass of the population. Sometimes these conditions led to competition among members of the working class, and hence to crime (Engels 1975a). In Marxian analysis these conditions led to massive demoralization. This psychological condition, in its turn, led either to crime or to rebellion.

The linking of crime and demoralization is a vivid and recurring theme in many of Marx and Engels's more polemical passages. Thus Engels wrote that the working class is

> cast out and ignored by the class in power, morally as well as physically and mentally. The only provision made for them is the law, which fastens upon them when

they become obnoxious to the bourgeoisie. Like the dullest of brutes, they are treated to but one form of education, the whip, in the shape of force, not convincing but intimidating. There is, therefore, no cause for surprise if the workers, treated as brutes, actually become such. (1975b:411–412)

In another passage, Engels blamed the appalling conditions at home and at work for the criminality of the working class in Manchester. These conditions produced demoralization that, in turn, fostered widespread "drunkenness, sexual irregularities, brutality, and disregard for the rights of property" (p. 421). Engels also suggested a different form that demoralization might take: "True, there are, within the working class, numbers too moral to steal even when reduced to the utmost extremity, and these starve or commit suicide; . . . numbers of the poor [actually] kill themselves to avoid the misery from which they see no other means of escape" (p. 412).

## Crime and Primitive Rebellion

One alternative to demoralization was rebellion. In *Capital* (1868), Marx documented the rebellion of the British working class against the harsh emergence of industrial capitalism. As a class, British workers first manifested opposition to the bourgeoisie by resisting the introduction of machinery; the Luddites even smashed it or attempted to assassinate manufacturers. "Theft," said Engels "was the most primitive form of protest" (1975b:502–503).

Although Marx and Engels identified certain working-class crime as rebellion, they did not look on it favorably. Doubtless they shared with their contemporaries a puritan assessment of the activities of the dangerous class. In addition, Marx and Engels condemned such forms of rebellion as having no value for working-class revolutionary consciousness. Thus Engels lamented that working-class crime is "the earliest, crudest, and least fruitful form of this rebellion" (p. 502). Elsewhere, Marx and Engels analyzed the class allies on which the working class could realistically depend for the growth of its revolutionary movement. Within that context, they complained: "The 'dangerous class,' the social scum, that passively rotting mass thrown off by the lowest layers of the old society, may, here and there, be

Friedrich Engels commented in harsh terms about the terrible effects of unbridled industrialization on the English working class in the 1840s: dangerous working conditions, poverty, open sewers, air- and water-borne diseases, and street crime.

swept into the movement by a proletarian revolution; its conditions of life, however, prepare it far more for the part of a bribed tool of reactionary intrigue" (1848:118).

## Evaluation of Marxism

Marx and Engels's writings are an important part of the development of sociological criminology. Their writings, like Durkheim's, have endured among criminologists because they offer a radical, sociological approach to crime in capitalist societies. Crime, in their view, is not caused by moral or biological defects in individuals but by fundamental defects in a society's social organization.

Marx and Engels saw crime, as Durkheim did, as an inevitable feature of existing social organization. Unlike Durkheim, they believed that crime is inevitable because it is an expression of basic social and class inequalities. Working-class crime, especially, results from demoralization and occasionally turns to primitive rebellion. The extent of crime and its forms, they suggested, should be understood in the context of the specific state, legal system, and class relationships associated with a given mode of production. Yet Marx and Engels did not explain crime simply by reference to economic factors. They clearly understood that crime involves a political process in which the state criminalizes certain conduct and in so doing often reflects the interests not of society as a whole but of certain groups within it. Crime, Marx and Engels sometimes suggested, was a form of rebellion against this process. This idea was taken up by criminologists in the 1970s and 1980s (see Chapters 13.3, 13.4).

Marx and Engels never seriously addressed certain basic questions about the nature of crime. Why, for example, are some actions defined as criminal but others are not? Because they did not consider this definitional question, Marx and Engels, like most of their Victorian contemporaries, tended to accept that crime is a violation of moral or good conduct. In arguing, therefore, that the lumpenproletariat and the unskilled working class engage in the great bulk of this conduct, they generally ignored the different types of crime committed by different classes. Finally, the writings of Marx and Engels contain no analysis of the links between crime and other forms of social inequality (see Chapter 3).

## Review

This chapter outlined the early forms of sociological criminology, which derived many theories and concepts from problems identified in the basic social organization of societies. This linking of crime and social organization was, and is, the key feature of sociological criminology. These ideas indelibly influenced the subsequent development of criminological theory.

## Toward a Social Psychology of Crime: Gabriel Tarde

1. Tarde developed a theory about the causes of crime that attempted to combine individualistic and sociological concepts. He was the leading critic of such biological theories of crime as Lombrosianism.

2. Tarde applied the concept of imitation to crime, thereby suggesting that, in addition to the importance of sociological factors, individual mental states contributed to the growth of crime.

3. Influenced by the growth of socialist and anarchist insurrections in France, Tarde pinpointed the imitative behavior of crowds and mobs as one of the leading causes of violence in modern societies.

## Toward a Sociology of Law and Crime: Émile Durkheim

1. Émile Durkheim was one of the founders of sociological criminology. His writings were an extremely successful attempt to integrate a theory of crime with a theory of law. His analysis of crime and punishment exerts great influence on modern criminology.

2. Durkheim's sociological method was based on the idea that societies can be fully understood only by the scientific method of positivism. Like Quetelet's social mechanics, Durkheim's criminology attempted to find regularities in criminal behavior.

3. Durkheim's criminology began with the belief that types of law and types of social solidarity were intimately connected. Mechanical solidarity is associated with repressive law; organic solidarity is associated with restitutive law. During the evolution from mechanical to organic solidarity, the volume of repressive law declines relative to other forms of law. This is one way of explaining the broad transformation in penal strategies that accompanied the Enlightenment and classical criminology (see Chapter 9.1).

4. Durkheim argued that the function of punishment is to maintain and strengthen social solidarity rather than to repress crime. Crime is a normal, inevitable, and useful form of social activity. Detailed analyses of crime in Durkheim's works concentrate on suicide and homicide. Both of these crimes testify to the sociological causes of crime and, especially, to the effects of anomie and egoism on them.

5. Durkheim argued that forms of punishment have varied in history according to two laws. Quantitatively, punishment has tended to be more repressive the less developed the society and the more absolute the power of the central authority. Qualitatively, the more developed the society, the more imprisonment tends to become its dominant form of social control.

## Classical Marxism: Marx and Engels on State, Law, and Crime

1. Marx and Engels's writings on state, law, and crime were set in the context of their sociological analysis of modern capitalist societies.

2. The key concepts of Marx and Engels's sociology are social classes, mode of production, means of production, social relations of production, and ideology. The articulation of these concepts defines the movement of social relationships throughout history, although their primary concern was with relationships in capitalist societies.

3. Marx and Engels generally insisted that the institutions of state and law, and the doctrines that emerge from them, serve the interests of the dominant economic class. The state arises from class struggles and gives the false appearance of independence from social classes. Law is endowed with several functions: It defends and enforces existing property relationships, and in class societies it does so in the context of unequal ownership of property; it acts as an ideological mechanism, promoting respect for private property; and in moments of acute class struggle, it acts as a mechanism of repression.

4. Marx and Engels offered a view of crime and capitalism that differed greatly from the social contract and free-will theorists of the Enlightenment. They defined crime in three ways: as a violation by the state of natural or human rights, as a result of the demoralization caused by the gruesome conditions of industrial capitalism, and as a form of primitive rebellion.

## Questions for Class Discussion

1. What did Durkheim mean when he said that "crime is normal"? Are societies with high crime rates necessarily worse off than societies with low crime rates?

2. Is crime inevitable? If so, under what circumstances?

3. Can you describe the social organization of a future society in which crime has disappeared entirely?

## For Further Study

### Readings

Garland, David. 2001. *The Culture of Control: Crime and Social Order in Contemporary Society.* Chicago: University of Chicago Press.

Greenberg, David F., ed. 1993. *Crime and Capitalism: Readings in Marxist Criminology.* 2nd ed. Palo Alto, CA: Mayfield.

### Websites

1. <http://www.relst.uiuc.edu/durkheim>: This site provides readers with biographical and academic summaries of Durkheim's work. Also listed is information about how to join an e-mail discussion list related to Durkheim.

2. <http://www.spu.edu/~hawk/marxh.html>: This site provides summaries of Marx's and Engels's writings, including *The Communist Manifesto.* There is also a useful link to "contemporary Marxism" for those who wish to explore the current state of Marxism.

3. <http://www.runet.edu/~lridener/DSS/DEADSOC.HTML>: This is a website funded by the American Sociological Association, the National Science Founda-

tion, and Radford University. It offers biographical information and summaries of the work of many of the key nineteenth-century and early twentieth-century sociologists in Europe and the United States.

4. <http://www.crimetheory.com>: This site is an elementary resource on criminology, and includes sections on learning, researching and teaching criminology. It is maintained by Professor Bruce Hoffmann of Ohio University.  ✦

# The Emergence of Criminology in the United States

## Preview

Chapter 11 introduces:

- Certain key themes and prejudices of the diverse analyses of crime that prospered in the United States before 1915.

- The social and intellectual factors that contributed to the emergence of criminology in the United States.

- The innovative methods and concepts of the Chicago school of social ecology, culminating in the findings of Shaw and McKay's *Juvenile Delinquency and Urban Areas* (1942).

- Merton's theory of "anomie," which offers a sociological explanation for the high rates of deviance and crime in the United States.

- The contributions of Edwin Sutherland—in particular, his theories of differential association and differential social organization, and his books *The Professional Thief* (1937) and *White Collar Crime* (1949).

## Key Terms

| | |
|---|---|
| anomie | rebellion |
| Chicago school of criminology | retreatism |
| conformity | ritualism |
| differential association | social disorganization |
| innovation | social ecology |
| institutionalized means | white-collar crime |
| norms | |

Chapters 9 and 10 introduced the most influential theories of crime fashionable in much of Europe at the dawn of the twentieth century. These theories are important not only because they acted as stepping-stones in the historical development of modern criminology but also because they exert a powerful influence on the ways in which we understand crime today.

Moreover, this historical introduction to criminological theory should provide a valuable lesson in intellectual humility: the sobering realization that our understanding of crime has not advanced much beyond that of theories put forward over 100 years ago. Yet this dubious progress is not peculiar to criminology. Taken as a whole, the social sciences have been notoriously unsuccessful in putting forward any confirmed generalization on social behavior! Criminology, then, shares its "failure" with other social sciences.

In this chapter, we continue our historical introduction by moving from Europe to the United States. We begin with certain of the diverse explanations of crime favored before 1915, just prior to the growth and professionalization of criminology in the United States.

## 11.1 The Early History of Criminology in the United States, 1895–1915

Prior to the emergence of the Chicago school of criminology in the decade after 1915, the study of crime had few institutional facilities with which to develop a systematic intellectual content. It is therefore hard to isolate a precise event or idea that marked the first appearance of a criminology indigenous to the United States.

Following the end of the Civil War in 1865, a multitude of published opinions concerning crime appeared. These views were voiced in amateurish ways by persons with vested interests in crime and criminality: prison reformers, medical doctors, psychiatrists, journalists, politicians, social reformers, philanthropists, and moral crusaders. Some treatises were enlightened for their era, such as the humanitarian proposals by the Pennsylvania Quakers for the reform of prisons and punishment, especially when compared with alternative proposals of the same era. Indeed, it is highly debatable whether the humanitarian basis of the modern penitentiary marks a real advance over pre-classical forms of punishment (see Chapter 9.1).

The ideological leanings of these early works have been usefully charted by Boostrom (1974). Behind these works, he suggested, lay four basic beliefs that paved the way for the development of a criminology whose focus would become the "correction of criminals" (pp. 2–3):

1. The idea that crime is an alien phenomenon in American society. Crime was claimed to be a phenomenon principally associated with alien, non-WASP groups. Crime was also seen as associated with the growth of urban-industrial centers stimulated by technological progress.

2. The effort of correctional reformers to dissociate their ideas and panaceas from those of radical groups such as socialists.

3. The effort to differentiate progressive correctional reform ideas from the perspective of Social Darwinism. Correctional reformers lobbied for creative government intervention (the positive state) to solve social problems while conservative Social Darwinists argued for the limitation of government to reactive police powers.

4. The establishment of the idea that the solution of the crime problem in modern society would require social support for special "scientific" expertise and intervention.

---

### Box 11.1    The Rise of Sociology in the United States, 1890–1910

Three major factors fostered the intellectual and institutional rise of sociology in the United States (Schwendinger and Schwendinger, 1974; Ross, 1991; Camic and Xie, 1994):

1. The Progressive Era (1890–1910)—a combination of secular and Christian (especially Protestant) reform movements inspired by the professional middle classes (lawyers, doctors, teachers, and so on) and designed to improve the lot of the poor in the wake of the problems associated with the ill effects of industrialization and urbanization.

2. The rapid expansion of the university system in the United States and the institutionalization of the social sciences and of statistics at elite universities (Columbia, Johns Hopkins, Yale, Harvard, Chicago) between the mid-1870s and 1915. The first course in sociology was probably offered in 1876 by Sumner; the first book on sociology was Lester Ward's *Dynamic Sociology* (1883). The first book on criminology to use sociology specifically as one of its multifactorial perspectives was probably Kellor's *Experimental Sociology* (1901).

3. The government's recognition, between 1865 and 1905, of new academic associations—including the American Social Science Association, the American Economic Association, the American Historical Association, and the American Sociological Society—for the professional security and advancement of the social science community.

Intellectually, the vast majority of writings on crime in the United States, up to and including the turn of the twentieth century, took the nature of crime and criminality entirely for granted. Crime was seen as a pathological activity unquestioningly committed by criminals. Sociological questions about the nature and possible normality of crime were neither raised nor even recognized as part of serious inquiry. Moreover, the understanding of crime, and especially of its causes, tended to be combined with the explanatory framework of whatever concepts seemed appropriate to the problems at hand. And these concepts tended to be borrowed piecemeal from those of European phrenology, medicine, and psychiatry. Biological concepts were especially in fashion, while Darwinism, degeneracy, imbecility, moral insanity, and, especially, Lombrosianism all exerted powerful influences on the public mind (Fink, 1938; Rafter, 1988, 1992). Indeed, long after its apparent discrediting in Europe, Lombrosianism retained a powerful hold on the American public's imagination.

The multifactorial thrust of much criminology of this era is exemplified by the work of Chicago sociologist Frances Kellor. Although Kellor's studies were unusual in that they addressed female criminality, her perspective conventionally combined Lombrosianism, psychology, and environmental sociology in the search for a scientific criminal sociology. In the 1890s, for example, Kellor visited female penitentiaries and workhouses to assess how well Lombroso's concept of "born criminality" applied to women. Aided by a mobile laboratory, Kellor (1899) compared 21 physical and psychological characteristics of 61 female criminals with those of 55 students. Regarding physical differences, although she largely disagreed with the assertions of the learned Italian doctor, Kellor concluded that female inmates were differentiated among themselves: "immoral women," such as prostitutes, were found "mentally and physically . . . more defective than the criminal" (p. 543).

Kellor also stressed the importance of sociological factors—including age, marital status, nationality, religion, occupation, and class origin—in understanding female criminality. For Kellor, these social and economic factors were almost always more critical than biological forces. For example, she found prostitution largely caused not by some innate female depravity but by limited economic circumstances. Kellor's multifactorialism led her to conclude that some women are criminal because of natural immorality, others because of domestic infelicity, and still others because of poor education; female recidivists tended to have "degenerate habits which enthrall them" (pp. 678–679).

In an important respect, all early studies of crime in the United States shared a common interest: their concern to correct and reform "criminals." Despite their paternalistic thrust, it was reformist motives that eventually led commentators on crime to become part of a wider and more recognized movement for the development of social science and, especially, sociology.

Criminology itself emerged from the Progressive Era's general concern with the alleviation of social problems. Criminology's position in universities across the United States derived from its inclusion within the movement for the expansion of sociology, and its voice was actively promoted by such professional associations as the National Prison Association and the National Conference of Charities and Corrections (later, of Social Work). This voice was enhanced in 1909 at a conference in Chicago, with the founding of the American Institute of Criminal Law and Criminology and of the *Journal of Criminal Law and Criminology*.

Between 1895 (the year Max Nordau's *Degeneration* was published) and 1915 (when John Gillin's *Social Pathology* was published), the vague subject matter of criminology was transformed by a deluge of empirical studies addressing the criminality of immigrants, of the dangerous classes, and of "Negroes." Intellectually, these studies involved a selective reliance on sociological perspectives that excluded everything in the realm of theoretical speculation. This was not the time, or so it must have seemed, to speculate on grandiose sociological questions—What is society? How is social order possible? Is crime "normal"?—even if they were asked by criminologists such as Cooley in the United States and Durkheim in Europe. Instead, there was a new emphasis on such empirical social categories as poverty, alcoholism, and family upbringing (Rafter, 1988). Each of these categories was seen as a potential factor in criminality in a continually expanding and, in principle, endless chain of causality. Typically, the various links in the causal chain were tied to the criminality of social, economic, political, and religious "outsiders": immigrants, persons of color, heretics, lunatics and imbeciles, the undeserving poor, the feebleminded, the naturally unfit, and others.

Titillated by the mass media and designed for popular consumption, pronouncements of criminologists on the causes of crime were naturally assured a large public audience. The focus on the individual as the appropriate object of study and on the legitimate goal of reforming the criminal character through the individualization of punishment assured criminologists of considerable financial support from both state and private agencies. By the end of World War I, criminology had gained a measure of support from the academic and scientific communities because of several criminology texts (for example, Parmalee, 1918) that urged the use of scientific principles as a basic method.

As a part of the movement for social reform, and as a fledgling member of the academic community, criminology was now charted on a respectable course. Next we consider the development of the Chicago school of criminology, the first U.S. "school" of criminology.

## 11.2 Crime and Social Ecology

By the term **social ecology** (or human ecology), we refer to a type of research that examines (1) various geographical areas within cities, communities, and neighborhoods and (2) the area concentrations, regularities, and patterns of social life in such fields as work/leisure, health/sickness, and conformity/deviance. In this section we outline the ecological approach to crime practiced by the **Chicago school of criminology** between the mid-1920s and early 1940s.

### Introduction to the Chicago School of Criminology

In Chapter 10 we identified two explanatory frameworks instrumental in the development of sociological criminology. First, a sociopsychological explanation focused on the individual and, specifically, on the ways in which society cultivates the latent tendencies of those individuals psychologically predisposed to crime (see Chapter 10.1). Second, a sociological explanation focused on the patterned and regular ways in which social structures themselves exert pressures on certain groups, making them more prone to commit crimes (see Chapter 10.2). The investigations of the Chicago school of criminology included both these frameworks.

Broadly, the Chicago school's work in the field of crime investigated: (1) the life histories of juvenile delinquents, interpreted both through personal accounts of their delinquent acts and with the aid of sociopsychological and, occasionally, clinical techniques, and (2) the geographical and social distribution of delinquents and delinquency rates. Many members of the Chicago school came from a common background that can be summarized as rural or small town, midwestern, Christian in upbringing, and reform-oriented or even liberal in its political views; their investigations therefore led directly to policies for social reform.

The Chicago school was part of the post-Progressive Era social science movement, many aspects of which evolved at the University of Chicago. Between 1915 and the early 1940s, sociological research in the United States was dominated by various academic disciplines at the University of Chicago, especially those of political science and sociology. This domination resulted from several factors, chief among them the nature of the city of Chicago itself. By the 1920s and 1930s, slightly more than a century after its founding, Chicago had changed beyond all recognition. From a small town of little more than two square miles and 200 inhabitants, Chicago expanded to become the second-largest industrial metropolis in the United States, with a corporate area of 211 square miles and a population of over 3.3 million. The city extended some 25 miles along Lake Michigan and from eight to 10 miles inland.

During this expansion, tremendous changes occurred in the social composition of many neighborhoods in the city. These changes were especially visible in neighborhoods in and adjacent to the central business district and in areas of rapid industrial growth. "About the only thing that could be thought beautiful about . . . Chicago," a Chicago sociologist commented pointedly, "was fresh and lively Lake Michigan" (Faris, 1970:21). To journalists, social reformers, and sociologists, the ever-changing and fascinating patterns of daily life in Chicago were a barometer of the human condition itself. German sociologist Max Weber, visiting the city in 1904, found it "incredible and compared it to a man whose skin had been peeled off and whose intestines were seen at work" (Bulmer, 1984:xvi).

In this stimulating atmosphere, many creative scholars combined their talents and applied their energies to a sociological analysis of the harsh consequences of "urbanism," and especially to those problems generated by living in the inner city. Prominent among them were such famous names as W. I. Thomas, Ernest Burgess, Robert Park, and George Herbert Mead. Affiliated with the department of sociology—as graduate students, teachers, and quasi-independent researchers under the leadership of Park and Burgess—were such criminologists as William Healy, Frederick Thrasher, Paul Cressey, John Landesco, Clifford Shaw, and Henry McKay (Bennett, 1981).

The Chicago school brought innovative, vigorous, and eclectic methods of analysis to its research on urbanism. In the history of empirical research, these methods fell, chronologically, midway between (although curiously unrelated to) investigations that

*Ellis Island official examining an immigrant: In the 1920s and 1930s, sociologists and criminologists in Chicago studied the many ways in which immigrants adapted to strains and stresses of social life in the United States.*

relied on large social surveys and those that used scientific measurement techniques. Members of the Chicago school used a dazzling array of methodological techniques in their research. Their quantitative methods included advanced statistical analyses. Their qualitative techniques included the use of life-history documents, case studies, investigative journalism, media materials, in-depth interviews, and participant observation. Above all, Chicago sociologists believed in following Park's recommendation to get their feet wet with real research (Bulmer, 1984); they took great pride in conducting research not in laboratories, faculty offices, or libraries but in "the open" or in "the field"—on the streets, in opium dens, in brothels, and in parks.

In effect, the Chicago school firmly believed that the new methodological techniques of fieldwork would provide the basis for a factual, theory-free analysis of society: "Facts speak for themselves" quite independently of theoretical interpretation. However, the Chicago school's "facts" did not speak for themselves. Behind their facts lay the guiding hand of an important theoretical assumption: that the social ecology of urbanism could proceed within the same framework as the ecological study of plant and animal life. This assumption was present, sometimes beneath the surface and sometimes quite overtly, in numerous writings of the Chicago school, from the early research of Park (1915) and Burgess (1925) on urban spatial analysis to Shaw and McKay's famous book *Juvenile Delinquency and Urban Areas* (1942). The assumption was used to help describe how industrial and commercial expansion invades and disturbs the "metabolism" of "natural areas" (local communities) in the city.

The guiding ecological assumption of the Chicago school is described well by Vold, Bernard, and Snipes (2002):

> The term *ecology*, as it is used today, is often linked to the idea of protecting the natural environment. In its original meaning, however, it is a branch of biology in which plants and animals are studied in their relationships to each other and to their natural habitat. Plant life and animal life are seen as an intricately complicated whole, a web of life in which each part depends on almost every other part for some aspect of its existence. Organisms in their natural habitat exist in an ongoing balance of nature, a dynamic equilibrium in which each individual must struggle to survive.

Ecologists study this web of interrelationships and interdependencies in an attempt to discover the forces that define the activities of each part. (pp. 117–118)

After World War I (1914–1918), Chicago sociologists turned their ecological attentions to a variety of social problems. Exacerbated by the severe hardships of the Great Depression, by Prohibition, and by the well-publicized rise of gangland warfare and union racketeering, crime itself came to be seen as a major social problem. Crime, therefore, was one of the chief topics studied by members of the Chicago school. For example, W. I. Thomas and Florian Znaniecki's *The Polish Peasant in Europe and America* (1918–1920) used personal documents and life histories to examine how hard it was for immigrants to adjust to life in America. W. I. Thomas's *The Unadjusted Girl* (1923) collected information from 3,000 interviews to establish that all social behavior, including that of female delinquency, apparently derived from one or all of four motives or "wishes": the wishes for new experience, for security, for response, and for recognition. As such, implied Thomas, delinquency and lawful activity were merely "functional alternatives" directed to the satisfaction of the same goals. *The Unadjusted Girl* marked a rare concern among criminologists with the behavior of young females. However, feminists find scant value in Thomas's book; the analysis is thoroughly sexist (females are entirely incidental to Thomas's concern with the four "wishes"). Thrasher's *The Gang* (1927) strongly implied that, although there are many gang types, delinquent gang activity represented a normal part of the process of adjustment between adolescence and adulthood. Delinquency, Thrasher found, was the best method of adjustment available to adolescents in deprived inner-city areas.

Clifford Shaw contributed two directions of research to the Chicago school before completing his famous *Juvenile Delinquency and Urban Areas* with Henry McKay in 1942. First, in *Delinquency Areas* Shaw (et al., 1929) argued that the physical destruction and social deterioration of inner-city areas leads to the disintegration of the community and, ultimately, to the loss of the community's ability to police itself. Social disorganization, in other words, causes increases in juvenile delinquency.

Second, Shaw showed how seemingly important it was for a researcher to listen to delinquents' own definitions of their activities. Why did juveniles, according to their own explanations, engage in delinquency? To answer this question Shaw collected more than 200 life histories of juvenile delinquents. In 1930, Shaw published *The Jack-Roller*, a widely read account of "a delinquent boy's own story." This book was followed by *The Natural History of a Delinquent Career* (1939), a book that contradicted the public condemnation of a convicted rapist and armed robber widely depicted as a brute and a beast. Instead, insisted Shaw, this felon should be understood in terms of the values transmitted to him by numerous juvenile institutions and by his economically insecure and disorganized community in Chicago.

Finally, we note *Brothers in Crime* (Shaw, McKay, and McDonald, 1938), an in-depth study of the social backgrounds, criminal careers, and personality characteristics of the five Martin brothers, children of foreign-born immigrants. This book was a sympathetic view of five "criminal careers" that had been determined by the cultural conflict into which immigrant families were thrust by poverty, lack of education, and the aggravating effects of such control agencies as juvenile institutions.

This sort of criminology was very different from much that had preceded it. Members of the Chicago school did not assume that those who committed crimes were malicious miscreants. On the contrary, they believed delinquents were normal juveniles in abnormal environments. In this, the Chicago school made considerable progress over the opinionated explanations of their predecessors.

We turn now to what was, in some respects, the greatest achievement of the Chicago school's contribution to criminology: Shaw and McKay's (1942) *Juvenile Delinquency and Urban Areas.*

## Shaw and McKay's *Juvenile Delinquency and Urban Areas* (1942)

Shaw and McKay's research applied to the city of Chicago the detailed statistical analyses pioneered a century earlier by Quetelet and Guerry (see Chapter 9.2). Its sophisticated analyses tried to untangle the links among the dynamics of urban growth, community problems, and rates of juvenile delinquency. Among the crucial questions about juvenile delinquency that Shaw and McKay sought to explore were:

1. Do juvenile delinquency rates and adult crime rates vary together in different types of cities?

2. Do rates of juvenile delinquency correlate with the rates of juvenile recidivism; with the economic, social, and cultural characteristics of local communities; and with patterns of immigration?

3. How do economic and social conditions influence the development of juvenile delinquency as a cultural tradition in certain neighborhoods?

4. How can juvenile delinquency be prevented and treated?

Shaw and McKay approached these questions in four stages. First, they identified various physical and sociodemographic changes in Chicago neighborhoods. On the one hand, the physical changes comprised such factors as the growth of the central business district and the invasion of traditional local communities in the course of industrial and commercial expansion. With this expansion, Chicago landlords typically failed to repair rented dwellings in surrounding areas because of expectations that rising property prices—caused by the increased demand of industry and commerce for scarce land—would eventually yield fat profits. As a result, "zones of transition" surrounding the central business district and the industrial developments of Chicago were subject to increasing physical deterioration that, in turn, was manifest in the number of substandard and dangerous buildings that survived in the zone of transition.

On the other hand, the changes in Chicago's social composition derived largely from the fact that from the 1880s to the 1930s the population in Chicago's zone of transition was in relative decline while the population in its expanding suburbs was increasing. Using census data, Shaw and McKay found that a disproportionate number of those in professional and clerical occupations resided in the affluent suburbs, far from the central business district and industrial development. Correspondingly, a disproportionate number of industrial workers and the poor were concentrated in areas of physical deterioration. These deteriorated areas also contained the greatest number of families on welfare.

In combination, the physical and social changes in Chicago led to a far-reaching geographic segregation of the population. Shaw and McKay discovered further that patterns of immigration were part of a related process of economic and occupational segregation. The native white population not only enjoyed the highest economic status but tended to live in comfortable suburban houses; the residents of deteriorated zones of transition tended to have the lowest economic status. This latter group included (1) white European immigrants (especially from Czechoslovakia, Germany, Greece, Italy, Ireland, Poland, and Russia) and (2) African Americans, many of whom were "internal immigrants" who had migrated to Chicago from rural areas in the South.

Each immigrant group tended to be concentrated in a particular section of Chicago, although African-American families were more dispersed throughout the deteriorated neighborhoods than were European immigrants. Upon arrival in the "New World," each impoverished immigrant group tended to be pushed into the areas of lowest economic status. Eventually, however, most groups (but not African Americans, Latinos, or Native Americans) worked their way to the suburbs; their places in the deteriorated neighborhoods were simply filled by subsequent arrivals. To paraphrase the jargon of social ecology: As industry and commerce extend their habitat, the metabolism of existing natural areas is dominated or destroyed; surviving areas, in succession, are organically reconstituted as part of another natural area. Shaw and McKay inferred that this complicated process led to differential rates of delinquents.

Second, Shaw and McKay focused on the distribution of delinquency in Chicago. The juveniles in their data were of three types:

1. Alleged male juvenile delinquents (namely, those under age 17) brought before the Juvenile Court of Cook County.

2. Juveniles actually committed to correctional institutions.

3. All boys dealt with by the juvenile police probation officers.

Although the objection could be made that these three types represented only a sample of those apprehended rather than of all juvenile delinquents, this sample was larger than any previous study. Moreover, the data were compiled from different periods of time: (1) 9,860 alleged Chicago juvenile delinquents for the period 1934–1940; (2) 8,411 for 1927–1933; (3) 8,141 for 1917–1923; and (4) 8,056 for 1900–1906. Their use of time-series data, Shaw and McKay reasoned, permitted comparisons of delinquency rates not only in the same area for different periods but also in other areas, some of which had undergone great sociodemographic changes and some of which had remained relatively stable.

Their findings, displayed with spectacular diagrams and shaded maps, were most revealing. Using a series of spot maps that located the homes of all the delinquent boys reported in their data, Shaw and McKay showed that certain areas of Chicago had large concentrations of juvenile delinquents, whereas in other areas the delinquents were greatly dispersed. The areas of heaviest concentration were generally those near the central business district or those within or near areas zoned for industry and commerce.

Shaw and McKay divided the map of Chicago into 140 units, each approximately one square mile in size. They then computed delinquency rates for each unit (a delinquency rate was the number of delinquent boys in any given unit expressed as a percentage of the total number of boys in that unit). Significantly, the units with the highest delinquency rates were found to be those near the central business district and those adjacent to areas zoned for industry or commerce.

Shaw and McKay showed further that delinquency rates throughout Chicago varied in a strikingly uniform pattern (see the zone maps in Figure 11.1): The center of the city had the highest delinquency rates and the units at the extreme periphery the lowest; in between, the rates decreased regularly the farther away from the center. This finding—that delinquency rates actually declined as one moved from the center to the periphery of the delinquency zones in Chicago—is analyzed in greater detail later in this section.

Third, Shaw and McKay showed that juvenile delinquency was not an isolated social problem: area by area, juvenile delinquency rates were strongly correlated with such other community problems as high rates of school truancy, young adult offenders, infant mortality, tuberculosis, and mental disorders. In other words, Shaw and McKay found that areas in Chicago with certain social problems also tended to have higher rates of juvenile delinquency. Moreover, these same areas had the highest juvenile recidivism rates and relatively more delinquents who were later arrested as adults (pp. 138-139).

Shaw and McKay stressed that their analyses were correlational, not causal. The high correlation between delinquency rates and certain sociodemographic characteristics of Chicago neighborhoods did not mean that these characteristics cause delinquency. For example, Shaw and McKay saw that although the proportion of the foreign-born and the African-American population was higher in areas with high delinquency rates, this fact did not mean that the delinquency rates of these populations were higher because they were foreign-born or African American. They were higher, in part, because the high turnover of immigrant populations caused a withdrawal of residents' identification with their community and, correspondingly, a lack of pride in their neighborhood. Curiously, areas with high delinquency rates continued to have high rates irrespective of which groups inhabited them. Thus, between 1884 and 1930, eight inner-city Chicago areas underwent no changes in delinquency rates relative to other areas, despite the fact that the dominant population in these eight areas changed from Germans, Irish, English/Scots, and Scandinavians to Italians, Poles, and Slavs. This stability in delinquency rates, in the face of changing ethnic compositions, meant that "the delinquency-producing factors are inherent in the community" (p. 315). The explanation of delinquency, Shaw and McKay insisted,

> must be in the first place, in the field of the more subtle human relationships and social values which comprise the social world of the child in the family and community. These more distinctively human situations, which seem to be directly related to delinquent conduct, are, in turn, products of larger economic and social processes characterizing the history and growth of the city and of the local communities which comprise it.

Finally, Shaw and McKay tried to extend the importance of the relationship between "social values" and "larger economic and social processes" to the causes of juvenile

**Figure 11.1    Male Juvenile Delinquency Rates, Chicago, 1900–1933**

MAP OF CHICAGO

Zone rates of male juvenile delinquents, 1900–1906 series

Zone rates of male juvenile delinquents, 1917–1923 series

Zone rates of male juvenile delinquents, 1927–1933 series

Source: Adapted from Shaw and McKay, 1969:69.

delinquency. In areas with low delinquency rates (i.e., generally middle-class areas and those with high economic status), on the one hand, Shaw and McKay suggested that there was a general consensus about conventional values and attitudes toward such things as the welfare of children, the desirability of education, constructive leisure-time activities, and conformity to law. In such middle-class areas, moreover, respect for social values was expressed and cultivated by a variety of voluntary social control organizations such as parent-teacher associations, women's clubs, service clubs, churches, and neighborhood centers. Children who lived in such environments tended to be insulated from direct contact with deviant forms of adult behavior and, in general, were "exposed to and participate[d] in a significant way in one mode of life only" (p. 171).

In areas with high delinquency rates (generally, working-class areas and those with low economic status), on the other hand, there was found to be wide diversity in norms and standards of behavior. This diversity resulted from the different cultural beliefs and practices of migrant groups and unassimilated immigrant groups, as well as from the moral values of predatory youth gangs and organized crime. Concerning these areas, Shaw and McKay summarized:

> Moral values range from those that are strictly conventional to those in direct opposition to conventionality as symbolized by the family, the church, and other institutions common to our general society. The deviant values are symbolized by groups and institutions ranging from adult criminal gangs engaged in theft and the marketing of stolen goods . . . to quasi-legitimate businesses and the rackets through which partial or complete control of legitimate business is sometimes exercised. . . . Thus, within the same community theft may be defined as right and proper in some groups and as immoral, improper, and undesirable in others. In some groups wealth and prestige are secured through acts of skill and courage in the delinquent or criminal world, while in neighboring groups any attempt to achieve distinction in this manner would result in extreme disapprobation. Two conflicting systems of economic activity here present roughly equivalent opportunities for employment and for promotion. (pp. 171–172)

For Shaw and McKay, in other words, areas with high delinquency rates were those whose children were exposed to (1) conflicting sets of moral values, (2) adult role models whose material success derived from participation in criminal activities, and (3) a social tradition of delinquency that was a hallmark of the life of the local community. Boys constantly surrounded by this social milieu were thus routinely exposed to delinquent lifestyles. However, the mere existence of criminal organizations did not explain why some boys were tempted to join and others were not. So, what causes juvenile delinquency?

In their conclusion, Shaw and McKay attempted to answer this question. Once again, they emphasized that the major difference between areas with high and low rates of officially recorded delinquency was that the former tended to be more impoverished and the latter more affluent. Despite this difference, boys in all areas of Chicago—both rich and poor—were "exposed [in school and elsewhere] to the luxury values and success patterns of our culture" (p. 319). However, success by legitimate means was difficult to achieve for boys in low-income areas because they usually lacked the opportunities and skills required to be successful. Boys from low-income families thus calculated that the best way to achieve success lay in acts of delinquency and crime. Juvenile delinquency is therefore rational activity, and delinquent boys are by no means necessarily disorganized, maladjusted, or antisocial. As Shaw and McKay explained:

> In the low-income areas, where there is the greatest deprivation and frustration, where, in the history of the city, immigrant and migrant groups have brought together the widest variety of divergent cultural traditions and institutions, and where there exists the greatest disparity between the social values to which the people aspire and the availability of facilities for acquiring these values in conventional ways, the development of crime as an organized way of life is most marked. Crime, in this situation, may be regarded as one of the means employed by people to acquire, or to attempt to acquire, the economic and social values generally idealized in our culture, which persons in other circumstances acquire by conventional means. (p. 319)

## Evaluation of the Chicago School

Shaw and McKay's findings in their famous study have had enormous influence on criminology, as has the methodological legacy of the Chicago school in general. Doubtless a tribute to Shaw and McKay's signal importance, the method and findings of *Juvenile Delinquency and Urban Areas* have been reinterpreted endlessly by successive generations of criminologists.

Now let us consider several criticisms, both empirical and theoretical, of Shaw and McKay's work. First, consider the relationship between the source of their data and their finding that rates of juvenile delinquency tend to be highest in the low-income and working-class neighborhoods of cities. These data came from records of such official agencies as juvenile courts and juvenile probation officers. Although Shaw and McKay realized that many juveniles commit serious offenses that go undetected or for which they are not apprehended, they did not acknowledge that crime rates are not pregiven, objective facts. Crime rates are always socially constructed (see Chapter 2). Delinquency rates, for example, reflect not only the illegalities of juveniles but also the reporting activity of the public and the decision to accept an act as an offense by a police officer. Delinquency is so often found in working-class areas partly because working-class adolescents are more likely to have their offenses reported to the police, and, if their offenses are reported, they are more likely to be arrested, to enter the criminal justice system, and to leave it as officially defined delinquents.

Moreover, recent self-report studies and victimization surveys show that although lower-class neighborhoods contain a disproportionate amount of violent crime, delinquency as a whole is not concentrated among working-class adolescents. Status offenses and property crimes, in particular, are far more evenly distributed throughout the class structure.

Second, consider that Shaw and McKay's data on delinquency distribution derived from the residences of juveniles who entered the criminal justice system. Subsequent research on urban social spaces, beginning with Newman's *Defensible Space* (1973) and moving on to today's focus on "crime hot spots" (see Chapter 14.1), has demonstrated the critical importance of the locations where crimes are committed rather than the residences of those who commit them—a fact of obvious importance in the case of syndicated, white-collar, and political crimes (see Chapters 7, 8, and 9).

Third, consider Shaw and McKay's claim that delinquency rates remained stable despite great changes in the social composition of Chicago neighborhoods. If we ignore such factors as class bias in the construction of delinquency rates, it is possible that this claim was true for the specific period investigated (namely, 1906–1940). Yet, there is no good reason to suppose, as Shaw and McKay did, that delinquency rates will be stable in other places and times (Lander, 1954). Indeed, it is likely that in Chicago itself delinquency rates after 1945 did not conform to the pattern predicted for them by Shaw and McKay (Bursik, 1984). Ultimately, we cannot be sure of the exact meaning of any claim about the stability of socially constructed crime rates. Does such a claim mean that the rate of actual illegalities remained stable? Does it mean, instead, that the actions of police officers remained constant? In posing these questions we are forced to raise anew a central question of the discussion in Chapter 2: What, precisely, do crime rates measure?

Theoretical criticisms of *Juvenile Delinquency and Urban Areas* tend to object that its findings are empiricist. Shaw and McKay believed mistakenly that their findings were strictly factual (essentially, that they existed independently of theoretical assumptions); actually their findings were deeply structured by theoretical assumptions that lurked below the surface of their argument (Valier, 2002).

Recall that social ecologists tend to see urban development as a process in which areas of industrial and commercial expansion interfere with the metabolism of adjacent areas. Certain natural areas of transition—those undergoing invasion, dominance, and succession—have high delinquency rates. As *Juvenile Delinquency and Urban Areas* attempted to show, this interference was manifest in the growth of juvenile delinquency and in other indexes of social disorganization in inner-city neighborhoods. However, Shaw and McKay also believed that, like the processes of change in plants and animal life, the surrounding areas would eventually return to a harmonious state of equilibrium through the mechanisms of natural selection and symbiosis. It was hypothesized that when and if immigrants acquired the skills required for survival in a hostile environment, they would move up the social ladder and then move out to the suburbs. When this move did not happen in Chicago, Shaw and McKay reasoned that it was because the inner-city areas lacked sufficient community controls to restore their

*Shaw and McKay theorized that juvenile delinquency would diminish as more conventional social structures replaced the 'disorganized' inner-city societies of new immigrants. Yet other factors were clearly in play as evidenced by the continued presence of juvenile delinquency throughout society.*

natural state. The sources of disorganization thus lay with the residents rather than with the profit-seeking decisions of industrialists.

However, quite aside from the difficulties of applying concepts about change in plant life to processes of change in social life, the concept of **social disorganization** remains unclear. Although Shaw and McKay were quite aware of the great diversity of lifestyles in Chicago, they nevertheless tended to start with an image of conventional lifestyles, then went on to describe those that deviated from convention as disorganized and, occasionally, as socially pathological. Sociologically, however, societies and communities can never be disorganized as such. *Disorganization* is a label that is always conceived of, explicitly or implicitly, in relation to some theoretically conceived yardstick of organization. Sometimes this conception is quite explicit (such as when someone says that unregulated industrial expansion is immoral because it destroys the communality of residential neighborhoods, or that, compared with the orderly lifestyles of the residents of Chicago's fashionable Gold Coast, life in the slums is disorganized). At other times, the concept of social organization is implicit only. Shaw and McKay assumed implicitly, and wrongly so, that the lifestyles and values of those in natural areas of transition were disorganized. Ultimately, Shaw and McKay assumed that juvenile delinquency was necessarily disorganized or deviant activity.

Moreover, their causal chain leading to delinquency suffered from theoretical confusion. Shaw and McKay made no attempt to follow through on the implications of their original insight—that industrial expansion, neighborhood destruction in zones of transition, and juvenile delinquency might be parts of the same causative process (Sampson and Wilson, 1995). In other words, although they correctly identified the socially harmful effects of unregulated industrial and commercial expansion on community life, they instead argued that these effects were generated by a breakdown in the values of the affected communities. For Shaw and McKay it was not dilapidated housing, overcrowding, poor hygiene, and inadequate leisure facilities (all effects of unregulated urban growth) that caused delinquency. Delinquency was caused by a breakdown in the values of the delinquents, in those of their families, and in those of their communities as a whole. Their analysis failed to view delinquency and capital movements as anything other than aspects of a temporary, coincidental process.

## 11.3 Social Structure, Anomie, and Deviance

In this section we outline a theory of crime and deviance that in certain ways marks a great advance on the school of social ecology: Merton's 1938 theory of social structure and anomie. Merton emphasized, or so it seemed, what Chicago criminologists generally had ignored—a theoretical explanation that linked deviance and crime to the class structure.

It is hard to exaggerate the importance of Robert Merton's 1938 article "Social Structure and Anomie." Strongly opposed to biological and individualistic explanations of deviance and crime, Merton focused on the rates of such conduct. In developing this focus, Merton relied on Durkheim's concept of **anomie** (see Chapter 10.2) to explain how and why "some social structures exert a definite pressure upon certain persons in the society to engage in nonconforming rather than conforming conduct"

(1969:255). But whereas Durkheim had stressed that anomic states arise from unregulated human desires, Merton pinpointed the importance of the relationship between means and goals.

Merton's central hypothesis was that, sociologically, deviant behavior is a symptom of a specific sort of social disorganization: a lack of fit between culturally prescribed aspirations and socially structured avenues for achieving them. Although his essay could in principle be applied to several societies, it is clear that Merton had in mind chiefly the United States and, especially, the goals enshrined in the "American Dream."

Merton's argument began with two important elements of social and cultural structures. The first element is made up of the culturally defined goals that are held out as legitimate objectives for all members of a society. These goals are "the things worth striving for." The second element is made up of the regulations, controls, and procedures for moving toward goals, which are termed **institutionalized means**, or **norms**. A well-regulated, or stable, society has a balanced equilibrium between means and goals. In a stable society, both means and goals are accepted by everyone and are available to all. Social integration occurs effectively when individuals are socialized into accepting that they will be rewarded for the occasional sacrifice of conforming to institutionalized means and when they actually compete for rewards through legitimate means. Malintegrated, or unstable, societies stress the goals without stressing the means, or vice versa. In some societies, institutionalized means are not integrated with important social values. In societies such as the United States, provisions for making the means of achieving the goals available to all are insufficient.

Certain means, such as vivisection or medical experimentation, although perhaps technically more efficient in achieving goals, are sometimes unacceptable. Yet people often turn to technically more efficient means if other institutionalized means are unavailable. The more widespread the practice of using noninstitutionalized means, the more a society destabilizes or, put another way, the more widespread anomie becomes.

Competitive sports illustrate the processes that lead to anomie. If success in sports is construed as "winning the game at all costs" rather than as winning by the rules, the use of illegitimate but technically more efficient means is more attractive to participants. As Merton put it:

> The star of the opposing football team is surreptitiously slugged; the wrestler incapacitates his opponent through ingenious but illicit techniques; university alumni covertly subsidize "students" whose talents are confined to the athletic field. The emphasis on the goal has so attenuated the satisfactions deriving from sheer participation in the competitive activity that only a successful outcome provides gratification. Through the same process, tension generated by the desire to win in a poker game is relieved by successfully dealing one's self four aces or, when the cult of success has truly flowered, by sagaciously shuffling the cards in a game of solitaire. (p. 259)

Moreover, Merton suggested that if "concern shifts exclusively to the outcome of competition, then those who perennially suffer defeat may, understandably enough, work for a change in the rules of the game" (p. 257). Merton believed that the United States is a society in which great emphasis is placed on certain success-goals without a corresponding emphasis on institutionalized means.

This lack of fit occurs in three ways. First, as in competitive sports, means are often elevated to ends (for example, money is commonly viewed as an end in itself rather than as a means to achieve a goal); moreover, its acquisition is a goal that can never be met. People in all income brackets want more money, and when they get more of it, they want still more. In other words, the goals of the American Dream are beyond nearly everyone's reach. Second, the lot of the multitudes who never achieve success-goals is made doubly worse because they not only fail to succeed but tend to endure penalties for such "failure." Through the socializing agencies of family, school, and peer groups we are bombarded constantly with such slogans as, "There is no such word as 'fail' "; "Never be a quitter"; and "You can make it if you try." Coupled with this pressure to maintain lofty goals are very real penalties paid by those who draw in or reduce their ambitions. The cultural manifesto, Merton argued, is clear: Never quit, never stop trying, never lower your horizons.

Merton never fully articulates the third description of the lack of fit between means and goals in the United States, although at several points it reaches the surface of his argument. Merton hints that because of a maldistribution of power certain segments of the population—such as individuals in the lower social strata—are continually denied access to legitimate, institutionalized means. Despite such slogans as "Anyone can be president" or "Work hard and you will be rewarded with monetary success," these goals are almost impossible to achieve for those at the bottom or at the margins of society. Tragically, failure tends to be defined as a consequence not of social inequality but of individual ineptitude or lack of ambition.

Merton's scenario of the American Dream contemplates a society that is egalitarian in its ideology but unequal in terms of the availability of the means of achieving success-goals. American society, therefore, is imperfect and badly integrated; its social and cultural structures inevitably produce strain and tension.

## Merton's Typology of Modes of Individual Adaptation

What are the consequences of this strain on the individual? Merton identified five responses to the strains and tensions of social life in the United States (see Table 11.1): conformity, innovation, ritualism, retreatism, and rebellion. We stress that Merton did not conceive of these responses as psychological conditions but as structural responses to the strain of anomie. The ways in which individuals respond to anomie in part vary, in Merton's formulation, according to their position in the class structure.

**I. *Conformity*. Conformity** is the most common practice. Although Merton did not explain why the majority of the members of society typically conform, he suggested that "were this not so, the stability and continuity of the society could not be maintained" (p. 264). However, Merton was concerned chiefly with the four deviant adaptations to the tensions generated by the gap between means and ends.

**II. *Innovation*.** The combination of a cultural emphasis on success-goals and the rigidity of the U.S. class structure, Merton insisted, produces an innovative deviant adaptation. **Innovation** is the most common deviant response and the most important for criminology. Innovation is deviant behavior that uses illegitimate means to achieve socially acceptable goals. Many crimes against property (such as burglaries, robber-

| Table 11.1 | A Typology of Modes of Individual Adaptation | |
| --- | --- | --- |
| Mode of Adaptation | Culture Goals | Institutionalized Means |
| I  Conformity | + | + |
| II  Innovation | + | − |
| III  Ritualism | − | + |
| IV  Retreatism | − | − |
| V  Rebellion | ± | ± |

Note: + signifies acceptance, − signifies rejection, ± signifies rejection of prevailing values and substitution of new values.

Source: Merton, 1969:263.

ies, and larcenies) are clear examples of innovative acts. Because innovative responses are distributed throughout the U.S. class structure, there is, Merton suggested, no simple correlation between crime and poverty. The pressures to succeed operate at all points in the class structure; innovative deviance occurs throughout the social structure—from robber barons and white-collar criminals to common criminals in the lower social strata. However, Merton continued, innovative deviance in the United States is concentrated largely in the skilled and unskilled working class. It is there, more than at any other class location, that the gap between goals (which all are urged to achieve) and means is most acute.

In his theory of innovative deviance, Merton assumed that innovators are persons who have been improperly socialized. Had they been socialized properly—had they internalized the need to follow institutionalized norms—their behavior would, by definition, be conformist. An alternative for those who have fully internalized the institutionalized values but who still crave the impossible-to-achieve aspirations of the American Dream is a dogged involvement with institutionalized norms at the expense of success-goals. This alternative Merton terms "ritualism."

**III. *Ritualism.*** Merton defined **ritualism** as "the abandoning or scaling down of the lofty cultural goals of great pecuniary success and rapid social mobility to the point where one's aspirations can be satisfied" (pp. 273–274). It is the response of conformist bureaucrats who "take no chances." Ritualism is expressed in such clichés as, "I'm not sticking my neck out" and "Aim low and you'll never be disappointed." Ritualism is practiced most often by members of the lower middle class, where "parents typically exert continuous pressure upon children to abide by the moral mandates of society, and where the social climb upwards is less likely to meet with success than among the upper middle class" (p. 275).

**IV. *Retreatism.*** **Retreatism** is an adaptation (or maladaptation) that relinquishes culturally prescribed goals and does not conform to institutionalized means. It is an escape mechanism that often arises when, after having internalized the importance of following legitimate means toward acceptable goals, an individual suffers repeated failure in goal achievement and is unable to resort to proscribed means. Retreatists constitute the "true aliens": they are "in the society but not of it" (p. 277). They include psychotics, autistics, pariahs, outcasts, vagrants, vagabonds, tramps, chronic drunkards, and drug addicts. The retreatist adaptation, Merton insists, is by and large a private and isolated response rather than a public one.

**V. *Rebellion.* Rebellion** involves alienation from legitimate means and values. In contrast to retreatism, rebellion is a collective activity. For a rebellious disposition to be transformed into organized political action, legitimate means and values must be viewed as arbitrary or mythical, loyalty to them must be withdrawn, and an allegiance must be developed to new groups possessed of a new myth. The new myth has two functions. First, it must identify the source of large-scale frustration in society itself rather than in the individual. Second, it must be directed to the founding of a society with closer links between merit, effort, and reward. The precise mix of these criteria, Merton could have added, is subject to almost infinite variety and includes anarchists, communists, and the Ku Klux Klan.

## Evaluation of Merton

Merton's analysis of the pressures and strains in the United States and of the way in which they lead to different deviant responses, including crime, is a brilliant polemic against those who believe that the causes of crime are found in such individualistic factors as defective personality or malformed biology. It is also a solid indictment of the rampant social inequality endemic to U.S. society (Sumner, 1994). Merton's argument about strain and anomie remains one of the most powerful sociological explanations of deviance and crime. As we learn in the remainder of this chapter, Merton's analysis has substantially influenced theories of delinquent subcultures (see Chapter 12.1, 12.2).

However, several criticisms must be made of Merton's analysis of the relations between social structure, anomie, and deviance. First, crucial parts of his argument hinge on unstated and unproven assumptions. For example, it is questionable whether acceptance of middle-class norms and values in U.S. society is as widespread as Merton depicts. Accepted by whom? For what reason? Are middle-class norms and values in Manhattan the same as those in rural Wisconsin? Again, Merton's argument that deviance is a response to structural strain assumes that no form of deviant activity has authenticity in its own right. Yet some deviant activities are engaged in for no apparent reason other than the fact that they are enjoyable.

Second, although Merton's analysis focuses on the psychic effects of strain on individuals at different points in the class structure, there is no indication of the structural causes of strain. Of course, we should not criticize Merton for not outlining something he never intended to examine—but this remains an important omission in his theory of social structure and anomie. It is especially important if we are concerned with issues of social policy and crime. If crime is caused by tensions and strain generated by a society that, for most people, routinely fails to deliver the promises of the American Dream, then how can crime be reduced? Should structural strain be seen as the starting point of a chain of causation that ends in crime and deviance? What are the causes of strain? Can nonconformist conduct be reduced by psychiatric counseling or prescription pills?

Third, recall that Merton's analysis was directed explicitly to success-oriented societies such as the United States. In such societies, the structural strain that produces nonconformist responses, and that culminates in anomie, derives from the gap between the availability of means and the ideology of equal opportunity. Strain is most intense for those with the least opportunity to partake in the promises of the American Dream (namely, lower-class individuals). Merton therefore suggests that nonconformist conduct (essentially, crime and deviance) is concentrated in the lower class. But this conclusion is at best tentative and, at worst, false. It is true that crimes of lower-class individuals are far more likely to be detected by the police and to lead to arrest (see Chapter 3.1). Yet only in this limited sense is the (property) crime rate of the lower class greater than that of other classes. This reality does not mean, however, that the actual volume of crime committed by the lower class is greater than that of other classes. Indeed, if the strains of life really operate as suggested, Merton is left with the problem of explaining why it is that most members of society engage in law-abiding activities far more than in deviance. To a certain extent, this very issue was the focus of the criminology of Merton's contemporary, Edwin Sutherland.

## 11.4 The Criminology of Edwin Sutherland

No introduction to modern criminology is complete without recognizing the enduring contributions made by sociologist Edwin Sutherland (1883–1950). He was raised in Nebraska and Kansas, his mother was active in Christian service, and his father was a Baptist minister and historian (Geis and Goff, 1983). By his own account, Sutherland began an academic career with primary training in political economy and political science and a major interest in the study of labor problems (1956). In 1906, Sutherland took a course in criminology at the University of Chicago, where the basic textbook was Henderson's *Dependent, Neglected, and Delinquent Classes* (1893). Then, as a sociologist at the University of Illinois, Sutherland taught courses in criminology. In 1921 he began serious work in criminology by drafting an overview of the field. This project led, in 1924, to the first reasonably systematic textbook in U.S. criminology, Sutherland's cautious yet progressive *Criminology*. In it, Sutherland claimed that the criminologist should not assume the correctness of such popular and legal categories as "crime," "criminality," and "crime rates." Instead, he argued, sociology should provide the primary perspective of criminology, the focus of which should be both law and crime.

Sutherland's sociological interest in such questions as "What is crime?" and "What is the relationship between crime and law?" was apparent throughout the main body of his work from the mid-1920s to the late 1940s. In what follows we divide his sociological criminology into four areas: differential association, differential social organization, his book *The Professional Thief*, and white-collar crime.

### Differential Association

In the early editions of *Criminology*, Sutherland stressed that the causes of crime are in principle infinite. However, his belief in multicausality weakened as further study convinced him to integrate existing findings about the causes of crime into a general theory of crime. In this regard Sutherland was greatly influenced by the pessimistic although, he largely agreed (Schuessler, 1973), correct findings of a widely read report released by the Rockefeller-funded Bureau of Social Hygiene in New York City. The report's most damning accusation (Michael and Adler, 1971) was that criminology in the United States was entirely lacking in scientific generalizations about the causes of crime. What Sutherland termed the theory (or "principle") of **differential association** resulted from his ambitious search for a general theory of the causes of crime.

The specific content of Sutherland's theory of differential association derived from Tarde's theory of imitation (see Chapter 10.1), from the Chicago school's concept of social disorganization, and from George Herbert Mead and W. I. Thomas's sociopsychological emphasis on the importance of meanings in social interaction. Although we do not address social psychology as such, it is worth quoting Vold, Bernard, and Snipe's (2002) summary of the elements in Mead's theory that influenced Sutherland's theory of differential association:

> In Mead's theory a cognitive factor—"meanings"—determines behavior. Mead then argued that people construct relatively permanent "definitions" of their situation out of the meanings they derive from particular experiences. That is, they generalize the meanings they have derived from particular situations, and form a relatively set way of looking at things. It is because of these different "definitions" that different people in different situations may act in very different ways. To cite an old example, two brothers may grow up in identical terrible situations, but one may become a drug lord while the other becomes a priest. (p. 161)

Sutherland meant for the theory of differential association to explain both the process by which a given person learns to engage in crime and also the content of what is learned.

The theory of differential association can be summarized as follows (Sutherland, 1947). First, criminal behavior is learned, like all other behavior, within intimate personal groups in an interactive process of communication. This means that criminality is not inherited biologically. Second, the learning of criminal behavior includes instruction in the techniques of crime and in the motivational values favorable to committing it. These values are learned from definitions that state whether legal codes are favorable or unfavorable. The principle of differential association asserts that a person becomes criminal when definitions favorable to the violation of law exceed the definitions unfavorable to violation and when contacts with criminal patterns outweigh contacts with anticriminal patterns. Exposure to such definitions and contacts varies in frequency, duration, priority, and intensity. Finally, wrote Sutherland:

> While criminal behavior is an expression of general needs and values, it is not explained by those general needs and values, since noncriminal behavior is an expression of the same needs and values. Thieves generally steal in order to secure money, but likewise honest laborers work in order to secure money. The attempts by many scholars to explain criminal behavior by general drives and values, such as the happiness principle, striving for social status, the money motive, or frustration, have been and must continue to be futile since they explain lawful behavior as completely as they explain criminal behavior. (p. 8)

Sutherland's theory has great appeal because its basic argument seems to offer a precise sociological explanation of why some people engage in crime and others do not. Persons commit crime because they have associated, socially and culturally, more (in frequency, duration, priority, and intensity) with procriminal patterns than with anticriminal patterns. Crime is thus a deviant action that is learned by normal persons who have been influenced by a specific cultural process.

Sutherland's theory of differential association has been, and continues to be, one of the most fertile causal accounts of crime. One of its great strengths is that it is a general theory that seeks to account for both criminal and noncriminal behavior. Analysis of criminal behavior is found especially in theories about the causal relationships between crime and subcultural ideas and values (see Chapter 12); theories of noncriminal behavior—specifically addressing the question, "Why do so many people not commit crimes?"—have focused on the behavioral processes of control and learning (see Chapter 12.3 and 13.1).

The theory of differential association has gained tremendous respect among criminologists, though it has also generated substantial controversy (Bernard and Snipes, 1996; Costello, 1997; Matsueda, 1997). Sutherland's collaborator, Donald Cressey, has argued persuasively that some of this controversy is quite unwarranted (Sutherland and Cressey, 1970). For instance, certain critics suggested mistakenly that the theory of differential association fails to realize that not all persons who associate with criminals actually become criminals themselves. Indeed, a careful reading of "Proposition #6" in Sutherland's theory suggests that it is not mere association with criminals and criminal patterns that causes crime. In fact, Sutherland fully realized that associating with criminals was not a sufficient condition for engaging in crime. Persons commit crime, Sutherland stressed, "because of an excess of definitions favorable to violation of law over definitions unfavorable to violation of law" (1947:6–7).

Some critics have suggested that Sutherland's theory does not apply to some sorts of crime, especially crimes, such as heroin addiction contracted in a hospital (Lindesmith, 1947), that involve no social milieu of procriminal associations. Gaylord and Galliher (1988) report that at one point Sutherland himself did not feel that "his theory could account for 'adventitious' crimes, criminal acts that were accidental, casual, or trivial in nature" (p. 151). But, they counter perceptively:

> It is unclear what these adjectives mean when applied to crimes. Is one to believe that Sutherland thought that they were accidental in the sense that they did not have causes? Or that they were engaged in by nonprofessional criminals? Or by persons lacking a criminal identity? (p. 151)

Behind the repeated misreadings of its basic terms lie three serious problems with the explanatory adequacy of differential association theory. First, the terms of the theory are so deliberately abstract that testing them has proven extremely difficult. How, for example, can we actually measure an "excess" of definitions favorable to violation of law over definitions unfavorable to violation of law? What, precisely, are "associations" with "criminal patterns"? Should such associations include the influence of deep-rooted, socially harmful tendencies such as racism and sexism—some of which have even been expressed in law and espoused by government officials and law enforcement officers? Questions such as these reveal clearly that the terms of Sutherland's theory are insufficiently precise.

Second, the actual causal chain in Sutherland's theory arguably rests on a tautology. Logically, if we assume that human beings are not automata, to say that crime is engaged in by persons who are motivated to engage in it or who learn to engage in it is not to say very much at all.

Third, the premises of Sutherland's theory are highly controversial. The image of the social actor postulated by Sutherland is that of an empty vessel with no history, no beliefs, no preferences, and no capacity for choice. Into this vessel Sutherland sought to pour "pro-" and "anti-" criminal tendencies. If (for some unstated reason) there is an excess of procriminal tendencies poured into this human vessel, then, the theory of differential association suggests, the vessel engages in crime. Because of this rigid determinism, the theory cannot explain why certain persons associate more with procriminal patterns than with anticriminal patterns. Yet this must certainly be incorporated into any theory that seeks to generalize about the causes of crime.

Sutherland was aware that his theory of differential association was seriously incomplete. He knew that individuals differed in their responses to procriminal patterns and that, therefore, elements of social psychology relating to differences in personality traits must be included in a revised version of the theory (Sutherland, 1956; Sutherland and Cressey [1949] 1970). He also knew that it was one thing to explain why a particular individual engages in crime but quite another to explain why some social groups have higher or lower crime rates than others. Eventually, Sutherland gave some indications of the direction in which he would have addressed this latter difficulty concerning his theory of differential association. These indications are found in his concept of "differential social organization" (or "differential group organization"). Because criminologists (including Cressey in Sutherland and Cressey, [1949] 1970) are tempted to read more coherence into this concept than Sutherland himself could give it, we proceed with considerable caution.

## Differential Social (Dis)Organization

Although his theory of differential association seemed to apply to the criminal behavior of individuals, Sutherland was also concerned with the question of why crime tended to be concentrated among certain groups in society. In his recollection of the development of the theory of differential association, Sutherland (1956) referred to the importance of three questions:

> One of these questions was, Negroes [sic], young-adult males, and city dwellers all have relatively high crime rates: What do these three groups have in common that places them in this position? Another question was, Even if feebleminded persons have a high crime rate, why do they commit crimes? It is not feeblemindedness as such, for some feebleminded persons do not commit crimes. Later I raised another question which became even more important in my search for generalizations. Crime rates have a high correlation with poverty if considered by areas of a city but a low correlation if considered chronologically in relation to the business cycle; this obviously means that poverty as such is not an important cause of crime. How are the varying associations between crime and poverty explained? (p. 15)

Sutherland ([1924] 1947) began to examine these sociological questions, albeit tentatively, in the context of his last version of differential association. Although almost wholly unintegrated, Sutherland's argument was that social organization in the United States had moved from a simple to a more complex and differentiated type as a result of the industrial revolution. At the same time, there had been a relaxation in the uniformity of social control. Traditional social controls, such as those exercised uniformly within the family and local community and by religion, were increasingly challenged by the rise of economic and political individualism, increased social mobility, and material acquisitiveness. In the United States this process of *social disorganization* or, more accurately, reorganization had been exacerbated by successive waves of immigration and had resulted in culture conflict between different communities. Crime was one expression of this conflict. Crime rates would be higher in communities that lacked traditional social controls and that contained some social groups organized for criminal behavior. Crime was also, therefore, an expression of such *differential social organization.*

Through these incoherent remarks, Sutherland was trying to convey the idea that differential social organization explains the origin of crime and that differential association explains its transmission from one person to another. A final twist appeared in Sutherland's last major book, *White Collar Crime* (1949), in which he attempted, briefly and tantalizingly, to integrate his incoherent combination of differential association and differential social (dis)organization with Merton's concept of anomie:

> Differential association is a hypothetical explanation of crime from the point of view of the process by which a person is initiated into crime. Social disorganization is a hypothetical explanation of crime from the point of view of the society. These two hypotheses are consistent with each other and one is the counterpart of the other. Both apply to ordinary crime as well as to white-collar crime.

> Social disorganization may be either of two types: anomie, or the lack of standards which direct the behavior of members of a society in general or in specific areas of behavior; or the organization within a society of groups which are in conflict with reference to specified practices. Briefly stated, social disorganization may appear in the form of lack of standards or conflict of standards. (1983:255)

## The Professional Thief (1937)

Sutherland's interest in the varying associations between crime and economic position led him to explore the crimes of those whose social position had little to do with poverty. This interest was expressed in his research on professional thieves and on white-collar crime.

Sutherland's book *The Professional Thief* was based on the recollections of Broadway Jones, alias "Chic Conwell," a professional thief, ex-drug addict, and ex-con from Philadelphia (or perhaps Boston) who had worked for twenty years as a pimp, pickpocket, shoplifter, and confidence man. Although most of the book was actually written by Conwell, Sutherland edited it for publication and wrote two interpretive chapters. Conwell's recollections provide a fascinating glimpse into the underworld of professional thieves and include details about criminal argot (slang), the roles of members in the mob (criminal group), rackets, the fix (techniques of avoiding conviction and/or doing time in prison), and thieves' images of the police, the law, and society at large. According to Conwell, the work habits of professional thieves are very similar to the practices of those engaged in lawful business activities:

> Professional stealing as a business is much like any other business. The conversation among thieves in a police station, prison, or hangout is concerned principally with their business, and it is no different in that respect from the conversation of monument salesmen in their meetings. Business possibilities, conditions, and returns are the foremost subjects of conversation, and just as the salesman learns of

fertile territory, new methods, new laws which affect the business, so does the thief. It involves as much hard work as any other business. There is little thrill about it. . . . It is no more thrilling than the work of the factory slave. (1937:140)

Sutherland's *The Professional Thief* is a classic in the history of criminology for two critical reasons. First, it provides an image of crime that is a decided alternative to the stereotypical picture of disreputable activities engaged in by poorer members of the working class. Indeed, Sutherland's portrayal of crime in this book points to the considerable skills and abilities needed to be a professional thief and to the code of ethics between professional thieves. This is a far cry from the popular image of criminals as mentally defective personalities or as biologically deformed individuals. In addition, it shows that the world of professional thievery is a fairly exclusive club, one to which all the learning principles of differential association fully apply. Second, the analysis in *The Professional Thief* carries through to its logical conclusion the Chicago school's theory that criminologists should investigate criminality "in the flesh" and "on the street" rather than in the comfort of their armchairs.

---

### Box 11.2 The Profession of Theft

According to Sutherland's analysis of Conwell's depiction of the professional thief, the profession of theft has five basic features: technical skill, status, consensus, differential association, and organization (Sutherland, 1937):

1. **Technical skill.** Like bricklayers, lawyers, and physicians, professional thieves have a stock of abilities and skills. Wits, front, speaking ability, manual dexterity, and specialization are all needed to plan and execute crimes, to dispose of stolen goods, and to fix those cases in which arrests occur.

2. **Status.** Like other professionals, the professional thief occupies a certain status based on such factors as ability, knowledge, dress, manners, wealth, and power. Professional thieves therefore often show contempt toward amateur, small-time, and "snatch-and-grab" thieves.

3. **Consensus.** Professional thieves usually share similar values that aid them in their criminal careers. Their reactions to certain things, including such things as prospective victims and squealing on other thieves, tend to be similar. "These reactions are like the 'clinical intuitions,'" Sutherland diagnosed, "which different physicians form of a patient or different lawyers form of a juryman on quick inspection" (p. 202).

4. **Differential association.** For reasons of security and safety, professional thieves often maintain a barrier between themselves and all others. They tend to associate chiefly with members of their own professional group. The group defines its own members because only professional thieves are received into it.

5. **Organization.** Because technical skills, status, consensus, and differential association form a core of knowledge informally shared by thieves in a network of cooperation, professional theft is organized crime (essentially, crime that is organized).

## White Collar Crime (1949)

We have seen how Sutherland (1949) argued that socially injurious acts (such as white-collar offenses) should be part of the proper subject matter of criminology regardless of how such acts are defined in legal terms (see Chapter 1.2). In this section we outline the findings of Sutherland's courageous book *White Collar Crime* (1949). This book amplified certain of his concerns in *The Professional Thief* and extended the scope of differential association theory to "white-collar crime," a term that Sutherland coined. It was Sutherland's last major venture in criminology, and it was to be his most important contribution.

Sutherland had become distressed, at least since the mid-1930s, that criminology had devoted nearly all its energies to analyzing the crimes of the poor (Geis and Goff, 1983). In the opening sentence of *White Collar Crime,* he remarked dryly that "criminal statistics show unequivocally that crime, as popularly understood and officially measured, has a high incidence in the lower socioeconomic class and a low incidence in the upper socioeconomic class" (Sutherland, 1983:3). Sutherland complained that official statistics of crime, most case studies, and Shaw and McKay-inspired analyses based thereon gave a distorted picture of the social distribution of criminality. These statistics and studies wrongly implied, for example, that poverty was the chief cause of crime. Yet Sutherland felt sure, from his preliminary studies of embezzlers and of the diverse crimes committed by large U.S. corporations, that criminality was far from being the preserve of the poor. Just as much as the poor, if not more so, it was the rich who committed crimes. In this attempt to reverse the familiar object of U.S. criminology—away from the crimes of the poor and toward those of the rich—lay the heart of Sutherland's revelations in *White Collar Crime.*

Sutherland defined **white-collar crime** as "a crime committed by a person of respectability and high social status in the course of his occupation" (1983:7). His studies of white-collar crime had two main thrusts, neither of which had been explored adequately before his description of them. The first was an estimate of the extent of white-collar crime, the second a theoretical explanation of the causes of white-collar crime.

The thesis of *White Collar Crime* is that persons of the upper socioeconomic class engage in much criminal behavior. His exposé of white-collar crime included a battery of staggering statistics provided by U.S. government agencies. For example, according to the U.S. Comptroller of the Currency, 75 percent of all banks that had been examined had violated banking laws. According to the Federal Trade Commission, commercial bribery was a prevalent and common practice of many industries. "The financial cost of white-collar crime," Sutherland estimated from the sparse data available prior to his study, "is probably several times as great as the financial cost of all the crimes which are customarily regarded as the 'crime problem' " (1983:9). However, the bulk of Sutherland's data in *White Collar Crime* consisted of decisions of federal, state, and municipal courts and administrative commissions involving the 70 largest manufacturing, mining, and mercantile corporations in the United States. Among the worst corporate offenders were such giants as American Sugar Refining; American Tobacco; Armour; DuPont; Ford; General Electric; General Motors; Gimbel; A&P; International Harvester; Loew's; Montgomery Ward; National Steel; Procter & Gamble; Sears, Roebuck; U.S.

Steel; Warner Brothers; Westinghouse Electric; and Woolworth. Sutherland reported in painstaking detail that in the preceding 20 years

> each of the 70 large corporations has one or more decisions against it, with a maximum of 50. The total number of decisions is 980, and the average per corporation is 14.0. Sixty corporations have decisions against them for restraint of trade, 53 for infringement, 44 for unfair labor practices, 43 for miscellaneous offenses, 28 for misrepresentation in advertising, and 26 for rebates. (p. 15)

Of the 70 largest industrial and commercial U.S. corporations, 97.1 percent were recidivists in that they had two or more decisions against them. In addition, Sutherland also revealed that the Federal Trade Commission, by order of Congress, reported that during the 1914–1918 and 1939–1945 world wars many corporations had violated wartime regulations. These violations included price regulation abuse, overcharging, and fraudulent profiteering in war-related materials, tax evasion, restraint of trade, illegal maintenance of competitive positions, violations of embargoes and neutrality, and even treason (for example, illegally revealing classified information to the enemy). As Sutherland concluded:

> The large corporations in time of war, when Western civilization was endangered, did not sacrifice their own interests and participate wholeheartedly in a national policy, but instead they attempted to use this emergency as an opportunity for extraordinary enrichment of themselves at the expense of others. (p. 191)

With these data Sutherland demonstrated that in order to maximize their profits, U.S. corporations routinely committed crimes against consumers, competitors, stockholders and other investors, inventors, employees, and the state itself. Corporations tended to commit more crimes the greater their age, the larger their size, and the more their economic position was monopolistic, anti-union, and dependent on advertising (pp. 258–263).

Sutherland complained vigorously that the criminal behavior of the lower socioeconomic class differs from the criminal behavior of white-collar and corporate offenders chiefly in the respective ways that society deals with them. The former are typically processed by the criminal justice system, the latter by quasi-judicial review boards and administrative agencies. The typical outcome for the former is prison, but for the latter it is a warning, an order to desist, or a fine. Indeed, these very different outcomes tend to hide the criminal nature of white-collar crime from the public, from the press, and from criminologists themselves.

We note also that in his explanation of white-collar crime, Sutherland preferred to ignore almost entirely both the economic form that this crime typically took and also the ways in which economic cycles (such as the Great Depression of the 1930s) stimulated economic and other abuses by the powerful. Sutherland attempted to explain the causes of white-collar crime in terms of his earlier general theory of crime. "The significant thing about white-collar crime," he emphasized, "is that it is not associated with poverty or with social and personal pathologies which accompany poverty" (1983:7). Because he had shown how white-collar crimes often occur, he believed that a general theory linking crime, poverty, and the poverty's related pathologies was entirely invalid.

The only factors common to the crimes of the rich and the poor, he theorized, were differential social organization and differential association.

Differential social organization fosters white-collar crime because it underpins the anomic ideology that free enterprise should not be regulated by government. Because of this ideology, neither the U.S. government nor the community is well organized to counter white-collar and corporate crime. Differential association fosters the transmission of white-collar crime because profit-seeking corporations rapidly mimic the techniques of their successful competitors and because specific techniques of violating the law are passed from one executive to another. These techniques are themselves part of a widespread corporate ideology favorable to violation of law, an ideology exemplified by such maxims as "We are not in business for our health" and "Business is business."

## Evaluation of Sutherland

Sutherland was a pioneer who contributed immeasurably to the development of criminology. His questioning of the basic subject matter of criminology—and its extension to social harms not always perceived, defined, or processed as crimes—was a valuable insight inadequately appreciated by many criminologists even today. His search for a general theory of crime was one of the first attempts by a criminologist to make explicit the ever-present role of sociological theory in all studies of crime. These two contributions guided Sutherland's search for the factual revelations in his books *The Professional Thief* and *White Collar Crime*, both milestones in criminology. As we shall learn, Sutherland's theoretical focus on the origin (differential social organization) and on the transmission (differential association) of criminal values was soon to influence new lines of inquiry in criminology, including the analysis of delinquent subcultures (see Chapter 12.1 and 12.2) and of the processes of control (see Chapter 12.3) and learning (Chapter 13.1).

## Review

This chapter outlined the early forms of criminological theory in the United States. The institutional position of criminology in the United States was dramatically transformed during the Progressive Era (circa 1890–1910). Before the Progressive Era, criminology was conducted in an unorganized and amateurish way; afterward, it found a secure and well-funded base in the universities. U.S. criminology rapidly gained global dominance, although its domination of criminological theory has created some hardship for the development of comparative criminology (see Chapter 15).

## The Early History of Criminology in the United States, 1895–1915

1. Intellectually, the vast majority of pre-1900 writings on crime took the nature of crime and criminality entirely for granted.

2. In addition to native concern with the crimes of immigrants, blacks, and other outsiders, early writings on crime borrowed piecemeal from European concepts of crime, especially those connected with biology.

3. Criminology emerged generally from the Progressive Era's (1890–1910) social reformism. It depended specifically on the support of the social science movement, the rise of various professional associations, and mass media stimulation of public interest in its pronouncements on the causes of crime. Gradually, criminology admitted the relevance of social factors to its investigations.

## Crime and Social Ecology

1. Initially, sociological criminology in the United States was almost exclusively identified with the perspective of social ecology developed by the Chicago school from 1920 onward. Chicago was an important site of the progressive movement, and the city naturally lent itself to the study of social problems, including crime.

2. The Chicago school adopted and spread several innovative research techniques, including both quantitative and qualitative methods. The latter involved life-history documents, case studies, investigative journalism, media materials, in-depth interviews, and participant observation. These methods, it was believed, would produce objective, value-free knowledge.

3. Shaw and McKay's *Juvenile Delinquency and Urban Areas* (1942) concluded that many social problems, including juvenile delinquency, were concentrated in zones of transition populated by white, lower-class immigrants and by blacks. This concentration was correlated with such factors as rates of adult crime, school truancy, disease, and mental disorders, and it remained highly stable despite resident turnover in the zones of transition. Certain of these problems, it was felt, could be alleviated by a change in the local community's values.

4. The Chicago school has been extremely influential in the development of sociological criminology. Nevertheless, it has been criticized for its factual errors and its empiricist theory.

## Social Structure, Anomie, and Deviance

1. This section examined Merton's influential article "Social Structure and Anomie" (1938). Merton's analysis of deviance and crime in part developed from the work of Durkheim and the Chicago school.

2. Merton argued that certain societies, such as the United States, are unstable because they fail to provide adequate means for achieving socially approved goals.

3. Failure to achieve socially approved goals leads to various structural responses: conformity, innovation, ritualism, retreatism, and rebellion.

4. Because it is based on various unproven assumptions, the validity of Merton's analysis of deviance is somewhat suspect.

## The Criminology of Edwin Sutherland

1. Sutherland tried to combine an explicit sociological theory of crime with detailed empirical analyses. Significantly, he attempted to extend the proper subject matter of criminology beyond state-defined categories of social injury.

2. Sutherland's general theory of differential association attempted to explain both conformity and deviation. It held that a person engages in crime because of an excess of definitions favorable to violation of law over definitions unfavorable to violation of law. Crime is thus learned behavior. By merging social disorganization theory with differential association theory, Sutherland attempted, largely unsuccessfully, to explain the origins of crime and its cultural transmission.

3. In *The Professional Thief* (1937) and *White Collar Crime* (1949), Sutherland pioneered analyses of certain crimes not often considered crimes either by the public or by criminologists, and often not processed as crimes by the criminal justice system. The first book examined the crimes and cultural world of professional thieves; the second book examined the occupational crimes routinely committed by white-collar executives in large corporations. Sutherland explained the transmission and persistence of these crimes with the theory of differential association.

4. Sutherland's theories of the causes of crime have proven difficult to test, largely because their content is imprecise and their scope is so general. Yet they remain the starting point for much analysis of crime today.

## Questions for Class Discussion

1. In the late 1920s, lawyer Jerome Michael and philosopher Mortimer Adler were commissioned by Columbia University Law School and by the Bureau of Social Hygiene in New York City to write a report on the desirability of establishing an institute of criminology in the United States. In their lengthy final report, Michael and Adler scrutinized the scientific status of existing criminology and concluded that "the work of criminologists has not resulted in scientific knowledge of the phenomena of crime" (1971:54). Do you agree with this claim?

2. Was Shaw and McKay's *Juvenile Delinquency and Urban Areas* (1942) scientific? How does a scientific explanation of crime differ from other types of explanation, such as a religious one? Are sociological and scientific explanations of the same sort? Can we understand the causes of social behavior (for example, crime) in the same way that natural scientists, such as physicists, for example, understand the behavior of molecules and gases?

3. When Shaw and McKay pinpointed the links between juvenile delinquency and the social organization of Chicago neighborhoods, were these links causative or correlational?

4. Does Merton's typology of deviance actually explain variations in crime rates?

5. Discuss the following (Sutherland, 1947:7–8): "The attempts by many scholars to explain criminal behavior by general drives and values—such as the happiness principle, striving for social status, the money motive, or frustration—have been and continue to be futile since they explain lawful behavior as completely as they explain criminal behavior. They are similar to respiration, which is necessary for

any behavior but which does not differentiate criminal from noncriminal behavior."

6. Why does the mass media not cover white-collar crime as much as it does some other types of crime, such as violent crime?

## For Further Study

### Readings

Gaylord, Mark S., and John F. Galliher. 1988. *The Criminology of Edwin Sutherland.* New Brunswick, NJ: Rutgers University Press.

Rafter, Nicole Hahn. 1997. Psychopathy and the Evolution of Criminological Knowledge. *Theoretical Criminology* 1 (2): 235–259.

Sumner, Colin. 1994. *The Sociology of Deviance: An Obituary.* New York, NY: Continuum.

Valier, Claire. 2002. *Theories of Crime and Punishment.* New York, NY: Longman.

### Websites

1. <http://www.sad.ch/sid/forschung/anomieresearch.html>: This site summarizes current research on anomie, as well as its application. Students should be able to see how a given theoretical perspective influences a particular social policy.

2. <http://www.seweb.uci.edu/about>: This is an overview of the study of social ecology provided by the School of Social Ecology at the University of California at Irvine. It traces the foundations of the ecological approach within sociology. ✦

# Delinquent Subcultures and Subcultures of Delinquency

## Preview

Chapter 12 introduces:

- The ways in which—beginning in the mid-1950s—criminologists have attempted to explain the origins, beliefs, and activities of male, lower-class, delinquent subcultures.

- Explanations of violent delinquent subcultures.

- The antipositivist theory of David Matza, which argues that delinquents are not nearly so committed to their activities as subcultural theorists have supposed.

* Social control theory as an explanation of delinquency.

## Key Terms

containment theory

control theory

drift

middle-class measuring rod

reaction formation

social control

status frustration

subculture

techniques of neutralization

## 12.1 Delinquent Subcultures

Chapter 11 examined Merton's (1938) theory of anomie and Sutherland's (1947) theory of differential association. Following the 1939–1945 war, these two theories exercised enormous influence over criminology. During the 1950s many criminologists examined the subcultural settings in which deviant values coexist with dominant social values. These subcultural theorists took their perspectives directly from the earlier writings of Merton and Sutherland. The central question of the subcultural theorists repeated Durkheim's question: Given the widespread persistence of deviance, what functions do deviant values serve for those who subscribe to them? This section outlines the key answers given to this question.

As research on delinquent subcultures developed during the 1950s, it gradually recognized the importance of a variable never properly examined by the Chicago school—the influence of social class. We begin our outline of subcultural theory with Albert Cohen's book *Delinquent Boys* (1955).

### A. K. Cohen's *Delinquent Boys* (1955)

Cohen's *Delinquent Boys* begins with the premise that juvenile delinquency is a major problem of every sizable American community. All attempts to control delinquency had failed, Cohen argued, because none had accurately identified its causes. Cohen stressed that the Chicago school had overemphasized the social disorganization of the zones of transition (see Chapter 11.2) and that these areas were not nearly as lacking in community spirit as researchers such as Shaw and McKay had imagined. Moreover, Cohen was critical of Mertonian anomie theory because it had failed to come to grips with the content of juvenile gangs. Cohen believed further that Merton had ignored the fact that delinquent gangs do not simply use deviant means to achieve culturally approved goals. Far from it, he insisted, delinquent gangs often seem to engage in violence simply for "the hell of it." And Sutherland's theory of differential association, too, failed to explain why some juveniles join gangs and others do not (see Chapter 11.4). Moreover, Cohen felt that Sutherland had taken for granted the existence of juvenile gangs and had failed to ask certain questions: Where do gangs come from? What are their origins? Why do delinquent gangs exist in some social settings but not in others?

About Sutherland, with whom he had done graduate study at Indiana, Cohen recorded his feeling that the theory of differential association

> has to do with how people come to acquire the delinquent or criminal culture through a process of association. But, I asked, Where does it come from? How do you explain the existence of the culture? . . . But [Sutherland] didn't think that was much of a question. Somewhere he said, actually he wrote it too, that the southern practice of dropping the r's is explained by the southern practice of dropping the r's—that's all you have to know—which incidentally is wrong. It sounds on the face of it that it might say something but the point is, some speech practices become extinct, others spread and you get novelties linguistically. Some catch on, others don't. So it really wasn't a very good answer. (quoted in Laub, 1983:189)

For Cohen, then, existing theories in criminology did not explain much about delinquent behavior. No theory had seriously examined the values and beliefs of juvenile gang members and the nature and causes of their activities. Why do some juveniles, and not others, join delinquent gangs? Why do gangs do what they do? Why do gangs persist in urban neighborhoods?

Cohen's *Delinquent Boys* tried to answer such questions by beginning with the idea that the world of juvenile delinquents is enveloped in a subculture. Although the term "subculture" had been in use among anthropologists at least since the 1870s, it was Cohen who first applied it to the study of delinquency (Wolfgang and Ferracuti, 1967). "Culture," for Cohen, refers to the knowledge, beliefs, values, codes, tastes, and prejudices that persist in the social relations people have regularly in their interactions with each other. A **subculture**, then, is a set of beliefs (and so forth) that differs in some way from the main or dominant culture. Taking part in delinquent acts is a major aspect of delinquent subcultures. As Cohen himself defined it, a delinquent subculture is "a way of life that has somehow become traditional among certain groups in American society. These groups are the boys' gangs that flourish most conspicuously in the 'delinquency neighborhoods' of our larger American cities" (1955:13).

Cohen reasoned that a good theory of delinquent subcultures must explain the existence of the six subcultural characteristics displayed in Box 12.1. But it must also explain why subcultures typically flourish where they do in the class structure.

Cohen argued that subcultures exist because they provide a solution to certain problems of adjustment shared by a group of individuals. Why, then, is the delinquent subculture found mostly in working-class environments? In his explanation, Cohen began with the position of the family unit in the local community. He noted that, although the boundaries between working-class and middle-class families are sometimes indistinct, childrearing practices do vary between different classes. Crucially, children are not equally prepared to satisfy the standards by which U.S. society evaluates their passage to adulthood. Working-class parents, for example, place less emphasis than middle-class parents on development of analytical skills, education, self-denying discipline, and long-term planning for adult status and career; they place more emphasis on physical prowess in groups and learning through "having fun." However, because all children are evaluated by middle-class standards, some children are doomed to be seen as failures in middle-class terms.

---

**Box 12.1　A. K. Cohen's Subculture of Delinquent Boys**

According to Cohen (1955), the subculture of delinquent boys has six major characteristics in the United States:

1. Its activities are *nonutilitarian, malicious,* and *negativistic:* Gang members are nonutilitarian because, for example, they sometimes steal simply for the hell of it; they are malicious because they take delight in others' discomfort, in terrorizing "good" children, and in flouting teachers and their rules (such as defecating on a teacher's desk); and they are negativistic because their delinquent conduct is right by the standards of the subculture precisely because it is wrong by conventional standards.

2. *Versatility:* Gang members rarely specialize in types of delinquent acts such as adult criminals and solitary delinquents do.

3. *Short-run hedonism:* Gang members have little interest in long-term goals, a fact that reflects their lower-class origins. Typically, they "hang around," "chew the fat," and "wait for something to turn up."

4. *Group autonomy:* Gang members are intensely loyal to their own gang, are very hostile to others, and resist even the efforts of their families to control them.

5. *Working-class membership:* Although cautious about relying on official crime statistics, Cohen nevertheless agrees that juvenile delinquency—especially the juvenile subculture—is overwhelmingly concentrated in the working class.

6. *Male:* Although Cohen recognized the existence of female gangs and of solitary delinquency engaged in by females, he agreed with official statistics showing that delinquent subcultures are male dominated.

---

The prevailing middle-class standards (the **middle-class measuring rod**) by which all children are evaluated, especially in schools, include ambition; individual responsibility; outstanding achievement, especially academic or athletic; industry and thrift; foresight; manners, courtesy, and personability; control of physical aggression; constructive leisure; and respect for property. Because middle-class children tend to acquire these skills from their parents and peers far more than working-class children do, most adolescent failures are drawn from the working class. Above all, it is in the school—that supremely middle-class institution—that working-class boys fail. Failure in school often results in **status frustration**, which causes feelings of "guilt, self-recrimination, anxiety, and self-hatred" (p. 126). Because the working-class boy finds himself at the bottom of the status hierarchy, he is now in the market for a solution.

According to Cohen, it is within the working-class delinquent subculture that the otherwise-unadjusted working-class boy finds a solution to his lack of status in middle-class life. The delinquent subculture, therefore, operates as an "adjustment mechanism" for many working-class adolescents. Adjustment occurs through a process of **reaction formation**, in which the academic success typically denied working-class boys is contemptuously redefined as the "bookish knowledge" of "sissies," whereas "street knowledge," which is learned from friends in the delinquent gang, is regarded as superior to other forms of knowledge. In general, the virtues of the working-class gang include the practices regarded by the middle class as vices: nonutilitarian, malicious, and negativistic activities. The gang confers a much-needed high status on members who practice these activities; this status is typically denied working-class adolescents when they participate in an alien middle-class world.

Additionally, Cohen addressed two further problems about delinquency that were almost completely ignored in his era and are largely so in ours: female delinquency and middle-class delinquency.

Regarding female delinquency, Cohen suggested that because females are not so-cialized into being successful in the male-dominated realms of society, young females do not have the adjustment problems characteristic of male, working-class "failures." Although young females can eventually find additional satisfaction in a career, success-ful relationships with the opposite sex are the primary means by which they derive sta-tus. Their activities focus, therefore, on popularity with boys, dating, beautification, charm, clothes, and dancing. Although involvement in a delinquent subculture can in-crease the masculine status of a boy, it can only do harm to the femi-nine status of a girl. Cohen con-cluded that for a boy the delinquent response, " 'wrong' though it may be and 'disreputable,' is well within the range of responses that do not threaten his identification of him-self as a male" (p. 140).

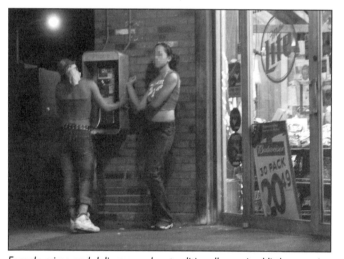

*Female crime and delinquency has traditionally received little attention from criminologists. Whereas the crimes of young males are often seen as reinforcing masculine values, those of young females are seen as less of a challenge to understand, or else ignored.*

Regarding middle-class delin-quency, Cohen rightly pointed out that its very existence must embar-rass those who argue that a poor or working-class background is the chief cause of delinquency in gen-eral. He therefore speculated that this embarrassment may stem from inadequate concepts of social class (namely, because lower-class and middle-class families may in fact be culturally closer to each other than is usually admitted, boys from both groups might be responding to the same cultural tensions). Another possibility, according to Cohen—which ties in well with other as-pects of his theory—is that middle-class delinquent subcultures respond to the same tensions of gender identification as their working-class counterparts. As Cohen argued in sociopsychological terms:

Because of the structure of the modern family and the nature of our occupational system, children of both sexes tend to form early feminine identifications. The boy, however, unlike the girl, comes later under strong social pressure to establish his masculinity, his difference from female figures. Because his mother is the object of the feminine identification which he feels is the threat to his status as a male, he tends to react negativistically to those conduct norms which have been associated with mother and therefore have acquired feminine significance. Since mother has been the principal agent of indoctrination of "good," respectable behavior, "goodness" comes to symbolize femininity, and engaging in "bad" behavior acquires the function of denying his femininity and therefore asserting his masculinity. This is the motivation to juvenile delinquency. (p. 164)

Consequently, Cohen reasoned that males from middle-class homes may join delinquent gangs as well.

It is appropriate now to mention three problems in Cohen's analysis. First, much of the importance of Cohen's work lies in the original way in which it extended to delinquent boys an explanation of Merton's category of the rebellious deviant. At root, however, both Merton and Cohen shared the view that deviance (Merton) and delinquency (Cohen) arise as a reaction of the lower classes to their failure in middle-class terms. In this view, working-class activities, such as boys' delinquency, are wholly parasitic on middle-class practices. Indeed, what this view of delinquency ignored was precisely what the Chicago school of ecology had emphasized (at least in principle): the importance of granting authenticity to the values of the deviants themselves. In other words, do working-class delinquents themselves regard their activities as a response to "failure"?

Second, like nearly all his contemporaries, Cohen did not refer to the importance of race in his explanations of juvenile subcultures in the United States. As Colin Sumner (1994) complains:

No one seemed to notice the point that if the delinquent culture was so common in U.S. cities perhaps it was not so "sub," and few made anything of the fact that its occupants were mostly black. Their blackness, and the blackness of the so-called subculture, was completely glossed over in the theory. . . . The subculture was truly an abstraction from reality. . . . There was to be a stark awakening in the sixties; one which would render the abstraction of the subculture somewhat farcical. (p. 181)

Third, Cohen failed to provide empirical evidence that working class delinquents accept middle-class success goals. In what sense, we are compelled to ask, does the subculture of working-class juvenile delinquency actually reject middle-class values? This question was soon addressed by other subcultural theorists, to whom we now turn.

## Delinquency and Lower-Class Culture

Cohen's *Delinquent Boys* rapidly stimulated numerous responses from criminologists and a wealth of new research into the diverse origins, functions, and forms of delinquent subcultures. We will outline the most influential arguments of this research.

The first major criticism of Cohen's findings was developed by Walter Miller in his article "Lower Class Culture as a Generating Milieu of Gang Delinquency" (1958). The bulk of Miller's data came from reports of daily contact with ghetto youth in a large eastern city during a three-year project into the control of juvenile delinquency. The subjects of the study were both black and white, male and female, and were in early, middle, and late adolescence.

Miller suggested that adolescent members of delinquent gangs, and of other forms of "street corner society," are not psychopaths, nor are they physically or mentally defective. Far from it. Gang members are often drawn from the most "able" sections of the community. Why, then, do they commit crimes? Reasoned Miller: "The most general answer is that the commission of crimes . . . is motivated primarily by the attempt to achieve ends, states, or conditions which are valued, and to avoid those that are disvalued within their most meaningful cultural milieu" (p. 346).

For achieving these ends, gang members tend to choose the most accessible means available. Miller argued that the lower-class way of life has a set of ends, or focal concerns, that include trouble, toughness, smartness, excitement, fate, and autonomy. These focal concerns differ greatly from those of the middle classes. For example, whereas the middle class might value achievement in high school examinations, the lower class values the smartness embodied in the capacity to outfox, outwit, or con others. The distinctive focal concerns of the lower class derive from aspects of its structural position in U.S. society. According to Miller, 40–60 percent of the United States is influenced directly by lower-class culture, and of this, 15 percent composes the "hard-core lower-class group." Above all, this latter group is characterized by its distinctive family unit—the female-headed household (see Chapter 3.2). The female-headed household is one that "lacks" a permanent male parent or that has no male parent involved in child care and family support.

According to Miller, the major factor that pushes lower-class boys into joining delinquent gangs is the widespread presence of female-headed households in their cultural milieu. Why is this so? Miller depicted the lower-class boy as the victim of a female web of neglect. Because he is surrounded by females, the lower-class boy suffers from acute identity crises, especially those crises associated with problems of gender-role identification (see Chapter 3.2). Miller argued that the female-headed household does not provide "a range of essential functions—psychological, educational, and others"—for the lower-class boy (p. 342). These functions, Miller concluded, are typically provided by the most accessible means available: the corner group and the gang. The focal concerns (such as smartness) of the gang parallel those of lower-class life in general. But the gang also embraces two further concerns that in combination explain their territoriality and their positive values: (1) belonging, or adherence to the rules of the gang, and (2) status (derived from smartness and related characteristics) as it is defined within the cultural framework of lower-class society.

Miller therefore reasoned that the delinquent gang functions to resolve crucial problems generated by the cultural, and especially the family, milieu of lower-class boys. But for Miller, unlike Cohen, the gang resolves these problems in its own cultural framework rather than in reaction to the cultural standards of the middle class. As an aside, we note that there is no evidence that boys in single-parent (female- or male-headed) households, for example, are more likely to be deprived emotionally or psychologically than boys in two-parent households (see Chapter 3.4).

Despite the antifeminist leanings of his argument, Miller casts serious doubt on the validity of Cohen's theory in one important respect. Recall that Cohen assumed that lower-class boys react to failure in middle-class worlds (such as school) and, as a result, seek status in the more familiar setting of the delinquent subculture. What Miller questions, quite correctly, is Cohen's assumption that the lower-class boy has no authentic values that identify gangs as good things to belong to simply because they are good things to belong to.

## Delinquency and Opportunity

Miller was part of a group of delinquency theorists (the Chicago school, Merton, and Cohen) who took the style and direction of delinquent subcultures, or gangs, very much for granted. However, this great simplification was uncovered by Richard Cloward and Lloyd Ohlin in their book *Delinquency and Opportunity* (1960). To explain why some juveniles violate conventional norms does not explain variations in the particular form of their deviant actions (such as theft, violence, drug use/abuse, and so forth). Why, for example, do some gangs allegedly focus on violence, some on theft, and still others on drug use/abuse? Following Merton's theory of anomie, Cloward and Ohlin asserted that delinquent subcultures arise because of a gap between the aspirations of lower-class youth and the possibility of their achieving those aspirations through legitimate means. However, the effects of the gap between aspirations and frustrated achievement vary from one individual to another. The direction of variation depends on two basic types of legitimate aspiration: aspirations for higher status (achieved by membership in the middle class) and for greater economic success. Table 12.1 outlines Cloward and Ohlin's four major categories of male lower-class youth.

According to Cloward and Ohlin, both Type I and Type II boys aspire to middle-class status. However, Type II boys regard a change in their reference groups as more important than greater economic success. Cloward and Ohlin agree with Cohen that when faced with frustrated opportunities for upward social mobility, boys of these two types are those most likely to react against middle-class values, because these boys are the ones who most want to be accepted by the middle class. Type III boys, who want more economic success (namely, money) but who are not interested in middle-class values or in becoming middle class, seek higher status in their own cultural milieu. They want " 'big cars,' 'flashy clothes,' and 'swell dames' " (p. 96). It is this group that composes the majority of delinquents. Type IV boys are street-corner

| Table 12.1 | Cloward and Ohlin's Classification of Lower-Class Youth | | |

| | Orientation of Lower-Class Youth | |
|---|---|---|
| Categories of Lower-Class Youth | Toward Membership in Middle Class | Toward Improvement in Economic Position |
| Type I | + | + |
| Type II | + | − |
| Type III | − | + |
| Type IV | − | − |

Source: Cloward and Ohlin, 1960:95.

boys who are not interested in social mobility in any sphere. These boys drop out, in other words, without dropping into anything else. Although they are sometimes criticized for lack of ambition, these boys rarely get into trouble with the law.

Cloward and Ohlin's astute analysis of delinquent subcultures clearly avoided an error made by Cohen. It did not assume, as Cohen's had, that the cause of most juvenile delinquency is the failure of lower-class youth to succeed in middle-class institutions such as schools. Even though they may fail, and even though they may be alienated from the school, lower-class delinquents do not become delinquent solely because of failure in school. The causative factors in delinquency are likely to be more complicated than the process suggested by Cohen. As Cloward and Ohlin indicated:

> Type III youth are alienated from the school because of a conflict regarding appropriate success-goals; this conflict simply reinforces their own definitions of criteria of success [i.e., making money versus making it into the middle class]. If these youngsters subsequently become delinquent, it is chiefly because they anticipate that legitimate channels to the goals they seek will be limited or closed. (p. 97)

Finally, Cloward and Ohlin argued that the illegitimate means of achieving success are not evenly distributed within working-class communities. They identify three sorts of delinquent subculture participated in by Type III boys:

1. *The criminal subculture.* The legitimate aspirations of delinquency-prone boys are satisfied illegitimately in neighborhoods where a criminal subculture already exists. A criminal subculture has its own success models, learning techniques, and gradations of status (mainly by age). Its leading members are also part of the conventional culture of the community, thus lending the subculture a measure of stability and legitimacy. Its focus is the rational, albeit illegal, provision of opportunities for income through activities such as theft. In areas where no established criminal subculture is available, the typical avenue for potential delinquents is membership in either a conflict or a retreatist subculture.

2. *The conflict subculture.* The environs of the conflict subculture are typically poor, disorganized, transient, and unstable. The activities of the conflict subculture make it extremely visible to the media and to the public. These activities focus on interpersonal violence, gang warfare, and the physical destruction of property.

3. *The retreatist subculture.* The retreatist subculture is the last avenue for boys who experience failure in both legitimate activities and in the illegalities of the criminal and conflict subcultures. The focus of the retreatist subculture is the retreat into persistent drug use/abuse. Of course, not all lower-class youth who experience status and economic deprivation engage in drug use/abuse. But those who choose to use and abuse drugs persistently are those who either (1) experience the double failure just described or (2) cannot revise their aspirations downward, yet continue to experience the strain of frustrated opportunities.

The apparent implications of certain of the findings of Cloward and Ohlin's study were actively pursued as policy by the federal government. As Vold, Bernard, and Snipes (2002; and see Einstadter and Henry, 1995) describe:

> After Robert Kennedy, who was then attorney general of the U.S., read Cloward and Ohlin's book, he asked Lloyd Ohlin to help develop a new federal policy on juvenile delinquency. The result was the passage of the Juvenile Delinquency Prevention and Control Act of 1961, which was based on a comprehensive action program developed by Cloward and Ohlin in connection with their book. The program included improving education, creating work opportunities, organizing lower-class communities, and providing services to individuals, gangs, and families. The program was later expanded to include all lower-class people and became the basis of Lyndon Johnson's War on Poverty. (pp. 144–145)

Billions of dollars were spent on the War on Poverty and other social welfare programs, but the war was eventually abandoned by President Nixon on the grounds that it showed no clear results. In fact, the reasons the program was abandoned are many and complex, including conservative objections that government should not be in the business of eliminating social inequalities. It must be considered seriously whether the subcultural theorists, because they had failed to identify the causes of juvenile delinquency, misunderstood the set of policies that should be implemented to contain it.

## Evaluation of Subcultural Theory

As noted, theories of delinquent subcultures arose in the 1950s largely as an attempt to answer various questions ignored by the Chicago school. Yet, like their predecessors in the Chicago school, the subcultural theorists continued either to ignore the delinquency of young females or typically to view it in masculine terms. Additionally, they ignored the delinquency of middle-class youth.

How much of an advance was the new subcultural criminology of the 1950s over the Chicago school? As David Matza (1964) reported, the sociologists of delinquent subcultures provided two basic insights about delinquency. First, they showed that it typically is not a solitary enterprise but a group activity. Second, they showed that delinquent activities, rather than being engaged in by biologically or psychologically deformed individuals, typically develop in the sociological context of particular territorial locales. Often they develop in neighborhoods with cultural traditions associated with established gangs.

The criminology of the subcultural theorists was a real advance over earlier work in at least two respects. First, the subcultural theorists explicitly raised what the Chicago school left dormant: the relation between lower-class opportunities and the social and economic inequality of the U.S. class structure. Moreover, the subcultural theorists implicitly condemned the economic inequalities, the blocked opportunities, and the strains that result from class structure. The problem remains, however, as to whether they were correct in concluding that benevolent social programs could contain the juvenile delinquency that resulted from these economic conditions. Second, in some cases subcultural theory displayed considerable sensitivity to issues not previously raised. It recognized, for example, that juvenile delinquency took a number of forms and was engaged in for a variety of reasons.

In assessing the merits of subcultural theory, we also note that its findings provoked widespread criticism. Certain early critics, in particular Kitsuse and Dietrick (1959), argued that Cohen, for example, overemphasized the extent to which the delinquency of lower-class boys is a reaction to failing in middle-class terms. Perhaps most working-class boys simply do not care about middle-class values. Do working-class boys have no authentic cultural traditions of their own? Other critics objected that the activities of delinquent gangs are utilitarian rather than nonutilitarian and are far more diverse than the subcultural theorists allowed. Still other critics objected that not enough emphasis had been placed on the deviant psychological characteristics of juvenile gang leaders. For example, Lewis Yablonsky (1962) charged (without evidence) that gang leaders are typically sociopaths.

Clarence Schrag (1962) argued that the theory of differential opportunity is too general in the face of real world complexities. Schrag objected that Cloward and Ohlin's theory fails to explain why, even in Type II and Type III communities, a substantial number of working-class boys do not join delinquent gangs. Why do some working-class boys join gangs, but not others? Schrag also pointed out that, especially in neighborhoods with high delinquency rates, delinquent gangs are far more diverse, more fluid, and less organized than Cloward and Ohlin maintain. Moreover, David Matza and Gresham Sykes (1961) disagreed with the subcultural theorists' portrayal of middle-class values as being centered on the Protestant ethic of hard work and abstemiousness. There are, they argued, numerous respectable subterranean values that both the middle class and the working class have in common, including the search for kicks and the identification of masculinity with toughness. In other words, Matza and Sykes questioned whether the activities of delinquent gangs really are deviant if those same activities find cultural support within the middle class.

## 12.2 Matza's *Delinquency and Drift* (1964)

In what at the time seemed to some criminologists a complete annihilation of subcultural explanations of delinquency, David Matza charged eloquently that subcultural theory failed altogether to understand the causes of juvenile delinquency. In his book *Delinquency and Drift* (1964), Matza forcefully attacked the core assumptions of the lengthy positivist tradition that stretched from Quetelet's social mechanics (see Chapter 10.2) to the ideas of the subcultural theorists. At the same time, in this book, as well as in his *Becoming Deviant* (1969) and in his writings with Gresham Sykes (Sykes and Matza, 1957; Matza and Sykes, 1961), Matza offered an alternative theory of delinquency.

The key concepts in Matza's theory of delinquency are (1) the "positive delinquent"; (2) the "subculture of delinquency"; and (3) "delinquency and drift " (neutralization, will, and preparation and desperation). To these we now turn.

### The Positive Delinquent

According to Matza, positivist criminology made three explicit assumptions about crime and criminality. Each assumption, he argued, was wrong. Matza pointed out that positivist criminology assumed that the proper focus of criminological study should be the criminal rather than the criminal law. This assumption had led to a search for all sorts of motivational and socioeconomic causes of crime. However, the assumption ignored that crime is, above all, not only an action but also an infraction (namely, law breaking). In neglecting to study the legal and other institutions that define certain actions as infractions (in essence, crime and deviance), positivist criminology had "for close to a century display[ed] little concern for the essence of crime-infraction" (1964:5).

Moreover, positivist criminology had been unduly preoccupied with copying the methods of the natural sciences. Rejecting the free-will philosophies of classical criminology (see Chapter 9.1), the positivists had assumed, as a matter of faith, that all human action is determined by scientific law and that, therefore, humans are largely incapable of choosing between different paths of action. "The positive delinquent does not exercise choice," Matza wrote, "his action is constrained [and he] must behave in a delinquent manner because of the determinants that have shaped him" (p. 11). Matza admitted that this approach of hard determinism, found especially in biological theories of crime, had given way in recent times to soft determinism. This modified analysis of delinquent subcultures endowed individuals with the capacity to exercise choice, but, Matza continued, advocates of soft determinism still basically believed that criminality is caused. This more subtle form of determinism is at the heart of linking crime with poverty, differential association, and the values of delinquent subcultures.

Further, argued Matza (1964), positivist criminology assumed that criminals are fundamentally different from the law-abiding citizenry. With the exception of eighteenth-century classical criminology, this assumption had been a central feature of all previous criminology. From this assumption it follows that criminals are thus constrained by a set of circumstances that simply do not apply to the law abiding. However, Matza objected: "A reliance on differentiation, whether constitutional, personal, or sociocultural, as the key explanation of delinquency has pushed the standard-bearers of diverse theories to posit what have almost always turned out to be empirically undemonstrable differences" (p. 12).

Matza concluded that this doomed attempt to distinguish between the criminal and the law-abiding had resulted in, or perhaps paralleled, several other errors by the positivists. Because subcultural theorists had assumed that the values of delinquents differ from those of nondelinquents, for example, insufficient attention had been paid either to the values of society at large or to smaller units within it, such as the family. To study crime, Matza implied, we must look far beyond the immediate social environment where infraction is detected. Moreover, positivist criminology accounted for too much delinquency. It had been an "embarrassment of riches" that predicted far more delinquency than actually occurs. If delinquents really were as different from the law abiding and as committed to the values of their subculture as the positivists had assumed, then

> involvement in delinquency would be more permanent and less transient, more pervasive and less intermittent than is apparently the case. Theories of delinquency yield an embarrassment of riches which seemingly go unmatched in the real world. This accounting for too much delinquency may be taken as an observable conse-

quence of the distorted picture of the delinquent that has developed within positive criminology. (p. 22)

Matza's criticisms of the positivists' skeletal assumptions are most revealing. *Delinquency and Drift,* however, did much more than simply criticize the explanations of subcultural theorists; as with several other texts in the emerging societal reaction and labeling perspectives (see Chapter 13.2), it also put forward an alternative image of delinquency.

## The Subculture of Delinquency

The basis of Matza's alternative theory of delinquency is that there is a subculture of delinquency but that it is not a delinquent subculture. Matza began by saying that subcultural theorists were wrong to see the relationship between the values of a subculture of delinquency and the values of mainstream culture as one of opposition. Things are not so neat and tidy. By and large, the vast majority of delinquents are children; it would therefore be surprising indeed if the subculture of delinquency were made up of children opposed strongly to the values of conventional mainstream culture. Matza believed, in other words, that juvenile delinquents are typically not very different from other juveniles and that their values are likely to be quite similar to nondelinquent youths.

These similarities between the conventional culture and the subculture of delinquency Matza termed "subterranean convergence." In many of their basic ideas the subculture of delinquency and the conventional culture converge: in cowboy masculinity, in the search for kicks and excitement, in the Bohemian celebration of the primitive, and in the persistence of territorial sentiments in certain localities of large cities.

Matza suggested that the subculture of delinquency is of two minds regarding delinquency: One frame of mind allows and encourages its members to behave illegally and to gain prestige from doing so; the other reveals that the subculture remains basically committed to the important values of conventional culture. Both frames of mind must be examined if the subculture of delinquency is to be understood accurately. Moreover, Matza continued, conventional culture is often not quite as conventional as it is made out to be. Conventional culture is complex and many-sided. Its features consist not only of ascetic puritanism, middle-class morality, the Boy Scout oath, and the like, but also of hedonism, frivolity, and excitement.

Matza suggested that the way to understand the two-mindedness of the subculture of delinquency is to assess the posture of delinquents in a variety of circumstances, especially in what he terms "the situation of apprehension" and "the situation of company." By the "situation of apprehension" Matza referred to the problem created if the subculture of delinquency and the conventional culture hold oppositional values: Delinquents will offer radical defenses of their activities when they are arrested by the police or when they are brought before a juvenile court. If the members of a subculture of delinquency are committed to their delinquent activities and values, they will feel almost no shame or guilt on detection by authority. Yet juveniles commonly express feelings of genuine contrition on apprehension. Such feelings cannot simply be dismissed as a manipulative tactic designed to appease authority. The contrition of juveniles, Matza concluded, "cannot be ignored if we are to avoid the gross stereotype of the delinquent as a hardened gangster in miniature" (p. 41). With the exception of a few bizarre oddities—regarded by ordinary delinquents as crazy—delinquents rarely desire either to attack the values of conventional culture or to defend those of the subculture of delinquency. Moreover, if delinquents are so different from nondelinquents, why do the vast majority of them desist from delinquency at the end of their adolescence?

By "the situation of company" Matza referred to the understanding of delinquents when in the company of their peers. Matza suggested that the values of the subculture of delinquency are far more fluid and less clear than usually thought. He argued that these values are not, as such, learned formally by novice delinquents, because there is no written or formal code of delinquent values to be learned. Actually, many things are not discussed openly and must be inferred (often wrongly!) by novices from the hints and cues of their friends. During entry into the subculture of delinquency, boys—there are very few females in Matza's *Delinquency and Drift*—suffer status anxiety about their masculinity. How can they learn the values of the subculture of delinquency without revealing that they are not yet the fully committed delinquents they believe all the other boys to be? Matza suggested that they do so by cautiously sounding out other boys about masculinity and appropriate delinquent acts. Thus: "Do I really like you? Yea, come here and such and I'll show you how much I like you." Or: "Do I think that stealing a car is a good thing? Man you a fag or something? Ain't you one of the boys?" Serious discussion of delinquency is almost always impossible for delinquents because of the anxiety it would produce about their own masculinity. Whatever the motive, Matza concluded, "The function of such remarks is to mislead the delinquent into believing that his subculture is committed to delinquency" (p. 54).

However, Matza was keenly aware that this comedy of errors cannot continue indefinitely. Most boys discover eventually, often from one close friend in whose company their anxieties can be relaxed, that almost no one is actually committed to the subculture of delinquency. They discover, in other words, that all along they were wrong to believe that delinquents are committed to their misdeeds. The importance of this eye-opening information is reinforced as juveniles become adults (as boys become "real men"). The achievement of real masculinity is marked by such new signs of status as jobs, wives, children, and mortgages. The acquisition of these "obvious" signs of masculinity allows the ex-delinquent to reject the values and activities of the subculture as "kids' stuff." Dwindling remnants of the old gang mix with the company of younger cohorts. But the great majority of members of the subculture of delinquency do not become adult criminals.

## Delinquency and Drift

Recall that, against the determinism of the positivist tradition, Matza was eager to assert the presence of a certain degree of choice and free will in human action. This assertion is found in his concept of **drift**. Matza suggested that the delinquent is committed neither to the subculture of delinquency nor to the conventional culture. Instead, the delinquent chooses, more or less consciously, to drift between the one and the other, often many times in the course of a single day:

Drift stands midway between freedom and control. Its basis is an area of the social structure in which control has been loosened [and where it is] coupled with the abortiveness of adolescent endeavor to organize an autonomous subculture. . . . The delinquent transiently exists in a limbo between convention and crime, responding in turn to the demands of each, flirting now with one, now with the other, but postponing commitment, evading decision. Thus, he drifts between criminal and conventional action. (p. 28)

Matza's theory of delinquency and drift has three components: neutralization, will, and preparation and desperation.

*Neutralization* is the process by which potential delinquents are freed from conventional social and moral controls, and because of which they are then able to engage in delinquency (Sykes and Matza, 1957). With Gresham Sykes, Matza argued that most juvenile delinquents are not nearly as committed to delinquent values and activities as subcultural theorists have supposed. Indeed, precisely because they are not really opposed to mainstream values, juveniles often display feelings of shame and guilt when their delinquency is detected and exposed. To shield novice delinquents from such feelings, experienced delinquents teach them a variety of techniques to rationalize and justify their behavior. For example, they teach them to say such things as, "I didn't mean it"; "I didn't really hurt anybody"; "They had it coming to them"; "Everybody's picking on me"; "I didn't do it for myself." These techniques operate to deflect or to neutralize the disapproval of such authority figures as judges, juvenile police officers, and probation workers.

**Techniques of neutralization**, then, generally reduce the effectiveness of social and moral controls (see Box 12.2). They allow juveniles to engage in delinquency despite the disapproval of authority figures or of their conforming peers. At the same time, Sykes and Matza were careful to note that such techniques are not powerful enough to shield all delinquents from feelings of shame and guilt. Moreover, some delinquents are so isolated from the conforming world of the dominant culture that neutralization techniques are not even useful.

Matza (1964) argued that the neutralization of the values of conventional culture is insufficient to ensure that a juvenile will actually drift into delinquency. For a delinquent

---

**Box 12.2    Techniques of Neutralization**

According to Sykes and Matza (1957), there are five basic techniques of neutralization:

1. **Denial of responsibility.** Insofar as the delinquent can define himself as lacking responsibility for his deviant actions, the disapproval of self or others is sharply reduced in effectiveness as a restraining influence. It may also be asserted that delinquent acts are due to forces outside of the individual and beyond his control, such as unloving parents, bad companions, or a slum neighborhood.

2. **Denial of injury.** The delinquent frequently, and in a hazy fashion, feels that his behavior does not really cause any great harm despite the fact that it runs counter to the law.

3. **Denial of victim.** Even if the delinquent accepts the responsibility for his deviant actions and is willing to admit that his deviant actions involve an injury or hurt, the moral indignation of self and others may be neutralized by an insistence that the injury is not wrong in light of the circumstances. The injury, it may be claimed, is not really an injury; rather, it is a form of rightful retaliation or punishment.

4. **Condemnation of condemners.** The delinquent shifts the focus of attention from his own deviant acts to the motives and behavior of those who disapprove of his violations. By attacking others, he feels the wrongfulness of his own behavior is more easily repressed or lost to view.

5. **Appeal to higher loyalties.** Internal and external social controls may be neutralized by sacrificing the demands of the larger society for the demands of the small social groups to which the delinquent belongs, such as the sibling pair, the gang, or the friendship clique. The conflict between the claims of friendship and the claims of law, or a similar dilemma, has of course long been recognized. If the juvenile delinquent frequently resolves his dilemma by insisting that he must "always help a buddy" or "never squeal on a friend," even when it throws him into serious difficulties with the dominant social order, his choice remains familiar to the supposedly law-abiding public.

act to occur, the juvenile must *will* it. Two factors that activate the will are preparation and desperation. Preparation provides the will to repeat old infractions of law; desperation provides the will to commit new ones.

By "preparation" Matza meant the skills a juvenile must have before committing a crime. To commit a robbery, for example, a youth must have a certain rudimentary level of strength, dexterity, speed, agility, and cunning to be successful. Also, a youth must not be apprehensive or "chicken" when about to violate the law; or, in the language of classical criminology, he must not be deterred by the threat of the imposition of law. Youths must believe that the police are relatively incompetent and that they are only relatively potent. In their preparation for delinquency, youths also learn that, even if their delinquency is detected, incarceration is unlikely.

By "desperation" Matza referred to what he suspected to be the primary motive in the will to delinquency: that youngsters feel they have no control over their lives. For youngsters with anxieties about their masculinity and about membership in their peer group, a mood of fatalism and desperation is the natural consequence of experiencing a lack of control. To assert control, a boy cannot just do anything ("Shit, man, anybody can do that"). He must master his fate. He must make something happen. Often the subculture of delinquency stresses the importance of delinquency as a means of making things happen; sometimes it stresses the time-honored method of exploiting and conquering females. However, Matza concluded, the will to crime may be "discouraged, deterred, or diverted by countless contingencies" (p. 191).

## Evaluation of *Delinquency and Drift*

One way of evaluating *Delinquency and Drift* is to see it as an attempt to restore to juveniles a degree of free will denied them by the determinism of the positivist tradition.

In criticizing the unwarranted determinism of positivist criminology, Matza tried to force us, instead, to appreciate the way in which deviants themselves view their activities. If certain youths consciously choose to drift between convention and delinquency, then clearly their accounts of why they drift become an essential part of explaining their actions. Deviants have voices that should be heard!

Although Matza's work has inspired few full-length studies, a notable exception is Jack Katz's phenomenological *The Seductions of Crime* (1988). Katz believes that positivist explanations that focus on "background" correlations—like socioeconomic factors or whether criminals were dropped on their heads when they were babies—do little to help us understand what motivates criminals to commit crime. As Katz wrote:

> The statistical and correlational findings of positivist criminology provide the following irritations to inquiry: (1) whatever the validity of the hereditary, psychological, and social-ecological conditions of crime, many of those in the supposedly causal categories do not commit the crime at issue, (2) many who do commit the crime do not fit the causal categories, and (3) what is most provocative, many who do fit the background categories and later commit the predicted crime go for long stretches without committing the crimes to which theory directs them. (pp. 3–4)

Expanding upon the work of Matza, Katz argued that we need to understand the "foreground" of experience, the thrill, the magic and emotions that "seduce" persons to commit crime. Katz extended his ethnographic method to such crimes as murder, robbery, and shoplifting.

Although Katz has managed to develop Matza's insights in important ways, the question remains: Is Matza's reformulation successful, or does his reformulation merely shift the causes of delinquency from one positivist area to another—from status frustration to masculine anxiety, for example? This is a difficult question. Although Matza's basic thesis that delinquents drift between conventional and delinquent activities has been tested extensively, generally these tests have focused on the importance that Matza has attributed to techniques of neutralization.

Using data on cannabis users from the European School Survey on Alcohol and Other Drugs, one study (Pereetti-Watel, 2003) of young French cannabis users has found that, in addition to Matza's techniques of neutralization, deviants may use three other techniques to deny that their behavior entails much risk. In particular, suggests Pereetti-Watel, cannabis users may scapegoat others, such as users of hard drugs such as heroin, cocaine, and crack cocaine; they may display self-confidence, particularly in their ability to control their own drug consumption; and they may offer comparisons between the low risks of cannabis use, and the higher risks of alcohol and other drugs.

But most tests of neutralization theory have explored two main questions: Do techniques of neutralization come before delinquent acts? Where do delinquents stand relative to delinquent and conventional values?

Some studies (e.g., Ball, 1966) have provided limited support for Matza's concept of techniques of neutralization. Others (e.g., Hamlin, 1988) have found that these techniques are motives that neutralize guilt after a delinquent act. Faced with this controversy, it is fair to conclude that some delinquents use techniques of neutralization before and others after their behavior has been detected and defined as deviant. For example, many people who cheat on their income tax returns rationalize their behavior beforehand by claiming, "Everyone else is cheating the IRS, and I'm stupid if I don't do it."

Carl Klockars (1974) and Darrell Steffensmeier (1986) have shown, in their biographical studies of professional fences, that certain thieves can neutralize their past and their future illegalities—if they are involved in a continuing criminal career—by reasoning, "I'm not hurting anyone when I steal, because insurance will always pay the loss" (and see Chapter 4.1). Listen to Sam, Steffensmeier's fence:

> I don't feel I hurt any little people 'cause most of the stuff did come out of business places and big places, which were insurance write-offs and which they will many times mark it double what it was. In a roundabout way, yes, the individual is going to pay for it, like with the higher transport and that. I would not feel bad about this. It's the same as, say, chiseling on income tax. You cheat Uncle Sam, but that's not the same as cheating this here person. (1986:241)

However, such partial confirmations of Matza's thesis on the use of neutralization techniques have been challenged by Michael Hindelang (1970, 1974). In his earlier study, Hindelang (1970) obtained the confidential information of 346 boys from a middle-class area of Oakland, California. In this study Hindelang asked his subjects to record the number of times they had committed any of 26 offenses (including theft, drug use/abuse, fighting, sexual deviance, and truancy) in the previous year. In addition, the youngsters were asked whether they strongly disapproved, disapproved, were indifferent to, approved, or strongly approved the act. If Matza was correct, and delinquents are not committed to their misdeeds, then delinquent approval of an act should be similar to approval expressed by nondelinquents. Hindelang found that 13 of 15 activities he examined showed a significant association between delinquent involvement and the approval of delinquent acts. These findings clearly contradict Matza's thesis that delinquents do not differ substantively from nondelinquents in their commitment to conventional culture.

Recall Matza's point that if delinquents really were so influenced by their subculture, it would be extremely difficult to explain the fact that most members of the subculture eventually abandon their delinquency. In other words, how can we account for the maturational reform of juvenile delinquents? Why do most juvenile delinquents become conformist adults? A possible explanation of maturation is in fact precisely the one suggested by Matza himself: Most delinquents are never seriously committed to their delinquency in the first place. But as David Greenberg (1993) has argued, it is in fact unclear why most subculture carriers abandon activities so highly prized within the subculture. Why do gang members eventually desist from delinquent activities? Greenberg is quick to point out that, as valuable as Matza's insight is, it opens up other nagging questions:

> Why does desistance from violen[t] offenses occur later and more slowly than [from] theft offenses? Why are some juveniles so much more extensively involved in delinquency than others? Matza's remarkable presentation of the subjective elements in delinquency must be supplemented by an analysis of the objective, structural elements in causation, if such questions are to be answered (p. 120; also see Chapter 3.4).

According to Greenberg, then, Matza did not adequately consider the relation between social class and socioeconomic status, on the one hand, and the distribution of values on the other. Are working-class youths, for example, more likely to engage in neutralization techniques than youths from other sections of society? If so, why? Indeed, why do some youths not commit delinquent acts? Or, to ask the same question differently, why do some youths conform to positive culture but others do not? This question has been explored within the context of control theory, to which we now turn.

## 12.3 Control Theory

The concept of "social control" was pioneered by Gabriel Tarde (see Chapters 9.3 and 10.1). In the United States it was used first by sociologists (e.g., Ross, 1901) and social psychologists (e.g., Mead, 1925). Early on, "social control" was understood broadly as all institutions and processes that guarantee social order. In some writings, it was depicted as a coercive device by which the will of the powerful was imposed on society. However, during the 1940s the concept of **social control** was given a much narrower reading. Two aspects of this narrower view were soon adopted as guiding themes in criminology. First, social control was stripped of its critical content and declared a functional necessity that contributed to the well-being of society. Without social control, functionalists claimed, anarchy and chaos would prevail in any society. Second, the concept was narrowed to include small groups (such as families, schools, and peers). The focus here was on how these groups socialized their members.

These narrower perspectives on social control are vividly present in the studies to which we now turn. These studies proceed on the central assumption that crime is likely to occur when the social bonds between an individual and society are weakened or severed. In what follows we present the two best-known versions of **control theory** in criminology: Walter Reckless's (1961) containment theory and Travis Hirschi's (1969) social control (or social bonding) theory.

### Containment Theory

Walter Reckless (1940) suggested that variation in the respective crime rates of different social groups was caused by variations in the ability to contain norm-violating behavior in the face of social change and cultural conflict. Reckless later developed this insight as **containment theory** in his book *The Crime Problem* (1961).

Reckless developed the theory of containment largely because of a major bias he detected in existing criminological theory. To Reckless's dismay, the vast majority of theories placed too much emphasis on the process of social disorganization as the cause of crime. To correct for this misplaced emphasis, Reckless argued that crime generally is prevented, or contained, as a result of two key processes: One occurs at the level of social organization, the other at the level of individual personality.

In attempting to correct what he saw as a misplaced bias toward factors of social organization at the expense of personality factors, Reckless (1961) relied on several new empirical studies of delinquency. According to these studies (Reiss, 1951; Nye, 1958), delinquents often came from broken homes and had not been properly socialized or controlled by their families, peer groups, schools, and adult friends. These studies also found that recidivists had weak egos and personal controls and poor self-concepts, whereas "good boys" (nondelinquents) tended to come from middle-class families or from families that were stable maritally, economically, and spatially. Moreover, good boys projected a good self-concept—namely, one that acts as an effective insulator against delinquency (Reckless, Dinitz, and Murray, 1956). The self-concept of good boys included law-abiding and obedient self-evaluations together with positive responses to family life and parental (especially maternal) control.

Reckless suggested that a good self-concept represents a favorable internalization of presumably favorable life-experiences, including an acceptance or incorporation of the proper concern that significant others have had for the person. It acts selectively on experience and holds the line against adversities (pressures), the subculture of delinquency, wrongdoing, and crime (pull), as well as discontent and frustrations (pushes). The poor self-concept is a residue of less favorable growth, the acceptance of less concern or a different concern (value-wise) of significant others.

Reckless's theory of containment is a hierarchical structure focusing on the ability of individuals to contain social and psychological conflict. For Reckless, inner and outer containments occupy a position between the pressures and pulls of the social environment and the inner pushes of the individual personality. At the top of the hierarchy is a layer of social pressures that bear down on the individual. These pressures include poverty, unemployment, economic insecurity, family conflict, minority group status, lack of opportunity, and class and social inequality. At the same level is a layer of social pulls that draw individuals away from their routines and accepted patterns of life. These pulls include influential deviants ("prestige individuals"), bad company, delinquent and criminal subcultures, and propaganda such as that purveyed by the mass media.

According to Reckless, immediately surrounding the individual is a barrier of outer containment. This barrier consists of effective family living and supportive groups and includes such factors as morality, supervision, discipline, reasonable norms and expectations, and safety valves to release tensions. If this barrier is weak, the individual is quite vulnerable to social pressures and pulls.

Inside the individual's consciousness is a barrier of inner containment. Deviance-prone individuals (essentially those with weak inner containment) are likely to have some combination of bad self-control, weak ego, underdeveloped superego (conscience), poor self-concept, low frustration tolerance, no sense of responsibility, and inadequate goal orientation. Inner containment is the last line of defense against internal and external pressures and pulls.

Finally, the bottom layer of the hierarchy consists of psychological pushes. These include varying degrees of hostility, aggressiveness, suggestibility, rebellion, guilt reactions, feelings of inadequacy and inferiority, sibling rivalry, and such organic difficulties as brain damage and epilepsy. According to Reckless, certain of these psychological pushes are usually too strong for inner as well as outer containment.

## Evaluation of Containment Theory

Several criticisms have been made of Reckless's theory. Some criminologists have rightly complained that important parts of his theory—such as a poor self-concept—are defined so vaguely that they are not testable (Schrag, 1962). What, precisely, is a poor self-concept? Is it, for example, the belief that one is no good? Or is it the belief that others believe that one is no good? How does one define "bad company"? How bad must company be for it to constitute bad company?

These difficulties notwithstanding, Reckless's containment theory fostered another, far more articulate theory of crime: Travis Hirschi's social control theory.

## Social Control Theory

Hirschi's *Causes of Delinquency* (1969) is a prominent landmark in the developing literature on the sociology and social psychology of social control. Hirschi thought that most sociological theories had failed to show that delinquency actually is caused by such factors as the strains of "sex, race, social class, neighborhood, mother's employment, the broken home, size of family, and so forth" (p. 65). Although these factors might be correlated with delinquency, Hirschi reasoned, there is no evidence they actually cause it. Instead of looking for the causes of delinquency, he argued, it is much more fruitful to look for the causes of conformity. Perhaps delinquency is merely an absence of the causes of conformity.

Hirschi therefore started with the seemingly biological proposition that most people have antisocial tendencies; however, these tendencies are actualized only if various sorts of social control are relaxed. Whether individuals are law abiding or deviant depends on the extent of variance from the four factors that are critical in bonding them to society: (1) attachment to parents, school, and peers; (2) commitment to conventional lines of action; (3) involvement in conventional activities; and (4) belief in conventional values.

First, Hirschi theorized, juveniles will be law abiding if they have strong attachments to positive role models or significant others—their parents, schoolteachers, and law-abiding friends. Weak attachments to expectations of significant others can derive from a lack of discipline by parents and teachers, poor intellectual and social skills exhibited by the juvenile, disrespect for or indifference to expectations and opinions of significant others, and differential association with juvenile delinquents.

Second, Hirschi maintained that for a system of social control to be effective, juveniles must fear punishment. He reasoned that delinquents are likely to be juveniles who, during their difficult passage to adulthood, are less committed to completing their education or achieving a high-status career.

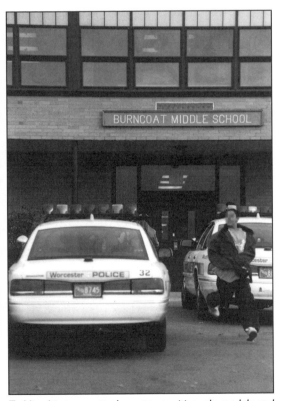

To Hirschi, strong attachment to positive role models and a commitment to conventional activities will decrease delinquency. Children reared without having had these values reinforced will be candidates for delinquency, regardless of their social and economic background.

Hirschi therefore disagreed with subcultural theories that identified frustrated aspirations as the main provocation for delinquency, although he did not identify the factors that cause variance in juvenile attachment to conventional lines of action.

Third, juvenile attachments and attitudinal commitments to positive role models and to conventional goals are likely to be reflected in the juvenile's daily involvement in conventional activities. The more juveniles are involved in such conventional activities as education and school-related activities, the more they are discouraged from engaging in delinquency, and vice versa.

Fourth, Hirschi argued that belief in the goodness of certain values—such as respect for the law and for the police and belief in the wrongness of such actions as juvenile delinquency—operates as a brake on delinquency. Finally, we note that Hirschi implied that all four factors (attachment, commitment, involvement, and belief) are strongly interrelated: "In general, the more closely a person is tied to conventional society in any of these ways, the more closely he is likely to be tied in the other ways. The person who is attached to conventional people is, for example, more likely to be involved in conventional activities and to accept conventional notions of desirable conduct" (p. 27).

In *Causes of Delinquency*, Hirschi attempted to test his theory empirically. His test was based on a study of school records, police records, and questionnaire responses gathered from a large sample of juveniles (stratified by race, sex, school, and grade) in the San Francisco-Oakland area in the mid-1960s. Self-report items included many questions about attitudes toward family, school, and peers. Six items in the questionnaire were meant to serve as an index of delinquency. Three questions asked whether in the last year the juvenile had stolen anything worth less than $2, worth $2–$50, and worth over $50. Three questions asked whether he or she had ever "taken a car for a ride without the owner's permission," "banged up something that did not belong to you on purpose," and (not counting fights with brothers and sisters) "beaten up on anyone or hurt anyone on purpose" (p. 54).

From these data Hirschi made a variety of generalizations about the links between social control and delinquency, each of which seemed remarkably at odds with previous theories. The seven most important of these generalizations are:

1. Juveniles engage less in delinquency the more they are attached to their families.

2. Juveniles engage less in delinquency the better they perform in school.

3. The greater a youth's stake in conformity, then, irrespective of the delinquency of his or her peers, the less likely he or she is to be delinquent.

4. Members of delinquent gangs do not have cohesive or warm associations with fellow gang members.

5. The importance of techniques of neutralization in delinquency is inconclusive.

6. There is no significant causal link between delinquency and social class.

7. In the United States, no section of society encourages delinquency more than any other.

Finally, we note that Hirschi later (1983) reformulated his theory somewhat and extended its scope to focus on child socialization rather than on adolescence. In this revised version Hirschi borrowed from the Oregon Social Learning Center's treatment of families with problem children. He reported the Center's "commonsense" finding that "children must be punished for their misdeeds" (p. 53). Continuing forcefully to reject theories of crime that stress such factors as poverty, social class, and unemployment, Hirschi asserted that good childrearing techniques and proper discipline are the chief ways to prevent or control juvenile delinquency. Good techniques include monitoring children, recognizing problems, and punishing misbehavior.

Thus, inadequate childrearing techniques and lax discipline are allegedly the chief factors in juvenile delinquency. These factors are especially present, Hirschi argued, among working mothers, in situations of child abuse, among parents with criminal records, in large families, and in single-parent families: "The single parent (usually a woman) . . . is less able to devote time to monitoring and punishment, and is more likely to be involved in negative, abusive contacts with her children" (p. 62).

Hirschi proposed, somewhat vaguely, three policies for the control of problem children. First, childrearing classes should be standard fare in high school so that future parents learn the rudiments of sound childrearing techniques. Second, parents and teachers should combine their knowledge and their supervisory roles in order better to address childrearing issues. Third, there must be appropriate governmental commitment to ensuring that families have incentives to raise law-abiding children. However, as Hirschi (1983) recognized, these proposals are highly controversial. For instance, should the government penalize parents (and guardians) who do not use sound childrearing practices? If so, how severe a penalty is appropriate? Where should the dividing line be drawn between family privacy and governmental responsibility?

## Evaluation of Social Control Theory

Among many criminologists, the control theory of crime continues to be extremely influential. In Hirschi's version (nowadays often referred to as "social bonding" theory), especially, it is a formalized theory whose several propositions lend themselves easily to empirical tests. It is a major source of current research and, until quite recently, has consistently received empirical support from researchers (Laub and Sampson, 1988; Voorhis, Cullen, Mathers, and Garner, 1988). Moreover, it has motivated other researchers (such as Toby, 1983) to pinpoint the apparent importance of strict control—and the dire consequences of lax discipline—in institutions such as schools.

However, certain research has shown that some of Hirschi's key concepts should be refined. For example, Stephen Cernkovich and Peggy Giordano (1987; and see Wells and Rankin, 1988) complain that Hirschi's concept of attachment is too vague. What exactly is attachment? How does one measure it? They suggest that to understand the subtle dynamics of family interaction, future researchers should (1) recognize the importance of different measures of attachment—including control and supervision, identity support (during adolescent crises), caring and trust, forms and degrees of intimate communication, parental disapproval of peers, and conflict—and (2) explore the effects on delinquency of the variety of intact and broken family units, including both-parent, mother-only, father-only, father/stepmother, and mother/stepfather homes.

The relation between Hirschi's concept of conformity, on the one hand, and his other key concepts (attachment, involvement, commitment, and belief), on the other, has also been criticized strongly. As discussed earlier, Hirschi asserted that juveniles are law abiding or conforming if they have strong attachments to their positive role models. But Hirschi's statement confuses a definition of conformity with an explanation of conformity. As Thomas Bernard (1987) wrote: "If conformity is defined as acts controlled by attachments, involvements, commitments, and beliefs, conformity cannot be explained by the same statement without simply restating the definition" (p. 417). In other words, Hirschi's reasoning appears to be circular. It is not at all clear that the concepts of control theory explain anything at all.

Other criminologists have raised serious doubts about the validity of Hirschi's findings. In his longitudinal study of 2,213 boys between 1966 and 1968, Robert Agnew (1985) found that Hirschi's theory cannot explain serious forms of juvenile crime. In other words, even if control theory can explain minor crimes such as petty theft, it does not and cannot explain why some juveniles commit very violent offenses. Some other explanation is needed of such crimes. Agnew also found that although at any given point in time delinquency may appear strongly correlated with Hirschi's control variables, in the long run, rather than delinquency being caused by weak social controls, delinquency itself can causally affect control! Agnew therefore concluded that "the explanatory power of Hirschi's social control theory has been exaggerated" (p. 58).

Criminologists have engaged in a heated dispute over the causal relationships indicated by theorists of control. There are essentially two sides to this dispute. According to conservatives such as Hirschi and his followers, the allegedly high and rising U.S. crime rates have been caused by the lax discipline and the cultural permissiveness of 1960s liberalism. In this view, rising crime rates have been caused by the general permissiveness of liberal parents, the decline of religious values, the collapse of order in the nation's high schools, governments that have been too generous with the poor and with welfare recipients, and criminal justice systems that are too soft on criminals. Thus, the solution to the problem of crime lies in greater social control. Typical conservative policies for controlling crime include compulsory religious instruction from the elementary school upward, restoration of strict discipline (including corporal punishment) in the nation's high schools, reduction or elimination of government welfare programs in order to cultivate individual responsibility and to foster initiative among the "undeserving poor," and increased severity of penal sanctions (such as longer prison sentences and determinate sentencing).

On the other side of this dispute are the liberal critics of control theory. Elliott Currie (1997), for example, has argued that the high violent crime rates in the United States have little to do with lax social control and much to do with the logic of free economic enterprise and its unfortunate consequences. Chief among these consequences are (Currie, 1997):

- The progressive destruction of jobs and livelihood.

- The growth of extremes of economic inequality and material deprivation.

- The withdrawal of public services and supports, especially for families and children.

- The erosion of informal and communal networks of mutual support, supervision, and care.

- The spread of a materialistic, neglectful, and "hard" culture.

- The unregulated marketing of the technology of violence.

- The weakening of social and political alternatives.

Moreover, liberal critics of control theory counter that strict discipline neither deters nor controls delinquency. Stricter discipline (including corporal punishment) may actually encourage delinquency, they continue, because its use teaches children that physical force is the appropriate way to solve interpersonal problems. It is no accident, the liberal argument concludes, that the United States has both the highest rate of violent crime and the highest rate of incarceration of all industrial nations. Punitive control and high rates of violent crime are both symptoms of the same problem: The United States is a thoroughly violent society, even, ironically, in its response to violent crime. In the liberal scenario, the causes of crime must be attacked by social policies that seek alternatives to imprisonment, that foster community spirit, that create employment for the poor, and that make adequate provision for the children of poorer families.

Although we do not explicitly assess the respective merits of the conservative and liberal viewpoints—admitting that the arguments supporting them are many and complex—we conclude this assessment of social control theory by noting one basic, perhaps fatal, criticism of the conservative viewpoint. Hirschi's theory of social control derives from an assumption about human nature that is probably undemonstrable and quite likely wrong: At the moment of birth, when society has not yet imprinted its values and its controls on our social characters, we are all aggressive and naturally violent animals. In this dark and pessimistic vision, as in the biblical theory of original sin, criminal behavior is something that parents, educators, and other agents of social control must work to avoid. But as Currie complains:

> Whatever one may think, on a purely philosophical level, about Hirschi's attitude toward human nature, it cannot tell us why some times, some places, and some groups are more criminal than others. In order to accomplish this, Hirschi must go on to blame a variety of changes in contemporary values and attitudes for weakening parents' capacity to quash their children's unruly impulses. (p. 187)

## Review

This chapter outlined subcultural perspectives on delinquency. First, we looked at the key themes emerging in the sociology of delinquent subcultures during the 1950s; this sociology was influenced strongly by earlier traditions of anomie and differential association. Second, we summarized David Matza's criticism of the positivist approach to juvenile delinquency. In his alternative formulation, Matza emphasized that juveniles consciously drift between the conventional culture and the subculture of delinquency. Third, we examined various theories that focus on the causal importance of the notion of control.

## Delinquent Subcultures

1. Beginning in the 1950s, Mertonian anomie theory led directly to further examination of the cultural settings that fostered juvenile delinquency.

2. Cohen's *Delinquent Boys* (1955) suggested that delinquent boys inhabit a subculture whose activities are nonutilitarian, malicious, and negativistic. Lower-class boys (rather than middle-class boys, or girls in general) are doomed to fail in terms of middle-class standards, especially in school, and they react by participating in the creation of a delinquent subculture or by joining a bearer group of such a subculture. This reaction provides the status that the middle-class world denies them.

3. Cohen's findings were criticized by numerous scholars, including Miller (1958) and Cloward and Ohlin (1960). Miller suggested that Cohen had overemphasized the extent to which lower-class youth internalized middle-class values. Lower-class delinquent subcultures should therefore be understood in terms of the focal concerns of lower-class life, especially the female-headed household.

4. In *Delinquency and Opportunity* (1960), Cloward and Ohlin responded that earlier theorists had simplified both the reasons that lower-class youth join delinquent subcultures and the variety of such subcultures. Delinquents tend to be boys who desire greater economic success but who, uninterested in becoming middle class, seek higher status in lower-class terms. Boys generally join a criminal subculture, if available; if not, they join a conflict subculture. Boys who fail in these subcultures, or for whom they are unavailable, tend to join the retreatist subculture.

## Matza's *Delinquency and Drift* (1964)

1. *Delinquency and Drift* offered powerful criticisms of the lengthy positivist tradition stretching from Quetelet's social mechanics of crime to the subcultural theories of delinquency discussed in this chapter. Matza argued that this tradition teaches wrongly that all activities of juveniles are determined by social and environmental forces over which they have absolutely no control. Matza claimed, rather, that juveniles exercise rational choice over their activities, whether delinquent or conformist.

2. Matza stressed the existence of a subculture of delinquency that is not a delinquent subculture. Because most delinquents are children, it is not surprising that the values of the subculture of delinquency are not opposed to those of the conventional culture. For this reason, most delinquents mature as conformist adults rather than as adult criminals.

3. Delinquents drift in and out of delinquency and conventional behavior. They rationalize their delinquent activity by means of five main techniques of neutralization: denial of responsibility, denial of injury, denial of victim, condemnation of condemners, and appeal to higher loyalties. These techniques are supplemented by situations of preparation and desperation.

4. Matza identified serious problems in the positivist tradition. However, there is little conclusive evidence that his image of a less-constrained deviant is actually closer to social reality. Some critics have suggested that Matza paid insufficient attention to constraints of social class and racial inequality.

## Control Theory

1. The two major forms of control theory are containment theory and social control (or social bonding) theory. Control theory assumes that crime is likely to occur when the social bonds between an individual and society are weakened or severed.

2. Reckless's theory of containment focuses on an individual's ability to contain social and psychological conflict. Inner and outer containments occupy a position between the pressures and pulls of the social environment and the inner pushes of the individual personality. Deviance-prone individuals tend to have weak inner and outer containments that result from a combination of factors such as bad self-control, weak ego, badly developed superego, and poor self-concept.

3. Containment theory has been criticized because several of its key concepts are either too vague or immune to empirical proof.

4. Hirschi's theory of social control is based on the idea that it is better to look for the causes of conformity than for the causes of delinquency. Delinquency is an absence of the causes of conformity. Whether individuals are law abiding or deviant depends on variation among four factors that bond them to society: attachment to parents, school, and peers; commitment to conventional lines of action; involvement in conventional activities; and belief.

5. Hirschi argued that good childrearing techniques and proper discipline are the chief means of preventing and controlling delinquency.

6. Although it has been criticized, Hirschi's theory remains influential today. As with containment theory, its concepts are rather vague and difficult to test.

7. The policy implications of control theory are the subject of heated debate among criminologists. Conservatives argue that stern discipline and family values are the best means of delinquency prevention; liberals reply that such discipline has never been shown to deter crime. Liberals argue that to reduce crime, we must attack its causes with policies that seek alternatives to prison, foster community spirit, create employment for the poor, and provide adequately for children of poorer families.

## Questions for Class Discussion

1. To what extent does Albert Cohen's *Delinquent Boys* (1955) represent a rejection of the findings of Clifford Shaw and Henry McKay's *Juvenile Delinquency and Urban Areas* (1942)?

2. How do the respective explanations of the causes of juvenile delinquency advanced by Walter Miller (1958) and Richard Cloward and Lloyd Ohlin (1960) represent an advance over Cohen's *Delinquent Boys*?

3. Do delinquents drift?

4. Can the assumptions of David Matza's *Delinquency and Drift* accurately be described as a return to the assumptions of classical criminology?

5. Which is more important as a cause of crime: lax social control or unregulated economic activity?

## For Further Study

### Readings

Sanchez-Jankowski, Martin. 2003. Gangs and Social Change. *Theoretical Criminology* 7 (2): 191–216.

Valier, Claire. 2002. *Theories of Crime and Punishment*. New York: Longman.

### Websites

1. <http://ojjdp.ncjrs.org/>: From the Office of Juvenile Justice and Delinquency Prevention, this site has useful information and links regarding official policies established to combat juvenile delinquency in the United States.

2. <http://www.iir.com/nygc/maininfo.htm>: This is the official website of the National Youth Gang Center. ✦

# Theoretical Diversity

## Preview

Chapter 13 introduces:

- The theoretical diversity in criminology that first appeared during the turbulent decade of the 1960s and that continues today.

- Five influential theories of crime: social learning theory, the labeling perspective, conflict theory, radical theory, and feminist theory.

## Key Terms

conflict theory

consensus theory

criminalization

deviance amplification

labeling perspective

liberal feminism

Marxist feminism

patriarchy

primary deviance

radical feminism

reinforcement

secondary deviance

social constructionism

social learning theory

socialist feminism

societal reaction

stigma

This chapter examines five theories of crime that matured during the 1960s and 1970s. In combination, these theories represent the beginnings of the theoretical diversity that now characterizes criminology. Social learning theory developed, in part, from much of the existing criminological theory examined thus far. The labeling perspective and conflict theory have been influenced less by existing theories of crime than by various social and political movements that flourished in the 1960s; these same movements also influenced radical theory and feminist theory.

## 13.1 Social Learning Theory

In Chapter 11.4 we examined Sutherland's focus on the origins and the transmission of delinquent values, and we learned that he stimulated new lines of inquiry, one of which is social learning theory. With Sutherland's original insight in mind, subsequent empirical studies indeed seemed to confirm that the more serious a juvenile's delinquent involvement, the more likely he or she will be to have friends who are also delinquent. This finding, however, does not explain how or why associational patterns influence delinquent involvement.

In arguing that Sutherland's theory of differential association and differential social organization cannot account for the process leading to individual criminality, Robert Burgess and Ronald Akers (1966:130) urged that criminologists try to use the genetic explanations of social behavior found in behavioral psychology. When these explanations are combined with structural explanations, such as subcultural and anomie theories, criminologists have termed them "social learning theory."

The basic premise of **social learning theory** is that social behavior is determined neither by inner personality drives nor by outer sociological and environmental factors. Rather, it is a cognitive process in which personality and environment engage in a continuous process of reciprocal interaction. Modern learning theory, especially the operant conditioning theory of such behavioral scientists as B. F. Skinner (1953), was pioneered in laboratory settings. Operant (or active) conditioning theory begins with the empirical fact that animal behavior is affected by its consequences, both negative and positive. Animals are easily trained to perform certain actions if they are rewarded for doing so. For example, dogs usually learn to sit following the command "Sit!" if, after every time they sit, they receive positive **reinforcement** in the form of a bone or a friendly pat from their trainer. Desired behavior, in other words, is reinforced through a process of conditioned learning that emphasizes rewards or (for dogs that do not sit on command) punishments.

However, Bandura (1973) has shown that the process of social learning would be extremely tiring and hazardous if it depended solely on rewards and punishments. Although some behavior patterns are acquired through the process of rewarding and punishing direct experience, other behavior patterns are acquired by observing the behavior of significant others (family and peer group).

## Differential Reinforcement

Several criminologists have indicated the importance of learning theory as an explanatory tool for understanding crime. For example, in a direct application of Skinnerian theory, Clarence Ray Jeffery (1965) claimed that, in any given social situation, whether someone commits a crime depends largely on his or her past conditioning history—namely, whether the individual has been reinforced (or rewarded) for crime. Jeffery's theory of *differential reinforcement* states: "A criminal act occurs in an environment in which in the past the actor has been reinforced for behaving in this manner, and the aversive consequences attached to the behavior have been of such a nature that they do not control or prevent the response" (p. 295).

Crime is therefore a response to reinforcing stimuli. For example, the crime of robbery may produce either money or imprisonment (and often both). If only money is produced, the behavior is likely to continue; if only imprisonment is produced, the aversive consequence is likely to deter the act. Thus, according to this explanation, crime depends chiefly on the process of differential reinforcement.

For Burgess and Akers (1966), social behavior (including criminal behavior) responds chiefly to a complicated network of rewards and punishments. Any given behavior is likely to continue or to increase if it is followed more by rewards than by punishments; the same behavior is likely to decrease or to end if it is followed more by punishments than by rewards. Paraphrasing Burgess and Akers (1966), criminal behavior is actually learned in seven stages (see also Akers, 1973; and Akers, Krohn, Lanza-Kaduce, and Radosevich 1979):

1. Criminal behavior is learned through direct conditioning or through imitation.

2. Criminal behavior is learned both in nonsocial reinforcing situations (for example, the physical effects of drug use) or nonsocial discriminative situations and through social interaction in which the behavior of others is either for or against criminal behavior.

3. The principal component of learning criminal behavior occurs in groups that compose the individual's major source of reinforcements: peer friendship groups, the family, schools, and churches.

4. Learning criminal behavior—including specific techniques, attitudes, and avoidance procedures—depends on effective and available reinforcers and the existing reinforcement contingencies.

5. The specific type and the frequency of learned behavior depend on the reinforcers that are effective and available and on the norms by which these reinforcers are applied.

6. Criminal behavior is a function of norms that are discriminative for criminal behavior, the learning of which occurs when such behavior is more highly reinforced than noncriminal behavior.

7. The strength of criminal behavior is a direct function of the amount, frequency, and probability of its reinforcement.

For Akers, all seven stages in this process must be examined. However, the central part of his theory lies in two factors that concern the learning of acts and definitions: (1) differential reinforcement and (2) positive and negative definitions (Akers, 1973; 1997). All social behavior is either strengthened by reward (positive reinforcement) and avoidance of punishment (negative reinforcement) or weakened by aversive stimuli (punishment) and lack of reward (negative punishment). Whether a deviant act or a conforming act occurs depends on differential reinforcement (essentially, the cumulative effect of past and present rewards or punishments both for the act and also for alternative acts). However, besides learning an act, a person also learns whether the act is defined as good or bad. The more a person defines an act as good or as justifiable, the more likely he or she is to engage in it and the less likely he or she is to engage in alternatives. As Akers summarized: "A person participates in deviant activity then to the extent that it has been differentially reinforced over conforming behavior or defined as more desirable than conforming alternatives, or at least justified" (1973:287–288).

As with Sutherland's theory of differential association, Akers's social learning theory is intended as a general theory of crime. The broad scope of this theory is best seen in Akers's book *Deviant Behavior: A Social Learning Approach* (1973). Here Akers tries to apply social learning theory to all deviant behavior—"the principal forms of which . . . [include] drug use and addiction; homosexuality; prostitution; white-collar, professional, organized, and violent crimes; suicide; and mental illness" (p. vii). In this book Akers applies the general principles of social learning theory to each aspect of deviance: (1) how a person first engages in the deviant act, (2) how that person progresses to more frequent engagement, (3) the substantive events that reinforce the act, and (4) the content of the definitions favorable to the act.

Consider two examples of Akers's use of learning theory: suicide and drug use. Suicide presents an interesting test case for a learning theory of deviance that relies on reinforcement as the major motivating element because, without exception, the act of taking one's own life cannot be reinforced for one's future behavior (one has none!). Moreover, on the whole, U.S. culture condemns suicide, which means that there are very few definitions favorable to it. But Akers is confident that the act of suicide is based on social learning, and he offers a four-stage model as evidence (1973):

1. People learn that suicide appears to be a solution to personal problems. Everyone knows, or learns, that some people eliminate their problems successfully by hanging themselves, jumping off bridges, or overdosing on drugs. A terminal illness, the loss of a loved one, financial ruin, and existential angst are all situations in which suicide can be rationalized, justified, excused, or

forgiven. These rationalizations are not defined as definitions favorable to the act of suicide, but they often operate to neutralize unfavorable definitions.

2. People learn about specific techniques of suicide. We learn that a drug overdose (which sometimes can be interrupted after the drug is taken) is less likely to be successful than suicide by shooting. We also learn, according to Akers, that certain techniques are considered more appropriate for one sex than another: the violence of shooting, for example, is a "masculine" technique, whereas a drug overdose is more "feminine."

3. People learn that the act of suicide receives considerable attention. Thus, some proportion of suicidal behavior is not actually intended to result in death but in gaining attention from loved ones. Suicide resulting from previously learned nonfatal suicidal behavior is common. In some cases of suicide without prior attempts, the act of suicide derives from imitation—psychiatrists, therefore, have high rates of suicide compared with most other occupations.

4. Whether a person tries to commit suicide again depends in part on the reaction of others. "They may increase their attention to him without necessarily solving the crises and thus reinforce further attempts, or they may reinforce his belief that there is no hope. In either case he is likely to attempt again, and one of these attempts may be fatal" (p. 251).

Another test of social learning theory was conducted by Akers et al. (1979) in a study of drug (marijuana) and alcohol use among teenagers. This study was based on a self-report questionnaire administered to 3,065 male and female teenagers attending grades 7 through 12 in seven communities in three Midwestern states. It strongly confirmed social learning theory: The probability of abstinence from drug and alcohol use decreased and the frequency of use increased when individual teenagers (1) associated more with using rather than abstaining peers and adults, (2) were more rewarded than punished for use, and (3) were exposed more to favorable than to unfavorable definitions of use. Akers and his colleagues concluded that these three factors explained 55 percent of the differences between users of and abstainers from alcohol, and 68 percent of the differences between users of and abstainers from marijuana. Another study (Wood et al., 1997) has claimed that criminal behavior recurs through a nonsocial learning process—that is, offenders (especially violent offenders) experience a neurophysiological sensation or "high" that reinforces their propensity to commit crime.

In a recent book—*Social Learning and Social Structure: A General Theory of Crime and Deviance*—Akers (1998) offers a useful personal history of the development of his theory and presents a slightly revised version of it. Here, Akers proposes a "social learning and social structure" (SSSL) model of crime. Figure 13.1 shows that social learning mediates the relationship between social structure (the independent variable) and criminal behavior and crime rates (the dependent variable). Although Akers acknowledges that many of the variables in this model have been tested extensively, he bemoans the fact that there has been little research on the relationship between social learning and social structure. He suggests, for example, that imitation will likely turn out to be a key factor in the learning of criminal behavior. Moreover, he points to the need for more research on social learning and serious crime, such as white-collar crime, in adult samples in many areas of noncriminal deviance, such as sexual deviance and problem drinking.

Finally, we note that Akers (1999; and see Akers and Jensen, 2003) and some critics have taken part in a a symposium on social learning theory in the journal *Theoretical Criminology*. Robert Sampson (1999), for example, who believes that social learning theory is deeply flawed, points out that empirical evaluations have concentrated too much on statistical modeling and not enough on the theoretical and conceptual aspects of their research designs. Interestingly, Sampson says that "[I]t is perhaps emblematic of the field of delinquency research that so much turns on semantics, renaming, and an ex post reading of what teenagers really mean when they agree that 'suckers deserve to be taken advantage of' " (Sampson, 1999:441).

Morash Merry (1999) criticizes social learning theory chiefly because its focus on individuals and on motivation has ignored the gender-related distribution of power, resources, and opportunities. She complains that "the research support for the connection of gender structure to social learning variables that are predictive of delinquency is quite incomplete, complex and controversial" (Morash, 1999:456).

Marvin Krohn (1999) is more supportive of the successes of social learning theory. At the same time, he hopes that more attention will be paid to the role of differential association within the theory, to integration with other theories (e.g., social control), and to the ability of the theory to grapple with its possible macrolevel implications."

Akers (1999) offers spirited replies to these critics. To Morash, for example, he responds that there is not much in his book about feminism because there is not much in the feminist literature about social learning theory. Moreover, Akers (1999) suggests there are three chief areas where the theory might be developed:

> First is the SSSL model going beyond links to the structural and sociodemographic covariates of crime to better propositional integration with theories such as social disorganization. Second is improved operationalization of the four major social learning concepts and of the structural concepts in further tests of social learning and the SSSL model. Third is going beyond these main concepts to specify additional social learning variables. (p. 492)

## Evaluation of Social Learning Theory

Apart from his own sustained research and that of a small group of followers, the basic principles of Akers's social learning theory, and its explanations of why some persons commit criminal and deviant acts, have still not been tested widely or deeply.

It is probable that some criminologists shy away from social learning theory because of the ethical difficulties associated with its policy implications. If criminal tendencies, including violence, are chiefly learned, it seems to follow that they can just as easily be unlearned through behavior modification. Controversial examples of behavior modification treatment include drug-based therapy, electrocardiac treatment, chemotherapy, and confrontational juvenile correctional programs such as Visionquest and boot camps. Although none of these strategies has proven very effective, all arouse widespread ethical controversy because they appear to foreshadow a return to the violent criminal justice system of the dark and distant past.

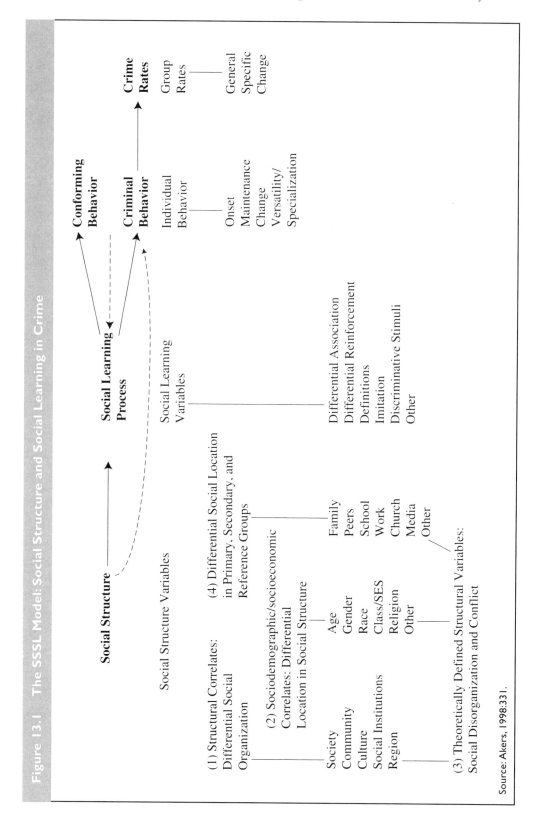

**Figure 13.1    The SSSL Model: Social Structure and Social Learning in Crime**

Social Structure ⟶     Social Learning     Conforming
                        Process             Behavior

                                            Criminal
                                            Behavior

Social Structure Variables     Social Learning
                               Variables

(1) Structural Correlates:     (4) Differential Social Location
Differential Social            in Primary, Secondary, and
Organization                   Reference Groups

    (2) Sociodemographic/socioeconomic
    Correlates: Differential
    Location in Social Structure

Society          Age          Family
Community        Gender       Peers
Culture          Race         School
Social Institutions  Class/SES    Work
Region           Religion     Church
                 Other        Media
                              Other

(3) Theoretically Defined Structural Variables:
Social Disorganization and Conflict

Differential Association
Differential Reinforcement
Definitions
Imitation
Discriminative Stimuli
Other

Individual
Behavior

Onset
Maintenance
Change
Versatility/
Specialization

**Crime
Rates**

Group
Rates

General
Specific
Change

Source: Akers, 1998:331.

Social learning theory arose when the notion of deterministic causation was unfashionable in criminology. Recall, for example, the devastating challenge posed by Matza's view that delinquency is not caused by deterministic forces but that juveniles episodically drift into (and out of) delinquency (Chapter 12.3). This detachment from deterministic theories was reinforced, in turn, by the tremendous popularity of the labeling perspective, which seemed to imply that crime should not be understood as having causes at all.

## 13.2 The Labeling Perspective

During the 1960s, the legitimacy of political authority was challenged by many college students, liberal intellectuals, women's movements, and members of minority racial groups. Questions about U.S. foreign policy in Vietnam and elsewhere, about domestic civil rights, and about the stark social, economic, racial, and gender inequalities in the world's richest society quickly filtered through to sociological perspectives on crime and criminal justice. Certain radical intellectuals (such as Marcuse 1964) argued that social inequality and injustice in the United States could be removed only by the powerless, deviant, outcast, criminal populations typically studied by criminologists. These populations, it was thought, had nothing to lose and everything to gain from a revolutionary overthrow of the existing social order. Reflecting this turbulent political climate, sociologists and criminologists opened a Pandora's box, using a key provided by Robert S. Lynd's (1939) famous question: "Knowledge for what?" In such an inegalitarian society as the United States, why is criminology typically concerned with crimes of the powerless rather than with crimes committed by the government, white-collar executives, and corporations? Who defines certain behavior as criminal? Whose side are we (the "we" who study crime with detached objectivity) on?

The criminologists who first examined such politicized questions were mainly younger scholars attached to the labeling perspective and conflict theory. As the labeling perspective developed, its neutral posture toward deviants became a celebration of deviant activity as evidence of the virtue of social diversity. Many deviant activities began to be seen in a different and more interesting light. The "opening up" and "demystifying" implied by the concept of deviance involves a very different relationship between the deviant and the student of deviance. In coming out of their criminological closets, labeling theorists tended to see in alcoholism, criminality, and mental illness, for example, individuals who are victimized by society and who are potential rebels against its values.

It is not easy to pin down the key concepts of the **labeling perspective**. There is even disagreement about the term itself. The labeling perspective has also been described as societal reaction, "sociology of deviance," "social interactionism," "the neo-Chicago school," and "the new deviancy theory." For convenience, we use "the labeling perspective" for all these terms.

Three key concepts are held by a majority of those using this perspective: (1) the social meaning of deviance, (2) societal reaction, and (3) stigma.

## The Social Meaning of Deviance

Following in the footsteps of the Chicago school of the 1920s and 1930s (see Chapter 11.2)—and drawing on the social psychology (phenomenology and symbolic interactionism) of George Herbert Mead, his student Herbert Blumer, and others—those researching deviance from the labeling perspective agree on the central importance of meanings in everyday life. Social reality itself is seen as an ongoing, fluid process that is constructed according to the outcome of the meanings that we attach to our interaction with others, on the one hand, and the meanings that they, on the other, attribute to us. Crime and deviance, then, are not pre-given, objective categories but negotiable statuses. Thus, in interactionist or participant observation studies, the researcher participates in the social interaction of drug users, alcoholics, mental patients, and others in order to "appreciate" the meanings that those people defined as deviant attribute to their own activities. As we saw in Chapter 12.2, this was partly the view of deviance advocated by David Matza.

The emphasis on meanings takes a number of twists and turns in the labeling perspective. At one level, the labeling perspective is skeptical that our knowledge can ever be objective and value-free. Because social behavior means different things to different people, one cannot have the sort of complete knowledge about social interaction that, for example, a natural scientist may have about the movement of inanimate objects such as billiard balls. Many of the studies in the labeling tradition have thus rejected the use of the scientific method. At another level, because they do not exist in a social vacuum, the meanings, perceptions, and opinions of certain individuals or groups are taken more seriously than those of others. Therefore, although reality is socially constructed, not all members of society have an equal voice in deciding precisely how it is constructed. Taking a sympathetic cue from the way in which society devalues deviants and outsiders, the labeling perspective typically sides with the underdog and the outcast.

A well-known example of the centrality of meaning in the labeling perspective is provided by Howard Becker's book *Outsiders* (1963). Becker argued (relying somewhat on learning theory) that marijuana users must learn to experience the meanings and effects of using marijuana if they are to get high "properly." He emphasized that social reality is constructed by the meanings embedded in everyday life. Indeed, Becker even claimed that the subjective experience of drugs is structured much more by social meanings and perceptions than by biological and pharmacological factors! If a situation is perceived and defined as real, then it is real in its consequences.

Moreover, as human and social beings, each of us differs in the meaning that we attach to our own behavior and to that of others. At different times, and to different people, our behavior (such as having a tattoo) may be perceived as interesting or exotic or daring. The very same behavior may also be seen as dangerous, abnormal, sick, delinquent, or criminal. The labeling perspective insists that such perceptions are the only real difference between normal and deviant behavior.

Becker argued that it is a mistake to see deviance simply as the breaking of some agreed-upon rule. To look at deviance in this way is to ignore the fact that what counts as deviance is largely a function of the ability of groups with political power to impose their concept of right and wrong on the behavior of other groups. Because great diversity exists in the values of groups with political power, great cross-cultural and cross-temporal variety exists in what officially (let alone unofficially) counts as deviance (see Chapter 15).

Homosexuality, for example, is perceived as morally deviant in some cultures but is tolerated in others; in still others, such as classical Greece and Rome, its practice was regarded as a positive virtue. In other words, suggested Becker, to understand deviance one must recognize that typically a given form of deviance is only statistically abnormal. As Becker argued:

> *Social groups create deviance by making the rules whose infraction constitutes deviance,* and by applying those rules to particular people and labeling them as outsiders. From this point of view, deviance is not a quality of the act the person commits, but rather a consequence of the application by others of rules and sanctions to an "offender." The deviant is one to whom that label has successfully been applied; deviant behavior is behavior that people so label. (p. 9, emphasis in original)

### Societal Reaction

In arguing that "deviant behavior is behavior that people so label," Becker does not claim that such acts as homicide would not exist without the label that is often attached to them. Rather, he points to the important role of **societal reaction** in the designation of certain acts as deviant or criminal. For example, although the act of killing another human being can occur without societal reaction to it, whether a given killing is labeled as murder, manslaughter, accidental death, or justifiable homicide depends crucially on the meaning attributed to it by a social audience. From Becker's perspective, it follows that society itself "creates" deviance because society defines it as such.

Half a century ago, Frank Tannenbaum (1938) pointed out that there is often a shift in society's reaction to delinquency and to delinquents, a process he described as the "dramatization of evil." Tannenbaum argued that the community's condemnation of delinquent behavior changes into a view of the offender as a delinquent person. Boys who vandalize schools are seen as "bad boys." In attempting to understand the mechanisms of this transformation, Edwin Lemert distinguished between primary and secondary deviance.

### Primary and Secondary Deviance

In his books *Social Pathology* (1951) and *Human Deviance, Social Problems, and Social Control* (1967), Lemert used the sociopsychological concepts of primary and secondary deviation to understand the process of deviance. Lemert proposed this distinction in order to draw attention to the difference between the "original" and the "effective" causes of the deviant attributes and actions "associated with physical defects and incapacity, crime, prostitution, alcoholism, drug addiction, and mental disorders" (1967:40).

According to Lemert, **primary deviance** can be caused by a host of social, cultural, and psychological events. Primary deviants undergo no change in their psychological makeup or in the way they act as members of society. **Secondary deviance** is caused by the way in which society reacts to some of the people who engage in primary deviance. After they are apprehended, primary deviants suffer a variety of consequences, many of which focus on the application to them of such deviant labels as "sick," "cripple," "criminal," "insane," and so on. Such labels can have important consequences—for friendship, for job opportunities, and for self-image. Sometimes the effect of deviant labels is so powerful—either through a self-fulfilling prophecy or through the negative consequences of stigmatization—that labeled individuals are forced to reorient their lives around the label. Secondary deviants accept their new identity as a "deviant" and act in accordance with the societal reaction to their primary deviance. Secondary deviance is thus a powerful tool for explaining recidivism.

Labeling theorists do not study the causes of crime in the same way that most theories we have examined thus far do. Indeed, labeling theorists tend to evade altogether questions of individual causation. It is clear that labeling theorists are concerned chiefly with the way society itself causes deviance. They are interested in how and why society labels certain behaviors deviant. Lemert, for example, argued that, whereas previous studies of deviance tended to rest heavily on the idea that deviance leads to social control, "I have come to believe that the reverse idea, i.e., social control leads to deviance, is equally tenable and the potentially richer premise for studying deviance in modern society" (1967:v).

According to the labeling perspective, the response to certain behavior is the crucial element in the designation of deviance. Much of the time the process of deviance creation is a routine and humdrum affair that commands little comment by the media. This is especially so for most property crimes and many crimes against public order. The great bulk of offenders processed by the criminal justice system—those accused of public drunkenness, larceny-theft and fraud, driving under the influence, and disorderly conduct—receive almost no attention in the media.

Every so often, however, a society becomes engrossed in a process of public frenzy directed toward certain forms of crime and deviance. Well-known examples of this intense process include the sixteenth- and seventeenth-century witch hunts in Europe and in colonial America, the moral crusade against prostitution between 1890 and 1920, the Nazi slaughter of Jews in the 1930s and 1940s, the McCarthyite search for communists in the 1950s, and the campaign against child abuse in the 1980s.

Lemert never suggested that societal reaction to primary deviance itself causes subsequent deviance, although he came close to this position. However, the diverse ways in which society reacts to and actually creates deviance have been examined in various other studies. Consider, for example, Stanley Cohen's (1972) research on how the media, the police, and various moral entrepreneurs conspired to create a panic over the activities of two youth gangs (the Mods and the Rockers) in southern England in the mid-1960s. Since the 1970s a similar, far more controversial panic has arisen over soccer hooliganism in Britain (Redhead, 1987). In each case the media and the agencies of social control acted in such a way as to fan out of all proportion what was originally a fairly small problem. This part of the process has been termed "deviance amplification" (Wilkins, 1964).

## Deviance Amplification

One well-known study illustrates the major features of the process of **deviance amplification** (Young, 1971). The subjects of Young's participant observation study were marijuana users in west London in the late 1960s. Young showed how the socially harmless activity of marijuana use was transformed into a social problem through the complicated web of interaction among the mass media, the public, the police, and the users themselves (see Figure 13.2).

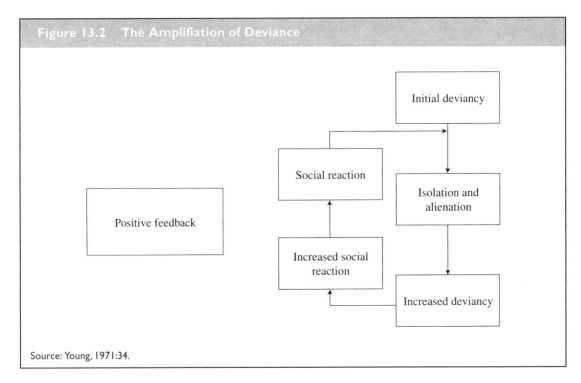

**Figure 13.2    The Amplifiation of Deviance**

Source: Young, 1971:34.

Young described how the mass media made marijuana use a social problem through sensationalistic and lurid accounts of the lives of marijuana users. The media's portrayal of marijuana users as sick, unwashed, promiscuous weirdos completely committed to drug use was a stereotype that inflamed popular indignation during 1967. Young showed how this media pressure led police to amplify the very problem they vigilantly sought to curb. Intensive police action led to an organized defensive posture in the drug-using community. Drug users united around a shared sense of injustice concerning harsh sentences and mass media stereotypes. Drug use became a symbol of defiance against an unjust and intolerant society.

The media used the rising number of drug convictions to fan public indignation about marijuana use even further. Increased pressure was then put on the police to stamp out this new evil. Expanded police drug units ensured greater detection of marijuana users. Once again the number of drug convictions soared. The vicious cycle was firmly established. Young's research demonstrated, then, that the police actually amplify the deviant activities they mean to control. Moreover, Gary Marx (1981) has shown that there are three types of interdependence between rule enforcers (such as police, prosecutors, and judges) and deviants that involve the possibility of deviance amplification: (1) escalation, (2) nonenforcement, and (3) covert facilitation.

First, the situation of *escalation* can arise from initial attempts at social control. Marx pointed out, for example, that "police involvement in family conflict, crowd, and automobile chase situations can contribute to violations where none was imminent, or it can increase the seriousness of these situations" (p. 223). The mere presence of police officers at the scene of a domestic disturbance, for instance, can easily escalate a potentially dangerous situation into an overtly violent one. High-speed police vehicle chases, which sometimes result in injuries or death, can lead to manslaughter charges where none would otherwise have existed.

Second, there is the situation of *nonenforcement,* which is less direct than escalation. According to Marx, the nonenforcement of rules is difficult to identify because it is often hidden and illegal. Marx documented that police may adopt a policy of nonenforcement with respect to informants, for example, who provide information about the law breaking of others or help facilitate a controlled commission of a crime, or with respect to vice entrepreneurs who agree to keep their own illegal behavior within agreed-on limits.

Third, in a situation of *covert facilitation,* rule enforcers take an active role in encouraging others to break rules. The police go undercover to buy or sell illegal goods and services, for example, or the police may pose as johns in order to arrest prostitutes or try to buy drugs in order to arrest drug dealers. Or the police may use a decoy, such as a female police officer in civilian clothes, to create a robbery or assault, or they may pose as the representatives of a foreign country in order to trap unwitting members of Congress taking a bribe to secure political influence in Washington.

## Stigmatization

As noted, whether or not individuals are regarded as deviant depends on societal reaction to their behavior. Moreover, partly because of this reaction to their behavior (primary deviance), some deviants are pushed into further (or secondary) deviance. This redirection of behavior occurs in a variety of ways. We now consider why societal reaction to deviance often results in, and can actually stem from, the fact that those who deviate from the norm tend to be stigmatized. Goffman (1963) related that, for the ancient Greeks, *stigma* referred to

> bodily signs designed to expose something unusual and bad about the moral status of the signifier. The signs were cut or burnt into the body and advertised that the bearer was a slave, a criminal, or a traitor—a blemished person, ritually polluted, to be avoided, especially in public places. Later, in Christian times, two layers of metaphor were added to the term: the first referred to bodily signs of holy grace that took the form of eruptive blossoms on the skin; the second, a medical allusion to this religious allusion, referred to bodily signs of physical disorder. (p. 1)

A **stigma** is therefore a sign of disgrace imposed on an individual. It is a way of spoiling a person's real identity, marking him or her as someone to be avoided. The stigmatizing process operates in numerous settings, and a stigma can be applied as a label to numerous persons: in medicine, to those with physical deformities (cripples, gimps, dwarfs, giants) or mental deviancy (weirdos, lunatics, crazies); in education, to those who achieve low grades in school (retards, dumbos, failures) or, sometimes, to those who achieve high grades (eggheads, nerds, brains); in religion, to those who do not believe in the "one and true" God (witches, heretics, pagans); and in the criminal justice system, to those convicted of crimes (ex-cons, recidivists, career criminals). In these examples a stigma is a sign denoting someone who is disqualified, by varying degrees, from full social acceptance. It can affect self-esteem, self-concept, and future behavior. Returning to the central importance of meaning, we emphasize that a stigma can vary in the meaning that it has both to the person stigmatized and to the social audience.

What are the effects of the stigmatizing process? According to one study (Schwartz and Skolnick, 1964), the effectiveness of legal sanctions against stigmatized individuals often varies with the social position of the defendant penalized. This study showed that unskilled workers suffer much more from the stigma that goes with accusations of assault than do doctors from the effects of accusations of medical malpractice. This finding is supported by a similar study in Holland (Buikhuisen and Dijksterhuis, 1971). This study found that two groups of convicts—one convicted once for theft, the other for drunken driving—received significantly less positive responses than nonconvicts in their job applications to 75 large companies.

However, another study, with a somewhat different focus, found that the effects of a stigma are not quite so straightforward. In this study Terance Miethe and Richard McCorkle (1997) set out to test whether prosecutors and judges are biased in their perceptions of gang members. If the "master status" of gang members includes their stereotypical designation as "vile, dangerous, detached, and unpredictable youths" (p. 411), as it did in this study of 168 gang and 202 nongang felony cases in Las Vegas in 1993, we would expect the criminal justice system to deal relatively harshly with gang members. The study found that the master status was at work in that sentencing decisions for gang members were far less likely to be affected by other offender and offense characteristics than for nongang members. But the study also found that charges against the sentencing of gang members were more lenient than in nongang cases! This is so, the authors speculated, because of additional images that are attached to the master status of gang membership. For example, prosecutors may be so keen to secure convictions of gang members that they "give up more" to do so, perhaps by plea bargaining or by being more likely to dismiss cases with unreliable witnesses.

What are the ways in which people respond to being stigmatized? How do stigmatized individuals—to pose Goffman's (1963) graphic question—"negotiate" their "spoiled identities" (p. 9)? Research addressing these two questions is inconclusive. The response to stigmatization clearly varies. Sometimes it is relatively easy for stigmatized individuals to hide or to "correct" their stigma. For example, persons with certain forms of deviant attributes, such as physical deformities or illiteracy, can seek surgical or educational remedies to reform or hide their apparent defects. However, as Goffman suggested, these strategies are not always completely successful: "Where such repair is possible, what often results is not the acquisition of fully normal status, but a transformation of self from someone with a particular blemish into someone with a record of having corrected a particular blemish" (1963:9).

The effects of a stigma also depend partly on the institutional context in which it is conferred. In his book *Asylums,* for example, Goffman (1961) reports that in "total institutions"—such as mental hospitals, where "a large number of like-situated individuals, cut off from the wider society for an appreciable period of time, together lead an enclosed, formally administered round of life" (p. xiii)—it is difficult to shrug off the effects of a stigma. Goffman reported that in the mental institution he studied for three years (St. Elizabeth's Hospital in Washington, D.C.), whenever patients exhibited "normal" behavior, the staff often interpreted that very normalcy as a sign that they were "abnormal"! According to some research (for example, Link, Cullen, Frank, and Wozniak, 1987), former mental patients often encounter public preconceptions that they are dangerous—not on the basis of their behavior but because of the label attached to them.

It is reasonable to conclude that responses to stigmatization are associated strongly with social class and relative powerlessness. The exact nature of this association, however, is unclear. Allen Liska (1981), for example, noted:

> Since blacks occupy a negative social status and are not well integrated into society, they are not very sensitive to official reactions of society. Labeling may have its maximum effect on people well integrated into society; hence, the effects of labeling should be maximal for first offenders, the middle class, and whites and minimal for prior offenders, the lower class, and blacks. (pp. 132–133)

However, although negative labeling arguably can be seen as affecting those with higher social status more than those with lower social status (for example, African Americans), it is also true that the former have greater resources for counteracting stigmatization. The question of whether certain social groups are better equipped to counteract the effects of labeling returns us to another question raised by Lemert's distinction between primary and secondary deviance: Is the person on whom the label "criminal" is conferred likely to be propelled into more crime or deterred from future criminal behavior?

## Evaluation of Labeling Theory

New empirical research on labeling has dwindled lately, but the labeling perspective remains quite influential in criminology (Triplett and Jarjoura, 1994; Victor, 2004). Its influence continues largely because it reminds us that labels such as "crime" and "deviance" are applied selectively to social phenomena. Moreover, the labeling perspective has uncovered the ironic ways in which the process of societal reaction sometimes amplifies the very problems it seeks to eliminate through the stimulation of moral panics and the effects of stigmatization.

A major difficulty with the labeling perspective is that its adherents have never pursued its own ambitious agenda. If terms such as "crime" and "deviance" are applied selectively to social behavior, it is crucial to explore the criteria of selection. Such an examination would involve thoroughgoing questions about the interests served by criminal law. In his book *Contrology*, Jason Ditton (1979) therefore complains:

> The total rejection of positivism by followers of the labeling perspective either had no effect at all on the institutionalized study of crime or, at best, the massive theoretical critique was distilled into an additional factor ("the reaction") to be henceforth co-opted in the unchanged rhetoric of mathematical calculation. It has always been content instead to snipe at convention from the theoretical sidelines—happy to stand on the lunatic fringe and lob distracting stories of strippers, nudists, gays,

teddy boys, nutters, dwarfs, and druggies at the central juggernaut of state-sponsored criminology. (p. 5)

In this assessment Ditton bemoans the fact that the labeling perspective never became the labeling theory. If criminal behavior really is what agents of social control define it as, then, concludes Ditton, the term "controlology," rather than "criminology," better reflects what we should be studying!

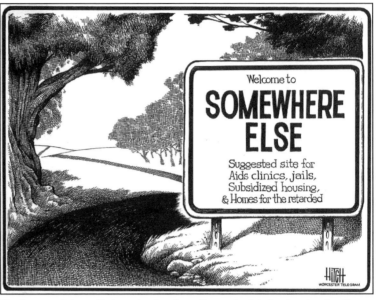

*The preconceptions of stigmatization: According to the labeling perspective, the societal reaction to deviance exacerbates problems of social isolation and exclusion.*

Although the labeling perspective has failed to travel as far as its logical conclusion—what Ditton refers to as "controlology"—nevertheless, its great insights continue to contribute to the development of criminology in at least two respects. First, because its emphasis on the harmful effects of labels has been widely recognized as correct, it has led, with mixed results, to certain changes in criminal justice policy. These changes embrace what Werner Einstadter and Stuart Henry (1995) have described as decriminalization, diversion, decarceration, and restitution (and see Henry and Milovanovic, 1996; Lanier and Henry, 1998). The changes also include the New Zealand–Australian-based movement toward "reintegrative shaming" and "restorative justice" (e.g., Braithwaite, 2002; Daly, 2002).

Second, because of its inclination to demystify powerful label-conferring institutions in areas such as criminal justice, mental health, and medicine, the labeling perspective nourishes a climate for the growth of "social constructionism" in criminology. **Social constructionism** encourages a healthy sociological disrespect for how knowledge of social problems such as crime is phrased, manipulated, defined, and disseminated in the mass media and in other public forums (see Chapter 1.2). In criminology its influence can be found in numerous studies of how moral entrepreneurs, social movements, and the mass media mold—or ignore—the public perception of the causes, prevalence, and seriousness of crimes such as serial murder, child abuse, drug use, prostitution, drinking and driving, and terrorism (e.g., Jenkins, 2003; Best, 2004). Like that of the labeling perspective, the motto of social constructionism might be "Question authority!"

## 13.3 Conflict Theory

In this section we examine conflict theory, a theory of crime that overlaps with the labeling perspective. To understand what conflict theory says about crime, criminalization, and criminal law, we review certain general ideas that conflict theorists hold about the nature of social conflict.

**Conflict theory** usually is approached by thinking of it in relation to its polar opposite, **consensus theory**. The debate over consensus and conflict theories pivots on three questions: How is social order possible? What is the nature of power? What is the nature of authority? The many answers given to these questions often hinge on the answers to certain other questions: What is human nature? What are the causes of social inequality? What is a "good" or a "just" society?

According to consensus theory, a democratic society is held together by its members' common acceptance of such basic values as virtue, honor, right, and wrong. These are the basic values on which most people agree most of the time. Because of this common agreement, social order proceeds in a harmonious and predictable fashion. This means that social change occurs only slowly and in a nondisruptive, evolutionary fashion. In such a situation power and authority tend to be invested in persons with intellectual or moral capabilities—persons knowledgeable about and attentive to the public good and the national interest.

According to conflict theory, on the other hand, there is little agreement on basic values. Society is made up of many competing groups, each with different interests. Conflict is the paradoxical feature of social order, and social change occurs in disruptive ways. Power and authority tend to be self-perpetuating domains of life that reflect deep-seated patterns of social, economic, and political inequality. In this conflict scenario, law is a weapon that the powerful use to enforce their private interests, often at the expense of the public interest.

## Crime and Criminalization

The best introduction to conflict criminology is the pioneering work of Thorsten Sellin. We have already noted (Chapter 1.2) the importance of Sellin's (1938) concept of conduct norms in the continuing debate over the proper definition of crime. We now focus on another aspect of Sellin's argument in his book *Culture Conflict and Crime*—namely, the role of conflict in understanding crime. Sellin suggested that the advance of civilization (i.e., of urbanization and industrialization) vastly increases the potential for social and cultural conflict. Instead of the well-knit social fabric of less technologically developed cultures, modern society contains many competing groups, poorly defined interpersonal relationships, and, especially in cities, social anonymity. The rules (conduct norms) of such a society increasingly lack the sort of moral force possessed by the rules that grow out of deep-rooted, unified community sentiments.

For Sellin, crime was one of the many consequences of the conflicting conduct norms and social disorganization of modern society. Culture conflict exists when a person is caught between conflicting cultural rules. Two forms of cultural conflict in particular tend to result in crime. *Primary culture conflict* arises when there is a clash between the norms of different cultures. This type of conflict can occur when the law of one group is extended to cover the territory of another group, or when members of one cultural group migrate to the territory of a different group. *Secondary culture conflict* arises from the process of differentiation and inequality in the parent culture. An example of secondary culture conflict is the clash between law enforcement and the second generation of immigrant families over the rules governing views of gambling, prostitution, and liquor.

Whereas Sellin emphasized the importance of cultural conflict as a cause of crime, George Vold (1958; and see Vold, Bernard, and Snipes, 2002) pointed to the role of what he termed "group conflict" and "political organization." Vold believes that in any society people in similar social situations group together to further their interests through collective action. Groups conflict with other groups when the goals of one can be achieved only at the expense of others: "The prohibitionist wishes to outlaw the manufacture and sale of alcoholic beverages; the distillers and brewers wish unrestricted opportunity to make and sell a product for which there is a genuine economic demand" (p. 208). In turn, distillers and brewers face competition over goals from other groups, such as trade unionists (who want to raise wages and improve working conditions) and environmentalists (who do not want distillery chemicals to pollute the atmosphere, the soil, or the land). Environmentalists, in turn, face competition from groups who claim that economic progress should not be restricted by undue government interference.

In a democratic society, says Vold, each of the many interest groups attempts to secure its own interests by lobbying the legislature to enact laws in its favor. Groups that muster the greatest number of votes effectively enact new laws that enforce their interests and that, at the same time, curb the behavior and goals of competing groups. In other words:

> The whole political process of law making, law breaking, and law enforcement becomes a direct reflection of deep-seated and fundamental conflicts between interest groups and their more general struggles for the control of the police power of the state. Those who produce legislative majorities win control over the police power and dominate the policies that decide who is likely to be involved in violation of the law. (p. 209)

For Vold, therefore, crime is behavior committed by minority groups whose regular actions and goals have not been secured by legislative process. Juvenile delinquency, for example, is minority behavior unacceptable to the more powerful adult world. Those who reject the majority view tend to be criminalized. Because patterns of criminalization reflect the different degrees of political power wielded by different social groups, Vold argued that much crime should be understood as having a political nature. This is obviously the case for crimes that result, for instance, from political revolution and social protest movements. But it is also true for other, less obvious cases, such as the clash of interests between management and workers and the struggle of racial minorities and women to secure their interests in racist and sexist societies. Vold concluded: "There are many situations in which criminality is the normal, natural response of normal, natural human beings struggling in understandably normal and natural situations for the maintenance of the way of life to which they stand committed" (p. 218).

Vold's focus on the role of power in the process of criminalization was expanded by the influential contributions to conflict theory of Richard Quinney (1970, 1977; Quinney and Wildeman, 1977). Quinney applied his theoretical perspective on the social reality of crime to a variety of situations: the religious and political foundations of criminal law; the behavior of judges, the judiciary, and the police; and such diverse conduct as that defined by the laws of theft, antitrust laws, food and drug laws, sexual psychopath laws, and legislation protecting morality and public order (see Box 13.1 and Figure 13.3).

---

**Box 13.1   Richard Quinney's Conflict Theory of Crime**

In his book *The Social Reality of Crime*, Richard Quinney (1970) stated the six propositions of his conflict theory of crime:

1. The defining quality of crime lies in the definition of crime rather than in criminal behavior as such. This definition is applied by legislators, police, prosecutors, and judges; it is always applied in the context of a society characterized by diversity, conflict, coercion, and change. Society is divided along political lines rather than being an entity based on consensus and stability. Persons become criminal when others define their behavior as criminal.

2. Criminal definitions exist because the interests of some segments (or groups) of society are in conflict with the interests of others. Segments with greater power can have their definitions formulated in law and imposed on those with lesser power. According to Quinney, the greater the degree of social conflict, the more likely it is that the powerful will criminalize the behavior of powerless groups that conflict with their interests.

3. The content of laws and their application tend to reflect the interests of the powerful because the powerful typically control or manipulate members of law enforcement and judicial machinery.

4. Different societal groups typically learn to do different things. The less frequently people engage in law making and law enforcing, the more frequently their actions are defined as criminal. Moreover, increased experience with criminal definitions increases the likelihood that people will do things that are subsequently defined as criminal.

5. There are many conceptions or opinions about which actions should be criminalized. However, Quinney pointed out that the opinions of the most powerful are in fact the most powerful opinions. Through the mass media the opinions of the powerful are communicated to others as the opinions that must be obeyed.

6. The social reality of crime is a composite of these propositions (see Figure 13.3).

---

Austin Turk has also made influential contributions to conflict theories of crime, especially in his book *Criminality and Legal Order* (1969). Turk's theory is most insightful in showing how conflict theorists understand the process of criminalization. Turk's complicated argument begins with the assumption that the social order of modern societies is based on the relationships of conflict and domination between authorities and subjects (1969). *Authorities* are those who make the most important legal decisions about the social order; *subjects* are those who have little or no influence on the process of decision-making or on its substantive content. Slum dwellers, for example, have virtually no control over decisions affecting their life chances in such vital areas as tenancy and welfare. Conflicts between authorities and subjects occur over a wide range of

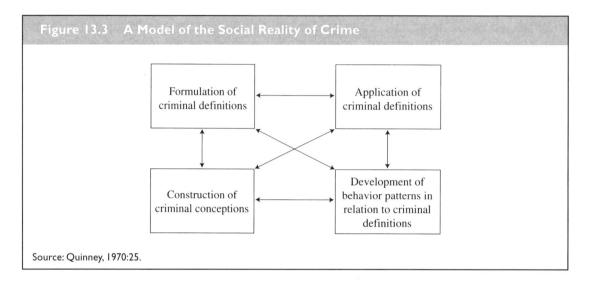

Figure 13.3    A Model of the Social Reality of Crime

Source: Quinney, 1970:25.

social and cultural norms. Law is a crucial mechanism for resolving (essentially, treating but not curing) many conflicts over acceptable values and behavior. **Criminalization** is the process by which authorities, for any reason, confer an illegal status on certain behaviors of subjects (resisters). Authorities are either first-line (police) or higher-level enforcers (prosecutors, trial court judges, and appellate court judges).

Turk's theory of criminalization is designed to answer two questions: (1) Under what circumstances do subjects become criminals? and (2) When are subjects dealt with harshly? Turk's answer to these questions has three parts. First, the more significant a law is to authorities, the more likely it is that resisters will be criminalized. This scenario, of course, assumes that the various enforcers agree to waive their respective discretionary powers not to arrest, not to prosecute, and not to find mitigating circumstances.

Second, Turk argued that the probability of criminalization varies according to the respective power of enforcers and resisters. Turk pointed out that "power differences between enforcers and norm resisters vary from relationships in which the enforcers are virtually all-powerful to cases where enforcers and resisters are about equal in resources, including effective organization, manpower, skills, funds, weaponry" (p. 67).

One would expect perhaps that the relatively greater the power of enforcers, the more likely they are to criminalize offensive behavior. Paradoxically, for Turk the probability of criminalization has a curvilinear relationship with power differences between enforcers and resisters. Turk suggested that the degree of criminalization of resisters depend largely on how threatened the enforcers feel by resisters. He argued that the greater the power of enforcers relative to resisters, the less likely it is that conflict results in criminalization; the closer their respective amounts of power, the more likely that the enforcers resort to criminalization.

Finally, Turk asserted that the probability of criminalization is influenced by what he termed "the realism of conflict moves." By this Turk meant that the criminalization of resisters' activities sometimes serves the interests of neither enforcers nor resisters. Because realism depends on knowledge of what it takes to be successful in a conflict, the act of criminalization is often a sign of failure. It would not be particularly astute on the part of the police, for example, if arrests created martyrs that increased the size of the opposition. By the same token, from the point of view of resisters, arrests might be very useful! Again, criminalization is less likely to occur the more sophisticated the resisters.

## Criminal Law and Crime

We have seen that criminalization is one of the key concepts of conflict theory. Crime is behavior that is criminalized through the application of criminal law. For conflict theory, then, we cannot understand crime without simultaneously understanding the role of criminal law in society (see Chapter 1.3). We now examine certain ways in which conflict theorists have understood criminal law.

One of the best-known conflict accounts of criminal law is contained in William Chambliss and Robert Seidman's *Law, Order, and Power* (1982). This book contains a comprehensive application of conflict theory to (1) the creation of law, (2) the general principles of law, and (3) the implementation of law. The analysis of law is approached with the underlying assumption that "the central myth about the legal order in the U.S. is that normative structures of the written law represent the actual operation of the legal order" (3). The law in the books, in other words, is not at all the same thing as the law in action. Chambliss and Seidman continued:

> This myth of the operation of the law is given the lie daily. We all know today that blacks and the poor are not treated fairly or equitably by the police. We know that judges have discretion and in fact make policy (as the Supreme Court did in the school desegregation cases). We know that electoral laws have been loaded in the past in favor of the rich, and the average presidential candidate is not a poor man, that one-fifth of the senators of the United States are millionaires.
>
> It is our contention that, far from being primarily a value-neutral framework within which conflict can be peacefully resolved, the power of the state is itself the principal prize in the perpetual conflict that is society. The legal order . . . is in fact a self-serving system to devise and maintain power and privilege. (p. 7)

As nineteenth-century philosopher Anatole France once remarked: "The majestic equality of the law allows both the rich and the poor to sleep under bridges if they so choose!"

Chambliss and Seidman's detailed analysis of the relationships between conflict, power, and the purposes of law is extended to such institutions as legislatures, appellate courts, and the police. But perhaps the most telling sections of their analysis concern appellate courts. Although many citizens see how easily the decisions of Congress can be swayed by lobbyists and special interest groups, most of us reject the idea that appellate courts are open to such persuasion. Yet Chambliss and Seidman suggested that the various inputs into the rule-making processes of the appellate courts are "necessarily biased in favor of ensuring that courts as institutions are more available to the wealthy than to the poor, and tend to produce solutions in the interests of the wealthy" (p. 113). These biases cluster around several variables, the two most important of which are (1) the selection of issues with which judges are confronted and (2) their personal characteristics and socialization.

Because most appellate cases are initiated by individual litigants, it follows that the majority of such appeals are actually brought by those with sufficient funds to afford them. Thus, most appellate cases, such as those in the area of trusts and corporate law, concern legal problems of the relatively wealthy. Conversely, legal problems of the poor rarely come to the attention of appellate courts. Nowhere is this bias reflected more than in the area of criminal law and police powers. The poor are arrested, interrogated, abused, and incarcerated more often than any other societal group (see Chapter 3.1). But the problems the poor routinely encounter throughout the criminal justice system almost never reach appellate courts. Moreover, the poor lack the funds to hire lawyers to initiate the necessary legal proceedings. Indeed, to protect themselves from the abuse of police powers, the poor must rely almost exclusively on the charitable endeavors of such groups as the American Civil Liberties Union.

For their accounts of the links among power, law, and crime, conflict criminologists have drawn examples from diverse historical periods and a variety of societies. An excellent example concerns a change in the law of theft in medieval England: the *Carrier's Case* of 1473, in which an English court in effect altered the definition of larceny in order to convict a cotton carrier of stealing the contents of several bales that he had been hired to transport.

The *Carrier's Case* is an example of the crude power and conflict that lie behind the majesty of the law. The case is important not only because it shows how judges in fact make law but also because it shows how extralegal factors influence judges when they make law.

Hall (1969) identified various political and economic conditions that thrust themselves on the court in the *Carrier's Case*. It is interesting to note that when the carrier was indicted for larceny, no specific mention was made of the contents of the bales he had opened. Hall produced evidence, however, to show that these contents were almost certainly either wool or cloth—no ordinary commodities during the fifteenth century. Indeed, wool and cloth were the products of the most important industry in England at that time, an industry encouraged by a king deeply committed to solidifying his rule at home by gaining the economic and political support of European merchants who traded in these commodities. According to Hall, King Edward IV (the reigning monarch of England) desperately needed to regulate and elevate the standards for security and honesty in the transportation of commodities bound for foreign markets. It is therefore quite likely that the king persuaded the court to expand the law of theft even though legal precedent did not permit it to do so.

Why did the judges expand the law? According to Hall, it was a matter of simple political expediency. During the fifteenth century the court of Star Chamber, like most other judicial bodies, was subject to the political will of the king. Thus, although judges at the time of the *Carrier's Case* wanted to assert their independence from the monarch, they were politically unable to do so. The result was a legal decision dictated by political interests.

The *Carrier's Case* illustrates the conflict theorists' claim that behind the majestic impartiality of the law often lies the power of an elite or a ruling class. When the situation requires, as in the *Carrier's Case,* and in numerous other cases from antiquity forward, the criminal law's thin veneer of neutrality is readily stripped away.

**Box 13.2   The *Carrier's Case***

As reported in Jerome Hall's account of the *Carrier's Case* of 1473 (1969; and see Chambliss, 1964), the facts of the case were as follows. A "carrier" had been hired as a bailee to transport certain bales of cotton to the English port of Southampton. However, during the journey he took the bales to another place, broke them open, and took the contents. The bailee was apprehended, charged, and convicted of larceny by a majority of judges in the Court of Star Chamber.

This innocent-looking case marked an important innovation in the English law of larceny. Prior to the *Carrier's Case*, the element of trespass had to be demonstrated by the prosecution in order for a defendant to be convicted of larceny. At that time, legal opinion agreed that (1) trespass was an essential element of larceny, (2) a person having possession of property could not commit a trespass upon that property, and (3) a bailee has possession (Hall, 1969). The common law recognized no criminal liability if a person who was legally entitled to the possession of an item later converted it to his or her own use (the rationale being that owners should protect themselves by selecting a trustworthy carrier). These three precedents therefore created a serious problem: Because the carrier had been legally consigned the bales, they were in his possession. There was, then, no legal precedent by which the carrier could be convicted of larceny! However, by clever intellectual juggling (known as a legal fiction), it was ruled that the mere opening of the bales ended the carrier's legal possession of them. In this way some of the most important English judges who were hearing the case ruled that the carrier was in fact guilty of larceny. The law of larceny was thus expanded to include this and similar factual situations.

## Toward an Integrated Conflict Theory

Recently a two-pronged tendency has appeared in order to integrate the many propositions of the conflict tradition and the empirical studies that have sought to test them. On the one hand, this integration has been furthered by a somewhat formal synthesis of the various concepts used in existing conflict theory. Thus Edmund McGarrell and Thomas Castellano's (1991) integrative model applies ideas about structural conflict, the influence of the mass media, fear of crime, and victimization to the formulation and enforcement of criminal law. Vold, Bernard, and Snipes (2002) have also offered a unified conflict theory of crime. This theory combines an understanding of how the diverse values and actions in modern societies intersect with political and economic power to influence the enforcement of criminal law and the distribution of official crime rates. On the other hand, especially in the work of John Hagan (1989), there is a movement to integrate aspects of existing conflict theory with concepts derived from the other traditions in criminology and elsewhere.

In his book *Structural Criminology,* Hagan (1989) and his colleagues developed what is variously termed "power-control theory" and "structural criminology." In his analysis of crime Hagan combined insights from the labeling perspective, control theory, Marxism, feminism, and a criminology that recognizes the importance of the macro level of social structure. Hagan's core claim is that the vertical relations of power (e.g., parents over children, men over women) are more important in understanding patterns of crime and exploitation than horizontal relations (e.g., peer pressure). In his book Hagan extended this core claim to white-collar and corporate crime; sentencing and punishment;

perceptions of (in)justice by different social classes and by race; and delinquency and the family.

One example of Hagan's approach was his integration of studies of labor force participation with those of household structures in order to examine why delinquency rates for males are almost universally higher than for females. Hagan argued that in Western industrialized societies, an instrument-object relationship exists between parents and children. Parents are the instruments of control, the objects of which are children. This relationship shapes gender patterns. However, these power relations vary with class and gender. In particular, Hagan noted, women gain new power in the family as they enter the labor market. He identified two family structures based on women's participation in the paid labor market: "patriarchal" and "egalitarian." In the former, the husband/father works outside the home in an authority position and the wife/mother works at home. Through socialization, daughters "focus their futures around domestic labour and consumption, as contrasted with sons who are prepared for participation in direct production" (p. 156). In the latter, the husband/father and wife/mother both work in authority positions outside the home. These egalitarian families "socially reproduce daughters who are prepared along with sons to join the production sphere" (p. 157).

Thus, although daughters are less delinquent than sons in both types of family because daughters are more controlled by their mothers, Hagan argued that daughters in patriarchal families are more often taught by parents to avoid risk-taking activities; in egalitarian families both daughters and sons are taught to be open to risk taking. It is this combination of the instrument-object relationship and the corresponding social psychology of risk taking that affects delinquency. According to Hagan, patriarchal families are characterized by larger gender differences in delinquency: "Daughters become more like sons in their involvement in such forms of risk taking as delinquency" (p. 158).

Hagan must be applauded for integrating some feminist insights into a framework for understanding girls' youth crime and for developing a theory that takes gender seriously as an explanatory variable. Although Hagan's original formulation of power-control theory seems to conclude that "mother's liberation causes daughter's crime" (Chesney-Lind, 1997:22), the theory is important because it demonstrates that gender is constructed differently in diverse family structures and social classes.

## Evaluation of Conflict Theory

Conflict explanations of crime, criminal law, and criminalization have been tested often and, to a certain extent, have been confirmed by criminologists. Confirmatory test cases include such diverse examples as laws concerning vagrancy, alcohol, drugs, prostitution, and bias in court decisions. In each case the ability of one segment of society to impose its moral view on another was a crucial element in the passage of a given law.

Consider, for example, David Jacobs and David Britt's (1979) study of police use of deadly force. This study addresses a crucial operational component of the criminal justice system: the relationship between inequality and officially sanctioned violent death. Jacobs and Britt attempted to test the proposition that violence, or the threat of violence, is the crucial element upholding the unequal relationships found in nearly all societies today. Controlling for such confounding factors as the police being more likely to use violence in areas with high rates of violent crime, they found that states with the most unequal income distribution were the most likely to have the highest number of police-caused homicides. Moreover, Steven Messner (1980; and see Chapter 15.3) has shown that a variation of this conflict hypothesis applies in many societies around the world. According to Messner, in a sample of 110 societies, high homicide rates were positively correlated with, and perhaps caused by, the social conflict that results from high levels of income inequality.

Finally, we note that it requires a great leap of faith to assume either that law always arises from conflict or that crime always expresses conflict, or that the process of criminalization always serves the interests of the powerful. Most criminologists today realize that arguments based on such general assumptions are seriously open to doubt. Moreover, conflict theory has rarely been precise in defining such crucial terms as "power" and "conflict." What, precisely, is "conflict"? Do all conflicts involve "power"? But quite apart from whether the claims of conflict theory should be seen as confirmed, disconfirmed, or simply too abstract to be testable, its chief legacy is its introduction of a political dimension largely lacking in earlier criminology.

## 13.4 Radical and Feminist Theories

Radical criminology and feminist criminology gained considerable importance in criminology in the 1970s and 1980s. In this section we introduce their respective theories and concepts.

### Radical Criminology

In Chapter 10.3 we outlined Marx and Engels's work on crime. As noted, neither Marx nor Engels devoted much time to the analysis of crime; however, several European socialist writers of the late nineteenth and early twentieth centuries did—attempting to apply Marxist theory to an understanding of crime. Foremost among these socialists was Willem Bonger, who published *Criminality and Economic Conditions* in 1905. Bonger reasoned that a capitalist economic system promotes egoism at the expense of altruism in all members of society and that certain people in all social classes develop a "criminal thought" from such egoism, which eventually leads to crime and to a criminal class. All crimes—economic, sexual, political, and pathological—committed by both the economically powerless and the powerful, Bonger argued, were the result of egoism engendered by a capitalist economic system.

Not until some 70 years later was Marxist theory first applied to an understanding of crime in the United States. Instrumental in the development of this "radical criminology" were a number of criminologists, including Herman and Julia Schwendinger (1975, 1977), William Chambliss (1975), Richard Quinney (1973a, 1973b), Tony Platt (1974), and Raymond Michalowski and Edward Bolander (1976). In Britain, Ian Taylor, Paul Walton, and Jock Young, in *The New Criminology* (1973), assembled a devastating critique of mainstream criminology and called for a social theory capable of explaining both the wider and immediate origins of the criminal act, as well as the effect of societal reaction on criminal behavior. Although it did not develop an explicit theory of its own, this book prompted theorists in the United States to form various radical perspectives on crime during the 1970s and 1980s.

Steven Spitzer (1975) devised probably the most intriguing Marxist theory of deviance. Assuming that capitalist societies are based on class conflict and that harmony is achieved through the dominance of a specific class, Spitzer reasoned that deviants are drawn from groups who create problems for those who rule. Although these groups largely victimize and burden people in their own classes, "their problematic quality ultimately resides in their challenge to the basis and form of class rule" (p. 640). In other words, populations become problematic for those who rule when they disturb, hinder, or call into question any of the following:

1. Capitalist modes of appropriating the product of human labor (called into question when the poor "steal" from the rich).

2. Social conditions under which capitalist production takes place (questioned by those who refuse or are unable to perform wage labor).

3. Patterns of distribution and consumption in capitalist society (questioned by those who use drugs for escape and transcendence rather than sociability and adjustment).

4. The process of socialization for productive and nonproductive roles (questioned by youth who refuse to be schooled or people who deny the validity of family life).

5. Ideology that supports the functioning of capitalist society (questioned by proponents of alternative forms of social organization).

Spitzer argued that problem populations are created in two ways: directly, through fundamental contradictions in the capitalist economy, and indirectly, through contradictions in social control institutions. An example of the direct creation of a problem population is the inherent production of surplus labor (as technological innovation replaces workers with machines) in capitalist economies. Surplus populations are necessary for capitalism because they help support continued capital accumulation. A surplus population provides a mass labor pool that can be drawn into wage labor when necessary and that simultaneously keeps wages down by increasing competition for scarce jobs. However, this surplus population is also problematic in that it must be neutralized and controlled (since it may rebel) if capital accumulation and, therefore, profit making are to continue. Thus, members of this group become eligible for processing as deviants.

Spitzer used mass education as an indirect example of the creation of a problem population. The widespread education of youth from all social classes was developed initially to withhold large numbers of young people from the labor market until they could later be absorbed into wage labor. Yet education simultaneously provides many youth with critical insights into the oppressive character of capitalism. These insights ultimately lead to hostilities toward the system and subsequent mobilization against it (for example, by dropouts and radicals). These youths then become eligible for deviant processing.

Spitzer identified two specific and discrete problem populations: social junk and social dynamite. "Social junk" refers to those who represent a control cost—the handicapped and mentally ill—but are relatively harmless to society. Their deviant status arises from their failure or inability to participate adequately in the capitalist marketplace. "Social dynamite" refers to those with the potential to challenge capitalist relations of production and who, therefore, represent a political threat to the capitalist class. An example of social dynamite is the Communist party.

Finally, Spitzer maintained a somewhat instrumentalist view of the state; such a view holds that the capitalist class dominates and utilizes the state as a vehicle for capital accumulation and the preservation of economic power. Thus, the institutions of the state are molded in accordance with the goals of the capitalist class. Spitzer argued that the institutions of the superstructure—of which the state is part—"originate and are maintained to guarantee the interests of the capitalist class" (p. 643).

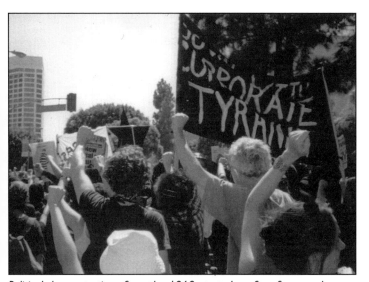

*Political demonstrations from the 1960s to today often focus on human-rights issues such as globalization, poverty, imperialist wars, homelessness, and racism.*

In *Class, State, and Crime*, Richard Quinney (1977) also developed a Marxist perspective on crime. He focused on four major areas. First, to understand crime we must study the development of the capitalist political economy, the forces and relations of production, the capitalist state, and the class struggle between the owners of capital and the working class. Second, we must uncover the systems of domination and repression historically used to benefit the capitalist class. Third, the forms of accommodation and resistance to capitalism by oppressed people must be revealed. Finally, the dialectical relationship of accommodation and resistance to the overall conditions of capitalist political economy must be disclosed, as it is there that we find the creation of crimes of domination and crimes of accommodation.

Quinney identified four types of crimes of domination that result from the reproduction of the capitalist system itself. "Crimes of control" include crimes by the police and the FBI, such as misdemeanors, felonies, brutality, illegal surveillance, and violation of civil liberties. "Crimes of government" involve political crime, such as the Watergate break-in and CIA assassinations of foreign political leaders. "Crimes of economic domination" consist primarily of corporate crimes ranging from price fixing to pollution but also including the close connections between syndicated crime and criminal operations of the state. Finally, "social injuries" are harms not defined as illegal in legal codes, such as the denial of basic human rights resulting from sexism, racism, and economic exploitation. "Crimes of accommodation" are acts of adaptation by the lower and working classes in response to the oppressive conditions of capitalism and the domination of the capitalist class. "Predatory crimes" are parasitical and include such acts as burglary, robbery, and drug dealing. "Personal crimes"—such as murder, assault, and rape—are directed at other members of the lower and working classes and result from the brutalized conditions of capitalism. Finally, "crimes of resistance" are actions conducted by members of the working class that are specifically directed at the workplace, such as sabotage and machine breaking. As Quinney summarized:

> Crimes of accommodation and resistance thus range from unconscious reactions to exploitation, to conscious acts of survival within the capitalist system, to politically conscious acts of rebellion. These criminal actions, moreover, not only cover the range of meaning but also actually evolve or progress from *unconscious reaction* to *political rebellion*. Finally, the crimes may eventually reach the ultimate stage of conscious political action—*revolt*. (p. 65–66, italics in original)

Thus, for Quinney, the crimes of domination seem to be the real societal harms, but they are not criminalized because they benefit the ruling class. Crimes of accommodation, on the other hand, range from simple adaptation to conscious political resistance. In fact, for Quinney some crimes and, therefore, criminals are admirable elements in the overall class struggle.

Quinney also took an instrumentalist view of the state, arguing that it promotes the interests of the ruling class and "is a device for controlling the exploited class, the class that labors, for the benefit of the ruling class" (pp. 44–45). Quinney maintained further that the "coercive force of the state, embodied in law and legal repression, is the traditional means of maintaining the social and economic order" (p. 45). Law, then, "is an instrument of the state that serves the interests of the developing capitalist ruling class" (p. 45).

Spitzer and Quinney developed their models of crime in the 1970s. In the 1980s, new models emerged. We summarize one of these, the work of William Chambliss.

William Chambliss (1988b) outlined a *structural contradictions* theory of crime. He argued that all historical eras and all societies, while constructing their means of survival, create contradictory forces, dilemmas, and conflicts. Under capitalism, the basic contradiction is between capital and labor. This contradiction results in worker demands for better working conditions and higher wages, even as capitalists resist these demands. The dilemma for capital, labor, and the state is how to reconcile the conflict, inasmuch as the fundamental contradiction is ignored. Resolving the conflict can result either in further conflicts—because the fundamental contradiction persists—or in an additional contradiction (as shown in Figure 13.4).

Chambliss also took a structuralist—rather than instrumentalist—position on the state. For structuralists, the state in capitalist societies takes a capitalist form not because of those who fill decision-making positions but because the state reflects capitalist economic relations; that is, the state is molded to fit and serve the interests of the capitalist economy regardless of those who fill its offices. For Chambliss, then, the law represents the state's response to various aspects of class struggle in a contradictory capitalist economy. Contradictions create dilemmas and conflicts—which those in state

**Figure 13.4    Structural Contradictions Theory**

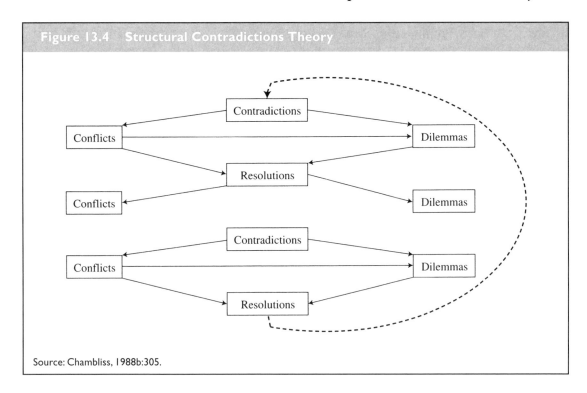

Source: Chambliss, 1988b:305.

positions attempt to resolve—leaving the contradictions in place. Although Chambliss agreed with instrumentalists that the capitalist class puts pressure on the state to pass laws that serve its interests (winning most of the time), resistance and pressure from other class forces are always present. When resistance leads to open conflict, the state responds through the law.

Chambliss also identified two fundamental contradictions in a capitalist political economy that lead to crime. The first is the "wages, profits, and consumption contradiction." If, on the one hand, workers have insufficient money to purchase commodities (because capitalists do not pay them enough in wages), the economy becomes sluggish. If, on the other hand, workers are paid high wages, this cuts into profits, and less money is available for reinvestment. This inherent contradiction of capitalism culminates in crime.

In addition, Chambliss identified a "wages-labor supply contradiction." Capitalism maintains a surplus labor force that helps keep wages down and provides a supply of labor from which capital can draw whenever the demands of workers threaten profits. The demanding workers are let go, and fresh labor is brought in. However, this reserve army of labor simultaneously "forms an underclass that cannot consume but nonetheless is socialized into a system in which consumption is the necessary condition for happiness. Criminal behavior offers a solution for the underclass: what they cannot earn legitimately they can earn illegitimately" (p. 309).

In sum, the above approaches employ Marxist theory to understand the relationship between the political and economic realms of a capitalist society. These perspectives advance our understanding of why certain behaviors are criminalized by the state whereas others are not, and of how a capitalist economic system itself generates certain class patterns of crime.

## Evaluation of Radical Theory

Using Marxist social theory, radicals in the 1970s and 1980s developed theories that give priority to historical and structural analyses of crime, focusing on economic relationships, class struggle, capital accumulation, and the role of the reserve army of labor.

Radical criminology, however, was not without its critics. For some, a radical criminology grounded in Marxist theory is actually impossible, inasmuch as crime is not an explicit Marxian concept like, for example, "mode of production" or "capital accumulation." Mainstream criminologists have criticized radical criminology for being unscientific (Turk, 1979), moralistic (Klockars, 1979; Toby, 1979), and utopian (Nettler, 1978). Radicals, however, have soundly addressed all these criticisms (Beirne, 1979; Greenberg, 1981).

Some of the most useful criticisms of radical criminology were made by radical criminologists themselves. For example, Spitzer (1980) argued that much of radical criminology is metafunctional. That is, capitalism is theorized "as 'needing' crime in order to justify its oppression of the masses" (p. 176). Radical criminologists have also identified problems with instrumental outlooks on the state. As noted, this position holds that the ruling class exercises state power directly through the manipulation of state policies. Critics have pointed out that neither the state nor the ruling class is monolithic—conflicts of interests exist within both the state and the ruling class, as well as between them (Spitzer, 1975; Beirne, 1979; Chambliss and Seidman, 1982).

Radical criminology has also been criticized for its one-dimensionality. Radical criminology, it is claimed, attempts to explain all crime in economic terms. This means that other social relations, such as gender and race relations, are at best secondary to class relations. This secondariness has been challenged by feminist criminologists and is discussed in the following section.

## Feminist Criminology

The feminist movement has had an important impact on the social sciences, including sociology and criminology. The term "feminist" is commonly and broadly used to refer to all those who consciously maintain that women are discriminated against because of their gender and who seek to end women's resulting subordination through social change.

Kathleen Daly and Meda Chesney-Lind (1988) have outlined five core elements of feminist thought that help distinguish feminism from other forms of social theory:

1. Gender is not a natural fact but a complex social, historical, and cultural product; it is related to, but not simply derived from, biological sex differences and reproduction capacities.

2. Gender and gender relations order social life and social institutions in fundamental ways.

3. Gender relations and constructs of masculinity and femininity are not symmetrical but are based on an organizing principle of men's superiority and social and political-economic dominance over women.

4. Systems of knowledge reflect men's views of the natural and social world; the production of knowledge is gendered.

5. Women should be at the center of intellectual inquiry, not peripheral, invisible, or appendages to men.

Contemporary feminist contributions to criminology can be divided into two phases; the first extends from the late 1960s to the mid-1980s and the second from the late 1980s to the present (Daly and Maher, 1998). We discuss the second phase in Chapter 14.4.

In the first phase, feminist criminologists concentrated on criticizing criminological theory for either being gender-blind or misrepresenting women. Feminist criminologists also conducted investigations of women's experiences as offenders, victims, and workers in the criminal justice system, and they used popular feminist theories of the time—liberal, Marxist, radical, and socialist—to explain women's and men's involvement in crime. Let us briefly consider the feminist theoretical perspectives on crime that emerged in the 1970s and 1980s.

As Jaggar and Rothenberg (1984) point out, **liberal feminism** has its roots in the eighteenth- and nineteenth-century social ideals of liberty and equality. Liberty came to be understood as freedom from interference by the state, primarily in the private sphere. The ideal of equality required that each individual should be able to rise in society just as far as his or her talents permit, unhindered by restraints of law or custom. What qualities should count as talents and how they should be rewarded is to be determined by the supply and demand for those talents within a market economy. To guarantee that the most genuinely talented individuals are identified, it is necessary to ensure that everyone has an equal opportunity to develop his or her talents. Within the liberal tradition, therefore, equality has come to be construed as equality of opportunity.

The formulation of the ideals of liberty and equality created the conditions that motivated women to demand that these ideals be applied to them as well as to men. From Mary Wollstonecraft's *A Vindication of the Rights of Women* in 1792 and John Stuart Mill's *The Subjection of Women* in 1851 to *Ms.* magazine and the publications of the National Organization for Women (NOW), the roots of women's subordination, for liberal feminists, are embedded in the denial to women of civil rights and social opportunities. Liberal feminists argue that women should receive the same rights and have the same opportunities as men. Women are oppressed because of gender discrimination, which deprives them of the same opportunities and rights that men enjoy. Consequently, women are effectively kept outside the mainstream of society (politics, business, finance, medicine, law, and so forth). Liberal feminists argue that this problem can be resolved by letting women into the mainstream. The liberal feminist program calls for state reform to bring about those changes necessary to promote women's rapid integration into the backbone of society.

One of the reasons for women's discrimination, according to liberal feminists, is gender-role socialization. Liberal feminists argue that conventional family patterns structure masculine and feminine identities. Girls and women, on the one hand, are socialized to be patient, understanding, sensitive, passive, dependent, and nurturing. The female role, liberal feminists continue, centers on functions reflecting these personality traits; such functions are found specifically in the family (women's identity resides in the domestic sphere) but also in the labor market, where women take gender-specific jobs such as clerical, service, and sales positions. Boys and men, on the other hand, are socialized to be self-confident, independent, bold, responsible, competitive, and aggressive. The male role reflects these traits, as a man is encouraged to find an identity in the public sphere (the workplace), thus providing money and security for "his" family. Because the role and the traits associated with femininity are defined as inferior, sexist ideologies arise that consider women to be second-class persons. Accordingly, because of the emphasis on both equality and socialization, liberal feminists have called for policies providing women with equal opportunities and androgynous socialization.

Some criminologists have used liberal feminist theory to explain the relationships between opportunity, socialization, and crime. Rita Simon (1975), for instance, argued that until the 1970s women's crime was quite limited because women's opportunities were restricted. With the rise of the second wave of the feminist movement in the 1960s and the subsequent liberated woman of the 1970s, women were provided with more opportunities to act like men. Simon alleged that this increased equality in the labor market resulted in increased opportunities for women to commit occupationally related crimes, such as embezzlement. However, as we note later, increased women's crime is made up primarily of nonoccupationally related crimes such as larceny (mostly shoplifting) and petty forms of fraud.

A more sophisticated formulation of liberal feminist opportunity theory was provided by Josephina Figueira-McDonough (1980), who hypothesized that similar levels of strain (resulting from high success aspirations and low legitimate opportunities) lead to similar criminal behavior patterns by both genders if they have equal knowledge of and comparable access to illegitimate means.

Liberal feminists also attempt to explain crime in terms of gender-role socialization. In the 1970s several liberal feminist writers emphasized the relationship between gender role and crime. For example, Dale Hoffman-Bustamante (1973) explained how patterns of crime are related to the different role expectations of men and women and thus to gender differences in socialization patterns. Ann Oakley (1972) was more explicit, contending that "the patterns of male and female crime are tied to cultural patterns of masculinity and femininity, so that the type and the amount of crime committed by each sex express both sex-typed personality and sex-typed social role" (p. 68). Oakley saw crime as specifically masculine, which helps explain women's lower crime rate:

> Criminality and masculinity are linked because the sorts of acts associated with each have much in common. The demonstration of physical strength, a certain kind of aggressiveness, visible and external "proof" of achievement, whether legal or illegal—these are facets of the ideal male personality and also of much criminal behavior. Both male and criminal are valued by their peers for these qualities. Thus, the dividing line between what is masculine and what is criminal may at times be a thin one. (p. 72)

Oakley went on to argue that although crime may be a specific manifestation of masculinity and, therefore, predominantly male, "the sex difference has narrowed considerably in recent years, suggesting that, as some of the differences between the sex roles are reduced by the conditions of modern life, the deviance of male and female becomes more alike" (p. 70). This point was later emphasized by Freda Adler in her book *Sisters in Crime* (1975). Adler argued that because of the women's movement, by the mid-1970s gender roles had so merged that women became more masculine and, thus, engaged in more violent crime.

Specific types of female crime have also been analyzed by liberal feminists in terms of gender-role socialization. For example, Karen Rosenblum (1975) argued that important parallels exist between the attributes of the female gender role and prostitution, so that the latter can be interpreted simply as a consequence and extension of fundamental aspects of the former. Women are defined as sex objects—either of lust or chastity—yet are socialized to be passive sexually and also to use sex as a means to status. Consequently, "the difference between the utilization of and expectations regarding sexuality is only one of degree. The decision to become a call girl simply requires an exaggeration of one aspect of the situation experienced as a nondeviant woman" (p. 180).

**Marxist feminism** differs considerably from liberal feminism. Marxist feminists theorize, following Engels (1970a), that the class and gender divisions of labor together determine the social position of women and men in any society, but they see gender division of labor as resulting from the class division of labor. According to Marxist feminists, as private property evolved, males began to dominate all social institutions. Thus Marxist feminists view the capitalist mode of production as the basic organizing mechanism of Western societies; this mode of production determines the social relations between classes and genders. Gender and class inequalities result from property relations and the capitalist mode of production.

For Marxist feminists, masculine dominance is an ideological manifestation of a class society in which women are primarily dominated by capital and only secondarily by men. The latter form of domination, however, results from the mode of production. Although most Marxist feminists examine masculine dominance and sexism in society, they comprehend the roles of men and women in relation to capital, not in relation to a separate system of masculine power and dominance. Women's labor in the home is analyzed not in terms of how it benefits men but, rather, how it provides profits for the capitalist class.

An excellent illustration of a Marxist feminist approach to crime is the work of Sheila Balkan, Ron Berger, and Janet Schmidt in their book *Crime and Deviance in America* (1980). Discussing women's crime, they argued that a capitalist mode of production "lays the foundation for a theory of women's criminality" (p. 211). To understand female criminality, they continued, we must understand the ideology of sexism and how it legitimizes the structure of the family under capitalism. By reason of the needs of a capitalist society—in particular the reproduction of labor power—women's social position has been centered on the family, sexuality, and the home. Sexism, they argued, is an ideological result of capitalist relations that structure women's position and women's crime. Consequently, nonviolent crimes by women—such as shoplifting and prostitution—reflect such conditions. Moreover, when women commit violent crimes such as murder, their victims are usually family members, relatives, or lovers. Women are also less likely to use guns and more likely to use such household implements as kitchen knives as weapons. Thus women's crime reflects their oppressed position in a capitalist economic system.

Similarly, Julia and Herman Schwendinger's (1983) Marxist feminist analysis of rape contended that the level of male violence in any society is determined primarily by class relations and the mode of production. The Schwendingers argued that societies without commodity production are gender egalitarian, women are deemed equal to men in most aspects of social life, and violence against women is almost nonexistent. When such societies begin to produce for exchange (either voluntarily or because of the imposition of colonial power), men control the production system and women are confined to the home. This new division of labor results in an increase in male authority, a decrease in women's social position, and violence against women. Hence, gender inequality and violence against women become closely tied to and rooted in the mode of production. Indeed, the Schwendingers concluded that exploitative modes of production in class societies either produce or intensify gender inequality and violence against women (p. 179).

Whereas Marxist feminism emphasizes the structural conditions of a class society (more specifically, a capitalist society) as the root cause of masculine dominance, women's special oppression, and thus crime, **radical feminism** sees masculine power and privilege as the root cause of all social relations and inequality. For radical feminists, the most important relations in any society are found in **patriarchy** (masculine control of the labor power and sexuality of women); all other relations (such as class) are secondary and derive from male-female relations. Radical feminists also assert the following (Jaggar and Rothenberg, 1984):

- Women were, historically, the first oppressed group.

- Women's oppression is the most widespread, existing in virtually every known society.

- Women's oppression is the deepest, in that it is the hardest form of oppression to eradicate and cannot be removed by other social changes such as the abolition of class society.

Catharine MacKinnon (1984), a prominent radical feminist, adds that the control of women's sexuality by men is central to masculine dominance. Sexuality, the primary social sphere of male power, entails the expropriation of women's sexuality by men, and this expropriation structures men and women as social and sexual beings within society. For MacKinnon, power is maintained over women through compulsory heterosexuality and sexual violence (rape, wife beating, sexual harassment, and pornography).

It follows that when discussing crime, radical feminists concentrate on violence against women. Certain segments of radical feminism emphasize biological determinism in their discussion of crime. For example, writing about rape, Susan Brownmiller (1975) argued that "by anatomical fiat—the inescapable construction of their genital organs—the human male was a *natural* predator and the human female served as his *natural* prey" (p. 16, emphasis added). For Brownmiller, gender inequality is the result of the anatomical and biological makeup of men and women. Male anatomy and biology provide men with the apparatus to rape women; by the very nature of their anatomy and biology, women "cannot retaliate in kind" (p. 14). Women's overall subordination and men's criminality—particularly male violence against females—result from these biological facts.

Many radical feminists disagree with Brownmiller's extreme biological determinism, arguing instead that women's victimization by men results from their social position rather than their biology. For example, Elizabeth Stanko (1985) argued in her book *Intimate Intrusions* that because of masculine dominance and female powerlessness, the "normal" male is physically aggressive and the "normal" female experiences this aggression in the form of sexual violence. For Stanko, violence against women seems to be universal across time and place: "To be a woman—in most societies, in most eras—is to experience physical and/or sexual terrorism at the hands of men" (p. 9). Thus, male violence is a reflection of the universality of male dominance and the secondary status of women.

Moreover, following MacKinnon's position on sexuality, Stanko argued:

Women learn, often at a very early age, that their sexuality is not their own and that maleness can at any point intrude into it. Sexuality, then, is a form of power, and gender, as socially constructed, embodies it, not the reverse. As such, male sexual and physical prowess takes precedence over female sexual and physical autonomy. (p. 73)

According to Stanko, women, as appendages to men, are "expected to endure or alternatively have been seen as legitimate, deserving targets of male sexual and physical aggression because that is part of what men *are*. Women, as connected to men, are then violated" (p. 74). Male violence is customary in patriarchal culture; therefore, it is also customary that women endure it. Thus, this ideology helps maintain male dominance and control over women. As Stanko concluded: "Forced sexuality for women is 'paradigmatic' of their existence within a social sphere of male power" (p. 75).

In short, radical feminists view the basic structure of social reality as a total system of male domination. This form of domination is constructed by men and enables them to control women's bodies and thereby to trap women as forced sexual slaves (Jaggar, 1983).

Finally, **socialist feminism** differs from both Marxist and radical feminism: It prioritizes neither class nor gender. Socialist feminists view both class and gender relations as interacting and co-reproducing each other in society. For socialist feminists, class and gender interact to determine the social organization of society at any particular time in history. To understand class, socialist feminists argue that we must recognize how it is structured by gender; conversely, to understand gender requires an examination of how it is structured by class. Consequently, people's overall life experiences are shaped by both class and gender relations, and the interaction of these relationships structures crime in society.

An example of a socialist feminist explanation of crime is James Messerschmidt's book *Capitalism, Patriarchy, and Crime* (1986b). Messerschmidt argued that the United States is a patriarchal capitalist society and that the interaction of patriarchy and capitalism patterns the types and seriousness of crime. This interaction creates a powerless group of women and the working and lower classes, on one hand, and a powerful group of men and the professional-managerial (traditional middle) and capitalist classes on the other. For Messerschmidt, power constituted by both gender and class is critical to understanding crime:

> It is the powerful (in both the gender and class spheres) who do most of the damage to society, not, as is commonly supposed, the disadvantaged, poor, and subordinate. The interaction of gender and class creates positions of power and powerlessness in the gender/class hierarchy, resulting in different types and degrees of criminality and varying opportunities for engaging in them. Just as the powerful have more legitimate opportunities, so they have more illegitimate opportunities. (p. 42)

Given that men and members of the professional-managerial and capitalist classes have the most power, they have greater opportunities to engage in crime, not only more often but also in ways that are more harmful to society. Males of all social classes therefore commit more crime than females, their class position determining the type of crime they may commit (for example, lower- and working-class males have no opportunity to commit corporate crimes, whereas professional- and managerial-class males have no need to resort to conventional crimes). In Messerschmidt's view, low female crime rates are related to women's powerless position in the United States. Their subordinate position relegates women to fewer legitimate as well as fewer illegitimate opportunities and to fewer resources with which to engage in serious forms of crime. Thus, overall, socialist feminists argue that crime is related to the opportunities a gender/class position allows, and they attempt a simultaneous explanation of the gender and class patterns of crime.

## Evaluation of Feminist Theory

Feminist criminology of the 1970s and 1980s made significant contributions to the field of criminology and, as we will see in Chapter 14.4, continues to flourish. Most concerns about first-phase feminist criminology centered on the feminist theories used to explain crime. For example, liberal feminism has been criticized for its inability to "explain the emergence of gender inequality, nor can it account, other than by analogy, for effects of race and class stratification on the conditions of women's lives. Its analysis for change tends to be limited to issues of equal opportunity and individual choice" (Andersen, 1993:318).

A critique of Rita Simon's position on crime supplies another example of the kind of criticism leveled at liberal feminism. Simon (1975) argued that the women's movement has increased women's opportunities in the labor market and that this advancement explains their increasing involvement in property crimes. But this argument ignores the fact that the sharpest increases in property crimes are found in nonoccupational theft, such as larceny (mostly shoplifting) and minor fraud (such as check and welfare fraud) (Chesney-Lind, 1997). Moreover, most female property offenders are adolescents who have had little or no contact with the labor market (Chesney-Lind, 1997).

The liberal feminist emphasis on gender-role socialization has also been criticized. Smart (1976) argued that liberal feminism failed to place the discussion of gender roles "within a structural explanation of the social origin of those roles" (p. 69). In other words, liberal feminists did not account historically, socially, and economically for women's subordinate position in the gender division of labor and, therefore, did not explain the broader reasons for the current patterns of socialization. Smart also criticized role theory for not discussing female motivation or intent. As she pointed out: "Role theory does not explain why, even though women are socialized into primarily conforming patterns of behavior, a considerable number engage in crime" (p. 69).

Both Marxist feminism and radical feminism have been criticized for being reductionist. Marxist feminists have been faulted for reducing all social phenomena—including male and female crime—to economic conditions and for being unable to explain gender divisions and power relations between men and women. Radical feminist theory has been criticized for its view that social classes are simply an epiphenomenon of gender inequality. Moreover, a major problem with radical feminist theory is that it assumes universal female subordination. Yet anthropological research has shown that in many gathering and hunting societies, gender relations were quite equal and men did not control the labor power and sexuality of women (Reiter, 1975; Shostak, 1983). Radical feminists have also been criticized for explaining male violence against women in biological terms or as simply a reflection of masculine power and dominance. Finally, the term "patriarchy," which both radical and socialist feminists use to label masculine dominance, has been criticized for its timeless characterization of masculine power and prestige. In other words, neither radical nor socialist feminists have adequately accounted for historical changes in patriarchy and its various forms.

## Review

This chapter examined five influential theories of crime: social learning theory, the labeling perspective, conflict theory, and radical theory and feminist theory. Each offers a different view of the processes that culminate in crime.

### Social Learning Theory

1. Social learning theory begins with the idea that social behavior is a cognitive process in which personality and environment interact reciprocally. It was pioneered in laboratory settings under the influence of B. F. Skinner's operant conditioning theory, according to which desired behavior can be reinforced by conditioned learning based on rewards and punishments.

2. Some criminologists have argued that whether individuals commit crime depends on their past conditioning history (namely, whether they have been reinforced [or rewarded] for having committed crime). Akers's social learning theory attempts to revise Sutherland's theory of differential association. Its major concepts are (1) differential reinforcement and (2) positive and negative definitions.

3. Social learning theory is a general theory of crime: It attempts to explain all crime.

### The Labeling Perspective

1. The labeling perspective claims that deviance and crime are in the eye of the beholder. It is not the quality of an act that makes it deviant or criminal but the

perception of it as such by a social audience. The labeling perspective is very much a creature of the social and political unrest of the 1960s.

2. Its underlying themes are a romantic attachment to the underdog, a reflexive concern with the role of the criminologist in an inegalitarian society, an opposition to scientism, and an emphasis on the importance of meanings in social interaction.

3. The distinction between primary and secondary deviance highlights how the societal reaction to deviance creates and amplifies the very behavior it seeks to control.

4. Deviance amplification also occurs through stigmatization. The stigmatizing effect of the label attached to primary deviation is one of the most important factors in secondary deviation. The handling of stigmatization requires skill and power that many individuals do not possess.

5. The labeling perspective has never been carried through to its logical conclusion. If crime and deviance are only categories conferred on behavior by agents of social control, then criminology should be reoriented "controlology."

## Conflict Theory

1. Conflict theory, often contrasted with consensus theory, overlaps with the labeling perspective. Its key idea is that to understand crime we must also understand the interests served by criminal law. On this view, crime is a category applied to some persons after a politico-legal process of criminalization. Theoretically, then, crime and criminal law are merely different sides of the same coin.

2. According to conflict theory, crime and criminal law are the two basic aspects of the process of criminalization. It is this process that criminologists should study.

3. The most influential examples of conflict theory are Vold's theory of group conflict and crime, Quinney's theory of the social reality of crime, and Turk's theory of criminalization.

4. Chambliss and Seidman have applied many insights of conflict theory in an attempt to understand the creation of law, the general principles of law, and the implementation of law. Law typically reflects the interests of the powerful.

5. Many assumptions of conflict theory have been revealed as overly generalized. Conflict theory, as such, has been most influential in the continuing popularity of the labeling perspective and in the emergence of radical criminology.

## Radical and Feminist Theories

1. Although Marx and Engels never gave crime concerted attention, several European socialist writers, such as Willem Bonger, applied Marxist theory to crime in the late nineteenth and early twentieth centuries.

2. It was not until the 1970s that a radical criminology emerged in the United States.

3. In the 1970s and 1980s, radical criminology developed various Marxist perspectives on crime and social control.

4. These approaches use Marxist theory to understand (1) why some behavior is criminalized and other behavior is not and (2) how a capitalist economic system generates class patterns of crime.

5. Feminist criminologists developed four major perspectives in the 1970s and 1980s—liberal, Marxist, radical, and socialist—that were used to explain crime. Each feminist perspective looks at gender relationships in a distinct way, asks different questions, and explains crime differently.

## Questions for Class Discussion

1. Can social learning theory adequately explain the causes of suicide?

2. In his book *Outsiders,* Howard Becker wrote that "deviance is not a quality of the act the person commits, but rather a consequence of the application by others of rules and sanctions to an 'offender' " (1963:9). Do you agree with Becker's view? Why? Why not?

3. Can crime be studied properly without simultaneously studying the process of criminalization?

4. Compare the various Marxist perspectives on crime with some of the other theories discussed in this book.

5. Choose several crimes (such as wife battering or prostitution) and show how the four feminist perspectives explain them.

## For Further Study

### Readings

Akers, Ronald L. 1998. *Social Learning and Social Structure: A General Theory of Crime and Deviance.* Boston: Northeastern University Press.

Daly, Kathleen, and Meda Chesney-Lind. 1988. "Feminism and Criminology." *Justice Quarterly* 5 (4): 101–143.

Lynch, Michael J., Raymond Michalowski, and W. Byron Groves. 2000. *The New Primer in Radical Criminology: Critical Perspectives on Crime, Power and Identity.* Monsey, NY: Criminal Justice Press.

Matza, David. 1964. *Delinquency and Drift.* New York: John Wiley.

Symposium on Social Learning Theory. 1999. Essays by Sampson, Morash, Krohn and Akers. *Theoretical Criminology* 3 (4): 438–493.

Vold, George B., Thomas J. Bernard, and Jeffrey B. Snipes. 2002. *Theoretical Criminology*. New York: Oxford University Press.

## Websites

1. <http://www.sonoma.edu/cja/info/Edintro.html>: This site is constructed in memory of Edwin Lemert and features a professional and personal biography of this influential criminologist.

2. <http://www.aber.ac.uk/media/sections/tv07.html>: This Media and Communication Studies site compiles information regarding television viewing and violent behavior, with links to social learning theory.

3. <http://www.critcrim.org>: A newsletter of the Division on Critical Criminology in the American Society of Criminology, this site provides summary essays about radical and feminist criminological perspectives.  ✦

# New Directions in Criminological Theory

## Preview

Chapter 14 introduces:

- The theory of routine activities and crime.

411

- Two general theories of crime and deviance: the theory of self-control and the theory of control balance.

- Two notable revisions to Mertonian strain and anomie theory: general strain theory and institutional anomie theory.

- Several varieties of critical criminology, including left realism, peacemaking, postmodernism, and feminism.

## Key Terms

| | |
|---|---|
| abolitionism | green criminology |
| anarchism | integrated theory |
| constitutive criminology | left idealism |
| control balance | left realism |
| control deficit | peacemaking criminology |
| control surplus | postmodernism |
| convict criminology | rational choice |
| cultural criminology | routine activities theory |
| feminism | self-control theory |
| general theory | strain |

In this chapter we outline the key aspects of several new theories in criminology. Each of these theories was developed at some point in the late 1980s or early 1990s. To a greater or lesser extent, each has been further elaborated and refined in response to scholarly criticism.

Although several of these theories embody a new movement toward "integrated" theory, the only accurate generalization that can be made about the theories discussed in this chapter is that they are extraordinarily varied in their basic assumptions about human sociality and in their substantive claims about crime. Some of them regard themselves as "general" theories of crime; that is, they attempt to explain all cases of the phenomena in their scope. Each has a somewhat different idea of the process of theory construction. Most of the theories discussed here differ from their competitors in what they identify as the causes of crime. Some of them believe that the search for the causes of crime is a futile enterprise doomed from the very outset. Moreover, critical criminology, which emerged from radical and feminist criminologies of the 1970s and 1980s, attempts to develop theoretical perspectives that contribute to the pursuit of positive social change and social justice.

## 14.1 Routine Activities and Crime

**Routine activities theory** reflects the apparent fact that high crime rates have become a normal part of life in the United States. The main features of routine activities theory derive from the insights of a number of other perspectives on crime and victimization. These perspectives include the free-will basis of human action (rational choice), allegedly popularized by the eighteenth-century classical criminology of Beccaria and Bentham (Cornish and Clarke 1986; and see Chapter 9.1); the Chicago school of ecology (see Chapter 11.2); and empirical studies showing that patterns of crime and victimization vary in time, in location, and in the social distance between offender and victim (see Chapter 3). The key claim of routine activities theory is that patterns of crime and victimization result from the everyday interaction in geographical space and in time of likely offenders, suitable targets, and guardians.

## The Chemistry of Crime

According to one of the earliest statements of the theory, routine activities include any "recurrent and prevalent activities which provide for basic population and individual needs, whatever their biological or cultural origins" (Cohen and Felson 1979:593). Routine activities may occur at home or away from home. Examples of these everyday activities include commuting to work and engaging in numerous activities associated with providing and acquiring food and shelter, sexual outlets, leisure, learning, and childrearing.

Figure 14.1 displays the three basic ingredients in routine activities theory, which Felson (2002) outlines under the general rubric of "the chemistry for crime":

1. *There must be a suitable target.* Targets may be either property or persons. Although the sociological characteristics of offenders are not a part of routine activities theory, the theory specifies four factors according to which the "suitability" of a target varies from the offender's perspective: its value, its inertia (how mobile or how easy it is to carry), its visibility, and its accessibility. Clearly, some targets, such as corner lots or public parks—called "hot spots"—are more vulnerable than others. Some targets are more suitable not only because they are worth more, for example, but also because no one is protecting them or looking out for them.

2. *There must be a target whose guardian or protector can be overcome by an offender.* A suitable target may be protected either by formal guardians such as police officers or, far more likely, by ordinary citizens such as property owners, neighbors, and pedestrians going about their everyday affairs.

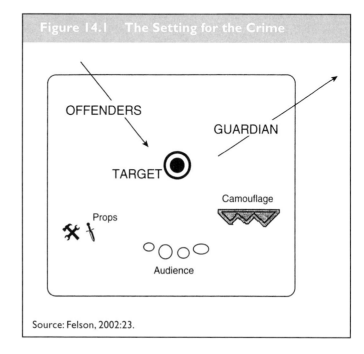

Figure 14.1  The Setting for the Crime

OFFENDERS

GUARDIAN

TARGET

Camouflage

Props

Audience

Source: Felson, 2002:23.

Their mere presence may deter a likely offender. Guardians may also include surveillance systems such as video security systems or burglar alarms.

3. *There must be a likely offender who may consciously plan to find a suitable target or else stumble across it.* Although the specific motivation of any given offender is irrelevant to routine activities theory, offenders tend to be opportunists who may choose to commit crimes either against property or against persons. In the case of the latter, offenders are more likely to pick victims who are physically weaker or who are outnumbered or otherwise at a disadvantage.

Besides these three "almost-always important" elements of a crime, crimes may be supplemented by three "often-important" elements. (Felson 2002):

- Any props that help produce or prevent a crime, including weapons or tools.

- Any camouflage that helps the offender avoid unwanted notice.

- Any audience the offender wants either to impress or intimidate.

In *Crime and Everyday Life,* Felson (2002) extends his analysis to the escalation sequence often involved in fights; to illegal markets for goods (e.g., drugs and stolen property), services (e.g., prostitution and contract killings) and persons (e.g., slaves, forced prostitution, illegal immigrants); and generally to youth crime, crime linkages, and recidivism. This analysis is clearly sympathetic to the "broken windows" theory (Kelling and Coles 1996), which suggests that, cumulatively, the presence of many minor crimes such as vandalism and graffiti creates a climate for the growth of serious crime. Indeed, Felson explicitly identifies a variety of ways in which one crime can feed into another. For example:

- There is sometimes an interplay of illegal markets, as when prostitutes sell drugs.

- One victimization sometimes leads to another (see the bicycle theft chain reaction in Figure 14.2).

- One crime might create the need for another, as when a burglar sets fire to a house to destroy evidence.

- Some crimes provide camouflage for others, as when a street-corner drug seller robs customers.

- One vulnerable target sometimes leads to another, as when a burglar discovers a woman inside an apartment and rapes her.

- Some offenders are vulnerable to victimization, as when a driver who goes through a red traffic light is attacked by another driver in a fit of road rage.

## A Routine Activity Approach to Crime Trends

Interestingly, Cohen and Felson have used some of the micro-level assumptions described above to explain changes in crime rates in the United States in two periods:

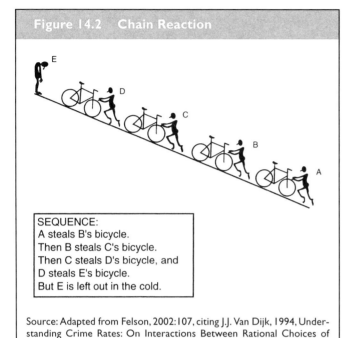

**Figure 14.2    Chain Reaction**

SEQUENCE:
A steals B's bicycle.
Then B steals C's bicycle.
Then C steals D's bicycle, and
D steals E's bicycle.
But E is left out in the cold.

Source: Adapted from Felson, 2002:107, citing J.J. Van Dijk, 1994, Understanding Crime Rates: On Interactions Between Rational Choices of Victims and Offenders, *British Journal of Criminology* 34(2):105-121.

1947–1974 and 1992–1996. Crimes in both periods are seen as normal events that matter-of-factly accompanied modernization and business growth. For the period 1947–1974 Cohen and Felson (1979) begin with the seeming paradox that during that time crime rates increased substantially even though there were, by some criteria, improvements in the economic conditions that many think are the breeding grounds of crime.

To explain this paradox they argue that some basic changes in the routine activities of the population led to an increase in the number of suitable targets and to a decrease in guardian presence; in combination, these changes produced an increase in the crime rate. They point out that during the period 1947–1974 some basic changes occurred in the routine activities of families and household members. Thus in the decade after 1960 the percentage of the population consisting of female college students increased by 118 percent, while married female labor force participation rose 31 percent. In other words, more households were empty during the day, which made them more vulnerable and, therefore, more suitable targets. Moreover, after 1960 there was a huge increase in the availability of and expenditures on durable consumer goods. Revolutions in the technology of durable consumer goods—especially electronic household appliances—made them lighter or smaller in size and, correspondingly, much easier to steal.

These fundamental changes in the circulation of goods and people, Felson and Cohen continue, were reflected in changes in crime rates during the 1960s. In particular,

- Personal and household victimizations increased faster than business victimizations.

- Shoplifting increased more rapidly than other types of thefts from businesses.

- Personal offenses by strangers outpaced such offenses by nonstrangers.

- Daytime residential burglaries increased more than those at night.

Felson (1997) has also used routine activities theory to explain the general decline of crime rates during the 1990s. As documented by the UCR, crimes reported to the police dropped by around 20 percent for robbery, burglary, and motor vehicle theft (1992–1996) and also for homicide (1993–1996). According to Felson, the major reason for the decline was a revolution in the use and movement of cash during the 1990s.

Specifically, from 1990 to 1994 there was a 57 percent increase in credit card spending, from $466 to $731 billion. With less cash in circulation, theft was far harder to accomplish successfully.

## Evaluation of Routine Activities Theory

With its great commonsense appeal, routine activities theory has been widely discussed and tested, and its implications have been applied as designs for local crime control.

But how well does routine activities theory explain crime? Several studies have confirmed aspects of the theory. It has been shown, for example, that reports of crime to Minneapolis police dispatchers came from only 3 percent of locations in the city (Sherman, Gartin, and Bueger, 1989). This seems to confirm that some locations are hot spots for crime. Another study found that, in the aftermath of Florida's Hurricane Andrew in 1992, the temporary absence of police briefly contributed to a rise in looting (Cromwell et al., 1995). This finding tends to confirm that the absence of capable guardians makes targets more suitable for offenders, which has also been largely substantiated by a cross-national study of burglary in England and Wales, the United States, and the Netherlands (Tseloni, Wittebrood, Farrell, and Pease, 2004).

However, serious doubt has been expressed about the core theoretical assumption of routine activities theory—namely, the rational choice perspective. Consider just one crime: robbery. According to Willem de Haan and Jaco Vos (2003; and see Exum, 2002), if robbers are depicted as operating only with a rational calculation of cost and benefit, we would miss much of the nuance of what they think, feel, and do when they rob. Robbers in fact often act impulsively, in inconsistent ways, with great displays of emotion.

Two further doubts must be raised about the explanatory power of routine activities theory. First, as Charles Tittle (1995) has complained, nowhere does the theory offer criteria to determine which routine activities are relevant to what criminal activity. For example, brushing one's teeth and reading the morning newspaper are routine activities, but presumably the theory would not say that these actions are relevant to crime. Why are some routine activities relevant to the understanding of crime but not others?

Second, routine activities theory is less a theory of the causes of crime than a statement about victimization—and a rather misleading one at that, because it fails to provide much or any of the sociological context of criminogenic situations, such as how and why crime is related to class, gender, race, and age. Consider just the area of gender and crime (Schwartz and Pitts, 1995; but see Felson and Messner, 1998). In arguing, for example, that an increase in female labor force participation leads to increases in crime because more households are unguarded during the day, the theory comes dangerously close to blaming females for precipitating their own victimization. Moreover, with its emphasis on a criminology of place rather than on sociological context, routine activities theory is quite silent about the fact that women are typically most in danger not from traveling to work but from their relationships with intimate males in their own households. Is patriarchy perhaps a routine activity?

About their lack of attention to the sociological contexts of crime, Tittle (1995) has concluded that **rational choice** theories in general, including routine activities theory, resemble little more than a mechanical gearbox that transforms inputs into outputs. "Without knowing how and why the inputs take on particular values," he points out, "understanding the gearbox is of limited use in explaining and predicting behavior" (p. 12). Some attempts (e.g., Wilcox, Land, and Hunt, 2003) are therefore now under way to develop routine activities theory by grafting other theories of criminal behavior onto it, such as theories of criminal opportunity and social disorganization.

## 14.2 Self-Control and Control Balance

We now describe two theories that are intended to be general theories of crime: the theory of **self-control** and the theory of control balance. Their common focus is the concept of control.

### Gottfredson and Hirschi's Theory of Self-Control

In recent years Travis Hirschi has radically narrowed or refocused, though not entirely abandoned, the theory of social control he presented in *Causes of Delinquency* (Hirschi, 1969; see Chapter 12.3). This change of emphasis was signaled in Michael Gottfredson and Hirschi's wide-ranging and influential book *A General Theory of Crime* (1990), in which they put forward a theory of self-control and crime.

Gottfredson and Hirschi argued that individual differences in criminal behavior stem from differences in "self-control." Finding much merit in classical criminology's emphasis on the relationships between pleasure and pain, they defined the problem of self-control as "the differential tendency of people to avoid criminal acts whatever the circumstances in which they find themselves" (1990:87). Low self-control coupled with opportunity increases an individual's propensity to commit crime, especially crimes involving force or fraud. High self-control effectively reduces the likelihood of committing crime. Moreover, those with high levels of self-control are significantly less likely throughout their lives to commit crime.

Clearly, this claim about the importance of self-control in the generation of crime has two crucial features: first, the characteristics of self-control and, second, the factors that promote or retard the level of self-control.

Gottfredson and Hirschi assumed that the characteristics of self-control can be derived from the nature of crime itself, which has five chief aspects:

1. Because crime offers immediate gratification of desires, people with low self-control wish to give in to their desires at once. They live in the here and now. For this reason, those with low self-control also tend to indulge in a variety of other immediate pleasures that are not criminal, such as smoking, drinking, using drugs, gambling, having illegitimate children, and engaging in illicit sex.

2. Because crime is exciting, risky, and thrilling, people with low self-control tend to be adventuresome, active, and physical rather than cautious, cognitive, and verbal.

3. Because crime provides few or meager long-term benefits and because engaging in crime interferes with jobs, marriages, family, and friends, people with low self-control tend to have marriages, friendships, and job profiles that are also unstable.

4. Because crime requires little skill or planning, people without self-control need not have or need not value cognitive or academic skills.

5. Because crime often causes victims pain or discomfort, people with low self-control tend to be self-centered and indifferent to others' suffering and needs.

To these five major characteristics of crime and self-control Gottfredson and Hirschi added that for those with low self-control, crime is not an automatic occurrence. For crime to occur, low self-control must be coupled with an opportunity to commit it. The opportunity for crime usually dictates whether any given person with low self-control actually commits a crime. Because crime is not a specialized activity, a potential criminal (in other words, a person with low self-control) will tend to commit a crime if the opportunity presents itself. Thus, a rapist is more likely than a nonrapist to (mis)use drugs and to commit robberies and burglaries. Moreover, if the opportunity to commit a crime is absent, persons with low self-control are more likely to engage in other acts that are "psychologically or theoretically equivalent to crime." Thus, in areas where property is secure and guarded, persons with low self-control will tend not to commit property crimes but are more likely than nonthieves to smoke, drink, and play truant from school.

What, then, are the sources or "causes" of low self-control? Gottfredson and Hirschi argued that the major cause is ineffective childrearing. As such, they continued, crime can be predicted from evidence of low self-control at very early stages in life. Children without self-control are children whose parents or guardians (1) do not monitor their behavior; (2) do not recognize deviant behavior when it happens; and (3) do not punish such behavior. By the time of the age of responsibility (eight years), most, if not all, children have attained—or failed to attain—a level of self-control that will remain constant for the rest of their lives:

> All that is required to activate the system is affection for or investment in the child. The person who cares for the child will watch his behavior, see him doing things he should not do, and correct him. The result may be a child more capable of delaying gratification, more sensitive to the interests and desires of others, more independent, more willing to accept restraints on his activity, and more unlikely to use force or violence to attain his ends. (p. 97)

Gottfredson and Hirschi asserted that many of the conventional causes of crime are in fact not causes of crime but consequences of low self-control. Persons with low self-control sort themselves into and are sorted into circumstances that are correlated with crime. For example, consider the longstanding finding that one of the causes of delinquency is that delinquents tend to have friends who are delinquent. This finding is rejected by Gottfredson and Hirschi; they believe that young persons with low self-control are attracted to the pleasures of delinquent activities and that the delinquent gang provides the opportunity for crime.

## Evaluation of Self-Control Theory

In formulating the theory of crime and self-control with Gottfredson in *A General Theory of Crime*, Hirschi apparently abandoned his earlier multifaceted theory of social control in favor of a monocausal theory whose core concept is intended to explain all crime. Hirschi and Gottfredson insisted that the theory of self-control can explain such diverse behaviors as delinquency, white-collar crime, and organized crime. The theory of self-control has been criticized because of this claim, among others. The never-ending search for a **general theory** is the Holy Grail of criminology. As such, it leaves itself open to the continuing objection that a theory that attempts to explain everything ultimately explains very little or even nothing at all.

Nevertheless, Gottfredson and Hirschi's theory of crime and self-control has led to some excitement among criminologists in the United States, and it has been subjected to considerable empirical testing (e.g., Burton et al., 1998; Gibbs, Giever, and Martin, 1998). The results have been mixed: Some researchers have rejected the theory; others have found that its key terms should be specified more clearly; and still others have lent it modest support (e.g., Pratt and Cullen, 2000). Perhaps a key reason for this mixed reception is that Gottfredson and Hirschi did not originally spell out precisely what they meant by "self-control" and by "opportunity" (Marcus, 2004). Moreover, the theory seems to be based on a tautology: If low self-control increases the propensity for crime, and if high propensity for crime is defined as low self-control, the theory is saying that low self-control causes low self-control (Hirschi and Gottfredson, 1993; Akers, 1997; Geis, 2000). What is needed, in short, are reliable indicators and measures of self-control that are separate from both the propensity to commit crime and crime itself. To this Hirschi and Gottfredson (2000) have replied that as logical systems, all theories contain tautologies and that the very heart of their theory contains not one but two "successful" tautologies: "deviant behavior predicts deviant behavior" and "self-control causes deviant behavior"!

Let us now point to three difficulties with self-control theory that return us squarely to important themes we raised earlier in the book.

First, crime is not simply an objective fact that can be identified and categorized in the same scientific way as rocks and butterflies. Crime is not only an action by an individual, a corporation, or a government but also a definition that is imposed on behavior by some lawful authority. Whether or not an action is a crime, in other words, hinges on the attitudes and reactions of powerful others. For example, we have described (Chapter 1.2) how the seafaring activities of Captain Kidd were transformed from being the praiseworthy and patriotic enterprise of a skilled sailor into the depraved and self-seeking illegalities of a pirate. Kidd's actions were criminal only because the British government so defined them and criminalized them as such!

Second, it seems impossible to characterize all criminal behavior as involving individuals with low self-control. Indeed, most criminologists would agree that persons with high levels of self-control who practice deferred gratification are precisely the individuals who engage in the numerous types of political, white-collar, and syndicated crime! At the very least, there are many crimes that require a specific rather than a general explanation and numerous others that have nothing to do with self-control (Reed and Yeager, 1996).

Third, if crime is an individual matter of self-control, how does one explain that some societies have much greater crime rates than others? Why does the United States have a homicide rate three to five times higher than the rate in most European countries (see Chapter 15)? Is it because the U.S. population somehow has less self-control, or does it have something to do with the nature of social organization in the United States?

We now turn to another recent exploration of the importance of the concept of "control": Charles Tittle's (1995) theory of control balance.

## Tittle's Theory of Control Balance

After the great success of labeling theory in the 1960s and 1970s, the concept of deviance did not play a significant role in the theoretical development of criminology. However, with Charles Tittle's book *Control Balance* (1995), the concept of deviance reemerged as an innovating force in criminology. Like Gottfredson and Hirschi's theory of self-control, Tittle's theory is focused on control, with an aim of nothing less than a general explanation of its subject matter. Indeed, the subtitle of his book is *Toward a General Theory of Deviance*. Tittle's theory tries to combine aspects of numerous other theories, including differential association, anomie, Marxism/conflict, social control, labeling, rational choice, and routine activities.

Tittle states that although what counts as deviance is subject to great variation, deviance is "any behavior that the majority of a given group regards as unacceptable or that typically evokes a collective response of a negative type" (p. 124). It is thus not the number of people who engage in an act that makes it deviant but the number of people who view it as such. Crime is merely a specialized form of deviance, one that is regarded as such by criminal law. Tittle identifies six forms of deviance, distinguished by how serious they are:

1. *Predation.* Acts of direct physical violence, manipulation, or property extraction, including theft, rape, homicide, robbery, assault, fraud, and individual price gouging, as well as acts such as parents' use of guilt to get a child's attention.

2. *Exploitation.* Acts of indirect predation, such as corporate price-fixing, unsafe workplaces, influence peddling, and contract killings.

3. *Defiance.* Acts of hostility or contempt for social norms—including vandalism, sullenness by a marital partner, and political protests—that bring the actor no obvious benefit.

4. *Plunder.* Acts of autocratic behavior, ethnic cleansing, and the destruction of the environment, rarely committed with an awareness of their harmfulness.

5. *Decadence.* Acts of undisciplined excess such as group sex with children, humiliating others for entertainment, sadistic torture.

6. *Submission.* Acts in which one allows oneself to be physically abused, humiliated, or sexually degraded.

Tittle's theory begins by accepting the basic premise of other control theories. This premise is that the main variable in explaining individual acts of deviance or crime is control of the ability to act. The theory's central premise is that "the amount of control to which an individual is subject, relative to the amount of control he or she can exercise, determines the probability of deviance occurring as well as the type of deviance likely to occur" (p. 135).

The "amount of control to which an individual is subject, relative to the amount of control he or she can exercise" is known as the "control ratio" for that individual. Individuals are in **control balance** if the amount of control that they exercise is the same as the amount of control that they experience. If one controls more than one experiences control, then one has a **control surplus.** If one experiences control more than one controls, then one has a **control deficit.**

Individuals with a control balance tend to conform. Those who have more control and those who have less control both tend to engage in more deviance than those in control balance—and the extent of their deviance is proportionate to how far out of balance they are. Individuals with control surpluses are likely to want to extend them; they will tend to do so by engaging in acts of exploitation, plunder, or decadence. Individuals with the smallest control surpluses are most likely to engage in exploitation, those with the largest surpluses (e.g., Nero, Howard Hughes, Michael Jackson) are most likely to engage in decadence. Those with control deficits are likely to wish to remove them or to minimize their effects; they will tend to do so by engaging in acts of predation, defiance, or submission. Individuals with marginal control deficits are most likely to engage in acts of predation; those with the most deficits, in acts of submission.

Under what conditions are individuals with an unbalanced control ratio motivated to engage in deviance? What provides the push, reason, impulse, or urge for them to deviate? Tittle says that motivating factors are of two basic sorts, one predispositional, the other situational. Predispositional factors include bodily and psychic needs; the desire for autonomy, which we all learn at a very early age; and the control ratio, which varies from one individual to another and depends on such factors as age, class, status, race, and gender.

But being predisposed to deviance does not necessarily mean that deviance will happen: "For deviant motivation to emerge, those predisposed toward it by an imbalanced control ratio must comprehend, or perceive, the possibility that deviance will alter their control ratios in an advantageous way" (p. 162). The situational influences on deviant motivation include provocations, such as verbal insults and racial slurs, and challenges from or displays of weakness by others. Adolescent subcultures, for example, are acutely aware of repression and encourage their members to resist it.

Tittle added a third and a fourth factor to this complex theory. The third is *constraint*, which refers to the probability, or perceived probability, that control will actually be exercised. Fourth, and finally, is *opportunity*. Clearly, one must have access to another person in order to assault him or her, and access to another's property in order to steal it.

## Evaluation of Control Balance Theory

Tittle's theory of control balance is clearly regarded by its author as a work in progress. Tittle himself has written that "it was unveiled like a roughly shaped clay statue with a sign saying 'bring your tools and your ideas and refine or reshape this' " (1997:99). In a broader context it must be seen as part of a movement in criminology toward an **integrated theory** (e.g., Braithwaite, 1989; Hagan, 1989; Vila, 1994; Bernard and Snipes, 1996; Barak, 1998), a key aspect of which is to model the process of theory building on the natural sciences. An integrated theory such as control balance seeks to be both as simple and as general as possible, which sometimes invites objections that its basic assumptions are too simple or wrong and that its scope is too general or too ambiguous (Short, Savelsberg, Jensen, and Tittle, 1999).

Modifications to some of the key components of control balance theory have been proposed by John Braithwaite (1997; and see Tittle, 1997, 1999; Piquero and Hickman, 1999). Braithwaite believes that the differences among exploitation, plunder, and decadence are not clearly defined. Moreover, there is perhaps no great difference between predation on the deficit side of control balance and exploitation on the surplus side. For example, predation might easily include shakedowns, bribery, extortion, and price-fixing. Indeed, Braithwaite recommended that most of Tittle's categories of deviance be abandoned in favor of a simplified theory of predatory deviance. In addition, Braithwaite (1997; and see Braithwaite and Pettit, 1990) advanced four implications of the theory of control balance, each of which makes an important statement about what a democratic and egalitarian society would look like:

1. Societies with greater equality of control will be better off because of reduced predatory deviance and reduced withdrawal from social and political life.

2. For any level of inequality of control, control that is exercised respectfully, without humiliation or debasement, will generate less predatory deviance.

3. When control is distributed with equity and exercised with virtuous respect, acceptance of that control is desirable because, especially for men, this acceptance will defuse predatory deviance.

4. When social bonds, social support, and communities are strong, equality of control is likely to increase, as is the respect with which control is exercised and the willingness of citizens to accept equitable, virtuous, and public-regarding controls.

## 14.3 Revised Strain Theory

The search for a general theory of crime is also present in various revisions to strain theory. We have already discussed Merton's arguments on **strain** and anomie, and we have seen how original and important they have been in criminology (Chapter 11.3). But we have also seen that crucial parts of Merton's arguments hinge on assumptions that are unstated and unproven. For example, it is highly questionable whether the acceptance of middle-class norms and values—whatever they might be—is as widespread in the United States as Merton depicted. Moreover, although Merton's analysis focused on the psychic effects of strain on individuals at various points in the class structure, he tended to assume that strain is unidimensional in its origins and that it transfers in a rather straightforward way from the social structure to individuals.

In what follows we outline the two most influential attempts to fill in some of the gaps in Merton's original formulation. These are, respectively, Robert Agnew's *general strain theory* and Steven Messner and Richard Rosenfeld's *institutional anomie theory*.

## Agnew's General Strain Theory

In his article "Foundation for a General Strain Theory of Crime and Delinquency," Agnew (1992) suggests that, with suitable revisions, strain theory has a central role to play in explaining crime and delinquency. Agnew tried to develop this role with new insights from research on stress in medical sociology and psychology, on equity and justice in social psychology, and on aggression in psychology. Agnew's approach focuses on the individual and his or her immediate social environment.

Whereas Merton's strain theory focused on the ways in which an individual is barred from achieving conventional goals, Agnew expands strain theory to include the analysis of "relationships in which others present the individual with noxious or negative stimuli" (p. 49)—relationships, for example, in which an individual is not treated in the way(s) she or he would like to be. Strain may therefore result from failure either to achieve conventional goals or to escape from painful relationships.

Agnew pinpoints three chief sorts of strain. First, strain can be brought on by *failure to achieve positively valued goals.* This failure can happen in many ways, including disjunctions between aspirations and expectations/actual achievements, disjunctions between expectations and actual achievements, and disjunctions between just/fair outcomes and actual outcomes. Adolescents may experience stress when they perceive their own position in life as unjust, for example, and as a result they may engage in delinquency in order to reduce their inputs (e.g., by playing truant) or to increase the inputs of others (e.g., by being disorderly). Alternatively, they may try to increase their outcomes (e.g., by theft) or to reduce others' outcomes (e.g., by vandalism, theft, and assault). Some individuals may perceive their situation as so unjust that they remove themselves altogether from it (by running away or, we might add, by suicide).

Second, strain results from *the removal of positively valued stimuli from the individual.* Examples of this situation include the loss of a boyfriend/girlfriend, a friend's serious illness or death, and the separation of one's parents. According to Agnew, such events can lead to delinquency "as the individual tries to prevent the loss of the positive stimuli, retrieve the lost stimuli or obtain substitute stimuli, seek revenge against those responsible for the loss, or manage the negative effect caused by the loss by taking illicit drugs" (p. 58).

Third, strain occurs through *the presentation of negative stimuli.* By "negative stimuli" Agnew means such stressful life events as child abuse/neglect, criminal victimization, verbal threats and insults, and negative relations with parents, peers, and at school. Each of these events can cause an aggressive response. Negative stimuli might also include physical pain, heat, noise, and pollution, all of which may be experienced as noxious for biological reasons.

Animal abuse is an example of crime to which Agnew (1998) applies his general strain theory. He suggests that strain may lead both directly and indirectly to animal abuse, particularly to its socially unacceptable forms. The negative behavior of our companion animals, such as when they bite us or chew our possessions, may sometimes cause us to be angry. Sometimes individuals who abuse animals do so to seek revenge on an animal that has caused them stress. At times, strain resulting in abuse may occur when animals threaten crops or livestock or when endangered species halt economic development.

Some of the animal abuse that is attributed to stress is often viewed as socially acceptable. How many of us protest farmers who shoot coyotes? Who spares the mosquito that bites one's arm?

Agnew argues that animal abuse, particularly of the type that most people believe to be unacceptable, may also be fostered by strain that is not caused by animals. This type of abuse occurs, first, when people are so stressed that their awareness of how they abuse has become dulled. Here, an individual might have a general propensity to lash out at all other beings, including animals. Second, animals may sometimes be used as weapons by one party against another in a domestic dispute, as has become quite well documented (see Chapter 5.2).

Two further aspects of Agnew's analysis of stress and animal abuse have considerable bearing on his general strain theory. The first is that Agnew recognizes that strain may sometimes reduce the likelihood of animal abuse. To illustrate this tendency, Agnew pointed out that some members of the eighteenth-century English working class were motivated out of sympathy—for creatures in similarly wretched conditions—to take part in the early anti-vivisection movement. We might note, as does Agnew himself, that nowadays feminist members of the animal protection community stress that they and animals often have a common oppressor (i.e., men).

Second, when he brings his theory of strain to bear on animal abuse, Agnew displays his willingness to admit the relevance of numerous other factors, both sociological and psychological (see Figure 14.3). Among these other factors—which might in principle be infinite—are an individual's social position; psychological traits, such as empathy; level of stress and strain; socialization; social control; and the nature of the animal under consideration. It remains to be seen whether this flexibility dilutes or strengthens the explanatory power of Agnew's general theory.

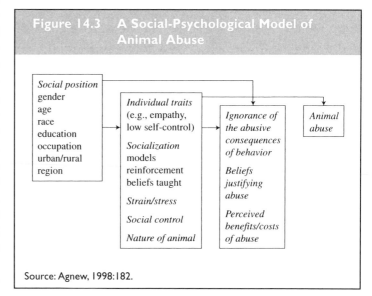

**Figure 14.3    A Social-Psychological Model of Animal Abuse**

Social position
gender
age
race
education
occupation
urban/rural
region

Individual traits
(e.g., empathy,
low self-control)

Socialization
models
reinforcement
beliefs taught

Strain/stress

Social control

Nature of animal

Ignorance of
the abusive
consequences
of behavior

Beliefs
justifying
abuse

Perceived
benefits/costs
of abuse

Animal
abuse

Source: Agnew, 1998:182.

## Evaluation of General Strain Theory

Some key problems exist both with how best to test Agnew's theory and with what its advantages are compared with Mertonian anomie theory. The scope of Agnew's general theory of strain and delinquency is much broader than earlier theories of anomie and strain. In particular, its reach extends far beyond the confines of social class. However, despite the narrow demographic makeup of the populations used to test his theory so far, it has gained some preliminary empirical support (Paternoster and Mazerolle,

1994; Agnew et al., 1996). For example, one study, which used data drawn from a nationally representative sample of 2,213 male public high school students, found that delinquent adolescents are more likely than nondelinquents to experience modest relief from strain's effects on anger, resentment, anxiety, and depression (Brezina 1996). Agnew (1995) has said that at heart his theory is very simple: "If we treat people badly, they may get mad and engage in crime" (p. 315), a conclusion that is similar to Christopher Jencks's (1987) finding that "adolescents who are treated like dirt will react accordingly" (p. 38). Few criminologists are likely to disagree.

## Messner and Rosenfeld's Institutional Anomie Theory

Whereas Agnew extends Merton's anomie theory by applying it at a social-psychological level, Steven Messner and Richard Rosenfeld have extended it to the macro level of social organization. In their book *Crime and the American Dream* (2001) Messner and Rosenfeld state that the American Dream refers to "a commitment to the goal of material success, to be pursued by everyone in society, under conditions of open, individual competition" (p. 5). The American Dream contains the basic values of American culture, in particular its commitment to achievement, individualism, universalism, and the glorification of materialistic success associated with the fetish for money. Messner and Rosenfeld claim that despite how it is filtered differentially through race and through gender, the American Dream is composed of values that are agreed on by a fairly high consensus of U.S. citizens.

Messner and Rosenfeld usefully extend Merton's analysis with their argument that U.S. society is unable to deliver the American Dream to a proportion of its citizens because in the United States—far more so than in other technologically developed societies—the capitalist economy has a lopsided dominance over all other major social institutions. This dominance of the economic realm in the institutional balance of power occurs in three interrelated ways.

First, *noneconomic institutional functions and roles are devalued.* Education, for example, tends to be seen not as end in itself but as a route to a well-paying job. Also, the chief tasks of families, such as parenting and nurturing, are not highly valued. Thus, homemakers do not have a high status; however, because of the fetish with material success, homeowners do, and, we might add, they are even rewarded with tax breaks by the government.

Second, *other social institutions are forced to accommodate to economic requirements.* For example, whereas societies such as Japan and some western European countries are strongly committed to family welfare, family life in the United States is dominated by the schedules and rewards of the labor market. Moreover, both schools and government depend heavily on private financial support.

Third, *economic norms penetrate most other institutional areas.* Thus "husbands and wives are 'partners' who 'manage' the household 'division of labor' in accordance with the 'marriage contract'" (p. 76). Schools are increasingly forced to be "accountable" to taxpayers, and students are sometimes described as "products" or even as "raw material" for the labor market.

Messner and Rosenfeld argue that the culture and the institutional structure of the United States—its social organization, in other words—lead directly to high levels of crime (see Figure 14.4 below). Crucially, the anomic forces in U.S. society that encourage crime are not opposed by the forces of social control that are meant to be nurtured by noneconomic institutions such as families and schools. Precisely because the power of capitalist economic values has devalued the prosocial messages of these noneconomic institutions, the latter are relatively powerless to create the sort of cooperative community that opposes crime. Hence, anomie is exacerbated and a vicious cycle occurs. According to Messner and Rosenfeld, the resultant generalized anomie helps explain not only the high rate of predatory crime in the United States but also white-collar and corporate crimes (and see Passas, 1990), as well as the pervasive inclination in the United States to own guns and to use them in illegal ways.

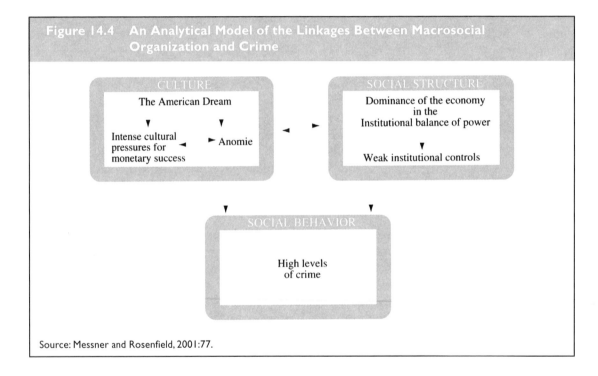

**Figure 14.4    An Analytical Model of the Linkages Between Macrosocial Organization and Crime**

Source: Messner and Rosenfield, 2001:77.

## Evaluation of Institutional Anomie Theory

Messner and Rosenfeld's account of the links among anomie, the decay of major social institutions, and the growth of crime in the United States in the 1990s and early 2000s has striking similarities to Durkheim's account of the same phenomena in France one hundred years earlier (see Chapter 10.2). Moreover, like Durkheim, Messner and Rosenfeld have responded to this crisis by searching for the causes of social order, and like Durkheim, they lament the rise of egoism, the decline of community, and the loss of faith in, or the lack of influence of, certain social institutions such as the family and the school. Messner and Rosenfeld's analysis is also similar to those conflict and Marxist explanations of crime that focus on the distorting effects on social life of the dominance of capitalist relations of production (see Chapter 10.3, 13.3, 13.4).

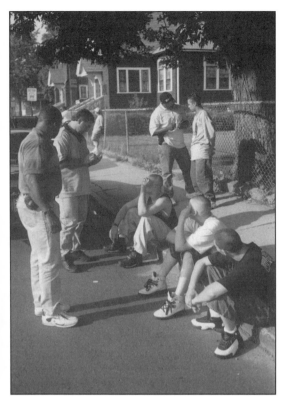

*The breakdown of social structures, particularly noneconomic ones, as a result of increasing emphasis on individualistic economic power has left upcoming generations with little community sentiment and few incentives to not break the law.*

Messner and Rosenfeld's solution to the problem of crime entails two broad movements for social change. In combination, these movements—one institutional, the other cultural—would amount to a radical restructuring of American society. The first is the rebalancing of the major social institutions so that the economy is no longer dominant—with the effect that the polity, the family, the school, and the system of social stratification are all democratized and given an egalitarian thrust. This is not a novel proposal, although it is an important one.

The second movement entails what Messner and Rosenfeld term "cultural regeneration"—a proposal that is, regrettably, found only rarely in contemporary criminology. Cultural regeneration involves a radical reappraisal of the American Dream. In order to reduce strain, money and material possessions must no longer serve as the chief gauges of social worth. Parenting, "spousing," teaching, learning, and serving the community must become meaningful ends in themselves. Moreover, Messner and Rosenfeld warn that such a society will have to develop a "cultural receptivity to restraints" (p. 109). By this they mean that significantly lower levels of crime are unlikely to occur unless we become less obsessed with individual rights, interests, and privileges and more concerned with collective obligations and mutual support.

## 14.4 Critical Criminologies

Critical criminology developed from the radical and feminist criminology of the 1970s and 1980s. It is an umbrella term for numerous perspectives that have emerged in the mid- to late 1980s and throughout the 1990s. Although these perspectives differ in significant ways—which we outline below—critical criminologies are similar in the sense that they uniformly question the following (MacLean and Milovanovic, 1998):

- The usage of the legalistic definition of crime—dominant conceptions of the "violent" offender that exclude many other agents of social injuries.

- Prevailing usages of linear, nondialectical notions of "causation."

- "Correctional" penal policy.

- The increasing investment of energy in more punitive responses to crime.

- The limited attention paid to political economy in the contribution to crime.

- The targeting of selected groups, informally or formally, for official police intervention.

- The resistance to entertaining (i.e., examining) gross inequalities in living standards, alienating working conditions, and dilapidated communities.

- The continued and often systematic practices of sexism, racism, and classism (and their intersecting effects) often disguised as neutral and objective or factual categories.

Critical criminologists are committed to theory construction that provides better conceptual tools for understanding "what is" and "what can be" and, in this way, contributes to the quest for positive social change and social justice. In this section we briefly summarize four critical criminologies: left realism, peacemaking criminology, postmodernism, and feminism.

## Left Realism

As we discussed more thoroughly in Chapter 3.1, conventional crime is predominantly an intraclass phenomenon. The conventional offender and victim are drawn from those classes—lower and working classes—that radical criminologists (see Chapter 13.4) tend to represent in their theorizing. In the mid-1980s, several radical criminologists attempted to develop a more coherent explanation of conventional crime than that offered by Marxist theory. In so doing, they advanced a critique of what they termed **left idealism.** According to this critique, left idealists argue that absolute economic deprivation (unemployment) drives people into crime and that the conventional criminal is somewhat of a rebel (Lea and Young, 1984). Indeed, some early radical criminologists of the 1970s (such as Quinney, discussed in Chapter 13.4; and see Greenberg, 1981), not only depicted the conventional criminal as a rebel but also argued that the criminal class, rather than the working class, was the vanguard of the revolution.

In his critique of left idealism, Jock Young (1986) added that for the left idealist, the conventional criminal sees through the inequitable nature of present-day society, and crime itself, in an attempt—however clumsy and ill-thought-out—to redress this balance. From this perspective, there is little need to have complex explanations for working-class crime; its causes are obvious. To blame the poor for their criminality is to blame the victim and to point moral accusations at those whose very actions are a result of their being social casualties. The real crime on which we should focus is that of the ruling class: the police, the corporations, and the state agencies. The ruling class causes real problems for the mass of people, whereas working-class crime is minor, involving petty theft and occasional violence and having little impact on working-class communities. To this portrayal of left idealism, Lea and Young (1986) added that left idealists provide no realistic solutions for crime, other than emphasizing "changing the social order."

According to this critique, left idealists adhere to a romantic image of the conventional criminal, make no attempt to understand the complex nature of conventional working-class crime, focus almost exclusively on the harms of the "ruling class," and ignore the development of a coherent program for curbing conventional crime.

Consequently, in the 1980s, left realists proposed the following as their program of **left realism**. First, conventional crime is a real problem for the working class. Rather than viewing crime as the result of absolute deprivation and as a form of rebellion, left realists argued that conventional crime is driven by relative deprivation as well as by reactionary, selfish, and individualistic attitudes (Lea and Young, 1984, 1986). Moreover, conventional crime has a disorganizing effect, pitting the poor against the poor. Rather than helping create a politically conscious community, conventional crime hinders working-class solidarity and thus "the ability to fight back" (1986:359). As Matthews (1987) put it, crime is not a heralded revolt but "tends to extend the fragmentation of urban life, mimic individualistic and acquisitive values, and limits public space and social and political participation" (p. 373). Because of this disorganizing effect, left realists argued that conventional crime must be examined seriously by radical criminologists.

Besides rejecting the Robin Hood image of the criminal and espousing the need for thoughtful empirical investigations of conventional crime, left realists also argue that crime control must be taken seriously. Rather than ignoring the conventional crime problem—as left idealists allegedly do—left realists argue for a concrete crime control program. Such a program first requires an honest assessment of the state, an assessment that, according to left realists, is lacking in left idealism. For left idealists, "the state is the direct instrument of the ruling class" and its ideological and repressive institutions "exist in order to maintain capitalism" (Lea and Young, 1984:101–102). Thus, left idealists argue that reform in such a state is impossible and will most likely backfire, turning against the working class. Left realists maintain that the state "represents very largely ruling-class interests," but they argue nonetheless that gains can in fact be "wrung out of it; reforms, however difficult to achieve, are possible and, in fact, relate to the state as in essence a site of contradictory interests" (p. 103). Therefore, the possibility of a concrete crime program does in fact present itself.

Certain elements of this program were outlined by Lea and Young (1986). First, they argue for *demarginalization*. Lea and Young propose that instead of marginalizing offenders in prison, we use such measures as community service orders, victim restitution schemes, and widespread decarceration. Second, they advocate *preemptive deterrence* (deterring crime before it is committed) through citizen groups who cooperate with the police, as well as through evening youth patrols such as the Guardian Angels. Third, Lea and Young argue for minimal use of prisons. They suggest that prisons, and thus custodial sentences, be used only in cases of extreme danger to the community. Fourth, they suggest that criminologists must look realistically at the circumstances of both offender and victim. Fifth, they argue that criminologists must be realistic about policing: The "police force" must be transformed into a "police service" accountable to the public. Finally, Lea and Young propose that criminologists must be realistic about the problem of crime in the present period. Because the degree of relative deprivation has risen continually, a situation of considerable discontent exists. Yet, concurrent with this rise of deprivation and discontent, no increase has occurred in working-class politics. The door is thus open for a criminal—rather than a political—response in working-class communities. Lea and Young advocate pursuing "alternative politics that harness the energies of the marginalized," helping create a "politics of crime control" that is part of other grass roots movements, and combating "the tendency of a divided and disillusioned public to move to the right" (p. 363).

In more recent work, left realists have argued that contemporary left idealism differs in form from the left idealism of the 1970s and early 1980s, which is not to say that it is any more palatable to the left realists. According to Jock Young (1997), current left idealists emphasize the biased nature of the criminal justice system, which is seen as more of a problem than crime itself. When left idealists do discuss crime, Young asserts, it is seen simplistically as the result of poverty and/or the "war" on drugs. Moreover, Young contends that left idealists see the increased use of incarceration not as the result of crime but as the result of "a moral panic about crime, created by conservative politicians, law enforcement agencies, and the mass media. . . . The public are lambasted by these writers as if they were cultural dupes whose attitudes and opinions are a product of watching too much TV" (p. 478). Thus, according to Young, current left idealists fail to "take crime seriously."

Young also extends the left realist position that the "potent" cause of crime is relative, as opposed to absolute, deprivation:

> Realist criminology points to relative deprivation in certain conditions as being the major cause of crime. That is, when people experience a level of unfairness in their allocation of resources and utilize individualistic means to attempt to right this condition, it is a reaction to the experience of injustice. One such individualistic response is "every man for himself," which is particularly prevalent in the U.S. Not surprisingly, the U.S. has the highest crime rate among advanced industrialized societies. (p. 488)

Moreover, Young (1999) argues that Western industrialized societies are "exclusive societies" in which large pockets of people are excluded from legitimate employment and the major institutions in their respective societies. Because the resulting combination of individualism and relative deprivation leads to much crime and violence in exclusive societies, left realists suggest the following policies to curb crime (Dekeseredy, 2003):

- Job creation and training programs, including publicly supported, community-oriented job creation.

- Higher minimum wage level.

- Government-sponsored day care so that poor single parents can work without the bulk of their paychecks going to pay for childcare; some unemployed single parents today do not look for work because they cannot afford child care.

- Housing assistance, which not only helps the poor but also enables abused women and children to escape their environments without ending up destitute and on the streets.

- Introduction of entrepreneurial skills into the high-school curriculum.

- Creation of links among schools, private business, and government agencies.

- Universal health care.

## Peacemaking Criminology

One of the distinctive products of the leftist concern with realism is a renewed attempt to humanize the institutions of criminal justice. This attempt is known as **peacemaking criminology,** an eclectic theoretical basis that lies in a loose mixture of religious humanism and feminism. This combination is most visible in Harold Pepinsky and Richard Quinney's edited book *Criminology as Peacemaking* (1991). At the beginning of their book, Pepinsky and Quinney declare:

> The peacemaking perspective is steadily making its way into criminology. In recent years there have been proposals and programs that foster mediation, conflict resolution, reconciliation, and community. They are part of an emerging criminology of peacemaking, a criminology that seeks to alleviate suffering and thereby reduce crime. This is a criminology that is based necessarily on human transformation in the achievement of peace and justice. (p. ix)

The various authors of the 20 chapters in this anthology address a wide variety of practical issues that converge on the need to use more humane and more caring approaches to the problem of crime. Although all the authors seem to agree with other critical criminologists that it is economic, political, and social inequalities that foster crime, the emphasis here is less on the causes of crime than on how to resolve the conflicts of which crime is an expression. The key policies of peacemaking criminology thus involve such terms as "responsiveness," "reconciliation," "conflict resolution," "harmony," and "community."

Some critical criminologists have expanded the peacemaking perspective. For example, Susan Caulfield and Angela Evans (1997) have argued that at its core "peacemaking has a reverence for life, for the connectedness of all beings" (p. 103). To help reduce human suffering, including the suffering that results from crime, Caulfield and Evans call for the criminal justice system to address the "essence," rather than the "appearance," of being human:

> Much of criminology and criminal justice focuses on the appearance of a human being: what they did, ascriptive characteristics, and the like. Rarely is there concern with understanding the essence of a person: how they feel, what they fear, how they see themselves in reference to the universe. We surmise, as do others, that this avoidance of one's essence is a part of self-defense or self-denial on the part of both individuals and criminal justice. . . . Knowing only the appearance, rather than the essence of harm, how can criminal justice keep from being fragmented and in search of some form of control, no matter how illusory? (p. 105)

According to Caulfield and Evans, peacemaking criminology, through an emphasis on cooperation, compassion, and respect for all species, allows for the examination of the essence rather than the appearance. Such an ideology, they argue, will move U.S. society toward peace and justice for all.

Similarly, Hal Pepinsky (1997) has argued that peacemaking criminology allows for the construction of a "compassionate discourse" that will "heal rifts in the social fabric" and weave all societal members "back into accepted, responsible, safe social relations, rather than identifying, condemning, punishing, and separating offenders from the community" (p. 109).

Richard Quinney (1997) has maintained that current responses to crime by the criminal justice system are a form of "negative peace." That is, the purpose of the criminal justice system is to deter or process acts of crime through the threat and application of force. Thus the criminal justice system's response to crime is a form of violence in itself, which subsequently begets further violence. Quinney therefore views peacemaking criminology as part of the movement toward "positive peace," which exists when the sources of crime—such as poverty, inequality, racism, and alienation—are no longer present. As Quinney concludes:

> There can be no peace—no positive peace—without social justice. Without social justice and without peace (personal and social), there is crime. And there is, as well, the violence of criminal justice. . . . Criminal justice keeps things as they are. Social policies and programs that are positive in nature—that focus on positive peacemaking—create something new. They eliminate the structural sources of violence and crime. A critical, peacemaking criminologist is engaged in the work of positive peace. (p. 117)

John Fuller (1998, 2003) has developed what he terms a "Peacemaking Pyramid Paradigm" as a first step toward a more coherent theory. This pyramid involves six stages that should be considered when constructing solutions to criminal justice system problems:

1. *Nonviolence.* Peacemaking criminology argues against state violence as a criminal justice policy, such as use of the death penalty.

2. *Social justice.* Peacemaking criminology opposes any form of racism, sexism, and classism in the criminal justice system, such as racial profiling.

3. *Inclusion.* The criminal justice system must be all-inclusive of community members, such as allowing a voice by family members of victims and offenders as well as other interested individuals from affected neighborhoods.

4. *Correct means.* It should be ensured that offenders and victims are not coerced into settlement of their cases—due process must be preserved.

5. *Ascertainable criteria.* It should be ensured that all parties involved in criminal justice proceedings understand the procedures, including clearly written legal guidelines.

6. *Categorical imperative.* Responses to crime should reflect a philosophy of nonviolence and social justice that is extended throughout the criminal justice system. All involved in the criminal justice process must be treated with respect and dignity.

## Postmodernism

At its most abstract level, **postmodernism** is a reaction to the scientific rationalism and positivist certainty of the Enlightenment. It rejects scientific notions of "cause" just as it rejects the idea that "crime" is a simple or fixed category. Henry and Einstadter (1998) summarize some of the common themes associated with postmodernism:

For postmodernists there are no eternal truths; indeed, any truth claims are subject to challenge and deconstruction. The emphasis is on what postmodernists term alternative discourse and meaning. Positivism is rejected in favor of subjectivistic accounts. There is no such thing as certainty, rather uncertainty is the order of the day. In its extreme form, no explanation of a phenomenon is superior to any other, a belief which, in the view of some, leads to nihilism. (p. 417)

Henry and Einstadter argue that postmodernist criminologists likewise challenge traditional (modernist) criminological "truths" yet must simultaneously reconstruct criminological discourse "along lines seen to better reflect the human condition, but always subject to change" (p. 417). Thus, postmodern criminologists argue for a "replacement discourse," or a method of "talking about crime, harm, and social justice that invests energy in displacing the negative discourse which feeds structures of oppression" (p. 417).

Bruce Arrigo (2003) has outlined a primer on postmodern criminological theory. He argues that three key issues principally inform postmodern thought in criminology:

1. *The centrality of language.* Written and spoken language shapes reality because it is the "source and product" of our social actions. Words define who we are, our interaction with others, and the institutions of society in which we participate. Language is not neutral but contains implicit values and hidden assumptions.

2. *Partial knowledge and provisional truth.* Because language structures thought and action in ways that are not neutral, the meanings of daily life are limited by the language in use. Inevitably, certain forms of understanding are devalued and what is regarded as meaningful is always already incomplete. Thus, "truth" and "knowledge" are at best partial and provisional.

3. *Deconstruction, difference, and possibility.* As language filters the way people think, feel, and act in partial and provisional ways, there exists a degree of "undeniable relativity" to being human. Deconstruction is a postmodern method used to decode a written or spoken text and thereby unveil the implicit values and hidden assumptions embedded in particular narratives. Deconstruction reveals the privileging in certain contexts of particular "truth claims" and how others are dismissed or ignored. Postmodernists attempt to embrace articulated differences by highlighting all voices involved in any social interaction.

The most thoroughgoing postmodernist position in criminology is **constitutive criminology,** an avowedly political position that seeks to get behind or to lay bare the rhetoric, the dogma, and the mystification that goes into the public discourse about crime. In other words, constitutive criminology examines how crime is constituted by public discourse. The chief authors of constitutive criminology are Stuart Henry and Dragan Milovanovic (1991, 1994, 1996, 2003). For present purposes, we can strip away the complex philosophical and linguistic wrappings of their labors and reduce constitutive criminology to three major propositions.

First, crime is not simply what the criminal law says it is. Rather, crime is the ability or the power to impose one's will on others in any particular social context: Crimes "are nothing less than moments in the expression of power, such that those who are subjected to them are denied . . . their own humanity, the power to make a difference" (1996:116). Henry and Milovanovic thus redefine crime "in terms of the power to create harm (pain) in any context" (p. 118). This redefinition of crime identifies two major forms of harm: "harms of reduction," which occur "when an offended party experiences a loss of some quality relative to their present standing," and "harms of repression," which occur "when an offended party experiences a limit or restriction preventing them from achieving a desired position or standing" (p. 103).

Second, Henry and Milovanovic reject modernist notions of causality, arguing that crime is "discursively constructed through human processes" in which "people lose sight of the humanity and integrity of those with whom they interrelate and whom their actions and interactions affect" (pp. 170, 175). The "psycho-socio-cultural matrix" provides the "discursive medium" through which individuals construct "meaningful harms to others" (p. x). In short, some individuals become "excessive investors" in the expression of power and control, resulting in "thought processes which objectify others as separate, dehumanized entities" (p. 175).

Finally, Henry and Milovanovic construct a policy for curbing crime. They argue that any human relationship that involves the actual or potential infliction of harm must be analyzed carefully in its discursive context, exposed, and restructured in nonharmful ways. Thus, their policy includes the development of alternative "replacement discourses" (primarily in the mass media) as well as "narrative therapies" in which excessive investors are assisted in developing "liberating life narratives" (p. 224).

Constitutive criminology, then, is an attempt to go beyond "modernism" and "skeptical postmodernism" by developing an "affirmative postmodern" approach to the study of crime and its control.

## Feminism

Contemporary contributions to criminology by **feminism** can be divided into two phases, the first extending from the 1970s and into much of the 1980s (see Chapter 13.4), and the second extending from the late 1980s to the present. In the first phase, feminist criminologists concentrated on criticizing criminological theory either for being gender-blind or for misrepresenting women. In addition, feminist criminologists conducted investigations of women's experiences as offenders, victims, and workers in the criminal justice system and used popular feminist theories of the time—liberal, radical, Marxist, and socialist—to explain women's (and men's) involvement in crime.

In the second phase of feminist contributions to criminology, two specific directions of theorizing about women and crime have occurred (Daly and Maher, 1998). These two directions involve (1) the examination of how women are constructed in and by particular discourses such as the law and (2) the exploration of women's actual lives and how their specific problems and responses to these problems influence involvement in crime. Daly and Maher contrast these two directions in feminist theorizing in the following way: The first "often characterizes women as effects of discourse" and the second "tends to characterize women as subjects of their own lives" (p. 4).

The work of Carol Smart (1998) is an example of what it means to examine the effects of discourse (language and symbolic representation) on women. Smart argues that the law can be understood as a discourse that produces gender identities. In particular, Smart shows that the law constructs both different "types of Woman" and "Woman as distinct from Man." Smart uses the example of the prostitute to explain this distinction more fully: "In legal discourse the prostitute is constructed as the bad woman, but at the same time she epitomizes Woman in contradistinction to Man because she is what any woman could be and because she represents a deviousness and a licentiousness arising from her (supposedly naturally given) bodily form, while the Man remains innocuous" (p. 28).

Smart also examines how legal discourse constructs the "bad mother." Taking us back to seventeenth-century England, Smart points to an Act of 1623 that made it unlawful for a mother to kill her bastard infant. With the introduction of this new law, the burden of proving innocence was placed on the mother alone. Then in 1803 the first statute on abortion was enacted in Britain, criminalizing abortion at any stage of pregnancy. In 1882 the age of consent was raised to 13 and in 1885 to 16, thus exposing young women who became pregnant—yet who were too young to marry—to legal control; and in 1913 the Mental Deficiency Act resulted in the incarceration of unmarried mothers on grounds of moral imbecility or feeble-mindedness. According to Smart, this set of laws established a type of woman (the bad mother) as well as Woman distinct from Man because motherhood was constructed as "natural":

> Means of avoiding motherhood were denied to women, and the inevitability of the link between sex and reproduction was established through the harsh repression of those deploying traditional means of rupturing this link. We see the rise of compulsory motherhood for any woman who was heterosexually active. The "bad mother" reinforced notions of proper motherhood and, therefore, is constructed by legal discourse as a type of woman. Yet simultaneously this legal discourse establishes the "bad mother" as Woman because "she invokes the proper place of Man." She is the problem (supposedly) because she does not have a man. (p. 30)

In contrast to Smart's postmodern feminism, the work of Meda Chesney-Lind explores women as subjects of their own lives. For example, in a study of gang members in Hawaii, she examined the personal and familial characteristics, self-reported delinquency, and the gang activities of both boys and girls (Joe and Chesney-Lind, 1998). The evidence (based on interviews) reveals significant differences between boy and girl gang members. Although both boys and girls came from high-crime and economically depressed neighborhoods, 75 percent of the girls (as opposed to 55 percent of the boys) reported being victims of parental physical and/or sexual abuse. Thus, although the gang provides a surrogate family role to most youth who join, this is especially so for girls who have been victimized by a family member. In other words, the reasons for joining a gang are not the same for girls and boys: Girls are more likely to be runaways from physical and sexual victimization at home who eventually approach a gang for solace as an alternative family. Chesney-Lind (1995, 1997) concludes that to understand female crime, it is important to focus on the "real" lives of women and girls and on how their real-life specific problems—based on gender, race, and class inequalities—and their response to these problems are related to eventual delinquent and criminal behavior.

Obviously, this focus is quite different than Smart's focus on women as the effects of discourse.

In the early 1990s, feminist scholars began to examine the relationship between masculinities and crime. Since then, numerous works have been published, from individually authored books (Messerschmidt, 1993, 1997, 2000, 2004; Polk, 1994; Collier, 1998; Winlow, 2001) to edited volumes (Newburn and Stanko, 1994; Bowker, 1998) to special academic-journal issues (Carlen and Jefferson, 1996). Like the work on girls and women by feminist criminologists, the examination of masculinities and crime has developed in two similar directions: men as effects of discourse and men as subjects of their own lives.

An example of the former is the work of Richard Collier's *Masculinities, Crime, and Criminology* (1998). The bulk of this book describes the ways in which various types of men—lawyers, criminologists, youth offenders, mass murderers, and fathers—have been constructed by discourse. As an example, Collier explores the discursive production of the "dangerous" male child in contemporary Britain. In particular, he focuses on how adolescent male offenders have been produced through discourse. Collier discusses the "rat boy" media discourse that emerged in Britain in the early 1990s because of growing concern over "what to do" with persistent adolescent male offenders. Rat boys would engage in "crime sprees" and then "hide in the maze of ventilation shafts, tunnels, and roof spaces . . . while trying to evade capture by the police"—hence, the name "rat boy." Various media discourses characterized these working-class boys as "monsters," "animals," "vermin," and "as beyond the social, outside society, as venal" (p. 91). According to Collier, what emerged through this characterization was an offending adolescent male who is simultaneously masculine "like other boys and yet, also appeared as other, as less than human, as *different* from other boys" (p. 91).

An example of exploring men as subjects of their own lives is the book *Crime as Structured Action* (1997) by James Messerschmidt. Here, Messerschmidt explores the relationship among masculinities as they are constructed by men differentiated through race, class, time, and social situation. As one example, Messerschmidt examines the changes in Malcolm X's masculine identity within a range of race and class contexts: a childhood in which he constantly battled for acceptance as a young man; a zoot-suit culture that embraced him without stigma as a "hipster" and "hustler"; and a spiritual and political movement that celebrated him as father, husband, and national spokesperson. Across these sites and through shifting currencies of his sense of masculine, race, and class identity, Malcolm X moved in and out of crime. Malcolm X simply appropriated crime as a resource for "doing masculinity" at a specific moment in his life, a period when gender, race, and class relations were equally significant. Thus, Messerschmidt provides information about why Malcolm X "chose" crime at a certain stage of his life and how that engagement relates to his gender, race, and class position in society.

As with feminist theorizing on women and crime, then, current efforts to theorize men and crime maintain two tendencies: Postmodern work investigates how men and boys are constructed by discourse, whereas other efforts explore men as active agents who construct masculinities and crime in particular social contexts.

Although the social construction of masculinities has now come under careful criminological scrutiny, in approaching the relationship between masculinities and crime, criminologists have concentrated on men and boys and ignored women and girls. Concentrating exclusively on men and boys neglects the fact that women and girls occasionally engage in masculine practices and crime. Given that masculinities and femininities are not determined biologically, it certainly makes sense to identify and examine possible masculinities by women and girls, and femininities by men and boys, and their relation to crime. Jody Miller (2001, 2002) has begun to do this in her important book *One of the Guys,* in which she shows that certain gang girls identify with the boys in their gangs and describe such gangs as "masculinist enterprises." These girls differentiate themselves from other gang girls by engaging in "gender crossing" and "embracing a *masculine* identity that they view as contradicting their bodily sex category (that is, female)" (Miller, 2002:443). Similarly, Messerschmidt's (2004) recent life-history study of adolescent assaultive violence—reported in his book *Flesh and Blood*—discovered numerous gender constructions by violent girls and found that some girls "do" masculinity by in part displaying themselves in a masculine way, engaging primarily in what they and others in their milieu consider to be authentically masculine behavior, and outright rejecting most aspects of femininity.

## Evaluation of Critical Criminology

In this section we have outlined the four chief perspectives of critical criminology: left realism, peacemaking, postmodernism, and feminism. These perspectives arose during the 1980s and 1990s and continue to flourish today. Each differs from the other three in its focus, method, and concepts, although overlap does occur—i.e., postmodernist feminism. Nevertheless, all four are united by their leftist and oppositional stance to many of society's master institutions and social inequalities.

This combination of diversity in perspective and leftist politics also lies at the heart of several other tendencies in critical criminology, which are either less widely supported or still in the process of emerging:

- **Abolitionism.** This perspective focuses on the oppressive and faulty logic of incarceration as a solution to the problem of crime. Here, prison and many other institutions of social control are typically seen not as a solution but as key parts of the problem (Bianchi and Van Swaaningen, 1986; de Haan, 1990; Hudson, 1997).

- **Anarchism.** This approach focuses on the state, its agencies and institutions, as the primary source of most social ills, including crime (Pepinsky, 1978; Tifft and Sullivan, 1980; Ferrell, 1997). Particular objects of attack include the machinery of prisons, police, courts, judges and lawyers.

- **Cultural criminology.** Often using ethnographic methodology, this perspective explores the political relationship between the constructions of meaning and the criminalization process (Ferrell and Sanders, 1995; Ferrell and Websdale, 1999; Ferrell, 2004). It has been used to examine the meaning and imagery of such diverse practices as base jumping, anti-abortion violence, media constructions of gender, drug dealing, and graffiti.

- **Convict criminology.** Most of this perspective's adherents are ex-cons who have become sociologists and criminologists (Ross and Richards, 2003). Its starting point is the horrendous size of the prison system in the United States and the misery that goes with it. Its humanist and ameliorative promise is to "tell it like it is" from the inside in ways that are not available to those who have never been incarcerated.

* **Green criminology.** The focus of this activist work-in-progress is the study of the crimes, harms, and abuses committed by humans against the environment, against nature, and against animals other than humans (Lynch and Stretsky, 2003; South and Beirne, 2005).

Let us now return to our assessment of left realism, peacemaking, postmodernism, and feminism.

The left-realist emphasis on taking street crime seriously and constructing anti-crime policy is an important contribution to criminology in general and critical criminology in particular. Nevertheless, some criminologists have criticized left realists for remaining unidimensional; that is, their concentration on "relative deprivation" is linked solely to social class, excluding any conceptualization of how gender and race might affect street crime. For example, given the fact that men perpetrate more street crimes and the more serious of these crimes than women, the logic of left realism requires that we conclude that men experience more relative deprivation than women. Thus, as Sandra Walklate (1998) has argued, left realists fail to explore how gender, race, and class interconnect and how this interconnection constructs crime differently. Recent writings by left realists have now attempted to overcome this criticism (see Young, 1999; DeKeseredy, 2003).

Peacemaking criminology sensitizes the discipline to the importance of humanistic approaches to crime and criminal justice. It emphasizes more humane and more caring approaches to the criminal justice system. Nevertheless, although laudable in its ideology, peacemaking criminology as yet offers no blueprint for achieving a humanistic criminal justice system. In other words, how does society move from a criminal justice system based on repression to one that concentrates on cooperation, compassion, and respect for all species? How do we actually move toward a "Peacemaking Pyramid"? One response to these questions has neatly been given by Kieran McEvoy (2003), who combines peacemaking criminology with a practical concern for human rights in attempting to reduce paramilitary violence in Northern Ireland.

Both constitutive criminology and postmodern feminist criminology pose a challenge to "modernist" criminology, especially to the concentration of conventional criminology on the "scientific" study of crime and social control. However, important questions remain about the writings of constitutive and postmodernist criminologists: Have they simply replaced a modernist truth with a postmodernist truth? For example, from a postmodernist position, constitutive criminology is simply a discourse in itself that (possibly unintentionally) declares that it frames the "true" picture of crime.

Finally, given the failure of criminology to theorize the best predictor of crime— "maleness"—current work on masculinities and crime is a welcome corrective to this past neglect. Indeed, this work has been located by criminologists "at the edge of criminological theorizing and empirical investigation" (Walklate, 1998:87) and is characterized as having "enormous intuitive appeal" (Cullen and Agnew, 1999:365). Nevertheless, this work is not without its critics. For example, Cullen and Agnew have criticized such efforts for maintaining a narrow definition of masculinity and for not easily explaining conformity among disadvantaged men.

## Review

In this chapter we have introduced a variety of criminological theories that have been developed in the last decade. Each will no doubt be developed further in the next decade. Several of these theories embody a movement toward general and integrated theory, yet they are remarkably diverse in their basic assumptions about human sociality and the causes of crime.

### Routine Activities and Crime

1. Crime should be understood in terms of the conjunction of the triangular relationships among likely offenders, suitable targets, and capable guardians.

2. Changes in crime rates are determined by fundamental changes of everyday patterns of life. These routine activities may occur in or outside households. Examples of routine activities include commuting to work and events associated with providing and acquiring food and shelter, sexual outlets, leisure, learning, and childrearing.

3. Despite its commonsense appeal, the theory offers no formal criteria about which routine activities are relevant to understanding crime. It also ignores the broader sociological context in which criminogenic situations occur.

### Self-Control and Control Balance

1. Gottfredson and Hirschi's theory of self-control suggests that individual differences in criminal behavior are the results of differences in "self-control." Low self-control coupled with opportunity increases an individual's propensity to commit crime, especially crimes involving force or fraud.

2. The major cause of low self-control is ineffective childrearing. The characteristics of self-control can be derived from the nature of crime itself, of which Gottfredson and Hirschi outline five chief aspects.

3. Empirical tests of self-control theory have had mixed results, with some critics characterizing its core proposition as a tautology.

4. The main premise of Tittle's theory of control balance is that the amount of control to which an individual is subject relative to the amount of control he or she can exercise determines the probability and type of deviance. The theory identifies six types of deviance: predation, exploitation, defiance, plunder, decadence, and submission.

5. Individuals are in control balance if the amount of control they exercise is the same as the amount of control they experience. If one controls more than one experiences control, then one has a control surplus. If one experiences control

more than one controls, then one has a control deficit. Individuals with a control balance tend to conform. Those who have more control and those who have less control both tend to engage in more deviance.

6. Some modifications to Tittle's theory have been proposed, including simplifying it into a theory of predatory deviance.

## Revised Strain Theory

1. Whereas Merton's strain theory focused on the ways in which an individual is barred from achieving conventional goals, Agnew expands strain theory to include the analysis of relationships in which others present the individual with noxious or negative stimuli.

2. Agnew's social-psychological theory pinpoints three chief sorts of strain: failure to achieve positively valued goals; the removal of positively valued stimuli from the individual; and the presentation of negative stimuli. Agnew has said that at heart his theory is very simple: "If we treat people badly, they may get mad and engage in crime."

3. In his analysis of animal abuse, Agnew admits the relevance of numerous other factors, both sociological and psychological. These include an individual's social position; psychological traits, such as empathy; level of stress and strain; socialization; social control; and the nature of the animal under consideration.

4. Despite the narrow demographic makeup of the populations that have been used to test it so far, Agnew's theory has gained some preliminary empirical support.

5. Messner and Rosenfeld's institutional anomie theory extends Merton's theory at the macro level. They argue that the American Dream in unachievable for some because of the lopsided dominance of the capitalist economy in the institutional balance of power.

6. This dominance of the economic realm occurs in three ways: noneconomic institutional functions and roles are devalued; other social institutions are forced to accommodate to economic requirements; and economic norms penetrate most other institutional areas. In combination, and in the absence of social control and cultural counterweights, this leads to high crime rates.

7. Messner and Rosenfeld's radical solution to the problem of crime in the United States involves both a rebalancing of the major social institutions and cultural regeneration.

## Critical Criminologies

1. Since the mid-1980s, some radical criminologists have developed a left-realist approach to crime. They argue that crime and its control must be taken seriously and have developed a program for curbing conventional crime.

2. Peacemaking criminologists attempt to humanize the institutions of criminal justice by emphasizing cooperation, compassion, and community rather than punishment, condemnation, and separation.

3. Constitutive criminology, a type of postmodernism, challenges modernist criminology in its definition of crime, in its arguments on causation, and in its policies
for curbing crime. Other forms of critical criminology include anarchism, abolitionism, convict criminology, cultural criminology, and green criminology.

4. In the second phase of feminist contributions to criminology, two specific directions of theorizing have occurred: the exploration of women's and men's actual
lives and an examination of how women and men are constructed in and by discourse. In addition, feminist criminologists have begun to examine the variable
relationship among masculinities, femininities, men, women, and crime.

## Questions for Class Discussion

1. In *Crime and Everyday Life,* Marcus Felson (2002) pinpoints the high risk of campus parking areas to property and violent victimization. Identify the assumptions
about social interaction and routine activities that he makes in recommending
each of the following designs for safer college campuses:
   - Arrange for night-time students and workers to have parking near
   building doors, but not so close that they block the view of the parking
   area from the building.
   - At low-use times, close off unneeded parking areas or sections of large
   parking areas to concentrate cars and people for supervision.
   - Require students and staff to sign up by name and have a sticker, even
   for nighttime or free areas.
   - Get visitors in cars to sign in and give them time limits.
   - Fence parking areas.
   - Eliminate nooks and corners in parking structures.
   - Build parking structures on slopes so people on foot will have clear
   sight lines.
   - Make parking structure stairwells easy to see into.
   - Orient buildings to face parking areas.
   - Trim hedges and the lower limbs of trees around parking areas, and
   avoid thick foliage.
   - Post signs and organize the flow of traffic so neither cars nor pedestri-
   ans will get lost.

2. Is suicide evidence of low self-control? Of high self-control?

3. Does the American Dream contribute to high crime rates?

4. Is a "Peacemaking Pyramid" actually possible in Western industrialized societies? Explain.

5. Discuss possible masculinities by women and femininities by men that may be
related to crime.

## For Further Study

### Readings

Messerschmidt, James W. 2004. *Flesh & Blood: Adolescent Gender Diversity and Violence.* Lanham, MD: Rowman & Littlefield.

Miller, Jody. 2001. *One of the Guys: Girls, Gangs, and Gender.* New York: Oxford University Press.

Schwartz, Martin D., and Suzanne E. Hatty, eds. 2003. *Controversies in Critical Criminology.* Cincinnati, OH: Anderson Publishing.

Short, James F. Jr., Joachim J. Savelsberg, Gary F. Jensen, and Charles R. Tittle. 1999. Symposium on Control Balance: Toward a General Theory of Deviance. *Theoretical Criminology* 3 (3): 327–352.

Tittle, Charles R. 1995. *Control Balance: Toward a General Theory of Deviance.* Boulder, CO: Westview Press.

### Websites

1. <http://www.ncjrs.org/works>: This is a Congressionally mandated report from the University of Maryland titled *Preventing Crime: What Works, What Doesn't, and What's Promising.* It is a good example of the relationship between theory and policy, especially rational choice and modern strain theories of crime.

2. <http://www.critcrim.org>: This is the Critical Criminology Homepage of the American Society of Criminology; it has links to a wide variety of data, current statistics, legal writings, and political resources.

3. <http://www.albany.edu/scj/jcjpc>: This is an electronic journal, the *Journal of Criminal Justice and Popular Culture.* When readers select the link to volume 3, they will find an article outlining cultural criminological theory. ✦

# Comparative Criminology

## Preview

Chapter 15 introduces:

- How comparative criminology helps us to understand crime in the United States.

- The chief sources of cross-national crime and victimization data.

- The problem of cultural relativism.

- The problem of globalization.

- Cross-national generalizations about countries with low crime rates, modernization and crime, and globalization and crime.

- The exceptional punitiveness of criminal justice in the United States.

## Key Terms

| | |
|---|---|
| comparative criminology | globalization |
| cultural relativism | methodological relativism |
| epistemological relativism | modernization thesis |
| ethnocentrism | transnational crime |

In many of the chapters of this book we have referred to crime in a variety of societies. In this chapter we explicitly compare crime and crime rates in the United States with the same phenomena in other parts of the world.

## 15.1 Approaching Comparative Criminology

Most theories about crime have been fashioned in the sociocultural context of just a handful of Western societies—especially societies where spoken English predominates. However, few such theories have been properly tested with evidence in other societies. Nevertheless, in the same way that all would-be scientific theories must be scrutinized under conditions that are as diverse as possible, so must theories regarding the causes of crime. Undertaken in a sensitive way, comparative criminology (or "cross-cultural" criminology) can remedy **ethnocentrism**, or the view that generalizations derived from one's own society necessarily apply to crime in all other parts of the globe. As the renowned anthropologist Margaret Mead reflected in her book *Coming of Age in Samoa* (1928), "As the traveler who has once been from home is wiser than he who has never left his doorstep, so a knowledge of one other culture should sharpen our ability to scrutinize more steadily, to appreciate more lovingly, our own."

### The Goal(s) of Comparative Criminology

**Comparative criminology** may be defined as the systematic and theoretically informed comparison of crime in two or more cultures. A comparative perspective should help us address a number of key questions about crime. How and why do some societies differ in their patterns of crime, whereas others are quite similar? Why do some countries have low crime rates? Can we generalize cross-nationally about the causes of crime? Can a criminological theory developed in one society explain patterns of crime in other societies? Why do some anticrime policies succeed in some societies yet fail in others?

In short, we need to explore how comparative criminology should proceed. The most popular procedural guidelines for constructing comparative generalizations regarding crime are essentially those offered some time ago by Clinard and Abbott (1973):

The goal of a comparative criminology should be to develop concepts and general-izations at a level that distinguishes between universals applicable to all societies and unique characteristics representative of one or a small set of societies. . . . Re-search should proceed . . . first in a single culture at one point in time, . . . second in societies generally alike, . . . and third in completely dissimilar societies. (p. 2)

In other words, comparative criminology should proceed in three stages. Any gener-alization about crime must be tested (1) in one culture at a single point in time; (2) across two cultures that share some common sociological feature—such as a similar level of technological development or a common type of political culture; and (3) across cultures that are completely dissimilar. Because this advice follows the course often used for testing generalizations in the natural sciences, it has much to recommend it. Clearly, it is easier to generalize about the United States and England, for example, than it is about the United States and Japan.

Moreover, and arguably following some long-established procedures in the natural sciences (physics, chemistry, etc.), we can point to various procedural rules to be fol-lowed in any attempt to make cross-cultural generalizations about crime. There are at least five of these procedural rules that we might apply in the search for generalizations about rising crime rates in different societies, for example:

1. Crime in different cultures can be compared only if the definition and mean-ing of criminal behavior in these cultures is the same.

2. An event $p$ (e.g., urbanization) is not the cause of rising crime rates if it occurs when rising crime rates do not occur.

3. $p$ is not the cause of rising crime rates if it does not occur when rising crime rates do occur.

4. $p$ is not the cause of rising crime rates if one or more other variables ($a$, or $a$, $b$ . . . $n$) are present in the same circumstances as $p$.

5. For the generalization "$p$ causes rising crime rates" to be intelligible, it must be explained by a theory.

Suppose that we wanted to explain why homicide rates might rise and fall over time. Ultimately we would want to test our theory of changing homicide rates across a range of societies. At some point, probably fairly early on, we would need to find some empiri-cal data about the raw number and rate (per 100,000) of homicides in various societies. One attempt to do this is represented by the data in Table 15.1.

According to these cross-national data, the United States has by far the highest ho-micide rate of all technologically developed societies. In the United States in 2001 the chance of being murdered was about three times greater than in Canada and Australia, three and a half times greater than in England and Wales, four times greater than in Ire-land, and five times greater than in Sweden.

However, rather than accept such data at face value, we must examine them more closely. Given that each country's homicide data in Table 15.1 (and see Chapter 2) are actually constructed by each country's police, how much confidence should we have in

| Table 15.1 | Homicide Rates in Selected Industrialized Countries, 1999–2001 | | | |

| Country | Number of homicides | | | Homicides per 100,000 population average per year |
|---|---|---|---|---|
| | *1999* | *2000* | *2001* | *1999–2001* |
| Austria | 60 | 82 | 158 | 1.23 |
| Australia | 386 | 346 | 340 | 1.87 |
| Belgium | 172 | 158 | . . . | 1.79 |
| Bulgaria | 305 | 318 | 282 | 3.87 |
| Cyprus | 12 | 8 | 9 | 1.39 |
| Czech Republic | 265 | 279 | 234 | 2.52 |
| Canada | 538 | 546 | 544 | 1.77 |
| Denmark | 53 | 58 | 52 | 1.02 |
| England/Wales | 766 | 850 | 891 | 1.61 |
| Estonia | 157 | 143 | 137 | 10.61 |
| Finland | 142 | 146 | 155 | 2.86 |
| France | 953 | 1,051 | 1,047 | 1.73 |
| Germany | 1,055 | 961 | 868 | 1.15 |
| Greece | 155 | 158 | 139 | 1.38 |
| Hungary | 253 | 205 | 254 | 2.34 |
| Ireland (Eire) | 47 | 56 | 59 | 1.42 |
| Italy | 854 | 818 | . . . | 1.50 |
| Lithuania | 343 | 398 | 378 | 10.62 |
| Netherlands | 230 | 226 | 264 | 1.51 |
| New Zealand | 99 | 99 | 93 | 2.50 |
| Northern Ireland | 34 | 48 | 52 | 2.65 |
| Norway | 37 | 49 | 41 | 0.95 |
| Poland | 741 | 854 | 776 | 2.05 |
| Portugal | 131 | 125 | 107 | 1.17 |
| Romania | 465 | 560 | 593 | 2.41 |
| Russia | 31,140 | 31,829 | 33,583 | 22.05 |
| Slovakia | 141 | 143 | 129 | 2.55 |
| Slovenia | 25 | 26 | 15 | 1.18 |
| Spain | 416 | 460 | 494 | 1.12 |
| Sweden | 108 | 90 | . . . | 1.11 |
| Scotland | 119 | 105 | 107 | 2.16 |
| South Africa | 23,823 | 21,683 | . . . | 55.86 |
| Switzerland | 89 | 69 | 86 | 1.12 |
| Turkey | 1,541 | 2,175 | 1,550 | 2.67 |
| United States | 15,522 | 15,586 | 15,980 | 5.56 |

Source: Adapted from Barclay and Tavares, 2003:10; LaFree and Drass, 2002.

their accuracy? Given this question, moreover, how meaningful are comparisons between crime rates in the United States and those in other parts of the world? Not the least of the obstacles facing comparative criminology is that societies vary in how their crimes are defined by their respective legal systems. Societies often vary, too, in how and how often crimes are reported to the police by the public and how the police record them. In addition, if homicides rates are so much higher in one society than another, why is this so?

As this chapter progresses we will see that some of these difficulties can, to a certain extent, be overcome. But first let us identify two other problems that raise further difficulties for comparative criminology. One concerns transnational crime; the other, cultural relativism. Each of these problems is linked to, and further complicated by, the mutual influence between globalization and crime.

## Transnational Crime

Consider the following examples of crime or possible crime, each from late 2004:

- Federal prosecutors in New York charged Ignacio Coronel Villareal, a suspected drug smuggler from Mexico who was working with Colombian drug organizations, with transporting tons of cocaine from Columbia and Mexico (Associated Press, October 28, 2004).

- Thousands of foreign would-be winners of the U.S. State Department's annual green card lottery were bombarded with swindling e-mail messages stating "Congratulations, you have won DV-2004-1005 USA National Visa Lottery!!!" The e-mail asked for personal information, a photo and $349.67 in fees (*New York Times*, October 28, 2004:A26).

- Federal prosecutors announced charges in New York against 51 alleged members of two Chinese gangs who were accused of attempted murder, immigrant smuggling, and trafficking in counterfeit clothing and purses. The gangs made tens of thousands of dollars a week, coordinating some of their crimes with associates in Asia (Associated Press, November 13, 2004).

- A Yemeni man, Mohamed Alanssi, who set himself on fire in front of the White House—and survived—was the main informer for federal prosecutors in a terrorism-financing case in Brooklyn, New York. Mr. Alanssi had been employed in an FBI antiterrorist "sting" operation and was about to testify against the Yemeni sheik Mohammed Ali Hassan al-Moayad, who had apparently boasted (in Germany and elsewhere) that he had ties to Al Qaeda and Hamas and that he had personally delivered $20 million to Osama bin Laden (*New York Times*, November 17, 2004:A260).

In none of the above cases is it quite clear where the crimes originated, in how many locations they were committed, and under which and how many jurisdictions they fell. Each of these cases involves **transnational crime**, which is crime committed across borders or across national boundaries (Loader and Sparks, 2002; Reichel, 2005).

Transnational crimes typically involve criminal syndicates and the trafficking of illicit drugs from one country to another. Especially under the powerful influence of globalization and the tremendous growth in the activities of transnational corporations, the numerous forms of transnational crimes—some well organized and some not (Sheptycki, 2003)—include terrorism, sometimes committed by individuals, sometimes by well-organized political or religious groups, and sometimes by governments themselves against the populations of other societies; trafficking in persons (slaves, women, and children, including outright kidnappings), in identities, in animals, and in human and animal organs; drug trafficking; money laundering and other financial crimes; environmental and green crime; espionage and the illegal gathering of information; and trafficking in stones, precious metals, art, and in archaeological artifacts. We may add, too, that governments sometimes commit transnational crimes: against other societies (as in the waging of unjust wars), against the populations of other countries, and against migrants and guest workers. Sometimes those responsible for patrolling borders and national boundaries themselves commit transnational crimes. Needless to say, local and national-based agencies of criminal justice are at a considerable disadvantage in dealing with transnational crime (Marx, 1997).

Sometimes, transnational crimes are committed in face-to-face encounters; at other times they are committed through flights or through airborne contaminants; in, under, or on the oceans; in cyberspace; and even in space itself. Ian Loader and Richard Sparks (2002) have aptly said that transnational crimes "routinely whirl across national borders" (p. 97). They summarize recent writing on transnational crime by stating that not only are transnational crimes extremely costly in financial terms—"money laundering by the hundreds of billions (maybe trillions) of dollars" (p. 97)—but successful postmodern organization and know how, coupled with alliances with premodern local identities and kinship networks—add to a generalized anxiousness about crime. Transnational crimes are, in other words, another rather large, often invisible object for the citizenry to worry about.

What does transnational crime imply for comparative criminology? Crucially, the networks, flows, and activities associated with transnational crime tend to blur or to make obsolete the traditional unit of comparative analysis: "societies," "nations," or "cultures." Transnational crime blurs the boundaries between these units by destroying their "purity" and their distinct identities. As such, it is becoming increasingly difficult to talk about crime "in the United States" or "in Canada" or "in Japan" without acknowledging that crimes in these countries sometimes originate in other countries, and vice versa. For good reason, therefore, the study of transnational crime is sometimes called "border-crossing criminology."

Although some authors believe that the study of transnational crime and comparative criminology are quite separate endeavors (e.g., McDonald, 1997), we are not convinced that this is really the case. It is true that, as it is conventionally seen, the job of comparative criminology is to compare aspects of crime in one society with those in another. It is also true that both transnational crime and the processes of globalization have muddied this "pure" comparison. But, as we will suggest, precisely how transnational crime and globalization affect different societies—in the same way, differently, or at some point in between—is also a very useful avenue of comparative enquiry. We might further enquire, for example, whether societies regarded as "failed states" are more vulnerable to transnational crime than more stable societies are. We might ask, too, whether transnational crime is more likely to penetrate societies with weak national militaries, corrupt politicians, weak informal social controls, and lengthy geographical borders.

## Cultural Relativism

Another major area of difficulty that confronts comparative criminology is cultural relativism. **Cultural relativism** has two forms: epistemological and methodological. **Epistemological relativism** involves the extraordinary claim that one can understand another culture only through the prism of one's own culturally determined system of values. It therefore implies the impossibility of meaningful comparative generalizations other than those that stem from ethnocentrism. Thus, if our concepts of crime differ from those of another culture, it is meaningless to say that an action does or does not seem criminal to the other culture in our terms. Although this conclusion has some logical and philosophical merit, it is so pessimistic—contradictory and self-refuting, even—that for practical purposes it can only be noted and then (not entirely with satisfaction) ignored.

**Methodological relativism**, on the other hand, is a strategy that operates as a sensitizing device to variation in the definition and meaning of crime in other cultures. It reminds us that, if we are about to make comparative generalizations about crime, we should first try to understand another culture's definition and construction of crime in its terms rather than our own. "Most knowledgeable observers agree," writes James Sheptycki (2005),

> that if anything, the methodological shortcomings of quantitative empirical data render sufficient grounds for caution. . . . In practice quantitative data can be pragmatically employed with due regard to their shortcomings, but in order to interpret such data it is necessary to place it in its social, cultural and historical context. By such methodological pragmatism comparative criminologists have attempted to reach out for a better understanding of their object of study. (p. 15)

The difficult issues of relativism can be better understood if we examine the methods and findings of a classic case study in the literature of comparative anthropology: Julia Brown's (1952) comparative study of deviations from sexual mores.

## A Case Study of Comparative Sexual Deviance

In her study, Brown proposed that every known society has a range of approved sexual practices and another range of practices subject to taboo. Those members of a society who faithfully follow the approved sexual customs are rewarded; those who deviate from such customs are punished. Brown focused on the following three problems: (1) the relative frequency with which specific types of sexual practices are considered deviant by different societies, where frequency is defined as the percentage of societies that forbids such practices; (2) the relative severity with which various deviant sexual practices are punished; and (3) the degree of correlation between the frequency and the severity of punishments.

Addressing the first two problems, Brown analyzed data in Yale University's Human Relations Area File, gleaning information about the sexual practices punished by 110 "simple" societies in Africa, North America, South America, Eurasia, and Oceania. (We note, in passing, that we do not agree with Brown's characterization of technologically undeveloped societies as "simple" because in many ways, especially in the realm of certain social relationships, such societies are actually quite "advanced.") Brown's findings are summarized in Table 15.2.

Brown next determined a punishment scale for deviant sexual practices. Her scale of ratings was based on a combination of the percentage of societies that forbade a specific practice and the intensity (mild, moderate, severe, very severe) of the punishment inflicted for each sexual deviation. The scale is summarized in Table 15.3.

Tables 15.2 and 15.3 contain at least two important findings. Examining the data in Table 15.2, we learn that the sexual practices most often forbidden in Brown's sample are incest, abduction, and rape. Those practices least often forbidden are premarital affairs and intercourse with one's fiancée. Second, from the data recorded in Table 15.3 and from a series of correlational analyses, Brown inferred that the more often a given sexual practice is forbidden, the more severely and the more often it is punished. Assuming that severity of punishment reflects the seriousness of an offense, as Brown did, we can infer that incest, abduction, and rape are generally viewed across cultures as the most serious offenses. However, Brown went beyond this

| Table 15.2 | Percentages of Societies Punishing Specific Sexual Practices | |
|---|---|---|
| Number of Societies | % Punishing | Practice and Person Punished |
| 54 | 100 | Incest |
| 82 | 100 | Abduction of married woman |
| 84 | 99 | Rape of married woman |
| 55 | 95 | Rape of unmarried woman |
| 43 | 95 | Sex during postpartum period |
| 15 | 93 | Bestiality by adult |
| 73 | 92 | Sex during menstruation |
| 88 | 89 | Adultery (paramour punished) |
| 93 | 87 | Adultery (wife punished) |
| 22 | 86 | Sex during lactation period |
| 57 | 86 | Infidelity of fiancée |
| 52 | 85 | Seduction of another man's fiancée |
| 74 | 85 | Illegitimate impregnation (woman punished) |
| 62 | 84 | Illegitimate impregnation (man punished) |
| 30 | 77 | Seduction of prenubile girl (man punished) |
| 44 | 68 | Male homosexuality |
| 49 | 67 | Sex during pregnancy |
| 16 | 44 | Masturbation |
| 97 | 44 | Premarital relations (woman punished) |
| 93 | 41 | Premarital relations (man punished) |
| 12 | 33 | Female homosexuality |
| 67 | 10 | Sex with one's betrothed |

Source: Brown, 1952:138, abridged.

inference: "The fact that these correlations exist is of interest since it tends to support the view that there may be generalized attitudes of permissiveness and punitiveness toward sexual activity" (p. 139).

How justified was Brown in her finding that different cultures have common attitudes toward sexual deviation? There are at least two problems with the method Brown used to arrive at this generalization: One problem involves the definition of certain behavior as criminal; the other involves the seriousness attached to such behavior.

Brown's assumption that all 110 societies criminalize sexual practices similarly is implausible. Consider incest. It is true that anthropologists have not discovered any place, past or present, where incest is tolerated in an entire society. But there are documented cases in which some cultures regard incest—however defined—as a necessary and obligatory social practice. For example, what we regard as incest seems to have been obligatory for members of royal families in Inca Peru, in Hawaii, and in ancient Egypt, where Cleopatra was the offspring of a brother-sister union (Guttmacher, 1951). In Bali, fraternal twins of the opposite sex have been permitted to marry because they had already been completely familiar in utero. Moreover, the Gusii of southwestern

| Table 15.3 | Mean Severity Values of Specific Punishments |
|---|---|

| Mean Severity Value | Specific Punishment |
|---|---|
| 1.0 | Small fine |
| 1.2 | Fistfight |
| 1.4 | Quarreling within family |
| 1.5 | Parental reproof |
| 1.8 | Beating by family member |
| 2.1 | Duel |
| 2.2 | Public ridicule and disgrace |
| 2.2 | Enforced marriage |
| 2.2 | Illness |
| 2.2 | Bad luck |
| 2.3 | Danger to near kin |
| 2.4 | Ceremonial penance |
| 2.4 | Lowered bride-price |
| 2.4 | Knifing |
| 2.5 | Temporary exile |
| 2.5 | Humiliation at wedding |
| 2.5 | Heavy fine |
| 2.5 | Enslavement of relative |
| 2.5 | Divorce, and return of bride-price |
| 2.5 | Public flogging |
| 2.6 | Difficulty in acquiring a husband |
| 2.6 | Failure of hunting or fishing |
| 2.6 | Desertion of spouse |
| 2.7 | Puniness of offspring, injury to child |
| 2.9 | Divorce with disgrace, no remarriage allowed |
| 2.9 | Facial mutilation |
| 2.9 | Multiple mutilation |
| 2.9 | Madness |
| 3.0 | Spearing of legs |
| 3.1 | Repudiation of bride by groom |
| 3.1 | Sorcery to injure or kill |
| 3.3 | Loss of virility |
| 3.4 | Public raping |
| 3.4 | Enslavement |
| 3.4 | Destruction of major property |
| 3.5 | Barrenness |
| 3.6 | Permanent exile |
| 3.7 | Life imprisonment |
| 3.7 | Torture, possibly resulting in death |
| 3.7 | Enforced suicide |
| 3.9 | Death |

Source: Brown, 1952:137, abridged.

Kenya will not proclaim it a sexual taboo if, during the ceremony of "taking by stealth," sexual intercourse occurs between kin as close as brother and sister (Mayer, 1953).

How do such counterexamples affect Brown's generalization about sexual practices in similar "simple" societies? As formulated—there are "generalized attitudes of permissiveness or punitiveness toward sexual activity"—Brown's generalization can be neither falsified nor confirmed by counterexamples. It cannot clearly be falsified because conditional clauses (of the sort "No society exerts incest taboos during the rainy season") could in principle account for any number of counterfactual cases. This limitation is shared by all scientific and sociological attempts to generalize.

Additionally, Brown's generalization cannot be confirmed. One of the necessary criteria for an intelligible generalization is that there be an identity between the practices within its scope. But there is no way of knowing from Brown's research, or from much data lodged in the Human Relations Area File, whether the sexual practices defined as incestuous are the same practices in the societies observed: Are they perhaps seen as similar only by the observer's own methodology? The sexual practices defined as incestuous by the Western observer inclined to generalizations, by the Sambia tribe in the highlands of New Guinea, and by travelers ("gypsies") in North America may in fact all be quite different.

The problem of the identity of social practices is probably acute for comparisons between simple societies. There is good reason to suppose that the problem is even more acute for comparisons between simple and modern societies, and even for comparisons between modern societies with similar legal cultures and traditions. Suppose, for example, that we wanted to compare incest rates between England and the United States. Under the Sexual Offences Act of 1956, it is an offense for a male in England to have sexual intercourse with a female whom he knows to be his granddaughter, daughter, sister, or mother. But in the United States, statutory incest refers to an additional range of behavior not prohibited by English law: sexual relations between males and their grandmothers, nieces, and aunts. Moreover, marriage between first cousins is not an uncommon practice in England; in the United States it is illegal in nearly half the states.

A second difficulty with Brown's generalization is the assumption that a rank order of punishment can be applied meaningfully across cultures. How items are entered in cross-cultural rankings in part depends on the values of those doing the ranking. How is an objective order of punishment to be devised? And by whom? Brown devised her rank order on the advice of "judges conversant with anthropological phenomena" (p. 137). Yet consider the item "death" as the most serious punishment in her scale. There are many cases recorded (in the Homeric myths, the Icelandic sagas, and others) where banishment or permanent exile is seen as a far more serious punishment than death. Moreover, in some modern cultures (for example, among the top levels of the Japanese military), enforced suicide is not a punishment but an honorable recourse to defeat in war. And in some cultures (for instance, in England among men of gentle birth and fashion until 1850 [Andrew, 1980]), a duel is not a punishment (as in Brown's scale) but the normal form of asserting honor or reputation following insult.

Let us return to the idea of exile to illustrate another point. Exactly how much of a punishment is exile? The effect of exile partly determines the answer to this question. Exile is culturally and subjectively variable; for example, to an Orpheus exiled to Hades (the Greek underworld), to Alexander Solzhenitsyn exiled from Russia to Vermont, and to Yasir Arafat exiled from his Palestinian homeland, expulsion certainly has very different meanings. The seriousness of expulsion depends partly "on how easy it is to attach oneself to another community and to what extent one is a second-class citizen in that community" (Moore, 1978:124): Does the exile become a refugee, a hero, an outlaw, or a welfare immigrant? The number of such complicating items can of course be multiplied greatly. But their message is a simple one: The severity of punishment attached to practices in a given society cannot simply be wrenched from its specific cultural context and inserted artificially into a rank order.

## Toward Uniform Cross-National Crime Statistics?

Now let us see what we can learn from one well-known attempt to measure cross-national crime rates: Marvin Wolfgang's (1967) classic study associated with methodological relativism. The major comparative problem identified by Wolfgang is the adequacy and reliability of international crime statistics. He noted correctly that statistical data produced by agents such as Interpol are based on an unwarranted assumption: that such crimes as homicide, robbery, and rape, for example, are regarded with the same degree of seriousness by all countries. This error is aggravated by wide cultural variation in legal definitions of crime and by differing attitudes toward the sanctity of life and property.

Wolfgang made several proposals to remedy this situation. The first relates to such official administrative policies as police efficiency, quality of criminal records, and discrepancies among countries for reported crimes, trials, and convictions. According to Wolfgang (1967), national police data must be standardized. These data could easily be made more reliable because "a team of experts from an international organization could, like the field representatives of the Department of Justice in the United States, help individual countries to set up and promote reliable reporting systems" (p. 66).

Wolfgang's second proposal is even more unconventional: the elimination of legal definitions of crime for purposes of comparative measurement of crime rates. The legal components of homicide, robbery, rape, and so forth would be replaced by requests for information about the type and extent of physical injury in violent crimes and/or the monetary value of property stolen or damaged. With this approach, Wolfgang argued, specific legal definitions of crime in national data would be eliminated but cultural integrity would be maintained.

Finally, Wolfgang proposed the use of a psychophysical weighting scale. A weighted crime for each participating country could thus be had by obtaining for each country the sum of the frequency of each measured crime, multiplying by its weight, then dividing by a constant population unit.

Would such a scale really permit a comparativist to assess the relative seriousness of crimes in different countries? We think not. Wolfgang's strategy contains a serious problem. Wolfgang's major proposal for comparative research is the elimination of legal definitions of crime. Behind this proposal lurks what should be the central theoretical problem of criminology as a discipline: If criminological generalizations are based solely on legal definitions, then criminology depends exclusively on the values enshrined in criminal law (see Chapter 1.2). But no criminologist enjoys the license to study solely the practices prohibited by criminal law.

Assume that the primary goal of criminology is the construction of sociological generalizations regarding the distribution and causes of antisocial practices. Some, but not all, of such practices will be forbidden by criminal law. If this is true, then the unqualified acceptance of legal definitions of crime makes criminology a parasitic affair at the very outset. On the other hand, if legal definitions of crime are eliminated from comparative criminology (as Wolfgang would have it), then much of what is most interesting and important about different cultures—why certain cultures define certain practices and not others as illegal, cultural variation in notions of right and justice, and different penal practices, to mention but a few—is wished away by fiat.

Wolfgang's strategy is not unlike that of students of religious practices who, in attempting to compare the extent of religious sentiments in different cultures, base their analyses exclusively on official statistics of baptisms, church attendance, and marriages. Perhaps such practices aid in understanding what people do but not necessarily in understanding why people do them or what they mean. Indeed, the replacement of legal definitions of crime by such "neutral" indicators as the assessment of bodily and monetary damages still results in a criminology based on definitions of criminal justice agencies, because these assessments are provided by national police agencies. By no stretch of sociological imagination can such indicators be termed "neutral." Additionally, if the legal definition of crime is abandoned entirely as the initial object of study, we risk describing social practices and relations not as they in fact are but only as we would like them to be.

## Evaluation of Comparative Criminology

Comparative criminology is important to the process by which monocultural theories of crime might be (dis)confirmed and falsified. It broadens our intellectual horizons. Yet, as we have seen, it is fraught with perils. For example, under the influence of globalization, one of the rapidly growing areas of crime is transnational crime—yet transnational crime blurs the pure image of a "society" or "culture" that is the traditional object of comparative criminology.

Moreover, and returning to Clinard and Abbott's third stage of comparative testing, what criteria allow us to identify cultures that are completely dissimilar? Such criteria are increasingly rare in the modern world, whose outermost reaches have been penetrated by the routine operations of transnational corporations and the processes of globalization.

Assume that what Clinard and Abbott actually meant was not "completely dissimilar societies" but societies as different as possible. What sociological properties would such societies have? No doubt these properties would include major differences in religious or scientific beliefs, economic systems, political structures, and degree of technological development. The greater the difference between any two cultures along such axes, one presumes, the more entitled we are to term them "dissimilar." But this assumption is not without difficulty. The more two cultures differ, the less likely it is that they have common items to compare and the less likely it is that verifiable generalizations can be made about them.

In the face of these difficulties we probably have little choice but to follow the practical advice of Keith Dixon (1977), who urges the criminologist to "maximize his understanding of alien cultures by honest-to-God fieldwork, moral charity, intellectual humility and a determination of the taken-for-granted assumptions of both his own and others' cultural milieu" (p. 76).

## 15.2 Comparative Crime and Victimization Data

Let's continue our exploration of comparative criminology with an outline of cross-national crime and victimization data. Most of these data are generated by large-scale international organizations such as the United Nations, Interpol, and the World Health Organization. Some, however, can be found in the reports of private human rights organizations, such as Amnesty International, Human Rights Watch, Oxfam, the International Red Cross, and Doctors Without Borders.

### Cross-National Crime Data

***United Nations.*** The United Nations has collected and analyzed comparative statistical data on crime since 1946. Although the United Nations's original concern was limited to a rather simplistic notion of the prevention of crime and the treatment of offenders, it now adopts a much broader policy toward crime. This larger view is clearly stated in Article 55 of the United Nations Charter (United Nations, 1983):

> With a view to the creation of conditions of stability and well-being which are necessary for peaceful and friendly relations among nations based on respect for the principle of equal rights and self-determination of peoples, the United Nations shall promote:
>
> A. Higher standards of living, full employment, and conditions of economic and social progress and development.
>
> B. Solutions of international economic, social, health, and related problems; and international cultural and educational cooperation.
>
> C. Universal respect for, and observance of, human rights and fundamental freedoms for all without distinction as to race, sex, language or religion. (p. iii)

This extension of the scope of the United Nations to encompass human rights resulted largely from the exposure of Nazi atrocities at the end of World War II. The perspective was extended first to war crimes and genocide and then to the widespread use of cruel, inhumane, or degrading treatment of political dissidents. It now includes the violation of human rights, political and economic abuses of colonial and institutional terrorism, and crime resulting from abuses of economic and political power by transnational enterprises. The complex organizational machinery (based in Geneva, Vienna, and New York City) of U.N. criminal policy includes the General Assembly, the Secretariat, the International Court of Justice, the Committee on Crime Prevention and Control, the Commission for Social Development, and various specialist bodies such as the Commission of Human Rights, the Commission on Narcotic Drugs, and the Centre for International Crime Prevention (now named the UNODC Crime Programme).

The United Nations has wrestled often with the need to provide adequate sets of international crime statistics. It has tried to collect and disseminate data in various ways. Let us mention three of these.

First, since 1955, U.N. congresses on crime prevention have been held every five years; Congress reports have sometimes appeared in the U.N. Crime Prevention and Criminal Justice booklets. These booklets have included reports on human rights, capital punishment, and torture; prison labor, aftercare, parole, and recidivism; economic development, crime, and colonialism; juvenile delinquency; and ethical standards in criminal justice. However, most of the articles in these booklets have provided data on only one country. As such, they would have to be significantly reinterpreted for comparative purposes.

Second, the United Nations has undertaken five Surveys on Crime Trends and Operation of Criminal Justice Systems (UNCJS). These surveys contain voluminous amounts of official data on crime, criminal justice and punishment. Recent data from the UNCJS and elsewhere have been compiled in the U.N. book *Global Report on Crime and Justice* (1999). Data for the much shorter sixth Survey, of 2000, has been supplemented by data from the International Crime Victim Survey, which we will discuss shortly.

Third, at its website, <http://www.uncjin.org/>, the United Nations operates a clearinghouse of statistics and links for the data that it generates itself and for other data generated by public and private bodies worldwide. These data are as meaningful as the sources from which they originate.

*Interpol.* The International Police Organization ("Interpol") is based in Lyon, France, and has published crime data bienially since 1950. In late 2004 Interpol had 182 member countries, the national police departments of each of which provided data on murder, sex offenses (including rape), serious assault, theft (of all sorts), fraud, counterfeiting, and drug offenses. In addition, in recent years Interpol has published occasional information on crimes against humanity, terrorism, and trafficking in children and adults.

In essence, Interpol is a clearinghouse of data collected by national criminal justice agencies. Each nation's crime data are, of course, collected in different ways. To take only the crime of murder, for example, some countries include attempted murder in their definition of murder; some fail to distinguish between murder and manslaughter; some base their homicide data on murders known to the police, others on convictions. Some countries, such as those in central Africa, do not even collect crime statistics.

Interpol's police-based data, in other words, are so plagued with national idiosyncrasies that they are of dubious value for purposes of comparative criminology.

*Comparative Crime Data File.* The centerpiece of Dane Archer and Rosemary Gartner's book *Violence and Crime in Cross-National Perspective* (1984; and see Bennett) is the CCDF, or Comparative Crime Data File. The CCDF lists the police-based data of 110 countries and 44 large cities up to 1982. It lists both the raw number of offenses and the offense rate (per 100,000) for murder, manslaughter, homicide, rape, assault, robbery, and theft, tabulating the data under their original legal labels.

The CCDF was an important stepping stone in the attempt to develop comparative crime data. Despite all the limitations of police-based data, the CCDF still has some limited historical value.

## Cross-National Victimization Data

As discussed in Chapter 2.3, victimization surveys offer a somewhat more reliable indicator of crime trends in the United States than police-based statistics such as the Uniform Crime Reports. Besides the National Crime Victimization Survey in the United States, national victimization surveys have also been conducted in many other societies. At first glance, the growth of these surveys offers a good source of comparative evidence about crime trends. Common sense tells us that if victims of crime are more willing to report their victimization to survey interviewers than to police officers, then victimization surveys should reveal more about the incidence of crime than police statistics.

Consider, for example, what we can learn from the comparative findings of victimization surveys conducted, respectively, in the United States and in England and Wales shown in Figure 15.1. We can see that, contrary to most popular opinion and media claims about where the United States stands in the league tables of crime, according to 1995 victimization surveys, the rates of robbery, assault, burglary, and motor vehicle theft were all higher in England and Wales than in the United States (Langan and

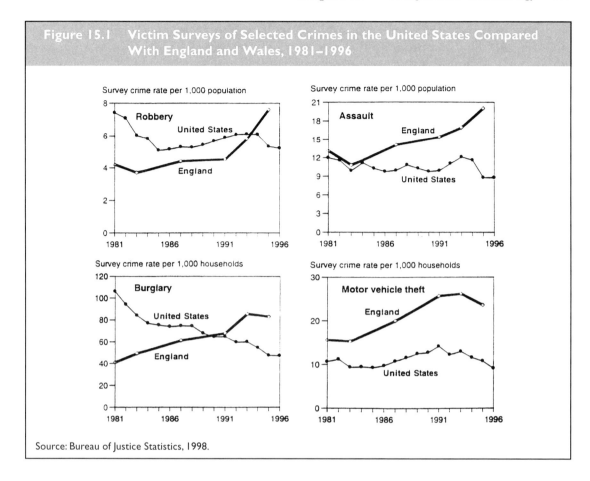

**Figure 15.1    Victim Surveys of Selected Crimes in the United States Compared With England and Wales, 1981–1996**

Source: Bureau of Justice Statistics, 1998.

Farrington, 1998). In addition, as one comparative study of crime on college campuses has tentatively found, victimization rates, including rates of sexual assault and theft, might well be higher on English campuses than those on U.S. campuses (Fisher and Wilkes, 2003). These—perhaps surprising—findings tend to have been confirmed by police statistics. Indeed, it appears to be true that compared with the rate in England and Wales, the homicide rate in the United States is the only exception to this trend in serious crimes. Moreover, even the difference in the homicide rate has been narrowing: Whereas during the 1980s the homicide rate in the United States was about 10 times that of England and Wales, by the mid-2000s it had become "only" three to five times higher.

Yet victimization surveys have their own peculiar methodological limitations that complicate their use in comparative analysis. Most surveys outside the United States, for example, have been very small, although it is possible that these small samples are as representative of the levels of victimization of their national populations as the large samples in the U.S. National Crime Victimization Survey. Furthermore, in some countries (such as the United States), victimization rates are calculated with households as the database; in other countries (for instance, Holland), rates are based on per capita victimizations. This difference casts some doubt on the validity of some comparative studies of victimization. Because household size tends to decline with affluence, different databases tend to obscure differences in the opportunity for crime that arise from variations in population size and household composition. Further problems arise from the wording of survey questions, which reflect legal definitions of crime that can vary from one country to another.

*The International Crime Victims Surveys.* Some of these problems have been overcome in the four sweeps of the International Crime Victim Surveys (ICVS), held respectively in 1989, 1992, 1996 and 2000 (Mayhew and Van Dijk, 1997; Van Kesteren, Mayhew, and Nieuwbeerta, 2000; Alvazzi del Frate and Van Kesteren, 2004). In general, the ICVS shows that victimization levels increased between 1988 and 1991, stabilized or fell in 1995, and then fell further in 1999.

Although there is little new in the format and methodology of the survey itself, the ICVS is unique in its use of standardized questionnaires, sampling methods, and data analyses and applying them to a large number of countries. In each country, 500–2,500 subjects are selected by random digit dialing telephone interviews (in studies of eastern Europe and of developing societies currently under way, the primary method of data collection is the face-to-face interview). Subjects are questioned about 11 main forms of victimization, divided into "household property crimes" and "personal crimes." Household property crimes include theft of, theft from, and vandalism to cars; theft of motorcycles; theft of bicycles; burglary with entry; attempted burglary; and break-ins to outbuildings. Personal crimes include robbery; theft of personal property, pickpocketing, and noncontact personal thefts; sexual incidents, sexual assaults, and offensive sexual behavior; and assaults/threats, assaults with force, and threats without force. If the subjects indicate that they had been victimized, more detailed questions are then asked about the event(s). Subjects are also asked a number of questions reflecting fear of crime and attitudes toward police. The data are weighted for gender, regional population distribution, age, and household composition, in order to make the samples as representative as possible of actual national populations age 16 or higher.

Among the key findings of the 2000 Survey of 17 industrialized countries are (see Table 15.4):

- In Australia, England and Wales, the Netherlands, and Sweden about 24 percent of the population were victimized by crime.

- In Canada, Scotland, Denmark, Poland, Belgium, France, and the United States, about 20–24 percent of the population were victimized by crime.

- In Finland, Catalonia (Spain), Switzerland, Portugal, Japan, and Northern Ireland fewer than 20 percent of the population were victimized by crime.

- Over 40 percent of ICVS crimes involved cars—theft of them and from them. The risk of having a car stolen was highest in England and Wales (2.6 percent of owners had a theft), Australia (2.1 percent), and France (1.9 percent). The lowest risks were in Japan, Switzerland, Catalonia, the United States, Finland, and the Netherlands, all of which had car thefts of 0.5 percent or less.

- For crimes involving physical contact (robbery, assaults with force, and sexual assaults involving women only), the highest risks (3 percent or more) were in Australia, England and Wales, Canada, Scotland, and Finland. These societies had more than double the rate in the United States Belgium, Catalonia, Portugal, and Japan. Japan had an especially low rate (0.4 percent).

- Women in Sweden, Finland, Australia, and England and Wales were most at risk of sexual assault. Women in Japan, Northern Ireland, Poland, and Portugal were least at risk. Women knew the offender(s) in about half of all sexual incidents (including sexual assault and the lesser crime of offensive sexual behavior), in a third they knew the offender by sight; and in about one-sixth they knew him by name.

- Support for imprisonment (for a recidivist burglar age 21) was the highest in the United States, the United Kingdom, and Japan (about half or more respondents chose it); it was lowest in Catalonia and France.

One of the most revealing findings of the 2000 Survey concerns the differing levels at which crimes are reported to the police. Based on the reporting of five crime types (theft from cars, burglary with entry, robbery, sexual incidents, and assaults and threats), the Survey found that the highest reporting rates (about 60 percent) were in Denmark, Sweden, Northern Ireland, and the Netherlands. Crimes were least often reported to the police in Portugal, Japan, Catalonia, and Poland (less than 40 percent). In Table 15.5 we can see the distribution of reasons for not reporting crimes to the police, which include the feeling that the crime was "not serious enough" or involved "no loss" or that the police could do nothing about it.

As interesting and suggestive as the ICVS data are, it must be stressed that their meaning is not altogether straightforward. As we already know (see Chapter 2.1), victimization surveys inevitably have their own methodological dilemmas. Thus, given that the rate of reporting crimes to the police varies from one country to another, there is no reason to suppose that the rate of reporting to survey interviewers is the same in each country. If a society has high reported victimization rates, does that mean that more persons are victimized there? Or do they mean that the citizenry there is more sensitive to violence—that they are more intolerant of intolerance—and therefore more likely to report it?

In short, we have good reason to be cautious about the meaning and usefulness of cross-national victimization surveys in comparative criminology.

## 15.3 Cross-National Generalizations Regarding Crime

Let us now examine three specific areas of crime about which comparative criminologists have sought to generalize:

- Countries with low crime rates.
- Modernization and crime.
- Globalization and crime.

### Countries With Low Crime Rates

Some of the most interesting questions for comparative criminology concern the nature of countries with low crime rates. Why do some countries consistently have

**Table 15.4   International Victimization Rates (1999); Percentage Victimized Once or More (Prevalence Rates)**

| | | 11 crimes | Car theft | Theft from car | Car vandalism | Motor-cycle theft | Bicycle theft | Burglary | Attempted burglary | Robbery | Personal theft | Sexual incidents | Assaults & threats |
|---|---|---|---|---|---|---|---|---|---|---|---|---|---|
| Australia | 1989 | 26.1 | 2.3 | 6.9 | 8.8 | 0.3 | 1.9 | 4.4 | 3.8 | 0.9 | 5.0 | 7.3 | 5.2 |
| | 1992 | 28.6 | 3.1 | 6.6 | 9.5 | 0.3 | 2.1 | 3.7 | 3.8 | 1.3 | 6.5 | 3.5 | 4.7 |
| | 2000 | 30.0 | 1.9 | 6.8 | 9.2 | 0.1 | 2.0 | 3.9 | 3.3 | 1.2 | 6.5 | 4.0 | 6.4 |
| Austria | 1996 | 18.8 | 0.1 | 1.6 | 6.7 | 0.0 | 3.3 | 0.9 | 0.5 | 0.2 | 5.0 | 3.8 | 2.1 |
| Belgium | 1989 | 17.7 | 0.8 | 2.7 | 6.6 | 0.4 | 2.7 | 2.3 | 2.3 | 1.0 | 4.0 | 1.3 | 2.1 |
| | 1992 | 19.3 | 1.0 | 3.9 | 6.1 | 1.1 | 2.8 | 2.1 | 1.6 | 1.0 | 3.1 | 1.4 | 1.8 |
| | 2000 | 21.4 | 0.7 | 3.6 | 6.1 | 0.3 | 3.5 | 2.0 | 2.8 | 1.0 | 4.1 | 1.1 | 3.2 |
| Canada | 1989 | 28.1 | 0.8 | 7.2 | 9.8 | 0.4 | 3.4 | 3.0 | 2.7 | 1.1 | 5.5 | 4.0 | 3.9 |
| | 1992 | 28.4 | 1.3 | 7.3 | 8.5 | 0.2 | 3.7 | 3.4 | 2.7 | 1.2 | 5.5 | 3.8 | 4.8 |
| | 1996 | 25.2 | 1.5 | 6.2 | 6.2 | 0.1 | 3.3 | 3.4 | 2.8 | 1.2 | 5.7 | 2.7 | 4.0 |
| | 2000 | 23.8 | 1.4 | 5.4 | 5.5 | 0.1 | 3.5 | 2.3 | 2.3 | 0.9 | 4.7 | 2.1 | 5.3 |
| Catalonia (Spain) | 2000 | 19.0 | 0.4 | 5.3 | 7.7 | 0.6 | 0.4 | 1.3 | 0.6 | 0.9 | 3.0 | 0.8 | 1.5 |
| Denmark | 2000 | 23.0 | 1.1 | 3.4 | 3.8 | 0.7 | 6.7 | 3.1 | 1.5 | 0.7 | 4.1 | 2.5 | 3.6 |
| England & Wales | 1989 | 19.4 | 1.8 | 5.6 | 6.8 | 0.1 | 1.0 | 2.1 | 1.7 | 0.7 | 3.1 | 1.1 | 1.9 |
| | 1992 | 30.2 | 3.7 | 8.6 | 10.6 | 0.4 | 3.0 | 3.0 | 2.9 | 1.1 | 4.2 | 2.1 | 3.8 |
| | 1996 | 30.9 | 2.5 | 8.1 | 10.4 | 0.2 | 3.5 | 3.0 | 3.4 | 1.4 | 5.0 | 2.0 | 5.9 |
| | 2000 | 26.4 | 2.1 | 6.4 | 8.8 | 0.4 | 2.4 | 2.8 | 2.8 | 1.2 | 4.6 | 2.7 | 6.1 |
| Finland | 1989 | 15.9 | 0.4 | 2.7 | 4.0 | 0.0 | 3.1 | 0.6 | 0.4 | 0.7 | 4.3 | 0.5 | 2.9 |
| | 1992 | 21.2 | 0.7 | 2.9 | 5.6 | 0.3 | 5.0 | 0.6 | 0.6 | 1.0 | 3.4 | 3.7 | 4.4 |
| | 1996 | 18.9 | 0.4 | 2.9 | 4.3 | 0.2 | 5.1 | 0.6 | 0.7 | 0.5 | 3.2 | 2.5 | 4.1 |
| | 2000 | 19.1 | 0.4 | 2.9 | 3.7 | 0.1 | 4.9 | 0.3 | 1.0 | 0.6 | 3.3 | 3.7 | 4.2 |
| France | 1989 | 19.4 | 2.4 | 6.0 | 6.4 | 0.6 | 1.4 | 2.4 | 2.3 | 0.4 | 3.6 | 1.1 | 2.0 |
| | 1996 | 25.3 | 1.6 | 7.2 | 8.3 | 0.8 | 2.8 | 2.3 | 2.2 | 1.0 | 4.0 | 0.9 | 3.9 |
| | 2000 | 23.4 | 1.7 | 5.5 | 8.2 | 0.3 | 1.8 | 1.0 | 1.3 | 1.1 | 3.0 | 1.1 | 4.2 |
| Germany (West) | 1989 | 21.9 | 0.4 | 4.7 | 8.7 | 0.2 | 3.3 | 1.3 | 1.8 | 0.8 | 4.0 | 2.8 | 3.1 |
| Italy | 1992 | 24.6 | 2.7 | 7.0 | 7.6 | 1.5 | 2.3 | 2.4 | 1.7 | 1.8 | 3.6 | 1.7 | 0.8 |
| Japan | 1989 | 8.5 | 0.2 | 0.7 | 2.5 | 0.2 | 3.5 | 0.7 | 0.2 | na | 0.2 | 1.0 | 0.7 |
| | 1992 | na | 1.1 | 2.3 | na | 3.2 | 9.6 | 1.1 | na | na | 1.3 | 1.8 | 0.5 |
| | 2000 | 15.2 | 0.1 | 1.6 | 4.4 | 1.0 | 6.6 | 1.1 | 0.8 | 0.1 | 0.5 | 1.2 | 0.4 |
| Netherlands | 1989 | 26.8 | 0.3 | 5.2 | 8.2 | 0.4 | 7.5 | 2.4 | 2.6 | 0.8 | 4.4 | 2.6 | 3.3 |
| | 1992 | 31.3 | 0.5 | 6.8 | 9.6 | 1.0 | 10.0 | 2.0 | 3.0 | 1.0 | 4.6 | 2.2 | 4.0 |
| | 1996 | 31.5 | 0.4 | 5.4 | 9.9 | 0.7 | 9.5 | 2.6 | 3.3 | 0.6 | 6.8 | 3.6 | 4.0 |
| | 2000 | 25.2 | 0.4 | 3.9 | 8.9 | 0.6 | 7.0 | 1.9 | 2.7 | 0.8 | 4.7 | 3.0 | 3.4 |
| New Zealand | 1992 | 29.4 | 2.7 | 6.9 | 7.9 | 0.3 | 4.4 | 4.3 | 3.6 | 0.7 | 5.3 | 2.7 | 5.7 |
| Northern Ireland | 1989 | 14.9 | 1.6 | 4.0 | 4.4 | 0.1 | 1.6 | 1.1 | 0.9 | 0.5 | 2.5 | 1.9 | 1.8 |
| | 1996 | 16.8 | 1.6 | 3.1 | 6.7 | 0.0 | 1.2 | 1.5 | 1.1 | 0.5 | 2.5 | 1.2 | 1.7 |
| | 2000 | 15.0 | 1.2 | 2.7 | 4.5 | 0.0 | 1.4 | 1.7 | 0.9 | 0.1 | 2.2 | 0.6 | 3.0 |

**Table 15.4  International Victimization Rates (1999): Percentage Victimized Once or More (Prevalence Rates), continued**

| | | 11 crimes | Car theft | Theft from car | Car vandalism | Motor-cycle theft | Bicycle theft | Burglary | Attempted burglary | Robbery | Personal theft | Sexual incidents | Assaults & threats |
|---|---|---|---|---|---|---|---|---|---|---|---|---|---|
| Norway | 1989 | 16.4 | 1.1 | 2.8 | 4.6 | 0.3 | 2.8 | 0.7 | 0.4 | 0.5 | 3.2 | 2.2 | 3.0 |
| Poland | 1992 | 27.0 | 0.7 | 5.3 | 4.7 | 1.0 | 4.2 | 2.1 | 2.3 | 1.7 | 8.1 | 3.6 | 4.2 |
| | 1996 | 22.9 | 0.9 | 5.7 | 5.4 | 0.3 | 3.2 | 2.0 | 1.8 | 1.8 | 5.6 | 1.5 | 3.7 |
| | 2000 | 22.7 | 1.0 | 5.5 | 7.0 | 0.1 | 3.6 | 2.0 | 1.3 | 1.8 | 5.3 | 0.5 | 2.8 |
| Portugal | 2000 | 15.5 | 0.9 | 4.9 | 6.3 | 0.3 | 0.8 | 1.4 | 1.2 | 1.1 | 1.9 | 0.6 | 0.9 |
| Scotland | 1989 | 18.6 | 0.8 | 5.4 | 6.5 | 0.3 | 1.0 | 2.0 | 2.1 | 0.5 | 2.6 | 1.2 | 1.8 |
| | 1996 | 25.6 | 1.7 | 6.6 | 9.8 | 0.1 | 1.9 | 1.5 | 2.4 | 0.8 | 4.5 | 1.3 | 4.2 |
| | 2000 | 23.2 | 0.7 | 4.2 | 9.0 | 0.1 | 2.0 | 1.5 | 1.9 | 0.7 | 4.6 | 1.1 | 6.1 |
| Spain | 1989 | 24.8 | 1.4 | 9.6 | 6.6 | 0.8 | 1.1 | 1.6 | 2.1 | 3.1 | 5.2 | 2.3 | 3.1 |
| Sweden | 1992 | 21.5 | 1.7 | 3.9 | 4.5 | 0.6 | 7.0 | 1.4 | 0.8 | 0.3 | 4.2 | 0.9 | 2.7 |
| | 1996 | 24.0 | 1.2 | 4.9 | 4.6 | 0.5 | 8.8 | 1.3 | 1.1 | 0.5 | 4.6 | 2.9 | 4.5 |
| | 2000 | 24.7 | 1.3 | 5.3 | 4.6 | 0.4 | 7.2 | 1.7 | 0.7 | 0.9 | 5.8 | 2.6 | 3.8 |
| Switzerland | 1989 | 15.6 | 0.0 | 1.9 | 4.1 | 1.2 | 3.2 | 1.0 | 0.2 | 0.5 | 4.5 | 1.7 | 1.2 |
| | 1996 | 26.7 | 0.1 | 3.0 | 7.1 | 1.4 | 7.0 | 1.3 | 0.1 | 0.9 | 5.7 | 4.6 | 3.1 |
| | 2000 | 18.2 | 0.3 | 1.7 | 3.9 | 0.2 | 4.7 | 1.1 | 1.8 | 0.7 | 4.4 | 2.1 | 2.4 |
| United States | 1989 | 28.9 | 2.1 | 9.2 | 8.9 | 0.1 | 3.0 | 3.8 | 5.4 | 1.9 | 4.5 | 4.5 | 5.4 |
| | 1992 | 26.1 | 2.6 | 7.0 | 8.0 | 0.4 | 2.9 | 3.1 | 3.9 | 1.5 | 5.3 | 2.3 | 4.7 |
| | 1996 | 24.2 | 1.9 | 7.5 | 6.7 | 0.2 | 3.3 | 2.6 | 3.0 | 1.3 | 3.9 | 2.5 | 5.7 |
| | 2000 | 21.1 | 0.5 | 6.4 | 7.2 | 0.3 | 2.1 | 1.8 | 2.7 | 0.6 | 4.9 | 1.5 | 3.4 |
| All countries | 1989 | 20.2 | 1.1 | 5.0 | 6.5 | 0.4 | 2.7 | 2.0 | 1.9 | 0.9 | 3.5 | 2.4 | 2.8 |
| | 1992 | 22.1 | 1.8 | 5.4 | 6.4 | 1.0 | 5.1 | 2.3 | 2.1 | 0.9 | 4.3 | 2.4 | 3.3 |
| | 1996 | 24.2 | 1.2 | 5.2 | 7.2 | 0.4 | 4.4 | 1.9 | 2.0 | 0.9 | 4.7 | 2.4 | 3.9 |
| | 2000 | 21.3 | 1.0 | 4.6 | 6.6 | 0.3 | 3.2 | 1.8 | 1.8 | 0.8 | 3.9 | 1.7 | 3.5 |

Source: Alvazzi del Frate and Van Kesteren, 2004:178–179.

lower crime rates than others? What, if anything, do these countries have in common? What can we learn from their experience? Let us briefly examine two countries with low crime rates: Japan and Ireland.

*Japan.* During most of the past century Japan had persistently low, stable, and occasionally declining crime rates. In 2001, for example, the Japanese homicide rate was 1.1 per 100,000 (or about one-sixth of the United States rate). When criminologists attempt to explain Japanese crime rates, they usually refer to the strong elements of informal social control in Japanese life, which tend to produce—from a Western perspective—a crushing conformity in social relationships. Such control, this explanation continues, is manifest in certain vital areas: the patriarchal nature of the family, the quality of formal education, the power of religion and, especially in urbanized areas, the surrogate family provided by economic corporations.

In such ways, Japanese life is controlled to such an extent that, to many citizens, crime and deviance are actually unthinkable. Additionally, these ordered features of Japanese life are themselves supplemented by an efficient police force that has an excellent rapport with the Japanese public (Bayley, 1991; Currie, 1998).

Moreover, while pointing to the harsher and more certain punishment awarded criminals

**Table 15.5   Reasons for Not Reporting Crimes to the Police, Based on Five Crimes: 2000 ICVS**

| | N | Not serious enough % | Solved ourselves % | Inappropriate for police % | Other authorities % | My family solved it % | No insurance % | Police could do nothing % | Police wouldn't do anything % | Fear/dislike of police % | Fear of reprisals % | Other reasons % | Don't know % |
|---|---|---|---|---|---|---|---|---|---|---|---|---|---|
| Australia | 603 | 47 | 9 | 4 | 4 | 1 | – | 8 | 6 | – | 3 | 32 | 2 |
| Belgium | 392 | 52 | 25 | 29 | 6 | 9 | 4 | 42 | 35 | 4 | 9 | 17 | 2 |
| Canada | 527 | 41 | 14 | 6 | 3 | 3 | 1 | 6 | 5 | 2 | 4 | 31 | 5 |
| Catalonia (Spain) | 447 | 51 | 7 | 5 | 2 | 1 | 2 | 10 | 17 | – | 2 | 13 | 3 |
| Denmark | 404 | 42 | 20 | 12 | 2 | 1 | 1 | 9 | 6 | 1 | 8 | 19 | 6 |
| England & Wales | 412 | 34 | 10 | 11 | 3 | 2 | 1 | 12 | 11 | 3 | 4 | 24 | 4 |
| Finland | 335 | 56 | 17 | 5 | 4 | 1 | 1 | 7 | 6 | – | 3 | 13 | – |
| France | 203 | 39 | 16 | 8 | – | 1 | 1 | 8 | 10 | 1 | 5 | 16 | 2 |
| Japan | 157 | 48 | 11 | 7 | 6 | 5 | – | 18 | 8 | 3 | 3 | 27 | 2 |
| Netherlands | 323 | 32 | 12 | 10 | 1 | 1 | – | 9 | 9 | – | 2 | 30 | 4 |
| Northern Ireland | 132 | 37 | 8 | 16 | 4 | 2 | – | 17 | 8 | 8 | 9 | 9 | 1 |
| Poland | 859 | 46 | 10 | 15 | 2 | 1 | 3 | 39 | 31 | 7 | 8 | 5 | 1 |
| Portugal | 348 | 41 | 10 | 10 | 1 | 2 | – | 13 | 10 | 2 | 3 | 11 | 1 |
| Scotland | 328 | 37 | 10 | 6 | 3 | 1 | – | 6 | 7 | 3 | 4 | 31 | 3 |
| Sweden | 357 | 34 | 14 | 18 | 1 | 4 | 2 | 11 | 11 | 2 | 3 | 16 | 2 |
| Switzerland | 553 | 42 | 14 | 12 | – | 1 | – | 11 | 5 | 3 | 5 | 10 | 5 |
| United States | 185 | 27 | 10 | 12 | 6 | 3 | – | 17 | 9 | 6 | 2 | 21 | 4 |
| All countries | 6,560 | 42 | 13 | 11 | 3 | 2 | 1 | 14 | 11 | 3 | 5 | 19 | 3 |

Source: Alvazzi del Frate and Van Kesteren, 2004:196.

in Japan—which Western commentators often do not see—the Japanese criminologist Setsuo Miyazawa (1993; and see Komiya, 1999) stresses that the push to conformity begins at an early age for Japanese children. This push toward conformity is then nourished through the combined power of education, work, family, religion, and ancestor worship. Miyazawa (1993) stresses how different the routines of Japanese childhood are compared with the daily lives of children in other parts of the world:

> The value of conformity is first taught at schools. For children, school epitomizes the conventional world. Japanese school children are among the busiest children in the world. A survey conducted by the Japanese government indicates that they do homework more than anyone else, play for a relatively short time, and sleep the least. . . . Japanese junior high school students spend six hours in the classroom each day and more than three hours in extracurricular activities and homework. (p. 98)

Before assessing the relevance of the Japanese experience to the possible understanding of crime in the United States, we note our disagreement with any explanation of Japan's low crime rate that begins and ends with the level of social control there. An inquiry into why Japan has relatively low rates of interpersonal crime should not be made at the expense of examining other forms of crime. It is quite possible that rates of white-collar crime, syndicated crime, and political corruption, for example, are higher in Japan than in most other industrialized societies. Thus, as some researchers have already pointed out, although the rate of individualistic forms of white-collar crime such as embezzlement may be quite low in Japan, white-collar crimes motivated for "the good of the company" may be very high there (Kerbo and Inoue, 1990).

The Japanese experience reflects the fact that high crime rates are by no means an inevitable feature of modernized societies. However, we believe that explanations of low Japanese crime rates inappropriately focus on the element of control in Japanese life. Two decades of failed get-tough conservative crime policies in the United States should tell us that control, as such, explains neither low nor high crime rates. In Japan's case the emphasis on control as an explanation of low crime neglects the ways in which Japanese society is more supportive of its citizenry than the United States in terms of providing social and welfare services. As many commentators on Japanese culture have pointed out, this supportive network is apparent in the relative absence in Japan of an underclass, in the fact of egalitarianism in income distribution, and in a complete absence of urban ghettos.

Time will soon tell whether the push toward lower crime rates occasioned by Japan's aging population—with relatively fewer young males—will be outweighed by recession-like economic conditions since the early 1990s (e.g., see Roberts and Lafree, 2004). Moreover, in trying to explain why Japan has relatively low crime rates, we need to look further afield than criminology's traditional focus on crime. Thus, it has been known at least since the time of Durkheim's (Chapter 10.2) analyses of homicide and suicide in France in the 1890s that any given social or personal crisis can lead to a variety of deviant responses, which themselves often vary by social class, gender, race/ethnicity, and age. If we examine in both societies the different responses over time to rising levels of unemployment, for example, we are likely to find rising homicide rates in the United States and rising suicide rates in Japan:

It is reasonably well established that the 50 percent increase, over a 10-year period, in the number of suicides (from approximately 21,000 in 1990 to in excess of 32,000 per annum by the end of the century) . . . was the product of economic stagnation and rising rates of unemployment. . . . Western criminologists conventionally look at how worsening economic indicators affect crime rates, but they seldom look at the act of suicide. . . . What is striking about the Japanese statistics is that crime rates do not seem particularly sensitive to shifts in the economic statistics (although this may also be changing). Rather, in Japan, where the cultural implications of "losing face" are more profound, and where losing one's employment amounts to a profound loss of face, the social impact of increasing numbers of men experiencing employment loss seems principally to be expressed in the dramatically rising number of suicides. (Sheptycki, 2005:14)

*Ireland.* Let us now shift our attention to the Republic of Ireland, another country with historically low crime rates. From the 1950s to the early 1970s, Ireland had exceptionally low and stable crime rates (McCullagh, 1996). However, by 1975 (approximately when Ireland became a fully industrialized society), there were five times as many recorded "shopbreakings," six times as many "housebreakings," and 29 times as many robberies as had been recorded in 1951. A substantial increase was also recorded for offenses against the person, with indictable assaults rising seven times over the same 25 years (Rottman, 1980). In the 1950s the average annual number of homicides was 7.2; in the 1960s it was 10.1; and from 1970 to 1975 it was 20.8. By 2001 the annual number of homicides had risen to 59 (see Table 15.1)—although compared with other industrialized countries, the rate of homicide was still very low at 1.42/100,000. Since 1995, the overall crime rate in Ireland has been declining (O'Donnell and O'Sullivan, 2003).

Such changes suggest that Ireland conforms to major strands of the modernization thesis yet also differs significantly from it. During the 1940s, the rapid decline of Irish agriculture—a decline that was not relieved but exacerbated by intensive industrialization during the early 1960s—created serious hardship among the Irish working class. Increased unemployment, in turn, led to enormous intrafamilial conflict and to other forms of dislocation, such as emigration. Rottman (1980) analyzed the changing Irish homicide patterns immediately after these great economic and social upheavals. He showed that after the early 1960s there occurred in Ireland a diminishing incidence of family homicide, an increasing proportion of homicides involving strangers, and more homicides in which females killed males. In these respects, Ireland appears to conform to the modernization thesis.

In other ways, however, Irish crime rates seem to contradict the modernization thesis. For example, after the industrialization of the 1960s, crime rates did not increase more in urban areas than in rural areas: The increase was diffuse rather than concentrated in cities (Rottman, 1980). Also, even though we are dealing with a small number of homicides, the rising percentage of men murdered by women—a 41.3 percent increase between the 1950s and the 1970s—is probably not typical of other modernized countries. Moreover, except for murder, rates of violent crime in Ireland may actually have declined between the early 1990s and the new millennium (O'Donnell and Sullivan, 2003). As three Irish sociologists have remarked concerning perceptions of crime in Ireland: "We have been encouraged to worry about a surge in crime, the appearance of which may have more to do with the growth of private insurance policies (and the need to report break-ins to the police before making a claim), than with any dramatic increase in criminal activity as such" (Tomlinson, Varley, and McCullagh, 1988:14).

It is fair to say, therefore, that Ireland is a real exception to the view that rising crime rates accompany modernization. Although there is as yet no sustained explanation of Ireland's persistently low crime rates, we note especially the powerful influence of Roman Catholicism in government, education, and family. An additional factor is undoubtedly the relationship between the Irish citizenry and the Garda, the Irish police force. According to the Irish Value Survey (cited in McCullagh, 1996), 85 percent of the Irish population has "a great deal" or "quite a lot" of confidence in the Irish police—more confidence, in fact, than in any other Irish institution. Moreover, similar levels of confidence in the police are exhibited by a remarkable 84.5 percent of Irish skilled and unskilled manual workers.

What do Japan and Ireland have in common? It's hard to say. One attempt to find commonalities among countries with low crime rates is Freda Adler's book *Nations Not Obsessed With Crime* (1983). Adler isolated five diverse "regions" in the world (European capitalist, European socialist, Latin America, Islam, and Asia) and then selected from each region two countries (respectively: Switzerland/Ireland, Bulgaria/German Democratic Republic, Costa Rica/Peru, Algeria/Saudi Arabia, and Japan/Nepal) with the lowest, or among the lowest, crime rates in its region.

Adler first tried to correlate each country's arrest rates with 47 socioeconomic variables, including age, occupation, national income, education, and patterns of consumer expenditure. From this correlational analysis Adler inferred that these 10 countries had no significant socioeconomic or cultural factors in common. At the same time, Adler identified some broad trends in the 10 countries:

> Most low-crime countries have in common lower-than-average population densities, lower-than-average urban populations, . . . lower-than-average population numbers which are economically active, a lower-than-average number of radio receivers and telephones, a higher-than-average population in agriculture. . . . and a higher than average crude death rate. (p. 10)

Still, there were startling sociocultural differences among these 10 countries. They had a variety of state structures, including military government, parliamentary democracy, popular democracy, and absolute and constitutional monarchies. Their economies ranged from subsistence agriculture (Nepal, Peru) to extensive industrialization (GDR, Switzerland, Japan). Some had urbanized slowly (Ireland, Switzerland), others quickly (Saudi Arabia, Japan). In some (Peru), unemployment rates were high; in others (GDR, Bulgaria, Japan, Switzerland) they were low. Some of the countries contained homogeneous populations, others were heterogeneous. Adler also outlined each country's formal and informal mechanisms of social control. Each appeared to have various systems of law, politics, and criminal justice. Each had differing levels of success in solving reported crimes, ranging from high (Japan, Saudi Arabia) to low. While actual support for human rights was difficult to measure, five countries retained the use of capital punishment.

Nevertheless, Adler claimed that she had found a common aspect among countries with low crime rates: popular involvement in—or popularity of—the criminal justice system. Six of the 10 countries—four highly industrialized (Japan, Switzerland, Bulgaria, and the GDR) and two underdeveloped (Nepal and Peru)—were "marked by an extraordinarily high degree of popular participation in crime control" (p. 128). Moreover, Saudi Arabia, Algeria, and Ireland had succeeded, despite foreign intervention, in maintaining the integrity of their indigenous systems of social control. Costa Rica (which has no standing army) had fostered local self-government and was actively popularizing its criminal justice system.

Adler also found that all 10 countries had strong elements of social control outside the criminal justice system. According to Adler, these elements did not exercise control by formal constraint; rather, "they transmit and maintain values by providing for a sharing of norms and by ensuring cohesiveness" (p. 130). First and foremost, her argument continued, was the survival of the power of the family, even during modernization. In each case the family, often patriarchal, remained a closely woven unit that exerted a powerful influence on its members. In societies where employment levels were high—with women composing a large segment of the labor force—strong efforts had been made to provide for children during work hours in day-care facilities and kindergartens. The retention of traditional family values was itself reinforced by a second system of control: religious, moral, or secular values. In all 10 countries—whether Islamic, Christian, or socialist—such values exhorted the citizenry to act for the common good; they "solidify the moral obligations of the community to reaffirm in common their common sentiments" (p. 132).

Remarkably, Adler's is the only study to have specifically examined how countries with high crime rates differ from those with low ones.

But we must note three criticisms of Adler's analysis. First, her study essentially avoided all thorny methodological and relativist problems of comparative research. She paid little attention, for example, to cross-national differences in history, law, and economy. Second, when examining non-Anglophone countries, Adler relied either on statements by native government officials or on secondary English-language commentaries. But interviewing government officials about such things as the popularity of the criminal justice system, for example, is not a very reliable way to gather information about crime in other (or any) cultures. Because she relied on secondary sources, we can determine neither the accuracy of their analyses nor the range of opinions they reflected. Finally, we must note that Adler's study, unique as it remains, has been quite overtaken by recent developments—especially the power of globalization and the tremendous increase in transnational crime.

## Modernization and Crime

Since the early 1960s, sociologists have argued that the mere fact of technological development produces common effects that tend, irrespective of different or even antagonistic political systems, to make all societies "converge." In this scenario, technology itself is seen as an even-handed factor that inevitably determines that all modern societies eventually converge on a common industrial model. This industrial convergence model, which in criminology is usually termed the **modernization thesis**, has eight characteristics (Lane, 1970, 1996):

1. Populations grow rapidly, family size falls, women are emancipated, and relationships between spouses become more equal.

2. Knowledge, wealth, political power, and human rights become more available to the entire population.

3. The division of labor is highly developed, and education and occupation determine individual positions in the social hierarchy.

4. Ideological differences are minimized and a premium is placed on hard work and economic productivity.

5. Legal systems apply a more-or-less common law to individuals of all social ranks.

6. Although political ideologies can be quite different, the central government organizes all of society.

7. Human relationships tend to be specific and achievement oriented rather than diffuse and ascribed.

8. Large-scale urbanism ensures that social relationships are impersonal, superficial, and differentiated.

In criminology the industrial convergence theory suggests that, as societies modernize, their homicide rates rise quite dramatically (Shelley, 1981; Beirne and Nelken, 1997). As they begin to industrialize and become more urbanized, in other words, societies of all social types often experience great social upheaval and dislocation, not the least because traditional patterns of family life are disrupted when young males move from rural areas to towns and to cities in search of work. Immense and rapid population growth in urban areas sometimes has explosive effects on infant mortality, health, sewage, food supplies, public order, and crime. It is violent crime in particular, including homicide, that escalates during the process of modernization. At the same time, this general social deterioration tends to be accompanied by the rise of the nation-state and its massive apparatuses of social control. The state tries to monopolize the use of violence through the development of formal institutions of social control, such as criminal law and police. The growth of a national network of these institutions is accompanied by the cultivation of less formal, but often very effective, processes of social control and moral regulation, which Elias (1978) has termed "the civilizing process."

The diverse signs of the civilizing process are said to include respect for individual rights; conscience; proper deportment in public places; the use of polite manners; rules for games and sports and the banning of most sports involving violence against animals; and the abolition of public executions and, eventually, of capital punishment altogether.

A central aspect of the "modernization and crime" thesis has been empirically tested by LaFree and Drass (2002). Their study is based on the assumption that if modernization is indeed accompanied by high homicide rates, industrializing societies are more likely than industrialized societies to have rapid and sustained homicide booms. Using

World Health Organization homicide data for 34 industrializing or industrialized nations from 1956 to 1998, LaFree and Drass found that 70 percent of the industrializing nations (seven of 10) but only 21 percent of the industrialized nations (five of 24) had homicide booms in this period (see Figure 15.2). This study therefore tends to support the modernization thesis.

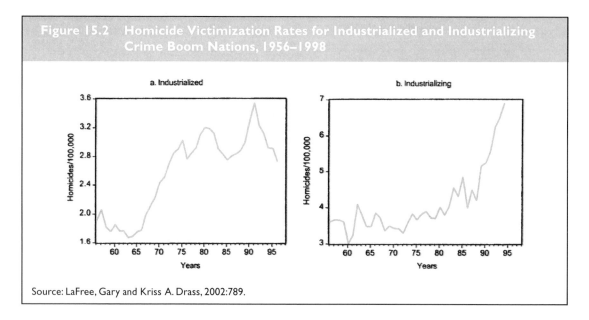

**Figure 15.2   Homicide Victimization Rates for Industrialized and Industrializing Crime Boom Nations, 1956–1998**

Source: LaFree, Gary and Kriss A. Drass, 2002:789.

Moreover, LaFree and Drass argue that several of the industrialized nations in their sample that had experienced homicide booms—such as the United States, Greece, and Spain, whose cases thus seemingly contradict the modernization thesis—were themselves suffering serious social disruption. In the 1960s and 1970, for example, the United States experienced widespread political turmoil. Rising homicide rates coincided in Greece with the fall of the military junta in 1974 and the rebirth of a democratic constitution. The rapid growth of homicide rates in Spain coincided with the death of dictator Francisco Franco in 1975. Further, unlike the persistent increase in homicide rates experienced by industrializing societies, the homicide rates of the United States, Greece, and Spain began to decline within two decades.

One of the most common plausible explanations of variation in homicide rates in industrialized societies concerns the importance of social and economic inequality. This explanation is especially applicable where inequality is accompanied by strain and a popular sense of injustice. One avenue of research found that in 34 industrialized countries, high homicide rates tended to be accompanied by high levels of income inequality and concentrated poverty (Rosenfeld and Messner, 1991; Neapolitan, 1997; Currie, 1998); this correlation holds even when controlling for variations in gross national product, population size, population density, and degree of urbanization. As Elliott Currie (1998) has stressed:

> The links between extreme deprivation, delinquency, and violence . . . are strong, consistent, and compelling. The effects are compounded by the absence of public

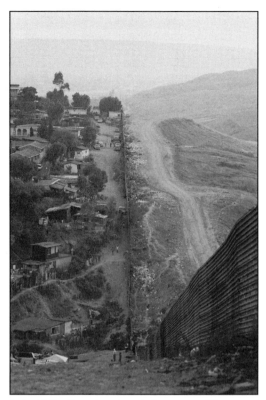

*Industrialization alone is not the cause of increased crime, but also the levels of economic deprivation and social inequality. The border to Tijuana shows the disparity between the poverty of Mexico and the opportunities of the United States—yet violent crime remains high in both due to structural inequities.*

supports to buffer economic insecurity and deprivation, and they are even more potent when racial subordination is added to the mix. And this—rather than "prosperity"—helps us begin to understand why the United States suffers more serious violent crime than other industrial democracies, and why violence has remained stubbornly high in the face of our unprecedented efforts at repressive control. (p. 131)

We must add, too, that one of the basic problems with existing modernization theory is that crime patterns in the Third World are not likely to repeat patterns of criminality in the more technologically advanced nations of the world. Criminality in the Third World is not simply a replay of the histories of more modernized nations. Indeed, many crimes committed in Third World countries actually originate in the First World and result in transnational crime.

Consider, for example, the worst industrial accident on record, which occurred when toxic gas leaked from a Union Carbide (now part of the Dow Chemical Co.) insecticide plant early on the morning of December 3, 1984, in the central Indian town of Bhopal (see Box 7.2):

Witnesses said thousands of people had been taken to hospitals gasping for breath, many frothing at the mouth, their eyes inflamed. The streets were littered with the corpses of dogs, cats, water buffalo, cows and birds killed by the gas, methyl isocyanate, which is widely used in the preparation of insecticides. Doctors from neighboring towns and the Indian Army were rushed to the city of 900,000, where hospitals were said to be overflowing with the injured. Most of the victims were children and old people who were overwhelmed by the gas and suffocated, Indian press reports said. (*New York Times*, December 4, 1989)

The Bhopal chemical leak resulted in the immediate deaths of 8,000 residents. By 2002, the death toll was well over 20,000, and it continues to rise by about 30 per month (Sarangi, 2002). About 120,000 survivors continue to press their injury claims outstanding in injury compensation courts for chronic exposure-induced diseases, including breathlessness, persistent cough, early-age cataracts, loss of appetite, menstrual irregularities, recurrent fever, back and body aches, loss of sensation in limbs, fatigue, weakness, anxiety and depression (Dinham and Sarangi, 2002). Despite extradition orders pending since 1992, by 2005 the Indian government had still failed to bring Union Carbide CEO Warren Anderson to trial.

---

### Box 15.1   DOW Looking Down the Barrel

An application was filed in the Chief Judicial Magistrate's Court today (February 27, 2004) requesting that the court proceed to issue a summons on the Dow Chemical Company to produce proclaimed absconder and wholly owned subsidiary Union Carbide to face trial in the ongoing criminal case. Holding banners that read "Bring Dow to the Court" and "Sheltering a murderer is equal to murder," more than 100 survivors held a demonstration outside the court as the application was filed. . . . UCC, Union Carbide Eastern and Warren Anderson have been charged with culpable homicide or manslaughter and were proclaimed absconders by the CJM's court . . . after they repeatedly failed to honour court summons.

Source: International Campaign for Justice in Bhopal, 2004:1.

---

What tragedies such as the Bhopal disaster imply is that societies "modernize" not according to some inner benevolent logic but, rather, according to the dictates of economic and political power within a global system of capitalist economies. Many patterns of crime and many large-scale acts of social harm cannot be understood if societies are viewed in isolation from each other.

### Globalization and Crime

Throughout this book we have referred to the growing importance of **globalization** in the understanding of patterns of crime in any given society, and we have only a little more to say about it here. In particular, we stress that there is no society in the world whose national boundaries are insulated from the economic and cultural processes of globalization. In a wonderfully apt phrase, Loader and Sparks (2002) describe globalization as a process of "divergent modernization" (p. 98). It is a worldwide process of sameness that is modified and contextualized by varying local circumstances. As Jock Young (2003) has written:

> Although the extent and level of economic globalization is debatable . . . the impact is worldwide. The First World poor are not left behind stranded in the inner cities deserted by capital, they live in intense and self-involved marketplaces and their eyes are on the outside world. The Third World peasant may not contribute much to the world economy and to the triad of the United States, Europe and Japan, but this does not mean that they are outside the forces of economic globalization: their coffee is sold on the world markets, they buy Coca-Cola at their local stall. (pp. 401–402)

Globalization affects not only how and under what conditions we work or are unemployed (Pastor and Alva, 2004; Welch, 2004), but also, culturally, it affects our identities: who "we" and who our "communities" are, where we live, and what our hopes are. Although globalization, as such, is not a part of comparative criminology as it has traditionally been understood, it is nevertheless a process that profoundly affects crime in any and all societies (Sparks and Loader, 2002; Young, 2003; Sheptycki and Wardak, 2005). Young (2003), in particular, has made six generalizations about the complex processes by which globalization fuels discontent worldwide—and hence leads to a variety of social and intersocietal problems, including crime:

1. Economically, globalization widens income differentials, both within the First World and between rich and poor countries.

2. Culturally, through mass media images of high levels of consumption, globalization generates aspirations among the First World poor and throughout the Third World that are blocked by structural inequality and unfairness. Globalization thus fuels relative deprivation.

3. Globalization creates a widespread crisis of identity, which is most obvious in rising unemployment and unstable families. The poor and minority groups, above all, suffer economic and political marginalization and feel disrespected.

4. Perceptions of great unfairness and feelings of insecurity provide a rationalization (or "technique of neutralization") for violence, for blaming others for one's own crises, and for dehumanizing them.

5. Given the crises of identity and of security brought about by globalization, minor differences between societies, and within societies, and between ethnic or racial groups, are exacerbated. Some of these differences are expressed in violent passionate conflict around masculinity and heroic myths.

6. Globalization leads to identity wars. These are found in crimes of passion, rage against humiliation, expressivity, and lifestyle. They are also found at the national level, where fundamentalist Western presidents and prime ministers wage holy wars against fundamentalist terrorists.

## 15.4 U.S. Crime in Comparative Perspective

Our chief focus in this chapter has been to supply a comparative dimension to comparative criminology. We have examined some of the major issues involved in actually doing comparative studies and have outlined some of the most common comparative generalizations on crime.

### Five Causes of High U.S. Crime Rates

Students often ask: "Why does the United States have one of the highest crime rates in the world?" Because it is so hard to offer good answers to this question, our only answer is, "We really don't know, precisely." However, if pressed to respond with a simple answer, we would reply that at least five factors distinguish the social structure of the United States from other comparable societies and that these factors contribute to its exceptional position in the world of crime and justice:

1. The United States has had one of the highest rates of structural unemployment since 1945.

2. The United States has the largest underclass of persons economically, socially, and politically discriminated against because of race and ethnic background.

3. The United States has inferior support systems of welfare, social security, health, and education.

4. The extreme and aggressive commercialism of U.S. capitalism provides incentives and motivations to circumvent acceptable (namely, legal) means of achievement.

5. The U.S. criminal justice system is one of the most punitive systems in the world.

We conclude this chapter with a brief outline of number 5 above, reviewing comparative evidence of the relationship between punitive penal policies and crime rates in the United States.

## Punitive Penal Policies

The comparatively high rates of personal and property crimes in the United States have been explained in numerous ways, but in recent times criminologists have tended to focus on the general climate of tolerance and permissiveness (whose roots go back to the turbulent liberalism of the 1960s) in the United States. It was not accidental, this explanation continues, that the turbulence and permissiveness of the 1960s coincided with unprecedented increases in the rates of violent crime. This permissiveness has become a favorite target of conservatives, and as an explanation of crime it surfaces in two major forms.

Both explanations of permissiveness focus on the consequences of the apparent weakening of social control in U.S. society. One explanation focuses on weakened control in such crucial socializing agencies as families, schools, and neighborhoods. For some people, therefore, the rise of permissiveness derives from liberal or weak-minded childrearing practices within families that are, in their turn, paralleled and reinforced by lax discipline in high schools. The other explanation refers to the loss of control, or the lack of punitiveness, in the criminal justice system and, specifically, to the mild or lax punishment apparently meted out to convicted criminals.

We firmly reject these explanations. The evidence simply does not support them.

Regarding the first explanation, it is difficult to support the argument that U.S. society has somehow become more permissive in its childrearing practices since the 1960s. Take only the example of corporal punishment of children. In Chapter 5 we outlined the extraordinary amount of physical child abuse in the United States, which is no doubt caused partly by the positive relationship demonstrated between the development of aggression in children and the use of corporal punishment (Straus, 2001). For us, the corporal punishment of children is a form of child abuse. About 75 percent of the U.S. public believes that physical punishment of children is acceptable behavior, and as many as 98 percent of parents in the United States sometimes "spank" their children. These figures contrast with Sweden, where the same belief is held by only about 25 percent of parents.

**Table 15.6** **Prison Populations in Selected Countries, 2001–2003**

| Country | Prison Population Total | Year(s) | Prison Population Rate (per 100,000 population) |
|---|---|---|---|
| Australia | 22,492 | 2002 | 115 |
| Austria | 8,114 | 2003 | 100 |
| Belgium | 9,253 | 2002 | 89 |
| Canada | 36,024 | 2001–02 | 116 |
| China | 1,512,194 | 2002 | 117 |
| Colombia | 54,034 | 2001 | 126 |
| Denmark | 3,439 | 2002 | 64 |
| England/Wales | 74,452 | 2003 | 141 |
| Finland | 3,617 | 2002 | 70 |
| France | 55,382 | 2003 | 93 |
| Germany | 81,176 | 2003 | 98 |
| Greece | 8,500 | 2002 | 80 |
| Iceland | 107 | 2002 | 37 |
| India | 304,893 | 2002 | 29 |
| Ireland | 3,366 | 2003 | 85 |
| Israel | 10,164 | 2002 | 163 |
| Italy | 56,574 | 2002 | 100 |
| Japan | 67,255 | 2002 | 53 |
| Netherlands | 16,239 | 2002 | 100 |
| New Zealand | 5,881 | 2002 | 155 |
| Nigeria | 39,368 | 2002 | 33 |
| Northern Ireland | 1,220 | 2003 | 70 |
| Norway | 2,662 | 2002 | 59 |
| Pakistan | 87,000 | 2002 | 59 |
| Portugal | 14,300 | 2003 | 137 |
| Saudi Arabia | 23,720 | 2000 | 110 |
| Scotland | 6,569 | 2003 | 129 |
| South Africa | 180,952 | 2003 | 402 |
| Spain | 56,140 | 2003 | 138 |
| Sweden | 6,506 | 2002 | 73 |
| Switzerland | 4,987 | 2002 | 68 |
| United States | 2,212,475 | 2003 | 714 |

Source: Adapted from Walmsley, 2004; Harrison and Harrison, 2004.

Evidence is also easy to provide that the U.S. criminal justice system is exceptionally punitive when compared with other societies. For example, the United States is now the only Western country that retains and uses the death penalty. Since 1997, an average of 75 people have been executed each year, a disproportionate amount of them persons of color (Deathpenaltyinfo.org/Fact Sheet.pdf).

Comparative evidence consistently reveals that the United States incarcerates more of its population than other Western countries (see Table 15.6). In 1995, 5.4 million persons in the United States were either in prison or under the supervision of the prison system, accounting for 5 percent of men age 18 and over, and for one in five African-American males (Wacquant, 1998). In 2003 the number of inmates in federal and state penitentiaries and in local jails soared to 2,212,475, up from 1,725,842 in 1997. In the same year the incarceration rate was 714 per 100,000 population, up from 601 in 1995 and 684 in 2000. Similar societies have far lower incarceration rates, with most clustering around 55–120 per 100,000; some are lower still, such as Iceland at 37, Japan at 53, Sweden at 73, and Ireland at 85 per 100,000. In 2004, almost 10 percent of all prisoners in the United States were serving life terms (Butterfield, 2004).

*We suggest that there is no evidence that the punitive nature of U.S. penal sanctions reduces the crime rate significantly. On the contrary: punitive penal policies are a violent part of the very problem they are apparently designed to solve.* Instead of pursuing ever-harsher penal policies, we should pursue reductions in the crime rate through social policies applied to the class structure itself. Certain societies in Western Europe have reported great success with a host of practical social policies.

In conclusion, we can do no better than repeat Elliott Currie's (1985, 1998; see also Savelsberg, 1998/1999) summary of these constructive policies:

- Exploration and development of intensive rehabilitation programs for youthful offenders, preferably in the local community or in a supportive institutional milieu.

- Community-based, comprehensive family support programs, emphasizing local participation and respect for cultural diversity.

- Improved family planning services and support for teenage parents.

- Paid work leaves and more accessible child care for parents with young children, to ease the conflicts between childrearing and work.

- High-quality early education programs for disadvantaged children.

- Expanded community dispute-resolution programs.

- Comprehensive, locally based services for domestic violence victims.

- Intensive job training, perhaps modeled along the lines of supported work, designed to prepare the young and the displaced for stable careers.

- Strong support for equity in pay and working conditions, aimed at upgrading the quality of low-paying jobs

- Substantial permanent public or public-private job creation in local communities, at wages sufficient to support a family breadwinner, especially in such areas of clear and pressing social need as public safety, rehabilitation, child care, and family support.

- Universal—and generous—income support for families headed by individuals outside the paid labor force.

## Review

In Chapter 2 we saw how hard it is to measure crime rates in the United States. We have now seen that it is just as hard—if not harder—to make intelligible comparisons between U.S. crime rates and those elsewhere.

This chapter has taught the importance of testing theories under conditions as diverse as possible, and, therefore, it has explored the crucial role of comparative studies for the theoretical development of criminology in the United States. The major task of this chapter has been to outline the key concepts, data, and findings of comparative criminology. It has done so in the expanding context of transnational crime and the processes of globalization.

## Approaching Comparative Criminology

1. Comparative criminology is the systematic and theoretically informed comparison of crime in two or more cultures. It should help us answer some key questions about crime, including why some countries have low crime rates and whether a criminological theory developed in one society can explain patterns of crime in other societies.

2. Transnational crime is crime committed across borders or across national boundaries. Examples include terrorism, trafficking in persons and identities, in animals, and in human and animal organs; drug trafficking; money laundering; environmental and green crime; espionage and the illegal gathering of information; and trafficking in stones, precious metals, art, and artifacts.

3. Cultural relativism has two forms. Epistemological relativism—which we recognized, then ignored—holds that because we can never understand the beliefs of cultures different from our own, we cannot compare our culture with such cultures. Methodological relativism is a strategy for comparing different cultures that, at the same time, attempts to respect the facts of cultural diversity. The precise difficulties presented by cultural relativism were illustrated by Brown's (1952) classic study of sexual deviance. We also examined Wolfgang's (1967) methodological strategy to standardize crime statistics.

## Comparative Crime and Victimization Data

1. The various sources of cross-national crime and victimization data include those of the United Nations, Interpol and other international agencies, and U.N.-sponsored victimization surveys. Other data, often on human rights violations, may be obtained from private organizations such as Amnesty International, Humans Rights Watch, Doctors Without Borders, and the International Red Cross.

2. For comparative purposes, using these sources entails the difficulty that societies define certain practices as crimes in different ways and also differ in the degree of seriousness that they attach to them. Each type of cross-national crime data is subject to at least the same limitations as the crime data generated in any given society.

## Cross-National Generalizations Regarding Crime

1. In this section several cross-national generalizations regarding crime were outlined. Each has its own merits.

2. We examined how countries with low crime rates might differ from ones with high crime rates. Little research has been completed on the sociological nature of societies with low crime rates. We outlined the available research, applied it especially to the cases of Japan and Ireland, and could offer only provisional answers. Among these are that societies with low crime rates are likely to be more egalitarian, less militaristic, and less urban.

3. We also examined the modernization thesis, which argues that generalizations can be made about the way in which industrialization and urbanization affect crime rates in all societies. The major problems with the modernization thesis are that it tends (1) to ignore relativist issues regarding differences in legal definitions of crime; (2) too often to be contradicted by empirical evidence; (3) wrongly to assume that criminality in Third World societies is a replay of the history of criminality in technologically advanced societies; and (4) to ignore the repressive colonial influence of First World countries and transnational corporations on the patterns of crime and globalization in the Third World.

4. We briefly outlined some generalizations that have been made about globalization and crime. Young's (2003) comments in this regard begin with the idea that globalization creates uncertainty and feelings of relative deprivation, which tend to lead to various forms of violence, including crime.

## U.S. Crime in Comparative Perspective

1. There are many reasons that the United States has one of the highest crime rates in the world. Our reasons tend to focus on inequalities and exclusion.

2. One reason for the high U.S. crime rates is that U.S. society, including its criminal justice system, is one of the most punitive in the world. Punitive penal policies are a violent part of the very problem they are apparently designed to solve.

3. To address the causes of high rates of crime, one must look beyond penal policies to fundamental and constructive changes in society itself.

## Questions for Class Discussion

1. Twenty-five hundred years ago, the Greek historian Herodotus (quoted in Feyerabend, 1987) recorded the following story:

   When Darius was king of Persia, he summoned the Greeks who happened to be present at his court, and asked them what they would take to eat the dead bodies of their fathers. They replied they would not do it for any money in the world. Later, in the presence of the Greeks, and through an interpreter, so that they could understand what was said, he asked some Indians, of the tribe called Callatiae, who do in fact eat their parents' dead bodies, what they would take to burn them. They uttered a cry of horror and forbade him to mention such a dreadful thing. (p. 42)

   What does this story tell us about the problem of cultural relativism?

2. Do crime rates in the Third World tend to repeat the patterns of recorded crime in countries such as the United States?

3. What lessons, if any, can U.S. policymakers derive from the incidence of crime in other countries?

4. Why are the rates of violent crime in the United States apparently so high in comparison with those of other modern industrialized countries?

## For Further Study

### Readings

Liddick, Donald R. Jr. 2004. *The Global Underworld: Transnational Crime and the United States.* Westport, CT: Praeger.

Nelken, David. 2003. Comparing Criminal Justice. In *The Oxford Handbook of Criminology,* edited by Mike Maguire, Rod Morgan and Robert Reiner, 175–202. Oxford: Oxford University Press.

Reichel, Philip, ed. 2005. *Handbook of Transnational Crime & Justice.* Thousand Oaks, CA: Sage.

### Websites

1. <http://www.ccurecweb.com/les/res/resour4.htm>: This website has links to a collection of numerous national and international criminal justice and law websites.

2. <http://www.hrw.org>: This is the website of the humanitarian organization Human Rights Watch, which monitors human rights, prison conditions, and prison abuses in some seventy countries worldwide.

3. <http://www.ifs.univie.ac.at/^uncjin /uncjin.html>: This is the homepage of the United Nations Crime and Justice Information Network. The site provides a mass of information regarding crime and justice on the national and international levels.

4. <http://www.unicri.it/icvs/data/index.htm>: This is the website of the International Crime Victimization Survey (ICVS).

5. <http://www.who.int/whosis/mort/mort.htm. At this website of the World Health Organization, coroner-based homicide and suicide data can be found. ✦

# Glossary

## A

***abolitionism*** A movement and theory whose aim is the abolition of most coercive state institutions of social control (e.g., prisons, police, the death penalty) because they are inherently repressive and harmful.

***age*** The length of time for which a human has existed. Economic benefits, social privileges, and political power are often based on age.

***aggravated assault*** An unlawful attack by one person on another for the purpose of inflicting severe or aggravated bodily injury.

***analogous social injuries*** Legally permissible and preventable acts or conditions caused by individuals or social institutions where consequences are similar to those of illegal acts.

***anarchism*** A multifaceted social movement united on the need to abolish the state. Nowadays, anarchist theory is most likely to inspire leftist globalization protesters, animal rights activists, and deep-green environmentalists.

***animal abuse*** Any act that contributes to the physical, psychological, or emotional pain, suffering, or death of an animal or that otherwise threatens its welfare. The act may involve active maltreatment or passive neglect or omission, and it may be direct or indirect, intentional or unintentional.

***anomie*** A condition of normlessness; a breakdown in the social order. A concept favored by Merton in his explanation of the high rate of crime and deviance in the United States.

***armed robbery*** The display of a deadly weapon to carry out a robbery.

***arson*** The willful or malicious burning of a house, public building, motor vehicle, aircraft, or other property of another.

***automobile theft*** The unlawful taking of, or the attempt to take, an automobile.

## B

***battering*** Slapping, shoving, pushing, and other violent acts that result in injury to the victim; it typically occurs for years.

***born criminal***  Cesare Lombroso's theory that physical attributes are associated with, or even cause, criminal behavior.

***bribery***  The giving of money or property to state officials in return for favors.

***burglary***  The unlawful entry into a house, business, or other structure with the intent to commit a felony.

## C

***carjacking***  The use of direct physical force to steal a motor vehicle from a driver.

***check fraud***  Deliberate deception for personal gain by the use of a counterfeit or forged check.

***Chicago school of criminology***  Part of the post-Progressive Era social science movement that evolved in Chicago between 1915 and the early 1940s.

***child abuse***  Intentional acts of a parent, relative, or guardian that result, or are likely to result, in physical, mental, or emotional injury or impairment of a child. Child abuse has four forms: physical abuse, sexual abuse, emotional abuse, and child neglect.

***civil disobedience***  A nonviolent action against the state or a refusal to obey certain laws considered unjust.

***classical criminology***  A criminology based on both free will and determinism and whose chief aim was to deter crime. It was part of the humanist reaction during the Enlightenment to the barbarities and inequities characteristic of feudal systems of justice. It was popularized by Cesare Beccaria and Jeremy Bentham.

***collective embezzlement***  Theft of funds from a savings and loan institution for personal gain, at the expense of the institution and with the approval of management.

***communism***  A theory advocating the elimination of private property. Its proponents believe that with the abolition of private property and with the disappearance of the class nature of the state, crime will almost disappear under communism.

***comparative criminology***  The systematic comparison of crime in two or more cultures.

***concepts***  Ideas that describe a property of an empirical datum or a relation among empirical data. They are usually a smaller part of a theory that is used to generate hypotheses.

***conduct norms***  Rules of behavior that embody the values of some powerful group in society.

***conflict theory***  An ancient theory that, when used in criminology, suggests that crime, criminalization, and criminal law must be seen in the overriding context of social, economic, and political inequality.

***conformity***  The most common (i.e., nondeviant and noncriminal) response in Robert Merton's typology of responses to frustrated opportunities.

***consensus theory***  Often juxtaposed with conflict theory to suggest that most people hold certain key values in common and that social structures are based on it.

***constitutive criminology*** The most thoroughgoing postmodern perspective in criminology; a political perspective that seeks to lay bare the rhetoric and mystification that enters public discourse about crime.

***containment theory*** A theory suggesting that variation in the crime rates of different social groups is caused by variations in the ability to contain norm-violating behavior in the face of social change and cultural conflict.

***control balance*** A theory claiming that the amount of control to which an individual is subject, relative to the amount of control he or she can exercise, determines the probability of deviance occurring, as well as the likely type of deviance.

***control deficit*** In Tittle's theory of control balance, if one is subject to control more than one controls, one has a control deficit.

***control surplus*** In Tittle's theory of control balance, if one controls more than one is subject to control, one has a control surplus.

***control theory*** A theory arguing that to find the factors leading to delinquency one must look for the causes of conformity; delinquency turns out to be merely an absence of the causes of conformity.

***convict criminology*** A humanist theory advanced by ex-prisoners who claim that only those who have been prisoners can fully understand the oppression and misery of prison life.

***corporate crimes*** Illegal or socially injurious acts of intent or indifference that are committed in order to further corporate goals and that physically and/or economically harm individuals in the United States and/or abroad.

***corporate theft*** Type of theft that differs from other forms of theft in that it does not entail face-to-face confrontation, it is not always readily apparent that a theft has occurred, and it serves the interest of the corporation.

***corporate violence*** Acts of violence committed by corporations against workers, consumers, or the public.

***corrupt campaign practices*** Various forms of illegal or unethical behaviors used to obtain political office, ultimately for the purpose of influencing state policy.

***credit-card fraud*** The use of stolen credit cards to purchase goods.

***crime*** In criminal law, crime is an action or omission that is prohibited by law, that is voluntary, and that coincides with a defendant's mental state. This book uses an eclectic and more sociological approach to crime, however, we view crime as a dynamic outcome of the relationship between the state and the social relations embedded in gender, race, age, and class. Crime can be seen as a violation of conduct norms, as a social harm, as a violation of human rights, and as a form of deviance.

***crime networks*** A loose affiliation of upperworld and underworld actors who cooperate in the provision of illegal goods and services for a profit.

***crime rate*** The prevalence of crime relative to the population.

*criminal justice system* The legally defined, authoritative system of surveillance, detection, policing, prosecution, and punishment of those who have committed crimes (and sometimes those who have not).

*criminal law* Rules enacted by legislatures or that result from judicial decisions that protect members of the public from state definitions of wrongdoing.

*criminal syndicates* Associations formed to conduct specific illegal enterprises for profit, whose members can include businesspeople, police, politicians, and criminals.

*criminalization* The process whereby criminal law is selectively applied to social behavior. It involves the enactment of legislation that outlaws certain types of behavior and provides for surveillance and policing of that behavior and, if the behavior is detected, for punishment.

*cultural criminology* Explores the political relationship between the constructions of meaning and the criminalization process, often with the aid of ethnographic material.

*cultural relativism* The philosophical and sociological claim that beliefs and practices in one culture may translate only roughly, or not at all, into those of another culture.

## D

*dangerous classes* A derogatory nineteenth-century term applied by law-abiding citizens to describe those members of the working classes, the unemployed, and the unemployable who seemed to pose a threat to law and order.

*deceptive advertising* Applied to advertisements that are misleading in a material respect; advertisers can make false statements as long as they are not deceptive.

*decriminalization* The removal of criminal prohibitions for certain behaviors while still regulating them.

*deviance* Any social behavior or social characteristic that departs from the conventional norms and standards of a community or society and for which the deviant is sanctioned.

*deviance amplification* The process whereby agencies of social control (e.g., the police) and the mass media create deviance.

*differential association* A theory that attempts to explain both the process by which a person learns to engage in crime and the content of what is learned.

*direct investment* A criminal syndicate's reinvestment of its profits from the illegal sale and distribution of goods and services into legitimate enterprises.

*drift* The lack of commitment to either the subculture of delinquency or conventional culture.

*dumping* A form of transnational corporate crime in which firms sell to other countries certain hazardous products banned or not approved for sale in the United States.

# E

***elder abuse*** Physical, sexual, and/or emotional abuse, as well as neglect, of elders. It is different from child abuse in that it also includes financial and/or material exploitation.

***election fraud*** A form of state corruption that includes illegal voting, false voter registration, and stuffing ballot boxes.

***embezzlement*** The taking of money from the workplace for one's personal use.

***employee theft*** Stealing merchandise or job-related items from the workplace.

***Enlightenment*** A philosophical and humanist eighteenth-century movement professing that reason and experience, rather than faith and superstition, must replace the excesses and corruption of feudal societies. It opposed cruel and inhumane punishments and challenged the prevailing views of the time concerning the relation between crime and punishment.

***epistemological relativism*** The extraordinary claim that one can understand another culture only through the prism of one's own culturally determined system of values.

***ethnocentrism*** The view that concepts and generalizations about one's own society necessarily apply to crime in other societies.

***eugenics*** The "science" of good genes and the basis of the eugenics movement (c.1870–1930) which argued that the socially useful citizens should be encouraged to have children; the socially and medically unfit should be isolated or forcibly prevented from breeding.

# F

***fear of crime*** A type of fear that has numerous forms and originates in the complex relationships among the media, crime itself, various sociological and psychological dimensions of people's lives, and modern-day anxieties.

***feminism*** A critical perspective that maintains that women are discriminated against because of their gender and that seeks to use social change to end women's resulting subordination.

***fencing*** Buying, selling, or dealing in stolen goods.

***financial fraud*** A form of fraud that serves the interests of the corporation.

# G

***gender*** Historically and culturally developed patterns of behavior resulting from relationships between males/males, females/females, and males/females.

***general theory*** A theory that is constructed according to the logic of the natural sciences and that seeks at once to be both as simple and as general as possible.

***globalization*** The worldwide process whereby individuals, peoples, economies, and states are becoming increasingly interconnected and interdependent.

***global conduct norms*** Rules of conduct, agreed on by the international community, that allow for prosecution of certain coercive relationships between a state and its citizenry and between one state and another.

***green criminology*** The study of crimes, harms, and abuses committed by humans against the environment, against nature, and against animals who are not human.

## H

***hate crimes*** Violence committed against people because of their race, ethnicity, disability, religion, or sexual orientation.

***human rights*** Natural and inalienable rights accorded to all human beings, such as the right to life, liberty, and happiness. They may also include rights essential to a dignified human existence, such as freedom of movement, free speech, a good education, employment, and so on.

## I, J

***identity theft*** Adopting another person's identity, usually to facilitate further crime.

***ideology*** Any set of structured beliefs, values, and ideas that can at once reflect social reality and distort it.

***illicit drug business*** The syndication of illegal drugs, such as heroin, cocaine, and marijuana, from the point of production, to importation, to wholesaling, to street sales.

***imitation*** Gabriel Tarde's idea that crime is influenced by the processes of imitation and that thereby people are socialized into criminality.

***individual/group terrorism*** Terrorism that occurs when individuals or groups who are not necessarily supported by a state engage in political assassination and/or domestic and international terrorist acts.

***income-tax fraud*** Cheating on one's income tax by, for example, underreporting wages.

***innovation***

***One of the four deviant or criminal responses in Robert Merton's typology of responses to frustrated opportunities.***

***insider trading*** Using information unavailable to the public to gain an advantage over others in the buying and selling of stock.

***institutionalized means*** Social regulations, controls, and procedures for moving towards and achieving goals and values.

***integrated theory*** A theory that combines some of the assumptions and propositions of two or more other theories into an explanatory framework with a broader scope.

***international law*** Various treaties, agreements, customary law principles, and general legal principles that serve to judge the actions and behavior of nation-states assenting to them.

***interpersonal coercion*** A woman's having sex with her husband or employer in the face of nonviolent threats.

## K, L

***labeling perspective*** A perspective suggesting that crime and deviance exist in the eye of the beholder.

***labor racketeering*** The infiltration, domination, and use of a union for personal benefit by illegal, violent, and fraudulent means.

***larceny*** The unlawful taking of property from the possession of someone other than one's employer.

***left idealism*** A type of critical criminology that focuses almost exclusively on the harms of the ruling class and that ignores the development of a coherent program for curbing conventional crime.

***left realism*** The view that conventional crime is driven by relative deprivation and by reactionary, selfish, and individualistic attitudes.

***legalization*** Complete removal of all criminal sanctions for certain behaviors without subsequent regulation.

***liberal feminism*** The view that women's subordinate status in society stems from socialization processes and from unequal opportunities and rights for women.

***life-course data*** Data about patterns of crime collected and interpreted over the course of offenders' lives, including official crime data, self-reports, psychological evaluations, IQ tests, criminal histories, court records, incarceration records, and coroners' reports.

***life-history data*** Collection of information to craft a rich document of offenders' changing personal choices and life experiences over time.

***loan sharking*** Financial loans at extremely high interest rates with rapid repayment required and violence as a potential sanction for nonpayment.

## M

***mafia*** A method or system of patron-client relationships; in Sicily it was a system dependent on patronage and the ability of a man of respect to use violence when necessary.

***manslaughter*** The killing of another person through gross negligence or without specific intent.

***Marxist feminism*** The view that class and gender divisions of labor together determine the social position of women and men in any society and that the gender division of labor derives from the class division of labor.

***mass murder*** This crime is committed when an individual kills two or more people at once, rather than singly over time.

***methodological relativism***  A strategy that operates as a sensitizing device to variation in the definition and meaning of crime in other cultures.

***methodology***  Techniques of measurement used to collect and manipulate empirical data.

***middle-class measuring rod***  Prevailing middle-class standards by which, in A. K. Cohen's theory of the origin of delinquent gangs, all adolescents are evaluated.

***mode of production***  A Marxist concept denoting the means of production and the social relations of production.

***modernization thesis***  The view that technological development produces common effects that tend to make all societies increasingly similar, irrespective of different or even antagonistic political systems.

***money laundering***  The process by which one conceals the existence, illegal source, or illegal application of income and then disguises that income to make it appear legitimate.

***motor vehicle theft***  The unlawful taking of or the attempt to take a motor vehicle such as an automobile, van, truck, or motorcycle.

***murder***  The willful killing of one human being by another, usually with premeditation.

## N

***neoclassical criminology***  The doctrinal and procedural compromise between classicism and positivism, devised roughly between 1890 and 1910, that has become the basis of criminal responsibility and punishment in most Western societies.

***norms***  Social regulations, controls, and procedures for moving toward and achieving goals and values.

## O

***occupational crimes***  Crimes committed by individuals in the course of their occupations for direct personal gain.

***occupational fraud***  A deliberate workplace deception practiced for personal financial gain.

***occupational theft***  An offense that stems from an abuse of trust between employee and employer; it includes employee theft and embezzlement.

***official crime data***  Data collected by the government and its official agencies.

## P, Q

***Panopticon***  Jeremy Bentham's "Inspection House" (c.1780), which was designed as an institution of social control for prisoners, workers, the insane, schoolchildren, soldiers, etc.

*patriarchy* Male control of the labor power and sexuality of women.

*peacemaking criminology* A critical perspective that examines the essence of the person charged with a crime and emphasizes cooperation, compassion, and respect for all species.

*physician fraud* A type of occupational fraud that involves writing pharmaceutical prescriptions, performing unnecessary surgical procedures, or overtreating Medicaid and Medicare patients.

*political bribery* The accepting of money or property by state officials for political favors.

*political crime* Includes crimes against the state (violations of law for the purpose of modifying or changing social conditions) and crimes by the state, both domestic (violations of law and unethical acts by state officials and agencies where victimization occurs inside the United States) and transnational (violations of domestic and international law by state officials or agencies where victimization occurs outside the United States).

*political repression* Illegal or unethical conduct by state officials or agencies for purposes of repressing political dissent.

*positivism* The belief that crime can be observed directly by using the procedures and explanatory logic of the natural sciences.

*positivist criminology* The second great theoretical movement in modern criminology, its method of analysis is based on the collection of observable scientific facts, and its aim is to uncover, to explain, and to predict the ways in which the observable facts of crime occur in uniform patterns.

*postmodernism* This theoretical movement challenges all truth claims, emphasizing alternative discourses, meaning, and subjectivist accounts.

*price-fixing* Violating antitrust laws through collusion to ensure profits above those that would be produced in a competitive industry.

*primary deviance* An original act of crime or deviance that may derive from a wide variety of social, cultural, psychological, and physiological events.

*professional murder* Killing another individual for profit.

*Prohibition* A period in the United States from 1920 to 1933 when the Volstead Act made it illegal to produce, distribute, or sell alcoholic beverages.

*property crime* The unlawful damage to or taking of the property of another.

*prostitution* The consensual grant of nonmonogamous sexual services to clients for payments.

## R

*race* Genetic differences in skin color, which only assume social significance when they are used to justify unequal treatment of one race by another.

***radical feminism*** The viewpoint that masculine power and privilege are the root of all social relations in any society; all other relations (such as class) are secondary and derive from gender relations.

***rape*** As traditionally defined in the criminal law, the carnal knowledge of a female forcibly and against her will, although an expanded definition is used in this book.

***rational choice*** Alleged basis of all calculated human action, including crime, that operates in some of the same ways as free will in theology.

***reaction formation*** A process of adjustment whereby, for example, the academic success typically denied working-class boys is contemptuously redefined as sissy and whereby street knowledge is regarded as superior.

***rebellion*** One of four deviant or criminal responses in Robert Merton's typology of responses to frustrated opportunities.

***reinforcement*** A key concept in social learning theory, which states that crime is largely a response to reinforcing stimuli. If individuals are rewarded for committing crimes, they are more likely to commit them again.

***repressive law*** In Durkheim's sociology, this type of law is religious in its origin and is associated chiefly with societies of mechanical solidarity. Its most common form is criminal law; its violation invites punishment.

***restitutive law*** In Durkheim's sociology, this type of law is associated chiefly with societies of organic solidarity. Its most common form is contract law; its violation invokes a demand to enforce the terms of a prior agreement.

***retreatism*** One of four deviant or criminal responses in Robert Merton's typology of responses to frustrated opportunities.

***ritualism*** One of four deviant or criminal responses in Robert Merton's typology of responses to frustrated opportunities.

***robbery*** The unlawful taking of, or the attempt to take, something of value from another person or persons by using violence or the threat of violence.

***routine activities theory*** A theory claiming that patterns of crime and victimization are the result of the everyday interaction of likely offenders, suitable targets, and guardians.

## S

***secondary deviance*** Society's reaction to some of those who engage in primary deviance, often causing them to accept their identity as a deviant.

***self-control theory*** The idea that individual differences in criminal behavior derive from differences in self-control.

***serial murder*** Killing of two or more people over a period of time by the same individual.

***sexual harassment*** An offense that occurs when the submission to or rejection of sexual advances affects one's employment or when it affects one's work performance by creating an environment that is intimidating, hostile, and offensive.

***shoplifting*** A type of larceny that entails the theft of property from a retail store by customers.

***social classes*** Groups of people who share the same position in the same production system.

***social constructionism*** The view that nothing in society is objective or factual, and that all aspects of society are to be understood as human creations.

***social coercion*** An offense that occurs when women feel that they should have sex with their husbands even if they do not want to because of social pressures—their wifely duty.

***social contract*** A doctrine created by Enlightenment philosophers (1750–1800) which asserted that society is held together by a mutually beneficial agreement between citizens, property owners, and the state.

***social control*** Occurring in both public and private realms, control that has ideological and repressive forms, including primary socialization within the family and secondary socialization within peer groups, the educational system, and the media.

***social disorganization*** A lack of fit between culturally prescribed aspirations and socially structured avenues for achieving them.

***social ecology*** A type of research that examines various geographical areas within cities, communities, and neighborhoods as well as the area concentrations, regularities, and patterns of social life in such fields as work/leisure, health/sickness, and conformity/deviance.

***social harm*** According to Edwin Sutherland, any illegalities that cause social harm should be studied by criminologists, whether or not they are defined by criminal law as such.

***social inequality*** The fact that critical aspects of life such as economic benefits, life chances, social privileges, and political power are unequally distributed in society.

***social learning theory*** This theory holds that social behavior is a cognitive process in which personality and social environment are involved in a continuous process of reciprocal interaction.

***social mechanics*** A nineteenth-century discourse based on the belief that the same lawlike regularity existing in the heavens and in nature also exists in society.

***social position*** One's individual location in society based on such social characteristics as class, gender, race, and age.

***social problem*** A social condition that is perceived as having harmful effects; opinions about whether a condition is a social problem vary among groups and depend on how and by whom the condition is defined and perceived in society.

***social solidarity*** Social order that is abstract and internal to consciousness and that is observable via other, more visible aspects of social life.

***socialist feminism***  The idea that the relationship of class and gender structures crime in society.

***societal reaction***  Part of the process of deviance by which society labels primary deviants, thus giving them an identity that leads them to act in expected ways, causing secondary deviance.

***sociological problem***  A sociological analysis of how patterns of crime arise from the interplay of political, economic, social, and ideological structures in society.

***stalking***  One or more individuals repeatedly pursuing someone in a harassing and/or threatening manner; it can take place offline (physically) or online (through the Internet).

***state, the***  The central political institution of a given society, whose major apparatuses are the government, the legal system, the military, and a variety of public bureaucracies.

***state-corporate crime***  Those illegal and harmful acts that occur at the intersection of state agencies and private corporations.

***state corruption***  The illegal or unethical use of state authority for personal or political gain.

***state terrorism***  Violations of international law that result in the use of force or violence to intimidate, coerce, or change a government or a civilian population for political reasons.

***statistics***  A set of techniques for the reduction of quantitative data to a limited number of more convenient and easily communicated descriptive terms.

***status frustration***  The lack of status in middle-class life, which causes negative feelings and the search for status in delinquent subcultures.

***stigma***  A sign of disgrace imposed on an individual.

***strain***  In Mertonian anomie theory, the many forms of response that one might have to the lack of fit between socially acceptable means and socially desirable goals.

***strong-arm robbery***  A robbery in which the offender does not use a weapon.

***subculture***  Applied to delinquency, a set of beliefs, values, codes, tastes, and prejudices that differs somehow from those of the main or dominant culture.


T


***techniques of neutralization***  The process by which potential delinquents are freed from conventional social and moral controls and because of which they are then able to engage in delinquency.

***terrorism***  The use of force or violence to intimidate, coerce, or change a government or a civilian population for political reasons.

***theories***  Sets of assumptions, mediated by concepts, that guide the interpretation of data and that try to explain both regularities and irregularities in data.

***transnational crime***  Crime committed across borders or across national boundaries.

***transnational corporate crimes*** Illegal behaviors of transnational corporations that conduct business in more than one country and that harm members of other societies; these crimes range from bribery to the export of hazardous products to dangerous working conditions.

***transnational political crimes*** Violations of international law by a state in which the resulting victimization occurs outside that state's territory.

## U

***unofficial crime data*** Nongovernmental data usually collected by private or independent agencies and researchers.

***utilitarianism*** The doctrine of free will that holds that all men rationally and freely choose to engage in the social contract and that those who challenge this contract, break its rules, or pursue harmful pleasures or wickedness are liable to be punished.

## V

***victimization surveys*** Surveys of representative samples of a general population that try to uncover what crimes have been experienced in a given period.

***victimless crimes*** Crimes created by the attempt to ban, through criminal legislation, the exchange of strongly desired goods and services between willing partners.

***victim precipitation*** Cited as a defense to a crime when the victim is said to be a direct, positive precipitator in the crime.

***white-collar crime*** The term first coined by Edwin Sutherland to describe a crime committed by a person of respectability and high social status in the course of his or her occupation. It typically takes an economic form and is stimulated by economic cycles.

## W

***wife rape*** Differs from rape in that women are raped only by a husband or an ex-husband. ✦

# References

Abadinsky, Howard. 1989. *Drug Abuse: An Introduction*. Chicago: Nelson-Hall.

Abt, Vicki, and Douglas J. McDowell. 1987. Does the Press Cover Gambling Issues Poorly? *Social Science Research* 71 (3): 193–197.

Adams, Carol. J. 1990. 'Deena'—the World's Only Stripping Chimp. *Animals Voice Magazine* 3, no. 1

Adler, Freda. 1975. *Sisters in Crime: The Rise of the New Female Offender*. New York: McGraw-Hill.

———. 1977. The Interaction Between Women's Emancipation and Female Criminality: A Cross-Cultural Perspective. *International Journal of Criminology and Penology* 5 (1): 101–112.

———. 1983. *Nations Not Obsessed with Crime*. Littleton, CO: Fred B. Rothman.

Adler, Jeffrey S. 1989. A Historical Analysis of the Law of Vagrancy. *Criminology* 27 (2): 209–229.

Adler, Patricia A., and Peter Adler. 1998. Foreword to *Ethnography at the Edge*, edited by Jeff Ferrell and Mark S. Hamm, xii–xvi. Boston: Northeastern University Press.

Ageton, Suzanne, and Delbert S. Elliott. 1974. The Effects of Legal Processing on Self-Concept. *Social Problems* 22 (1): 87–100.

Agnew, Robert. 1985. Social Control Theory and Delinquency: A Longitudinal Test. *Criminology* 23 (1): 47–61.

———. 1992. Foundation for a General Strain Theory of Crime and Delinquency. *Criminology* 30 (1): 47–87.

———. 1995. Strain and Subcultural Theories of Criminality. In *Criminology: A Contemporary Handbook*, edited by Joseph F. Sheley, 305–327. Belmont, CA: Wadsworth.

———. 1998. The Causes of Animal Abuse: A Social-Psychological Analysis. *Theoretical Criminology* 2 (2): 177–209.

Agnew, Robert, Francis T. Cullen, Velmer S. Burton, T. David Evans, and R. Gregory Dunaway. 1996. A New Test of Classic Strain Theory. *Justice Quarterly* 13 (4): 681–704.

Akers, Ronald L. 1973. *Deviant Behavior*. Belmont, CA: Wadworth.

———. 1997. *Criminological Theories*. Los Angeles: Roxbury.

———. 1998. *Social Learning and Social Structure: A General Theory of Crime and Deviance*. Boston: Northeastern University Press.

———. 1999. Social Learning and Social Structure: Reply to Sampson, Morash and Krohn. *Theoretical Criminology* 3 (4): 477–493.

Akers, Ronald L., and Gary F. Jensen (eds.). 2003. *Social Learning Theory and the Explanation of Crime: A Guide for the New Century*. New Brunswick, NJ: Transaction.

Akers, Ronald L., Marvin D. Krohn, Lonn Lanza-Kaduce, and Marcia Radosevich. 1979. Social Learning and Deviant Behavior: A Specific Test of a General Theory. *American Sociological Review* 44 (4): 636–655.

Albanese, Jay. 1985. *Organized Crime in America*. Cincinnati: Anderson.

———. 2004. *Organized Crime in Our Times*. Cincinnati, OH: Anderson.

Albini, Joseph L. 1971. *The American Mafia: Genesis of a Legend*. New York: Appleton-Century-Crofts.

Alvazzi del Frate, Anna, and J. N. Van Kesteren. 2004. Criminal Victimization in Urban Europe. Key Findings of the 2000 International Crime Victims Survey, available at <www.unicri.it/icvs/publications/pdf_files/key2000i/index.htm>.

Amnesty International. 1998. *USA—Rights for All*. London: Amnesty International Secretariat.

———. 2004. *Clouds of Injustice: Bhopal Disaster 20 Years On*. London: Amnesty International Publications.

Anderson, David C. 1999. The Aggregate Burden of Crime. *Journal of Law and Economics* 42 (2): 611–642.

Anderson, Elijah. 1999. *Code of the Street*. New York: W.W. Norton & Company.

Anderson, Margaret L. 1993. *Thinking About Women: Sociological Perspectives on Sex and Gender*. New York: Macmmillan.

Anderson, Sarah, and John Cavanagh. 2000. *Top 200: The Rise of Corporate Global Power*. Washington, D.C.: Institute for Policy Studies.

Andrew, D. T. 1980. The Code of Honour and Its Critics: The Opposition to Duelling in England, 1700–1850. *Social History* 5 (3): 409–434.

Archer, Dane, and Rosemary Gartner. 1984. *Violence and Crime in Cross-National Perspective*. New Haven: Yale University Press.

Archer, John E. 1985. 'A Fiendish Outrage'? A Study of Animal Maiming in East Anglia: 1830–1870. *Agricultural History Review* 33 (Part II): 147–157.

Arluke, Arnold, Jack Levin, Carter Luke, and Frank Ascione. 1999. The Relationship of Animal Abuse to Violence and Other Forms of Antisocial Behavior. *Journal of Interpersonal Violence* 14 (9): 963–975.

Arrigo, Bruce A. 2003. Postmodern Justice and Critical Criminology: Positional, Relational, and Provisional Science. In *Controversies in Critical Criminology*, edited by Martin D. Schwartz and Suzanne E. Hatty, 43–55. Cincinnati, OH: Anderson.

Ascione, Frank R. 2001. *Animal Abuse and Youth Violence*. Washington, D.C.: U.S. Department of Justice, Office of Juvenile Justice and Delinquency Prevention.

Asinoff, Robert. 1985. India Accident Raises Questions of Corporate Responsibiility. *In These Times* December 19–January 8: 10.

Aulette, Judy Root, and Raymond Michalowski. 1993. Fire in Hamlet: A Case Study of State-Corporate Crime. In *Political Crime in Contemporary America: A Critical Approach*, edited by Kenneth Tunnell, 171–206. New York: Garland Press.

Avakame, Edem F., James J. Fyfe, and Candace McCoy. 1999. Did You Call the Police? What Did They Do? An Empirical Assessment of Black's Theory of Mobilization of Law. *Justice Quarterly* 16 (4): 765–792.

Bachman, Ronet. 1994. *Violence and Theft in the Workplace*. Washington, D.C.: Bureau of Justice Statistics.

———. 2001. Assault (Context of in the United States). In *Encyclopedia of Criminology and Deviant Behavior*, edited by Clifton D. Bryant, 37–40. New York: Brunner-Routledge.

Bailey, William C., and Ruth D. Peterson. 1987. Police Killings and Capital Punishment: The Post-Furman Period. *Criminology* 25 (1): 1–25.

———. 1995. Gender Inequality and Violence Against Women: The Case of Murder. In *Crime and Inequality*, edited by John Hagan and Ruth D. Peterson, 174–205. Stanford, CA: Stanford University Press.

Baldry, Anna C. 2003. Animal Abuse and Exposure to Interparental Violence in Italian Youth. *Journal of Interpersonal Violence* 18 (3): 258–281.

Balkan, Sheila, Ronald Berger, and Janet Schmidt. 1980. *Crime and Deviance in America: A Critical Approach*. Monterey, CA: Wadsworth.

Ball, Richard A. 1966. An Empirical Exploration of Neutralization Theory. *Criminology* 4 (2): 22–32.

Bandura, Albert. 1973. *Aggression: A Social Learning Analysis*. Englewood Cliffs, NJ: Prentice-Hall.

Barak, Gregg. 1998. *Integrating Criminologies*. Boston: Allyn and Bacon.

———. 2001. Crime and Crime Control in an Age of Globalization: A Theoretical Discussion. *Critical Criminology* 10 (1): 57–72.

Barclay, Gordon, and Cynthia Tavares 2003. International Comparisons of Criminal Justice Statistics 2001, *Home Office Bulletin* no. 12/03.

Barlow, Melissa Hickman. 1998. Race and the Problem of Crime in Time and Newsweek Cover Stories, 1946 to 1995. *Social Justice* 25 (2): 149–183.

Barry, Kathleen. 1979. *Female Sexual Slavery*. Englewood Cliffs, NJ: Prentice-Hall.

Bartol, Anne M. 2001. White-Collar Crime. In *Encyclopedia of Women and Crime*, edited by Nicole Hahn Rafter, 284–285. Phoenix, AZ: Oryx Press.

Basile, Kathleen C. 1999. Rape by Acquiescence: The Ways in Which Women 'Give in' to Unwanted Sex With Their Husbands. *Violence Against Women* 5 (9): 1017–1035.

Battle, Joyce. 2003. *Shaking Hands with Saddam Hussein: The U.S. Tilts toward Iraq, 1980–1984.* Washington, D.C.: National Security Archive.

Bayley, David H. 1991. *Forces of Order: Policing Modern Japan.* Berkeley: University of California Press.

Beaty, Jonathan, and S. C. Gwynne. 1991. *The Dirtiest Bank of All.* Time, July 29, 42–47.

Beccaria, Cesare. [1764] 1963. *Of Crimes and Punishments.* Translated by Henry Paolucci. Indianapolis: Bobbs-Merrill.

Becker, Howard S. 1963. *Outsiders: Studies in the Sociology of Deviance.* New York: Free Press.

Beckett, Katherine, and Theodore Sasson. 2004. *The Politics of Injustice: Crime and Punishment in America.* 2nd edition. Thousand Oaks, CA: Sage.

Beirne, Piers. 1979. Empiricism and the Critique of Marxism on Law and Crime. *Social Problems* 26 (4): 373–385.

———. 1987. Adolphe Quetelet and the Origins of Positivist Criminology. *American Journal of Sociology* 92 (5): 1140–1169.

———. 1993. *Inventing Criminology: Essays on the Rise of* Homo Criminalis. Albany: State University of New York Press.

———. 1994. The Law Is an Ass: Reading E. P. Evans, *The Medieval Prosecution and Capital Punishment of Animals. Society and Animals* 2 (1): 27–46.

———. 1999. For a Nonspeciesist Criminology: Animal Abuse as an Object of Study, *Criminology,* 37 (1): 117–148.

———. 2002. On the Sexual Assault of Animals: A Sociological View. In *The Animal/Human Boundary: Historical Perspectives,* edited by Angela N. H. Creager and William Chester Jordan, 193–227. Rochester, NY: Rochester University Press and Davis Center, Princeton University.

———. 2004. From Animal Abuse to Interhuman Violence? A Critical Review of the Progression Thesis. *Society & Animals* 12 (1): 39–65.

Beirne, Piers, and David Nelken, eds. 1997. *Issues in Comparative Criminology. International Library of Criminology and Criminal Justice.* Aldershot: Dartmouth.

Belknap, Joanne. 2001. *The Invisible Woman: Gender, Crime, and Justice.* Belmont, CA: Wadsworth.

Bell, Daniel. 1961. *The End of Ideology.* New York: Collier.

Bellis, David J. 1981. *Heroin and Politicians: The Failure of Public Policy to Control Addiction in America.* Westport, CT: Greenwood.

Bennett, James. 1981. *Oral History and Delinquency: The Rhetoric of Criminology.* Chicago: University of Chicago Press.

Bennis, Phyllis. 2003. *Before & After: U.S. Foreign Policy and the September 11th Crisis.* New York: Olive Branch Press.

Benson, Donna J., and Gregg E. Thompson. 1982. Sexual Harassment on a University Campus: The Confluence of Authority Relation, Sexual Interest, and Gender Stratification. *Social Problems* 29 (3): 236–251.

Benson, Michael L., and Greer Litton Fox. 2004. *When Violence Hits Home: How Economics and Neighborhood Play a Role.* Washington, D.C.: National Institute of Justice.

Bentham, Jeremy. [1780] 1973. *An Introduction to the Principles of Morals and Legislation.* New York: Hafner Press.

Bergen, Raquel Kennedy, ed. 1998. *Issues in Intimate Violence.* Thousand Oaks, CA: Sage.

Bernard, Thomas J. 1983. *The Consensus-Conflict Debate: Form and Content in Social Theories.* New York: Columbia University Press.

———. 1987. Structure and Control: Reconsidering Hirschi's Concept of Commitment. *Justice Quarterly* 4 (3): 409–424.

Bernard, Thomas J., and Jeffrey B. Snipes. 1996. Theoretical Integration in Criminology. In *Crime and Justice: A Review of Research,* edited by Michael Tonry, 20:301–348. Chicago: University of Chicago Press.

Berry, Steve. 1998. Special Report: Time-Honored Oath to 'Whole Truth' May Be Losing Aura. *Los Angeles Times,* August 9.

Best, Joel, ed. 2001. *How Claims Spread.* New York: Aldine de Gruyter.

———. 2004. *More Damned Lies and Statistics: How Numbers Confuse Public Issues.* Berkeley: University of California Press.

Bianchi, Herman, and Rene Van Swaaningen, eds. 1986. *Abolitionism: Towards a Nonrepressive Approach to Crime*. Amsterdam: Free University Press.

Black, Donald. 1970. Production of Crime Rates. *American Sociological Review* 35 (4): 733–748.

———. 1976. *The Behavior of Law*. New York: Academic Press.

———. 1989. *Sociological Justice*. New York: Oxford University Press.

Black, George. 1981. *Triumph of the People: The Sandinistas Revolution in Nicaragua*. London: Zed Press.

Blau, Judith R., and Peter M. Blau. 1982. The Cost of Inequality: Metropolitan Structure and Violent Crime. *American Sociological Review* 47 (1): 114–129.

Block, Alan. 1979. The Snowman Cometh: Coke in Progressive New York. *Criminology* 17 (1): 75–99.

———. 1983. *East Side, West Side: Organizing Crime in New York, 1930–1950*. New Brunswick, NJ: Transaction.

———, ed. 1991. *The Business of Crime: A Documentary Study of Organized Crime in the American Economy*. Boulder, CO: Westview Press.

Block, Alan, and William J. Chambliss. 1981. *Organizing Crime*. New York: Elsevier.

Block, Maggie, Rosa Bernstein, Penny Ciancanelli, Gay Ferguson, Alan Howard, Kathy Huenemann, Marta Sanchez, Bob Seltzer, Julio Velazquez, and Sol Yurick. 1972. Nixon and Organized Crime. *North American Congress on Latin America (NACLA)* 6: 3–17.

Blok, Anton. 1974. *The Mafia of a Sicilian Village*. 1860–1960. New York: Harper and Row.

Blumstein, Alfred. 2000. *Effects of NIBRS on Crime Statistics, NCJ-178890*. Washington, D.C.: U.S. Department of Justice.

———. 2002. Why Is Crime Falling—Or Is It? *Perspectives on Crime and Justice, National Institute of Justice 2000–2001 Lecture Series* 5: 1–34.

Boeringer, S. D. 1996. Influences of Fraternity Membership, Athletics and Male Living Arrangements on Sexual Aggression. *Violence Against Women* 2 (2): 134–147.

Bonger, Willem. 1905. *Criminality and Economic Conditions*. Bloomington, IN: Indiana University Press.

Boostrom, Ronald L. 1974. *The Personalization of Evil: The Emergence of American Criminology, 1865–1910*. Ph.D. diss. University of California, Berkeley.

*Boston Herald*. 1988. *7 Cops Guilty in Racketeering Case*. September 4, 10.

Bourgois, Philippe. 1996. In Search of Masculinity: Violence, Respect, and Sexuality Among Puerto Rican Crack Dealers in East Harlem. *British Journal of Criminology* 36 (3): 412–427.

Bowker, Lee (ed.). 1998. *Masculinities and Violence*. Thousand Oaks, CA: Sage.

Bowker, Michael. 2003. *Fatal Deception: The Untold Story of Asbestos*. New York: St. Martins.

Box, Steven. 1983. *Power and Mystification*. New York: Tavistock.

———. 1987. *Recession, Crime, and Punishment*. London: Macmillan.

Brady, James P. 1983. Arson, Urban Economy, and Organized Crime: The Case of Boston. *Social Problems* 31 (1): 127.

Braithwaite, John. 1979a. Transnational Corporations and Corruption: Towards Some International Solutions. *International Journal of the Sociology of Law* 7 (2): 125–142.

———. 1979b. *Inequality, Crime, and Public Policy*. Boston: Routledge and Kegan Paul.

———. 1981. The Myth of Social Class and Criminality Reconsidered. *American Sociological Review* 46 (1): 36–57.

———. 1984. *Corporate Crime in the Pharmaceutical Industry*. Boston: Routledge and Kegan Paul.

———. 1989. *Crime, Shame, and Reintegration*. Cambridge: Cambridge University Press.

———. 1997. Charles Tittle's Control Balance and Criminological Theory. *Theoretical Criminology* 1 (1): 77–97.

———. 2002. Setting Standards for Restorative Justice. *British Journal of Criminology* 42 (3): 563–577.

Braithwaite, John, and Philip Pettit. 1990. *Not Just Deserts: A Republican Theory of Criminal Justice*. Oxford: Oxford University Press.

Branfman, Frank. 1978. South Vietnam's Police and Prison System: The U.S. Connection. In *Uncloaking the CLA*, edited by Howard Frazier, 110–127. New York: Free Press.

Bray, Howard. 1980. *Pillars of the Post*. New York: W.W. Norton.

Breacher, Edward M. 1972. *Licit and Illicit Drugs*. Boston: Little, Brown.

Brecher, Jeremy. 1980. *Strike!* Boston: South End Press.

Brenner, M. Harvey. 1976. *Estimating the Social Costs of National Economic Policy*. Joint Economic Committee of the U.S. Congress. Washington, D.C.: U.S. Government Printing Office.

Brezina, Timothy. 1996. Adapting to Strain: An Examination of Delinquent Coping Responses. *Criminology* 34 (1): 39–60.

Britt, Chester L. 1997. Reconsidering the Unemployment and Crime Relationship: Variations by Age Group and Historical Period. *Journal of Quantitative Criminology* 13: 405–428.

Brody, Reed. 1985. *Contra Terror in Nicaragua: Report of a Fact-Finding Mission, September 1984–January 1985.* Boston: South End Press.

Brogden, Mike, and Preeti Nijhar. 2000. *Crime, Abuse, and the Elderly.* Portland, OR: Willan.

Broidy, Lisa, and Robert Agnew. 1997. Gender and Crime: A General Strain Theory Perspective. *Journal of Research in Crime and Delinquency* 34 (3): 275–306.

Brown, Julia S. 1952. A Comparative Study of Deviations from Sexual Mores. *American Sociological Review* 17 (2): 135–146.

Browne, Angela. 1995. Fear and Perception of Alternatives: Asking 'Why Battered Women Don't Leave?' Is the Wrong Question. In *The Criminal Justice System and Women,* edited by Barbara Raffel Price and Natalie J. Sokoloff, 228–245. New York: McGraw-Hill.

Brownmiller, Susan. 1975. *Against Our Will: Men, Women, and Rape.* New York: Simon and Schuster.

Bruce, Marino, and V. Roscigno. 2003. 'Race Effects' and Conceptual Ambiguity in Violence Research: Bringing Inequality Back In. In *Violent Crime: Assessing Race and Ethnic Differences,* edited by D. Hawkins, 238–254. New York: Cambridge University Press.

Bruce, Marino A., Vincent J. Roscigno, and Patricia L. McCall. 1998. Structure, Context, and Agency in the Reproduction of Black-on-Black Violence. *Theoretical Criminology* 2 (1): 29–55.

Buder, Leonard. 1986. In Partial Verdict, U.S. Jury Finds 6 Radicals Guilty of 2 Bombings. *New York Times,* March 5, B3.

Buergenthal, Thomas and Sean D. Murphy. 2002. *Public International Law.* St. Paul, MN: West Publishing.

Buikhuisen, Wouter, and Fokke P. H. Dijksterhuis. 1971. Delinquency and Stigmatisation. *British Journal of Criminology* 11 (2): 185–187.

Buitrago, Ann Mari. 1988. *Report on CISPES Files Maintained by FBI Headquarters and Released Under the Freedom of Information Act.* New York: Fund for Open Information and Accountability, Inc.

Bulmer, Martin. 1984. *The Chicago School of Sociology: Institutionalization, Diversity, and the Rise of Sociological Research.* Chicago: University of Chicago Press.

Bureau of Justice Statistics. 1989a. *New Directions for the National Crime Survey.* Report NCJ-115571. Washington, D.C.: U.S. Department of Justice.

———. 1993a. *Highlights from 20 Years of Surveying Crime Victims.* Report NCJ-144-525. Washington, D.C.: Department of Justice.

———. 1998. *Crime and Justice in the United States and in England and Wales, 1981–1996.* Report NCJ-173402. Washington, D.C.: U.S. Department of Justice.

———. 2000. *Effects of NIBRS on Crime Statistics.* NCJ-178890. Washington, D.C.: U.S. Department of Justice.

———. 2004a. *Crime and Victim Statistics: Summary Findings.* <http://www.ojp.usdoj.gov/bjs/cvictgen.html>.

———. 2004b. *Criminal Victimization.* <http://www.ojp.usdoj.gov/bjs/cvictgen.htm>.

Burgess, Ann W., and Linda L. Holmstrom. 1983. *The Victim of Rape.* New Brunswick, NJ: Transaction Books.

Burgess, E. W. 1925. The Growth of the City: An Introduction to a Research Project. In *The City,* edited by Robert E. Park and E. W. Burgess, 47–62. Chicago: University of Chicago Press.

Burgess, Robert L., and Ronald L. Akers. 1966. A Differential Association-Reinforcement Theory of Criminal Behavior. *Social Problems* 14 (2): 128–147.

Burgoon, Brian. 1996. Job-Destroying Villain: Is It NAFTA or the Mexican Currency Crisis? In *Real World International,* edited by Marc Breslow, David Levy, and Abby Scher, 14–18. Somerville, MA: Dollars and Sense.

Burman, Michele, Susan Batchelor, and Jane Brown. 2001. Researching Girls and Violence: Facing the Dilemmas of Fieldwork. *British Journal of Criminology* 41 (3): 443–459.

Bursik, Robert J. 1984. Urban Dynamics and Ecological Studies of Delinquency. *Social Forces* 63 (2): 393–413.

Burton, Velmer S., Francis T. Cullen, T. David Evans, Leanne Fiftal Alarid, and R. Gregory Dunaway. 1998. Gender, Self-Control, and Crime. *Journal of Research in Crime and Delinquency* 35 (2): 123–147.

Butterfield, Fox. 2004. Almost 10% of All Prisoners Are Now Serving Life Terms. *New York Times* May 12, p. A.15.

Bynum, Timothy. 1987. Controversies in the Study of Organized Crime. In *Organized Crime in America: Concepts and Controversies,* edited by Timothy Bynum, 3–11. Monsey, N.Y.: Willow Tree Press.

Cain, Maureen, and Alan Hunt. 1979. *Marx and Engels on Law.* London: Academic Press.

Calavita, Kitty, Henry N. Pontell, and Robert H. Tillman. 1997. *Big Money Crime: Fraud and Politics in the Savings and Loan Crisis.* Berkeley: University of California Press.

Cameron, Mary Owen. 1964. *The Booster and the Snitch.* New York: Free Press.

Camic, Charles, and Yu Xie. 1994. The Statistical Turn in American Social Science: Columbia University, 1890 to 1915. *American Sociological Review* 59 (5): 773–805.

Campbell, Elaine. 2004. Police Narrativity in the Risk Society. *British Journal of Criminology* 44 (5): 695–714.

Cantor, David, and James P. Lynch. 2000. Self-Report Surveys as Measures of Crime and Criminal Victimization. *Criminal Justice* 4: 85–138.

Caputi, Jane. 2000. Call Girls. In *Encyclopedia of Women and Crime,* edited by Nicole Hahn Rafter, 18–19. Phoenix: Oryx Press.

Carlen, Pat, and Tony Jefferson, eds. 1996. Masculinities and Crime. Special Issue of the *British Journal of Criminology* 33 (6).

Carlson, Susan M., and Raymond J. Michalowski 1997. Crime, Unemployment and Social Structures of Accumulation: An Inquiry into Historical Contingency. *Justice Quarterly* 14: 101–133.

Carson, Taj C. 2000. Organized Crime (The Mafia). In *Encyclopedia of Women and Crime,* edited by Nicole Hahn Rafter, 160. Phoenix, AZ: Oryx Press.

Caulfield, Susan L., and Angela R. Evans. 1997. Peacemaking Criminology: A Path to Understanding and a Model for Methodology. In *Thinking Critically About Crime,* edited by Brian D. MacLean and Dragan Milovanovic, 102–108. Vancouver, B.C.: Collective Press.

Center for Constitutional Rights. 1988. Political Spying and the Central America Movement. *Movement Support Network News* 4: 13.

Center for Economic and Social Rights. 2003. *Tearing Up the Rules: The Illegality of Invading Iraq.* New York: Center for Economic and Social Rights.

———. 2004. *Beyond Torture: U.S. Violations of Occupation Law in Iraq.* New York: Center for Economic and Social Rights.

Cernkovich, Stephen A., and Peggy C. Giordano. 1987. Family Relationships and Delinquency. *Sociological Quarterly* 20 (2): 131–145.

Chambliss, William J. 1964. A Sociological Analysis of the Law of Vagrancy. *Social Problems* 12 (1): 67–77.

———. 1975. Toward a Political Economy of Crime. *Theory and Society* 2 (Summer): 149–170.

———. 1988a. *On the Take: From Petty Crooks to Presidents.* Bloomington: Indiana University Press.

———. 1988b. *Exploring Criminology.* New York: Macmillan.

Chambliss, William J., and Robert B. Seidman. 1982. *Law, Order, and Power.* Reading, MA: Addison-Wesley.

Chancer, Lynn S. 1998. *Reconcilable Differences: Confronting Beauty, Pornography, and the Future of Feminism.* Berkeley: University of California Press.

Chang, Nancy. 2001. *The USA PATRIOT Act: What's so Patriotic about Trampling on the Bill of Rights?* New York: Center for Constitutional Rights.

Chapkis, Wendy. 1997. *Live Sex Acts: Women Performing Erotic Labor.* New York: Routledge.

Chepesiuk, Ron. 1999. *Hard Target: The United States War Against International Drug Trafficking, 1982–1997.* Jefferson, NC: McFarland and Company.

Chermak, Steven. 1994. Body Count News: How Crime Is Presented in the News Media. *Justice Quarterly* 11 (4): 561–582.

Chesney-Lind, Meda. 1995. Girls, Delinquency, and Juvenile Justice: Toward a Feminist Theory of Young Women's Crime. In *The Criminal Justice System and Women,* edited by Barbara Raffel Price and Natalie J. Sokoloff, 71–88. New York: McGraw-Hill.

Chesney-Lind, Meda, and Lisa Pasko. 2004. *The Female Offender.* Thousand Oaks, CA: Sage.

Chesney-Lind, Meda, and Randall G. Shelden. 2004. *Girls, Delinquency, and Juvenile Justice.* 3rd edition. Belmont, CA: Wadsworth/Thomson.

Chevalier, Louis. 1973. *Laboring Classes and Dangerous Classes in Paris During the First Half of the Nineteenth Century.* Translated by Frank Jellinek. Princeton: Princeton University Press.

Chomsky, Noam. 2002. *9-11.* New York: Seven Stories Press.

———. 2003. *Hegemony or Survival: America's Quest for Global Dominance.* New York: Metropolitan Books.

Chomsky, Noam, and Edward S. Herman. 1977. The United States Versus Human Rights in the Third World. *Monthly Review* 29 (July-August): 22–45.

———. 1979. *The Washington Connection and Third World Fascism.* Boston: South End Press.

Church Committee. 1975. Select Committee to Study Governmental Operations with Respect to Intelligence Activities. *Alleged Assassination Plots Involving Foreign Leaders.* Washington, D.C.: U.S. Government Printing Office.

———. 1976. Select Committee to Study Governmental Operations with Respect to Intelligence Activities. *Intelligence Activities and the Rights of Americans.* Washington, D.C.: U.S. Government Printing Office.

Churchill, Ward, and Jim Vander Wall. 1988. *Agents of Repression.* Boston: South End Press.

Clarke, Richard. 2004. *Against All Enemies: Inside America's War on Terror.* New York: Free Press.

Clarke, Ronald V., and Patricia M. Harris. 1992. Auto Theft and Its Prevention. In *Crime and Justice: A Review of Research,* edited by Michael Tonry, 16: 1–54. Chicago: University of Chicago Press.

Claybrook, Joan. 1984. *Retreat From Safety.* New York: Pantheon.

———. 1986. White-Collar Crime. *Trial* April, 35–36.

Clinard, Marshall B., and Daniel J. Abbott. 1973. *Crime in Developing Countries: A Comparative Perspective.* New York: John Wiley.

Clinard, Marshall B., and Richard Quinney. 1973. *Criminal Behavior Systems.* New York: Holt, Rinehart and Winston.

Clinard, Marshall B., and Peter C. Yeager. 1980. *Corporate Crime.* New York: Free Press.

Cloward, Richard A., and Lloyd E. Ohlin. 1960. *Delinquency and Opportunity: A Theory of Delinquent Gangs.* New York: Free Press.

Cohen, Albert K. 1955. *Delinquent Boys: The Culture of the Gang.* New York: Free Press.

———. 1965. The Sociology of the Deviant Act: Anomie Theory and Beyond. *American Sociological Review* 30 (1): 5–14.

Cohen, Lawrence E., and Marcus Felson. 1979. Social Change and Crime Rate Trends: A Routine Activity Approach. *American Sociological Review* 44 (4): 588–608.

Cohen, Stanley. [1972] 1980. *Folk Devils and Moral Panics: The Creation of the Mods and Rockers.* New York: St. Martins Press.

Coleman, James. 1994. *The Criminal Elite.* New York: St. Martins Press.

———. 2002. *The Criminal Elite: Understanding White-Collar Crime.* New York: Worth.

Collier, Richard. 1998. *Masculinities, Crime, and Criminology: Men, Heterosexuality, and the Criminal(ized) Other.* Thousand Oaks, CA: Sage

Conklin, John. 1972. *Robbery and the Criminal Justice System.* New York: Lippincott.

———. 2003. *Why Crime Rates Fell.* Boston: Allyn and Bacon.

Cook, Philip J., and Gary A. Zarkin. 1985. Crime and the Business Cycle. *Journal of Legal Studies* 14 (1): 115–128.

Cooley, John. 2000. *Unholy Wars: Afghanistan, America, and International Terrorism.* London: Pluto Press.

Copes, Heith and Samuel E. Wallace. 2001. Motor Vehicle Theft. In *Encyclopedia of Criminology and Deviant Behavior,* edited by Clifton D. Bryant, 393–396. New York: Brunner-Routledge.

Corbett, Claire. 2003. *Car Crime.* Portland, OR: Willan.

Corn, David. 1988. Bush's CIA: The Same Old Dirty Tricks. *The Nation* August 27–September 3, 157–160.

———. 2003. *The Lies of George W. Bush: Mastering the Politics of Deception.* New York: Crown Publishers.

Cornish, Derek B., and Ronald V. Clarke. 1986. *The Reasoning Criminal: Rational Choice Perspectives on Offending.* New York: Springer-Verlag.

Costello, Barbara. 1997. On the Logical Adequacy of Cultural Deviance Theories. *Theoretical Criminology* 1 (4): 403–428.

Cressey, Donald. 1969. *Theft of the Nation.* New York: Harper and Row.

Criminal Justice Collective. 2000. *Investigating Difference: Human and Cultural Relations in Criminal Justice.* Boston: Allyn & Bacon.

Cromwell, Paul F., Roger Dunham, Ronald Akers, and Lonn Llanza-Kaduce. 1995. Routine Activities and Social Control in the Aftermath of a Natural Catastrophe. *European Journal on Criminal Policy and Research* 3: 56–69.

Cromwell, Paul F., and Jason Jolicouer. 2001. Burglary. In *Encyclopedia of Criminology and Deviant Behavior*, edited by Clifton D. Bryant, 50–53. NY: Brunner-Routledge.

Cromwell, Paul F., James N. Olson, and D'Aunn Wester Avary. 1991. *Breaking and Entering: An Ethnographic Analysis of Burglary*. Newbury Park, CA: Sage.

Crosset, Todd, J. Ptacek, M. McDonald, and Jeffrey Benedict. 1996. Male Student Athletes and Violence Against Women: A Survey of Campus Judicial Affairs Offices. *Violence Against Women* 2 (2): 163–179.

Crosset, Todd, Jeffrey R. Benedict, and Mark McDonald. 1995. Male Student Athletes Reported for Sexual Assault: A Survey of Campus Police Departments and Judicial Affairs Offices. *Journal of Sport and Social Issues* 19 (2): 126–140.

Cruz, Michael J. 2000. Gay Male Domestic Violence and the Pursuit of Masculinity. In *Gay Masculinities*, edited by Peter Nardi, 66–82. Thousand Oaks, CA: Sage.

Cullen, Francis T., and Robert Agnew, eds. 1999. *Criminological Theory, Past to Present: Essential Readings*. Los Angeles: Roxbury Publishing.

Cullen, Francis, William J. Maakestad, and Gray Cavender. 1987. *Corporate Crime Under Attack*. Cincinnati: Anderson.

Cullen, Francis, John Wozniak, and James Frank. 1985. The Rise of the Elderly Offender: Will a New Criminal Be Invented? *Crime and Social Justice* 23: 151–165.

Current Population Reports. 1997. *The Black Population in the United States*. Washington, D.C.: Census Bureau.

———. 2004. *Projections of the Population of the U.S. by Age, Sex, and Race: 2004 to 2080*. Washington, D.C.: U.S. Government Printing Office.

Currie, Elliott. 1985. *Confronting Crime: An American Challenge*. New York: Pantheon.

———. 1997. Market, Crime, and Community. *Theoretical Criminology* 1 (2): 147–172.

———. 1998. *Crime and Punishment in America*. New York: Metropolitan.

Curry, Timothy. 2000. Booze and Bar Fights: A Journey to the Dark Side of College Athletics. In *Masculinities, Gender Relations, and Sport*, edited by Jim McKay, Michael Messner, and Donald Sabo, 162–75. Thousand Oaks, CA: Sage.

Dadds, Mark R., Cynthia M. Turner, and John McAloon. 2002. Developmental Links Between Cruelty to Animals and Human Violence. *Australian and New Zealand Journal of Criminology* 35 (3): 363–382.

Dahmer, Lionel. 1994. *A Father's Story*. New York: W. Morrow.

Daly, Kathleen. 2002. Restorative Justice: The Real Story. *Punishment and Society* 4 (1): 55–79.

Daly, Kathleen, and Meda Chesney-Lind. 1988. Feminism and Criminology. *Justice Quarterly* 5 (4): 101–143.

———. 1988. Battered Women: Implications for Social Control. *Contemporary Crises* 12 (4): 345–372.

Daly, Kathleen, and Lisa Maher, eds. 1998. *Criminology at the Crossroads: Feminist Readings in Crime and Justice*. New York: Oxford University Press.

de Haan, Willem. 1990. *The Politics of Redress: Crime, Punishment, and Penal Abolition*. Boston: Unwin Hyman.

de Haan, Willem, and Jaco Vos. 2003. A Crying Shame: The Over-Rationalized Conception of Man in the Rational Choice Perspective. *Theoretical Criminology* 7: 29–54.

DeFronzo, James. 1983. Economic Assistance to Impoverished Americans. *Criminology* 21 (1): 119–136.

DeKeseredy, Walter. 2003. Left Realism on Inner-City Violence. In *Controversies in Critical Criminology*, edited by Martin D. Schwartz and Suzanne E. Hatty, 29–41. Cincinnati, OH: Anderson.

Dekkers, Midas. 2000. *Dearest Pet*. London: Verso.

Department of Justice. 2003. *Sourcebook of Criminal Justice Statistics*. Washington, D.C. Department of Justice.

Department of Labor. 1988. *Labor Force Statistics Derived From the Current Population Survey, 1948–1987*. Washington, D.C.: U.S. Government Printing Office.

———. 1998. *News*. Washington, D.C.: Bureau of Labor Statistics.

Desroches, Frederick J. 2002. *Force and Fear: Robbery in Canada*. Toronto: Canadian Scholars' Press.

———. 2003. Drug Trafficking and Organized Crime in Canada: A Study of High-Level Drug Networks. In *Critical Reflections on Transnational Organized Crime, Money Laundering, and Corruption,* edited by Margaret E. Beare, 237–255. Toronto: University of Toronto Press.

Diamond, Stanley. 1973. The Rule of Law Versus the Order of Custom. In *The Social Organization of Law,* edited by Donald Black and Maureen Mileski, 318–334. New York: Seminar Press.

DiCristina, Bruce. 2004. Durkheim's Theory of Homicide and the Confusion of the Empirical Literature. *Theoretical Criminology* 8 (1): 57–91.

Dinges, John. 2004. *The Condor Years: How Pinochet and His Allies Brought Terrorism to Three Continents.* New York: W.W. Norton.

Dinham, B., and S. Sarangi. 2002. The Bhopal Gas Tragedy, 1984—The Evasion of Corporate Responsibility. *Environment and Urbanization* 14 (1), April.

Ditton, Jason. 1977a. *Part-Time Crime.* New York: Macmillan.

———. 1977b. Perks, Pilferage, and the Fiddle: The Historical Structure of Invisible Wages. *Theory and Society* 4 (1): 39–71.

———. 1979. *Controlology.* London: Macmillan.

———. 2000. Crime and the City: Public Attitudes Towards Open-Street CCTV in Glasgow. *British Journal of Criminology* 40 (4): 692–709.

Dixon, Keith. 1977. Is Cultural Relativism Self-Refuting? *British Journal of Sociology* 28 (1): 75–88.

Dobash, R. Emerson, and Russell P. Dobash. 1979. *Violence Against Wives.* New York: Free Press.

Donaldson, Stephen. 2001. A Million Jockers, Punks, and Queens. In *Prison Masculinities,* edited by Don Sabo, Terry A. Kupers, and Willie London, 118–126. Philadelphia: Temple University Press.

Douglas, Jack D. 1977. Watergate: Harbinger of the American Prince. In *Official Deviance,* edited by Jack D. Douglas and John M. Johnson, 112–120. New York: Lippincott.

Douglas, Jack D., and Paul K. Rasmussen, with Carol Ann Flanagan. 1977. *The Nude Beach.* Beverly Hills: Sage.

Dowie, Mark. 1979. The Corporate Crime of the Century. *Mother Jones* 4 (9): 23–25, 37.

Doyle, Jack. 2004. *Trespass Against Us: Dow Chemical and the Toxic Century.* Monroe, ME: Common Courage Press.

Duesterberg, Thomas J. 1979. Criminology and the Social Order in Nineteenth-Century France. Ph.D. diss., Indiana University.

Duhart, Detis T. 2001. *Violence in the Workplace, 1993–99.* Washington, D.C.: U.S. Department of Justice.

Durkheim, Émile. 1948. *The Elementary Forms of Religious Life.* 1912. Translated by Joseph W. Swain. Glencoe, IL: Free Press.

———. 1951. *Suicide: A Study in Sociology.* 1897. Translated by J. A. Spaulding and G. Simpson. New York: Free Press.

———. 1958. *Professional Ethics and Civil Morals.* 1900. Translated by Cornelia Brookfield. Glencoe, IL: Free Press.

———. 1982. *The Rules of Sociological Method.* 1894. Translated by W. D. Halls. London: Macmillan.

———. 1983. [1901]. Two Laws of Penal Evolution. In *Durkheim and the Law,* edited by Steven Lukes and Andrew Scull, 102–132. Translated by T. Anthony Jones and Andrew Scull. New York: St. Martin's Press.

———. 1984. *The Division of Labor in Society.* 1893. Translated by W. D. Halls. New York: Free Press.

Duster, Troy. 1987. Crime, Youth Unemployment, and the Black Underclass. *Crime and Delinquency* 33 (2): 300–316.

Dwyer, Lynn E. 1983. Structure and Strategy in the Antinuclear Movement. In *Social Movements of the Sixties and Seventies,* edited by Jo Freeman, 148–161. New York: Longman.

Egger, Steven A. 2001. Homicide, Serial. In *Encyclopedia of Criminology and Deviant Behavior,* edited by Clifton D. Bryant, 278–280. New York: Brunner-Routledge.

Einstadter, Werner, and Stuart Henry. 1995. *Criminological Theory.* Fort Worth: Harcourt Brace.

Eisnitz, Gail A. 1997. *Slaughterhouse.* New York: Prometheus.

Elias, Norbert. 1978. *The Civilizing Process.* Oxford: Oxford University Press.

Elliott, Caroline, and Dan Ellingsworth. 1997. Exploring the Relationship Between Unemployment and Property Crime. *Applied Economic Letters* 5: 527–530.

Elliott, Delbert S., and Suzanne S. Ageton. 1980. Reconciling Race and Class Differences in Self-Reported and Official Estimates of Delinquency. *American Sociological Review* 45 (1): 95–110.

Elliott, Delbert S., and David Huizinga. 1983. Social Class and Delinquent Behavior in a National Youth Panel: 1976–1980. *Criminology* 21 (2): 149–177.

Emerson, Steven. 1988. *Secret Warriors: Inside the Covert Military Operations of the Reagan Era.* New York: G. P. Putnam.

Engels, Friedrich. [1885] 1975c. *Anti-Dühring.* London: Lawrence and Wishart.

———. [1886] 1970a. Ludwig Feuerbach and the End of Classical German Philosophy. In *Karl Marx and Frederick Engels: Selected Works,* 3: 337–376. Moscow: Progress Publishers.

———. [1888] 1970b. The Role of Force in History. In *Karl Marx and Frederick Engels: Selected Works,* 3: 377–428. Moscow: Progress Publishers.

Epstein, Samuel. 1978. *The Politics of Cancer.* San Francisco: Sierra Club Books.

Ericson, Richard V., Patricia M. Baranek, and Janet B. L. Chan. 1980. *Visualizing Deviance.* Toronto, Ontario: University of Toronto Press.

Eschholz, Sarah. 2002. Racial Composition of Television Offenders and Viewers' Fear of Crime. *Critical Criminology* 11 (1): 41–60.

Eschholz, Sarah, Ted Chiricos, and Marc Gertz. 2003. Television and Fear of Crime: Program Types, Audience Traits, and the Mediating Effect of Perceived Neighborhood Racial Composition. *Social Problems* 50 (3): 395–415.

Evans, Ernest. 1983. The Use of Terrorism by American Social Movements. In *Social Movements of the Sixties and Seventies,* edited by Jo Freeman, 252–261. New York: Longman.

Exum, M. Lyn. 2002. The Application and Robustness of the Rational Choice Perspective in the Study of Intoxicated and Angry Intentions to Agress. *Criminology* 40 (4): 933–966.

Ezzati, Majid, and Alan D. Lopez. 2003. Estimates of Global Mortality Attributable to Smoking in 2000. *The Lancet* 362 (September) 13: 847–852.

Fagan, Jeffrey. 1994. Women and Drugs Revisited: Female Participation in the Cocaine Economy. *Journal of Drug Issues* 24 (2): 179–225.

Faris, Robert E. L. [1967] 1970. *Chicago Sociology, 1920–1932.* Chicago: University of Chicago Press.

Farrall, Stephen, and David Gadd. 2004. The Frequency of the Fear of Crime. *British Journal of Criminology* 44 (1): 127–132.

Farrell, G., and Ken Pease. 2001. *Repeat Victimization.* Monsey, NY: Criminal Justice Press.

Farrington, David P. 2002. In *The Oxford Handbook of Criminology,* 3rd edition, edited by M. Maguire, R. Morgan, and R. Reiner, 657–701. Oxford: Clarendon Press.

Farrington, David P., and Jeremy W. Coid. 2003. *Early Prevention of Adult Antisocial Behaviour.* Cambridge: Cambridge University Press.

Federal Bureau of Investigation. 1998. *Uniform Crime Reports, 1997.* Washington, D.C.: U.S. Government Printing Office.

———. 2004a. Crime Reporting in the Age of Technology. *CJIS Newsletter* 4 (1).

———. 2004b. *Uniform Crime Reports.* Washington, D.C.: U.S. Government Printing Office.

Felson, Marcus. 1997. A 'Routine Activity' Analysis of Recent Crime Reductions. *The Criminologist* 22 (6): 1–3.

———. 1998. *Crime and Everyday Life.* 2nd edition. Thousand Oaks, CA: Pine Forge Press.

———. 2002. *Crime and Everyday Life.* 3rd edition. Thousand Oaks, CA: Pine Forge Press.

Felson, Marcus, and Ronald V. Clarke. 1997. *Business and Crime Prevention.* Monsey, N.Y.: Willow Tree Press.

Felson, Richard B., and Steven Messner. 1998. Disentangling the Effects of Gender and Intimacy on Victim Precipitation in Homicide. *Criminology* 36 (2): 405–423.

Ferrell, Jeff. 1997. Against the Law: Anarchist Criminology. In *Thinking Critically About Crime,* edited by Brian D. MacLean and Dragan Milovanovic, 146–154. Vancouver, B.C.: Collective Press.

———. 2004. Boredom, Crime and Criminology. *Theoretical Criminology* 8 (3): 287–302.

Ferrell, Jeff, and Mark S. Hamm, eds. 1998. *Ethnography at the Edge: Crime, Deviance, and Field Research.* Boston: Northeastern University Press.

Ferrell, Jeff, and Clinton R. Sanders, eds. 1995. *Cultural Criminology.* Boston: Northeastern University Press.

Ferrell, Jeff, and Neil Websdale, eds. 1999. *Making Trouble: Cultural Constructions of Crime, Deviance and Control.* New York: Aldine de Gruyter.

Ferri, Enrico. [1884] 1917. *Criminal Sociology.* Translated by J. I. Kelly and J. Lisle. Boston: Little, Brown.

Feyerabend, Paul. 1987. *Farewell to Reason.* London: Verso.

Figueira-McDonough, Josephina, with Elaine Selo. 1980. A Reformulation of the Equal Opportunity Explanation of Female Delinquency. *Crime and Delinquency* 26 (3): 333–343.

Finch, Emily. 2003. What a Tangled Web We Weave: Identity Theft and the Internet. In *Dot.cons: Crime, Deviance and Identity On the Internet,* edited by Y. Jewkes, ***NEED PAGE #S***. Portland, OR: Willan.

Findlay, Mark. 1999. *The Globalization of Crime.* Cambridge: Cambridge University Press.

Fink, Arthur E. 1938. *Causes of Crime: Biological Theories in the United States, 1800–1915.* Philadelphia: University of Pennsylvania Press.

Finkelhor, David, and Kersti Yllö. 1985. *License to Rape: Sexual Abuse of Wives.* New York: Holt, Rinehart and Winston.

Fisher, Bonnie S., and Andrew R. P. Wilkes. 2003. A Tale of Two Ivory Towers: A Comparative Analysis of Victimization Rates and Risks between University Students in the United States and England. *British Journal of Criminology* 43 (3): 526–545.

Fishman, Mark. 1978. Crime Waves as Ideology. *Social Problems* 25 (5): 535–543.

Flavin, Jeanne. 2003. Feminism for the Mainstream Criminologist: An Invitation. In *The Criminal Justice System and Women,* 3rd edition, edited by Barbara Raffell Price and Natalie J. Sokoloff, 31–48. New York: McGraw Hill.

Flynn, Clifton P. 2000. Battered Women and Their Animal Companions: Symbolic Interaction Between Human and Nonhuman Animals. *Society & Animals* 8 (2): 100–127.

Foucault, Michel. 1979. *Discipline and Punish: The Birth of the Prison.* Translated by Alan Sheridan. New York: Vintage Books.

———. 1980. *Power/Knowledge: Selected Interviews and Other Writings, 1972–1977.* Translated by Colin Gordon et al. New York: Pantheon.

Frank, Nancy K., and Michael J. Lynch. 1992. *Corporate Crime, Corporate Violence.* Albany, N.Y.: Harrow and Heston.

Friedman, Robert I. 1984. Senator Paul Laxalt: The Man Who Runs the Reagan Campaign. *Mother Jones* 9 (7): 32–39.

Friedrichs, David O. 1996. *Trusted Criminals: White-Collar Crime in Contemporary America.* Belmont, CA: Wadsworth.

———. 2004. *Trusted Criminals: White-Collar Crime in Contemporary Society.* Belmont, CA: Wadsworth.

Fritner, M. P., and L. Rubinson. 1993. Acquaintance Rape: The Influence of Alcohol, Fraternity Membership, and Sports Team Membership. *Journal of Sex Education and Therapy* 19 (4): 272–84

Fuller, John. 1998. *Criminal Justice: A Peacemaking Perspective.* Boston: Allyn & Bacon.

———. 2003. Peacemaking Criminology. In *Controversies in Critical Criminology,* edited by Martin D. Schwartz and Suzanne E. Hatty, 85–95. Cincinnati, OH: Anderson.

Fuller, Lon L. 1949. The Case of the Speluncean Explorers. *Harvard Law Review* 62 (4): 616–645.

Gadd, David, and Stephen Farrall. 2004. Criminal Careers: Interpreting Men's Narratives of Change. *Theoretical Criminology* 8 (2): 123–156.

Gallup, George, Jr. 2004. *The Gallup Poll: Public Opinion 2003.* Wilmington, DE: Scholarly Resources.

Galton, Francis. 1869. *Hereditary Genius.* London: Macmillan.

———. 1889. *The Politics of Corruption: Organized Crime in an American City.* New York: Russell Sage.

Gardiner, John. 1970. *The Politics of Corruption: Organized Crime in an American City.* New York: Russell Sage.

Gareau, Frederick. 2004. *State Terrorism and the United States: From Counterinsurgency to the War on Terror.* London: Zed Books.

Garitty, Michael. 1980. The U.S. Colonial Empire Is As Close As the Nearest Reservation. In *Trilateralism: The Trilateral Commission and Elite Planning for World Management,* edited by Holly Sklar, 238–688. Boston: South End Press.

Garland, David. 1985. *Punishment and Welfare: A History of Penal Strategies.* Aldershot, U.K.: Gower.

———. 1990. *Punishment and Modern Society.* Chicago: University of Chicago Press.

———. 1997. 'Governmentality' and the Problem of Crime: Foucault, Criminology, Sociology. *Theoretical Criminology* 1 (2): 173–214.

———. 2001. *The Culture of Control: Crime and Social Order in Contemporary Society.* Chicago: University of Chicago Press.

Garofalo, Raffaele. 1885. *Criminologia.* Turin: Bocca.

Garrow. David. 1981. *The FBI and Martin Luther King, Jr.* New York: Penguin.

Garry, Eileen M. 1997. *Juvenile Firesetting and Arson*. Washington, D.C.: Office of Juvenile Justice and Delinquency Prevention.

Gasiorowski, Mark J., and Malcolm Byrne, eds. 2004. *Mohammad Mosaddeq and the 1953 Coup in Iran*. Syracuse: Syracuse University Press.

Gaylord, Mark S., and John F. Galliher. 1988. *The Criminology of Edwin Sutherland*. New Brunswick, NJ: Transaction Books.

Geis, Gilbert. 2000. On the Absence of Self-Control as the Basis For a General Theory of Crime. *Theoretical Criminology* 4 (1): 35–53.

Geis, Gilbert, and Colin Goff. 1983. Introduction to *White Collar Crime: The Uncut Version*, by Edwin H. Sutherland, ix–xxxiii. New Haven: Yale University Press.

General Accounting Office. 1988. *Controlling Drug Abuse: A Status Report*. Washington, D.C.: GAO/GGD.

Gibbons, Don C. 1994. *Thinking About Crime and Criminals*. Englewood Cliffs, NJ: Prentice-Hall.

Gibbs, John J., Dennis Giever, and Jamie S. Martin. 1998. Parental Management and Self-Control: An Empirical Test of Gottfredson and Hirschi's General Theory. *Journal of Research in Crime and Delinquency* 35 (1): 40–70.

Gibson, Mary. 2002. *Born to Crime: Cesare Lombroso and the Origins of Biological Criminology*. Westport, CT: Praeger.

Gill, Martin. 2000. *Commercial Robbery*. London: Blackstone Press.

Glassner, Barry. 1999. *The Culture of Fear*. New York: Basic Books.

Glueck, Sheldon, and Eleanor Glueck. 1930. *500 Criminal Careers*. New York: A. A. Knopf.

———. 1950. *Unraveling Juvenile Delinquency*. New York, NY: The Commonwealth Fund.

Godfrey, Barry, Clive Emsley, and Graeme Dunstall. 2003. *Comparative Histories of Crime*. Portland, OR: Willan.

Goetting, Anne. 1999. *Getting Out: Life Stories of Women Who Left Abusive Men*. New York: Columbia University Press.

Goetz, Barry. 2001. Arson. In *Encyclopedia of Criminology and Deviant Behavior*, edited by Clifton D. Bryant, 24–28. New York: Brunner-Routledge.

Goffman, Erving. 1961. *Asylums*. New York: Anchor Books.

———. 1963. *Stigma*. Englewood Cliffs, NJ: Prentice-Hall.

———. 1967. *Interaction Ritual: Essays on Face-to-Face Behavior*. Garden City, N.Y.: Doubleday.

Goode, Erich. 1984. *Drugs in American Society*. New York: Alfred A. Knopf.

Goring, Charles. 1913. *The English Convict: A Statistical Study*. London: M.M.S.O.

Gottfredson, Michael R., and Travis Hirschi. 1990. *A General Theory of Crime*. Stanford, CA: Stanford University Press.

Gould, Larry A. 2000. White Male Privilege and the Construction of Crime. In *Investigating Difference: Human and Cultural Relations in Criminal Justice*, edited by Criminal Justice Collective, 27–43. Boston: Allyn & Bacon.

Graber, Doris A. 1980. *Crime News and the Public*. New York: Praeger.

Graham, James M. 1975. Amphetamine Politics on Capitol Hill. In *Whose Law? What Order? A Conflict Approach to Criminology*, edited by William J. Chambliss and Milton Mankoff, 107–122. New York: John Wiley.

Grauerholz, Elizabeth, and Amy King. 1997. *Prime Time Sexual Harassment*. Violence Against Women 3 (2): 129–148.

Green, Mark, and John Francis Berry. 1985. *The Challenge of Hidden Profits*. New York: William Morrow.

Green, Mark, Beverly C. Moore, and Bruce Wasserstein. 1972. *The Closed Enterprise System*. New York: Bantam Books.

Greenberg, David F. 1977. Delinquency and the Age Structure of Society. *Contemporary Crises* 1 (2): 189–224.

———, ed. 1981. *Crime & Capitalism: Readings in Marxist Criminology*. Mountain View, CA: Mayfield.

———. 1983. Crime and Age. In *Encyclopedia of Crime and Justice*, edited by Sanford Kadish, 1: 30–35. New York: Macmillan.

———. 1985. Age, Crime, and Social Explanation. *American Journal of Sociology* 91 (1): 1–21.

———. 1988. *The Construction of Homosexuality*. Chicago: University of Chicago Press.

———, ed. 1993. *Crime and Capitalism: Readings in Marxist Criminology*. 2nd edition. Palo Alto, CA: Mayfield.

Greenberg, Jerald. 1997. The STEAL Motive: Managing the Social Determinants of Employee Theft. In *Antisocial Behavior in Organizations,* edited by Robert A. Giacalone and Jerald Greenberg, 85–108. Thousand Oaks, CA: Sage.

———. 2002. Who Stole the Money, and When? Individual and Situational Determinants of Employee Theft. *Organizational Behavior and Human Decision Processes* 89 (1): 985–1003.

Greer, Scott, and John Hagan. 2001. Crime as Disrepute. In *What Is Crime?,* edited by Stuart Henry and Mark M. Lanier, 207–226. Lanham, MD: Rowman and Littlefield.

Gurr, Ted Robert, Peter N. Grabosky, and Richard C. Hula. 1977. *The Politics of Crime and Conflict.* Beverly Hills: Sage.

Gutman, Roy. 1988. *Banana Diplomacy: The Making of American Foreign Policy in Nicaragua, 1981–1987.* New York: Simon and Schuster.

Guttmacher, Manfred Schanfarber. 1951. *Sex Offenses.* New York: W.W. Norton.

Hacker, Andrew. 1988. *Black Crime, White Racism.* New York Review of Books 35 (3): 36–41.

Hagan, Frank E. 1997. *Political Crime: Ideology and Criminality.* Boston: Allyn and Bacon.

Hagan, John. 1974. Extra-Legal Attributes and Criminal Sentencing: An Assessment of a Sociological Viewpoint. *Law and Society Review* 8 (3): 357–383.

———. 1989. *Structural Criminology.* New Brunswick, NJ: Rutgers University Press.

———. 1991. Destiny and Drift: Subcultural Preferences, Status Attainments, and the Risks and Rewards of Youth. *American Sociological Review* 56 (5): 567–582.

Hagan, John, and Bill McCarthy. 1997. *Mean Streets: Youth Crime and Homelessness.* New York: Cambridge University Press.

Hagan, John, Bill McCarthy, and Holly Foster. 2002. A Gendered Theory of Delinquency and Despair in the Life Course. *Acta Sociologica* 45: 37–46.

Hagan, John, and Patricia Parker. 1999. Rebellion Beyond the Classroom: A Life-Course Capitalization Theory of the Intergenerational Cases of Delinquency. *Theoretical Criminology* 3 (3): 259–285.

Hagan, John, and Ruth D. Peterson, eds. 1995. *Crime and Inequality.* Stanford, CA: Stanford University Press.

Hall, Jerome. 1952. *Theft, Law, and Society.* New York: Bobbs-Merrill.

———. 1969. Theft, Law, and Society: The Carriers Case. In *Crime and the Legal Process,* edited by William J. Chambliss, 32–51. New York: McGraw-Hill.

Haller, Mark. 1976. Bootleggers and American Gambling, 1920–1950. In *Gambling in America,* Commission on Review of National Policy Toward Gambling, 102–143. Washington, D.C.: U.S. Government Printing Office.

Halliday, Denis. 2004. US Policy and Iraq: A Case of Genocide? In *Genocide, War Crimes, and the West,* edited by Adam Jones, 264–269. London: Zed Books.

Hamilton, Lee H. 1993. Case Closed. *New York Times* January 24, 17.

Hamlin, John E. 1988. The Misplaced Role of Rational Choice in Neutralization Theory. *Criminology* 26 (3): 425–438.

Hamm, Mark S. 1993. *American Skinheads: The Criminology and Control of Hate Crime.* Westport, CT: Praeger.

Harrison, Allen J., and Paige M. Harrison. 2004. Prisoners in 2003. *Bureau of Justice Statistics,* Bulletin no. NCJ 205335, p. 1.

Hawkins, Darnell F. 2003. *Violent Crime: Assessing Race and Ethnic Differences.* New York: Cambridge University Press.

Hay, Douglas. 1975. Property, Authority, and the Criminal Law. In *Albion's Fatal Tree,* edited by Douglas Hay, Peter Linebaugh, John G. Rule, E. P. Thompson, and Cal Winslow, 17–63. New York: Pantheon.

Head, William B. 2001. Fences and Fencing. In *Encyclopedia of Criminology and Deviant Behavior,* edited by Clifton D. Bryant, 226–229. New York: Brunner-Routledge.

Heath, Linda, and Kevin Gilbert. 1996. Mass Media and Fear of Crime. *American Behavioral Scientist* 39 (4): 379–386.

Heidensohn, Frances. 1985. *Women and Crime: The Life of the Female Offender.* New York: New York University Press.

Held, David, Anthony McGrew, David Goldblatt, and Jonathan Perraton. 1999. *Global Transformations: Politics, Economics, and Culture.* Stanford, CA: Stanford University Press.

Helmer, John. 1975. *Drugs and Minority Oppression.* New York: Seabury Press.

Henderson, Charles Richmond. 1893. *Introduction to the Study of the Dependent, Defective, and Delinquent Classes.* Boston: D.C. Heath.

Henry, Stuart. 1976. The Other Side of the Fence. *Sociological Review* 24 (November): 793–806.

———. 1977. On the Fence. *British Journal of Law and Society* 4 (1): 124–133.

———. 1978. *The Hidden Economy.* London: Martin Robertson.

———. 1987. The Political Economy of Informal Economies. *Annals of the American Academy of Political and Social Science* 493 (September): 137–153.

Henry, Stuart, and Werner Einstadter, eds. 1998. *The Criminology Theory Reader.* New York: New York University Press.

Henry, Stuart, and Mark M. Lanier. 2001. *What Is Crime?* Lanham, MD: Rowman and Littlefield.

Henry, Stuart, and Dragan Milovanovic. 1991. Constitutive Criminology: The Maturation of Critical Criminology. *Criminology* 29 (2): 293–315.

———. 1994. The Constitution of Constitutive Criminology: A Postmodern Approach to Criminological Theory. In *The Futures of Criminology,* edited by David Nelken. London: Sage.

———. 1996. *Constitutive Criminology: Beyond Postmodernism.* London: Sage.

———. 2003. Constitutive Criminology. In *Controversies in Critical Criminology,* edited by Martin D. Schwartz and Suzanne E. Hatty, 57–69. Cincinnati, OH.: Anderson.

Herman, Edward. 1982. *The Real Terror Network.* Boston: South End Press.

Hess, Henner. 1973. *Mafia and Mafioso: The Structure of Power.* Lexington, MA: D.C. Heath.

Hewitt, Christopher. 2003. *Understanding Terrorism in America: From the Klan to Al Qaeda.* New York: Routledge.

Hier, Sean P. 2003. Risk and Panic in Late Modernity: Implications of the Converging Sites of Social Anxiety. *British Journal of Sociology* 54 (1): 2–20.

Hills, Stuart, ed. 1987. *Corporate Violence.* Totowa, NJ: Rowman and Littlefield.

Hills, Stuart L., and Ron Santiago. 1992. *Tragic Magic: The Life and Crimes of a Heroin Addict.* Chicago: Nelson-Hall.

Hinckle, Warren, and William Turner. 1981. *The Fish Is Red: The Story of the Secret War Against Castro.* New York: Harper and Row.

Hindelang, Michael J. 1970. The Commitment of Delinquents to Their Misdeeds: Do Delinquents Drift? *Social Problems* 17 (4): 502–509.

———. 1974. Moral Evaluations of Illegal Behaviors. *Social Problems* 21 (3): 370–385.

———. 1979. Sex Differences in Criminal Activity. *Social Problems* 27 (2): 143–156.

Hirschi, Travis. 1969. *Causes of Delinquency.* Berkeley: University of California Press.

———. 1983. Crime and the Family. In *Crime and Public Policy,* edited by James Q. Wilson, 53–68. San Francisco: Institute for Contemporary Studies.

Hirschi, Travis, and Michael Gottfredson. 1983. Age and the Explanation of Crime. *American Journal of Sociology* 89 (3): 552–584.

———. 1993. Commentary: Testing the General Theory of Crime. *Journal of Research in Crime and Delinquency* 30 (1): 47–54.

———. 2000. In Defense of Self-Control. *Theoretical Criminology* 4 (1): 55–69.

Hirschi, Travis, and Michael J. Hindelang. 1977. Intelligence and Delinquency: A Revisionist Review. *American Sociological Review* 42 (4): 571–587.

Hobsbawn, Eric. 1959. *Primitive Rebels.* New York: W. W. Norton.

Hoffman, Abbie, and Jonathan Silvers. 1988. An Election Held Hostage. *Playboy* 35 (10): 73–74.

Hoffman-Bustamante, Dale. 1973. The Nature of Female Criminality. *Issues in Criminology* 8 (2): 117–132.

Hollinger, Richard C., and John P. Clark. 1983. *Theft by Employees.* Lexington, MA: Lexington Books.

Hollway, Wendy, and Tony Jefferson. 1997. The Risk Society in an Age of Anxiety. *British Journal of Sociology* 48 (2): 255–266.

Holmes, Ronald M., and James E. DeBurger. 1988. *Serial Murder.* Beverly Hills: Sage.

Holtfreter, Kristy, Michael Reisig, and Merry Morash. 2004. Poverty, State Capital, and Recidivism Among Women Offenders. *Criminology and Public Policy* 3: 185–208.

Honegger, Barbara. 1989. *October Surprise.* New York: Tudor Publishing.

Hooton, Ernest Albert. 1939. *Crime and the Man.* Cambridge, MA: Harvard University Press.

Hopkins, Elaine. 1988. A Matter of Conscience for a G-Man. *The Progressive* 52 (3):14.

Howe, Laura K. 1977. *Pink-Collar Ghetto.* New York: G. P. Putnam.

Hudson, Barbara. 1997. Punishment or Redress? Current Themes in European Abolitionist Criminology. In *Thinking Critically About Crime,* edited by Brian D. MacLean and Dragan Milovanovic, 131–138. Vancouver, B.C.: Collective Press.

Human Rights Watch. 2005a. *Afghanistan.* New York: Human Rights Watch.

———. 2005b. *Guantanamo: Three Years of Lawlessness.* New York: Human Rights Watch.

Humphreys, Laud. 1970. *Tearoom Trade: Impersonal Sex in Public Places.* Chicago: Aldine.

Hunt, Alan. 1978. *The Sociological Movement in Law.* London: Macmillan.

Hunter, Mic. 2000. Sexual Abuse of Children. In *Encyclopedia of Women and Crime,* edited by Nicole Hahn Rafter, 238–239. Phoenix, AZ: Oryx Press.

Huston, Aletha C., Halford H. Fairchild, and Edward Donnerstein. 1992. *Big World, Small Screen: The Role of Television in American Life.* Lincoln: University of Nebraska Press.

Iadicola, Peter, and Anson Shupe. 1998. *Violence, Inequality, and Human Freedom.* Dix Hills, N.Y.: General Hall.

Ignatius, David. 1986. The Contrapreneurs: Skirting Congress and the Law for Years. *Washington Post,* December 7, D1, D2.

Inciardi, James A., Dorothy Lockwood, and Anne E. Pottieger. 1993. *Women and Crack Cocaine.* New York: Macmillan.

International Campaign for Justice in Bhopal. 2004. Available at <http://www.bhopal.net/index.php>, p. 1.

*Internet Fraud Report.* 2003. Federal Bureau of Investigation and National White-Collar Complaint Center, Internet Fraud Center, available at <http://www1.ifccfbi.gov/index.asp>.

Jacobs, Bruce A. 2000. *Robbing Drug Dealers.* New York: Aldine de Gruyter.

Jacobs, David. 1981. Inequality and Economic Crime. *Sociology and Social Research* 66 (1): 12–28.

Jacobs, David, and David Britt. 1979. Inequality and Police Use of Deadly Force: An Empirical Assessment of a Conflict Hypothesis. *Social Problems* 26 (4): 403–412.

Jaggar, Alison M. 1983. Feminist Politics and Human Nature. *Totowa, NJ: Rowman and Allanheld.*

Jaggar, Alison M., and Paula Rothenberg, eds. 1984. *Feminist Frameworks.* New York: McGraw-Hill.

Jefferson, Tony. 1996. From 'Little Fairy Boy' to the 'Compleat Destroyer': Subjectivity and Transformation in the Biography of Mike Tyson. In *Understanding Masculinities: Social Relations and Cultural Arenas,* edited by M. Mac an Ghail, 153–167. Buckingham: Open University Press.

Jeffery, Clarence Ray. 1965. Criminal Behavior and Learning Theory. *Journal of Criminal Law, Criminology, and Police Science* 56 (3): 294–300.

Jehl, Douglas, Steven Lee Myers, and Eric Schmitt. 2004. G.I.'s Prison Abuse More Widespread, Says Army Survey. *New York Times* May 26, A1.

Jencks, Christopher. 1987. Genes and Crime. *New York Times Review of Books,* February 12, 33–34.

Jenkins, Philip. 1984. Varieties of Enlightenment Criminology. *British Journal of Criminology* 24 (2): 112–130.

———. 1988. Myth and Murder: The Serial Killer Panic of 1983–1985. *Criminal Justice Research Bulletin* 3 (11): 1–7.

———. 1994. *Using Murder: The Social Construction of Serial Homicide.* New York: Aldine de Gruyter.

———. 2003. *Images of Terror: What We Can and Can't Know About Terrorism.* New York: Walter De Gruyter.

Jesilow, Paul D., Henry N. Pontell, and Gilbert Geis. 1993. *Prescription for Profit: How Doctors Defraud Medicaid.* Berkeley: University of California Press.

Joe, Karen A., and Meda Chesney-Lind. 1998. 'Just Every Mother's Angel': An Analysis of Gender and Ethnic Variations in Youth Gang Membership. In *Criminology at the Crossroads: Feminist Readings in Crime and Justice,* edited by Kathleen Daly and Lisa Maher, 87–109. New York: Oxford University Press.

Johansen, Bruce, and Roberto Maestas. 1979. *Wasicbu: The Continuing Indian Wars.* New York: Monthly Review Press.

Johnson, Michael P. 2001. Conflict and Control: Symmetry and Asymmetry in Domestic Violence. In *Couples in Conflict,* edited by Alan Booth, Ann C. Crouter, and Mari Clements, 95–104. Mahwah, NJ: Lawrence Erlbaum Associates.

Johnson, Michael P., and Kathleen J. Ferraro. 2000. Research on Domestic Violence in the 1990s: Making Distinctions. *Journal of Marriage and the Family* 62 (November): 948–963.

Johnstone, John W. C., Darnell F. Hawkins, and Arthur Michener. 1994. Homicide Reporting in Chicago Dailies. *Journalism Quarterly* 71 (4): 860–872.

Jones, Adam (ed.). 2004. *Genocide, War Crimes, and the West: History and Complicity*. London: Zed Books.

Joseph, Janice. 2003. Cyberstalking: An International Perspective. In *Dot.cons: Crime, Deviance, and Identity on the Internet*, edited by Yvonne Jewkes, 105–125. Portland, OR: Willan.

Judis, John. 1988. The Big Sleazy: A New Era of Government Corruption. *In These Times*, July 20-August 2, 7.

Junger-Tas, Josine. 1994. Delinquency in Thirteen Western Countries: Some Preliminary Conclusions. In *Delinquent Behavior Among Young People in the Western World: First Results of the International Self-Report Delinquency Study*, edited by Josine Junger-Tas, Gert-Jan Terlouw, and Malcolm W. Klein, 370–385. Amsterdam: Kugler Publications.

Jurik, Nancy, and Peter Gregware. 1992. A Method for Murder: The Study of Homicides by Women. *Perspectives on Social Problems* 4 (2): 179–201.

Katz, Jack. 1988. *The Seductions of Crime*. New York: Basic Books.

Keat, Russell, and John Urry. 1975. *Social Theory as Science*. London: Routledge and Kegan Paul.

Kefauver Committee. 1951. *Special Committee to Investigate Organized Crime in Interstate Commerce*. Washington, D.C.: U.S. Government Printing Office.

Kelling, George L., and Catherine M. Coles. 1996. *Fixing Broken Windows: Restoring Order and Reducing Crime in Our Communities*. New York: Martin Kessler Books.

Kellner, Douglas. 2003. *From 9/11 to Terror War: The Dangers of the Bush Legacy*. New York: Rowman & Littlefield.

Kellor, Frances A. 1899. Psychological and Environmental Study of Women Criminals. Parts 1 and 2. *American Journal of Sociology* 5 (4): 527–543; 5 (5): 67–182.

———. 1901. *Experimental Sociology: Delinquents*. New York: Macmillan.

Kelly, Orr, and Ted Gest. 1982. Reagan Revolution Takes Firm Hold at Justice. *U.S. News and World Report*, April 26, 24–26.

Kendall-Tackett, Kathleen. 2000. Incest Victims. In *Encyclopedia of Women and Crime*, edited by Nicole Hahn Rafter, 114. Phoenix, AZ: Oryx Press.

Kendall-Tackett, Kathleen, and Roberta Marshall. 1998. Abuse. In *Issues in Intimate Violence*, edited by Raquel Kennedy Bergen, 47–63. Thousand Oaks, CA: Sage.

Kerbo, Harold, and Mariko Inoue. 1990. Japanese Social Structure and White-Collar Crime. *Deviant Behavior* 11 (2): 139–154.

Kimmel, Michael S. 1993. Does Pornography Cause Rape? *Violence Update* 3 (10): 18.

Kimmel, Michael S., and Matthew Mahler. 2003. Adolescent Masculinity, Homophobia, and Violence: Random School Shootings, 1982–2001. *American Behavioral Scientist* 46 (10): 1439–1458.

King, Harry, and William J. Chambliss. 1984. *Box Man: A Professional Thief's Journey*. New York: John Wiley.

Kitsuse, John I., and Aaron V. Cicourel. 1963. A Note on the Uses of Official Statistics. *Social Problems* 11 (2): 131–139.

Kitsuse, John I., and David C. Dietrick. 1959. Delinquent Boys: A Critique. *American Sociological Review* 24 (2): 208–215.

Klanwatch. 1989. *Intelligence Report: Special Report on Hate Crime in 1988*. Montgomery, AL: Southern Poverty Law Center.

Kleck, Gary. 1997. *Point Blank: Guns and Violence in America*. New York: Aldine de Gruyter.

Kleck, Gary, and Ted Chiricos. 2002. Unemployment and Property Crime: A Target-Specific Assessment of Opportunity and Motivation as Mediating Factors. *Criminology* 40: 649–680.

Klemke, Lloyd W. 1992. *The Sociology of Shoplifting: Boosters and Snitches Today*. Westport, CT: Praeger.

———. 2001. Shoplifting. In *Encyclopedia of Criminology and Deviant Behavior*, edited by Clifton D. Bryant, 469–472. New York: Brunner-Routledge.

Klockars, Carl B. 1974. *The Professional Fence*. New York: Free Press.

———. 1979. The Contemporary Crises of Marxist Criminology. *Criminology* 16 (3): 477–515.

Knapp Commission. 1972. *Knapp Commission Report on Police Corruption*. New York: Braziller.

Komiya, Nobuo. 1999. A Cultural Study of the Low Crime Rate in Japan. *British Journal of Criminology* 30 (3): 369–390.

Kornbluh, Peter. 2003. *The Pinochet File: A Declassified Dossier on Atrocity and Accountability*. New York: W.W. Norton.

Koss, Mary P., and Sarah L. Cook. 1998. Facing the Facts: Date and Acquaintance Rape Are Significant Problems for Women. In *Issues in Intimate Violence,* edited by Raquel Kennedy Bergen, 147–156. Thousand Oaks, CA: Sage.

Koss, Mary P., and J. Gaines. 1993. The Prediction of Sexual Aggression by Alcohol Use, Athletic Participation, and Fraternity Affiliation. *Journal of Interpersonal Violence* 8 (1): 94–108.

Kramer, Ronald C. 1992. The Space Shuttle Challenger Explosion: A Case Study of State-Corporate Crime. In *White-Collar Crime Reconsidered,* edited by Kip Schlegel and David Weisburd, 214–243. Boston: Northeastern University Press.

Kramer, Ronald C., and Raymond J. Michalowski. 1990. *Toward an Integrated Theory of State-Corporate Crime.* Unpublished manuscript.

———. 2004. *War, Aggression, and State Crime: A Criminological Analysis of the Invasion and Occupation of Iraq.* Unpublished manuscript.

Krohn, Marvin D. 1999. Social Learning Theory: the Continuing Development of a Perspective. *Theoretical Criminology* 3 (4): 462–476.

Kruger, Henrik. 1980. *The Great Heroin Coup.* Boston: South End Press.

Kruttschnitt, Candace. 1982. Women, Crime, and Dependency. *Criminology* 9 (4): 495–513.

Kunstler, William. 1978. FBI Letters: Writers of the Purple Rage. *The Nation,* December 30, 721–722.

Kunze, Michael. 1987. *Highroad to the Stake.* Translated by William E. Yuill. Chicago: University of Chicago Press.

Kuo, Lenore. 2002. *Prostitution Policy: Revolutionizing Practice Through a Gendered Perspective.* New York: New York University Press.

Kupers, Terry A. 2001. Rape and the Prison Code. In *Prison Masculinities,* edited by Don Sabo, Terry A. Kupers, and Willie London, 111–117. Philadelphia: Temple University Press.

Kurtz, Howard. 1988. E. F. Hutton to Plead Guilty. *Washington Post,* April 2, A3.

LaFree, Gary. 1999. Declining Violent Crime Rates in the 1990s: Predicting Crime Booms and Busts. *Annual Review of Sociology* 25: 145–169.

LaFree, Gary, and Kriss A. Drass. 2002. Counting Crime Booms Among Nations: Evidence for Homicide Victimization Rates, 1956 to 1998. *Criminology* 40 (4): 769–800.

LaFree, Gary, and Michelle Hussong. 2001. Race and Crime. In *Encyclopedia of Criminology and Deviant Behavior,* edited by Clifton D. Bryant, 441–448. New York: Brunner-Routledge.

Lamour, Catherine, and Michael R. Lamberti. 1974. *The International Connection: Opium from Growers to Pushers.* New York: Pantheon Books.

Lander, Bernard. 1954. *Towards an Understanding of Juvenile Delinquency.* New York: Columbia University Press.

Lane, David. 1970. *Politics and Society in the USSR.* London: Weidenfeld and Nicolson.

———. 1996. *The Rise and Fall of State Socialism.* Cambridge: Polity Press.

Lane, Jodi, and James W. Meeker. 2003a. Ethnicity, Information Sources, and Fear of Crime. *Deviant Behavior* 24 (1): 1–26.

———. 2003b. Women's and Men's Fear of Gang Crimes: Sexual and Nonsexual Assault as Perceptually Contemporaneous Offenses. *Justice Quarterly* 20 (2): 337–371.

Langan, Patrick A., and David P. Farrington. 1998. *Executive Summary to Crime and Justice in the United States and England and Wales,* 1981–96. Report NCJ-173402. Washington D.C.: Bureau of Justice Statistics.

Lanier, Mark M., and Stuart Henry. 1998. *Essential Criminology.* Boulder, CO: Westview.

Laub, John H. 1983. *Criminology in the Making: An Oral History* Boston: Northeastern University Press.

———. 2004. The Life Course of Criminology in the United States: The American Society of Criminology 2003 Presidential Address. *Criminology* 42 (1): 1–26.

Laub, John H., and Robert J. Sampson. 1988. Unraveling Families and Delinquency: A Reanalysis of the Gluecks Data. *Criminology* 26 (3): 355–380.

———. 1993. Turning Points in the Life Course: Why Change Matters to the Study of Crime. *Criminology* 31: 301–325.

———. 2001. Understanding Desistance From Crime. In *Crime and Justice,* edited by Michael Tonry, 1–69. Chicago: University of Chicago Press.

Lea, John, and Jock Young. 1984. *What Is to Be Done About Law and Order?* New York: Penguin.

———. 1986. A Realistic Approach to Law and Order. In *The Political Economy of Crime: Readings for a Critical Criminology,* edited by Brian MacLean, 358–364. Englewood Cliffs, NJ: Prentice-Hall.

Lee, Matthew R., and William B. Bankston. 1999. Political Structure, Economic Inequality, and Homicide: A Cross-National Comparison. *Deviant Behavior* 19: 27–55.

Lee, Murray. 2001. The Genesis of 'Fear of Crime.' *Theoretical Criminology* 5 (4): 467–485.

Lefkowitz, Bernard. 1997. *Our Guys: The Glen Ridge Rape and the Secret Life of the Perfect Suburb.* New York: Vintage.

Lemert, Edwin M. 1951. *Social Pathology: A Systematic Approach to the Theory of Sociopathic Behavior.* New York: McGraw-Hill.

———. 1967. *Human Deviance, Social Problems, and Social Control.* Englewood Cliffs, NJ: Prentice-Hall.

Lens, Sidney. 1973. *The Labor Wars: From the Molly Maguires to the Sitdowns.* New York: Doubleday.

Levin, Jack, and Jack McDevitt. 1993. *Hate Crimes: The Rising Tide of Bigotry and Bloodshed.* New York: Plenum Press.

Liebert, Robert M., and Joyce Sprafkin. 1988. *The Early Window: Effects of Television on Children and Youth.* New York: Pergamon.

Lifschultz, Lawrence. 1988. Inside the Kingdom of Heroin. *The Nation* November 14, 477, 492–496.

Lindesmith, Alfred R. 1947. *Opiate Addiction.* Bloomington, IN: Principia Press.

Linebaugh, Peter. 1976. Karl Marx, the Theft of Wood, and Working Class Composition. *Crime and Social Justice* 6 (Fall/Winter): 5–16.

Link, Bruce G., Francis T. Cullen, James Frank, and John F. Wozniak. 1987. The Social Rejection of Former Mental Patients: Understanding Why Labels Matter. *American Journal of Sociology* 92 (6): 1461–1500.

Liska, Allen E. 1981. *Perspectives on Deviance.* Englewood Cliffs, NJ: Prentice Hall.

Loader, Ian, and Richard Sparks. 2002. Contemporary Landscapes of Crime, Order, and Control: Governance, Risk and Globalization. In *The Oxford Handbook of Criminology*, 3rd edition, edited by Mike Maguire, Rod Morgan, and Robert Reiner. Oxford: Oxford University Press.

Loeber, R., and David P. Farrington, eds. 2001. *Child Delinquents: Development, Intervention and Service Needs.* Thousand Oaks, CA: Sage.

Lombroso, Cesare. 1876. *L'uomo delinquente (Criminal Man).* Milan: Hoepli.

———. 1918. *Crime: Its Causes and Remedies.* 1902. Translated by Henry P. Horton. Boston: Little, Brown.

Lombroso, Cesare, and William Ferrero. 1895. *The Female Offender.* 1893. Reprint, London: T. Fisher Unwin.

Lombroso-Ferrero, Gina. [1911] 1972. *Lombroso's Criminal Man.* Montclair, NJ: Patterson Smith.

Luckenbill, David F. 1977. Criminal Homicide as a Situated Transaction. *Social Problems* 25 (2): 176–186.

———. 1981. Generating Compliance: The Case of Robbery. *Urban Life* 10 (1): 25–46.

Lyman, Michael D., and Gary Potter. 2004. *Organized Crime.* Upper Saddle River, NJ: Prentice Hall.

Lynch, Michael, and Paul Stretsky. 2003. The Meaning of Green: Contrasting Criminological Perspectives. *Theoretical Criminology* 7 (2): 217–239.

Lynch, Michael J., Paul Stretesky, and Paul Hammond. 2000. Media Coverage of Chemical Crimes, Hillsborough County, Florida, 1987–97. *British Journal of Criminology* 40 (1): 112–126.

Lynd, Robert S. 1939. *Knowledge for What?* Princeton: Princeton University Press.

Maas, Peter. 1986. *Manhunt.* New York: Random House.

MacIntyre, Alasdair. 1981. *After Virtue.* Notre Dame: University of Notre Dame Press.

MacKinnon, Catharine A. 1984. Not a Moral Issue. *Yale Law and Policy Review* 2 (2): 32–145.

MacLean, Brian D., and Dragan Milovanovic, eds. 1998. *Thinking Critically About Crime.* Vancouver, B.C.: Collective Press.

Mahajan, Rahul. 2002. *Full Spectrum Dominance: U.S. Power in Iraq and Beyond.* New York: Seven Stories Press.

Maher, Lisa. 1997. *Sexed Work: Gender, Race, and Resistance in a Brooklyn Drug Market.* New York: Clarendon Press.

Maher, Lisa, and Richard Curtis. 1992. Women on the Edge of Crime: Crack Cocaine and the Changing Contexts of Street-Level Sex Work in New York City. *Crime, Law, and Social Change* 18 (2): 221–258.

Maher, Lisa, and Kathleen Daly. 1996. Women in the Street-Level Drug Economy: Continuity or Change? *Criminology* 34 (4): 465–491.

Mahoney, Patricia, Linda M. Williams, and Carolyn M. West. 2001. Violence Against Women by Intimate Relationship Partners. In *Sourcebook on Violence Against Women,* edited by Claire M. Renzetti, Jeffrey L. Edleson, and Raquel Kennedy Bergen, 143–178. Thousand Oaks, CA: Sage.

Maier, Mark, and James W. Messerschmidt. 1998. Commonalities, Conflicts, and Contradictions in Organizational Masculinities: Exploring the Gendered Genesis of the Challenger Disaster. *The Canadian Review of Sociology and Anthropology* 35 (3): 325–344.

Majendie, Paul. 2004. Iraqi Prison Photos Mar U.S. Image. *Reuters* April 30.

Mandino, Carole. 2000. Old Enough to Know Better? Aging and Criminal Justice. In *Investigating Difference: Human and Cultural Relations in Criminal Justice,* edited by Criminal Justice Collective, 161–170. Boston: Allyn & Bacon.

Mann, Coramae Richey, and Marjorie S. Zatz, eds. 1998. *Images of Color, Images of Crime: Readings.* Los Angeles: Roxbury Publishing.

Manning, Peter K. 2003. *Policing Contingencies.* Chicago: University of Chicago Press.

Marcus, Bernd. 2004. Self-Control in the General Theory of Crime. *Theoretical Criminology* 8 (1): 33–55.

Marcuse, Herbert. 1964. *One Dimensional Man.* Boston: Beacon Press.

Markowitz, Gerald, and David Rosner. 2002. *Deceit and Denial: The Deadly Politics of Industrial Pollution.* Berkeley, CA: University of California Press.

Mars, Gerald. 1983. *Cheats at Work.* Boston: Unwin.

Marshall, Johnathan, Peter Dale Scott, and Jane Hunter. 1987. *The Iran-Contra Connection.* Boston: South End Press.

Martin, Susan E. 2001. Hate Crimes. In *Encyclopedia of Criminology and Deviant Behavior,* edited by Clifton D. Bryant, 254–257. New York: Brunner-Routledge.

Marx, Gary T. 1981. Ironies of Social Control: Authorities as Contributors to Deviance Through Escalation, Non-Enforcement, and Covert Facilitation. *Social Problems* 28 (3): 221–246.

———. 1997. Social Control across Borders. In *Crime and Law Enforcement in the Global Village,* edited by William F. McDonald, 23–39. Cincinnati, OH: Anderson.

Marx, Karl. [1842] 1975a. Comments on the Latest Prussian Censorship Instruction. In *Karl Marx/Frederick Engels Collected Works,* 1: 109–131. London: Lawrence and Wishart.

———. [1842] 1975b. Proceedings of the Sixth Rhine Province Assembly. Debates on the Law on Thefts of Wood. In *Karl Marx/Frederick Engels: Collected Works,* 1: 224–263. London: Lawrence and Wishart.

———. [1848] 1969a. The Communist Manifesto. In *Karl Marx and Frederick Engels: Selected Works,* 1: 108–137. Moscow: Progress Publishers.

———. [1852] 1969b. The Eighteenth Brumaire of Louis Bonaparte. In *Karl Marx and Frederick Engels: Selected Works,* 1: 398–487. Moscow: Progress Publishers.

———. [1853]. 1956. Capital Punishment. In *Karl Marx: Selected Writings in Sociology and Social Philosophy,* edited by T. B. Bottomore and Maximilian Rubel, 228–230. New York: McGraw-Hill.

———. [1857–1858] 1973. *Grundrisse: Introduction to the Critique of Political Economy.* Translated and introduced by Martin Nicolaus. New York: Vintage.

———. 1859. Population, Crime, and Pauperism. *New York Daily Tribune,* September 16.

———. [1859] 1969c. Preface to A Contribution to the Critique of Political Economy. In *Karl Marx and Frederick Engels: Selected Works,* 1: 502–506. Moscow: Progress Publishers.

———. [1868] 1967. *Capital.* 3 vols. New York: International Publishers.

———. [1871] 1969d. The Civil War in France. In *Karl Marx and Frederick Engels: Selected Works,* 2: 190–244. Moscow: Progress Publishers.

Marx, Karl, and Friedrich Engels. [1845] 1976. *The German Ideology.* Moscow: Progress Publishers.

Mathews, Roger. 2002. *Armed Robbery.* Portland, OR: Willan.

Mathiesen, Thomas. 1997. The Viewer Society: Michel Foucault's 'Panopticon' Revisited. *Theoretical Criminology* 1 (2): 215–234.

Matsueda, Ross L. 1997. 'Cultural Deviance Theory': The Remarkable Persistence of a Flawed Term. *Theoretical Criminology* 1 (4): 429–452.

Mattera, Philip. 1985. *Off the Books.* New York: St. Martin's Press.

Matthews, Roger. 1987. Taking Realist Criminology Seriously. *Contemporary Crises* 11 (4): 371–401.

Matza, David. 1964. *Delinquency and Drift.* New York: John Wiley.

———. 1969. *Becoming Deviant.* Englewood Cliffs, NJ: Prentice-Hall.

Matza, David, and Gresham M. Sykes. 1961. Juvenile Delinquency and Subterranean Values. *American Sociological Review* 26 (5): 712–719.

Mawby, Rob. 2001. *Burglary.* Portland, OR: Willan.

Mayer, P. 1953. Gusii Initiation Ceremonies. *Journal of the Royal Anthropological Institute* 83:9–36.

Mayhew, Pat, and Jan J. M. Van Dijk. 1997. *Criminal Victimization in Eleven Industrialised Countries: Key Findings from the 1996 International Crime Victims Survey.* The Hague: Ministry of Justice and University of Leyden. No. 162.

McCaghy, Charles H., Peggy C. Giordano, and Trudy Knicely Henson. 1977. Auto Theft: Offender and Offense Characteristics. *Criminology* 15 (3): 367–385.

McClennen, Joan C. 2005. Domestic Violence Between Same-Gender Partners: Recent Findings and Future Research. *Journal of Interpersonal Violence* 20 (2): 149–154.

McClintock, Michael. 1985. *The American Connection: State Terror and Popular Resistance in Guatemala.* London: Zed Books.

McCorkle, Jill. 2003. Embodied Surveillance and the Gendering of Punishment. *Journal of Contemporary Ethnography* 32 (1): 41–76.

McCoy, Alfred. 1972. *The Politics of Heroin in Southeast Asia.* New York: Harper and Row.

McCullagh, Ciaran. 1996. *Crime in Ireland: A Sociological Introduction.* Cork: Cork University Press.

McDevitt, Jack. 1989. The Study of the Implementation of the Massachusetts Civil Rights Act. Unpublished paper.

McDonald, William F. 1997. Crime and Justice in the Global Village: Towards Global Criminology. In *Crime and Law Enforcement in the Global Village,* edited by William F. McDonald, 3–21. Cincinnati, OH: Anderson.

McEvoy, Kieran. 2003. Beyond the Metaphor: Political Violence, Human Rights, and 'New' Peacemaking Criminology. *Theoretical Criminology* 7 (3): 319–346.

McFarlane, Judith M., Jacquelyn C. Campbell, Susan Wilt, Carolyn J. Sachs, Yvonne Ulrich, and Xiao Xu. 1999. Stalking and Intimate Partner Femicide. *Homicide Studies* 3 (4): 300–316.

McGarrell, Edmund F., and Thomas C. Castellano. 1991. An Integrative Conflict Model of the Criminal Law Formation Process. *Journal of Research in Crime and Delinquency* 28 (2): 174–196.

McIllwain, Jeffrey Scott. 1999. Organized Crime: A Social Network Approach. *Crime, Law & Social Change* 32 (3): 301–323.

McIntosh, Mary. 1973. The Growth of Racketeering. *Economy and Society* 2 (1): 35–69.

McNulty, Thomas, and Paul Bellair. 2003. Explaining Racial and Ethnic Differences in Serious Adolescent Violent Behavior. *Criminology* 41: 709–749.

McSherry, J. Patrice. 2001. *Operation Condor: Deciphering the U.S. Role.* Crimes of War Project. <http://www.crimesofwar.org>.

Mead, George Herbert. 1934. *Mind, Self, and Society: From the Standpoint of a Social Behaviorist.* Chicago: University of Chicago Press.

Mead, Margaret. 1928. *Coming of Age in Samoa.* New York: Blue Ribbon Books.

Meier, Robert F., and Gilbert Geis. 1997. *Victimless Crime? Prostitution, Drugs, Homosexuality, Abortion.* Los Angeles, CA: Roxbury.

Merton, Robert K. [1938] 1969. Social Structure and Anomie. In *Delinquency, Crime, and Social Process,* edited by Donald R. Cressey and David A. Ward, 254–284. New York: Harper and Row.

Messerschmidt, James W. 1986a. *The Trial of Leonard Peltier.* Boston: South End Press.

———. 1986b. *Capitalism, Patriarchy, and Crime: Toward a Socialist Feminist Criminology.* Totowa, NJ: Rowman and Littlefield.

———. 1987. Feminism, Criminology, and the Rise of the Female Sex Delinquent, 1880–1930. *Contemporary Crises* 11 (3): 243–263.

———. 1993. *Masculinities and Crime: Critique and Reconceptualization of Theory.* Lanham, MD: Rowman and Littlefield.

———. 1997. *Crime as Structured Action: Gender, Race, Class, and Crime in the Making.* Thousand Oaks, CA: Sage.

———. 2000. *Nine Lives: Adolescent Masculinities, the Body, and Violence.* Boulder, CO: Westview.

———. 2004. *Flesh & Blood: Adolescent Gender Diversity and Violence.* Lanham, MD: Rowman & Littlefield.

Messner, Michael A. 2002. *Taking the Field: Women, Men, and Sports.* Minneapolis: University of Minnesota Press.

Messner, Michael A., and Mark Stevens. 2002. Scoring Without Consent: Confronting Male Athletes' Sexual Violence Against Women. In *Paradoxes of Youth and Sport,* edited by Margaret Gatz, Sandra Ball Rokeach, and Michael A. Messner, 225–240. Albany: State University of New York Press.

Messner, Steven F. 1980. Income Inequality and Murder Rates. *Comparative Social Research* 3: 185–198.

Messner, Steven F., and Richard Rosenfeld. 1998. *Crime and the American Dream.* 2nd edition. Belmont, CA: Wadsworth.

———. 2001. *Crime and the American Dream.* 3rd edition. Belmont, CA: Wadsworth/Thomson Learning.

Michael, Jerome, and Mortimer J. Adler. [1933] 1971. *Crime, Law, and Social Science.* Montclair, NJ: Patterson Smith.

Michalowski, Raymond J. 1985. *Order, Law, and Crime.* New York: Random House.

Michalowski, Raymond J., and Ed Bolander. 1976. Repression and Criminal Justice in Capitalist America. *Sociological Inquiry* 46 (2): 99–110.

Michalowski, Raymond J., and Ronald C. Kramer. 1987. The Space Between Laws: The Problem of Corporate Crime in a Transnational Context. *Social Problems* 34 (1): 34–53.

Mieczkowski, Thomas. 1986. Geeking Up and Throwing Down: Heroin Street Life in Detroit. *Criminology* 24 (4): 645–666.

———. 1994. The Experiences of Women Who Sell Crack: Some Descriptive Data from the Detroit Crack Ethnography Project. *Journal of Drug Issues* 24 (2): 227–248.

Miethe, Terance D., and Richard C. McCorkle. 1997. Gang Membership and Criminal Processing: A Test of the 'Master Status' Concept. *Justice Quarterly* 14 (3): 407–427.

Mill, John Stuart. [1851] 1970. *The Subjection of Women.* New York: Source Book Press.

Miller, Eleanor. 1986. *Street Women.* Philadelphia: Temple University Press.

Miller, Jody. 1995. Gender and Power on the Streets: Street Prostitution in the Era of Crack Cocaine. *Journal of Contemporary Ethnography* 23 (4): 427–52.

———. 1998. 'Up It Up': Gender and the Accomplishment of Robbery. *Criminology* 36 (1): 37–66.

———. 2001. *One of the Guys: Girls, Gangs, and Gender.* New York: Oxford University Press.

———. 2002. The Strength and Limits of 'Doing Gender' for Understanding Street Crime. *Theoretical Criminology* 6 (4): 433–60.

Miller, Jody, and Dheeshana Jayasundara. 2001. Prostitution, the Sex Industry, and Sex Tourism. In *Sourcebook on Violence Against Women,* edited by Claire M. Renzetti, Jeffrey L. Edleson, and Raquel Kennedy Bergen, 459–480. Thousand Oaks, CA: Sage.

Miller, Karla S., and John F. Knutson. 1997. Reports of Severe Physical Punishment and Exposure to Animal Cruelty by Inmates Convicted of Felonies and by University Students. *Child Abuse & Neglect* 21 (1): 59–82.

Miller, Walter B. 1958. Lower Class Culture as a Generating Milieu of Gang Delinquency. *Journal of Social Issues* 14 (3): 5–19.

Milovanovic, Dragan, and Stuart Henry. 1991. Constitutive Penology. *Social Justice* 18 (3): 204–224.

Mintz, Morton. 1985. At Any Cost: Corporate Greed, Women, and the Dalkon Shield. *The Progressive* 49 (11): 20–25.

———. 1986. A Crime Against Women: A. H. Robbins and the Dalkon Shield. *Multinational Monitor,* January 15, 17.

Miyazawa, Setsuo. 1993. The Enigma of Japan as a Testing Ground for Cross-Cultural Criminological Studies. *Annales Internationales de Criminologie* 32: 81–102.

Moffitt, Terrie E. 1993. Adolescence and Life-Course-Persistent Antisocial Behavior. *Psychological Review* 100: 674–701.

Mokhiber, Russell. 1999. *Corporate Predators: The Hunt for Mega-Profits and the Attack on Democracy.* Monroe, ME.: Common Courage Press.

Mokhiber, Russell, and Robert Weissman. 2004. The Ten Worst Corporations of 2004. *Multinational Monitor* 25 (12): 1–26.

Moore, Sally Falk. 1978. *Law as Process.* London: Routledge and Kegan Paul.

Moore, William. 1974. *The Kefauver Committee and the Politics of Crime, 1950–1952.* Columbia: University of Missouri Press.

Morash, Merry. 1999. A Consideration of Gender in Relation to Social Learning and Social Structure: A General Theory of Crime and Deviance. *Theoretical Criminology* 3 (4): 451–462.

Morgan, Phoebe A. 2001. Sexual Harassment. In *Encyclopedia of Women and Crime,* edited by Nicole Hahn Rafter, 241–242. Phoenix, AZ: Oryx Press.

Morgan, Robin. 1980. Theory and Practice: Pornography and Rape. In *Take Back the Night: Women on Pornography,* edited by Laura Lederer, 134–147. New York: William Morrow.

Moyers, Bill. 1988. *The Secret Government: The Constitution in Crisis.* Washington, D.C.: Seven Locks Press.

Mullins, Christopher, and Richard Wright. 2003. Gender, Social Networks, and Residential Burglary. *Criminology* 41: 813–839.

Musto, David F. 1973. *The American Disease: Origins of Narcotic Control.* New Haven, CT: Yale University Press.

Nash, Nathaniel. 1985. Capitalist Punishment. *The New Republic* May 27, 56.

National Center on Child Abuse and Neglect. 2003. National Child Abuse and *Neglect Data Systems Working Paper 2.* Washington, D.C.: U.S. Department of Health and Human Services.

National Center on Elder Abuse. 2004. *Elder Abuse Statistics.* Washington, D.C.: National Center on Elder Abuse.

National Church Arson Task Force. 1997. *First Year Report for the President.* Washington, D.C.: U.S. Government Printing Office.

National Coalition of Anti-Violence Programs. 2004. *Anti-Lesbian, Gay, Bisexual, and Transgendered Violence in 2003.* New York: NCAVP.

National Commission on the Causes and Prevention of Violence. 1970. *Final Report: To Establish Justice, To Insure Domestic Tranquility.* New York: Bantam Books.

National Crime Survey. 2004. *Criminal Victimization in the U.S., 2003.* Washington, D.C.: U.S. Department of Justice.

Neapolitan, Jerome L. 1997. *Cross-National Crime: A Research Review and Sourcebook.* Westport, CT: Greenwood Press.

Nelken, David. 2003. Comparing Criminal Justice. In *The Oxford Handbook of Criminology,* edited by Mike Maguire, Rod Morgan, and Robert Reiner, 175–202. Oxford: Oxford University Press.

Nelli, Humbert S. 1981. *The Business of Crime.* Chicago: University of Chicago Press.

———. 1987. A Brief History of American Syndicate Crime. In *Organized Crime in America: Concepts and Controversies,* edited by Timothy S. Bynum, 15–29. Monsey, New York: Willow Tree Press.

Nerenberg, Lisa. 2002. *Abuse in Nursing Homes.* National Center on Elder Abuse. Washington, D.C.: National Center on Elder Abuse.

Nettler, Gwynn. 1978. *Explaining Crime.* New York: McGraw-Hill.

*New York Times.* 1998. August 3: A1.

Newburn, Tim, and Elizabeth A. Stanko. 1994. *Just Boys Doing Business? Men, Masculinities, and Crime.* New York: Routledge.

Newman, Oscar. 1973. *Defensible Space: Crime Prevention Through Urban Design.* London: Macmillan.

Nixon, Howard L. 1997. Gender, Sport, and Aggressive Behavior Outside Sport. *Journal of Sport and Social Issues* 21 (4): 379–391.

Nye, F. Ivan. 1958. *Family Relationships and Delinquent Behavior.* New York: John Wiley.

O'Donnell, Ian, and Eooin O'Sullivan. 2003. The Politics of Intolerance—Irish Style. *British Journal of Criminology* 43 (1): 41–62.

O'Neil, William L. 1969. *The Woman Movement: Feminism in the United States.* New York: Barnes and Noble.

O'Toole, Laura L., and Jessica R. Schiffman. eds. 1997. *Gender Violence: Interdisciplinary Perspectives.* New York: New York University Press.

Oakley, Ann. 1972. *Sex, Gender, and Society.* New York: Harper and Row.

Oberdorfer, Don, and Patrick E. Tyler. 1983. U.S.-Backed Nicaraguan Rebel Army Swells to 7,000 Men. *Washington Post* May 8, A1, A10, A11.

Ohmae, K. 1995. *The End of the Nation State.* New York: Free Press.

Ortega, Suzanne T., Jay Corzine, Cathleen Burnett, and Tracey Poyer. 1992. Modernization, Age Structure, and Regional Context: A Cross-National Study of Crime. *Sociological Spectrum* 12 (3): 401–406.

Ortiz, Roxanne Dunbar. 1977. *The Great Sioux Nation.* Berkeley: Moon Books.

Paolucci, Henry. [1764] 1963. Translator's introduction to *On Crime and Punishments,* by Cesare Beccaria, ix–xxiii. Indianapolis: Bobbs-Merrill.

Parenti, Michael. 1983. *Democracy for the Few.* New York: St. Martin's.

———. 2002. *Democracy for the Few*. 7th edition. New York: Wadsworth.

Park, Robert E. 1915. The City: Suggestions for the Investigation of Human Behavior in the City. *American Journal of Sociology* 20 (5): 577–612.

Parker, Donn B. 1976. *Crime by Computer*. New York: Charles Scribner.

Parmalee, Maurice. 1918. *Criminology*. New York: Macmillan.

Passas, Nikos. 1990. Anomie and Corporate Deviance. *Contemporary Crises* 14 (2): 157–178.

———. 2003. *International Crimes*. Dartmouth, Kent: Ashgate.

Pastor, Manuel, amd Susan Alva. 2004. Guest Workers and the New Transnationalism: Possibilities and Realities in an Age of Repression. *Social Justice* 31 (1–2): 92–111.

Paternoster, Raymond, and Robert Brame. 1997. Multiple Routes to Delinquency? A Test of Developmental and General Theories of Crime. *Criminology* 35 (1): 49–80.

Paternoster, Raymond, and Paul Mazerolle. 1994. General Strain Theory and Delinquency: A Replication and Extension. *Journal of Research in Crime and Delinquency* 31 (3): 235–263.

Paulsen, Derek J. 2003. Murder in Black and White: The Newspaper Coverage of Homicide in Houston. *Homicide Studies* 7 (3): 289–317.

Peacock, Patricia. 1998. Marital Rape. In *Issues in Intimate Violence*, edited by Raquel Kennedy Bergen, 225–235. Thousand Oaks, CA: Sage.

Pearce, Frank. 1976. *Crimes of the Powerful*. London: Pluto Press.

Pearce, Frank, and Steve Tombs. 1999. *Toxic Capitalism: Corporate Crime and the Chemical Industry*. Toronto: Canadian Scholars' Press.

Pearson, Karl. 1919. Charles Goring and His Contribution to Criminology. In *The English Convict: A Statistical Study*, xv–xx. Abridged version. London: M.M.S.O.

Peelo, Moiro, Brian Francis, Keith Soothill, Jayn Pearson, and Elizabeth Ackerley. 2004. Newspaper Reporting and the Public Constructon of Homicide. *British Journal of Criminology* 44 (2): 256–275.

Pepinsky, Harold E. 1978. Communist Anarchism as an Alternative to the Rule of Criminal Law. *Contemporary Crises* 2 (3): 315–334.

———. 1997. What Is Peacemaking? In *Thinking Critically About Crime*, edited by Brian D. MacLean and Dragan Milovanovic, 109–114. Vancouver, B.C.: Collective Press.

Pepinsky, Harold E., and Richard Quinney, eds. 1991. *Criminology as Peacemaking*. Bloomington: Indiana University Press.

Pereetti-Watel, Patrick. 2003. Neutralization Theory and the Denial of Risk: Some Evidence From Canabis Use Among French Adolescents. *British Journal of Sociology* 54 (1): 21–42.

Perry, Barbara J. 1998. Defenders of the Faith: Hate Groups and Ideologies of Power in the United States. *Patterns of Prejudice* 32 (3): 32–54.

Petit, Jacques G. 1984. The Birth and Reform of Prisons in France. In *The Emergence of Carceral Institutions: Prisons, Galleys, and Lunatic Asylums, 1550–1900*, edited by Pieter Spierenburg, 125–147. Rotterdam: Erasmus University.

Pfohl, Stephen. 1984. The Discovery of Child Abuse. In *Deviant Behavior*, edited by Delos Kelly, 45-65. New York: St. Martins.

Pfost, Donald. 1987. Reagan's Nicaraguan Policy: A Case Study of Political Deviance and Crime. *Crime and Social Justice* 27/28: 66–87.

Phillipson, Coleman. [1923] 1975. *Three Criminal Law Reformers: Beccaria, Bentham, Romilly*. Montclair, NJ: Patterson Smith.

Piquero, Alex, and Matthew Hickman. 1999. An Empirical Test of Tittle's Control Balance Theory. *Criminology* 37 (2): 319–341.

Platt, Tony. 1974. Prospects for a Radical Criminology in the United States. *Crime and Social Justice* 1 (Spring/Summer): 2–10.

Platt, Tony, and Cecilia O'Leary. 2003. Patriot Acts. *Social Justice* 30 (1): 5–22.

Pogrebin, Mark, ed. 2004. *About Criminals: A View of the Offender's World*. Thousand Oaks, CA: Sage.

Polk, Kenneth. 1994. *When Men Kill: Scenarios of Masculine Violence*. New York: Cambridge University Press.

Porterfield, Austin L. 1946. Delinquency and Its Outcome in Court and College. *American Journal of Sociology* 49 (3): 199–208.

Potter, Gary. 1994. *Criminal Organizations: Vice, Racketeering, and Politics in an American City*. Prospect Heights, IL: Waveland.

Prados, John. 1986. *President's Secret Wars*. New York: William Morrow.

Pratt, Travis C., and Francis T. Cullen. 2000. The Empirical Status of Gottfredson and Hirschi's General Theory of Crime: A Meta-analysis. *Criminology* 38 (3): 931–964.

President's Commission on Law Enforcement and the Administration of Justice. 1967a. *The Challenge of Crime in a Free Society.* Washington, D.C.: U.S. Government Printing Office.

Presidential Commission. 1986. *Report on the Space Shuttle Challenger Accident.* Washington, D.C.: U.S. Government Printing Office.

Ptacek, James. 1998. Why Do Men Batter Their Wives? In *Issues in Intimate Violence,* edited by Raquel Kennedy Bergen, 181–195. Thousand Oaks, CA: Sage

Public Citizen. 2004. *The Ten Year Track Record of NAFTA: The Mexican Economy, Agriculture and Environment.* Washington, D.C.: Public Citizen Global Trade Watch.

Quetelet, Adolphe. [1831] 1984. *Research on the Propensity for Crime at Different Ages.* Translated by Sawyer Sylvester. Cincinnati: Anderson

———. 1842. *A Treatise on Man.* Translated by R. Knox and T. Smibert. Edinburgh: Chambers.

———. 1848. *Du systéme social et des lois qui le régissent.* Paris: Guillaumin.

Quinney, Richard. 1965. Suicide, Homicide and Economic Development. *Social Forces* 43 (3): 401–406.

———. 1970. *The Social Reality of Crime.* Boston: Little, Brown.

———. 1973a. There's a Lot of Us Folks Grateful to the Lone Ranger: Some Notes on the Rise and Fall of American Criminology. *Insurgent Sociologist* 4 (Fall): 56–64.

———. 1973b. Crime Control in Capitalist Society: A Critical Philosophy of Legal Order. *Issues in Criminology* 8 (Spring): 75–79.

———. 1977. *Class, State, and Crime.* New York: Longman.

———. 1997. Socialist Humanism and Critical/Peacemaking Criminology: The Continuing Project. In *Thinking Critically About Crime,* edited by Brian D. MacLean and Dragan Milovanovic, 114–117. Vancouver, B.C.: Collective press.

Quinney, Richard, and John Wildeman. 1977. *The Problem of Crime.* New York: Harper and Row.

Rafter, Nicole Hahn, ed. 1988. *White Trash: The Engenic Family Studies, 1877–1919.* Boston: Northeastern University Press.

———. 1992. Criminal Anthropology in the United States. *Criminology* 30 (4): 525–545.

———. 1997. Psychopathy and the Evolution of Criminological Knowledge. *Theoretical Criminology* 1 (2): 235–259.

Rafter, Nicole Hahn, and Mary Gibson. 2004. Editors' Introduction. In *Criminal Woman, the Prostitute, and the Normal Woman,* by Cesare Lombroso and Guglielmo Ferro, translated by Rafter and Gibson, 3–33. Durham, NC: Duke University Press.

Ranelagh, John. 1987. *The Agency: The Rise and Decline of the CIA.* New York: Simon and Schuster.

Ray, Oakley. 1983. *Drugs, Society, and Human Behavior.* St. Louis: C. V. Mosley.

Reckless, Walter C. 1940. *Criminal Behavior.* New York: McGraw-Hill.

———. 1961. *The Crime Problem.* New York: Appleton-Century-Crofts.

Reckless, Walter C., Simon Dinitz, and Ellen Murray. 1956. Self-Concept as an Insulator Against Delinquency. *American Sociological Review* 21 (6): 744–746.

Redhead, Steve. 1987. *Sing When You're Winning: The Last Football Book.* Manchester: Manchester University Press.

Reed, Gary E., and Peter Cleary Yeager. 1996. Organizational Offending and Neoclassical Offending: Challenging the Reach of a General Theory of Crime. *Criminology* 34 (3): 357–382.

Reichel, Philip (ed.). 2005. *Handbook of Transnational Criminal Justice.* Thousand Oaks, CA: Sage.

Reiman, Jeffrey. 2004. *The Rich Get Richer and the Poor Get Prison: Ideology, Class, and Criminal Justice.* Boston: Allyn & Bacon.

Reiner, Robert. 2002. Media Made Criminality. In *The Oxford Handbook of Criminology,* edited by Mike Maguire, Rod Morgan, and Robert Reiner, 376–416. Oxford: Oxford University Press.

Reisner, Marc. 1991. *Game Wars: The Undercover Pursuit of Wildlife Poachers.* New York: Viking.

Reiss, Albert J., Jr. 1951. Delinquency as the Failure of Personal and Social Controls. *American Sociological Review* 16 (2): 196–207.

Reiter, Rayna. 1975. *Toward an Anthropology of Women.* New York: Monthly Review Press.

Renzetti, Claire M. 2000. Lesbian Partner Battering. In *Encyclopedia of Women and Crime,* edited by Nicole Hahn Rafter, 148–149. Phoenix: Oryx Press.

Ritchie, Robert C. 1986. *Captain Kidd and the War Against the Pirates.* Cambridge, MA: Harvard University Press.

Roberts, Aki, and Gary LaFree. 2004. Explaining Japan's Postwar Violent Crime Trends. *Criminology* 42 (1)179–209.

Rosen, Ruth. 1982. *The Lost Sisterhood: Prostitution in America, 1900–1918.* Baltimore: Johns Hopkins University Press.

Rosenblum, Karen. 1975. Female Deviance and the Female Sex Role: A Preliminary Investigation. *British Journal of Sociology* 25 (2): 169–185.

Rosenfeld, Richard, and Steven F. Messner. 1991. The Social Sources of Homicide in Different Types of Societies. *Sociological Forum* 6 (1): 51–70.

Rosoff, Stephen M., Henry N. Pontell, and Robert Tillman. 1998. *Profit Without Honor: White-Collar Crime and the Looting of America.* Upper Saddle River, NJ: Prentice-Hall.

———. 2004. *Profit Without Honor: White-Collar Crime and the Looting of America.* Upper Saddle River, NJ: Prentice Hall.

Ross, Dorothy. 1991. *The Origins of American Social Science.* Cambridge: Cambridge University Press.

———. 1992. *Confronting Drunk Driving: Social Policy for Saving Lives.* New Haven: Yale University Press.

Ross, E. A. 1901. *Social Control.* New York: MacMillan.

Ross, Jeffrey Ian, and Stephen C. Richards, eds. 2003. *Convict Criminology.* Belmont, CA: Wadsworth/Thomson Learning.

Rottman, David. 1980. *Crime in the Republic of Ireland.* Paper no. 102. Dublin: Economic and Social Research Institute.

Ruggiero, Vincent. 2002. 'Attac': A Global Social Movement? *Social Justice* 29 (1/2): 48–61.

Russell, Diana E. H. 1986. *The Secret Trauma: Incest in the Lives of Girls and Women.* New York: Basic Books.

———. 1990. *Sexual Exploitation.* Beverly Hills: Sage.

———. 1998. The Making of a Whore. In *Issues in Intimate Violence,* edited by Raquel Kennedy Bergen, 65–77. Thousand Oaks, CA: Sage.

Russell, Dick. 1988. Welcome to Dioxinville, Arkansas. *In These Times,* March 9–15, 8–13.

Saleilles, Raymond. 1911. *The Individualization of Punishment.* 1898. Translated by Rachel Szold Jastrow. Boston: Little, Brown.

Sampson, Robert J. 1999. Techniques of Research Neutralization. *Theoretical Criminology* 3 (4): 438–451.

Sampson, Robert J., and John H. Laub. 1993. *Crime in the Making: Pathways and Turning Points Through Life.* Cambridge, MA.: Harvard University Press.

———. 2003. Life-Course Desisters? Trajectories of Crime Among Delinquent Boys Followed to Age 70. *Criminology* 41 (3): 555–592.

Sampson, Robert J., and William Julius Wilson. 1995. Toward a Theory of Race, Crime, and Urban Inequality. In *Crime and Inequality,* edited by John Hagan and Ruth D. Peterson, 110–125. Stanford: Stanford University Press.

Sanchez-Jankowski, Martin. 2003. Gangs and Social Change. *Theoretical Criminology* 7 (2): 191–216.

Sanday, Peggy. 1981. The Socio-Cultural Context of Rape: A Cross-Cultural Study. *Journal of Social Issues* 37 (1): 5–27.

———. 1996. *A Woman Scorned: Acquaintance Rape on Trial.* New York: Doubleday.

Sarangi, Satinath. 2002. Crimes of Bhopal and the Global Campaign for Justice. *Social Justice* 29 (3): 47–52.

Sasson, Theodore. 1995. *Crime Talk: How Citizens Construct a Social Problem.* New York: Aldine de Gruyter.

Savelsberg, Joachim. 1998/1999. Controlling Violence: Criminal Justice, Society, and Lessons from the United States. *Crime, Law, and Social Change* 30 (2): 185–203.

Scarpitti, Frank R., and Carol Calwin Lenhart. 2001. Credit Card Fraud. In *Encyclopedia of Criminology and Deviant Behavior,* edited by Clifton D. Bryant, 106–109. New York: Brunner-Routledge.

Scheffer, David J. 1987. U.S. Law and the Iran-Contra Affair. The American *Journal of International Law* 81 (3): 696–723.

Schrag, Clarence. 1962. Delinquency and Opportunity: Analysis of a Theory. *Sociology and Social Research* 46 (2): 167–175.

Schrager, Laura Shill, and James F. Short. 1978. Toward a Sociology of Organizational Crime. *Social Problems* 25 (4): 407–419.

Schuessler, Karl. 1973. Introduction to *Edwin H. Sutherland on Analyzing Crime,* edited by Karl Schuessler, ix–xxxvi. Chicago: University of Chicago Press.

Schur, Edwin M. 1968. *Law and Society: A Sociological View.* New York: Random House.

———. 1988. *The Americanization of Sex.* Philadelphia: Temple University Press.

Schwartz, Martin D., and Carol A. Nogrady. 1996. Fraternity Membership, Rape Myths, and Sexual Aggression on a College Campus. *Violence Against Women* 2 (2): 148–163.

Schwartz, Martin D., and Victoria L. Pitts. 1995. Exploring a Feminist Routine Activities Approach to Explaining Sexual Assault. *Justice Quarterly* 12 (1): 9–31.

Schwartz, Richard D., and Jerome C. Miller. 1964. Legal Evolution and Societal Complexity. *American Journal of Sociology* 70 (2): 159–169.

Schwartz, Richard D., and Jerome H. Skolnick. 1964. Two Studies of Legal Stigma. In *The Other Side,* edited by Howard S. Becker, 103–117. New York: Free Press.

Schwendinger, Julia, and Herman Schwendinger. 1974. *The Sociologists of the Chair: A Radical Analysis of the Formative Years of North American Sociology (1883–1922).* New York: Basic Books.

———. 1975. Defenders of Order or Guardians of Human Rights? In *Critical Criminology,* edited by Ian Taylor, Paul Walton, and Jock Young, 113–146. London: Routledge and Kegan Paul.

———. 1977. Social Class and the Definition of Crime. *Crime and Social Justice* 7 (Spring/Summer): 4–13.

———. 1983. *Rape and Inequality.* Beverly Hills, CA: Sage.

Sciolino, Elaine. 1988. Fighting Narcotics: U.S. Is Urged to Shift Tactics. *New York Times* April 10, A1, A10.

Scott, Walter. 1988. Personality Parade. *Parade Magazine* October 30, 2.

Seager, Jodi. 1993. *Earth Follies: Coming to Feminist Terms With the Global Environmental Crisis.* New York: Routledge.

Sellin, Thorsten. 1938. *Culture Conflict and Crime.* New York: Social Science Research Council.

Shaw, Clifford R. 1930. *The Jack-Roller: A Delinquent Boy's Own Story.* Chicago: University of Chicago Press.

———. 1939. *The Natural History of a Delinquent Career.* Chicago: University of Chicago Press.

Shaw, Clifford R., and Henry D. McKay. [1942] 1969. *Juvenile Delinquency and Urban Areas.* Chicago: University of Chicago Press.

Shaw, Clifford, Henry D. McKay, and James F. McDonald. 1938. *Brothers in Crime.* Chicago: University of Chicago Press.

Shaw, Clifford R., et al. 1929. *Delinquency Areas: A Study of the Geographic Distribution of School Truants, Juvenile Delinquents, and Adult Offenders in Chicago.* Chicago: University of Chicago Press.

Sheehan, Daniel. 1988. *Inside the Shadow Government.* Washington, D.C.: Christic Institute.

Shelley, Louise I. 1981. *Crime and Modernization: The Impact of Industrialization and Modernization on Crime.* Carbondale: Southern Illinois University Press.

Shenon, Philip. 1988a. Enemy Within: Drug Money Is Corrupting Enforcers. *New York Times* April 11, A1, A2.

———. 1988b. North, Poindexter, and Two Others Indicted. *New York Times* March 17, A1, D27.

Sheptycki, James. 2003. Against Transnational Organized Crime. In *Critical Reflections on Transnational Organized Crime, Money Laundering and Corruption,* edited by Margaret E. Beare, 120–144. Toronto: University of Toronto Press.

———. 2005. Relativism, Transnationalization and Comparative Criminology. In *Transnational and Comparative Criminology,* edited by J. Sheptycki and A. Wardak, 69–90. London: Glasshouse Press.

Sheptycki, James and Ali Wardak, eds. 2005. *Transnational and Comparative Criminology.* London: Glasshouse Press.

Sherman, Lawrence W., Patrick R. Gartin, and Michael E. Bueger. 1989. Hot Spots of Predatory Crime: Routine Activities and the Criminology of Place. *Criminology* 27 (1): 27–55.

Shihadeh, Edward S., and Graham C. Ousey. 1998. Industrial Restructuring and Violence: The Link Between Entry-Level Jobs, Economic Deprivation, and Black and White Homicide. *Social Forces* 77: 185–206.

Short, James F., Jr., Joachim J. Savelsberg, Gary F. Jensen, and Charles R. Tittle. 1999. Symposium on Control Balance: Toward a General Theory of Deviance. *Theoretical Criminology* 3 (3): 327–352.

Shostak, Marjorie. 1983. *Nisa: The Life and Words of a !Kung Woman.* New York: Vintage Books.

Shover, Neal. 1996. *Great Pretenders: Pursuits and Careers of Persistent Thieves.* Boulder, CO: Westview Press.

Sick, Gary. 1991. *October Surprise: Americas Hostages in Iran and the Election of Ronald Reagan.* New York: Times Books.

Sidel, Ruth. 1998. *Keeping Women and Children Last.* NY: Penguin.

Simon, Carl P., and Ann D. Witte. 1982. *Beating the System: The Underground Economy.* Boston: Auburn House Publishing.

Simon, David R. 2001. Prostitution-Female. In *Encyclopedia of Criminology and Deviant Behavior,* edited by Clifton D. Bryant, 264–266. New York: Brunner-Routledge.

———. 2002a. *Tony Soprano's America: The Criminal Side of the American Dream.* Boulder, CO: Westview.

———. 2002b. *Elite Deviance.* Boston: Allyn & Bacon.

Simon, David R., and D. Stanley Eitzen. 1986. *Elite Deviance.* Boston: Allyn & Bacon.

Simon, Jonathan. 2002. The Land of the Free and the Home of the Fearful: Governing America Through Fear of Crime Before 9/11 and Since. Available in part in *War on Crime Adversely Affects War on Terrorism, Professor Says Kevin Bergquist,* at <http: //www.umich.edu/~urecord/0102/Oct14_02/g_simon.shtml>.

Simon, Rita. 1975. *Women and Crime.* Lexington, MA: D.C. Heath.

Simon, Thomas, and James Mercy. 2001. *Injuries From Violent Crime, 1992–1998.* Bureau of Justice Statistics, NCJ-168633.

Singer, Peter. 1990. *Animal Liberation.* New York: Avon Books.

Skinner, B. F. 1953. *Science and Human Behavior.* New York: Macmillan.

Smart, Carol. 1976. *Women, Crime, and Criminology: A Feminist Critique.* Boston: Routledge and Kegan Paul.

———. 1979. The New Female Offender: Reality or Myth? *British Journal of Criminology* 19 (1): 50–59.

———. 1998. The Woman of Legal Discourse. In *Criminology at the Crossroads: Feminist Readings in Crime and Justice,* edited by Kathleen Daly and Lisa Maher, 21–36. New York: Oxford University Press.

Smith, Douglas, and Christy A. Visher. 1980. Sex and Involvement in Deviance/Crime: A Quantitative Review of the Empirical Literature. *American Sociological Review* 45 (4): 691–701.

Smith, Dwight. 1976. *The Mafia Mystique.* New York: Basic Books.

Sokoloff, Natalie. 1980. *Between Money and Love.* New York: Praeger.

South, Nigel, and Piers Beirne (eds.). 2005. *Green Criminology.* London: Taylor and Francis.

Spano, Richard. 2003. Concerns About Safety, Observer, Sex, and the Decision to Arrest: Evidence of Reactivity in a Large-Scale Observational Study of Police. *Criminology* 41 (3): 909–932.

Sparks, Richard F. 1981. Surveys of Victimization: An Optimistic Assessment. *Crime and Justice: An Annual Review of Research* 3: 1–60.

Spitzer, Steven. 1975. Toward a Marxian Theory of Deviance. *Social Problems* 22 (5): 638–651.

———. 1980. Left-Wing Criminology: An Infantile Disorder. In *Radical Criminology: The Coming Crises,* edited by James A. Inciardi, 169–190. Beverly Hills: Sage.

St. James, Margo. 1987. The Reclamation of Whores. In *Good Girls/Bad Girls: Feminists and Sex Trade Workers Face to Face,* edited by Laurie Bell, 81–87. Seattle: Seal Press.

Stack, Steven, and Mary Jeanne Kanavy. 1983. The Effect of Religion on Forcible Rape: A Structural Analysis. *Journal for the Scientific Study of Religion* 22 (1): 67–74.

Stanko, Elizabeth. 1985. *Intimate Intrusions: Women's Experiences of Male Violence.* Boston: Routledge and Kegan Paul.

———. 2000. Victims R Us: The Life History of 'Fear of Crime' and the Politicization of Violence. In *Crime, Risk and Insecurity,* edited by Tim Hope and Richard Sparks, 13–29. London: Routledge.

Stanton, Duncan. 1976. Drugs, Vietnam, and the Vietnam Veteran: An Overview. American *Journal of Drugs and Alcohol Abuse* 3: 557–570.

*Statistical Abstract of the United States.* 2003. Washington, DC: U.S. Government Printing Office.

Stead, Philip John. 1983. *The Police of France.* London: Macmillan.

Steel, Ronald. 2004. Totem and Taboo. *The Nation* 279 (8): 29–35.

Steffensmeier, Darrell J. 1983. Organization Properties and Sex Segregation in the Underworld: Building a Sociological Theory of Sex Differences in Crime. *Social Forces* 61 (4): 1010–1032.

———. 1986. *The Fence: In the Shadow of Two Worlds.* Totowa, NJ: Rowman and Littlefield.

Steffensmeier, Darrell, and Emilie Anderson Allan. 1995a. Criminal Behavior: Gender and Age. In *Criminology: A Contemporary Handbook,* edited by Joseph Sheley, 83–114. Belmont, CA: Wadsworth.

———. 1995b. Age-Inequality and Property Crime: The Effects of Age-Linked Stratification and Status-Attainment Processes on Patterns of Criminality Across the Life Course. In *Crime and Inequality,* edited by John Hagan and Ruth D. Peterson, 95–115. Stanford, CA: Stanford University Press.

Steffensmeier, Darrell J., and Jeffrey T. Ulmer. 2004. *Confessions of a Dying Thief.* Hawthorne, NY: Aldine de Gruyter.

Stevenson, Richard W. 2004. President Offers Defense on Iraq and the Economy. *New York Times* February 9, A1, 19.

Stolzenberg, Lisa, Stewart J. D'Alessio, and David Eitle. 2004. A Multilevel Test of Racial Threat Theory. *Criminology* 42 (3): 673–698.

Strange, S. 1996. *The Retreat of the State: The Diffusion of Power in the World Economy.* Cambridge: Cambridge University Press.

Straus, Murray A. 2001. *Beating the Devil Out of Them.* New Brunswick, NJ: Transaction Books.

Sumner. Colin. 1994. *The Sociology of Deviance: An Obituary.* New York: Continuum.

Surette, Ray, ed. 1984. *Justice and the Media.* Springfield, IL: Charles C. Thomas.

———. 1992. *Media, Crime, and Criminal Justice.* Pacific Grove, CA: Brooks/Cole.

———. 1998. *Media, Crime, and Criminal Justice.* 2nd edition. Belmont, CA: West/Wadsworth.

Sutherland, Edwin H. 1937. *The Professional Thief: By a Professional Thief.* Chicago: University of Chicago Press.

———. [1924] 1947. *Criminology.* Philadelphia: J. B. Lippincott.

———. [1942] 1956. Development of the Theory. In *The Sutherland Papers,* edited by Albert Cohen, Alfred Lindesmith, and Karl Schuessler, 13–29. Bloomington: Indiana University Press.

———. [1949] 1983. *White Collar Crime.* New Haven, CT: Yale University Press.

Sutherland, Edwin H., and Donald R. Cressey. [1949] 1970. *Criminology.* Philadelphia: L. B. Lippincott.

Sykes, Gresham M., and David Matza. 1957. Techniques of Neutralization: A Theory of Delinquency. *American Sociological Review* 22 (6): 664–670.

Tallmer, Matt. 1987. Chemical Dumping as a Corporate Way of Life. In *Corporate Violence,* edited by Stuart Hills, 111–120. Totowa, NJ: Rowman and Littlefield.

Tannenbaum, Frank. 1938. *Crime and the Community.* Boston: Ginn.

Tappan, Paul W. 1947. Who Is the Criminal? *American Sociological Review* 12 (1): 96–102.

Tarde, Gabriel. 1884. Qu'est-ce qu'une société? *Revue philosophique* 18: 501.

———. 1886. Problémes de penalité. In *La criminalité comparé,* 122–211. Paris: Alcan.

———. [1886] 1902. *La criminalité comparé.* Paris: Alcan.

———. [1890] 1903. *The Laws of Imitation.* Translated by F. Parsons. New York: Henry Holt.

———. 1892. Les crimes des foules. *Archives de l'anthropologie crininelle* 7: 353–386.

———. 1893. Foules et sectes au point de rue criminal. *Revue des deux mondes* 120: 349–387.

———. 1912. *Penal Philosophy.* 1890. Translated by R. Howell. Boston: Little, Brown.

Taylor, Ian, Paul Walton, and Jock Young. 1973. *The New Criminology.* London: Routledge and Kegan Paul.

Taylor, Laurie. 1984. *In the Underworld.* Oxford: Basil Blackwell.

Thomas, William I. 1923. *The Unadjusted Girl: With Cases and Standpoints for Behavior Analysis.* Boston: Little, Brown.

Thomas, William I., and Florian Znaniecki. 1918–1920. *The Polish Peasant in Europe and America.* Chicago: University of Chicago Press.

Thorbek, Susanne, and Bandana Pattanaik, eds. 2002. *Transnational Prostitution: Changing Global Patterns.* New York: Zed Books.

Thornberry, Terence, and R. L. Christenson. 1984. Unemployment and Criminal Involvement: An Investigation of Reciprocal Causal Structures. *American Sociological Review* 49 (3): 398–411.

Thornberry, Terence P., Marvin D. Krohn, Alan J. Lizotte, Carolyn A. Smith, and Kimberly Tobin. 2003. *Gangs and Delinquency in Developmental Perspective.* Cambridge: Cambridge University Press.

Thrasher, Frederic Milton. 1927. *The Gang: A Study of 1,313 Gangs in Chicago.* Chicago: University of Chicago Press.

Thurman, Quint, and Brenda Vose. 2001. Tax Fraud. In *Encyclopedia of Criminology and Deviant Behavior,* edited by Clifton D. Bryant, 490–493. New York: Brunner-Routledge.

Tifft, Larry L., and Dennis C. Sullivan———. 1980. *The Struggle to Be Human: Crime, Criminology, and Anarchism.* Orkney, U.K.: Cienfuegos Press.

———. 2001. A Needs-Based, Social Harms Definition of Crime. In *What Is Crime?,* edited by Stuart Henry and Mark M. Lanier, 179–203). Lanham, MD: Rowman and Littlefield.

*Time.* 1983. *Wife Beating: The Silent Crime.* September 5, 23.

Tittle, Charles R. 1975. Labeling and Crime: An Empirical Evaluation. In *The Labeling of Deviance,* edited by Walter R. Gove, 241–263. Beverly Hills: Sage.

———. 1995. *Control Balance: Toward a General Theory of Deviance.* Boulder, CO: Westview.

———. 1997. Thoughts Stimulated by Braithwaite's Analysis of Control Balance Theory. *Theoretical Criminology* 1 (1): 99-110.

———. 1999. Continuing the Discussion of Control Balance. *Theoretical Criminology* 3 (3): 344–352.

Tjaden, Patricia, and Nancy Thoennes. 1998. *Prevalence, Incidence, and Consequences of Violence Against Women.* Washington, D.C.: U.S. Department of Justice.

Toby, Jackson. 1979. The New Criminology Is the Old Sentimentality. *Criminology* 16 (3): 516–526.

———. 1983. Crime in the Schools. In *Crime and Public Policy,* edited by James Q. Wilson, 69–88. San Francisco: Institute for Contemporary Studies.

Tombs, Robert. 1980. Crime and the Security of the State: The Dangerous Classes and Insurrection in Nineteenth-Century Paris. In *Crime and the Law: The Social History of Crime in Western Europe Since 1500,* edited by V. A. C. Gatrell, Bruce Lenman, and Geoffrey Parker, 214–237. London: Europa.

Tomlinson, Mike, Tony Varley, and Ciaran McCullagh. 1988. Introduction to *Whose Law and Order? Aspects of Crime and Social Control in Irish Society,* edited by Mike Tomlinson et al., 9–20. Belfast: Sociological Association of Ireland.

Tomsen, Stephen. 2002. *Hatred, Murder and Male Honour: Anti-Homosexual Homicides in New South Wales, 1980–2000.* Caberra: Australian Institute of Criminology.

Totten, Mark. 2000. *Guys, Gangs, and Girlfriend Abuse.* Toronto: Broadview Press.

Triplett, Ruth, and Roger Jarjoura. 1994. Theoretical and Empirical Specification of a Model of Informative Labeling. *Journal of Quantitative Criminology* 10: 241–276.

Tseloni, Andromachi, and Ken Pease. 2003. Repeat Personal Victimization: 'Boosts' or 'Flags'? *British Journal of Criminology* 43 (1): 196–212.

Tseloni, Andromachi, Karin Wittebrood, Graham Farrell, and Ken Pease. 2004. Burglary Victimization in England and Wales, the United States and the Netherlands: A Cross-National Test of Routine Activities and Lifestyle Theories. *British Journal of Criminology* 44 (1): 66–91.

Tunnell, Kenneth D. 1992. *Choosing Crime: The Criminal Calculus of Property Offenders.* Chicago: Nelson-Hall.

Turk, Austin T. 1969. *Criminality and Legal Order.* Chicago: Rand McNally.

———. 1979. Analyzing Official Deviance: For a Nonpartisan Conflict Analysis in Criminology. *Criminology* 16 (3): 459–476.

———. 2000. Political Offenders. In *Encyclopedia of Women and Crime,* edited by Nicole Hahn Rafter, 87–88. Phoenix, AZ: Oryx Press.

Tushnet, Mark. 1988. *Central America and the Law: The Constitution, Civil Liberties, and the Courts.* Boston: South End Press.

U.S. Department of Health and Human Services. 2004. *National Household Survey on Drug Abuse.* Washington, D.C.: Department of Health and Human Services.

U.S. Department of Labor. 2004a. *Bureau of Labor Statistics: Injuries, Illnesses, Fatalities, 2002,* available at <http://stats.bls.gov/iif/oshsum.htm#02Summary%20News%20Release>.

———. 2004b. *Incidence Rates of Nonfatal Occupational Injuries by Industry and Case Types, 2002.* Available at: <http: //www.bls.gov/iif/oshwc/osh/os/ostb1244.pdf>.

U.S. House Subcommittee on Crime. 1980. *Increasing Violence Against Minorities.* Washington, D.C.: U.S. Government Printing Office.

U.S. Senate Subcommittee on Terrorism, Narcotics, and International Operations. 1989. *Drugs, Law Enforcement, and Foreign Policy.* Washington, D.C.: U.S. Government Printing Office.

UNICEF. 1999. *Child and Maternal Mortality Survey.* New York: UNICEF.

United Nations. 1983. *Human Rights: A Compilation of International Instruments.* Publication E.83.XIV.1. New York: United Nations.

———. 1986. *Demographic Yearbook, 1984.* New York: United Nations, Department of International Economic and Social Affairs, Statistical Office.

———. 1999. *Global Report on Crime and Justice,* edited by Graeme Newman. New York: Oxford University Press.

———. 2004. *Afghanistan: Opium Survey 2004.* New York: United Nations.

Valier, Claire. 2002. *Theories of Crime and Punishment.* New York, NY: Longman.

Valukas, Anton R., and Ira Raphaelson. 1988. Judicial Corruption. In *Prosecution of Public Corruption Cases,* edited by U.S. Department of Justice, 1–15. Washington, D.C.: Department of Justice.

van Dijk, Jan. 2000. Implications of the International Crime Victims Survey for a Victim Perspective. In *Integrating a Victim Perspective Within Criminal Justice,* edited by Adam Crawford and Jo Goodey, 97–121. Aldershot, NH: Ashgate.

Van Kesteren, J. N., P. Mayhew, and P. Nieuwbeerta. 2000. *Criminal Victimization in Seventeen Industrialised Countries: Key Findings from the 2000 International Crime Victims Survey.* The Hague, Ministry of Justice.

Vayrynen, Raimo. 2004. *Anti-Globalization Movements at the Crossroads.* University of Notre Dame: Kroc Institute for International Peace Studies.

Victor, Jeffrey S. 2004. Sluts and Wiggers: A Study of the Effects of Derogatory Labeling. *Deviant Behavior* 25 (1): 67–85.

Vila, Brian. 1994. A General Paradigm for Understanding Criminal Behavior. *Criminology* 32 (3): 311–360.

Vinton, Linda. 2001. Violence Against Older Women. In *Sourcebook on Violence Against Women,* edited by Claire M. Renzetti, Jeffrey L. Edleson, and Raquel Kennedy Bergen, 179–192. Thousand Oaks, CA: Sage.

Vold, George B. 1958. *Theoretical Criminology.* New York: Oxford University Press.

Vold, George B., Thomas J. Bernard, and Jeffrey B. Snipes. 2002. *Theoretical Criminology.* 4th edition. New York: Oxford University Press.

von Hirsch, Andrew. 1976. *Doing Justice: The Choice of Punishments.* New York: Hill and Wang.

Voorhis, Patricia Van, Francis T. Cullen, Richard A. Mathers, and Connie Chenoweth Garner. 1988. The Impact of Family Structure and Quality on Delinquency: A Comparative Assessment of Structural and Functional Factors. *Criminology* 26 (2): 235–261.

Wacquant, Loic. 1998. Imprisoning the American Poor. *Manchester Guardian Weekly* 159 (12): 8–9.

Walker, Samuel. 1980. *Popular Justice: A History of American Criminal Justice.* New York: Oxford University Press.

Walklate, Sandra. 1998. *Understanding Criminology: Current Theoretical Debates.* Philadelphia: Open University Press.

———. 2004. *Gender, Crime, and Criminal Justice.* Portland, OR: Willan

Walmsley, Roy. 2004. World Population List. *Home Office Research Findings,* no. 234.

Walsh, Dermot. 1986. *Heavy Business: Commercial Burglary and Robbery.* Boston: Routledge & Kegan Paul.

Walsh, Marilyn E. 1977. *The Fence.* Westport, CT: Greenwood Press.

Warr, Mark. 2001. Age and Crime. In *Encyclopedia of Criminology and Deviant Behavior,* edited by Clifton D. Bryant, 4–6. New York: Brunner-Routledge.

———. 2002. *Companions in Crime.* New York: Cambridge University Press.

Washington, James Melvin, ed. 1986. *A Testament of Hope: The Essential Writings of Martin Luther King, Jr.* New York: Harper and Row.

Waters, Malcolm. 2001. *Globalization.* New York: Routledge.

Weis, Joseph G. 1976. Liberation and Crime: The Invention of the New Female Criminal. *Crime and Social Justice* 6 (Fall): 17–27.

Welch, Michael. 2004. Quiet Constructions in the War on Terror: Subjecting Asylum Seekers to Unnecessary Detention. *Social Justice* 31 (1–2): 113–129.

Welch, Michael, Melissa Fenwick, and Meredith Roberts. 1998. State Managers, Intellectuals, and the Media: A Content Analysis of Ideology in Experts' Quotes in Feature Newspaper Articles on Crime. *Justice Quarterly* 15 (1): 219–241.

Weld, William F. 1988. Introduction: Why Public Corruption Is Not a Victimless Crime. *Prosecution of Public Corruption Cases,* edited by U.S. Department of Justice, i–v. Washington, D.C.: Department of Justice.

Weldon, W. F. R. 1894–1895. An Attempt to Measure the Death-Rate Due to the Selective Destruction of Carcinus Moenas with Respect to a Particular Dimension. *Proceedings of the Royal Society of London* 57: 360–382.

Wells, L. Edward, and Joseph H. Rankin. 1988. Direct Parental Controls and Delinquency. *Criminology* 26 (2): 263–285.

Weyler, Rex. 1982. *Blood of the Land.* New York: Everest House.

Whitt, Hugh P. 2002. Inventing Sociology: André-Michel Guerry. In *Essay on the Moral Statistics of France* (1833), by André-Michel Guerry, edited and translated by Hugh P. Whitt and Victor W. Reinking, pp. ix–xxxvii. Lewiston, NY: Edwin Mellen.

Wilcox, Pamela, Kenneth Land, and Scott A. Hunt. 2003. *Criminal Circumstance: A Dynamic Multicontextual Criminal Opportunity Theory.* New York: Aldine de Gruyter.

Wilkins, Leslie T. 1964. *Social Deviance: Social Policy, Action, and Research.* London: Tavistock.

Williamson, Celia, and Terry Cluse-Tolar. 2002. Pimp-Controlled Prostitution: Still an Integral Part of Street Life. *Violence Against Women* 8 (9): 1074–1092.

Wilson, James Q. 1985. *Thinking About Crime.* New York: Vintage.

Wilson, James Q., and Richard J. Herrnstein. 1985. *Crime and Human Nature.* New York: Simon and Schuster.

Winlow, Simon. 2001. *Badfellas: Crime, Tradition and New Masculinities.* New York: Berg.

Wise, David. 1976. *The American Police State.* New York: Random House.

Wolak, Janis, David Finkelhor, and Kimberly Mitchell. 2004. Internet-Initiated Sex Crimes Against Minors: Implications for Prevention Based on Findings From a National Study. *Journal of Adolescent Health* 35 (5): 424–433.

Wolfe, David A. 1985. Child-Abusive Parents: An Empirical Review and Analysis. *Psychological Bulletin* 97 (3): 462–482.

Wolfgang, Marvin E. 1958. *Patterns in Criminal Homicide.* Philadelphia: University of Pennsylvania Press.

———. 1967. International Criminal Statistics: A Proposal. *Journal of Criminal Law, Criminology, and Police Science* 58 (1): 65–69.

Wolfgang, Marvin E., and Franco Ferracuti. 1967. *The Subculture of Violence.* London: Tavistock.

Wollstonecraft, Mary. [1792] 1975. *A Vindication of the Rights of Women.* New York: W. W. Norton.

Wood, Peter B., Walter R. Gove, James A. Wilson, and John K. Cochran. 1997. Non-Social Reinforcement and Habitual Criminal Conduct: An Extension of Learning Theory. *Criminology* 35 (2): 335–366.

Wright, Gordon. 1983. *Between the Guillotine and Liberty: Two Centuries of the Crime Problem in France.* New York: Oxford University Press.

Wright, James, Peter H. Rossi, and Kathleen Daly. 1983. *Under the Gun: Weapons, Crime, and Violence in America.* New York: Aldine.

Wright, Richard T., and Scott H. Decker. 1994. *Burglars on the Job: Streetlife and Residential Break-ins.* Boston: Northeastern University Press.

———. 1997. *Armed Robbers in Action: Stickups and Street Culture.* Boston: Northeastern University Press.

Wyden, Peter. 1979. *Bay of Pigs: The Untold Story.* New York: Simon and Schuster.

Yablonsky, Lewis. 1962. *The Violent Gang.* New York: Macmillan.

Yates, Roger, Chris Powell, and Piers Beirne. 2001. Horse Maiming In the English Countryside: Moral Panic, Human Deviance, and the Social Construction of Victimhood. *Society & Animals* 9 (1): 1–23.

Yin, Peter. 1985. *Victimization and the Aged.* Springfield, IL: Charles C. Thomas.

Young, Jock. 1971. The Role of the Police as Amplifiers of Deviancy, Negotiators of Reality, and Translators of Fantasy. In *Images of Deviance,* edited by Stanley Cohen, 27–61. Harmondsworth, U.K.: Penguin.

———. 1986. The Failure of Criminology: The Need for a Radical Realism. In *Confronting Crime,* edited by Roger Matthews and Jock Young, 4–30. Beverly Hills: Sage.

———. 1997. Left Realist Criminology: Radical in Its Analysis, Realist in Its Policy. In *Oxford Handbook of Criminology*, edited by Mike Maguire, Rod Morgan, and Robert Reiner, 473–498. Oxford: Clarendon Press.

———. 1999. *The Exclusive Society*. Thousand Oaks, CA: Sage.

———. 2003. Merton With Energy, Katz With Structure. *Theoretical Criminology* 7 (3): 389–414.

Zimring, Franklin E., and Gordon Hawkins. 1997. *Crime Is Not the Problem: Lethal Violence in America*. New York: Oxford University Press. ✦

# Photo Credits

Page 7: Knickerbocker Design; page 20 AFP/Behrouz Mehri/Getty Images; page 64: Mark C. Ide; page 68: Roxbury Publishing; page 74: Roxbury Publishing; page 84: www.corbisimages.com; page 91: Mark C. Ide; page 103: Photodisc; page 111: Photodisc; page 118: DigitalStock; page 127: Reuters; page 131: DigitalStock; page 141: Photodisc; page 154: Photodisc; page 162: www.corbisimages.com; page 165: www.corbisimages.com; page 168: www.corbisimages.com; page 176: Photodisc; page 180: DigitalStock; page 187: courtesy of Ronald Reagan Library; page 196: Roxbury Publishing; page 207: Roxbury Publishing; page 210: www.corbisimages.com; page 224: Roxbury Publishing; page 228: DigitalStock; page 237: The Granger Collection; page 257: Photodisc; page 266: Piers Beirne, courtesy of Bowdoin College; page 269: Piers Beirne; page 271: University College London Library; page 277: The Lilly Library, Indiana University, Bloomington, Indiana; page 291: Getty Images; page 292: Stock Montage; page 306: The Granger Collection; page 317: Keystone-Mast Collection, UCR/California Museum of Photography, University of California at Riverside; page 325: DigitalStock; page 347: photo illustration by Mark C. Ide; page 363: photo illustration by Mark C. Ide; page 386: David Hitch/Worcester Telegram; page 397: Roxbury Publishing; page 427: Mark C. Ide; page 469: DigitalStock. ✦

# Author Index

## A

Abadinsky, Howard, 246
Abbott, Daniel J., 444, 454
Ackerley, Elizabeth, 11
Adams, Carol J., 157
Adler, Freda, 403, 465, 466
Adler, Mortimer, 13, 331
Adler, Patricia, 55
Adler, Peter, 55
Ageton, Suzanne S., 49
Agnew, Robert, 71, 366, 422, 423, 424, 425, 439, 440
Akers, Ronald, 372, 373, 374, 375, 376, 377, 407, 419
Albanese, Jay, 77, 165, 169, 171, 172, 179, 188
Albini, Joseph L., 160, 161, 168, 169, 170, 190
Allan, Emilie Anderson, 71, 87, 89
Alva, Susan, 470
Alvazzi del Frate, Anna, 458, 461, 462
Amnesty International, 214, 216, 248
Anderson, David, 4
Anderson, Sarah, 212, 213
Andrew, D. T., 452
Archer, Dane, 456
Archer, John E., 150
Arluke, Arnold, 151
Arrigo, Bruce, 433
Ascione, Frank R., 148
Asinoff, Robert, 214
Associated Press, 150, 447
Aulette, Judy Root, 241, 242
Avary, D'Aunn Wester, 104, 115

## B

Bachman, Ronet, 129
Bailey, William C., 78, 285
Baldry, Anna C., 148
Balkan, Sheila, 403
Ball, Richard A., 359
Balzac, Honoré de, 274
Bandura, Albert, 373
Bankston, William B., 68
Barak, Gregg, 22, 422
Baranek, Patricia M., 11
Barclay, Gordon, 56, 446
Barlow, Melissa Hickman, 11
Barry, Kathleen, 182
Bartol, Anne M., 74
Basile, Kathleen C., 138
Batchelor, Susan, 52
Battle, Joyce, 254
Bayley, David H., 462
Beccaria, Cesare, 266–269, 272, 273, 284, 285, 413
Beck, 473
Becker, Howard, 379, 380, 409
Beckett, Katherine, 10
Beirne, Piers, 21, 149, 150, 152, 264, 265, 274, 283, 400, 438, 467
Belknap, Joanne, 72, 75, 77, 134, 138, 139, 142
Bell, Daniel, 169
Bellair, Paul, 83
Bellis, David J., 247, 251
Bennett, James, 316, 456
Bennis, Phyllis, 254
Benson, Donna J., 153
Benson, Michael L., 139
Bentham, Jeremy 269–272, 273, 285
Bergen, Raquel Kennedy, 132, 137, 138, 139, 141, 145
Berger, Ron, 403
Bernard, Thomas J., 300, 317, 332, 333, 352, 366, 388, 393, 421

Berry, John Francis, 207
Berry, Steve, 141
Best, Joel, 5, 386
Bianchi, Herman, 437
Black, Donald, 16, 43
Black, George, 249
Blau, Judith R., 68
Blau, Peter M., 68
Block, Alan, 162, 166, 167, 169, 186
Block, Maggie, 187
Blok, Anton, 160, 161
Blumer, Herbert, 379
Blumstein, Alfred, 46
Boeringer, S. D., 136
Bolander, Edward, 395
Bonger, Willem, 395, 408
Boostrom, Ronald L., 313
*Boston Herald*, 230
Bourgois, Philippe, 78
Bowker, Michael, 204, 436
Box, Steven, 77, 203
Brady, James P., 119
Braithwaite, John, 63, 67, 205, 213, 214, 386, 421, 422
Brame, Robert, 49
Branfman, Frank, 247, 248
Bray, Howard, 237
Breacher, Edward M., 172
Brecher, Jeremy, 224
Brenner, M. Harvey, 66
Brezina, Timothy, 425
Britt, Chester L., 67
Britt, David, 394
Brody, Reed, 250
Brogden, Mike, 91
Broidy, Lisa, 71
Brown, Jane, 52
Brown, Julia, 449, 450, 451, 452, 475
Browne, Angela, 140
Brownmiller, Susan, 404, 405

527

# Subject Index

## Z